Ham Spray House
Hungerford, Berks.

Mrs Quentin Bell

SPAIN.

GIBRALTAR

BIRRELL & GARNETT
ENGLISH AND FOREIGN BOOKSELLERS
30 GERRARD STREET
LONDON W.

Frances Partridge

Frances Partridge

The Biography

Anne Chisholm

Weidenfeld & Nicolson

LONDON

First published in Great Britain in 2009
by Weidenfeld & Nicolson

1 3 5 7 9 10 8 6 4 2

A CIP catalogue record for this book
is available from the British Library.

ISBN: 978 0 297 64673 0

Typeset by Input Data Services Ltd, Bridgwater, Somerset

Printed in Great Britain by CPI Mackays, Chatham ME5 8TD

The Orion Publishing Group's policy is to use papers that
are natural, renewable and recyclable products and made
from wood grown in sustainable forests. The logging and
manufacturing processes are expected to conform to
environmental regulations of the country of origin.

Weidenfeld & Nicolson

An imprint of the Orion Publishing Group Ltd
Orion House, 5 Upper Saint Martin's Lane, London, WC2H 9EA
An Hachette Livre UK Company

www.orionbooks.co.uk

To Michael, 1924–2005
and to
Jesse, 1970–2002

Contents

List of Illustrations   ix

Foreword   xi

1   Bedford Square and Tweenways   1

2   Bedales and Cambridge   22

3   The Bookshop and Bloomsbury   38

4   The Making of Ralph Partridge   54

5   Trouble at Tidmarsh Mill   70

6   Frances and Ralph   84

7   Journey to Spain   96

8   Gordon Square and Ham Spray   106

9   Darkness at Ham Spray   123

10   Marriage and Motherhood   146

11   Ostrich Tendencies   164

12   Trials of War (1)   181

13   Trials of War (2)   200

14   Problems of Peace   215

15   Facing Fear   237

16   Return to London   257

17   Towards Recovery   276

18   Bloomsbury Revisited   298

19 Travelling and Writing   320
20 So Old and Still Alive   344

    Afterword   364
    Appendices   371
    Note on Sources, and Acknowledgements   373
    Source Notes   377
    Index   389

Illustrations

All illustrations are taken from the albums in the Frances Partridge archive and are used with permission of the Literary Executor of the Frances Partridge Estate and the Provost and Fellows of King's College, Cambridge, with the following exceptions:

Section One

In the nursery with Nan (Richard Garnett album)
Will and Margaret Marshall (Richard Garnett album)
In the Lake District (Richard Garnett album)
David Garnett, by Lady Ottoline Morrell, 1920 (National Portrait Gallery, London)
Lady Ottoline Morrell, Ralph and Michael Llewelyn Davies, by Philip Edward Morrell, 1920 (National Portrait Gallery, London)
At Tidmarsh Mill, by Lady Ottoline Morrell, 1923 (National Portrait Gallery, London)

Section Three

Nigel Nicolson and Frances, by Susan Fox
Frances in her bedroom, by Julia Hedgecoe, 1997 (National Portrait Gallery, London)
At the Bloomsbury Gallery, by Susan Fox
Frances at 90, by Snowdon (Camera Press, London)

While every effort has been made to trace copyright holders, if any have inadvertently been overlooked the publishers would be happy to acknowledge them in future editions.

Foreword

Not long before her ninety-ninth birthday, I went to call on Frances Partridge at her flat in West Halkin Street to talk about the possibility that I might write her biography. It was not the first time that we had met; that had been when she was in her eighties, when we had been at the same dinner table two or three times, and I had exchanged a few words with her at crowded literary gatherings. I remember wondering how someone so old and slight could face the noisy throng; she would stand slightly to one side, looking small and bird-like, observant and amused.

I knew little then about her early life, apart from the fact that she had been closely connected to the Bloomsbury group. My knowledge of her came from the diaries of her life in the 1960s and 1970s, which I had reviewed for *The Times Literary Supplement* when they were published during the 1990s, and which I, like many others, had greatly admired. Her connection with Bloomsbury interested me less, at that time, than her gift for friendship, her sharp eye for the vagaries of human behaviour and her ability to survive loss and grief. 'Like all diaries,' I had written in 1990 of *Hanging On*, in which she recounted her struggle to rebuild her life after the death of her husband in 1960, 'this record ... cannot be judged simply as a book. Character, behaviour and qualities of heart as well as mind make diaries worth reading quite as much as literary skill.'

Frances had liked my reviews, but another point in my favour was the fact that I was far from being what she called a Bloomsbury hound. By the time I came along, she had earned the right to be seen not as a minor character on the Bloomsbury stage but standing at the centre of her own. What became known during the 1920s as the Bloomsbury group, a loose collection of friends involved in intellectual, literary and artistic life, known for their progressive opinions and complicated love affairs, had only really begun when the Stephen sisters, later Vanessa Bell and Virginia Woolf, moved from Kensington to Gordon Square in 1904 when Frances was four. She was thus a generation younger than the people she herself called Old

Bloomsbury, whose careers as writers and artists and unconventional private lives were in full swing long before she grew up and came within their orbit. Then, as now, not everyone admired or liked Bloomsbury; but Frances had always acknowledged a great debt to them all, for helping her to think for herself. Long afterwards, she had been much involved in the process whereby Bloomsbury, after decades of obscurity, had been rediscovered and re-evaluated. In writing about her, I hoped to find out what effect Bloomsbury attitudes and values had had on the life of one woman and to learn what it was like to live long enough to see the friends of your youth turned into material for biographers and film-makers. Above all, though, I was interested to discover how and why Frances Partridge's private diary, her intimate record of living through the twentieth century, had, when published in her old age, brought her such recognition and acclaim.

Frances lived longer in Belgravia than in Bloomsbury. Arriving for the first time at her flat in West Halkin Street, on the first floor of a substantial white-pillared house between Belgrave Square and Sloane Street, I saw that she had settled in an opulent part of London very different in atmosphere and tradition from the grey Georgian squares in the shadow of the British Museum and London University. Her flat was not large, but it did not feel cramped; there was a wide hall, and the main room at the front had high ceilings, good proportions and two handsome French windows opening onto a balcony full of plants and small shrubs. This sitting room was painted a dull pink, with two walls hung with bookshelves picked out in mustard yellow. There were large painted ceramic plates on the top shelves, and some handsome Staffordshire figures. Over her desk hung a glowing portrait of Lytton Strachey reclining, painted by Dora Carrington in 1916, his long fingers holding his book up to his bearded face. The fireplace was filled in with a bright mosaic, made for her by the Russian artist Boris Anrep, showing a black cat staring into leaping flames; over it hung a tranquil picture of a classical head and flowers by Duncan Grant, while above her work table by the window was Grant's large painting of a juggler and an acrobat. There was a framed black and white photograph of her husband, Ralph Partridge, in his thirties and wearing a sailor's hat, and a portrait of her son Burgo as a small boy, his dark eyes bright and his black curls glossy. Her mantelpiece was thick with cards and invitations. The bedroom was a cool grey, with a large tapestry cat in a walnut frame over the bed, water-colours of flowers, more books, and family photographs of her grand-daughter and great-granddaughters. In the bathroom was a drawing of a sprawling odalisque by Augustus John. The flat felt full of the past but not at all shrine-like, calm and warm, with its well-used furniture, jugs of flowers and scattering of books and papers.

Frances, who still lived alone, would greet visitors over the intercom, her light, high voice lifting on the second syllable of 'Hello', and then be waiting at the open door of her flat. She always wore loose trousers, dark blue or sometimes plaid, a shirt, a jersey or two, and neat slippers. I never saw her without her heavy silver necklace with its dangling pointed beads, and her favourite bracelet, a wide, convex band of silver with a faint inlaid gold pattern, which would slip round her twig-like wrist like the antique rings on her tiny fingers.

Frances was considered a beauty in her youth, with a wide forehead, lustrous dark eyes and hair and smooth olive complexion. Now her hair was sparse and grey, her skin blotched with the brown marks and bruises of age and her face was deeply wrinkled; nevertheless, when she smiled or laughed, which she did often, her great charm made her beautiful again and her eyes shone with intelligence and humour. She had always been a small woman, with delicate wrists and ankles and a neat, athletic figure, and full of energy: a keen skater, a tennis-player, a great walker and swimmer and a famously good dancer. Now she was smaller than ever, but straight-backed and upright and still able to manage the stairs unaided; she sometimes used a stick, but was deeply resistant to wheelchairs. But to embrace her was to feel bone; it was not surprising to learn that she could be, and had been, blown over by a puff of wind. Physically insubstantial, she was still a considerable presence. Her mind and her memory were sharp, she was disconcertingly perceptive and she never uttered a dull sentence.

Our first appointment went easily. She had already decided that the time had come for her to co-operate with a biographer, and the fact that she knew me a little, and that I had the support of her agent and friend Gill Coleridge, and one of her oldest and closest male friends, Robert Kee, meant that she was already inclined to accept me. We discussed my previous books, especially *Faces of Hiroshima*, an account I had written of a group of girls injured when the Americans dropped the bomb in 1945. This interested her because she assumed, rightly, that I had wanted to remind readers of the human consequences of nuclear war. Herself a lifelong pacifist, she wondered where I stood; I said that I was on the fence, often drawn to pacifism while unable to see how Hitler could have been stopped without war. She said that in her opinion, war solved nothing and only led to more war. When I asked her what she thought a biography of her could add to what had already been written, and especially to what she had published about herself, she did not hesitate: 'I would like you to get Ralph right,' she said at once. 'No-one ever has.' I knew from her diaries how deeply she had loved him and missed him; otherwise all I knew about Ralph Partridge came from Michael Holroyd's biography of Lytton Strachey, which portrayed him as the somewhat surprising love object of Strachey and husband of his companion Dora Carrington. All I could do was to say that I would do my best to understand and present him afresh. We then talked a little about marriage; Frances considered a happy marriage not only the greatest blessing in life, but one of the most interesting of relationships. 'People think marriage is dull,' she said. 'They are quite wrong.'

In the wake of this meeting, when I realised that as far as she was concerned the sooner we started work the better, I began to visit her regularly with my notebook and tape recorder. We began at the beginning, with her parents' marriage and her early life, as even though she deplored biographies that start by plunging into genealogy – 'Ancestors are hell, don't you think?' – and considered friends at least as important as family, she conceded that some account of her origins and background was required.

On that first visit, she had taken me into her bedroom and showed me the walnut cupboard in the corner by the window, told me it had been brought back from France in the 1920s by Lytton Strachey and that it now contained all her diaries, letters and papers. They were organised in large battered box files and looked in good order. In the drawers beneath were heaps of photograph albums, not just hers but those left by Lytton and Carrington. 'You can have all this, of course,' she said, adding she would instruct all her friends and family to help me. I could ask them, and her, anything I wanted. 'You see,' she said, 'I have always believed in the truth.'

One

Bedford Square and Tweenways, 1900–1914

Frances was never greatly interested in her forebears, or the family legend that her father could trace his family back to John of Gaunt; but she liked to recall that both her parents had Irish connections, and that her mother had been born in New Zealand. She herself was born in London, on 15 March 1900, the sixth and last child and fourth daughter of William Cecil Marshall and his wife Margaret Anne, whose maiden name was Lloyd. Her mother was thirty-six when she had Frances, and her father fifty-one; looking back, Frances remembered him as elderly and remote and she would speak of him in a fond but detached way. Her mother, on the other hand, always known to her children as Mam (her initials after she married were M.A.M.), she remembered with emotion. 'I was always much more interested in my mother than my father. She was a very good mother and as a child I loved her passionately.'

As it happens, Margaret Anne Marshall can speak for herself. She left a detailed account of the first half of her life, her marriage, the birth of all her children and their domestic and social life; ending in 1914, it provides an unusually intimate account of the building of a late-Victorian family. Written in her old age as a record for her family, it conveys the character of a positive, sweet-natured, humorous woman with a mind of her own, a woman of spirit with a social conscience who nevertheless was happy to build her life almost entirely around her husband and children. Thanks to her, it is possible to see in close-up the private world into which Frances arrived as the twentieth century began, and to learn about the values and characteristics of the family surrounding her as she grew up.

Mam's own childhood was shadowed by loss and grief. With a striking lack of self-pity she describes in her memoir how by the time she was twelve, both her parents were dead. Her father was Anglo-Irish, the son of one Provost of Trinity College, Dublin, and the younger brother of another; a clergyman, he had been out in New Zealand some twelve years when he married Sarah Green, from County Armagh. Margaret Anne was their fourth child, and she was born in the vicarage of St Paul's, Auckland, in July 1863.

Frances enjoyed Mam's tales of her 'fearless' grandfather's adventurousness and courage, how he travelled through Spain in the 1830s and then in New Zealand became chaplain to the army during the Maori Wars. Later, he helped to nurse 'the natives' of Norfolk Island through a smallpox epidemic. Frances' grandmother was impulsive, warm-hearted, impatient and musical, with a good singing voice. Like all the children of the Empire, Mam grew up thinking of England as home; unlike most of them, she was separated from her parents not by being sent back to school but by their early deaths. Her mother died in 1875 from heart disease, aged forty-seven. Mam recalled seeing her unconscious on her deathbed and hearing the death rattle in her throat; she wrote of her painful regret that 'the undemonstrative habits of our family' had made it impossible for her to express her feelings. Eight months later, her father was also dead. Of his seven children, the oldest was twenty-one, the youngest only four. It was soon decided that the four youngest, including Mam, would be adopted by their uncle Humphrey Lloyd, the Provost of Trinity College, Dublin, and his wife Dora, who was over fifty and childless.

Life at the Provost's Lodgings in Dublin was secure but subdued; the orphaned children's aunt and uncle, though kind, were strict, and brought in a detested German governess. 'I remember vowing that if I had children they should not be handed over to governesses,' wrote Mam. In adolescence she was found to have a curved spine, and made to spend several hours a day in bed; she describes herself at around this time as 'exaggeratedly religious and morbidly sensitive'. She must also have been resilient, as she survived, it seems, without physical or emotional damage, and in 1881, after Humphrey Lloyd's death, she and her sister Edith went back to England to live with yet another set of relations in Brighton. The Lloyds had a strong sense of family; Mam was especially fond of her bookish sister Alice, who went to Newnham College, Cambridge, and her slightly raffish soldier brother, Charlie. By this time a new life had opened up for her; her spinal problem was cured, she visited Paris and Italy, and had a romantic interlude with a violin teacher. Photographs show her to have been small, trim and dark-haired, not a beauty, but full of an attractive eagerness and vitality.

Then, in the winter of 1886, when she was twenty-three, Margaret Anne Lloyd met William Cecil Marshall, a tall, fair-haired, blue-eyed architect of thirty-eight. He seems to have swept her off her feet; after a rush of picnics, theatres, and dinners with his many friends, he proposed to her in a hansom cab on the way back from the theatre. Six weeks later they were married in the small church at Shottermill, near Hindhead in Surrey, where Will had already worked on several houses. It was not a grand or formal wedding; Mam describes it as 'very like a picnic', with only a handful of friends and relations present. Her aunt Dora, who Mam felt was much relieved to see one of her adopted nieces so suitably wed, gave her away, and as the couple left for their honeymoon in a large and well-staffed house lent by a client of Will's in nearby Liphook aunt Dora was heard to say, 'I suppose I ought to cry, but I really don't see why I should.'

Mam's account of the man she married is admiring and affectionate. He was the youngest son of Henry Cooper Marshall of Derwent Island, Keswick, and belonged to a large and well-established Lake District clan. A Marshall forebear had made a small fortune out of cloth and linen manufacturing in the Yorkshire Dales and Leeds, and his descendants had moved out to the Lake District, where they built themselves several substantial High Victorian houses on the shores and islands of Derwentwater. Will's grandfather was an MP for Yorkshire in the early nineteenth century, and an uncle had become Father of the House of Commons. Will Marshall's mother had aristocratic connections: she was Catherine Spring Rice, daughter of an Irish peer. The Marshalls and the Spring Rices were linked by other marriages, and one of Will's grandmothers was the daughter of an Earl of Limerick.

By the standards of the day Mam had done rather well for herself. Not only was her new husband's family prosperous and well-connected, but he had already established himself as a successful architect, with a thriving practice. Educated at Rugby and Trinity College, Cambridge, he had at first wanted to be a painter, but was persuaded by his father that architecture was a more reliable profession; he drew so well, according to Mam, that some of the drawings he made in Italy were admired by Ruskin. He loved poetry, and could recite Swinburne, Browning and Tennyson at length. He also had a keen interest in natural history, and had come to know Charles Darwin towards the end of the great man's life, when he had been commissioned to build a new study at Down House in Kent. Will Marshall collected moths and butterflies, and even made a contribution to Darwin's study of the fertilisation of orchids.

He was also vigorous and athletic. He played real tennis for Cambridge and built several real tennis courts around England. Later he took up lawn tennis, and was runner-up in the first English championship at Wimbledon in 1877. Above all, he loved walking, swimming and skating in the Lake District, where he went as often as possible. 'He would go any distance for good ice ... and I have heard him speak with enthusiasm of skating on

Derwentwater by moonlight'. He even published a small handbook on figure skating. Good with children, he was a great favourite with his younger relations; and within a year of their marriage, Margaret and Will Marshall were expecting their first child.

Frances' parents, as they embarked on creating the family into which she was to be born, sound both typical of their time and class and yet agreeably free of some of that time and class's limitations. They were unpretentious but confident Late Victorians, reasonably well-off without being glaringly rich, securely upper-middle-class without being grand, interested in art and literature without being especially intellectual or creative. They were not narrow-minded, but neither were they consciously unconventional. They believed in social progress and in education, for girls as well as boys.

At first, the couple lived in Will's bachelor studio in Torrington Place, off Gower Street, while they looked for a house together. On 15 January 1888 they moved into one of Bloomsbury's most handsome and substantial houses in its most splendid square. No. 28 Bedford Square was a finely proportioned, solid and elegant five-storey Georgian house, with its grey stonework set off by black railings and white decorations. Mam in her memoir calls it a 'palatial abode', and admits that she was daunted at first by the responsibility of running such an establishment. The house had been in bad shape when they bought it; they put in new drains, a decent bathroom and a new kitchen at the back with a study over it. Will must have been doing well to afford all this, as well as raising some of the ceilings on the upper floors, furnishings, complete redecorations, including the delicate painting of the fine Adams mouldings in the main room in Wedgwood colours, and much fashionable William Morris wallpaper. It was Mam's duty to deal with the eight servants they required, which she did not at first find at all easy. 'I still remember', she wrote, 'how terror overcame me when I had to dismiss a cook, and I gave her notice through the speaking tube, not daring to face her.'

There was much entertaining in their impressive new home, with its twenty-six-foot drawing room and double doors through to a huge room at the back; their house-warming party included dancing and amateur theatricals, and they soon embarked on a round of dinners, dances and suppers. As a bride, Mam had to make and receive endless calls and wear her bridal dress to dinner. Formal dinners meant ten courses, but she and her husband both preferred more relaxed evenings, which would begin with an 'At Home', and proceed to a cold supper and dancing. 'Sixty people came,' she wrote in her diary after one such evening. 'Turned into a dance.'

Many of their friends had artistic or intellectual leanings, like their

Bedford Square neighbours the Asquiths, the literary critic Walter Raleigh, the actor Johnston Forbes-Robertson. Mam became especially fond of the classical scholar Jane Harrison, already an academic star. And the young Marshalls soon came within the orbit of the founding families of what had not yet become the Bloomsbury group; the Stephen family were still firmly based in Kensington in the 1880s and 1890s. However, Will was already a member of Sir Leslie Stephen's group of serious walkers, who would set off regularly for 'Sunday tramps' in the countryside near London, and Virginia and Vanessa Stephen's half-brothers, George and Gerald Duckworth, were, Mam wrote, 'great stand-byes at parties'.

Both the Marshalls had a social conscience, and although they loved to enjoy themselves they were not frivolous. Mam in particular felt it was her duty to improve the lives of the less fortunate. Early in their marriage, she records, she and her husband helped at a college for working men and women in Queen Square; Willie taught mathematics and she German, Jane Austen and music.

Will worked hard. He frequently had to go out of London to visit a site or meet clients, often to Cambridge, the Hindhead area or as far away as the Lake District. On Sundays he would take their dog Pan, a woolly poodle given to them as a wedding present, and set off to join Leslie Stephen's walkers. Mam needed a day of rest, but even when she was pregnant and not feeling at all well she was expected to visit the Lake District with him. 'I met so many new relations during these visits that I gave up as hopeless the attempt to disentangle them,' she wrote, after mentioning six different sets of Marshalls, mostly amiable, some quite eccentric, all curious about the new bride.

The Marshalls' first child, Horace, was born in early April 1888, at home in Bedford Square, like all their children. Mam stayed in bed for the customary three weeks; but by 1 June she was considered strong enough to go down to Hindhead, to stay with their friend Edward Nettleship, the distinguished ophthalmologist (he operated on Gladstone's cataracts in 1894) in the house Will had built for him there. 'I think it was during this visit,' wrote Mam, 'that we decided to buy a piece of land for ourselves.' Will Marshall had long dreamed that one day he would be able to build a house for a family of his own.

In the late nineteenth century Hindhead, then a village on a hill beside the London-to-Portsmouth road, was sometimes referred to as Mindhead. The area had a reputation as a retreat for writers, scientists and other professionals, drawn there by the spectacular scenery around the Devil's Punch Bowl, the bracing air, the fine walks through gorse and rough

woodland, the excellent golf course and the comparatively easy com-
munications with London. Will already knew the area, and it was not long
before he had found the perfect spot: about eleven acres of copse and heather
near the top of the steep hill leading up from Haslemere towards Hindhead
itself, at the junction of three roads – hence the sugary name he and Mam
chose for the house, Tweenways, a source of embarrassment to Frances in
later life. Mam always remembered how one day, when they were exploring
the site, 'Alfred Tennyson appeared in his cloak and soft felt hat. He told us
he had nearly bought this piece himself but had decided in favour of a piece
on Blackdown, further from main roads and traffic.' He liked the look of
their dog, 'and stooped to pat him, saying in his deep growl "What! The
great god Pan!"'

Several of the new residents around Hindhead were unconventional by
Victorian standards; one or two, like George Bernard Shaw, were positively
subversive. He once told a class of local schoolchildren that the first duty of
a child is to disobey its parents. The Russells, an aristocratic family with
strong intellectual characteristics and a tendency to reinvent the social rules,
were already established in the area by the time the Marshalls arrived. It was
Rollo Russell, a shy, humorous man interested in meteorology, epidemiology
and drains, who introduced his nephew, the brilliant young philosopher
Bertrand Russell, to the Pearsall Smiths, a family of rich Quakers from
Philadelphia, who had settled not far away. In 1894, Bertrand Russell married
his first wife, Alys Pearsall Smith.

Tweenways was ready for occupation in the spring of 1889. The Hindhead
of those days, according to Mam, was a beautiful stretch of heather-and-
gorse-covered common and deep valleys thick with trees. There were very
few houses on their hillside. Just above them was an eccentric scientist,
Professor Tyndall, a keen mountaineer who saw the area as the English
Switzerland and erected an enormous brushwood fence to keep out the
neighbours. More friendly locals included, as well as the Nettleships, the
family of Sir Frederick Pollock, Professor of Jurisprudence at Oxford and
another keen mountaineer. At first, life at Tweenways was refreshingly
simple. There was no water supply and no drainage system; 'we all sank our
wells, and had earth closets, and were lit by oil lamps and candles'. The red-
brick, red-tiled house the Marshalls called a cottage was in fact quite
substantial, with a large drawing room overlooking the garden, gabled roof,
four bedrooms, servants' quarters and stables. They brought maids down
from London to help, as well as an Irishwoman called Mary, 'rescued'
according to Mam from an East End infirmary, to be resident caretaker.
Soon they had to buy a pony and trap to transport them all the two and a

half miles from the station; 'Mary-pony', a small grey, half Arab and half New Forest, always remembered with amused affection by Frances, was bought from the Tennysons. Apart from planting bulbs during the winter before they moved in, the Marshalls did little to the garden at first; in due course they acquired a skilful and devoted, if completely illiterate, gardener, George, who later married one of the housemaids. There was a fine old oak in the middle of what later became the lawn.

Before long, Aunt Dora had moved nearby, to a house built for her by Will. 'By degrees, the colony grew,' wrote Mam. Will joined the golf club, and golf, along with bridge and tennis, became one of his passions. She made a conscious effort to keep their life at Hindhead less formal than in London; the Marshalls and their circle made a point of never wearing 'real evening clothes', and Mam recalled Christy Minstrel parties 'to soften up grand newcomers', when she would appear in short trousers, a little red coat and cap, and black make-up. 'It used to be said that no-one was quite accepted at Tweenways till their faces had been blackened.' In 1893, Mam acted 'The Coming Woman' to a large audience in Hindhead, 'wearing checked bloomers and trying to puff a cigarette'.

Mam was on the side of the Coming Woman, and it was around this time that she encountered two of the most formidable pioneers of votes for women, Miss Garrett and Mrs Fawcett, who lived round the corner from the Marshalls' London house. Through them, she was drawn into being an active worker for women's suffrage. Up till then neither she nor her husband had paid much attention to politics. Will was, and remained, a Liberal Unionist, but was really more interested in the Eugenics Society, which sounds sinister today but then was regarded as a progressive cause, and also with the Society for Psychical Research, to which he had been introduced by his cousin from Cambridge, Frederic Myers. Unlike many Victorian husbands he did not at all mind his wife becoming involved in the suffrage campaign. Mam loved and admired Mrs Fawcett, a small, dynamic woman of great energy and humour, and attended meetings and rallies as often as she could, although, as she writes, 'It did not come easy to me to walk in processions through crowded streets or to face jeering or hostile audiences ... The tendency at that time was to consider the whole thing slightly ridiculous, and questions as to who was minding the baby or cooking the dinner were considered highly humorous and always raised a laugh.' It was not until her family was complete and her children growing up that Mam became seriously involved with the suffrage campaign, both in London and as secretary and later chair of the Haslemere Branch of the National Union of Women's Suffrage Societies.

Mam was no feminist, but she was undoubtedly a woman with her own opinions and a disinclination to follow the social rules if she felt them inhumane. While discussing the plight of an unmarried friend one day, 'I shocked Willy', she wrote cheerfully, 'by declaring that single women who wished to have children should do so without any sort of stigma. Willy said that for a British Mother . . . I was the most immoral woman he knew! I was quite serious about this, and I don't suppose very many people would disagree with me nowadays.' This was certainly an advanced view in the 1890s, and not all that prevalent in the 1930s, when she was writing, either.

Although the Marshalls spent as much time as possible at Tweenways, for twenty years it remained their weekend and holiday retreat. The big house in Bedford Square was the centre of their busy family and social life during the last decade of the nineteenth century and the early years of the twentieth. Mam led what she calls, wryly, 'a fairly strenuous existence'; running two establishments and entertaining in both, she also produced five children in nine years: Horace in 1888, Julia (Judy) in 1890, Rachel (Ray) in 1891, Thomas (Tom) in 1893 and Eleanor in 1897. Perhaps because of her own family history, she was an unusually attentive and careful mother; when any of her children fell ill, she took pride in nursing them herself. Of course she had help; soon after Horace's birth the household was joined by Elizabeth Croucher, always known as Nan, who took charge of each baby in turn and remained a central presence in Marshall family life for nearly fifty years.

Mam was lucky to find Nan, and she knew it. Nan was a Londoner with a strong cockney accent, a small, thin woman who had been looking after children since she was twelve. Mam regarded her as 'a born nurse, devoted to children, ready to give up her afternoon out if they seemed to need her, endlessly ingenious at keeping them occupied and amused, and at managing them without battles . . . her whole life was bound up in the nursery and in her home'.

Thanks in large part to Nan, Mam was able to enjoy her London life to the full while her children were young. Will played bridge, and though Mam did not she was happy to provide bridge suppers at Bedford Square. Although she loved music, and taught all her children to do so too, he did not enjoy concerts much; but they went often to the theatre, especially to see their friend and neighbour Johnston Forbes-Robertson, whose Hamlet Mam saw repeatedly and considered the best that could be imagined. They had several painter friends, too, and used to join in 'Picture Sundays', which involved a round of studios inspecting paintings due to be submitted to the Royal Academy's summer show. She was also amused to visit Edward

Nettleship's son-in-law Augustus John, married to Ida Nettleship and living in a studio not far from Bedford Square, even though she and Will found the bohemian squalor and lavish drinking of the John establishment unnerving.

In the last years of the nineteenth century, just before Frances was born, Will Marshall was at the peak of his career; in the late 1890s he won several big public commissions, including a new wing of the East London Hospital, the Botanical Laboratory at Cambridge and the Alexandra Hospital for Children with Hip Disease in Queen Square, opened in 1897 by the Prince of Wales. Mam attended the ceremony. 'I am afraid I was not impressed. The Prince was not good to look at and he spoke like a foreigner.' The Marshalls were a popular couple; as Mam put it, Will's clients nearly always became his friends. They could afford to give parties, go regularly to the theatre – Will invested in a theatre company with Forbes-Robertson – take family holidays in the Lake District and in Ireland, and visit fashionable Biarritz in winter for the sea air. The Marshalls were doing well.

Early in 1900, when Mam was six months pregnant with Frances, her sixth and last child, she uncharacteristically took to her bed for a fortnight. She was exhausted by the recent visit to Bedford Square of her brother Fred and his family (making, as she noted, a total of seven children and four parents in the house); and she was still recovering from the strain of appearing in court before Christmas on behalf of one of her maids, who had begun proceedings against a man who had made her pregnant and then refused to marry her. According to the judge, who awarded the woman damages, Mam's testimony had made all the difference. She was also much preoccupied with the Boer War; not only did she have relations in South Africa, but Will was working on a building for Tremayne Buller, brother of the war's leading General, Sir Redvers Buller, VC, and brought home frequent news of the situation. As Mam recalled, everyone assumed that the Boers could never stand up to the British, and it was a shock when the news showed that indeed they could. In the weeks before Frances was born the whole family was longing for good news from South Africa. When Lady-smith was finally relieved, the Marshall children rushed to tell their mother. 'Ray brought me the news,' she wrote, 'and Tom cried because she got to me first with it ... People in the street began to cheer, flags were waved, and hung out from the houses, and at night windows were lighted up and cheering crowds filled the street.'

It was into this mood of imperial rejoicing, in the last days of the reign of Queen Victoria, that Frances Catherine Marshall was born, on 15 March 1900. She was not quite what her mother had expected; the Marshalls had hoped for a third son to balance their family evenly between the sexes. 'I had made up my mind that this child should be a small, dark, curly-haired boy, and be named Tony.'

Never, in recalling her childhood, did Frances convey any sense that she was a disappointment to her parents, because of her sex or for any other reason. On the contrary, she demonstrated, all her life, the benefits – a positive, optimistic outlook on life, emotional security, a certain basic social and intellectual confidence – of being the much loved youngest child of a large, busy, cheerful Victorian professional family. She and her sister Eleanor, the closest to her in age, were known as The Little Ones. By the time she was born, the older children were at school: Horace and Tom, to their mother's sorrow (Mam was not a great believer in boarding schools), went away to prep school and then to Marlborough and Rugby respectively, while the girls were first taught at home and then moved on at five to Queen's College, Harley Street, where they remained as day girls. At 28 Bedford Square the top two floors were the children's territory; as the youngest, Frances shared a bedroom with Nan. In Mam's view, it was good for children to be able to lead their own lives in their own part of the house when they were small, though she was relieved that Nan, unlike many of her profession, was never put out when she appeared. All the Marshall children had meals in the nursery (carried up four flights from the kitchen) until they could feed themselves, when they would sometimes go downstairs for lunch; but every evening, in their best clothes, they would visit their parents in the handsome drawing room on the first floor, for an hour of music and games before bed.

In the first years of Frances' life, two dramas affected the family at 28 Bedford Square – one public, the other domestic. On 21 January 1901 Queen Victoria died; it was a great shock, wrote Mam, and yet she could not help thinking it was time for a new monarch. She and Will took the older children, wearing black, to a memorial service and also to join the thousands lining the streets to watch the funeral procession cross London. That winter, Frances developed scarlet fever, then a terrifyingly dangerous and infectious childhood disease. Mam coped splendidly: she sent the other children down to Tweenways, sealed off the top floors of the house and nursed her youngest daughter for six weeks. When a sanitary inspector called and told her that he had come to take the child away to an isolation ward, the family doctor supported her in refusing to allow him to do so. Frances survived, and was taken down to Tweenways to recover.

In the summer of 1902, the whole family – a group of eleven, including Nan, a cook and a parlourmaid, accompanied by two puppies, several pet rats and some caged birds – removed to the bracing seaside air of Sheringham in Norfolk. Here, Mam records with some pride, 'Baby bathed beautifully'. Swimming was to become a special passion of Frances', and her earliest memory was of being lowered into the sea, and of her father's bearded face in the water, waiting for her to swim to him.

When she came to write about her childhood, Frances described her father affectionately while not pretending that they had been close. She respected his enquiring mind, his commitment to 'eugenics, agnosticism and the march of science' while recognising that he was in many ways a conventional man, for whom the pattern of 'class distinctions courteously observed' was important. She fondly recalled his physical strength and vigour, his blue eyes and his 'old-fashioned elegance' – he would wear a strip of silk brocade pulled through an opal ring as a tie – but what she most appreciated in him, looking back, was his great love of landscape and natural beauty. From as early as she could remember, she had 'very strong feelings for nature, woken by my father' and she would describe with lyrical precision how she felt about the Lake District, where holidays with her father and many Marshall relations were one of her childhood landmarks. It was there that she 'first discovered the intense pleasure which could be got from the natural world, and which is still one of my strongest emotions: it had its origins for me in that clean chilly light, the all-pervading greyish greenery, the steel surface of the lake, the hollow wooden sound of oars in rowlocks, and the pebbles seen through the clear water as I dangled my hand over the side of the boat'. Being, as a small child, 'so fortunately close to the ground, I rapturously responded to the look of smooth grey rocks emerging from close cropped turf, or springs threading through mossy stones, the smell of earth and wet bracken, and the intricate details of ferns and fronds'.

Although Bedford Square garden, with its huge plane trees and dusty bushes, was not at all the same thing, and Frances much preferred the comparative wilderness of Hindhead, she retained equally precise memories of the London of her Edwardian childhood, the games in the Square, the sound of horses' hooves, the strange shouts of the hansom cab drivers, the water-sprinkling carts trundling round the Square, the delicious smell of melted chocolate from a local shop. Above all she remembered Nan, and how she would lie snugly in bed watching her get dressed in the morning in long frilled drawers and flannel petticoats: 'what reassurance her whole appearance gave me!' Nan, she knew instinctively, was on the children's side, whatever they did. Every evening when he was at home, she and Eleanor would go to visit their father in his study, where he would give them pencils, one red and one blue, to draw with while he read to them from Dickens or Scott; but it was her mother who taught Frances to read, at about the age of four, from a book called *Reading Without Tears*, and she enjoyed the whole process so much that she longed to go to school, 'avid for knowledge of the world as well as books'. Later came the magic moment when, in a white silk embroidered frock, she would be allowed into the drawing room for a game of cards or spillikins until her mother, by playing 'Wee Willie Winkie' on the piano, indicated that it was time to go up to bed. Frances for some years was afraid of the dark, and disliked the black shadows on the landings between the drawing-room floor and her bedroom; she recalled bursting into tears regularly when the time came to leave her mother, the glowing lamps and the brilliant chandelier and brave the darkness, even with Nan beside her.

Inexorably, the safe, magic circle of home began to let in other people and the outside world. The small Frances was sensitive, observant and precise; for her third birthday, she recalled, the cook by mistake decorated the birthday cake with an iced figure of eight; 'I knew my numbers, and I thought that was wrong.' However, it was at the same party that she first remembered being admired: 'I was wearing a pink silk dress with white chiffon over it, and a small boy told me I was lovely.' Her first day at school, when she was five, was less pleasing; off she went, her hair tied back in a tidy pigtail, to the Infants Department at Queen's College, wearing a brown skirt and a scarlet jumper. At the end of the day, a group of older girls grabbed her new satchel and made her cry by telling her she looked like a mutton chop with blood running out of it. 'I think this was the moment', she wrote, some eighty years later, 'when room had to be found in my scheme of the universe for the hostility of the outside world.' Another strange and unfriendly remark lodged in her memory: Mam was determined that all her children should learn a musical instrument, in hopes of a family string quartet, and Ethel Nettleship, Augustus John's sister-in-law, came to Bedford Square to teach Eleanor the cello and Frances the violin. One day, Frances overheard the adored music teacher praising Eleanor to Mama and then announcing 'but Frances is just spoiled blackberry jam'. She was still wondering what this could have meant at the age of a hundred. She preferred another mysterious memory, of being embraced at a tender age by a tall man with a pink face who, she was later told, was Henry James, a friend of her aunt Alice, who had made friends with him in Rye.

In 1908, as he approached the age of sixty, Will Marshall decided that it was time to give up the London house and his architectural practice and retire with his family to Hindhead. He had already extended Tweenways once; now, intending to spend the rest of his life there and with six children between the ages of nineteen and eight to accommodate, he did so again, adding an enormous new drawing room along the garden side. After two decades of regular and often prolonged stays in the area it was hardly a dramatic or unexpected move for the family, and Mam records no regrets at leaving Bedford Square; as for Frances, she felt nothing but delight that they were going to live full-time in the country. But Bedford Square was her first home, and London was always to be familiar territory.

With the move to Tweenways, the first part of Frances' childhood was over. A certain simple, unquestioning happiness had by that time come to an end, symbolised for her by the withdrawal of physical affection by her mother. As a small child she had found her father, with his bristly beard, 'un-nuzzleable against'; it was her mother's warmth and softness she revelled in and missed when 'the delightful hugs and snugglings on her lap of early childhood came to a sudden stop'. Just as Mam in her memoir deplored the emotional straitjacket of her upbringing, so Frances, looking back, described her mother as 'rigorously undemonstrative'. She never doubted her mother's love, but she came to deplore the way her parents, like the English Victorians that they were, believed in concealing their emotions. When she was still a child, her mother said to her one day: 'You should never cheapen your feelings for people by letting them be seen.' Frances came to believe that this stricture, which she never forgot, did her emotional development some damage; 'Her shattering remark ate into me like rust, and I brooded for a long time over the possibility of accepting it as a formula for behaviour.' Nevertheless, asked if she felt that she had been a fortunate child, that her early years were safe and happy, and that she grew up feeling loved and secure, she considered the matter and then agreed that this was so.

From 1908 until 1915, Tweenways and the sandy hills and heather of Hindhead were Frances' childhood paradise. Later, she would call it, coolly, 'our Surreyfied domain with its bracken-filled corners, its sloping lawns and conifers' but also remembered 'countless magical delights – the hot smell of ponies, or of being in the middle of a head-high forest of bracken'. She loved the secret corners of the garden where children could disappear for hours, the animals they all adored – rabbits, a hare, guineapigs, white mice, pet rats, canaries, dogs, cats, her mother's chickens and the ponies. Will built the younger children a special hut where they could play and make a mess, and put in a tennis court for the older ones and their friends. As for the house itself, she remembered with particular nostalgia the riot of her mother's favourite dark, glowing William Morris wallpapers, and with amazement the fact that there was only one family bathroom. She was less in favour of the enormous painted and moulded plaster scene from *As You*

Like It designed by her father to go above the large fireplace in the new drawing room.

Moving to the country meant a new school. Brackenhurst, at Hindhead, was a small girls' school with about twenty pupils, both boarders and day girls; it was run by two women, Miss Gruner and Miss Gibbings, and was favoured by the neighbourhood's more intellectual parents. Frances and Eleanor were driven there each morning in the pony and trap by one of the gardeners, and collected again each afternoon. Miss Gruner was German, fierce and beady-eyed; Miss Gibbings was soft-hearted, lame and, according to Frances, 'one of the best teachers I ever came across'. Miss Gibbings even made her feel she loved geometry; above all, she realised, 'I loved to learn'. And it was at Brackenhurst, where she spent the next seven years, that she first experienced the joy of friendship, when she met a girl just over a year younger than she was, Julia Strachey, who was to delight, puzzle and occasionally torment her for the rest of her life.

Because her mother had made the acquaintance in London of three of Julia's aunts – Pippa, Marjorie and Elinor, all keen suffragists – Frances' world had always contained Stracheys; and, as she later wrote, 'one Strachey led to another'. A family with powerful Anglo-Indian connections, Julia's father, Oliver, her suffragist aunts and her uncles Lytton and James were among the ten children of Sir Richard Strachey and his wife Jane, who had returned from India to live in Bayswater. Frances soon realised that they all, especially the women, tended to be unusual, strong-minded, opinionated people; she was astonished to overhear Elinor say to Will Marshall one day, 'I don't believe a SINGLE word you say'. She was also struck by the distinctive, swooping Strachey voice, characteristic of both sexes and very unlike the hearty booming tones of the Marshall men. Julia was not to be the only member of the clan to become part of Frances' life, but she was the only one to become an intimate friend. Their backgrounds were socially similar, but in all other ways their childhoods could not have been more different; where Frances was part of a cheerful, ordinary family, Julia was a solitary child, neither of whose parents appeared to want her very much, passed from one relative to another in a way designed to create anxiety and insecurity in later life.

Julia's father Oliver was the third of the five sons of Sir Richard and Lady Strachey. After Eton and Balliol he was sent round the world in an attempt to cure him of homosexual tendencies that he did not actually have; he then lived in Vienna, studying music and hoping to be a professional pianist. Later, like his brother Ralph, he followed family tradition and went out to India; there he married a pretty German-Swiss girl called Ruby Mayer, whom his family suspected might be unsuitable. They turned out to be right; when Julia was five, her mother became pregnant by another man and Julia was sent back to her father's family in England. Ruby effectively vanished from Julia's life overnight, as did all the warmth and happiness of her Indian childhood; her clever, eccentric, womanising father was not inclined to give her a home. Julia never recovered from the shock of losing the people and the place she loved most. 'I had been packed off to travel half across the globe,' she wrote, 'bundled away from my well-loved home in my parents' bungalow, to be boarded out with an old English aunt, in order to be turned into a civilised, hardworking, dowdy English lady like all my other Strachey aunts.' She lived, at first, with her aunt Elinor, now Lady Rendel, in a large house in Kensington, looked after by the family's grim Scottish nanny; she was desperately unhappy, and could not under-stand why her parents did not come and rescue her. Her Rendel cousins were already young adults; they tried to be kind to her, but she was inconsolable. By the time she was eight, when her aunt told her in hushed tones that her parents had been divorced and that she would not see her mother again, she was resigned to her fate. 'I had well and truly grasped that I had been deserted and betrayed by the two people I loved most, whom I had trusted absolutely.'

By the time Frances and Julia met, Oliver Strachey had returned from India and Julia's life had changed again. He fell in love with Ray Costelloe, a close friend of his sister Elinor's daughter Ellie; they decided to marry, and Julia was sent as a boarder to Brackenhurst. She would spend the holidays not with her father but with her stepmother Ray's eccentric Quaker aunt Alys, known to Julia as Aunty Loo, who after the collapse of her marriage to Bertrand Russell set up house near Midhurst with her brother, the man of letters Logan Pearsall Smith.

Frances was unaware of her new friend's difficult childhood until much later; all she knew was that she had found a soulmate. Mam, who had recommended Brackenhurst to Lady Rendel in the first place, promised to keep an eye on her, and soon Julia became part of the family, spending every weekend at Tweenways. For Julia, to have a close friend of her own and to become part of a family must have been a comfort. For Frances, who took the company of her brothers and sisters for granted, Julia was always special. All her life, friendship was to be one of her guiding stars, and 'Julia', she later wrote, 'became my first real friend. She was tall for her age but slim as a reed ... her face was a perfect oval, her wideset eyes of an unusual sea-blue colour, and her mouth so small that she used to complain she could only open it vertically when she laughed or smiled. I remember her trying to expand it sideways with my mother's glove-stretchers. We passed happy days, and hardly ever quarrelled.'

The two girls could hardly have looked more different. Frances was small and neat, dark-eyed, with a broad forehead, thick, glossy dark hair and a full mouth; she also had a decided chin, while Julia's was small and slightly receding and her long fairish hair was scraped back from her oval face in two long plaits. Julia's natural expression tended to be solemn, even melancholy; she was frequently urged by bustling, extrovert Aunty Loo to look more cheerful. Frances was described by her mother as a happy child, with her 'dark eyes that seemed always ready to smile'.

During their school holidays Frances paid several visits to Julia at Ford Place, a romantic, rambling Elizabethan house with a walled garden where they were allowed to dress up in Aunty Loo's old clothes and paint all over the attic walls. Eventually, she came to think that perhaps Julia had been a bit hard on Uncle Logan and Aunty Loo, who did their best to amuse their young charge and her friends; but there was no doubt that the Pearsall Smiths were a peculiar bunch. Frances recalled how she and Julia would lie for hours giggling on their beds imitating Aunty Loo's peculiar Quaker speech (she used 'Thee' and 'Thou'). At Tweenways, they would climb trees and spend happy hours in the hayloft above the stable, having 'long secret conversations flavoured with the scent of hay and harness'. They only joined the grown-ups for meals; otherwise they were left alone, in accordance with Mam's principles.

When she was ten or eleven Frances began, with Julia's help, to think for herself about serious matters such as love, sex and the existence of God. Over breakfast one day at Ford Place she overheard a 'rather ribald' conversation about God between Adrian Stephen, the younger brother of Virginia Woolf and Vanessa Bell, and the girl he was soon to marry, Karin Costelloe, Ray Strachey's sister. They discussed his character and appearance just as if he were a human being; but it was 'the tone rather than the content of what they said that flashed its message into my mind like the beam of a lighthouse'. She understood in a flash that these two clever grown-ups simply did not believe in God; so why then should she? 'I only had to ask myself the question to realise that I no longer did, and I was conscious of an immense sense of liberation which was purely pleasant, nor did I ever feel the least temptation to believe in God again.' She knew instinctively, however, that while it was fine to analyse such matters in secret with Julia they were best not mentioned in public, even in the family circle. Her parents were not particularly fervent believers, but they went through the motions and rituals of Anglican observance, and had their children baptised and confirmed. To the end of her days Frances would relate how, one night while staying in a house the family had taken for a holiday in the Isle of Wight, she announced to her sister Eleanor, as she jumped into bed, 'Eleanor, you know I don't believe in God.' Her sister was deeply shocked, but Frances never recalled an attempt by her parents, or indeed anyone else, to get her to change her mind.

Then there was sex. Naturally, as they moved towards adolescence, Frances and Julia became curious, and Frances, an observant child, was surrounded by older brothers and sisters moving towards love and marriage. She recalled feeling annoyed at being excluded from the glamorous tennis parties, dances and flirtations going on around her; 'in this scintillating atmosphere of gaiety and romance I was definitely out of things; looks were exchanged and words flew over my head'. She always maintained that her first love was the dashing young Dick Rendel, Julia's cousin and Aunt Elinor's eldest son, who was often at Tweenways in pursuit of her eldest sister, Judy. Their marriage, in 1911, formally linked the Strachey and the Marshall families, and took place at the same small church in Shottermill where Mam and Will had married. Far from being jealous, Frances was thrilled: 'there would now be more opportunities for my doting contemplation'.

In time-honoured fashion, Mam did nothing to enlighten her youngest daughter about the facts of life except leave a book called *How We Are Born* on a convenient bookshelf. This informed her about childbirth but left the act leading to pregnancy unexplained, as did the various dictionaries and medical books she and Julia consulted. They tried to imagine what married couples of their acquaintance might do to produce children; this did not get them very far, especially as one husband they considered turned out to be given to exposing himself, as his unfortunate wife one day confided to Mam. Frances, sitting reading on the window seat, overheard the conversation but found it unhelpful. Eventually, during the school holidays, she received a thrilling letter from Julia. '"I've found out how ladies are fertilised for babies. You simply won't believe me when I tell you." When next term came, she did tell me, and indeed I hardly could.' Thus the mystery was resolved, but there was an awkward postscript to the story: Mam found Julia's letter and felt it her duty to make sure that Frances had the facts straight. Neither she nor her daughter enjoyed the talk that ensued. In fact, Frances was left with the impression that sex was not all that much fun. 'I felt Mam didn't much care for it; you had to put up with it if you wanted children.'

What stayed with Frances all her life about the first years of her friendship with Julia Strachey was the sheer delight of finding someone with whom she could argue, laugh and above all discuss topics, often abstract, of keen mutual interest. She always knew that Julia was the more imaginative, even fantastical, of the two of them; she saw herself, even at that age, as by nature realistic and sceptical. To have a companion outside the family was vital to her; it was not that she disliked any of them, although as the youngest she did sometimes feel a bit surrounded; but she discovered early on that she needed something more than her family could provide. In her old age, asked to describe her brothers and sisters as children, she did so succinctly and with no hint of family piety. Horace and Judy, she said, were so much older that she hardly knew them as people; Horace in particular she thought was probably always a rather conventional character. Ray was always her favourite sister; she was much the most original, and a talented artist who went to study at the Central School in 1912. Ray was also adventurous; in 1913, when she was twenty, she went on a trip to Russia with a woman friend, where she rode around the Caucasus and learned Russian songs and dances. Frances' brother Tom was 'obviously my mother's favourite ... he was the cleverest of us, and I was possibly the next'. As for Eleanor, they were not really close. Her main childhood memory of Eleanor was of furious arguments on the way home from school.

With the family settled at Tweenways, and all of them at school or university, Mam had more time and energy for her own interests, and soon began to stir up Hindhead and Haslemere society. Always keenly concerned about maternal and child welfare, she ran the Mothers' Union, became a manager of a local school and started a Health Society in Shottermill. Will, in his retirement, also did his bit, becoming a leading light in the Golf Club, where he played regularly with his new friend and neighbour Sir Arthur Conan Doyle. He also started a Dental Clinic, served on the Parish Council and set up a local branch of the Eugenics Education Society. It turned out that Mam was too liberal-minded for the Mothers' Union committee members, who asked her to organise a protest meeting against any liberalisation of the divorce laws in favour of women. This she refused to do, offering instead to hold a discussion at which they could all say what they thought. 'As this did not satisfy the committee I resigned,' she wrote, adding cheerfully, 'I seem to have been a disturbing element on several committees.' She also protested strongly when she discovered that the district nurse was not allowed to attend any unmarried woman having a baby. Her daughter noticed, and admired, her unconventional opinions.

Soon Mam was more and more caught up with campaigning for votes for women. As chair of the local suffrage association, she had to address public meetings; at her first, 'nearly all the family was in the hall, even Frances who had threatened to become an anti if she was not allowed to come'. Not everyone in the neighbourhood liked the idea of women having the vote; Mrs Beveridge, whose son was to play such a big part in the founding of the welfare state, actually started an anti-suffrage society. Mam and her supporters were undaunted. They rented space in the local news-paper, and filled it with facts and figures about the movement every week. All her life, Frances was proud of the way her mother stood up for her convictions. She enjoyed recalling that she had paraded with a 'Votes for Women' banner at the age of six.

Most of all, looking back, Frances acknowledged the importance of her mother's passion for music, which was to be one of her own greatest pleasures. They were a musical family; Mam played the piano, Eleanor the cello, and Tom and Frances the violin, so that Mam's dream of a family string quartet occasionally came true. They sang together, too; Frances remembered 'slightly comic' times when she and Tom sang 'Là ci darem la mano' from Mozart's *Don Giovanni* in the drawing room after tea. Eleanor had a good enough voice to consider becoming a professional singer, and Frances always thought Tom could have chosen a career in music. From the age of nine or ten, she would accompany Mam to the excellent concerts held in Haslemere; she remembered being greatly impressed by the beautiful d'Aranyi sisters, who played the Bach Double Violin Concerto together, and above all by the cellist Pablo Casals, whom she loved for his 'bold attack, marvellous phrasing and even his gentle snoring'. She would imitate the sound he made with glee. 'Musical masterpieces that have eaten their way into the soul at a tender age bite very deep.'

In 1914, Julia was moved from Brackenhurst to the most celebrated of progressive boarding schools: Bedales, at Steep outside Petersfield, a few miles from Tweenways. Frances missed her friend badly; 'I pined for her; I mooned about; my mother laughed at me and tried to rally my spirits.' She begged to be allowed to go to Bedales herself, and although her parents had never thought boarding school a good idea for girls, they went to see the school and eventually decided to let their youngest daughter have her way.

Mam's memoir, which peters out during the war, shows very clearly how the Marshall family, like most of the nation, remained happily oblivious of the coming convulsion until virtually the last moment of peace. Frances' childhood was coming to an end just as Western Europe slid into carnage and destruction. But 1914, for the Marshalls, opened cheerfully enough. Tweenways was full of young people, and they arranged a series of parties and dances. By this time Horace, now twenty-five, had left Cambridge and joined an engineering firm based in Newcastle and was engaged to the daughter of some Hindhead neighbours; Julia Strachey was staying, as was Ray's ebullient Russian friend and some young Lloyd cousins, the children of Mam's soldier brother Charlie. There were three separate dances: one for the adults, one for the young people and one for the servants, which was attended by forty-seven guests.

As the last summer of peace approached, Mam was more preoccupied than ever with family matters. Will's health had been causing concern; now in his mid-sixties, he was showing signs of arterial disease. In May the Marshalls, accompanied by their friend Jane Harrison and Horace's fiancée Rachel, went over to Paris to consult a heart specialist who treated his patients with currents of electricity. While Will was submitting to this, Mam bought a smart dress and an umbrella for Rachel; she also, through mutual Hindhead friends, went to have tea with Gertrude Stein, whom she found to be 'large and handsome and brown and cheerful'. That June, Horace and Rachel were married in Grayshott Church, with a reception held nearby. The two families were photographed together, looking oddly serious; Frances, in a white lace frock and a hat, is staring at her feet. Soon afterwards Mam organised a happy, busy musical weekend, with tea for some ninety-five people on the terrace overlooking the garden, followed by a concert in the big room with the *As You Like It* relief over the fireplace. Mam had a beautiful new Steinway grand piano, chosen for her by a musician friend, the pianist Louis Edgar. He, Tom and two of Tom's Cambridge friends, Howard and Kennard Bliss (younger brothers of Arthur) played Bach, Beethoven, Brahms, Schumann and Chopin. The house was full, and in between the concerts there were charades and tennis parties. 'I think of those few days of gaiety and enjoyment', wrote Mam, looking back twenty years on, 'as the last of the carefree gatherings of the old life that was soon to be a thing of the past. I remember vividly the impression made by that striking group of gifted young men.' All of them were old enough to go to war.

And then, on 21 July 1914, Mam saw Tom off on a train to Germany without a qualm. The most academic as well as the most musical of the family, he had obtained a First in Part 1 of his History Tripos at Cambridge and was destined for the Foreign Office. He had spent part of the previous summer in Tours to improve his French; now, he went off to study German in Dresden.

By 27 July the rumours of war were so loud that Willie and Mam realised that Dresden was not the right place for Tom to be. For several days they sent telegrams and pulled strings. Frances and Eleanor, meanwhile, went off to Sussex to spend the first part of the summer holidays with Uncle Charlie and their Lloyd cousins.

War was declared between England and Germany on 4 August; in the middle of that night a telegram arrived saying that Tom could not leave because the German army had mobilised. All the Marshalls knew was that Tom was in the hands of the German authorities. At Tweenways, 'exhausted physically and mentally', Mam waited for news. It was not until almost the end of the month that news came via Switzerland that Tom was safe. Interned with other civilian prisoners, he spent the next four years of war in a camp at Ruhleben, near Berlin, where he was able to send letters and postcards and receive parcels. It cannot have been long before Mam and Will realised how lucky they were. Horace, as an engineer, was in a reserved occupation. Not many families with two sons of an age to be called up got off so lightly. The impact of that terrible war was felt less intimately by the Marshall family than by many others, but for all of them, and perhaps especially for their youngest daughter, the years of safety and confidence were gone for ever.

Two

Bedales and Cambridge, 1915–1921

When Frances remembered the beginning of the First World War, what first came to her mind was a sense of embarrassment, even of shame, at the recollection of how she had been stirred, at the age of fourteen, by patriotic songs like 'Land of Hope and Glory' and the waving of flags. She found the memory valuable, as it taught her how easy it is to be moved by mass emotion. By the time she came to write about that war some sixty years later, her long-established pacifist views coloured her recollections; but she did not pretend that at the age of fourteen she understood what pacifism was. She could not recall arguments at home about pacifism, which suggests that it was not discussed, let alone supported, although one of her first cousins, Will Marshall's energetic suffragist niece Catherine, took up the anti-war cause. Catherine Marshall was in fact a leading light in the pacifist movement, and helped to found the British section of the Women's International League for Peace and Freedom, which has been described as 'the most solid achievement of the feminist pacifists to emerge from the war'. She ran the No Conscription Fellowship office in London, and worked closely with Bertrand Russell, one of the most distinguished and prominent of the peace campaigners; but she was never part of Frances' life, then or later.

When the war began Frances was with her young Lloyd cousins, Winnie and Maurice, who were twins, at the aptly named Battle Farm, near Hastings. She recalled walking with Winnie across the Sussex fields under evening skies ominously tinged with red; Uncle Charlie had been a regular soldier, and he and his wife were 'staunchly patriotic' and sure that the war would soon be won. Frances had rather a crush on Maurice, who was not much older than she was and a naval cadet, and was taken aback when he was immediately recalled to his ship; she was also, she wrote, 'almost shocked – probably quite unfairly' by the apparent eagerness with which her aunt sent her only son to war. Maurice was to be killed at Zeebrugge in 1918.

Back at Tweenways, Frances found her mother frantic with anxiety over Tom, until the news of his internment set her mind at rest. From then on her two brothers were safe, but all around the Marshall circle other young men, relations and friends, were going off to war. Her sister Judy's husband Dick Rendel, so much admired by Frances, was soon with the British Expeditionary Force in France; their daughter Jill, the first Marshall grand-child, was just over a year old and Judy was pregnant with her second baby. Judy and her children were to spend much of the war at Tweenways, so Frances would have seen the anguish of a young woman with a husband in the front line. But despite the fact that the Marshalls' world overlapped with Bloomsbury, which was overwhelmingly pacifist during the First World War, Frances' immediate family was not that way inclined.

Before long, the Marshalls were doing what they could to help. First there were the Belgian refugees; Tweenways took in a number of them, including a charming Captain and his wife who stayed for some time; they also took on a refugee as a kitchenmaid. The initial wave of sympathy for the brave Belgians, fed by lurid atrocity stories, gave way before long to irritation; Mam describes one character who 'grumbled about the food, tried to make love to his hosts' housekeeper and went round the place looking for a house he would like to live in and boldly asking for it'.

By October 1914 Tweenways was entertaining 'soldier parties' from the camps set up among the gorse and pines nearby. All through the war waves of grateful officers and men, Scots, English and later Canadians, would escape the bleak and muddy conditions for a few hours to have tea, a hot bath and a sing-song with the friendly, hospitable Marshalls, who set aside 'a room with a good fire, a piano, books and games and writing materials'. Sometimes the soldiers would arrive with a sackful of socks to be washed and mended; often, after tea Mam would play the piano for them in the big drawing room; the men would sing their favourite songs and the maids as well as the family would join in. Frances never forgot how the giant Cameron Highlanders, kilts swinging, reduced everyone to tears with their renditions of 'My Bonnie Lies Over the Ocean' and 'Will Ye No' Come Back Again'. 'When they left for the front,' she wrote, 'their Pipe Major gave us an earsplitting concert on the bagpipes, marching round and round our long drawing room as a gesture of farewell.' She did not record, as her mother did, how the Belgian kitchenmaid, tears streaming down her face, watched them leave the house and called after them: 'Kill! Kill much Germans!'

Once the soldiers and the Belgian refugees were absorbed into life at Tweenways, Frances was surprised by how little difference the fact that the country was at war seemed to make. But she understood that all was not as it seemed, and she clearly remembered the underlying sense of strain. 'We carried on our normal existence among cross-currents of violently repressed emotion, but there was an almost complete failure to communicate between the young men returning on "weekend leave" from the unspeakable horror of the trenches, and those who remained undislodged from their comfortable peacetime furrows'. Many years later, Dick Rendel told her how he had been 'physically incapable' of telling his pregnant wife anything at all about what he was going through when he came home on leave; and she never forgot 'the expression on the face of this returning ghost let out briefly from hell' when a neighbour, getting up from the bridge table, said to him cheerfully that she supposed he must be longing to get back to the front. It was, wrote Frances, 'an expression of agony, hastily twisting itself into a mask representing the reaction she expected'.

So everyone at Tweenways kept the flags flying, and put on a brave face; but perhaps, in fact, Mam understood more than Frances realised. The war years, she wrote towards the end of her memoir, 'are merged in a sense of overwhelming horror, which never lifted. What was happening "out there" and in that German prison camp overshadowed everything. Even the weather was only important because of what it meant to those "out there". At first one said "It cannot last" – and then later on "Will it ever end?"'

Meanwhile, Frances was getting used to her new school. Bedales, where she arrived in the autumn of 1915, was founded in 1893 and had been established outside the small village of Steep since 1900, the year she was born. John Haden Badley, the founder and headmaster, known as the Chief (or, according to Frances, as the Chump) was himself the product of an entirely conventional education, at Rugby and Cambridge; but, influenced by Ruskin, the Arts and Crafts movement and others with the urge to build high-minded communities, Badley turned against the public-school ethos and decided to set up a different kind of school. It would be co-educational, there was to be no compulsory chapel, and no corporal punishment. The emphasis was to be on simplicity, austerity and the outdoor life. 'Jaws' on Sundays replaced Chapel. Badley and his wife had a touching belief in 'wholesomeness, cleanliness, naturalness' and the innate innocence of adolescent boys and girls, who could, if properly handled, surely live together without the 'silliness' of sexual feelings. All these progressive notions appealed to the clever, progressive families of the early-twentieth-century intellectual aristocracy, the Darwins, Huxleys and Wedgwoods, the Stracheys and the Trevelyans. Old Bloomsbury had strong Bedales connections: Roger Fry sent his children there.

As it happened, the Marshalls and the Badleys already had a certain amount in common. He was married to a niece of Mam's suffragist friend,

Millicent Fawcett; Mrs Badley herself was Secretary of the Petersfield Suffragists and so a natural ally of Mam's. Both families had a passion for the Lake District. But although the Marshalls were evidently not put off by the unconventional aspects of Bedales, they did not decide to send their youngest daughter there for ideological reasons. Nor did Frances ever imply that it was a desire for a better or different kind of education that made her beg to go there. She simply wanted to be with her best friend Julia and, after all, the school was only a few miles down the road from home. Mam, busier than ever running Tweenways in wartime, was no doubt glad to have Frances nearby and safely looked after.

The Bedales Frances joined in 1915 was a cluster of red-brick, gabled, Arts and Crafts buildings set in a still unspoiled Hampshire valley, with a fine hall, an outdoor swimming pool, its own farm and a reputation for sandal-wearing earnestness. The school had grown impressively since 1900; by 1914 it contained 482 boys and 203 girls. For all its experimental side, Bedales provided a serious education for those who wanted to learn; the school had been recognised by the Board of Education since 1911. The collapse of Europe into war was felt as a particular blow, as the school had from the start prided itself on being 'international in outlook and membership', and was tolerant, if not encouraging, towards pacifism. When the war began, Badley 'resisted', according to the school's historians, all requests to allow military training at Bedales. As it happened, several former pupils, and one teacher, were fighting on the German side. When Herr Hinne was killed, Badley wrote solemnly in the school Record that 'although he died fighting in the ranks of our enemies, none will think of him as anything but a true Bedalian'. During Frances' time there, boys leaving the school went straight into the army, reappearing in khaki to say goodbye on their way to the front. It was all dramatic, painful and confusing. Just before Frances arrived, one of Bedales' outstanding old boys, Ferenc Békássy, a Hungarian who had gone on to King's College, Cambridge, to become an Apostle, a poet and a friend of Maynard Keynes and Rupert Brooke, was also killed fighting for the other side. He was twenty-two, and his younger sister Eva was still at Bedales, where the Badleys looked after her until the war was over.

Frances, when she came to write about her Bedales years, never presented her teenage self as preoccupied by the war. At the time, she had more selfish concerns. Having never been away from home for long, she was appalled by the ugliness and discomfort of institutional life: the cold, the primitive lavatories, the nasty food. 'My heart sank. So boarding school was this bleak place of cold baths, unpleasant smells and above all no privacy ... Oh for the warmth, the Morris wallpapers, chocolate cake for tea, and scrupulously suppressed signs of parental love which I nevertheless knew to be there!' She found her dormitory, with its six hard beds and sickly colour scheme, hideous and comfortless. She disliked the school's idiom, the way the boys all called each other 'you great lout' and how any girl who bothered about her appearance was referred to as 'being silly'. Above all, she did not care for the Chief, who always had a favourite among the girls and made a point of overseeing naked (though not mixed) swimming. She did not complain at the time, but she did not forget either. 'An old hypocrite and a far from admirable character,' was her final verdict on him.

But after this unpromising start, Frances soon found that Bedales was not all bad. Although the difference in their ages meant that she did not see as much of Julia as she had hoped, she quickly made another lasting friend, Margaret Leathes, a clever half-Russian girl from a distinguished medical family, and started to enjoy herself. A few letters to her favourite sister Ray from the start of her time at Bedales have survived; they are brisk and cheerful, and while hardly showing signs of writing talent, indicate that Frances, by the age of fifteen, had a positive attitude to life and a capacity for enjoyment. 'I like the people here, most of them, immensely,' she wrote. 'This afternoon, being Saturday, is free except for singing which I like very much, we are doing the Elijah with great brilliance and are going to perform it soon.' She also, she informs her sister, does a lot of dancing, including 'extraordinary country dances', goes to cooking lessons ('rather fun') and learns how to prune apple trees; she has joined the lettering class with Julia, and even been to a lacrosse match; 'we all watched and ate buns and shouted through megaphones'.

While Frances always maintained that she resisted all attempts to make her into a good Bedalian, she was better schoolgirl material than her friend Julia. Frances was never to be attracted to institutions, but she was never a deliberate rebel either; she may not have been impressed by Bedales' rules and rituals, but she knew instinctively how to make the best of the place. She would recall that the teaching was 'patchy', but the fact remained that during her time there she was introduced to two subjects which were to fascinate and entertain her all her life: botany and philosophy. Not caring for chemistry or physics, she chose to study botany instead, along with 'a host of other girls and one rather sheepish, red-faced boy'. They were well taught, and she loved learning about the anatomical structure and reproductive behaviour of plants. As for philosophy, she paid tribute always to one teacher in particular, Mr Heath, 'a clever dwarf with a basso profundo voice and a furious temper when roused'. It was Mr Heath who introduced her to logic, and also to a book which made a lifelong impression on her:

Bertrand Russell's *The Problems of Philosophy*. She was struck by 'the lucid, straightforward style' of the writing, and in particular the thrill of first being made to follow abstract arguments. Apparently she also met Russell around this time, on one of her visits to the Pearsall Smiths at Ford Place. He was, she recalled, 'a slight figure who held himself erect and spoke in clipped tones. His head was large and his forehead sloping. He reminded me forcibly of the Hatter in Alice in Wonderland.' Russell remained one of her heroes. Mr Heath went on to become Professor of Philosophy at Swansea.

She enjoyed these classes, and she also appreciated the freedom Bedales allowed. She and her friends were able to ride their bicycles around the countryside, and to go tobogganing and skating in the winter; they would talk about everything, 'profane and serious', hold debates on serious matters like censorship, and it was even 'the done thing' to walk around with your nose in a book. Before long, of course, the 'great louts' began to take an interest her; Frances was growing up to be a very pretty girl, with her neat figure, glossy dark hair, vitality and ready smile. For all the Badleys' efforts to make flirtation seem silly, there was plenty of scope for romantic friendships between boys and girls, all, in Frances' memory, innocent enough; her own score was one kiss in two years. 'Our tentativeness may now be seen as a waste of time,' she wrote, 'but I don't believe the muffled state of our passions made them less important to us.'

Inevitably, the war loomed over these early attachments, 'like some pitiless guillotine waiting to fall'. The list of names inscribed in gold on the Roll of Honour steadily grew. 'Oh when would it stop? ... selfishly we thought of the war for the most part as a dark, threatening cloud overhanging the otherwise enchanted landscape of youth, and fervently longed for it to be over.' Frances always felt that it was during her time at Bedales that the seeds of her pacifism were sown; but it was not only the horror of the war itself, from which she was still largely protected, that influenced her. She would also recall with disgust seeing two boys battering each other during a boxing match; it was not so much the thick blood as the 'naked, murderous hatred' in their eyes that upset her, and contributed to her growing conviction 'that physical violence was indefensible – and indirectly that war was never justifiable'. She was also impressed by the 'sanity' of the Lansdowne Letter to *The Daily Telegraph* in 1917, which called for a truce to discuss peace terms. 'I was immensely impressed by this brave move – which needless to say was received with howls of outrage, and it certainly influenced me to decide, after a good deal of thought, that I was a pacifist.'

Her friend Julia, meanwhile, found Bedales far less congenial. In fact, at Bedales certain fundamental differences in their natures emerged. Somehow,

Frances kept out of trouble; Julia found herself drawn to it. According to Margaret Leathes, who was also one of Julia's close friends, 'Poor Julia lived in an aura of disapproval from the staff.' Always more interested in her own appearance and her effect on the opposite sex than Frances, Julia frequently demonstrated 'silliness'; she was constantly the victim of 'little talks' on the subject from teachers or older pupils. She was particularly sensitive to cold; Frances remembered her as 'spending most of her time wrapped in coats, rugs and scarves in one of the practising rooms, bouncing up and down over the piano keys as she miraculously poured forth a stream of improvised jazz'. Folk dancing and gardening were not for her; she loved dressing up and acting, and loathed all outdoor activities. But perhaps what divided her most seriously from both Frances and Margaret was that for all her quick wit she disliked lessons and showed little or no inclination to learn, and unlike them she had no interest in going to university. She remained a regular visitor to Tweenways; but Margaret Leathes' parents disapproved of her – perhaps because she kept powder and rouge in her navy blue elasticated knickers.

Meanwhile at Tweenways Mam continued to hold open house for the soldiery, even though Will Marshall's health was not good and they were always anxiously awaiting news from Tom in Ruhleben or Dick Rendel in France. The only one of their children to be directly under threat from the enemy was Ray, who found herself cowering under the glass roof of her art school during a Zeppelin raid on London. In 1916 Eleanor went up to Cambridge, to study Mathematics at Newnham; but after getting a Third in Part 1 in the summer of 1918 she left, her heart set on a musical career, perhaps as a singer. The three Marshall girls must have been a large part of the attraction at Tweenways gatherings, and other social events organised for the men stationed around Hindhead. Frances particularly enjoyed the dances, and realised later that after she had followed the latest fashion and bobbed her thick hair, she probably seemed older and more sophisticated than she really was. 'Our escorts were mainly Canadians, and considerably less backward than the Bedales boys . . . I had quite a success, including a serious suitor who pursued me with appallingly dull letters and suggestions of visits when I went back to school.' Her mother, wary of her daughter's Canadian admirer, intercepted these letters and got rid of him. 'I regret to say that I took an inquisitive but completely detached interest in the business of being courted, while not caring a pin for the Captain himself.'

In the spring of 1918 Frances took the entrance examinations for Newnham, one of the two women's colleges at Cambridge. She had to write an essay and do two three-hour papers on either Maths, Classics or History, two on Modern Languages, and one on Natural Sciences; there was also an interview, and 'references satisfactory to the Principal' were required. None of this presented a problem, and she left Bedales knowing that she would be going up to Cambridge in October 1918.

Not long before she left school, Frances experienced what she later described as 'a moment of truth'. It had nothing to do with religion; she was walking along a nondescript stretch of road near Tweenways when she suddenly realised, 'as if a flash of lightning had penetrated my brain', that her mind and her thoughts were her own, and that 'no-one and nothing could make me think against my own grain, or divert my beliefs from their chosen channel'. This revelation was intensely exciting to her; it remained with her for life.

That summer, she and her sister Eleanor went off together to do their bit for the war effort by working as land girls at Castle Howard in Yorkshire, an experience that left her with a strong distaste for 'the intolerable boredom of land work' and for the arrogant aristocracy. Her grand hostess-cum-employer was Rosalind, Countess of Carlisle, and she was there because two of the Countess's granddaughters were Hindhead neighbours and friends of the Marshalls. They were staying in the palatial Castle Howard, while Eleanor and Frances were installed as lodgers with a farmer's family, where they shared a four-poster bed and were served huge meals in silence. The work was gruelling; they sweated away hoeing turnips and 'singling' mangel-wurzels, their faces covered with flies. But there were compensations; Frances rather enjoyed haymaking, especially riding on the horse rake, and helping with the harvest, gathering and arranging the sheaves of corn. Above all she relished the evenings when they met the Howard girls at the lake, tore off their clothes and plunged into the dark green water. She began, for the first time, to keep a diary, but after the farmer's wife found it hidden on top of her best hat, it was abandoned and lost.

At weekends they would be graciously invited up to the Castle for a bath and dinner, followed by parlour games and charades. There Frances observed how the dumpy, irascible Countess, a fierce teetotaller, terrorised her family and guests, including her son-in-law, the gentle, scholarly Gilbert Murray, then Professor of Classics at Oxford. Frances remembered being impressed by his curiously successful mind-reading demonstrations.

When Frances went up to Cambridge in October 1918, the war was almost over. Cambridge was family territory; her father and both her brothers had been there, as well as her aunt Alice and her sister Eleanor. Moreover, both the women in charge of Peile Hall at Newnham, where Frances spent the next three years, were known to the family. The Principal of the Hall was Pernel Strachey (later the college Principal), recalled by Frances as somewhat remote and resembling 'a shy, faintly amused giraffe', and her deputy was Mam's friend Jane Harrison, whom Frances had known all her life.

To begin with, Frances found the college depressing. It was the first time she had been in an all-female environment, and she was not sure she cared for it; the war years had frozen the place into a bleak formality, so that it was only after asking each other 'May I Prop?' that the girls used each others' Christian names, and friendships out of your own year were discouraged. The other 'freshers' seemed to her to scuttle around like 'dowdy, frightened mice'. But, as with Bedales, it did not take her long to find her feet. Her Cambridge years, she told a younger friend sixty years afterwards, were 'wildly happy'.

She was lucky, she reckoned, to be at Newnham, which was within walking distance of the Cam, the backs and all the most beautiful college buildings, rather than at Girton, which was a forbidding Victorian pile several miles out. She was also lucky to arrive when she did; the university, like the whole country, felt a surge of relief and hope when the war was finally over. According to the college magazine, Newnham held its own Armistice Day celebrations that November, the month after Frances arrived: 'Trees, red buildings, Clough's stiff windows lit up by a leaping bonfire; round it a swirl of dancing figures, cadets, Newnham in thinnest evening frocks, a wild medley made grotesque and beautiful by the blaze that leaped and faded.' The 'Present Students Letter' in the College Roll for 1918 announced 'a great quickening in Newnham. Not only is it full, but it is seething with intense vitality. The sap of youth and energy is running very strong.' Change and renewal were in the air, and young women, especially, were beginning to appreciate the recognition, speeded up by the war, that they were entitled to more freedom. Frances was less politically inclined than her mother, and was not involved, either at Cambridge or later, in campaigns for women's rights; but she was naturally inclined to take advantage of the postwar mood.

Not that change was imminent in Cambridge; in 1918 'duly qualified women' were admitted to the University Parliamentary Franchise and given the vote but, as elsewhere in the country, only at the age of thirty; and in 1919, when Girton and Newnham women's colleges asked whether, 'at a time of general reconstruction', it was not time for them to be recognised at last as full members of the University (Oxford had just done so), their request was turned down. 'We must believe that this check is for a time only,' wrote the Newnham Principal, sadly. Frances always felt that it was hardly fair for women to be denied formal degrees when they had taken the same courses and exams as the men; but she was too busy enjoying herself to feel angry. The *Cambridge Review's* comment indicated the general University view. 'Not that we wish in any way to appear unchivalrous or to minimize the good work often done by women students; but "so long as the sun and moon endureth" Cambridge should remain a society for men.' It was not until 1948 that Cambridge, the last university in England to hold out so long, gave women equal status.

The main event of her first year was the return to Cambridge of young men, many of them, Frances recalled, 'anxious to make up for lost time, and more interested in dancing and taking girls out than in swotting for their degrees. Among those who appeared were some ex-Bedales boys, my brother Tom and a lot of naval officers on a course.' The return of Tom Marshall from four years in the German prison camp was thrilling, but also disconcerting. His experiences had greatly changed him; Frances never forgot meeting him at the railway station, and realising that her favourite brother was no longer a high-spirited boy but a serious, rather withdrawn young man. He seemed afraid of emotion; this she regarded as not just the characteristic Marshall fear of showing feelings but something deeper. 'He was very shaken by his time in Germany ... when he came back he was embarrassed, a different person in a way. He had been debonair, flighty, cheerful; he came back rather grave and shy.' Tom himself always felt that it was the reading and thinking he did to survive the boredom and passivity of camp life that led him to take life seriously and to turn away from comfortable middle-class values and expectations. But for all his new ser-iousness, it was agreeable for Frances to have a brother at Trinity. She was allowed to visit him in college, and a number of his friends soon became hers.

Soon Frances found a friend of her own at Newnham. Julia Strachey by this time was living with the Pearsall Smiths in London, studying Com-mercial Art at the Slade; inevitably they saw much less of each other. During her time at Cambridge Frances' best friend was a lively, funny Scottish girl with fair hair and pink cheeks called Dot Mackay, also reading English, with whom she discussed free will and free love and whether it was right to inherit wealth (Frances had just had £2,000 – the equivalent of about £150,000 today – settled on her by her father and was supposed now to manage her own finances, which she was not finding easy). She did not take her work very seriously during her first two years, although she never forgot the impression of original thinking conveyed by the critic and literary scholar I.A. Richards, who encouraged and inspired her. The musical life of Cambridge attracted her; she joined the Newnham Musical Society, the Bach choir and Boris Ord's madrigal singers; she had a good voice, and was occasionally prevailed upon to sing solo, although she was 'petrified with terror'. She preferred play-readings, where she met brilliant young men like the future Nobel Prize winner Patrick Blackett and the future English don and Shakespearean expert George Rylands, nicknamed Dadie, a handsome fair-haired charmer who became a friend for life. Frances was full of physical energy, and played lacrosse, tennis and went swimming, boating or walking whenever she could. She also discovered at Cambridge how much she loved dancing, and that she had a real talent for it.

In the wake of the war, as Frances observed, 'all England had gone dancing mad and so had Cambridge'. As one of her fellow undergraduates wrote with some astonishment, in the autumn of 1918 something hitherto unheard of occurred: 'For the first time on record Newnham is giving a Dance, a real dance in that men are being invited ... this dance is important. It shows that Newnham is beginning to shake off prejudice and nervous convention and broaden its mind at last.' Frances and her friend Dot were founder members of the Quinquaginta, a new club which organised weekly dances to an undergraduate jazz band, where the prettiest girls – another regular, was the beautiful Rosamond Lehmann, who arrived at Girton in 1920 – and the most socially desirable young men would meet and dance together in a cheerful frenzy. Frances could recall seeing both the Prince of Wales and his brother Prince Albert there, and the Princes' friend Dickie Mountbatten was one of her most frequent partners. Frances and Dot were among the star performers; their programmes were filled up a week ahead, and Frances, not boastful by nature, looked back with pleasure on her dancing prowess at Cambridge to the end of her life.

Of course these dancing marathons led to flirtations, but Frances was always quite clear that romance was not really the point. Nor was conversation; 'all we cared about in our partners was their technical ability – they had to be first-rate performers – and such young men were often great bores to talk to'. Eventually she and Dot paired off with two 'totally a-sexual dance partners' who took them to May Balls when May Week, suspended during the war, resumed in 1920. Frances was surprised when her partner, with whom she could only recall the most superficial conversation, later became Lord Chief Justice Parker of Waddington.

In fact, though Frances had plenty of dancing partners and admirers at Cambridge, some of whom made 'amorous advances' to her, she did not take any of them seriously. She enjoyed male company, and admiration, and she found Newnham's rules about chaperones absurd; she solved the problem by inventing a suitable married woman, 'Mrs Kenyon', to chaperone her, as women undergraduates were not supposed to entertain a man in their room without one. She always felt that the Principal, Pernel Strachey, knew perfectly well what was going on when she asked Frances one day to tell her all about Mrs Kenyon. Slowly, the chaperones faded out; although women were still forbidden to visit any man except a brother in his college, by May 1919 they were permitted to meet a man in a teashop, and in 1920 to go punting on the river in mixed groups.

Despite her own disinclination to allow a man to do more than kiss her, which she felt was typical of her generation of Cambridge women ('there was a lot of kissing, but absolutely no affairs'), Frances did leave Cambridge with at least one serious suitor. This was a very tall man called Geoffrey Sieveking, nicknamed the Mast. She felt, looking back, that she knew all along that she did not really want to marry him, but he pursued her for some time. She was also greatly admired by another man, Raisley Moorsom, who was nine years older than she was and had been at King's before going into the army. Educated, like her, at Bedales, he was the more intellectual of the two, and a friend of an older King's generation: E.M. Forster, Maynard Keynes and Francis Birrell.

In the summer of 1920, after getting a respectable Second in the first part of her degree (despite leaving one examination early in order to watch a tennis match), Frances realised that the thought of another year reading English bored her; she particularly disliked the idea of *Beowulf* and Anglo-Saxon. She decided instead that what really interested her was philosophy, and so changed to Moral Sciences, determined to accomplish the two-year course in one. For all her self-proclaimed frivolity and passion for dancing, she was intellectually curious and not afraid of hard work, and the year she spent reading Moral Sciences shaped her mind for life. She found she had a natural aptitude for philosophical debate, and that she greatly enjoyed abstract argument. She always recalled with great clarity and humour both the ideas and the personalities she encountered; they were her intellectual benchmarks.

In 1920, the Moral Science tripos consisted of four subjects: Philosophy, Psychology, Logic and Ethics. Her knowledge of philosophy and logic was confined to what she had learned at school and her reading of Russell's *Problems of Philosophy*; now she plunged eagerly into deeper waters. The great philosophical guru of an earlier generation of undergraduates, G.E. Moore, whose *Principia Ethica*, published in 1903, had been such a crucial and formative influence on Maynard Keynes, Lytton Strachey and their circle, was still very much a presence in Cambridge although he no longer taught there; he did, however, sometimes attend the Moral Sciences Club, where Frances once observed him. The club met of an evening in one of the men's colleges, where 'undergraduates and their betters argued in blue clouds of pipe smoke'. Moore was no longer the slender, handsome man whose appearance and charm, as well as his liberating theories concerning the ethical primacy of 'the pleasures of human intercourse and the enjoyment of beautiful objects', had so overwhelmed his admirers. He had become 'a middle-aged, middle-sized, greyish man, who sat on the hearthrug holding his ankles in both hands and tying himself in knots, while he endeavoured to explain "what one *exactly* meant when one said one was going to Madingley that afternoon".' She was amused at the way he and the other great men of philosophy made such minor matters appear significant; but she found she too had a taste for such 'profitable mole-like tunnelling in all directions'. On the same occasion she noticed 'a tall, cadaverous man with a noble forehead, goggle glasses and an inconspicuous nose' who was not afraid to argue with Moore; this was Harry Norton, a brilliant, if neurotic, mathematician and close friend of Lytton Strachey and his younger brother James.

It was still obligatory to read *Principia Ethica*, and Frances duly did so, but found herself underwhelmed. 'J.S. Mill and Bentham were among my heroes,' she recalled, 'and I didn't find his attempt to demolish their theories convincing.' J.M.E. McTaggart had been another target of Moore's, but Frances, who attended his lectures on Hegel, considered him 'an outstanding thinker', if hard to follow. She found him personally both kindly and engaging and was amused by the way he reminded her of a barrage balloon as he floated into the lecture room, his big round head always tilted to one side. But her favourite among the philosophy dons was undoubtedly W.E. Johnson, known as Willy, the chief lecturer in Logic. A brilliant thinker, said to have greatly influenced Maynard Keynes, he was, she wrote, 'a very shy but affectionate man and a born teacher'. He made a point of asking all his students to tea, but seems to have been particularly taken with Frances. He loved music, especially Mozart; when he realised Frances' musical bent, he asked her to musical evenings and even prevailed upon her to sing to his accompaniment. 'In my mental picture of Willy Johnson he is enthusiastically performing a Mozart piano sonata, his white head bending forward and peering at the music. Then, suddenly, leaning back, he raises his right hand high in the air and brings the little finger down with a triumphant ping on the highest note. I am turning over for him, and wondering which are the yellower – the piano keys or his false teeth, and his tall gaunt sister Fanny stands listening with a plate of cucumber sandwiches in her hand.' He took her work seriously, offered her extra tutorials and tried to help her sort out her thoughts on free will and determinism, with which she was much preoccupied at the time. She was drawn towards belief in causality, but at the same time felt sure that she was free to think whatever she wanted. He tried to convince her that freedom in fact depended on determinism – that an individual's choices were both free and also 'the product of a long causal chain forged from heredity and environment'. She continued to ponder the matter all her life, but she remained sure of one thing: 'I really loved Willy Johnson'.

Among her fellow Moral Sciences students was a man who, like Dadie Rylands, was to become part of her life, though at the time she only observed him with interest. This was Sebastian Sprott, an undergraduate at King's and a special favourite of Keynes. Frances noticed his elegant appearance, cameo ring and swirling cloak; she was also, despite her earlier exposure to it among her mother's friends, greatly struck by his voice, which reminded her 'of all the Stracheys I had ever known' with its ascent from low and soft to 'a faint scream' and habit of emphasising words like 'sublime'. In fact, she later realised, she encountered in Sprott, 'without being able to diagnose them, some symptoms with which I was later to become very familiar ... the disease he was suffering from was, of course, incipient Bloomsbury'. During her Cambridge years, Frances, directly or indirectly, was in touch with many of the people who were to affect her life the most. The world of the Apostles, the homoerotic atmosphere still surrounding Keynes at King's, the influence of Lytton Strachey, her Principal's brother, who would some-times take tea at Newnham, all became part of her landscape.

Another of the Moral Sciences group was a girl whom Frances had known at Bedales, Lettice Baker. They had not really taken to each other there – Frances found her a bit hearty – but working together brought them closer, and when in due course Lettice married one of the cleverest of the younger Cambridge philosophers, Frank Ramsey, Frances made great friends with him too. It was to be through Frank that she got to know Wittgenstein. Thus she encountered several of the leading philosophers of the twentieth century, and their ideas, as well as their personalities, remained with her.

When Frances was in her last year at Cambridge, her father, whose health had been deteriorating for some time, died at the age of seventy-three. She always maintained that his death was neither unexpected nor especially upsetting; even so, it seems extraordinary that she did not, apparently, attend his funeral. His slow decline after a series of strokes had overshadowed life at Tweenways, where Mam looked after him with relays of nurses.

During his last year or two, his daughter Ray, who was beginning to make a name for herself as an artist and illustrator, brought to the house the young man she was to marry, David Garnett, nicknamed Bunny, who later described his visits to Tweenways in unflattering terms. He found the household gloomy and subdued, and ascribed the atmosphere not just to Will Marshall's illness but to the Marshall family's tendency 'to what they very rightly called "mouldiness"' – their word for melancholy and low spirits. He was always relieved when Dick Rendel was there; his humour and high spirits lightened the atmosphere. 'They were not an effusive family,' he wrote, 'and I was grateful to Dick Rendel who woke them up.' He had not yet met Frances, and Ray, the Marshall he had fallen in love with, was unusually quiet and shy; he described her himself as 'the most silent woman I have ever known'. Bunny himself was as fair-haired and blue-eyed as she was dark, and although he too could be shy, had no inclination whatever to 'mouldiness'.

Frances took her Finals that summer, and emerged with a very creditable 2:1. Her Cambridge years ended with a delicious flurry of May Balls and a proposal of marriage from Geoffrey Sieveking, which she half accepted, against her better judgement. By the 1920s girls had begun to realise that life held many possibilities. She was more concerned with finding a job than with marriage; life in London beckoned. Her mother – for whom, Frances later thought, Will's death was something of a liberation – had already decided to sell Tweenways and move back to Bloomsbury, where she intended to find a house big enough to accommodate Eleanor and Frances. Meanwhile, David Garnett and Ray were living in rooms above the bookshop he had set up with his friend Francis Birrell in Taviton Street, round the corner from Gordon Square. When Frances started job-hunting, she needed somewhere to stay; as Bunny later recalled, 'our first meeting was in 19 Taviton Street. You had arrived from Cambridge and I found you a bed for the night. You were the most lovely creature I had ever seen.' Frances in due course described her brother-in-law more calmly. 'He was then a well-built, fair-haired man of about thirty and I liked him immediately.' He let her use his room; she was surprised, but agreeably so, by its lack of furniture. Apart from a bed and a wooden chest, all it contained was 'an early Duncan Grant of a nude sponging herself in the bath, and one nail hammered into the wall from which a large bunch of ties was suspended. I felt I was glimpsing a new, strange world.'

Although she did not have a clear idea about what she wanted to do, Frances was not at first aiming for the literary world; she was interested in the comparatively new field of applied psychology, but when she suggested this to her mother's friend, the 'arch feminist' Pippa Strachey, who had started an employment bureau for women, she found her discouraging. She sought out an expert in the field, Cyril Burt, who could only offer her unpaid research giving intelligence tests to nine-year-olds, which she rather enjoyed; he then found her a paid job testing Lyons Corner House waitresses to discover why they broke so much china. At this point, in the late autumn of 1921, another job came up which she accepted with alacrity. Through David Garnett she became 'accountant, delivery girl and dogsbody' at Birrell and Garnett's bookshop.

Three

The Bookshop and Bloomsbury, 1922–1923

When Frances arrived at Birrell and Garnett, the 'New, Foreign, Antiquarian and Second-hand Booksellers' occupied the ground floor at 19 Taviton Street, a short walk from her mother's new establishment at 27 Brunswick Square. The upper floors were divided into lodgings; the shop had only been in existence for a couple of years, but already it had an unusual clientele and a reputation for amiable eccentricity. The two founders were great friends; both pacifists, they had first thought of starting a bookshop together during the long, grim months they spent with a Quaker relief mission during the war, rebuilding villages in northern France. For Frances, Birrell and Garnett was to be the stage where the cast of characters who shaped her future made their appearance while, at first, she quietly played her subordinate role, observing them all perform.

When she started to work for him, she still hardly knew David Garnett, as during his courtship of her sister Ray she was still at Cambridge; she could not have had any idea how intimately he was involved with Old Bloomsbury. Bunny, as he was usually known to his friends and relations, was the only child of parents for whom the term 'low living and high thinking' could have been invented. Edward Garnett was the most respected publisher's reader and editor in London. Bunny's mother, Constance, was a small, shortsighted woman some years older than her husband, a gifted translator who had done more than anyone to introduce the great Russian writers of the nineteenth century to the British public. She translated Chekhov, Turgenev and Dostoevsky; she met Tolstoy in Russia and the young Lenin in London. The Garnetts built themselves a wood-and-stone Arts and Crafts house, The Cearne, in the woods near Edenbridge in Kent, where they lived in rustic discomfort. Bunny, who acquired his nickname because as a small child he used to wear a rabbit-skin cap, grew up familiar with Russian exiles and his parents' writer friends: Conrad, Galsworthy and D.H. Lawrence.

A solitary boy, he roamed the woods around the Cearne and developed a passion for natural history. Sometimes he would sleep outdoors for fun;

he was taught at home until he was thirteen, when after a long trip to Russia with his parents he was sent to University College School, where, not surprisingly, he failed to fit in. His early interests were more scientific than literary, and at eighteen he went on to Imperial College to study botany. Although he was based at his parents' Hampstead flat, he soon branched out into a life of his own.

Bunny was strong and well-built, with a steady blue gaze and a slow, thoughtful way of talking. He had a full, sensual mouth; his nature was affectionate and strongly sexual. As a young man he was attractive to, and attracted by, both sexes. He had not been brought up with conventional moral attitudes; he could never recall his parents sharing a bedroom, and his mother accepted his father's love affairs. Before long, he had drifted into the fringes of Bloomsbury's younger set, where Francis Birrell, who had been a favourite of Keynes at King's, became his first homosexual friend. Soon, Bunny was meeting Lytton Strachey, Clive and Vanessa Bell, as well as the painter Mark Gertler and the artistic girl he loved, Dora Carrington. He also took up with Virginia Woolf's younger brother, Adrian Stephen, who gave regular parties in Gordon Square where Young Bloomsbury would flirt and play poker.

At one of these gatherings, in late 1913 or early 1914, Bunny met Duncan Grant, the handsome young painter who had already been the lover of Lytton Strachey and then of Maynard Keynes. Before long Duncan was deeply in love with him, and within a few months they were having an affair which lasted, despite Bunny's flings with women and Duncan's furious jealousy, until around the middle of 1919.

Soon after the war began Bunny decided he was a pacifist, like Duncan, Francis Birrell and most of his new circle. After his stint with the Quakers in France, he returned to England where he and Duncan avoided conscription by working on the land, ending up at Charleston in Sussex, the farmhouse under the downs near Lewes found as a refuge from the war by Vanessa Bell in 1916. She lived there with her two sons, Julian and Quentin, while, by mutual consent, their father Clive led his own life in London. Vanessa had herself been in love with Duncan Grant for some years, and they slept together occasionally; but she knew he preferred men, and she and Bunny soon formed their own mildly amorous friendship. In December 1918 Angelica, her daughter by Duncan Grant, was born; Bunny admired the baby in her cradle, speculated about marrying her when she grew up and probably saved her life by sending for a doctor when she fell ill. Clive Bell accepted her as his daughter.

When Frances joined the bookshop in 1921, her job at first temporary,

Bunny had only been married to her sister Ray for a few months. They had met after Bunny took a room in the communal household at Taviton Street where Ray was also a lodger; she was working as an assistant on the *Burlington Magazine*. The romance surprised his friends, who found Rachel Marshall odd-looking and uncommunicative; but he saw in her a true original, with a gentle charm all her own. She was round-faced, with dark eyes and even darker hair, which she wore bobbed with a fringe. Her natural expression was melancholy, but her long silences were punctuated with outbursts of laughter and high spirits, known to her family as 'Ray going mad again'. To many people, and especially to Bunny, she was like 'a woodland creature', shy, easily wounded but with the capacity for great love and loyalty. They had their travels to Russia in common, and also a passion for the countryside. How much she, and her family, knew about Bunny's confused love life before they married is impossible to tell. There is no evidence that any of the Marshalls disapproved of him, although Bunny later wrote, without being specific, 'Nobody was at all enthusiastic about our marriage'.

Mam, at any rate, was determined to make the best of it. After reminding Mrs Garnett of various previous connections between the two families – Mam had been taught mathematics as a girl by Constance's brother – she went on: 'I have seen your son several times. And he has met all my family, and we all feel his charm and attraction, and believe that he and Rachel really suit each other ... about her feelings for him there can be no doubt – she is genuinely in love, I believe for the first time in her life.' Mam's main concern was financial; had her husband been alive, she wrote, he would have 'made careful enquiries into future income'. Tweenways had not yet been sold when she wrote (on 17 March 1921) but eventually, she reckoned, Ray would have some £300 a year of her own (£14,000 today). Evidently, she was hoping that the Garnetts would also help the young couple. 'I shall be so glad to hear from you – David has been warmly welcomed into this family, and I hope you feel that you can welcome Rachel.' Some months after the register office wedding, which was not attended by any Marshalls or Garnetts, Bunny and Ray went to live in Brunswick Square with Mam, Eleanor and Frances. They had one of the large rooms on the ground floor and a bedroom upstairs.

To some of Old Bloomsbury Bunny's marriage represented defection. The homosexuals were not pleased. Lytton Strachey, writing to his brother James, was savage: Bunny's marriage 'has raised a universal howl of exe-cration – in which my voice has loudly joined. It seems quite maniacal. The female (do you know her?) is hideously ugly and mute as a fish.' It was rumoured, he went on, that Ray would not 'grant the last favour' outside marriage – 'and so he, like an idiot, gave way ... Francis [Birrell] is in despair. Duncan callous. I, personally, am a little put out.'

Duncan Grant, in fact, was angry and upset. He told Bunny that marriage was 'a reality in the eyes of the world of the most odious sort' and hated the idea of the young couple having children. However, urged by Bunny, who wanted them to be friends, he painted Ray's portrait, remarking enigmatically that she sat for him 'like cream cheese on a plate'. He had done many erotically charged paintings and drawings of the golden-haired Bunny; his portrait of Bunny's wife is sombre-toned and more formal, showing a composed, expressionless girl with sad eyes. It is likely, in fact, that Ray was pregnant when they married in March 1921, as during the autumn she had a stillborn child. The baby was born in Brunswick Square; Frances never forgot the horror of this tragedy and Ray's terrible grief. In time, however, the young Garnetts were to have two healthy sons. Bunny was not faithful by nature; it was not long before he made advances to his pretty sister-in-law, but she evaded them with ease and never held it against him. She was always much closer to Bunny and Ray than to any of her other siblings.

Frances soon became fond, too, of her other boss, Francis Birrell, whose father, Augustine Birrell, was a renowned wit and man of letters who had been Secretary of State for Ireland during the war. His son was more frivolously inclined. According to Frances, he became known as Frankie to avoid confusion over their names; 'a substitution which I don't think he liked, but which he took as good humouredly as he did most things'. She found him 'irresistibly loveable'. He was ten years older than she was, a 'short, rather square figure with a large head ... thinning brown curls clustered around a fine brow, schoolboy-style spectacles sat on his short nose, and his wide mouth stretched wider still in an engaging grin, accompanied by a continuous rattle of amusing talk and little explosions of laughter'. He was exceptionally well-read, especially in history and French, and 'loved gossip whether of the present age or of the age of St Simon'. He was not, however, always amiable to new customers, who could suddenly be confronted by 'a small tousled figure suggesting a wire-haired terrier, who would bark sharply "YES! What do you want?" though no rudeness was intended, and the customer would hurry quickly away'.

Bunny and Frankie needed a calm and efficient assistant. As Bunny acknowledged, 'Frankie and I were, of course, totally unsuited to running any kind of business, and in particular a shop where close attention to detail is essential.' Lytton Strachey described the shop as 'a queer business: but somehow it subsists, though how, one hardly knows, considering the extreme dreaminess of the shopmen'. Various friends, notably Keynes, gave them financial advice; in the end they put in £900 capital between them, and paid themselves, and Frances, £3 a week. When the Omega Workshop, Bloomsbury's commercial experiment in art and design, closed in 1919, Roger Fry gave them some useful tables, and the partners' fathers, Augustine Birrell and Edward Garnett, contributed sets of classic works from their own libraries. Frances recalled shelves full of Constance Garnett's Russian translations, publications from Leonard and Virginia Woolf's Hogarth Press, and new French novels – including *À la recherche du temps perdu* by Marcel Proust, which she soon caught up with and read, in French, as each volume appeared. The first volume came out in 1913; the second in 1919, and the remaining six between 1920 and 1927, during her bookshop years. Bloomsbury admired Proust, and Frances reread him, in French and English, to the end of her days. The shop also had a profitable line in first editions of Henry James, and E.M. Forster brought them good business by putting them in touch with one of his grand Indian friends who ordered quantities of books to be sent out to Hyderabad in tin boxes.

Frances' duties were varied. She found herself keeping the accounts, compiling catalogues, writing letters, doing up parcels and running errands to publishers – taking it in turns with Frankie 'to go by bus or tube to collect books ... or deliver them to London addresses'. In 1922 the shop moved to new premises in Gerrard Street in Soho, and a small boy called Reggie was employed to carry books around town by tricycle, with Birrell and Garnett painted on the red box behind the saddle. 'Six Seducers!' he would shout cheerfully at the trade counter when picking up copies of *Seducers in Ecuador* by Vita Sackville-West.

Frances enjoyed her work, and Frankie, though punctilious about correspondence and correct forms of address, was not a hard taskmaster. A lot of time was spent reading the new books, placing bets on horses, and playing a game which involved awarding each other marks for qualities like elegance and originality. At the end of a hard day they would sink into some nearby pub and drink whisky, for which Frances developed quite a taste. Mam was unnerved when Frankie gave her daughter a bottle of whisky for Christmas, and warned that one of her aunts had taken to drink. Frances did not pay much attention; she went on liking whisky, but she was never to be a serious drinker.

Later in 1922, Bunny Garnett gave up working at the bookshop to concentrate on writing. That year he published his first book, *Lady into Fox*, the strange and haunting tale of a woman who turns into a vixen, inspired and delightfully illustrated by Ray and prominently displayed in Birrell and Garnett's window. A surprise success, the novel won the Hawthornden Prize and made his name overnight. But he still visited them regularly, as the shop had become a place for friends to meet and gossip; various new partners and assistants came and went, but as Frances recalled the atmosphere remained the same. The customers consisted almost entirely of 'friends and friends of friends, and were for the most part denizens of Bloomsbury, physically and spiritually . . . They all bought their books from us – the Woolves, the Bells, Duncan Grant, Maynard Keynes, the Desmond MacCarthys, the Adrian Stephens, the Stracheys, Anreps and Saxon Sydney Turner.' Thus she came into easy and regular contact with the people who had been at the heart of Old Bloomsbury for over twenty years. She found them more and more attractive. 'These, I reflected, were the sort of people I would like to know and have friends among, more than any others I had yet come across. I was instantly captivated and thrilled by them. It was as if a lot of doors had suddenly opened out of a stuffy room which I had been sitting in far too long.'

It may seem odd, given that Frances' life so far had not been particularly stuffy, that she should find her first independent contact with them all so exciting. But she was ready, at twenty-one, to branch out and find her own way. In many ways, she and Bloomsbury were a natural fit. Her background and education commended her to them; she was not an outsider – and they could be chilly to outsiders. As a tribe they were not strange to her; at the same time they were different enough to be exciting. What she liked best about them, she always said, was their passion for talk and ideas and their preference for unconventional thinking and behaviour. Their outspokenness about their views and emotions was a revelation to her and made her family seem buttoned-up, even philistine by comparison. 'In my home circle even the more civilised had shied away from words like "good" and "beautiful" and would veil their appreciation of works of art in phrases such as "That's rather a jolly bit" or "Isn't this amusing?"' Her new acquaintances were not afraid of enthusiasm, or criticism, and always said what they thought; 'they didn't keep afloat in a social atmosphere by the wing-flapping of small talk. If they were bored by the conversation they showed it.' It took time for Frances to become absorbed into this new world – perhaps more time, and with more hesitation along the way, than she later remembered. But by 1922 she had met, through the bookshop, two people in particular who were to change her life.

Dora Carrington, the painter, and her husband, Ralph Partridge, then working for Leonard and Virginia Woolf at the Hogarth Press, were neither a conventional nor a faithful couple. They shared a house with Lytton

Strachey, to whom they were both devoted, at Tidmarsh Mill outside Pangbourne in Berkshire, but were frequently in London; Ralph visited the shop regularly on Hogarth Press business, and Carrington, who had known Bunny since 1915, also had dealings with them over books and used them occasionally to sell her glass and silver paper pictures. She and Frances were in touch in November 1921 over a missing parcel sent out to the Partridges' great friend Gerald Brenan in Spain; by mid-1922, when Carrington wrote to congratulate Bunny on *Lady into Fox*, she was sending greetings to 'that beautiful sister-in-law'. Ralph Partridge, meanwhile, had not failed to notice the bookshop's attractive new assistant; and she had noticed him. Indeed, she realised that she had seen him before, in a rather different context, during the summer of 1920, when she had been invited to Henley and watched Ralph row in the Christ Church boat that won the Ladies Cup. He had joined her group for strawberries and cream; she did not speak to him, but admired from afar his ebullience and strong rowing man's physique.

By the early 1920s, Frances was living in two worlds at once: the safe, familiar world of her family and Cambridge friends, and her new and more risky world at work in bohemian literary London. She was attracted to the free-thinking, free-living circle that frequented the bookshop, but her ties to the more traditional standards of her upbringing remained strong – not least because of her devotion to her wise, and notably unstuffy, mother, who never seems to have tried to control her children or criticise their way of life.

For most of her life, Frances kept two kinds of diary. There was a small engagement book, containing events, appointments and arrangements, and then, from her late twenties onwards, there was her diary proper, in which she wrote freely and at length about her thoughts and emotions as well as her doings. Her engagement book for 1922 shows Frances still much involved with her family; Mam had succeeded in making 27 Brunswick Square home for her two unmarried daughters and her son Tom, although by 1921 he was a lecturer at Trinity College, Cambridge, and contemplating a political career. She left them all free to come and go, and to decorate their bed-sitting rooms – Frances painted hers bright green and hung Russian magazine illustrations given to her by Ray on the walls. At Brunswick Square she was able to be both independent and protected; Nan, for whom Frances always remained the favourite, youngest charge, had moved back to London with them to help run the household, along with a cook and three maids. Mam had brought her grand piano from Tweenways, and there were soon regular musical evenings again, when Eleanor (whose attempt at a professional career as a singer was foundering because of acute stage fright), Tom and Frances would perform; 'people to tea and music' appears in the engagement book several times. The Marshalls also held play-readings and organised tennis and swimming parties; Frances went to concerts, the ballet and the opera (Chaliapin, like Casals, was a hero; in her nineties she would chant 'Chaliapeeeeeen' with shining eyes). The postwar craze for jazz and dancing was at its height; Frances would demonstrate her skilful Charleston at popular dance halls like the Palais de Danse or the Criterion where, as in Cambridge, she was never short of a partner.

She was still, in fact, juggling her two most persistent Cambridge suitors, Geoffrey Sieveking and Raisley Moorsom; sometimes she saw them on the same day, one for lunch and one for dinner. Geoffrey was pressing her to get married; in a letter to her mother she protests about Mam's anxiety about her health ('I'm very fit really – why did you think I looked ill? I've really felt better since we've been in London than I have for some time') and her love life. 'Don't worry about Geoffrey and me – we haven't had any sort of crisis – and really I don't feel it is a strain, except at times.' This ambiguous response cannot have reassured Mam; and although the romance teetered on the brink of becoming a formal engagement, Frances really knew, as the year wore on, that it would not do. He was too straightforward, somehow, and not at all in tune with the bookshop cast of characters. She felt awkward when he called on her there, and then guilty; as she could not face telling him the truth she simply withdrew into the Marshall shell until eventually Geoffrey left the stage.

As for Raisley Moorsom, she dismissed him too around the middle of the year. He kept a handful of her letters; they convey quite clearly that she was not in love with him. In March 1922 he sent her a ring for her birthday; she wrote to thank him, saying she knew she shouldn't really keep it, but did, adding 'I don't really think I shall like being 22 at all – it's an insipid sort of age.' He made her feel guilty, too. The black border to her Brunswick Square writing paper, presumably dating from her father's death, she described airily as an indication that she was in mourning 'for my state of mind ... ungrateful pig you must think I am'. He offered to buy her a fur coat, and pressed her to marry him, but she kept him at arm's length. 'Don't think I take things for granted. I don't, but am as you know incapable of expressing myself.' In September, after she returned from a walking holiday in the Dolomites with her sister Eleanor and her friend Dot Mackay, they evidently had some kind of showdown. She told him she hoped they could stay friends, and wrote him one or two more letters about the bookshop, and how her job there was to be permanent, and the move to Gerrard

Street – 'I look forward to it with mingled pleasure and annoyance' – and about what she thought of *Lady into Fox* – 'a very queer story and I think rather good'; but although they remained in occasional touch after he went to work for the League of Nations in Geneva, the friendship faded away.

In May, Frances attended the new series of lectures given by Roger Fry, along with all Bloomsbury; in June she was back in Cambridge for the weekend to see Tom, went dancing, and boating on the river. Back in London she had tea with old Lady Strachey, and dinner on the same day with Frankie Birrell. On 2 October the pocket diary notes 'Back to Bookshop'. On 15 November she records the election and also 'Dinner and Dance at the Criterion'. Tom was not elected and decided that politics were not for him. He was to move on from Cambridge to the LSE, where he had an influential career as a pioneer in sociology; he always remained the most left-wing of the Marshalls, though Mam herself, after her husband died, started to vote Labour and Frances would always consider herself left-of-centre.

Two days later, on 17 November 1922, her engagement book records Frances' first Bloomsbury gathering: 'Party, Duncan's studio, 8.30.' In 1921 Duncan Grant had taken on a studio at 8 Fitzroy Street, previously used by Whistler, Augustus John and Sickert, which was to be one of Bloomsbury's social centres for twenty years. Built onto the back of the main house, it was ideal for parties, being forty feet long and as high as it was wide. Frances described it as 'a vast, mysteriously shadowy apartment, reached by a metal staircase and corridor apparently suspended in space, which clanked under our footsteps, and on which one or two amorous couples would be standing enlaced. Inside the studio, Chinese or Spanish pottery, draped stuffs and dusty still lives stood about on tables, leaving a large central space for dancing and performances.' There was a lot of drinking but not, to her knowledge, any drug-taking; a great deal of excitable, intense conversation, 'a certain amount of casual love-making and above all continuous, passionate dancing, dancing of a high standard, whether Blues, Charleston or Black Bottom'. These parties were thrilling and different, with a hint of danger, 'an element of orgy' and more than a touch of camp. Couples of the same sex would dance together and flirt, heterosexual men would sometimes dress as girls and girls as men; it was all very unlike May Balls or the Quinquaginta, let alone Tweenways or Brunswick Square. Among the young men who were often at such gatherings was Ralph Partridge, dancing expertly and energetically with both men and women, sometimes accompanied by Carrington, sometimes not.

During the first half of 1923, with the heady bohemian world of her new bookshop friends opening up before her, Frances gained two new admirers, both of them well-connected, promising and eligible young men. Neither of them was in the least bohemian, but both were highly intelligent and well-read. Philip Nichols, brother of the poet Robert Nichols, had joined the Diplomatic Service after Winchester, Balliol and a brave wartime career. Colin Mackenzie was an Etonian whose time at Cambridge reading Economics had been interrupted by an even more harrowing war, in which his two best friends were killed; he himself lost a leg. They were both in London that summer, Philip at the Foreign Office and Colin on leave from his job representing a Scottish company in Milan. Colin was in the throes of a romantic friendship with Iris Origo, an intense, cultivated young American woman recently married to an aristocratic Italian and living in Tuscany; they wrote to each other regularly, and his letters show how struck he was with Frances Marshall, whom he met at a party at Lord's for the Eton and Harrow cricket match.

At Cambridge, Colin Mackenzie had been a pupil of Keynes, who thought well of him; and he knew Tom Marshall, whom he described to Iris as 'a brilliant young history don at Trinity, a good violinist and a defeated Labour candidate'. When he met Frances, she was with three of her less conventional Cambridge friends, the glamorous Dadie Rylands, the enigmatic Adrian Bishop and the distinguished musician Boris Ord; 'she was the only member of the party new to me,' wrote Colin, 'and also the only female on this side of the channel who has roused in me a flicker of interest ... attractive, bobbed hair, decidedly "modern" with a strong taste for alcohol!' They all had dinner together at the Café Royal, traditionally the place where bohemia met high society, after which Colin, sounding faintly disapproving, described how Frances 'lay about the place in a restoration type frock – a picture of frustrated desire ... but she really is extremely nice'. Before he left London for Scotland he went to Birrell and Garnett's to say goodbye to her, bought some books and encountered Bunny Garnett and also Lytton Strachey. He was still emotionally caught up with Iris; but Frances Marshall stayed in his mind. He would take her out whenever he came to London, and a plan developed for them to travel to Italy together with Tom.

Meanwhile, though, Ralph Partridge had begun to pursue Frances in earnest. In the late summer of 1923 there was another party; they danced together all evening and Frances found herself the target of 'a long, high-powered and concentrated courtship such as I had never been subjected to before'. The young man who was now pursuing her was experienced, determined and at the heart of the world she found so excitingly different.

In the summer of 1923, Ralph Partridge was twenty-eight. He had been closely involved with Lytton Strachey and Dora Carrington for five years; before that, his world had been far removed from Bloomsbury. The man who now set his heart on Frances was more complicated than he appeared. By the time he met her, three experiences had altered his life and affected his character: his service in the army, his love for Dora Carrington and his friendship with Lytton Strachey.

Ralph's background was deeply respectable and solidly Anglo-Indian. He was born in India in 1894; his father, Reggie, the clever, ambitious son of a Devon solicitor, had come top of his year in the ferociously competitive examination for the Indian Civil Service and gone out to Bengal in 1883 at the age of nineteen. There, at a tennis party, he met Jessie Sherring, from a family of clerics and missionaries based in Benares; they were married at Naini Tal, one of the hill towns favoured by the British, in 1888. Reggie's career flourished until a fall left him with concussion and damaged his eyesight; instead of his influential job in the Bengal secretariat he found himself back in the hills, at Pauri, 5,400 feet up in the foothills of the Himalayas, in charge of a district twice the size of Devon and five miles' hard travel from the nearest British neighbour.

By the time Ralph was born at Pauri, and christened Reginald Sherring (though always known to his family as Rex), he already had two older sisters: Dorothy and Jessie. Dorothy left an account of her family, including a description of life in India and of her adored younger brother. It was a typical, and in some ways, at first, idyllic, Anglo-Indian childhood; she recalled the views of the mountains, the devoted ayahs and mahouts, the elephants, the doolies, the fruit. 'The pigs were fed on apricots . . . and the strawberry season lasted two months.' The Partridges had brought Nursie from Budleigh Salterton to look after the children; despite her fear of finding a leopard under her bed, she was 'the greatest comfort and the most faithful servant'. Everyone doted on Ralph, who was known as Sonny Sahib.

Like all Anglo-Indian families of the time, the Partridges had to face separation when their daughters grew old enough to go to school; the damage done to family relationships was much less worrying than the likelihood that their health and character, not to mention their accent, would be ruined by growing up in India. Ralph's parents decided, in 1897, that Reggie should take them all home, and leave them there while he went back to continue his work. So from the age of three until he was sixteen, Ralph barely had a father. Reggie, as Dorothy put it, 'returned on leave every three years to be introduced to his children afresh'. Their mother, too, spent long periods away, back in India during the winter. 'A reliable person was put in charge of us while Mother was away and we disliked every one.'

While Ralph was growing up, the family was based in a small house in Bristol. According to his sister, Ralph was 'a delightful little boy . . . vigorous, interested in everything, indefatigable and very truthful'. He did well at school, and won a scholarship to Westminster, where he arrived at thirteen, already six foot tall and with a mind of his own. He refused to play games, but even so ended up as Head Boy. In due course he went up to Christ Church, Oxford, in 1913, on a closed scholarship to read Law. He was broad and strong by this time, as well as tall, and was soon rowing for the College.

Even allowing for sisterly adoration, it sounds as if Ralph Partridge, in his first year at Oxford, was a splendid specimen of straightforward young English manhood, with his keen brain, strong build, flashing blue eyes and abundant energy. 'I, his sister, loved and admired him intensely,' Dorothy wrote. 'I could not think of anyone more wonderful.' According to her, he had already fallen seriously in love, and his family thoroughly approved the girl of his choice: Pamela Horsley, the 'gentle and charming and intelligent' daughter of Sir Victor Horsley, a distinguished brain specialist. But Ralph, like all the young men of his generation, was approaching the edge of a precipice. In the summer of 1914, as Europe blundered towards disaster, he was coming up to twenty, and about to start his second year at Oxford. As soon as war was declared, he joined the rush to serve his country.

Ralph Partridge made a very good soldier, although it took him, and the army, a little time to find this out. Having joined the Royal Warwickshire Regiment, he found himself seconded to the 48th Division Cyclist Company, a new unit whose role was to move around the battlefield at high speed, carrying despatches and supporting the cavalry. After a year with the Cyclists in northern France Ralph had done well enough to be recalled to his regiment in the spring of 1916. Thereafter he distinguished himself during the appalling carnage of the Somme, and rapidly became commander of a company (with a life expectancy, according to Dorothy, of three weeks), a Captain and then, at the age of twenty-three, a Major. His family always proudly believed that he was the youngest Major in the entire army.

Like all those who survived the Somme, Ralph endured unspeakable horrors. His worst experience was being buried alive; he wrote Dorothy an account of 'what it feels like to die'. He was in a forward trench with his company when a shell burst and he was submerged in rubble and mud. They were under fire, but his batman 'rushed to the heap and began scraping and scooping away . . . at last he uncovered a head. Rex was unconscious and his eyes were glazed and his tongue black and sticking out.' They poured brandy down his throat and revived him; all he remembered was that he could not move and that when he tried to breathe his lungs filled up with earth and grit. His batman was given the DCM; Ralph himself was awarded the MC and the Croix de Guerre.

A couple of affectionate letters from Ralph to his 'darling Dorothy' have survived. The first, before he was sent to the front, is humorous, and tells of saving a cow's life by steering her past sentries to get to a vet. The second, dated Christmas Day 1916, is angry. After describing his Christmas dinner (half a sucking pig and seven other courses), he goes on: 'I'm well personally but spirits are not in the ascendant. It makes me sick to see what the politicians half a million men have fallen for this year have to say for their beastly selves.' He was not so caught up in soldiering that he could not criticise the direction of the war and the willingness of generals and politicians to sacrifice the lives of younger men.

Despite the horrors, the danger and the anger, there was much about being a soldier that he enjoyed. One of the best accounts ever written of how war can be exciting, even enjoyable, as well as terrible was written by one of Ralph's fellow Cyclists, whom he met while training in England. This was Gerald Brenan, whose complex, at times explosive friendship with Ralph began during the war.

Gerald Brenan was the same age as Ralph, and like him was born overseas into a family serving the Empire. Unlike him, he was also born a natural rebel. His father was a soldier, and set on Sandhurst and a military career for his son; he was not best pleased when, aged seventeen, Gerald, who loved poetry and hated conventions, ran away to walk to Afghanistan. He got as far as Bosnia before the winter and poverty drove him home, where his father forced him to agree to studying for the Indian police. He was still planning to escape this fate when the war began.

Gerald's view of Ralph during the war cannot, for reasons that will become apparent, be swallowed whole; but it should not be dismissed either. His first sight of Ralph was reading *The Times* 'with an air of great concentration . . . suddenly he dropped the sheet which concealed him with a deep, hearty laugh and I saw a good-looking man of powerful build with the brightest, bluest eyes I had ever beheld in my life'. Gerald thought him a born leader, and could not understand what he was doing with the Cyclists, until he got to know him better, when he realised that Ralph 'was very sure of himself and did not easily submit to authority that he regarded as stupid or incompetent'.

From the start, Gerald liked and admired Ralph, but his admiration was tinged with envy. He recognised Ralph as a stronger character than he was, a man able to dominate other men and to seduce women. Gerald was himself dominated by his peppery father, and was, unlike Ralph, squeamish and uneasy about sex. He would find himself left holding the ladder while Ralph made love to a girl in the hayloft at the farm where they were billeted, or hanging around while his friend flirted with waitresses in Armentières or visited a brothel in Amiens. Gerald, looking back (he was to write several accounts of Ralph), made up for these humiliating memories by recalling his friend as a bit of a philistine, who never read a book, whereas he himself was obsessed with Rimbaud, Flaubert and Baudelaire. 'I could not share with him my feelings about poetry or the inner life,' he wrote, 'but on a more mundane footing we were good companions. I found his rollicking high spirits and zest for life irresistible ... There was always an element of hero worship in my liking for him. I admired his sexual prowess and I admired still more his obvious superiority as a soldier.'

Gerald was certainly more literary and imaginative than Ralph, but Ralph's education and good mind meant that they were intellectual equals. As time would show, Gerald was more creative – he was a born writer – but Ralph had a keen scholarly and critical intelligence; it was their temperaments that were entirely different. Both were capable of deep feeling, but Gerald was the more nervous and emotional, and while Ralph loved a good argument, Gerald would retreat at the first sign of one. Both were in fact romantics, but where Gerald was tortured and diffident Ralph was straightforward and robust. Their time together in the war was the beginning of a lifelong involvement, a rare example of an intense, articulate friendship between men not afraid to acknowledge their feelings.

Gerald recorded his new friend's attitude to the war in letters home. He encountered Ralph several times during 1916, once in July leading his battalion up the line on his grey mare Bucephala. They visited the town of Ypres together on a hot afternoon, and on their way back had a fierce argument (Gerald wrote that Ralph was always irritable when he was hot) in the course of which Ralph 'said that pacifists were skulkers and ought to be shot while I had defended their right to think as they did'. Later, Gerald came across Ralph in command of a company after the battle of Ovillers, having lunch in a trench (tinned Hungarian goulash, German champagne and a cigar). 'The further end of the trench he was occupying was held by the Germans. What was needed, he said, was to bomb up it so as to reach a machine gun that was holding up our advance, but his men were tired and not out for taking risks. He himself seemed to be completely in his element.'

After lunch, with the stench of decomposing bodies kept at bay by Ralph's cigar, Gerald found his friend 'more serious and gloomy ... As usual, he said, the staff was execrable.' Orders were arriving too late, and made little sense when they did. Lives were being lost unnecessarily. Even so, as Gerald admitted in a long and somewhat confused letter to his father, both he and Ralph were often exhilarated by battle. 'Although, I wrote, everything one could see was horrible, I could not help liking it. Partridge, when he was out in rest, always longed to get back and had even said that he wished the war would go on for ever.' Gerald was not the only one of the two to be confused, but he was the one to realise it.

Gerald tried to explain why they had such mixed feelings. 'I feel sure', he wrote, 'that Ralph thought, as I did, that war was horrible and looked forward to its end. But the young love to test themselves and a battle is a great challenge. Anyone who feels himself rising superior to that challenge experiences a sense of power and elation, and he had risen so far above it that he must at times have felt that war was his true vocation. For this reason I envied him for being in the thick of things while I was still an embusqué.'

Ralph was awarded the MC in February 1917, and the bar added after he was wounded later in the same year. According to the citation, 'when acting second in command of the battalion under dangerous conditions ... he was wounded while helping men out of their assembly trenches. His sound judgment and unfailing courage were of the greatest assistance.' After a period of home leave in the summer of 1918, Ralph's war came to an end on 5 November in northern Italy, where his regiment had been sent to support the Italians against the Austrians.

Another letter, treasured by his proud family, shows what the men who served with him thought of Major Partridge. After he had called on the mother of one of them, a Mrs Nicholls of Dawlish, during his last leave she reported the visit to her son, who wrote back: 'I am so glad Major Partridge has called Mother ... He is one such as one rarely finds nowadays, an officer and a gentleman.' After praising Ralph's courage and leadership, and saying how popular he was with the men, who had given him a hero's welcome when he caught up with them in Italy, he summed Ralph up as 'A man true to his traditions and straightforward in every way.' She sent this tribute to the Partridges.

There is no doubting the sincerity of this letter, which was not written to be seen by Ralph's family, and even allowing for the mood and idiom of the time it indicates that he was an outstanding officer. According to Dorothy, after the war 'the War Office offered him a permanent commission but he refused it'. The fact was that in 1918, during the same leave when he visited Mrs Nicholls, he had come into the orbit of Dora Carrington and Lytton Strachey, two people for whom soldiering was not a career to be admired. He would not remain 'true to his traditions and straightforward' for very much longer.

Four

The Making of Ralph Partridge, 1918–1920

When Frances began to fall in love with Ralph in the summer of 1923, the bookshop network would have ensured that she knew his marriage was unusually stormy and that he and his wife shared a house in the country with Lytton Strachey. But she could hardly have realised the extent to which any relationship with him would be conditioned by his commitment not just to Carrington but also to Lytton and the way of life the threesome had built at Tidmarsh. This commitment was to have a profound effect on Frances' future; to understand how and why requires a look back at the origins and nature of the ménage, and especially at the emotional balance between Lytton, Ralph and Carrington at the point when Frances arrived on the scene.

Before Ralph Partridge entered their lives in 1918, Lytton and Carrington had only known each other for three years, and it was less than a year since they had set up house together. When they first met, it had been Lytton who made the first move: he tried to kiss Carrington while out walking, which she did not appreciate – especially when she was informed that he was homosexual. There followed the famous, and clearly symbolic, episode when she crept into his bedroom intent on punishing him by cutting off his beard while he slept. As she leaned over him with the scissors he opened his eyes, and she fell in love.

Lytton Strachey was ten years older than Carrington and thirty-two when they met. He was tall, thin and dark, with spidery limbs and the swooping Strachey voice; a founder member of Bloomsbury since making friends with Thoby Stephen at Cambridge in 1903, he was the eighth child and fourth son in the family, a cultivated, waspish, witty man much loved and admired by his friends. His first book, *Eminent Victorians*, published in the spring of 1918, made his name, changed the art of biography for ever and established him as the leading iconoclast of his day. In his own circle he was openly homosexual, but had close friendships with women; his great early love had been his cousin Duncan Grant, who broke his heart by taking up with Maynard Keynes.

Dora Carrington, who dropped her first name at eighteen, studied at the Slade before the war, where she won prizes, bobbed her hair, dressed up as a boy and broke a few hearts herself. Like Lytton's, her background was Anglo-Indian; but while his parents were part of the elite, and intellectually inclined, hers were more modest. Her father was an engineer who worked for the railways; when he returned from India, still a bachelor at fifty, he married a family governess. Carrington grew up in Bedford, a town favoured by retired Anglo-Indians; she adored her father, but rebelled early against her mother's prudish attitudes. Carrington was smallish, slightly clumsy and pigeon-toed, with thick fair hair, bright blue eyes and a pink and white complexion. Her childish air and small breathless voice concealed a wilful, original character. Although she was attractive to men she found sex unappealing; the prospect of marriage and children horrified her. By the time she met Lytton several fellow art students had been desperately in love with her, and the young Jewish painter from the East End, Mark Gertler, had been driven nearly mad by her refusal to sleep with him. Her first contact with the world of Bloomsbury was through Gertler, who had been taken up by the generous, eccentric and flamboyant Lady Ottoline Morrell during the war; Lytton, before they met, had taken rather a fancy to Gertler himself. Carrington's virginity became a favourite topic of speculation at Garsington, the Morrells' country house near Oxford, but she apparently held onto it until she went to bed with Lytton Strachey in a hotel at Glastonbury in the summer of 1916.

Their sexual relationship, hardly surprisingly, did not endure; but the intimacy and affection between them was to grow. Lytton was a natural teacher, and Carrington became his devoted and enthusiastic pupil. Together they read English and French history, Shakespeare, the metaphysical poets; above all, she loved to listen to him read his own writing. He encouraged her to work; during 1916 she painted his portrait lying back on a cushion, reading. It is an image of reverence for an intellectual, a bearded, bespectacled man deep in his book; his skin glows and his beautiful translucent hands with their slender fingers are painted with veneration as well as skill. The notion that Lytton never really loved Carrington, that she thrust herself on him and then clung to him like a leech, has been rejected by both their biographers. In his way, as his many letters to her show, he cared about her; but although early on he allegedly told Bunny Garnett (never the most reliable of reporters) that he was indeed 'in love' with Carrington, this was not so for long. He remained fond of her and, crucially, entertained by her. She, on the other hand, was truly in love with him for the rest of her life, obsessed with his physical presence as well as his subtle, humorous mind. From 1916 onwards her life revolved around looking after him; her happiness depended on his. She found the Mill at Tidmarsh as a refuge for him from London, did all the hard work of decorating and furnishing it, and organised life there to suit Lytton's habits and wishes. Her own needs, and her own work, always came second.

By the summer of 1918 she must have realised that he was unlikely to be happy, in the long term, without a handsome young man around. She and Lytton had found other sexual partners since 1916; she had finally given in to Gertler, while Lytton was always on the lookout for a new adventure. Their affairs were no secret; each of them was amused, and titillated, by confiding their desires and amours to the other. Their letters are sprinkled with suggestive jokes and innuendos, and Carrington's with sly references to male beauty, erections and little drawings of cocks and pussies. Her sex life may have been problematic, but she was nevertheless sexually and emotionally highly charged; increasingly she was drawn to beautiful young women. She loved Lytton for understanding this and because he made no physical demands on her, but she still needed the sense of power that being wanted by a man provided; and her ability to attract young men could only increase her charm for Lytton. Carrington, like Vanessa Bell before her, had to accept that she could only share a homosexual man's life if she was prepared not just to tolerate but to welcome his male lovers.

There were other reasons why it suited Lytton well to have Carrington part of his domestic life. The way Bloomsbury chose to live, with same-sex affairs conducted alongside heterosexual relationships, was not just unusual and, to the conventional majority, shocking and distasteful, but dangerous, as homosexuality was against the law. Respectable people shuddered at the name of Oscar Wilde, whose trial and humiliation had taken place only a generation earlier. For an active homosexual there was a lot to be said for setting up house with a devoted and open-minded young woman to keep scandal and criminal proceedings at bay. It would, of course, be even better if she brought attractive young men within reach.

At the same time, Lytton did not want to be the sole focus of Carrington's affections. He was always nervous of her becoming too dependent on him; Virginia Woolf noted this in her diary soon after the move to Tidmarsh, when Lytton said to her: 'That woman will dog me'. Virginia felt proprietary about Lytton, her old admirer (he had once proposed marriage to her) and the great friend of her husband's youth, and admitted to jealousy at Carrington's intimacy with him; but she was not the only one with reservations about Lytton's new liaison. Old Bloomsbury in general was surprised and not altogether pleased by the relationship. When the Tidmarsh ménage began, during the winter of 1917, both Lytton and Carrington were shy about it, and took steps to placate their friends and families. She told her parents that she was to share the house with other young women from the Slade; and Lytton made much of the fact that Tidmarsh was really a joint enterprise with several friends and his brothers Oliver and James.

In the summer of 1918, as the war entered its closing stages, two important events took place in the lives of Lytton and Carrington, and both were to prove significant for the future of Frances Marshall, then working away as a land girl at Castle Howard before going up to Cambridge. The publication of *Eminent Victorians* in May made Lytton Strachey rich and famous, and in August Ralph Partridge made his first visit to Tidmarsh Mill.

Ralph arrived on the Tidmarsh stage at a promising moment. Carrington's affair with Mark Gertler was finally over; in February of that year, after discovering that she had been lying to him about the extent of her involvement with Lytton, Gertler had attacked him in a London street and written her a series of vitriolic letters. So Carrington was now without a lover; and Lytton's new fame meant that he was being courted by society and spending a lot of time away from Tidmarsh in grand country houses or London drawing rooms. Carrington was not included in his new social life; as Bunny Garnett wrote of the hostesses, like Maud Cunard and Margot Asquith, who pursued him, 'they would no more have thought of including Carrington than of asking him to bring his housekeeper or his cook'. The charms of Tidmarsh would be enhanced for them both by the presence of someone new. Again, Virginia Woolf encouraged Lytton to express his uneasiness. Her diary for July 1918, just before Ralph came on the scene, records Lytton's response when she told him that she felt his influence on Carrington had improved her. 'Ah, but the future is very dark' was his reply. 'I *must* be free. I shall want to go off.' Virginia was beginning to feel for Carrington, 'so dependent on Lytton, and having so openly burnt the conventional boats'.

Carrington met Ralph first, through her brother Noel, who knew him from Westminster and Oxford. Also on leave from the army, Noel was keen to introduce his bohemian sister to his gallant soldier friend. He arranged a walking tour to Scotland; they set off from London, and Carrington wrote Lytton an excited first impression. 'I found Partridge shared all the best views of democracy and social reform, wine and good cheer and operas. He adores the Italians and wants after the war to sail in a schooner to the Mediterranean islands and Italy, and trade in wine without taking much money and to dress like a brigand. I am so elated and happy.' She had reservations, though, about his looks: 'Not very attractive to look at. Immensely big. But full of wit and reckless.' Already she was wondering how he would strike Lytton and fantasising about future jaunts. On 6 July she wrote more suggestively: 'We have just had a lovely swim in the lake ... what a superb creature is a youth nude.' She was revising her initial impression, though, feeling her way towards the view that fitted best with her devotion to Lytton: that Ralph was physically attractive, but dull. This view of him was to prove tenacious. 'I suppose two years ago I should have enjoyed the company of these two,' she added, of her brother and his friend, 'but their conversation seems so pointless and there seem to be no activities – or did I detect something attempting to rise under his bathing garment – but I fear that merry acrobat will get little pleasure this holiday!'

Before long, her mood changed. The rain poured down and, as always when they were apart, she missed Lytton. He had written back to her, clearly intrigued: 'The existence of Partridge sounds exciting. Will he come down here, when you return, and sing Italian songs to us, and let us dress him as a brigand? I hope so; but you give no suggestion of his appearance – except that he's "immensely big" which may mean anything.' Later in the same letter, which was long, funny and affectionate, informing her that the kitchen garden was quite beyond him ('The beans frighten me'), he returned to the Partridge possibilities. 'And what's his address? So that I may send him a wire and ask him down for a bathe in the Roman Bath? Why not, pray? Oh, I forgot, it will take a week before I can get anything out of you, and by that time I shall be entirely absorbed by the Duchess of Marlborough, Mr Astor and Lord X. How unfortunate!'

Their first meeting, however, was a notable failure. On 10 August 1918 Ralph was invited to spend a day at the Mill. After the undergraduates and soldiers he was used to, Ralph was bemused by Lytton, who in turn found Major Partridge altogether too belligerent. Ralph held forth about the war, announcing to Lytton and Carrington, just as he had to Gerald, that pacifists ought to be shot. Carrington was appalled; Lytton said little. Afterwards, Carrington wrote crossly to her brother deploring his friend's lack of interest 'in books or poetry or painting', while Ralph told Noel that 'Old Man Strachey with his billowing beard and basso-falsetto voice did not play a great part'. Carrington's notion that she and Ralph had similar ideas about changing the world after the war did not last long, and Ralph was more puzzled than attracted by Carrington, who was not at all the kind of girl he was used to, being neither an easy conquest nor a respectable marriage prospect. Soon afterwards he had to go back to Italy and the war. The man

Carrington and Lytton first met was a serving officer, who took his duties to his men very seriously.

After the war was over, Ralph returned to Christ Church. Noel Carrington was also back at Oxford; his sister told Lytton that she found the prospect of their company tedious. She seems to have felt the need to remind him regularly that handsome, conventional young men were of no interest to her; perhaps she was also fending off the realisation that they were likely to be of great interest to him. 'He (Noel) sprang on me last night that the Major was in England having been demobbed and might come down today (Jan 16) ... I pull a face of anger and suppressed rage. *Two* young men talking about Oxford and the Civil Service.' Carrington was worried that even if Lytton appreciated her admirer's looks, he might be bored by his conversation. However, the next few months, while Ralph resumed undergraduate life at Oxford, were to see the flowering of the relationship between all three of them, and the start of the transformation of Reginald Sherring Partridge, known as Rex, from a straightforward young man with a good brain but limited emotional and intellectual experience into a more complicated and surprising character. By the time he left Oxford in the summer of 1920, he would have a new name – Lytton having decided that Rex had imperial overtones – new views on politics and pacifism and above all have rejected, once and for all, traditional attitudes to family, career, sexual morality and marriage. In the disillusioned aftermath of the war, Lytton and Carrington between them turned Major Partridge into the man Frances Marshall would come to love.

The process was neither quick nor smooth. By the Easter vacation, in March 1919, Carrington had decided to join her brother Noel, Ralph and his sister Dorothy for another journey, this time to Spain. Every step of the way, she wrote to Lytton. Her mood, as the foursome set off from London on a steamship, was unromantic: 'I shall I see be thrown into the arms of the Major Bird simply out of sheer boredom and cold.' She had to share a cabin with Dorothy: 'how revolting women are'. Dorothy Partridge, who adored her brother just as he was, found the peculiar new girl in his life disconcerting. She tried offering Carrington advice. 'Her generalisations on life made me boil with rage inside. She said people ought not to be unhappy or morbid but ought to control their feelings.' As for Ralph, he was argumentative, and when they went for a walk together in the romantic Alhambra he was a disappointment. 'He's even a bore at such moments ... Still it doesn't really matter as after this I shall probably never see him again. Miss DP has confided to me she doesn't like me or my philosophy as it has a bad effect on her brother. Dear, dear.'

There were, however, more promising moments, especially when they went walking in the hills around Ronda and slept on the floor by the fire in a shepherd's hut. In Madrid the Goyas in the Prado took her breath away. By the end, she had rather come round to Ralph: 'I must say the young man improves a good deal when one knows him. He is softer and more human.' She was also gratified to notice that he was showing distinct signs of irritation with his sister.

Back in England, Ralph became a regular presence at Tidmarsh during the summer term. He would bicycle the ten miles from Oxford through the green and golden countryside, arrive hot and dusty and cool off by swimming naked in the small pool known as the Roman Bath. Then he would make himself useful; as Carrington put it, he joined her 'minor battalion of slaves in the garden'.

The developing relationship between the three of them can be traced through Lytton and Carrington's correspondence. Letters capture a flicker of a thought, reflect a passing mood, are often written (especially by these two) as much to amuse as to reveal or conceal; each had their reasons for disguising the truth of their feelings for Ralph from the other. But gradually he became not just an occasional amusement but a vital presence in their lives.

An interested observer of the Tidmarsh ménage at this early stage was Gerald Brenan, who caught up with Ralph and his new girl during the summer of 1919. Later, Gerald would maintain that, having heard about Carrington during the war, he entertained hopes of capturing her for himself; certainly as soon as he saw her he was bewitched.

'It was one of those heavily overcast English summer days,' he wrote. 'The trees and the grass were steeped in a vivid green, but the purplish clouds overhead shut out the light and made the interior of the house dark and gloomy.' Carrington reminded him of one of the lute-playing angels in Piero della Francesca's *Nativity*, with 'her restless blue eyes and her golden brown hair cut in a straight page-boy bob'. Lytton was sitting in a deep armchair. Peering into the gloom, Gerald saw 'an extraordinary figure' who at first put him in mind of 'a darkly bearded he-goat glaring at me from the bottom of a cave. Then I saw that it was a man and took in gradually the long, relaxed figure, the Greco-ish face, the brown sensitive eyes hidden behind thick glasses, the large, coarse nose and ears, the fine, thin, blue-veined hands.' He was also struck, of course, by the voice: 'both very low and in certain syllables very high pitched, and which faded out at the end of the sentence, sometimes without even finishing it'.

They had a proper tea in the dining room – honeycomb, home-made cakes and jam, served in a pink lustre tea service. Ralph joined them – Gerald noted his dirty white shorts, nondescript shirt, and then rather stylised way of speaking which contrasted with the Rabelaisian laugh, rolling blue eyes, and baritone voice in which he sang a jazz song or a ballad'. Carrington and Lytton seemed from another world, she 'with her simple pre-Raphaelite clothes and her coaxing voice and smile that concealed so many intense and usually conflicting feelings; Lytton, elegant in his dark suit, gravely remote and fantastic, with something of the polished and dilettante air of a sixteenth century cardinal. It was not any similarity of temperament or upbringing that had brought these three together.' So what was it? Gerald wondered (and was to go on wondering for the rest of his life). More and more he came to feel that Carrington belonged with him and not with Ralph. He was bemused to see the man so much less bohemian and bookish than himself on intimate terms with her and with Lytton. He was also, of course, sexually jealous. Once again Ralph had the girl and he was left outside.

All that summer, Carrington and Lytton maintained to each other that while Ralph was amiable, useful, entertaining and above all physically splendid, he was unfortunately rather a bore. They both took increasing pleasure in his company and were coming to depend on it; but it was some time before either could admit the fact. In June, Lytton was away for a while, but Carrington's letters kept him in the picture. 'The young man Partridge came over Saturday after lunch and spent his afternoon in the Bath, and reading volumes from our sex library on the lawn.' She had taken to using him as a model: 'I've been drawing RP naked in the long grass in the orchard. I confess I got rather a flux over his thighs and legs.' A week later, he was, to her surprise, getting on rather well with her Slade friend Alix Sargent Florence, once a lover of Bunny Garnett's and now in hot pursuit of Lytton's brother James (himself previously infatuated with Rupert Brooke). 'The Major Bird', she reported, was chatting to Alix about 'every subject under the sun from buggery to trade unions' (neither of them subjects much discussed, one imagines, in Ralph's home circle or among the rowing fraternity at Christ Church).

Sometimes Carrington went into Oxford to see Ralph. They swam in the river by the Trout Inn, and she helped him with a lunch party in his rooms ('cocktails and salmon'). After lunch, 'Noel went back to his studies and I continued my investigations'. At this point she added a small drawing of an erect penis.

Later, she went on, they bicycled to Garsington for tea, where they found a large group of guests including Lytton's Apostle friend from Cambridge,

Goldsworthy Lowes Dickinson. Ralph went for a swim in the ornamental pool on the lower lawn; again, his physique was much admired. 'Goldie was completely bowled over by the major's blue eyes and pestered me with questions about him!!! Ottoline now raves about his appearance and even Alix.' As for Carrington herself: 'I remain adamant, and admit – to you – that his thighs are elegant, his private parts enorme, his deltoids as white as ivory – but his face the face of a Norwegian dentist.' (Previous writers have quoted her remark about his face but delicately omitted the rest.)

This letter ends: 'Oh Lytton I love you almost to bursting point'. Carrington was impressed by Ralph's strength and virility; but she had not lost her distaste for sex, nor her fear of being dominated by a man, and she wanted always to remind Lytton that it was him she truly loved. As far as sex was concerned, though, Ralph was not accustomed to taking no for an answer, and as they started to plan a holiday in Devon she knew that they would end up sharing a bed. The prospect of a sexual relationship with Ralph was deeply unnerving; she made light of her fears to Lytton, while at the same time sensing that the voyeur in him would enjoy hearing about it, and perhaps value her more because of it. But with Ralph constantly at Tidmarsh, she sometimes resented his presence; it interrupted her precious time alone with Lytton.

Lytton played the game too. When she told him, after he had given a talk in Oxford to a group of undergraduates, that Ralph was worried that he did not like him, he replied, 'The Partridge was quite wrong. I really liked him more than anyone else – he seemed so modest; but I wish he had rather more forehead.' By this time 'the Partridge' was affectionately, if also teasingly, known as the Major, or Majorio, or the Major Bird, or, more daringly, La Majora; and Carrington several times referred to him as Nos Roi (he was, after all, still called Rex). He did not become Ralph in Carrington's letters before early 1920.

By mid-July Carrington was telling Lytton from Cornwall that the Major was 'a most excellent bedfellow' despite the distasteful matter of contraception and the problem of his still unreconstructed opinions. 'The evening was spent quarrelling vigorously over the war and CO's,' she wrote on 14 July, 'until I became so tired and angry that I gave it up. The night was pleasant, but ... The major remains exactly the same. I'm afraid there is no chance of him ever becoming less dull.'

By now, though, Lytton himself indicated his interest in the Major's physical charms. At first, the game was played, like many of his and Carrington's best games, on paper. He pretended to be left out, even a touch jealous: 'Lord! Why am I not a rowing blue, with eyes to match, and 24? ... I suppose he would be shocked if I suggested that you should give him a kiss from me.' Quickly, the whole thing became a plaintive joke, often used to sum up Bloomsbury's approach to sexual complexity: 'The world is rather tiresome I must say – everything at sixes and sevens – ladies in love with buggers, and buggers in love with womanisers, and the price of coal going up too. Where will it all end?' But the joke pointed the way to something serious. After the Cornwall holiday, when Carrington was back at Tidmarsh and Ralph was starting his final year at Oxford, Lytton began to fall in love with the Major in earnest. Carrington, characteristically, was now in retreat. The fact that she was sleeping with Ralph meant that he felt he owned her; she was determined that he should not. Both of them cried on Lytton's shoulder; the emotional atmosphere intensified. At some point, emotional excitement took physical form.

The question of whether or not Lytton Strachey and Ralph Partridge, who certainly came to love each other dearly, were also lovers in any physical sense has up till now always been answered firmly in the negative. 'Hopelessly heterosexual' was how Frances would describe her husband. During her lifetime, that was the accepted view of him. Now, the likelihood can be acknowledged that there was, for a time, a sexual aspect to the relationship. By early 1920 Lytton had established an extraordinary hold over Ralph, part intellectual, part emotional, and taught him that just as there are many different kinds of love, so there are many varieties of sexual pleasure and that most people can experience more than one.

As for Ralph, like most public schoolboys and undergraduates he would have known all about homosexual impulses by the time he left Oxford for the war. Only Lytton's openness about his preference and about sexual matters in general would have been new to him. From childhood, Ralph had lacked a father, which may have helped to make him open to Lytton's influence; after Reggie Partridge retired and returned to England their relationship was not good. The family was never really reunited; his father lived in Devon, while his mother and sisters, who adored Ralph and expected much of him, were mostly in London. Given the alacrity with which he moved away from their circle of influence and into Lytton's, he may well have been longing, consciously or not, to break out and discover another, freer self. Above all, for him, as for many of his generation, the war changed everything. After his experiences in France, where enjoyable but unromantic episodes of sexual bravado took place alongside painful responsibility for his men and the loathing aroused by the death and squalor all around him, he returned a willing pupil for all that Lytton had to teach him. Rejecting his family's standards and adopting Lytton's (including, before long, his pacifist beliefs) was Ralph Partridge's way of recovering from all that he had seen and done at the front. The war had proved, Michael Holroyd has written, 'a catalyst on *Eminent Victorians* which began without a hero but acquired a theme'. It had also acted as a catalyst for the transformation of Dorothy's Rex into Lytton and Carrington's Ralph.

Lytton now had on his hands a more challenging pupil than the young men from King's. In fact, in Ralph Partridge it was as if all the traditions and virtues Lytton had so brilliantly subverted in *Eminent Victorians* were embodied in the opinionated but essentially undeveloped character of Carrington's latest conquest. Lytton found himself presented with the opportunity to remake a classic product of Victorian values in his own image, to turn a sturdy young Englishman's assumptions inside out while acquiring, for himself as well as for Carrington, a love object and a congenial, practical companion.

From the start, there was a lot of innuendo and sexual playfulness, as Carrington and Lytton found that Ralph was quite willing to join in their games and jokes and dressing up. Lytton's letters of 1919 and 1920 are sprinkled with suggestive references to punishing him for bad behaviour – 'probably by being put in the stocks when you next appear' – or thanking him for a present of a list, in French, of strange Christian miracles and relics. This tribute went down well. 'Bye the bye,' mused Lytton, 'why is it that the relics of the holy are never of the more intimate regions of the body? Surely Christ's prick would be highly edifying, and the buttocks of St John the Divine would attract many worshippers.' Soon he is writing to 'Dearest Redgie', hoping that the portrait he has asked Carrington to paint is coming along and adding, 'I have discovered some earrings for you to wear at the dance and I must request you to set about at once learning the hornpipe.' Ears were the focus of many of Lytton's erotic impulses and fantasies.

In the meantime, Carrington had begun to write long confiding letters to Gerald Brenan, by this time back in Spain. She had found him a romantic figure, and also felt that they were fellow artists with much in common. It was her suggestion that they write to each other – and as he was safely removed from the scene, and loved writing letters even longer than hers, he was the perfect correspondent for her. Since childhood, Carrington had been naturally secretive, and the more anyone tried to pin her down the more devious she became. Determined not to surrender her independence to Ralph, and perhaps unsettled by the growing intimacy between him and

Lytton (she had asked Lytton not to let Ralph read her letters), she set out to make Gerald her own.

At first, her references to Ralph are studiedly neutral. She calls him 'the young man' and says he comes to Tidmarsh most weekends, and that he has given up Law for English Literature, under Lytton's influence. As with Carrington, Lytton loved to read the classics with Ralph, especially Shakespeare and the metaphysical poets. 'I like him more than I did,' she went on. 'It's difficult not to when anyone is so excessively kind and digs my potato patch and sits for my pictures.'

But less than a month later, on 15 December, her tone changes. This letter suggests that relations between the Tidmarsh trio had intensified, and that their flirtatious games had become something more. Perhaps this was when the more intimate 'triangular trinity of happiness' was formed. 'Oh a great deal has happened in this Mill since you last set foot in it!', she wrote:

> What fun to write a letter which would incriminate everyone, and be a lasting testimony to these strange times and the nakedness of a female's mind. But I can't . . . I've become much fonder of RP. He has become so much more charming and has given up his slightly moral character which used to tire me. So we never quarrel now and have become a perfect pair of pigeons in our affections. I certainly will never love him but I am extremely fond of him – I believe if one wasn't reserved, and hadn't a sense of 'what is possible' one could be <u>very</u> fond of certainly two or three people at a time.

This letter has usually been read in the context of Carrington's need to ensure Gerald's devotion; but it could also reflect the altered situation between Lytton, herself and Ralph. What follows sounds like Lytton speaking. 'To know a human being intimately, to feel their affection, to have their confidences is so absorbing that it's clearly absurd to think one only has the inclination for one variety.'

The extent to which the ménage à trois included sex would not much matter except for the fact that Ralph always maintained that his friendship with Lytton was only that, and that Frances believed him. His truthfulness, especially in affairs of the heart, was one of the things she admired and treasured in him. Perhaps a bit of sexual play did not, for Ralph, really count, if that was all that went on in the big bed at Tidmarsh where, as a later letter from Carrington mentions, at least once they were 'all three together'. Or it could be that whatever details Ralph shared with Frances about Lytton and Carrington and himself did not signify much to either of them and were forgotten as time went by. Although Ralph was to have many warm friendships with homosexual men, and was always keenly interested in their lives and loves, there was never any hint of homosexual behaviour from him apart from during the years he was closest to Lytton. Lytton himself, looking back, would recall those years, and the letters Ralph wrote him, with the wistful regretfulness of a former lover. Perhaps the way to regard this episode in Ralph's life is that it was natural, given that Lytton, Carrington and he were living under the same roof and bound together by love, for them occasionally to give that love physical expression. When, at the end of her life, it was suggested to Frances that this might well have happened, she agreed.

Sex or no sex, there can be no doubt that by early 1920 Lytton was deeply in love with Ralph. In his letters, Ralph is his dearest creature, his angel, his sweet Ralph; he wants to know what goes on at Bloomsbury parties in London when he is not there – 'Is Duncan talking fantastically, and is Maynard ogling you? . . . It's been such a delightful heavenly time . . . I think you know how much I love you.' He minded when Ralph was away from the Mill: 'It seems so good when we're all three together that I grudge every minute that keeps us apart,' he wrote, adding that if he doesn't turn up that week 'I shan't see you for a hundred years, it seems to me. My beard will be snowy white, and your ears will have grown so intolerably perky for want of pulling that they'll have to be clipped by the executioner.' Sometimes Lytton went to Oxford himself, to give Ralph lunch, with 'a bottle of the best claret to keep you warm for your towpath'. He was hoping for time alone with Ralph, without Carrington. Clearly, they had become very close. Lytton was never robust, and Ralph had voiced his concern. 'My dearest creature,' he wrote back, 'Don't bother too much about my health. The exhaustion that shatters is the kind that's caused by miserable baffled desires – in a black period of my life I was nearly killed by it; but now, dear, I am buoyed up and carried along by so much happiness!' Such desires were apparently baffled no longer.

The happy times at the Mill were too good to last; but the poem Lytton wrote to his two companions on the occasion of his fortieth birthday, on 1 March 1920, testifies to how good they were. Lytton tells them how he would reply should the gods offer him anything he wanted. Friends, he said, a country house, books, 'a little art; perhaps a little fame as well'. What else? the gods ask him. 'Look round, be bold, and choose some more!'

Hum! I should pause; reflect; then 'Yes!'
Methinks I'd cry, I see, I see.

> What would fill up my happiness?
> Give me a girl to dwell with me . . .

The girl's charms are warmly listed: her 'genial' beauty, her warm and loving heart. And then –

> Enough! But hush! – if once again
> Once more the Gods the gates of joy
> Threw wide, and bade me take! – Ah then
> I'd whisper 'Let me have a boy!'
>
> Yes, Yes, a charming boy, whose soul
> With tenderest affection flows,
> Young, yet not too young – the rich whole
> Of manhood blooming in youth's rose;
>
> Gentle as only strength could be;
> With something of a Grecian grace,
> And sweeter, fairer still to me
> The loved light of an English face.

While this tender set of verses should not be given huge weight, the emphasis is very much on the girl's love for the writer, while the boy's attributes are described with true passion.

Lytton was not just drawn to Ralph's blue eyes and broad shoulders; he had come to realise that Ralph had a strong, clear mind that, once opened up, was responsive, quick and eager for information and argument. He was also full of energy, humour and common sense, and everyone who knew him well always remarked on his warmth and kind-heartedness. As for Ralph, he found Lytton's combination of wit and erudition and his sympathetic, non-judgemental attitude to sexual and emotional matters irresistible; and the fact that Carrington loved Lytton meant that Ralph either had to compete with him for her love or accept and share it. For Carrington, as ever, what mattered most was that Lytton got what he wanted. Lytton's need for Ralph's company suited her well.

For a few weeks early in 1920 the balance between the three of them was exactly right. 'I danced most of the evening with our Ralph,' wrote Carrington to Lytton happily after another Oxford party; they visited Cambridge together in February (where Frances was halfway through her second year at Newnham) and they met Frances' brother Tom, whom Carrington found 'rather intelligent and dominating'. As the Easter vacation approached, the trio were making plans to travel to Spain and visit Gerald Brenan. When Ralph was asked to row for Oxford in the first Boat Race to be held after the war, he declined; he would rather go abroad with Lytton and Carrington. Not many young men, then or now, would turn down a chance to row in the Boat Race for personal reasons. Lytton and Carrington must have been proud of 'our Ralph'. His family must have been appalled. Seventy years later, a niece of Ralph's, his sister Dorothy's daughter, still felt outrage at the way Lytton and Carrington had changed him. The word she used was 'depraved'.

But Carrington was restless, and her interest in Gerald Brenan was growing. She and Ralph, who was also eager to see his friend on his Spanish mountainside, were sure Lytton would love Spain and Gerald as they did. Ralph took charge, and as travelling around Spain was uncomfortable, and Carrington fretted about Lytton's well-being and objected to being bossed about, they quarrelled a good deal. Eventually they struggled up to Yegen, the primitive village high up in the Alpujarras in Andalucia where Gerald Brenan had settled. From there Lytton described to his cousin and confidante, Clive Bell's mistress Mary Hutchinson, the rigours of the journey and 'emotional crises, too, of the strangest sort – until finally we arrived in pitch darkness and almost dead at our singular destination – the abode of an amiable lunatic by name Brenan ... Well, I hardly guessed that I should ever live to be led to such a spot by the beaux yeux of a major!'

Gerald's own account induces sympathy for all concerned: Lytton had to keep getting off his mule because of agonising piles; his digestion could not tolerate the oily Spanish food and rough wine; he was so exhausted when they reached Yegen that he did not go out for several days and hardly spoke. When he did venture forth, it was to sit sidesaddle on a mule, 'bearded, spectacled, very long and thin, with his coarse red nose, holding an open sunshade above him'. Only on his last evening, 'cheered by the thought that his visit was drawing to an end', did he relax enough to show how charming he could be, and 'the great gentleness of his tone and manner when he was with people whom he liked'.

Back in England, a crisis loomed: the first of many. Carrington's emotional elusiveness drove Ralph mad; he began to press her to marry him. Pressure simply made her more elusive; with the end of his time at Oxford approaching, no clear idea of what he would do next and Carrington refusing to commit herself, Ralph boiled over and threatened to leave her, Lytton and Tidmarsh altogether. It is hardly surprising that he should sometimes rebel against the emotional and erotic tangle around him; his position at Tidmarsh was both ambiguous and subordinate. His attempt at self-assertion, however, was short-lived. Between them, Lytton and Carrington reeled him in.

And so the trio settled down again, for the time being. Ralph rowed for Christ Church with Lytton's rather vague encouragement – 'I hope you'll get a bump very quickly every time' – and made the most of his last weeks at Oxford. 'Am I never to see you again?' wrote Lytton plaintively. 'You vanish in a mist of dances, Garsington, portraits, motors, and next, I'm told, there's Henley ... so the Lord alone knows when I shall be able to pull your wicked orejas.' There was indeed Henley, where Ralph the victorious athlete caught Frances Marshall's eye; meanwhile Lytton was doing his best to find his young friend a congenial occupation.

Lytton and Carrington were determined not to lose their playmate to some dreary job that would take him away from their world. Lytton, after a brief flutter of frivolity – 'a touch of rouge, and Piccadilly?' – took the matter seriously, and consulted Leonard Woolf, who suggested Ralph apply for a job with the Labour Party. Curiously, one of his rivals for the post was Frances' first cousin, the serious-minded pacifist Catherine Marshall. 'She is all that is most unpleasant,' wrote Lytton, 'pale, enthusiastic, with a projecting tooth ... Her revoltingness alone will recommend her to those gloomy persons who decide.' Ralph was duly turned down; but through Lytton's good offices, it was soon agreed that on 1 September 1920 he should start work with the Woolfs at the Hogarth Press.

Five

Trouble at Tidmarsh Mill, 1921–1923

Virginia and Leonard Woolf were two of the most influential and critically stringent members of Old Bloomsbury, and over the next two years they observed Ralph Partridge closely. The series of emotional dramas that was to change the course of his life and, before long, Frances Marshall's, took place while he was under their eye, and their view of him has had a lasting effect on his reputation. Ralph appears frequently in Virginia Woolf's diaries of the early 1920s, shown in flashes of curiosity, sympathy and exasperation; Leonard's view, written four decades later, is more considered. Ralph was the third of a succession of assistants at the Press, all of whom arrived with high hopes and none of whom lasted very long (Carrington's friend Alix lasted one day). He joined the Woolfs at a crucial moment, when they realised that their enterprise, started in a small way in 1917 – Leonard called it their hobby – could not grow and flourish without help.

By 1920, the Hogarth Press had published only five books, two written by the Woolfs (the others by T.S. Eliot, Katherine Mansfield and John Middleton Murry) and all of them printed and bound by themselves in the afternoons, after they had finished their own work for the day. They both worked very hard. Virginia was writing her third novel, *Jacob's Room*, and reviewing for *The Times Literary Supplement*; Leonard was editing the *International Review*, contributing regularly to the *New Statesman* and contemplating standing for Parliament. He went to his office in Fleet Street three or four days a week; otherwise they lived and worked at Hogarth House, the beautiful eighteenth-century house in Richmond they had rented since 1915. Although Virginia rather pined for Bloomsbury and social life she had already suffered a serious mental breakdown and Leonard was determined to ensure that she led a calm and regular life. The Woolfs felt that it would be better for Virginia, who dreaded the moment when she had to submit her writing to an editor, if the Hogarth Press remained her publisher. Thus Ralph joined them at a moment of some tension, with expectations running high. All concerned recognised that it was entirely Lytton's recommendation that got him the job.

Leonard knew all about what he called 'the strange ménage à trois' at Tidmarsh, and regarded Carrington as having 'one of those mysterious, inordinately female characters made up of an infinite series of contradictory characteristics'. Ralph he considered not as straightforward as he looked. 'On the surface he was typical public schoolboy, Oxford rowing blue, tough, young blood ... a great he-man, a very English Don Juan. But beneath this façade of the calm unemotional public school athlete there was an extraordinary childlike emotional vulnerability.' He wondered if this 'emotionalism' was perhaps hereditary, after learning that Ralph's father had worked himself up into a suicidal state over a debt to the Inland Revenue. Ralph, who had found a loaded revolver at his father's house, asked the Woolfs if he could bring him to dinner to distract him; Leonard found Partridge senior 'like his son, a very large man with a surface of rugged imperturbability'. In Leonard's view, Ralph himself was not the type to contemplate suicide, but 'beneath the rather ebullient, hail-fellow-well-met, man of the world façade there was a curious stratum of emotionalism not unlike Mr Partridge's. He was easily moved to tears.'

The idea was that Ralph would eventually, after a trial period, become a partner. Meanwhile he was to work two or three days a week, and be paid £100 a year and fifty per cent of the net profits. As well as helping with the Press, he was appointed Leonard's secretary. From the first, there was confusion about what Ralph's role really was. Leonard saw him primarily as someone who would share the physical work of printing, and he and Virginia soon taught Ralph how to set up a page of type and machine it.

As for Virginia, she was impressed with Ralph but also uneasy. She was stirred by his physical splendour and perhaps a touch envious of his robust good health. 'The young man, aged 26, just left Oxford, is a superb body – shoulders like tough oak; health tingling beneath his skin. Merry shrewd eyes ... I'm shy of stupid young men; but P hasn't that stupidity anyhow. He has been religious; is now socialistic; literature I don't suppose counts for much ... Well, how will it turn out? What shall we print?' If he was by now 'socialistic', it is probably safe to assume that he was a pacifist. It had taken Lytton and Carrington three years to change his mind about war for ever.

The working relationship between Ralph and the Woolfs, while increasingly fractious, was productive. 'The effect of Ralph's joining the Hogarth Press can be seen in the rapid expansion of our list to six books in 1922 and thirteen in 1923,' wrote Leonard. Meanwhile Virginia soon realised that the emotional situation between Ralph and Carrington was coming to the boil. Ralph wanted to move on; he had a job, now he needed a wife. He pressed

Carrington so hard that she and Lytton agreed that the only solution was for her to live in London with Ralph during the week and come to Tidmarsh only at weekends. As it happened, Lytton's brother James had just married Carrington's friend Alix Sargent Florence; soon afterwards they both left London for Vienna to study psychology under Freud himself. Their rooms at 41 Gordon Square were empty, and Ralph and Carrington set up house there in October 1920. Ralph was happy to have won this partial victory, presumably unaware that she was writing mournful letters to Gerald and to Lytton, who told his brother James that the move was in the nature of an experiment and that 'the emotional complexities are considerable'. He informed Virginia that Carrington had promised Ralph to make a final decision about marriage after Christmas.

At first, Ralph got on rather well with Virginia, who was struck by the way he put 'his ox's shoulder to the wheel'. She was curious about his sexual and emotional life and encouraged him to talk; he alarmed Carrington by reporting 'amazing conversations' about masturbation. 'I am sure it's all very dangerous,' she wrote to Lytton, 'and she'll worm all sorts of things out of him.' (Clearly there was something to worm.) Virginia's own sexuality was restricted by her husband's agreement with her doctors that sex, like motherhood, would threaten her mental stability; but she liked to be admired and it amused her to flirt with him a little. 'I have just kissed Ralph on the neck,' she informed her sister Vanessa; 'It's these elderly passions that are so dangerous.' Ralph probably flirted too; he liked to recall how angelic she looked, coming down the stairs at Hogarth House in her nightdress, with bare feet. Nevertheless, she deplored his crude and old-fashioned attitude to women. He was, she decided, 'an indomitable, perhaps rather domineering young man; loves dancing; in the pink of health; a healthy brain. He described a brothel the other night – how, after the event, he and the girl sat over the fire discussing the coal strike. Girls paraded before him – that was what pleased him – the sense of power.'

Not long before Christmas she discussed the Carrington–Ralph impasse with Lytton, who told her he was tiring of the recurrent crises. When she said that she could never have married a man like Ralph, whom she considered 'a despot', his reply was: 'True. But what's to happen to Carrington? She can't live indefinitely with me – perhaps with him?' Soon afterwards, when the Woolfs visited Tidmarsh in January 1921, Lytton was even more pessimistic. 'Perhaps after all,' said Lytton, 'one oughtn't to allow these attachments. Our parents may have been right.' He was careful not to let Virginia know how much he himself cared for Ralph.

Early in the New Year, Lytton decided that he too would spend more time in London; his mother had just moved to 51 Gordon Square, and his new book, *Queen Victoria*, dedicated to Virginia (and mostly typed out by Ralph) was about to be published. The marriage decision had been postponed yet again; he told James, who did know his brother's feelings, that 'RP continues to be very charming, and I don't think oppresses her with maritalism too much'. But by the spring, the situation had deteriorated. Stalled by Carrington, Ralph was increasingly frustrated at the Hogarth Press. Leonard was punctilious and fierce about time-keeping. Ralph was often late; he found the work boring. Cross and distracted, he started to make mistakes; one of his duties was to send books out for review, and Virginia was not pleased when *Monday or Tuesday* was sent to *The Times* without the date of publication. Under strain all round, Ralph blew up, threatening that if Carrington would not marry him he would become a sheep farmer in South America. Observing his assistant in a state of 'almost hysterical craziness', Leonard advised him 'to put a pistol at her, not his head'. Even Virginia felt that Carrington should make up her mind, but that although she probably was, as Ralph said, 'selfish, untruthful and quite indifferent to his suffering', she should beware of marrying a man who was, as she told him to his face, 'a bit of an ogre and tyrant' who wanted to control 'the body and mind and time and thoughts of his loved. There's his danger and her risk.'

Finally, in May 1921, after writing Lytton one of the saddest letters in the history of love, Carrington gave in. She could not bear seeing Ralph so wretched; he appeared on the brink of a complete breakdown. Again, she told Lytton that it was him she loved, not Ralph, but that she thought she could make Ralph happy, although 'he knows that I am not in love with him'. She said too that recently Ralph had told her, 'because he was jealous and wanted to hurt me', that as well as fearing her dependence, Lytton had disliked her showing him physical affection. When Lytton replied, he was as affectionate and reassuring as he could be: but the damage was done. And it was clear that he thought she had made the right decision for all three of them. He wrote tenderly to Ralph, restating his dependence on the Tidmarsh triangle. On 21 May 1921, Carrington and Ralph were married. In Cambridge, Frances Marshall had just done her Finals and was being much sought after at May Balls.

Carrington had her reward: the threesome was hardly suspended at all. The honeymoon journey to Italy began with quarrels and ended by meeting Lytton in Venice; Carrington had already managed to lose her wedding ring. The reaction against Ralph for bullying her into marriage was not long in coming. Gerald Brenan, in Spain, received a letter hinting that she might well have preferred to marry him, assuring him that the marriage meant little and that she would never change her name to Partridge. In August, Gerald joined them on a holiday in the Lake District, where he and Carrington fell into each other's arms behind the bushes while Ralph went fishing. After Watendlath, they considered themselves in love. That autumn, Ralph spotted Frances at Birrell and Garnett's bookshop.

Within the year both Ralph's marriage and his job were in jeopardy. He and Leonard were constantly at odds; he would rush off to a party leaving the Woolfs to clear up after him, and they had decided he was both arrogant and sloppy, a deadly combination. When the next storm blew up they were much less sympathetic.

The storm, which became known as the Great Row (Frances always called it that, though she knew nothing about it at the time), struck in the summer of 1922 when Ralph finally found out about Gerald and Carrington. His rage and indignation were not at all muted by the fact that he was himself having a passionate affair at the time with Valentine Dobree, another Slade friend of Carrington's (and a woman to whom Carrington had announced herself to be strangely attracted) who by now was married to the man of letters Bonamy Dobree. Valentine, who was darkly beautiful and considered a femme fatale, precipitated the Row. She could not resist telling Ralph that she had agreed to distract him during a visit to the Dobrees' house in the Pyrenees earlier that year, so that Carrington could be alone with Gerald, and that everyone except him knew that his new wife was carrying on with his best friend. The Great Row took place mostly at Tidmarsh; it was tearful, prolonged and extremely painful, as Ralph backed Carrington into a corner, exposed her deceptions and berated Gerald for his treachery. Despite the civilising influence of Bloomsbury, represented by Lytton, who did his best to calm them all down, Ralph was beside himself with rage and jealousy. Virginia Woolf was scathing about his ugly, irrational behaviour. 'For the last few days we have had a mad bull in the house,' she wrote, 'an Englishman in love, and deceived.'

Although, through Lytton's efforts and Gerald's withdrawal to Spain, the marriage limped on, it was fundamentally damaged. Ralph's affair with Valentine continued for some months but petered out during the autumn, to Lytton and Carrington's great relief; although Ralph brought her to Tidmarsh she was not at all the kind of woman who would ever fit in there. Carrington wrote Gerald a long, secret account of the Great Row's aftermath: Valentine, she had concluded, 'cannot be a citizen in a civilised world. In other words she can't share our lives. And I don't believe it is possible for Ralph to have very intimate relations with a third person who is hostile to his other friends ... he never sees her but he comes back cynical about Tidmarsh, suspicious and cynical about me, and even about Lytton ... Lytton and me seem "cold fishes" to use her favourite expression.'

The more Ralph bullied and interrogated Carrington, the more devious she became. They all wrote each other immensely long explanatory letters, Gerald's often with secret postscripts that Carrington would smuggle up to her bedroom. Ralph informed Gerald that it was intolerable for him to share Carrington because her sexual appetite was much weaker than his; meanwhile he continued to carry on openly with other women. He maintained that it was her deceit, not her infidelity, that meant he could never trust her again. Lytton regarded Ralph's obsession with Carrington's 'virtue' as half crazy, but he advised her, if she wanted to keep him, to be very careful. The transformation of Ralph Partridge, where sexual mores were concerned, was evidently only skin-deep. However, no-one in Bloomsbury circles, where the situation was naturally much discussed, appears to have challenged Ralph's assumption that he could take lovers while expecting Carrington to be faithful, although on the whole their sympathies were with her.

By November, Carrington was beginning to feel secure again. 'Ralph agreed yesterday', she told Lytton, 'that nothing mattered compared to our triangular trinity of happiness.' As for Lytton himself, he had steered them all through another hurricane of emotion. He was always, in his subtle way, self-serving; but then he was still in love with Ralph himself. 'I can't say how happy your decision to try going on here has made me,' he wrote to Ralph. 'I suppose I could face life without you, just as I could face life without one of my hands cut off ... I sympathise with you so absolutely, so completely, my dear, dear love. Sometimes I feel as if I *was* inside you! Why can't I make you perfectly happy by waving some magic wand? Keep this letter to yourself.'

By the end of the year Leonard and Virginia had decided that Ralph would have to go. He was neither surprised nor upset, and after weeks of negotiation and discussion, with Lytton much in play, the parting was agreed in December and took place in March 1923. All concerned behaved well, and there was no open breach of friendship, but the Woolfs were left feeling annoyed by Ralph's uncouth behaviour and the way he seemed to them to exploit his relationship with Lytton. There was even talk of him starting a Tidmarsh Press of his own, on the back of Lytton's reputation. Ralph wrote to Gerald in Spain asking him for something to publish; he summed up the position crisply. 'The temperament of Leonard, the sensibility of Virginia and my own pigheadedness now admit the impossibility of coalition. I didn't comprehend them and they didn't comprehend me, two years ago, or we should never have embarked on partnership.' That spring, the Woolfs themselves set off to Yegen; Ralph issued a warning, uneasy at the prospect of Virginia and Gerald discussing the Great Row. 'I used to make confidences to her,' he wrote, 'but when I saw how little she thought confidences confidential I drew back. She can be charming at moments and perfectly odious at others though it's hard to believe the last, until you've heard her insulting people to their faces just because she thinks them stupid ... I don't want them to make any mischief between us and Virginia might easily try to get up some excitement for herself at our expense.'

Ralph threw away an opportunity when he left the Hogarth Press – even though it was never easy to work for the Woolfs. In theory, a career in publishing could have suited him well; he had a flair for business, a talent for organisation and a good critical intelligence. In practice, encouraged by Lytton and Carrington, who preferred him at their beck and call, he was never to take a job again. Thereafter, one way or another Lytton kept him afloat: Ralph became his secretary (Carrington called him the secretary bird), managed his finances and took on most of his professional correspondence. Nothing came of the Tidmarsh Press; Ralph took up bookbinding instead.

Far from strengthening Ralph's position and reputation with Old Bloomsbury, his two and a half years working for the Woolfs did much to undermine it. On the surface, they remained friendly enough; but the notion of Ralph as idle, selfish and a bit of a bully had taken root. Vanessa Bell, in particular, who in her quiet way was just as important an arbiter within Bloomsbury as her sister, took strongly against him. Ralph Partridge was never a welcome visitor to Charleston.

Ralph's traces at the Hogarth Press faded fast, but can just be discerned in *Mrs Dalloway*, the novel Virginia Woolf was working on during his time there. In the novel, she deals with the after-effects of the war on one young man who had endured it, the shattered, shell-shocked Septimus, and drew on her knowledge of Ralph Partridge and his friend Gerald Brenan. These two young men, although they had not been driven out of their minds, had certainly been profoundly shaken by their experience in the trenches. In her notes for *Mrs Dalloway* she indicated that Septimus would be 'partly R, partly me' and might also have 'something of GB in him?' Between them they suggested to her 'The young man who has gone into business after the war: takes life to heart: seeks truth – revelations.' As her biographer remarks, 'Together, these young men out of the war, with their disturbingly intense emotional lives and their uncertainty about the future, seemed to her to represent the postwar trauma of a whole generation.'

Against this background of personal and professional muddle and humiliation Ralph Partridge became increasingly interested in pretty, clever Frances Marshall, who was so attractive, so easy to find in Birrell and Garnett's bookshop (by now in Gerrard Street in Soho) and above all so very different from Carrington. For five years, he had been caught up in sexual and emotional complexities which were not only new but in some ways foreign to him. He may have been liberated by Lytton and Carrington, but he had also been lured out of his depth. Now he began to discover a girl whose nature was to be straightforward. Carrington's and Frances' characters were as different as their appearance. Carrington was golden-haired, blue-eyed and pink-cheeked; her toes turned in like a little girl's, she was rounded and she could look clumsy. Frances had lustrous dark hair, brown eyes and creamy skin; she was slender and light on her feet. Carrington had a fantastical, whimsical cast of mind; Frances was rational and liked argument. Where Carrington was naturally devious, Frances was naturally truthful. Where Carrington was full of doubts and insecurities, Frances had a certain fundamental confidence in who she was. Where Carrington was afraid of sexual passion, drawn to women and averse to dominant men, Frances, although sexually inexperienced, was at ease with male company and attention. Moreover, unlike Carrington, she could not be patronised, either intellectually or socially, being, through her family connections, already linked to Bloomsbury. She was not only attractive, she was suitable; and although she still lived with her mother, she was very much a girl of her times, enjoying the new postwar freedoms, working, drinking, dancing, uninterested in sitting at home waiting for a husband. For the moment, though, she was not Ralph's only romantic interest. To Gerald, still pining for Carrington on his Spanish hilltop, Ralph boasted of his new freedom to play the field – a not very subtle way of re-establishing his sexual superiority. 'I keep seeing new people, a younger generation than Bloomsbury. There is Marjorie Joad, who has taken up my duties at Hogarth: Frances Marshall, who sits in Birrell and Garnett's shop; various Cambridge young men with good looks and posts at the Nation; rising talent, dancers and partygoers; the 1917 Club, new faces, with a hope of new minds.' He claimed to be carrying on five intrigues with five different women.

But before long Ralph began to concentrate on Frances. He would make a beeline for her at parties, dance with her all night if she would let him and he bombarded her with letters. The first of the many letters from Ralph that Frances kept to the end of her life is dated 2 August 1923, and it is an apology for misbehaviour at a party the night before. 'Have I committed an atrocity ... I didn't mean to hurt you in any way and you became so aloof.' He flattered and teased her and tried to win her good opinion. 'The first thing I heard about you was that Pernel Strachey said Cambridge was full of young men whose hearts you had broken, but "she's got her head screwed on the right way".' Ralph added, 'I generally prefer the wrong way.' He told her his real name, adding: 'Perhaps you hate the name Rex – I could change it again if you like. In the war I was Raoul in France and Rinaldo in Italy but I'd go further than that to give you satisfaction.' He soon settled back to being Ralph, but perhaps, with this particular girl, his instinct was to revert to a pre-Strachey self. Soon, however, she became Francesca to his Paolo and his letters became more ardent and more confident. 'You've got me upon my knees ... I think you are an absolute darling ... I like talking to you, telling you stories about other people, watching your face, holding your hands, dancing with you, going for walks with you.' He wanted them to share their life stories. He told her who his 'enemies' in the Bloomsbury circle were, as if warning her not to listen to what they said about him: Mark Gertler, Ottoline Morrell, Clive Bell – and possibly Bunny Garnett. When Bunny realised what was going on, he did indeed warn Frances that Ralph was a great seducer. By now he was having a fling with the young woman who had taken over from him at the Hogarth Press, Marjorie Joad, the consort of the philosopher. But although Frances was beginning to respond to Ralph, she was not about to go to bed with him.

That autumn, as well as having dates in London for lunch, dinner and, especially, dancing, at which they both excelled, she was invited to Tidmarsh for the weekend. This was her first experience of Lytton, Carrington and Ralph at home, and the prospect made her nervous. Carrington was charming to her, but it must have been strange to be looked after by her admirer's wife; she was awed by Lytton's erudition and thankful to find the friendly, eager, young Raymond Mortimer, already a rising critic, among the guests along with E.M. Forster and a strange French doctor. This was the start of a long, sunny friendship between Frances and Raymond; she did not much care for the louche Frenchman, who after dinner tried to make them all describe how they had lost their virginity. 'I felt too embarrassed and ashamed to write "Never"!' she later recalled. The mysterious doctor appears in a photograph of Ralph, broad-shouldered in a beret, Forster, neat in a flat cap, the bearded Strachey in a battered trilby, and Frances, her small face just visible between a large dark hat and her coat collar, standing in a row on a bridge over the river.

By the time Frances visited Tidmarsh, though, the ménage was on the move. Perhaps because its harmony had been damaged by the Great Row, perhaps because the damp was not good for Lytton, the place had begun to lose its charm for all three of them. Carrington had long loved the Wiltshire downs, where the sky was bigger and the horizon wider than in the Thames Valley; she went house-hunting, and in October 1923 took Ralph and Lytton to see a house outside the small village of Ham, near Hungerford. She described the discovery to Gerald: first they walked past a lodge, then down a long avenue of lime trees, past some barns and then 'the back of a rather forbidding farm house. We walked to the front of it and saw to our amazement in the blazing sun a perfect English country house with a superb view across fields to the downs.' This was Ham Spray House, and they decided they must try to buy it. At £3,000 the price was steep; Ralph started negotiating with the agents. The plan was that Lytton would provide most of the cash, that Ralph would contribute what he could (his father had recently died and he had some capital of his own) and the house would be bought in Ralph's name.

As Ralph was aware, he was not the only man eager for Frances' company that autumn. She had three other eligible admirers: Philip Nichols from the Foreign Office, who was increasingly interested in her; Geoffrey Sieveking who had still not given up hope; and Colin Mackenzie, now based in Glasgow and making his way in business. She did not keep any of Colin's letters to her; but he kept hers, and they show her in close-up at this critical moment, when she was making up her mind whether to allow Ralph Partridge into her life. Later, she chose not to recall much about him and the part he had played; now, he can perhaps be seen to have stood for her pre-bookshop world, the world in which she had grown up, which had always been progressive enough to be interesting while remaining respectable enough to be safe.

In her letters to Colin, usually written from work, Frances sounds amused but far from overwhelmed by Bloomsbury, its characters and its parties. During 1923, as well as giving him provocative descriptions of Bloomsbury gatherings ('a charming fancy dress party yesterday. Lytton Strachey was there as Jesus') and teasing him about his grand friends, like the Douros of Stratfield Saye, she told him how much she longed to travel abroad, especially to Italy, the country he knew so well. She had just glimpsed it on her walking tour in the Dolomites that summer with two friends from Newnham. When he promptly suggested they plan a trip there together, she prevaricated. 'Of course I want to come to Italy with you – but will it be possible is the question. You seem to forget I have a mama who is not quite but nearly as conventional as most other mamas.' However, she added,

'I do believe in training one's parents to realise one is a free agent . . . there's nothing in the world that bores me so utterly as all this propriety business and my mama is the only person in the world for whom I would take it into account at all.' Later in the year, Bloomsbury was getting on her nerves. 'Really the Bloomsburians – they pall after a bit. I went to a Bloomsbury party last night at which there were so many intrigues and jealousies going on, they were like strings across the room, all twined up, one felt bewildered . . . I hate all this footling waste of energy.'

Perhaps emboldened by this outburst, he suggested they visit Eton together. He wanted to show Frances his old school and perhaps the famous Wall Game. She wrote back cheerfully to accept, adding 'I don't believe I've ever seen a public school' (which seems odd given she had two public-school brothers). As it happened, the Eton outing took place the weekend after her visit to Tidmarsh, which she described to Colin without mentioning Ralph, telling him how she had feared she would not be up to the intellectual level but in the end had a surprisingly good time, and that a drunken French doctor had asked everyone 'embarrassing questions'. Later, she was to turn against public schools; but she wrote Colin an enthusiastic thank-you letter.

Ralph's attitude to Frances' other admirers was simple but effective. He declined to take them seriously, gave them dismissive nicknames – Sieveking was Longlegs, Colin was the Gentleman from Glasgow – and teased her about them, but he was uneasy about the competition. They had the great advantage of being unmarried, and it was so easy to find Frances at the bookshop. 'Who was the spruce gentleman who pretended he'd come to buy a book when his one wish was to feast his rather bloodshot eyes on you?' Sometimes when he looked in, to collect the latest instalment of Proust (like Frances, he and Lytton were eagerly reading each volume as it appeared) he felt unwelcome. 'Will you tell me if they want me to keep away from the bookshop? Did you feel the strain as acutely as I did?' Bunny and Frankie were both protective of Frances and suspicious of Ralph's intentions. His letters became more ardent and intense. He did not conceal from her that he was carrying on with Marjorie Joad; he believed in complete candour in such matters. He pressed her to trust him and confide in him. 'You don't treat me yet as part of yourself. That is my object – the very depths of intimacy . . . I want you to be perpetually happy and never unhappy, only I haven't discovered the secret of perpetual happiness myself . . . as for your beauty, I can't stand up to it at all . . . it prostrates me at your feet.' Ralph also introduced her to his mother; in a letter to Lytton, Carrington described a musical evening chez Mrs Partridge senior, who had taken a flat in Bloomsbury herself, which included Lytton's sister Marjorie and Ralph's sister Dorothy. Ralph sang Spanish ballads, 'sweet Frances sang Purcell'. None of Ralph's family cared for Carrington, who seemed to them a very odd sort of wife; and they did not understand either why Ralph was not pursuing a career rather than running errands for Lytton Strachey.

But on the Tidmarsh front, Carrington was plotting her next move. She began to talk about a winter visit to Gerald in Spain. There was no question of Lytton going with them this time; apart from his fear of discomfort, there was the matter of Ham Spray to pursue. For once, Carrington was prepared, even eager, to go somewhere without him. The more she sensed that Ralph was seriously interested in Frances, the more she needed to revive her own romance; and what better way to prove that the horrors of the Great Row had receded than for all three of them to be together again in Yegen? And surely it would not be hard now for them to spend time alone together, given Ralph's new attachment. 'Ralph', she wrote to Gerald on 20 November, 'is in love with a black-haired beauty and thinks life is perfect ... a beautiful Princess that lives in Birrell and Garnett's bookshop. So you need not fear that there will be any more glooms.' She herself, on the other hand, she went on, was in love with a house – Ham Spray. Lytton, with some misgivings, agreed to the plan. She and Ralph would travel out to Yegen before Christmas.

Ralph was perfectly amenable, not least because he had devised a plot of his own. He wanted to get Frances away from her other admirers. Why should she not join them for a few days, perhaps in Paris, where they would surely be pausing on their way home in January? He suspected that he would find it easier to capture her away from London.

Frances was tempted, but the plan was not confirmed when Ralph and Carrington set off the week before Christmas. She spent the weekend before they left at Tidmarsh, and saw them off on the train, as a postscript at the end of Ralph's letter from Paris shows. 'It was charming of you to come and see us off this morning,' wrote Carrington. 'It made the exit much less unpleasant ... I hope you will come to Tidmarsh again directly we get back. I loved having you this weekend so very much, My love, Carrington.' From then on, Carrington often added a few lines or a drawing to Ralph's letters to Frances. Her messages were always affectionate, but they also served to remind Frances of her presence and her claims on Ralph.

Frances liked Carrington, but Ralph was well on the way to winning her heart. Her first letters to him have a very different tone from those she was writing simultaneously to Colin. She calls him her dearest Paolo, describes her doings in detail – the hectic Christmas rush in the bookshop – 'we work all day like niggers, and have had to lay in a special stock of whisky to take before we go home as we are too exhausted otherwise to face the horrors of the tube' – and another musical evening, this time at Brunswick Square, where Marjorie and Oliver Strachey performed comic turns and she and her brother Tom sang Mozart arias. She and Ralph invented mocking nicknames for the Marshall family: they became the Gorillas, and Mam the Queen of the Forest. She tells him she has found someone to stand in for her if she comes to Paris and urges him to write her another letter quickly; 'Tell me about all your young ladies. I hear no gossip now you are gone.' She finished the letter in bed. 'My eyelids are dropping, but in spite of that I love you. Your Francesca.'

From Spain, Ralph wrote Frances a stream of long, loving, pressing letters. He described their journey and life in Yegen in vivid detail – these are good letters, observant and well-written – and they prove his need to hold Frances' attention and his increasing anxiety lest she not after all meet him in Paris. Her letters were shorter and less frequent than his, the post in Spain was erratic, and he began to wonder if it had been a mistake to leave her. He sensed trouble ahead: 'I can't define the events that are to harrow us or one of us, and yet that makes me panicky, the pervading unhappiness of so many other people might stick a spoke in us somehow.' At the same time he wrote affectionate, reassuring letters to Lytton, encouraging him about Ham Spray, urging him to join them in Paris, as if he needed to let Lytton know that Frances was no threat. 'I never thought Frances would be able to come actually, when I said I'd like to see her in Paris . . . I'm longing to see her, but I'm longing to see you, dearest, too.'

As the Woolfs had realised, Ralph, beneath the ebullient, confident surface, was easily rattled. He told Frances every exotic detail of their Yegen Christmas – how they drank green chartreuse and smoked Moorish tobacco said to be half hashish, but which to his disappointment produced no erotic dreams – and hinted at long, significant walks and talks with Gerald and Carrington, but 'topics become so delicate so far away and when I can't watch your face'. Bunny Garnett's annoying success with *Lady into Fox* was discussed; Gerald threatened, Ralph wrote, to emulate the muezzins' call to prayer and shout 'A Pox on *Lady into Fox*' from the Yegen rooftops.

Any endearments in her letters delight him. 'You called me dearest one at the beginning, my dear once in the middle and said you still loved me at the end – you're darling.' He sent her elaborate advice about travel arrangements and how and where to meet them, and asked her to wire her plans: 'If you say "not coming" I shall hardly get over it.' When her letters seem cool, he starts to panic. Has she changed her mind? Does she still love him?

Has he upset her? Why are her letters so guarded? He sits in the primitive bathroom to write to her during a crashing thunderstorm, while Gerald and Carrington read Baudelaire to each other very loudly. 'If I don't get a letter from you at Madrid I shall become a sodomite and have done with it.'

Frances, meanwhile, had not greatly enjoyed her own Marshall Christmas. From the first, she and Ralph encouraged each other in the Bloomsbury tendency to find family life comic at best and boring and depressing at worst. Christmas Eve in the shop was fun; they gave each other presents, and 'finished the day having drinks at the Criterion and went home cheerful and tipsy'. But otherwise – 'You would have hated the sort of time I've been having – children seething everywhere, ceaseless noise, nothing in particular to do, and yet impossible to go and read in peace, over-eating, bad temper.' She tries to reassure him, while not quite committing herself to Paris. 'Yes, I still love you just as much, but you seem rather like a stranger because the life you're leading is so utterly and absolutely different from mine – with your Goyas and Grecos, monkeys and dons – but I love you.'

Finally, on 3 January, she wrote the letter he was longing for. Paris was going to come true. 'Of course I'm going to come.'

Six

Frances and Ralph, 1923–1925

When she decided to join Ralph in Paris, Frances took an important step; but she could not have failed to realise how strongly he remained committed to Lytton and Carrington. While she was making up her mind, and he was fretting in Spain, another significant decision was taken which he instantly relayed back to Frances. 'We have just had a wire from Lytton,' he wrote on 7 January. 'He has bought Ham Spray for £2,300.' Ralph sounded both pleased and anxious:

> We shall have to move – we shall be thrust into a hostile country remote from a railway station, with no electric light, no drains, poisonous water, no servants, insufficient furniture, leaky roof, the clergyman will call, the county will cut us, the sheep will eat the fuschias, the elms will fall on the scullery, the tennis lawn will go to rack and ruin, the rhubarb will be nipped by the frost, the Labour Party will bring in the capital levy, my mother will live to be 100, Lytton will be prosecuted for raping Annie, I shall go to gaol for sodomy and you will find some wretched excuse for not coming to Paris.

His fear was unfounded. Frances reached Paris first, on 12 January 1924, and awaited the travellers in the Hôtel des Saints Pères. The next day Ralph and Carrington arrived, laden with Spanish pottery, carpets and a particularly beautiful, carefully chosen red silk embroidered shawl as a present for Frances from them both. Ralph had booked a room for himself and Carrington next door to Frances, and for the next few days he showed her round Paris. Frances was thrilled to be taken to good restaurants, to spend a day at the Louvre, to see a Racine play at the Comédie Française and to hear Mistinguett. It was her first taste of sophisticated travel. She enjoyed it all greatly. Carrington was not happy. Having allowed her two weeks of Gerald's company in Spain, Ralph had no compunction about leaving her on her own. She pretended she did not mind, but in fact she did; she relieved her feelings by grumbling to

Gerald. 'Since Ralph and Frances will be quite happy by themselves I shall go to galleries all day by myself. She is very charming and looked exquisite in her red shawl, and yet how curious it all is. Ralph said to me "of course I would rather be alone in Paris with Frances, but I see she half wants you to stay here because of her people, so you had better stay, only I must see her alone. You weren't very tactful this morning" ... how easy it is for him and what a long time it was before we were alone together at Yegen.' It cannot have taken Carrington very long to realise that in Frances, Ralph had found someone much more suitable for him than the dramatic, demanding Valentine, someone indeed who could perhaps fit in with Lytton and herself; but she was wary. Could the triangle ever really change and absorb a fourth person? And was Frances perhaps too good to be true? 'She is a very delightful companion,' Carrington told Gerald. 'Perhaps almost too perfect, beautiful and unselfish. I think I would like her better if I could detect one fault.'

As for Frances, never, in her letters of the time or in anything she wrote or said later, did Ralph's marriage to Carrington seem to trouble her in any conventional sense. She accepted from the start what he told her, that although he was committed to their joint life with Lytton, the marriage was neither close nor passionate, and that both partners were free to form other relationships. Early on, too, he told her that Carrington's true love was not him, but Lytton. She realised that Ralph was likely to go on sleeping with his wife as well as other women when it suited him; she certainly knew all about Marjorie Joad and, as he soon told her about the Great Row, about Valentine. Unless she started to sleep with him herself, she was not in a position to object, and there is no evidence that she did. He told her that he would always tell her the truth, and she believed he always did, comfortable or not. Bloomsbury believed in truth-telling and on the whole behaved accordingly, and Frances respected them for it. Eighty years on, she would say with admiration that Ralph was the most completely truthful person she had ever known.

Meanwhile, with the final details of the purchase of Ham Spray still uncertain, Lytton was not at all sure that he would be able to join them, and Carrington began to talk of hurrying back to England. This prospect annoyed Ralph and unnerved Frances; to be alone in a Paris hotel with Ralph would be asking for trouble. But the purchase of Ham Spray was clinched, Lytton arrived triumphant and their last three days in Paris were spent as a foursome. Frances was struck by how Lytton, so familiar with French literature, declined to speak a word of French or to make any decisions or arrangements. 'He left all such practical matters to Ralph.' By 21 January they were all back in England.

Their time in Paris had brought Frances and Ralph much closer. Their letters after the return are protestations of love. 'Oh my dearest, my love, I miss you,' wrote Ralph from Tidmarsh, in the intervals of unpacking the Spanish pottery (much of it in pieces). He was to see her two days later, but it seemed too long to wait. Back under her mother's roof in Brunswick Square she was writing to him, 'I'm quite sure I love you more since Paris than I did before.' Meanwhile Carrington had taken to her bed with a feverish cold, from whence she wrote an aggrieved ten-page letter to Gerald. To him, she had no need to conceal her reservations about Frances, or her feelings about Frances' effect on Ralph.

'He is of course fascinating about his lady. He tells me everything, and goes into her most minuet [sic] actions ... I feel personally a slight gulf of age between her and myself [Carrington was seven years older than Frances, thus thirty-one to her twenty-four, and a year older than Ralph]. She has so obviously never loved, or felt anything passionately. She has also never suffered. She clearly thinks we make rather a fuss over life; I think it's a too big difference between us. Even Ralph admitted it made a limitation to her understanding. She is also ruthlessly egotistical, that is rather terrifying.' Carrington was irritated by Ralph's insistence that she should become Frances' friend, just as Gerald, in spite of everything, was his, and his assumption that because he shared the details of his new love with her, she should do likewise. 'He tried to make out I wasn't friendly to his liaison and that I hadn't tried to make friends with her. This was too childish, for I was only twice alone with her for a few minuets and it was perfectly clear she was engrossed in R and hadn't the slightest desire to be my most intimate friend.' Ralph went on to tax her with being secretive. She quoted him verbatim to Gerald. '"I tell you all about my feelings for Frances, and go into details of our relations, and what we discuss, and my lusts for her. You never tell me anything about yourself and Gerald ... I never know what your physical relations are ... would you, if I said I didn't mind, like to go to bed with him?"' Poor Carrington, whose sexuality was uneasy, could not bear these interrogations and knew perfectly well that Ralph was seeking justification, if not permission, for his increasingly serious feelings for Frances. Gerald's love balanced the situation; but she much preferred it on paper, where she could make promises without having to fulfil them. 'I will be more intimate with you in April ... Please always remember Ralph reads my letters. Dearest Gerald I love you so much.'

Thus the stage was set for the next few months, with Frances and Ralph exchanging loving letters, meeting whenever Ralph was in London – he was taking a bookbinding course – and occasionally at Tidmarsh for a weekend, when Carrington would be as charming and welcoming to Frances as she could manage before retreating to write secret letters of complaint to Gerald. Ralph's affair with Marjorie Joad petered out; Frances was not best pleased when her brother Tom married Marjorie in 1925. Ralph kept up the pressure on Frances; his letters became more and more ardent, sometimes anxious, above all determined to get her to open up to him, emotionally as well as sexually. Frances was sometimes evasive or slightly defensive; self-revelation was new to her. She told him about her slightly awkward relations with Bunny – himself just back from a visit to Gerald with Ray – about meetings with her old school and Newnham friends, and what she was reading – Chekhov (in Bunny's mother's translation), Proust and *Les Liaisons dangereuses*, a book which with its cool, explicit approach to complex sexual relationships was a great favourite with Bloomsbury. 'Tell me exactly what you thought of the account of the seduction,' wrote Ralph eagerly. 'I was so filled with horror at the one-sidedness of it.' (Frances' reply has vanished.) He loved her 'without a single misgiving or qualification'. Carrington 'wants you to know that she loves you too'. As well as being truthful by nature, Frances was not suspicious. She believed, perhaps too readily, that Carrington (and indeed Lytton, who was watching and waiting) meant what they said and enjoyed her company.

Ralph left Frances in no doubt about his eagerness to get her into bed. After a weekend at Tidmarsh, he raved about her physical beauty – her black hair, her delicious freckles, her apricot skin – and teased her about sex. He was busy educating her in Bloomsbury's taste for outspoken jokes and innuendos, and wrote her a rude limerick:

> There was a young lady from Newnham
> Who declared that men's balls were albumen;
> She regarded the foreskin
> As part of a whoreskin
> And was thought very knowing – at Newnham.

After which, fearing his vulgarity might displease her, he recounted how he dreamed of her dancing in Paris at a party given by Proust's Madame Verdurin.

Ralph's keen interest in sex verged on exhibitionism, which sometimes went too far even for Bloomsbury, pioneers in taboo-breaking and saying the hitherto unsayable. At a Gordon Square party given by Marjorie and

Alix Strachey in the summer of 1924, he and Marjorie acted a scene from
Schnitzler's *La Ronde*. Perhaps it was just as well that Frances was away at
the time; Vanessa Bell described it to Roger Fry as a copulation scene and
found it painfully embarrassing. The audience talked louder and louder,
trying to drown the 'very realistic groans made by Partridge . . . I don't think
anyone enjoyed it. It was a great relief when Marjorie sang hymns.' (Her
favourite comic turn was to make hymns and nursery rhymes sound
obscene.) The Woolfs were also present for this treat; afterwards, according
to Virginia, 'Leonard went home and contemplated, seriously, some
scientific form of suicide'.

Frances' virginity was evidently a topic for discussion. Bloomsbury was
not impressed by women who were suspected of clinging to theirs (such as
Carrington and Frances' sister Ray). 'Is it true that you'd rather not talk
about your virginity?' Ralph enquired. 'It seemed to me at one minute that
you were bridling last night, and didn't want to have to think about what
I was saying.' He promised to leave the topic alone, but 'We'll have a grand
discussion when you feel in the mood and get rid of all the suppressions'.
Frances found this sort of thing, and Ralph's constant scrutiny of her moods,
a bit much. Then she would become remote, which he found disconcerting.
He himself, he told her, 'would go to any lengths of exposing myself to
someone I love. I would go much further with you and I intend to, only
I see your barricades go up and I often lose my nerve.' He insisted on telling
her about his previous loves; sometimes she could not conceal her dislike
of the way he had treated them. In turn, he expected her to tell him about
the other men in her life; but when she did, he did not much like it. 'The
Gentleman from Glasgow arrived yesterday,' Frances wrote cheerfully, 'and
we visited the Savoy, Claridges and the Café Royal. I will not deny that he
has suddenly begun making up to me.' Although her next sentence was
'I want to see you again very very much' Ralph felt threatened, and it did
not help that plans for Frances and Colin to travel to Italy together in the
summer were taking shape. Always more volatile emotionally than he
appeared (and certainly more so than Frances), he renewed the pressure on
her to sleep with him; if Frances gave in to him physically he would have
won. He knew that the strength of his desire frightened, even repelled her.
'Sometimes too I think you dislike my interest in the bodily part of lust –
you think I give too much attention to it – you see it has a certain point
but not all the point I give it.' Frances shared some of her family's dislike of
emotional or physical demonstrativeness and although Ralph assured her
that lust for 'her lovely body' was the least of what he felt for her – 'you
could have two wooden legs tomorrow and get jaundice and I wouldn't care

a jot less for you' – he sometimes pushed her too hard. After one evening had ended badly he was dejected: 'Your last words to me were "oh do leave me alone" and you said them as if you had been meaning them for some time.'

Apart from enjoying the treats Colin offered her, Frances had begun to use him as a safety valve. It is impossible now to know what, if anything, she told her family or women friends about Ralph – although her family were certainly curious, as she learned from Lytton, who had been approached by Bunny to find out what the position was. But to Colin, she started to mention someone she called 'The B ... y [i.e. Bloomsbury] young man', and the dilemma she was in. 'The trouble is', she wrote around Easter 1924, 'that I'm faced with two alternatives which seem equally intolerable – either marrying the BY or a complete split.' At this point, the awkward fact that the BY already had a wife was not mentioned. 'I wish he was the sort of character who took things lightly,' she went on, 'but he's not. Both his character and the history of his loves make him take these things desperately hardly.' She was really not romantically interested in Colin at all, but she liked him and could not help teasing him. 'I love sliding down towers on a mat,' she informed him, in the same letter. 'Find a Freudian significance if you dare ... the BY arrives to take me to dinner any minute. Here he is – goodbye.'

During that spring Frances' mind was briefly taken off her romantic problems by her first appearance in print, in the pages of the *New Statesman*. She was asked to review a book entitled *Bedales: A Pioneer School* by her old headmaster, J.H. Badley. Her short, unsigned review with its provocative headline 'The Pleasures of Ignorance' appeared on 8 March 1924; she took a spirited, critical line about her old school. She praised it for being co-educational and for allowing pupils enough spare time: 'it is a relief to see the importance of learning how to dispose of freedom recognised for once'. However, she took exception to the way that almost all school activities – farming, weaving, music, arts and crafts – seemed to count more than actual learning; and here a private joke against Ralph can surely be discerned. 'Bookbinding and vegetable growing can after all be as great tyrants as Latin and Greek, and are of no greater use in after life.' Her final blast was challenging: Bedales, she suggested, while professing to be unconventional, was inclined to substitute one kind of convention for another. 'Doubtless it produces healthy, open-air, no nonsense people with a love of country life and of doing things with their hands, but can it produce anything else?' Two weeks later, a furious letter signed by 'twenty-one readers' appeared, accusing the anonymous reviewer of 'a shameful number of mistakes'; Frances wrote insouciantly to Ralph, 'I might have known what a hornet's nest I would set going.'

As summer approached, the move to Ham Spray gathered momentum. Frances was involved every step of the way, helping with the packing-up of one house and the removal to the other, as well as with the redecorating that followed. She was at Tidmarsh for the last weekend of all, and Ralph wrote to her half an hour before they finally left, on 17 July. Both Lytton and Carrington were sad to go, wondering if they would ever be as happy again as they had all been at the Mill House; and Ralph admitted he felt 'uprooted, like a tree' and worried that he was 'engaged on something that you can't really share with me'.

Frances was not always as amenable as she appeared. Her way of showing Ralph that he could not take her for granted was to press ahead with plans to travel to Italy in the late summer with Colin, along with her brother Tom and the new bookshop assistant, Jane Norton, who was in love with him, en route to a Marshall family gathering in Venice. Ralph's response was predictable. 'The BY young man is still a source of trouble,' she told Colin. He had asked her to marry him (still no mention of Carrington) and she had declined, but he was refusing to take this as final. When Frances suggested a pause in their relationship, Ralph's reaction frightened her. 'He said he would do something desperate and made me promise not to ... I wish I knew what to do.' The parallels with Ralph's behaviour towards Carrington three years earlier are striking. Once again, his emotionalism surged out of control; once again he was determined to get what he wanted.

At Ham Spray that summer the move had stirred up a certain amount of sexual restlessness. Lytton's early passion for Ralph had waned, though he remained loving and dependent on him; but he was seriously attracted by two new young men, Philip Ritchie and Roger Senhouse. Carrington was tormenting Gerald Brenan, on a visit from Spain and desperately in love, by refusing to sleep with him and pursuing an affair with Henrietta Bingham, the bisexual daughter of the American Ambassador to London. Sex with Henrietta was a revelation to Carrington; she realised – and told poor Gerald, though not apparently Ralph – that she had finally found sex more pleasurable than disgusting. Perhaps to show off, or to titillate Ralph and Lytton, Carrington began to proclaim her desire for Frances. One of her postscripts read, 'R wants me to add that I am going to have a desperate assault on you next time, so come armed with a Sapphic belt, if you value your virginity, that's to say if you have the article, but Sapphic virginity aint ... Oh no no, I assure you.' Frances was not shocked, but neither did she respond; she was never in the least physically drawn to women and always made the fact quite plain. There might have been three in a bed on occasion at Tidmarsh, but such sport had no appeal to Frances.

In late August the Italian party set off on their journey, from Genoa to Lucca and through Tuscany to Pisa, Florence and Siena. Frances loved the sunshine, the landscape and the paintings, San Gimignano's towers by moonlight, the Duccios in Siena and the Giottos in Padua. She wrote to Ralph as often as she could, referring breezily to avoiding being alone with Colin ('poor little Glasgow') and assuring Ralph of her love – 'I feel a bit loose in the soul though not a bit in the body' – but not as often or as fully as he wrote to her.

Ralph may have bullied Frances face to face, but now his letters were loving, gossipy and entertaining, as if he wanted to make Ham Spray and its doings irresistible to her on her respectable Italian holiday. He paints a picture of considerable emotional and sexual complexity: Lytton was infatuated with Philip Ritchie, Carrington with Henrietta Bingham, and Noel Carrington with a girl called Catherine, as beautiful as a Bellini Madonna, whom Ralph is not allowed to meet. Gerald Brenan is wretched, and Raymond Mortimer has been to bed with Nancy Cunard.

His main titbit, however, concerned E.M. Forster, and was of particular interest to Frances. Having just finished *A Passage to India*, and needing to escape from his own demanding mother in Weybridge, Forster had become Frances' mother's lodger in Brunswick Square. It had been Vanessa Bell's idea; Ray and Bunny Garnett, now with two small sons, had moved to a house of their own, Hilton, near Cambridge. Frances had written a disrespectful account of Forster to Colin Mackenzie when he moved in, remarking on his 'twisty nose, and little giggle' and deploring his choice of 'pathetically suburban looking furniture'. In a typically Bloomsbury manoeuvre, Forster had recently told Carrington, who told Ralph, that he felt Ralph, so agreeably friendly at Tidmarsh in the pre-Frances era, now ignored him; so after a short 'explication' they went for a long walk on the downs. Ralph's letter is a good example of his shrewdness, as well as his taste for openness in such matters.

'I like him for liking me, but I'm completely in the dark as to his real character. His language is so linked up with his mother and his aunts that it is like a dialect which I can't talk. I agreed that I'd behaved badly to him on his previous visits . . . We talked about friendship, but not with conviction or much interest. He likes it without intimacy, I with, or otherwise it seems to me almost too mild. He asked me to kiss him – which I did – his cheek is rough and smells of nothing at all, more like cardboard than flesh, his hands on the other hand are rather soft and female.' Ralph's friendship with

Forster soon faded away; Forster and Frances never really took to each other, and his books were never among her favourites.

Ralph also reported in some detail to Frances on the Carrington and Gerald situation. He told her how detached he now felt; even when Carrington told him, 'rather timidly', that she and Gerald had been to bed together he did not mind. As Ralph explained, he was well aware that Carrington's sexual interest in him had been revived by his interest in Frances. 'C declared she had wanted me to have her more often these last months – at the same time I'm certain she's not any more physically excited by me than she ever was … I think C wanted me not so much for the excitement as the reassurance … she said she thought I was more beautiful than before.' As for Gerald, 'I never minded him wanting to have her, but objected to her wanting to be had by him.' But now, his objections had vanished. 'I don't feel in the least isolated and unhappy because I love you so much.' A few days later – after recounting a stuffy occasion where Ralph in a dinner jacket and Carrington in black velvet made a rare appearance as Major and Mrs Partridge to dine at Ham Manor, only to learn 'that the village views us as Bohemians and therefore as foreigners' – he returned to this theme. 'A triangular relation can be perfectly all right I think only one doesn't talk about certain subjects to the other side of the triangle … Carrington said she knew that the reason why I wasn't jealous now was because I didn't want so much to go to bed with her, which is true enough.' Meanwhile, he had been out partridge-shooting. 'You've shot the fattest of the day with your bright brown eye,' he told Frances, 'only you haven't bothered to take him home with you.'

The Italian journey ended in Venice, where Frances and Tom rejoined their family; Colin had gone to visit Iris Origo in Tuscany. 'He kept saying he wanted to talk to me and I feel rather guilty because it's true I was practically never alone with him and when we were I was embarrassed in a curious way,' Frances told Ralph. She was right to feel uncomfortable; she was not being honest with Colin, and he was beginning to think himself in love with her. Indeed, before long he told her so, and that it had occurred to him to ask her to marry him but then he had decided against it. Frances was unmoved. 'I think you are very sensible in not wanting to marry me. For the very good reason that I think I should be a dismal failure as a married lady and unless a cataclysm occurs I think I shall probably avoid that state for life.'

Back at the bookshop that autumn, her letters to Colin show that she was beginning to find the situation with Ralph more and more of a strain. 'It began when I went to a dance one night, not knowing the BY man was to be of the party. He made rather a scene. I didn't mind his abuse so much at the time but when I got home it somehow weighed on my mind and I didn't get to sleep till 7.' She took to bromide every night 'like a drug fiend'. What she did not tell Colin was that Ralph was now becoming violently jealous of Philip Nichols. He had reason; Frances was much more attracted to Phil than to any of her other admirers. Tall, civilised, humorous, he was heir to a handsome house in Essex and all set for a distinguished career in the Foreign Office; he was also, unlike Colin with his wooden leg, a brilliant dancer, and as Ralph knew that was a way to Frances' heart. Ralph, as she later wrote, 'was much too acute not to realise that here was a more serious rival than the others I went out with; he questioned me closely, and I couldn't conceal anything from him.' Now subjected to the full force of Ralph's emotional bullying, she found herself in rather a state. 'If he loved you,' she said, looking back, 'you felt his power.'

Ralph and Ham Spray, though, claimed Frances for Christmas 1924, celebrated by a play called 'A Castle in Spain', written by Lytton and starring himself, Ralph and Carrington, Roger Senhouse, Dadie Rylands and Frances. Frances described it to Colin as 'a fantastic and rather obscene little play ... I have to be a young lady dressed up as a man and make violent love to Dadie who is a young man dressed up as a lady'.

Meanwhile Carrington had started to paint a portrait of Frances, at Ralph's request. It was not going well. 'Something awful has happened to the head of you,' Ralph told her. 'The paint's sunk in, and your cheeks are hollow and your eyes wild and your jaws like lanterns, but DC says it's all for the best and will recover.' This portrait, if it was ever finished, did not survive; nor did any portraits of Ralph himself. Outwardly friendly, Carrington's reservations about Frances continued. She described her to Alix Strachey as 'rather a dim character. I mean she never behaves differently and one never gets to know anything more about her. But considering how lovely she is, and how spoiled by hundreds of young men, and the dullness of the bookshop, I think she remains very intelligent.' Carrington was intellectually diffident, and beginning to worry about getting middle-aged and plain. Frances' brains and beauty, as well as the steadiness of her character, were unnerving.

In fact, at the beginning of 1925 Frances was in an uncharacteristic state of emotional indecision, unable to commit herself fully to Ralph by going to bed with him, comforted by Colin's concern and affection, and on the verge of becoming seriously involved with Phil Nichols. Her letters to Ralph sound guilty and unhappy. After one particularly muddled week, when she had put him off because she already had dates with Colin, Sieveking and

Nichols, a reproachful letter from him made her wretched. 'I'm so upset I've told Glasgow I can't have dinner tonight, but must go and succour Jane in distress, a most elaborate plot. Glasgow is angry, everything's awful. I'm so tired, though, I simply want to collapse into bed – too tired to talk even to you my darling. But I don't don't don't want, and can't bear you to be unhappy, and through my stupidity. You will have lunch with me on Wednesday and dinner, and lunch on Thursday? But oh I have to have dinner with PN on Thursday, but I'm coming for the weekend on Saturday.' Around this time Ralph sent her a drawing showing her juggling four little male dolls. Underneath he wrote: 'This lady is attempting a difficult feat. You notice it is not merely balls she is juggling with, but unwieldy and intractable young men.' One, he explained, had 'an exceptional length of leg'. Another, a leg made of wood. A third, a Foreign Office type, was sporting a top hat and a cigar. 'It is of the essence of the performance that no two should ever come into contact with each other, which would undoubtedly happen if she paused for a moment.' There is a 'spare' figure on the floor, Ralph himself; will she succeed in bringing him into play, so that she is juggling four men, 'an even greater test of her skill?'

A complicated life did not really suit Frances; her uncertainties over Ralph were real, not tactical. Sometimes she needed to escape from his intensity and accept Colin's invitations to Claridge's, or go for a walk in the country with Phil. As the year wore on, Phil began to gain ground. She went on a walking weekend alone with him, reporting to Ralph that he had wanted her to sleep with him, but that she had refused; she accepted an invitation to go to his home in Essex, Lawford Hall, and meet his family. Over Easter, she and Ralph met in France but she was travelling with two Newnham friends and Ralph was with Lytton and Carrington. They must both have realised that they would have to manage some time alone together if their relationship was to survive. After France, Ralph wrote: 'Will you please reserve me next Christmas and next Easter, and Easter 1927–1977, and Christmas 1927–77 . . . I shall have a little printed slip made out: "Mr Partridge and Miss Marshall do NOT go to bed together but that is no reason why they shouldn't occasionally be left alone".'

By the summer, Ralph had a plan. He began to concentrate on persuading Frances to travel alone with him to Spain. At the time, she did not acknowledge that by agreeing, she was burning her boats; later, she saw things rather differently. 'Purely tactically it was a brilliant move . . . it seemed at the time to be shelving the decision and I agreed with a feeling of relief. But I think I subconsciously knew that it was more than that – I was making it.' By this time, she had told Colin who the BY was, and that he was married; now she tried to present the Spanish journey as just a holiday with a great friend. She wrote to him the night before they left, asking him to write to her, as she would to him. 'You, I know, think I'm foolish in the way I sometimes ignore what people may say and think.' He was away himself, so she was spared any awkward scenes; it was trickier with Philip, but she reported to Ralph that she was managing to avoid explanations. The other person she needed to reassure was Mam, who sensibly let her off the hook. 'Last night I talked to mother a good deal, never mentioning who my companion was, though we got out maps etc. She never asked me, and I don't believe she will, unless at the very last moment. I must say I think it is remarkable of her.' On the eve of her departure, Frances sounded happy and confident, above all relieved to be leaving the muddle and recriminations of the past months behind. 'Oh my darling,' she wrote, 'we talk about nothing but me – it's intolerable. When we get to Spain let's talk about nothing but you.'

As for Lytton and Carrington, they had seen how unsettled and unhappy Ralph had been and come to realise that he needed Frances if he was to become their reliable companion again. And Ralph himself must have known he had won. On 12 September 1925 he wrote to Frances: 'This is the last day I shall be separated from you for over a month . . . do you mind my spending the first week crying with relief with my head in your lap?'

Seven

Journey to Spain, 1925–1926

By leaving for Spain alone with Ralph in the autumn of 1925 Frances made the most important decision of her life. She saw this clearly later, but at the time it was not quite so obvious, to her, to her family, or to the other men who loved her. In her heart she knew that she and Ralph would, at last, become lovers; and no doubt this aspect of the journey had been comprehensively discussed at Ham Spray. In future years, Ralph would inform his closest friends, whether to raise a sympathetic laugh or to impress them with his beloved's virtue and strength of mind, that far from falling rapturously into bed as soon as they left England Frances made him wait until they reached Cadiz; by which time they had already visited Segovia, Madrid, Toledo, Córdoba and Seville. Gerald Brenan later maintained that he had warned Ralph that the journey would make or break them.

In fact, their time in Spain was intensely happy and harmonious and proved them to be excellent travelling companions. Ralph had beguiled Frances with tales of the country's power and beauty; she found it mesmerising from the moment they got off the train in Segovia in the dark, and smelled the aromatic plants, charcoal fires, cooking oil and hot dust. From then on Spain became her preferred European country, as it was his. They travelled by train and bus, staying in cheap hotels where they were glad of the mosquito net brought with them from the Army & Navy Stores, along with eight volumes of *Clarissa* which they intended to read aloud.

Frances kept up a correspondence with both Colin and Phil from Spain. 'I do miss you – and I'm jealous of the Bird,' wrote Phil in late September. 'Say you like Cadiz – it was your going there with him that hurt most.' She told him when she and Ralph started sleeping together; his reaction was that he had expected this would happen, but that he was not giving up. With Colin, she was more circumspect, writing a cagey answer to a letter from him asking her what she thought she was doing. 'I didn't come to Spain with R through any ulterior motive, marriage or its equivalent,' she wrote back, stiffly. 'I came with him because we are very great friends and because I am very fond of him ... I will not deny that I was rather pleased to be able to go alone with him.' Spain was all she had hoped, and Cadiz 'a snow white town that nearly makes you blink – a deep blue sea and sky. We shall stay here some time I think and lead an idle life and find somewhere nice to bathe.' She had hardly looked at a book (so much for *Clarissa*). Something in Frances still needed to keep up appearances.

Another view of Frances and her Spanish adventure comes from the perceptive Iris Origo, to whom Colin was by now forwarding Frances' letters. 'Whatever she feels about the other man,' wrote Iris, 'she does care, quite a lot, about your judgment and opinion of her.' She agreed with him that Frances' attitude was 'half defiance, half apology, with rather more of the latter'; as for whether she would be 'swept off her feet' (and into bed), Iris deduced that she had not set off having taken any final decision. Her verdict was that there was 'a strong element of defiance of convention' involved, but also 'a certain wistfulness and longing for "safety first"'. Far from advising Colin to give up, she encouraged him to believe he might yet win Frances. She was wrong only on this last point.

When Frances and Ralph travelled back to England in late October they had decided they wanted to live together. There were, however, great difficulties in their way; as soon as they separated in London the golden glow of Spain faded fast. Frances had committed herself to a man who was still committed elsewhere; his ties to Lytton and Carrington were even more powerful than the ties of a conventional marriage. Frances understood that such interwoven lives and loves could not be disentangled by a simple divorce.

At first, she was able to cling to her recent happiness and not think about the rest. 'My darling sweet angel lovie,' she wrote from the bookshop, 'I am happy and love you.' Her mother and Nan had been at Brunswick Square to greet her, bursting into the hall when she arrived; she talked at length about her doings, and again, although she kept saying 'we', her mother did not ask who her companion had been. But Frances soon heard from Frankie Birrell that Mam had been ringing round everyone, Tom and Marjorie (they had married in 1924), Jane Norton, Ray and Bunny, asking if they knew who her daughter's travelling companion was. It seems almost impossible that Mam had not discovered the truth, but if she had she did not confront her daughter with it.

Frances had a much harder time with Philip Nichols and Colin Mac-kenzie. She found a letter from Phil asking her to dinner immediately; 'I don't know what I shall say to him but I think as near the truth as possible will be best.' Whatever she told him, he did not give up. As for Colin, he

was furious, less with her than with Ralph. To both men, Ralph looked like
the classic cad, compromising Frances while he still had a wife, and apparently not even proposing to divorce. Colin was so blunt that Frances felt
she never wanted to see him again.

Meanwhile, affectionate messages and even a present arrived from Carrington at Ham Spray, where the hope was that Ralph would soon settle
down. By clinging to her virtue Frances had kept him on tenterhooks; now,
with any luck, she would be a soothing influence. Lytton and Carrington
needed Ralph calm and cheerful, not distracted and restless.

The trouble was that before long Frances realised that she could not carry
on as before. Something in her nature refused to fudge the issue; she wanted
to share Ralph's life as an equal, not as an occasional junior partner. Such
clarity was uncomfortable, but it also gave her great strength. She believed
he felt the same way, but while she was a free agent, he was not.

For the next weeks and months, as 1925 ended and 1926 began, the
situation was wretched. Frances could not face Ham Spray, as Lytton and
Carrington had made it clear that if he set up house in London with her,
she would not be welcome there. They were putting up, she wrote later, 'a
strong wall of agitated and articulate opposition to our plans'. When she
met Ralph in London, agonising discussions led nowhere and reduced her
to tears. He sent her apologetic letters telling her how much he loved her
and hated making her unhappy; but he seemed incapable of taking action.
Instead, he told her she had three courses to choose from: to live with him,
to revert to seeing him occasionally or to stop seeing him. 'I agree to
whichever you choose, because I don't know what will make you happiest.'
This attitude was not much help, as Frances told him. 'Dearie it is hopeless
to talk to me of choosing courses. I didn't feel, don't you see, as if any
decision I should make would be a valid one and especially as I was to make
it alone.'

They exchanged letters full of longing and indecision. Their new intimacy
is reflected in nicknames and endearments; she was his own darling angel,
his snippet: he was her darling sweet angel love, her chubb. Then Ralph
told her that Lytton had decided to intervene. 'He's gone off to town today
with the intention of an interview with you, dearest, which I expect has
already come off. I've no idea what he'll say or what you'll feel about it, but
he said he hoped it might clear up his and the Ham Spray position with
you easier than through me.' She described their meeting at the Oriental
Club to Colin, anxiously awaiting the latest developments. 'On Friday I had
a curious interview with Lytton. We sat alone in the lounge of his Anglo
Indian Club and discussed the whole question ... He was very nice but the

conversation was fruitless, I'm afraid, only proving how impossible the present position is to solve.'

Frances' later account of this crucial conversation, which took place in the one room in the club 'allowed to be sullied by the presence of females', fully conveys how determined she was 'to stand up for what I believed to be the right Ralph and I possessed to our joint happiness'. She did not see why, if they set up house together in London, Ralph should not remain part of Ham Spray life or why she should not be able to visit 'as often as they liked'. She had no wish, she assured Lytton, to seduce Ralph away from his dearest friends (nor, she always added, did she ever try to do so).

Lytton heard her out, and then dropped his bombshell. As always, he combined intelligent sympathy with self-interest. He could not, he told Frances, promise that if she and Ralph lived together in London he would continue at Ham Spray with Carrington. He was fond of her, of course, but she did tend to lose her head: 'I rely very much on Ralph's practical support, sound sense and strength of character.' He was, in effect, threatening to abandon Carrington and break up Ham Spray. 'I left the Oriental Club pierced by a poisoned dart,' wrote Frances. 'So far I had not felt I was acting like a criminal.' How could she possibly inflict such a blow on Carrington? She felt more trapped and unhappy than ever, but her own position did not change. Lytton must have realised, at this meeting, if he had not done so before, that Frances was more formidable than she appeared.

Both her chivalrous suitors, seeing her love affair stalled and she herself plainly miserable, tried to distract her with invitations and outings. She saw the New Year in at a nightclub in a party with Phil who, she informed Ralph, pressed her to marry him immediately. She prevaricated, feeling 'awful'; but she did not altogether dismiss the idea. In the first week of January, she saw Phil twice, Ralph twice and had three dates with Colin, for whom her feelings were cooler, and so simpler. Having consulted Iris, Colin suggested a weekend at Stratfield Saye. Frances found his loyalty comforting, and soon forgave him for the harsh things he had said about Ralph. Over the weekend she talked to him fully about her dilemma for the first time. For the next three months or so, he reported what she told him to Iris. The more he learned the truth about Frances' plight, the more he decided he loved her and ought to rescue her.

Colin and Frances also saw three possible solutions. She could break off the relationship with Ralph, or insist on a divorce so that they could marry, or live with him without a divorce. Colin found Carrington (Mrs P as he preferred to call her) a puzzling figure. 'Both Frances and P say they are fond of her, an affection she is supposed to return. But for semi-material reasons if for no other she would naturally prefer a status quo.' Apart from the emotional damage, how would Carrington, who had no money, no job and no claim on Ham Spray except as Ralph's wife, support herself? Frances, he continued, 'is by no means certain what she wants to do and I think she at last bitterly regrets having got herself into this position. P seems to be rather leaving her to choose which may be unselfish but seems to me to show a lamentable lack of backbone. He is, however, to his credit uncomfortable about the third solution. This Frances refuses to be – arguing that it would not be the same among the people she habitually mixes with'. Colin found her near breaking point, exhausted, overworked at the bookshop, and hardly sleeping at all; he advised her not to decide anything until she felt better. As for his own views, the divorce court would be bad enough, but the idea of her living in sin with Ralph drove him mad. 'I was pretty beastly,' he admitted. 'She has never exactly lied to me but she has been needlessly evasive.' He lectured her mockingly on 'the imprudence of our intelligentsia . . . she made hardly any effort to defend herself and just looked unutterably weary.'

No doubt to Frances' relief, Colin returned to Glasgow where he fell into deep gloom. Iris sent him a telegram – 'Courage my friend' – and advised him to stand back, and encourage the idea of divorce. She pointed out that 'a woman's happiness does not necessarily depend on the character of the man she cares for'. This was not much comfort for Colin. 'I love her more than ever now she has run herself into this tangle.' Previously, her control over her emotions had seemed a little inhuman; now he saw her as 'a shuttlecock of fortune like most of the rest of us'.

By now, Lytton and Carrington had been forced to accept that Frances was not going to give in. Faced with losing Ralph altogether, Carrington at first tried to convince him that she was still in love with him, and eager to sleep with him; when this failed, she and Lytton came up with a compromise. They suggested that Frances should move out of Brunswick Square and share a flat with a friend, so that she and Ralph could see each other in London; he would divide his life between her and Ham Spray. Carrington wrote surreptitiously to Julia Strachey to advance this plan; she had no compunction about using Frances' oldest friend to get what she wanted, but the possible flat fell through.

Gradually, all concerned understood that Frances was not prepared to settle for a divided life. If they were to have a future together, Ralph now had to put her first. She wanted him to live with her and visit Ham Spray, not the other way round; but at the same time, she knew that to force him to abandon not just Carrington but Lytton and Ham Spray would cause immense unhappiness, to him as well as to the other two. No wonder she was paralysed and sleepless.

At the beginning of February she decided to take Colin's advice and go away by herself and think things over at Owley, her sister Judy Rendel's fine old moated house in Kent. Ralph agreed, reluctantly – but persuaded her to spend a few days with him on the Dorset coast first. Having told him not to telephone her at Owley, or write, she could not resist writing to him. She lay in bed late while her sister brought her breakfast in bed; she sat by the fire and read Chekhov's letters. The reeds in the moat reminded her of Ralph's 'sweet head'. She had received a resentful letter from Philip. 'Darling,' she wrote, 'Some of the time at Bridport [where they had entered, and won, a tango competition] I was as happy as I've ever been.' But their brief respite had ended with more painful conversations. Was it wrong and selfish of her to plead her own cause?

In the end, the impasse was resolved by a remarkable exchange of letters between Carrington and Frances. Carrington wrote first. Her letter is gentle, sad and contains no hint of hostility. After all the emotional confusion of the recent months, now 'The Treaty has to be drawn up. I have to face that owing to a situation, which cannot be got over, I must give up living with Ralph.' In return, she begged Frances 'to still let me keep some of my friendship with R'. She tried to explain her feelings: 'I do love R, only in a different way, just as you love him. It isn't any easier for me to give him up than it would be for you.' She explained that if Ralph were to leave Ham Spray, her life with Lytton would be wrecked. 'I am obliged to accept this situation, you must see that. All I can do is to beg you to be, any rate at first, a little generous ... You see, Frances, you can afford to be lenient because R is so completely yours in his affections – in spite of all your difficulties, and unhappiness, you are a gainer, we losers.' If Frances could not bring herself to let Ralph continue sharing life at Ham Spray, then that life would have to end; but 'If you can, you must know it would mean everything to Lytton, and me.' Carrington's letter ended 'I send you my love. I hope you are happier.'

Frances' response was immediate and generous. It was a great relief to be able to communicate directly with Carrington at last, rather than through Ralph. 'You have always been such an angel to me,' she wrote, 'and I am so fond of you that it makes it all the more intolerable, this horrible knot in which our happinesses have got involved.' Then in two sentences she unties the knot. 'I never never never feel that if R should live with me I should want him not to see you very often and go on being fond of you. My greatest hope, but I've feared an unreasonable

one, was that living with me he should still be able to see you continually
and eventually that we should all be able to meet together without any
of our present awful feelings.' Frances was clear-sighted. She knew that
Carrington and Lytton remained hugely important to Ralph. She had
rejected the 'half and half life' suggested by Lytton, she explained, because
the strain on everyone would be as great, if not greater, than before,
especially for Ralph, and that 'it really is necessary (for practical reasons
such as work incidentally as well) to have roots in one place and not
two'. Finally, 'Because I love R and want to live with him, and want him
to share my life instead of being a visitor into it – I can't see how I could
find this incompatible with his being fond of you and seeing you every
day of his life.' Perhaps only that final phrase was unrealistic.

After this exchange, the way ahead was clear at last. Frances and Ralph
would find a flat in London; Ralph would continue to share Ham Spray
with Lytton and Carrington, and Frances would be welcomed there with
him at weekends. In the euphoria of that spring, no-one felt the need to be
precise about Frances and Ham Spray, either about how much time she
would spend there or what her position in the household would be. It was
assumed that sometimes she would want to spend a weekend or holiday
elsewhere; Ralph no doubt assured Lytton and Carrington that they would
often be a threesome, and that Ham Spray life would expand to take in
Frances, but not change. It was the best that could be managed, a generous,
civilised arrangement, in which all concerned obtained much, if not quite
all, they wanted. No doubt Lytton had influenced Carrington's attitude and
her letter; no doubt Ralph had convinced them both that his love for
Frances was not negotiable. But it was Frances' strength of mind and realistic
appraisal of the situation that had won the day.

Now Frances had some awkward letters and conversations ahead. She
wrote to Colin on 1 March 1926, a firm, clear letter marking the end of her
years of living in two worlds. She had made, she told him,

the decision I know you hoped I wouldn't make ... Ralph and I have
decided that we are going to live together as soon as a suitable flat can be
found ... You see I've got to that feeling of certainty when I'd rather think
about being dead than not seeing R again. I can't face it, I find, and so
I sacrifice my desire not to make Carrington unhappy, and show myself
in my usual selfish colours. It seems to me to try and stop R from seeing
her would be the most uncivilised thing I could do. I don't believe her
present degree of being in love with R is anything more than a temporary
state, but I think her affection for him is real and permanent.

Lytton, she went on, 'is fonder of Ralph than of anyone else in the world', and she could not justify taking Ralph away from him and Ham Spray as well as from Carrington. These were 'the reasons which decide me against a divorce'. Later on, perhaps, 'one might reconsider the question'.

Finally, though she was sorry to hurt him and others she cared about, and was not looking forward to breaking the news to her mother, 'that this move will be for my own happiness I no longer have any doubts. You said you hoped I would be happier when I'd decided – so I will tell you that I am as happy as I've ever been in my life.'

She also wrote to Phil Nichols, who had recently been sent off to Mexico by the Foreign Office, and had written to tell her that he now wished he had tried harder to stop her going to Spain. Now, he felt 'broken' and as if he never wanted to return to England; he admired her courage, but 'I see no hope of ceasing to love you'. Both Philip and Colin were seriously hurt, but remained her friends and, in time, accepted Ralph; but for the time being, Colin told Frances, he could not trust himself to meet Ralph, adding rather pompously that to do so would be to betray his principles. To Iris he wrote that although he found it hard, he would go on seeing Frances because he did not want her to feel abandoned when she was most in need of support. (Colin's heart mended; but in 1927 it was broken again by Iris herself, when after having a passionate affair with him she realised that she could not leave her husband and children.)

Now Frances had to face up to her family. She decided to write to them explaining her decision as clearly as possible, much as she had done to Colin. Ray and Tom, the closest to her and to Bloomsbury, were the least surprised or shocked; she told Ralph that she was hoping that Eleanor, her youngest sister and the only one still living at Brunswick Square, would help reassure Mam. Only Horace, the eldest brother (nicknamed Great Growly by Frances, indicating a formidable presence), is still remembered in the family as expressing serious disapproval of his sister's conduct – which never seems to have bothered her in the least.

When finally she and Mam had the conversation Frances had been dreading, she found her mother remarkably tolerant and accepting. 'Obviously my mother would have preferred us to get married after a divorce,' she wrote later. 'Yet when I explained the position to her she accepted it valiantly ... She had I think expected me to marry one of the eligible suitors who used to call to take me out.' Mam comes well out of all this, and her youngest daughter always respected and loved her for accepting her decision with so little fuss. 'Fortunately,' wrote Frances firmly, 'my mother became extremely fond of Ralph, as he did of her.'

There was only one person to whom Frances still could not bear to tell the truth: her old nanny. Nan was fragile now, and deeply religious, and would have been terribly distressed to learn that Miss Frances, the beloved youngest of her charges, was to be living in sin with a married man. So a secret marriage was invented, and Frances was woken on her 'wedding morning' by a tearful Nan and six teaspoons.

As for Ralph himself, having the decision made for him left him, he wrote, light-headed. 'O, I've been so wretched and miserable – day after day and night after night, and nothing to think of except that my love had gone and I couldn't go to her, and she was curing herself of being fond of me, while I couldn't cure myself of loving her so much I wanted to die.' Given that he had only been out of touch with her for about a week – 'this hideous week' – his reaction indicates that he really had thought he might lose her; it also shows what Lytton, Carrington, the Woolfs and Gerald Brenan already knew – that Ralph was easily swamped by self-doubt and self-pity. If ever a man needed a constant lover, it was he.

Now events moved quickly. On 6 March Frances was back at Ham Spray; on the 25th Ralph dined at Brunswick Square. The next step was for him and Frances to find a flat. As it happened, James and Alix Strachey were again looking for tenants at 41 Gordon Square. Another kind of girl might have baulked at the prospect of having Lytton's brother as landlord and of starting what she regarded as married life in the same rooms where Ralph had persuaded Carrington into a trial marriage six years earlier, but that sort of thing did not bother Frances. She was sure of her feelings for Ralph and of his for her and never, then or later, was one to look for trouble. Gordon Square was familiar territory and she loved the large light rooms on the first floor looking over the plane trees in the square. They painted one room pink and the other green, bought a large double bed at Heal's and covered a dresser with handsome Spanish plates. There were more weekend visits to Ham Spray and Hilton, meetings with Gerald and for Frances a slightly awkward dinner at Claridge's with Colin, after which he took her, rather appropriately, to Gershwin's *Lady Be Good*. He told Iris he felt sorry for Frances, but they were friends again.

While Frances and Ralph furnished their flat, Lytton and Carrington made the best of things. Carrington told Julia that now the treaty was drawn up 'a good deal of the horrors will be mitigated for everyone'; Lytton, replying to a letter of commiseration from Sebastian Sprott (who had recently endured the marriage of his lover Maynard Keynes to the Russian ballerina Lydia Lopokova), described the circumstances leading to the new arrangement as 'shattering' both to Carrington and to himself. 'Everyone has behaved with great magnanimity, and I don't see that blame attaches anywhere – but it's unfortunate.' James Strachey, visiting Ham Spray soon after Frances' reappearance, saw 'the situation' rather differently. He wrote afterwards to Alix: 'I thought Carrington seemed in rather a bad way ... The Major's young lady was there as usual, and they were as usual absorbed in each other; and it looked as if Carrington was verging towards active hostility towards them – for which I shouldn't blame her. Lytton of course is serenely unaware (or pretends to be) of every difficulty.' Everyone was trying hard, but it was not easy.

Meanwhile, national politics (which did not often impinge on Ralph and Frances' life) had taken a dramatic turn, and even in mid-move they were caught up in the General Strike during the first week of May 1926. They both considered themselves left-wing, and at the bookshop (now being run by a declared Communist, Graham Pollard), Frances was surrounded by excited young men predicting revolution. 'The air was dense with emergency,' she wrote. Ralph helped Leonard Woolf gather writers' and artists' signatures for a petition (suggested by the Archbishop of Canterbury) urging the government to negotiate with the strikers; according to Virginia, he and Gerald Brenan were their 'emissaries'. Ralph and Frances, returning by train after a visit to Bunny and Ray, became minor casualties of the strike when their amateur train driver (obviously a strike-breaking undergraduate, Frances concluded) caused a crash at Audley End. Three people died, and Frances was badly shaken; for some years afterwards she would feel terror and claustrophobia, 'as if a demon had been let out of my unconscious', in tunnels or on the tube.

At last, on 14 May, they moved in. And now, setting up house for the first time in Gordon Square, Frances arrived in the social heart of Bloomsbury.

Eight

Gordon Square and Ham Spray, 1926–1928

By 1926, it was over twenty years since Vanessa Stephen had bought No. 46 Gordon Square and led the way across London from respectable Kensington, away from white stucco and Hyde Park to the grey Georgian terraces and garden squares of the more raffish district between the Tottenham Court and Gray's Inn roads. By the 1920s, the north-east side of Gordon Square was almost all Bloomsbury territory. Lytton, whose mother had moved there from Belsize Park in 1920, likened the square to a Cambridge college; he occasionally stayed with her at No. 51, which was also home to his sisters Pippa and Marjorie and a London base for Pernel during her Newnham years. Life at 51 remained old-fashioned while Lady Strachey was alive. Frances, who was sometimes invited for tea, recalled her as monumental, 'as solid and rugged as a Rodin statue'. A maid in a white cap would answer the front door, there was a board in the hall saying who was In or Out, and on the servants' day off one of the younger Strachey great-nieces, like Janie or Julia, would be summoned to light the gas cooker and heat up the evening meal.

Julia herself had moved in with her father, Oliver, at No. 42, and so became Frances' next-door neighbour. Thus, as Frances put it, her old ally came back into her life and stayed there. Their close friendship, in abeyance while Frances was at Cambridge, revived after she began working in London; the fact that Carrington had set out to captivate Julia, and succeeded, could have been tricky, but Frances never appeared to mind. Julia, by now working as a model, was at her most dashing: slim, elegant, with long legs and a fashionable Eton crop. She was keenly interested in clothes and her appearance, and would urge Frances, who was not, to take more trouble. Luckily Ralph was fond of her, and they amused each other. She was often short of money and led a complicated love life; Frances and Ralph became a stable, comforting element in her life. She fought a good deal with her eccentric and strikingly unpaternal father, Oliver, who was hopelessly susceptible to pretty girls; he had a succession of mistresses and soon saw nothing wrong with expressing his attraction to Frances. No-one took this at all seriously, least of all Frances. During the war Oliver had found his métier, and was working as a cryptographer for the Foreign Office. He and his wife Ray were on good terms, but led largely separate lives.

Another Gordon Square resident who conceived a brief passion for Frances was the immensely tall, melancholy-looking Adrian Stephen, Vanessa and Virginia's younger brother, who lived at No. 50. Both he and his clever, deaf wife Karin (Ray Strachey's sister) were aspiring psychoanalysts; Frances would observe them walking round the square under the plane trees, deep in discussion. His sister, Vanessa Bell, when she was not at Charleston, occupied No. 37, as did Duncan Grant; Clive Bell kept rooms at No. 46, where his landlord was Maynard Keynes.

Thus Frances, glowing with love for Ralph, was admired by a number of the male residents of Gordon Square, for whom a marriage, let alone what Virginia Woolf referred to as a 'lefthanded establishment', was no barrier to dalliance. She soon became a particular favourite of Clive Bell, who nick-named her Fanny and would say wistfully that she had the best legs in Bloomsbury; he took her to lunch at the Ivy, the restaurant off St Martin's Lane popular with well-heeled intellectuals and his favourite haunt, and included her in dinner parties in his rooms, often without Ralph. From the start, it was understood that invitations to one of them did not have to include the other. Alongside panels painted by Duncan Grant, Clive's walls were hung with remarkable works by Juan Gris, Vlaminck and Picasso (a friend from pre-war Paris). He would preside over dinner wearing a purplish suit with black frogging, sprinkling his conversation with French, running his hands anxiously through his tufty reddish hair and fiddling compulsively with his sock suspenders. Frances became very fond of him, finding him 'an eighteenth-century character, part country squire and part man of letters' and a generous host with the gift (rare in Bloomsbury) of encouraging his guests to shine rather than intimidating them with his wide knowledge of French literature and art. After dinner he would offer her, as well as the men present, brandy and a cigar, and she would often accept.

Above all, the move to Gordon Square led to Frances winning the friendship of James and Alix Strachey. It did not happen overnight; their loyalty to Lytton and Carrington was long established, and both of them had heard all too much about Ralph's previous emotional upheavals. Alix was one of Carrington's oldest friends and confidantes; James was wary of anyone or anything that could upset Lytton. But Frances came to trust them and was always grateful to them for, as she put it, 'the help they quietly gave Ralph and me in welding our lives together'.

James and Alix were a curious couple. Devoted to each other, their relationship was never exclusive – James had been hopelessly in love with Rupert Brooke at Cambridge and later took up with Brooke's beloved, Noel Olivier; and Alix, whose early lovers had included Bunny Garnett, was strongly drawn to women both before and after she married James in 1920. It was Alix who made the marriage happen; she rented No. 41 Gordon Square in 1919 and invited James to live there with her. Eight years older than Frances, she too had been educated at Bedales and Newnham; she was six foot tall, lean and dark, with strong features, big hands, a melancholy temperament and a passion for logical argument. Frances considered that she had 'the more remarkable mind', but also appreciated her unexpected bursts of enthusiasm for ice cream, champagne, motorbicycling and ballroom dancing. James was also tall, but slight, with a round pink face and silky white hair; Frances found him highly emotional, and inclined to passionate outbursts if anyone dared venture the smallest criticism of his three heroes, who to him could do no wrong: his brother Lytton, Mozart and Freud. Like Lytton, they were both atheists and firm pacifists.

By the time Frances knew them, they had returned to London as dedicated followers of Freud. Freud had already asked them to translate one of his papers; this was the start of fifty years of work as Freud's leading translators into English. As well as working on translations, James practised as a psychoanalyst in his sitting room on the floor directly above Frances and Ralph's flat; anxious-looking characters would hover by the front door, and James found it prudent to ask Ralph to be ready to run upstairs if a patient turned violent. 'All this', Frances observed, 'gave No. 41 an interesting but slightly psychopathic atmosphere.'

Through James and Alix, Frances found herself as close to the beginning of Freudian practice in London as it was possible for someone not directly involved in the study or application of Freudian psychology to be. It was not until much later that she herself played a part in the dissemination of Freud's ideas, when she took on the massive task of indexing the Hogarth Press edition of the *Collected Works*, but from her mid-twenties on she lived in a world where those ideas were constantly discussed, and increasingly taken for granted. Bloomsbury and Freud were linked from the beginning.

The arrival of Freudianism in England was an erratic process, but by the mid-1920s it had been well under way for at least ten years. Before that, in turn-of-the-century Cambridge, the Society for Psychical Research, supported by Frances' father, Will Marshall, and his cousin and friend F.W.H. Myers (father of the writer Leo Myers, another of Frances' admirers) had discovered Freud while pursuing research into the supernatural. Freud himself contributed a paper on the unconscious to the Society in 1912, by which time James Strachey had become a member. The first of Freud's books to attract the interest of the general reader were *The Interpretation of Dreams*, published in English in 1913, and *The Psychopathology of Everyday Life* in 1914; the first article on Freud for the general reader to appear in English was written by Leonard Woolf for *The Nation* in 1914. Later, the Hogarth Press was to become Freud's English publisher. By 1924, *The Nation* was still hotly debating Freud, but progress had been made since an article of 1913 deplored the morbid atmosphere of sex and suggested that Freud's introspection betrayed his 'Oriental heredity'.

Among the problems exercising James and Alix when Frances got to know them, the questions of infantile sexuality, the Oedipus complex, penis envy, sublimation and the unconscious were prominent. These concepts, and the terms in which they were discussed, are commonplace today; but in the 1920s they were still fresh and disturbing. Not many people would have applied them to their own lives, and Bloomsbury on the whole did not. James and Lytton were close, and supported each other always, but even James felt a surge of irritation after a lunch with his brother (at the Oriental Club, again) dissecting sexual and emotional complexities. 'Why', he wrote to Alix, 'can't these asses read the Professor's works?' As for Frances and Ralph, there is no evidence that they were reading them either; but the concepts and above all the language they were exposed to by their proximity to the Stracheys began to have an effect as they took up their lifelong habit of analysing their own and their friends' behaviour not just as gossip but in terms of general principles. Neither of them ever contemplated analysis for themselves. As for Old Bloomsbury, Lytton Strachey persisted in regarding attempts by homosexuals to get themselves 'cured' by psychoanalysis or anything else as ridiculous and retrograde, and neither Leonard nor Virginia Woolf, despite being his English publishers, regarded Freud or his followers as having anything to offer to help them deal with her bouts of insanity.

During their first year in Gordon Square, Frances, who only knew them from the bookshop, had two social encounters with the Woolfs. As if to emphasise that they still considered Ralph a friend, and accepted his new situation, they invited him and Frances to dinner; her pocket diary shows that they went to Hogarth House on 21 July after playing tennis from six to seven p.m. Virginia's diary mentions the occasion without comment; she was tired, and on the verge of a much-needed summer retreat to Rodmell. On 23 November Frances and Ralph asked them back to Gordon Square. On both occasions Frances was struck by Virginia's need to challenge the younger generation. 'She often launched these attacks on the young; I think they came from a sort of jealousy,' wrote Frances. 'Young writers and poets were particularly in danger.' When Alix and Julia Strachey joined the party after dinner, Virginia was delightful to Julia, whom she considered frivolous and hence no competition, and concentrated her fire on her clever, serious-minded sister-in-law. '"Oh yes, Alix, I know all about you," Virginia said. "You simply spend your whole time dancing, and sink further into imbecility every minute."' But Alix then drew Virginia into an argument about psychoanalysis, and not surprisingly got the better of her. It was left to Leonard, whom Frances always found easier than his wife, to make the evening end amiably. 'Come on, Virginia,' he said as they got up to go, 'don't disgrace the older generation.' Virginia was preoccupied at the time with writing *To the Lighthouse*, and with her new friendship with Vita Sackville-West, and Frances and Ralph in their happiness would not have been of much interest to her. The Woolfs were to remain background figures in Frances' life, and she came to share Ralph's mixed feelings about them.

It was a novelty for Frances to be a hostess, and she enjoyed it. Not that she did any cooking herself; for that there was Mabel, their first servant, who kept house for them, cooked breakfast and would return to cook dinner if required. During their first year together they entertained Frankie Birrell and Ralph Wright from the bookshop, the Desmond MacCarthys (Molly, who first coined the term Bloomsbury, and her pretty daughter Rachel were becoming great friends), Frances' mother and, in August, Philip Nichols – by this time in the picture, but not, apparently, having given up hope. Frances was not after all married, nor apparently likely to be; and she continued to make dates for dinners at the Café Royal or Claridge's, followed by theatres or the opera, with both Colin and Philip.

In September 1926, almost exactly a year after their journey to Spain, Frances and Ralph spent a month in the newly fashionable South of France, where they developed a passion for sunbathing and swimming, preferably naked. There they were observed by Gerald Brenan, who found their blissful happiness hard to bear and wrote Carrington a letter which shows him torn between envy and contempt. 'Ralph and Frances are here and seem perfectly happy. They bathe, eat a large dinner, lie flat on the beach, solve a crossword puzzle, read *The Times*, bathe again, eat another large dinner and go to bed. One would think that no shade of unhappiness and difficulty had ever crossed their lives ... A week of such a life would drive me to suicide ... Love and affection are the great stupefiers and soporifics.' True artists, he maintained, avoid such traps. Suddenly Ralph seemed 'rather pathetic. It is as though in a world where everyone is walking about he had somehow sunk down into a deep armchair, and could not get up, and knew that he could not.'

Frances and Ralph's evident happiness was bound to irritate those around them who were less lucky, and Carrington most of all. It was hard for her to see Ralph so absorbed in someone else, not just because she was used to being more important to him than anyone but because she was afraid that Lytton would be upset by Ralph's preoccupation with Frances. When they were all together at Ham Spray (Frances' pocket diary shows that she spent thirteen weekends there between March and December 1926) Ralph was inevitably less available to them than he used to be, and the atmosphere was different. There are frequent pointed references in Carrington's letters to Frances' high spirits, and how she and Ralph would insist on playing ping-pong or dancing to the radio after dinner, so that Ham Spray saw fewer of the quiet evenings Carrington loved when they would listen to classical music or Lytton would read aloud. As it happens, both Frances and Carrington left private records of Ham Spray life and how they felt about it in the late 1920s.

Frances described a typical day at Ham Spray in May 1927. It was a weekend; Alix Strachey, Julia and her new young man, Stephen Tomlin, known as Tommy, a complicated, attractive sculptor of interest to both Lytton and Carrington as well as to Julia, were also staying. Nothing in particular happened; Virginia Woolf's new novel, *To the Lighthouse*, was discussed over breakfast on the verandah, badminton was played, Lytton worked in the morning and rested after lunch, Carrington and Julia teased each other, Ralph and Frances sat in a field and discussed why some people like to keep secrets, while Carrington (a prime example) rode her white pony, Belle, on the downs. Lytton took Tommy for a walk, and after dinner he read *Henry V* aloud. The kitten peed on Ralph's trousers: '"POOR little puss," murmured Carrington, "he didn't dare ask to be excused"'. In bed, Frances tried in vain to get Ralph interested in discussing Byron. 'And then an ordinary but happy day ended in sleep.'

This short piece of writing marks the first appearance of Frances as a diarist, and already has her characteristic tone, with its delicate balance of humour, reflection and precise observation. She notices the sun on the wind-blown aspen leaves outside her bedroom window, Julia's mauve silk dressing gown, the careful way Lytton slipped his feet into his shoes. Emotional tensions are hinted at: will Julia mind Lytton's attentions to Tommy? What are the prospects, if any, for Gerald and Carrington?

Her day revolves around a series of conversations with Ralph. She wakes up wanting to talk to him, and they discuss themselves, their friends and ideas that occur to them all day long. They wonder, for example, why people in love always want the beloved to change, but resist doing so themselves: 'Ralph said, 'No-one can alter his or her character. And I: Possibly not, but they can sometimes modify their behaviour.' After her working week in London (she was the only one of the party who kept office hours) Ham Spray provides rest, country quiet and the company of friends. There is a lot of argument and a lot of laughter; Frances would always recall that Bloomsbury gatherings were full of people laughing their heads off. Although the impression she creates is delightfully harmonious, a cooler note is struck from time to time. Carrington is a funny and energetic presence, but her role is presented as domestic; Frances' day starts when, still in her four-poster bed, she hears Carrington calling the household to breakfast, and while Frances plays badminton Carrington is bent double in the garden. Over the meals she has organised, if not cooked, Carrington's part in the conversation is minimal. There is no hint that she is a painter.

Above all, Frances' attitude to Lytton suggests some ambivalence. After dinner, she wants to go on with her book (*Astarte*, by Lovelace). 'Oh how I hope there's no reading aloud, I thought, and just then Carrington said in her most coaxing tone "Lytton, would you read to us, do you think?"' At first Lytton demurs; but, pressed by one and all apart from Frances, he gives in. She soon finds herself caught up by the performance: he reads 'with gusto, his voice now deep and rich as velvet, now soaring to near treble, while all the time his long elegant left hand made pouncing movements in the air'. Shakespeare and Lytton between them won her over; but something in her resisted the atmosphere of Lytton worship. Something in him was equally, if not more, resistant to her; he did not dislike her but she was not really his kind of person, being, his biographer remarks, 'too unrealistically straightforward and remorselessly well balanced.' These were, of course, the very qualities that made her ideal for Ralph.

It was in everyone's interest to make sure that the weekend foursome at Ham Spray worked, and as the diary Frances had begun to keep shows, during 1927 and 1928 it worked well enough. Their weekends were full of other people, Dadie Rylands and Lytton's new love Roger Senhouse as well as James and Alix Strachey and Julia and Tommy (who married in the summer of 1927). But in London, although she and Ralph went out and about, to parties, films and lectures, her favourite evenings were spent quietly at home, playing with their black kitten (they both loved cats), reading (Frances was deep in Carlyle) and, above all, talking. Thanks to Ralph, Frances felt the Marshall family's tendency to emotional inhibition crumbling away; she could hardly wait to share all her thoughts and feelings with him. 'I am infinitely grateful to Ralph', she wrote, 'for the way he has patiently worn down the invisible walls of reserve with which I have surrounded myself for so long.' He had a gift for emotional intimacy, unusual in a man of his background; although she felt he did not acquire it directly from Lytton or Carrington, it was perhaps a quality released in him by the general Bloomsbury passion for discussing thoughts and emotions.

Frances had complete confidence in Ralph's love for her and his essential reliability. This was just as well, because even some of their close friends felt compelled, from time to time, to point out to her the drawbacks of her position. She did not care what conventional people thought; it must have been harder to ignore warnings from those she thought of as unconventional. Leo Myers was one: over lunch (oysters, chicken and pears in chocolate sauce) he told her what his friends were saying. 'Oh, Frances Marshall, yes, isn't that the girl who went to live with Ralph Partridge? *What* a pity! So dreadful for her parents!' She was considered an 'infatuated idiot' and Ralph a cad; the fact that they frequented Ham Spray, under the same roof as Ralph's wife, was regarded as the most shocking fact of all. Even Clive Bell would remind her about the social perils of living in sin, while, like Leo, harbouring designs on her himself; according to Gerald, Clive boasted to Vanessa that he still anticipated making Frances one of his mistresses. Gerald, as Frances knew, tended to exaggerate, embroider and even invent, not out of malice but out of over-excitement. He only really annoyed her when he told her that their friends were divided into those, like Tommy Tomlin, who took Carrington's side and those, like Eddie Sackville-West, who took Frances'. 'I don't want my part taken!' wrote Frances in a fury. 'I haven't got a part. I hate the stupid geometrical figures by which people try to understand the emotions of others, imposing hard straight lines – or "sides" as they call them – onto tender curvaceous human beings who have none.' She was fond of Gerald, but wary of him.

By the end of 1927, Frances had come to feel, after six years, that the time had come to leave Birrell and Garnett. Ralph encouraged her, and she longed to be released from the nine-to-five routine, but 'the idea of freedom is almost alarming. Moreover I tremble at the thought of disturbing the equilibrium of the last few months, which have been as happy as any in my life.' But on 21 December she took the plunge; it was agreed that she should leave in the spring. That night, she and Ralph went to a Christmas party given by Maynard and Lydia Keynes; feeling like 'a small boat pushing out into a very large sea', Frances found 'a familiar island' in Adrian Stephen and another in Frankie Birrell, who had just been offered a job at the Hogarth Press. 'I hadn't the heart to be as damping as I felt.' She drank champagne with Roger Senhouse, talked to Roger Fry about chess, and sat with Ralph and Ottoline Morrell to watch Duncan Grant imitating Caruso; but the Keynes' house was unbearably cold, and she and Ralph moved on to No. 37 where they found the MacCarthys, the Bell boys and Dadie Rylands complaining that Cambridge undergraduates regarded him as an old fogey (he was twenty-five).

A few days later, she took the evening train to Hungerford with Ralph, Julia and Tommy. Christmas and New Year were to be spent at Ham Spray. The weather was ominous, and Frances had a bad cold. It snowed heavily; the house was icy; soon Carrington had a cold as well. James Strachey arrived; Carrington waited on Julia hand and foot; Ralph found Tommy irritating. The sun came out, the snow-covered garden and the downs were magically beautiful and Frances went tobogganing with Ralph, but, she wrote, 'something seemed wrong with us all'. Conversations were 'unreal; laughter was 'half-hearted'. As soon as Christmas was over, Lytton, 'boyishly eager' to keep a date with Roger Senhouse in London, insisted on walking to Hungerford station through the deep snow. They all went with him in a bizarre procession, with Lytton in a big fur coat, Ralph with a rucksack, long boots and crimson fur-trimmed hat and James with a scarf wound round his head. Lytton's train took him away and the others repaired to the Bear Hotel and drank too much brandy. Then they plodded back 'along the shining road with its sugar icing banks, while the sky turned an exquisite clear yellow and the snow a delicate purplish pink'.

By 30 December Frances was hoping to be able to leave along with James, Julia and Tommy, but the problem was Carrington, who could not make up her mind what she wanted. 'Ralph was exasperated with her, saying that she would bear us a grudge whatever we did.' The others left; Frances and Ralph stayed behind. That night, there was another heavy fall of snow.

Neither Frances nor Carrington were at all happy that New Year's Eve. Both of them recorded, without comment, how Ralph brought in a part-ridge, frozen to death. Carrington described the ominous dead bird in her first entry in a new notebook (her married name misspelled on the cover as D.C. Partride) and retreated to her studio all day while Frances and Ralph went tobogganing. While they were out she extracted a letter from Gerald from Ralph's pocket and read it with distaste. Increasingly, she disliked her situation. 'The year ended rather melancholy. The great distinction suddenly seemed to appear between couples supporting each other – and isolated figures unattached . . . felt rather removed from R and F.' Their high spirits, their jokes and the way they never stopped talking to each other irritated her. She missed Julia, and above all she missed Lytton. The wind howled,

Frances, aged ten

Her parents: Will
and Margaret Marshall,
c. 1890

In the nursery with Nan

In the garden at Tweenways, 1912: (left to right) Frances, Eleanor, Ray, Judy, Mam, Will, Horace, Dick Rendel, Tom

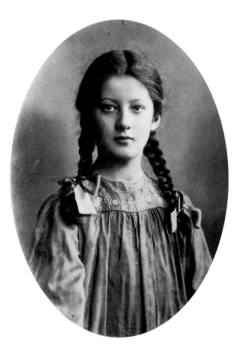

Her first friend: Julia Strachey, c. 1910

In the Lake District, 1912: Frances is third from left

First term at Cambridge, October 1918

Three Newnham girls: Frances is on the right

In the Dolomites, summer 1921

David Garnett, soon to be her brother-in-law, 1920

Major Reginald Sherring Partridge (Ralph), 1918

Ralph at Garsington, on Ottoline Morrell's right, 1920

At Tidmarsh Mill, 1923: (left to right) Carrington, Ralph, Lytton Strachey, Oliver Strachey, Frances

Near Tidmarsh, 1923: (left to right) Ralph, E.M. Forster, Lytton, French doctor, Frances

Philip Nichols, late 1920s

In Italy, summer 1924, with Tom Marshall (left) and Colin Mackenzie

Frances and Ralph in Gordon Square, summer 1926

Carrington and Lytton at Ham Spray, 1920s

Drinks on the lawn at Ham Spray: (left to right) Carrington, Marjorie Strachey, Frances, Ralph

In the Spanish mountains, 1929: Ralph (front) and Gerald Brenan

Gerald in Spain

In bed at Ham Spray, late 1920s

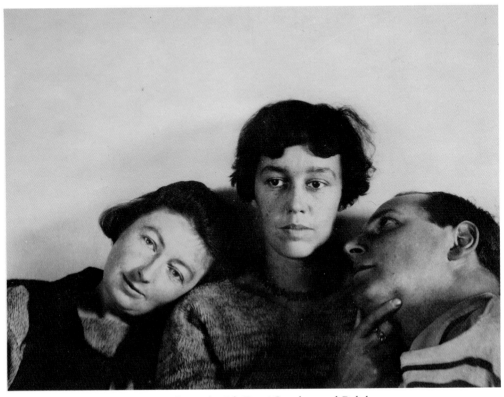

Frances (centre) with Esmé Strachey and Ralph

the snow was succeeded by rain, no-one slept well. Carrington took to her bed, and dreamed she called to Ralph in terror but he could not hear her as he was talking to Frances about Ibsen. When she woke up she heard the couple discussing how to cook pigeon; later she noted with some satisfaction that the result was tough. No wonder Frances, according to her diary written the same day, could think of nothing but 'Shall we get away to London tomorrow?' One almost feels sorry for Ralph.

But Frances' diary was not the only outlet for her feelings that New Year. She was still in touch with Phil Nichols, who was about to be sent to New Zealand for two years by the Foreign Office; she was sad to see him go. The letter she wrote him over New Year at Ham Spray must have encouraged him to think that there was still a chance he might win her. 'It's certainly most odd', she wrote, 'that what one might consider as an agreeable holiday with a little tobogganing thrown in quickly turns into a penance, when one longs to get away at all costs.' She felt 'a horrible sense of unreality'. She wondered if she might be suffering from 'Robert's disease' – Phil's brother, the poet Robert Nichols, was known to suffer from bouts of depression – which she described as 'feeling one's not living but only existing, getting through the days like so many hunks of tinned beef'. She wanted very much to see something of him before he left for the Antipodes at the end of the month.

It was a relief all around when, on 3 January 1928, Frances and Ralph finally left Ham Spray. Carrington got up early to light the stove; she took a cup of coffee back to bed with the cat, where they were joined by Ralph, 'rather like a general filled with a sort of excitement at going off'. She made breakfast for him and Frances, and waved them goodbye; later she noted that there had been 'a tiresome air of something', and resented being cast as a martyr. Over the next few days, she tried to recover herself and accept the fact that she was going to have to get used to spending more time on her own.

In the diary extracts she eventually published, Frances dealt with Phil Nichols' departure for New Zealand in a few composed lines. They had a private goodbye dinner at Boulestin's, with very good champagne. Two days later there was a large farewell party at Claridge's, where Frances wore a white velvet dress and yellow orchids and found herself sitting next to Robert Nichols, 'likeable but a little mad', at dinner. Arnold Bennett, at the height of his renown as a novelist and critic, was among the guests; he was taken with Frances and asked her to dance, which she greatly enjoyed despite his 'ebullient vulgarity', cockney accent and prominent teeth. They discussed French novels, including *Les Liaisons dangereuses*, as they whirled around the floor.

Again, her letters to Phil show that she was not as composed as she seemed. She scribbled a pencil note to thank him for their dinner, saying that she had been too 'émue' at leaving him that night to do so. 'I think about you and feel about you without stopping but it seems impossible to put anything into words except how much I want you to be happy.' She knew all his friends hated her: 'Well let them – I hate myself.' A few days later he was gone, and within the week Frances was writing him the first of the many letters she sent to New Zealand over the next two years. On the morning of his departure she had salted her boiled egg with tears: 'you'll probably laugh – but I'm glad I didn't come to the station to see you off as I should have disgraced myself'. As for news, she fears that hers will seem very dull and predictable. Her new admirer Arnold Bennett had invited her to dinner but she had not been able to go; anyway 'It's fatal to be a success the first time one meets someone – one is only a more crushing failure by contrast the second.' The bookshop, now that she is leaving, is rather fun, and she has played a great joke on Graham Pollard, the earnest Communist, by writing him a note on scented mauve paper purporting to be from a woman requesting an assignation. She thinks Phil might like *The Wayzgoose* by Roy Campbell; shall she send it? She wants him to write to her with every detail of his new life; above all, she wants him to be happy. Although her tone is resolutely cheerful, she does not sound all that happy herself.

Anyone, even someone as naturally truthful as Frances, when writing to a rejected lover is likely to understate current happiness with that lover's successful rival. Frances' letters to Phil during 1928 never show disappointment in her life with Ralph; she never complains, or criticises him, nor Lytton or Carrington. She describes her life in positive terms, almost consistent with the diary she published later. But the small inconsistencies are significant, because they show her as she was still adjusting to Ralph and the life she had chosen, the life she was later to chronicle and celebrate, at a time when she was still able to look over her shoulder at other possibilities and other points of view.

Usually, she set out to entertain Phil with tales of her London social life; she especially enjoyed telling him about the evening she eventually spent at dinner with Arnold Bennett and his actress mistress Dorothy. The other guests were Frankie Birrell, the Hutchinsons and an Australian couple; Frances declared herself more 'in love' with Bennett than ever, especially with his 'fascinating, scratchy, crooning voice'. She was surprised that neither the food nor the champagne were good, and did not much care for being led upstairs by Dorothy with the other women while Frankie and the Australian argued hotly about pacifism. 'It would rouse your satirical amusement', she told Phil, 'the imperceptible loosening of the stays, pulling up the skirts figuratively and actually … taking on an air of selfconsciously false camaraderie and warmth.' Frances always had a sharp eye for falseness; but she rather admired the unselfconscious way Dorothy lay on the floor to demonstrate stomach exercises.

A week later there was another dinner party, rather more to her taste. She was the only woman at a gathering of Clive Bell's, along with Roger Fry, Peter Lucas and Raymond Mortimer; Frankie Birrell and Lionel Penrose came in later, and there was an 'absolutely Cambridge conversation lasting into the small hours and starting with philosophy and ending up with Love'. Clive was hopelessly romantic, Lucas cynical – 'One only has to go to bed with someone two or three times and one finds their conversation too utterly boring to be endured' – while Roger Fry 'maintained a splendid optimistic realism' despite his advanced age. 'I listened enthralled, but I didn't give my view of the question, and hardly knew what it was.' What she did know, however, and noted in her diary, was that she much preferred this conversation to the 'women's talk' at Arnold Bennett's dinner. 'Even Clive seemed to forget I was a female, which flattered me.'

As the date of her departure from the bookshop drew nearer Frances' spirits rose. 'To be free in May seems the most hysterically delicious thing that could ever happen.' Having successfully fooled Graham Pollard with the fake love letter, she now played an equally satisfactory trick on Frankie by writing him a Valentine purporting to come from one of his heroes, the writer Humbert Wolfe. She could not believe it would work, but it did. There were more jokes and tricks on April Fool's Day at Ham Spray: the breakfast eggs were hollow, and painted shells were placed in birds' nests in the trees. It took three months for her to get a letter back from Phil; by this time she had left the bookshop and was planning a summer of freedom with Ralph, although they were feeling poor after losing money on their investments – her only reference to the economic crisis of that year. Both of them had some capital, and Ralph was good at managing it, but she would miss her regular earnings. Bunny Garnett, now at the Nonesuch Press, had offered her work correcting proofs; it would be dull, but the money was welcome. She wanted to try writing some short stories, while doubting that she was really creative. 'Actual experience is the only thing that seems to stimulate my imagination.' When she deduced that Phil had not found congenial company, let alone someone to love in New Zealand, she advised him to come home and marry the charming and loveable Rachel

MacCarthy. Frances knew that Ralph had taken a great fancy to Rachel and she could see why; for Phil and Rachel to marry would bind them all together and increase the sum of everyone's happiness. Perhaps, subconsciously, she also wanted Rachel to find a man of her own.

By this time, it had been agreed that Frances would join Ralph in a major new task: helping Lytton prepare the first complete edition of the great Victorian diarist, Charles Greville. With work due to start in September, this gave her a summer of freedom – the first she had had since leaving Cambridge in 1921. As an experiment – and to leave Ralph free to travel with Lytton and Carrington – Frances went away on her own. She told Phil she had enjoyed her 'strange week of solitude', spent in a bedsitting room in Lymington in the New Forest, five shillings a day all told, working on her story, reading and walking. In July, she and Ralph took the two young MacCarthys, Rachel and her brother Michael, to Brittany with them on holiday. The weather was perfect; they basked and swam naked and ate delicious seafood to their hearts' content.

On her return, Frances found a letter from Phil that was not easy to answer. He was missing her so badly that on 21 June he wrote her a further declaration of love, and urged her to give up Ralph, whom he described as 'a fat man of sycophantic (so I am informed) inclination', and marry him. He was not sober when he wrote, and suggested that she try getting drunk before answering.

Frances replied from Hilton on 12 August. Her tone is cool. She cannot do as he asks for two reasons: 'there is nothing to drink, and there is no answer to be made'. He maintains that he cannot love anyone but her; she disagrees. 'You somehow feel that you can't give your mind to the idea of living with someone else because you'd rather it was me – and don't you see that that's absolutely not true.' Again, she urges him to come back to England, marry Rachel 'and be happy, and realise as quickly as possible what a disagreeable crotchety character I am'. She wants them to be friends. 'CCs, though disagreeable as companions for any long streak of time and intolerable as wives, may be very nice in their curious way as old Cronies, Confidants and Correspondents. And there Phil, that is all the answer I can give to your letter, and like it please, as much as you can.'

After turning to other topics – she is starting work for Bunny on the proofs of the Nonesuch Plutarch, her sister Ray, 'polished by the Riviera sun', is looking 'beautiful in a half savage way' and her nephews William and Richard 'are enchanting enough to make anyone wish they had children, and nuisance enough to make anyone thankful they have none' – she finally, at the end of her letter, gets to the heart of the matter. 'I must just say at the risk of being disagreeable (but it is something I have suppressed so often on previous similar occasions that it must come out at last) – I am just as much in love with R now as I was 2 years ago when I first began to live with him – and the result is that when other people say disagreeable things about him, it happens that I think worse of them and not of him.' Phil's attack on Ralph had been a mistake. 'I simply state this, it is a fact and perhaps a natural one, but I rather particularly dislike these remarks beginning rather insidiously "I am told that he" or "everyone says that"'. Nevertheless, 'I am very fond of you, and, do you know, I miss you immensely – your Frances.' The trouble was that she was not his Frances, she was Ralph's and she would not, from the time she committed herself to him until the end of her days, hear a word against him.

After this awkward exhange, her letters continued as before. The next came from Charleston, where she was invited by Clive and without Ralph. 'It's the first time I've been down here,' she wrote on 24 August, 'which I've always considered the heart and fortress of Old Bloomsbury, and I'm so fascinated by observation I can hardly remember to do anything else.' Her description of the scene is affectionate, amused and precise. 'I sit out, though a coldish wind blows and the sky is grey, in front of the sitting room, faced by a jungle of apple trees. Hollyhocks and immense dahlias; and Raymond [Mortimer] has just been stung by a wasp on his finger so he sits gloomily rubbing himself with an onion. From the studio come sounds of the painters painting – the painters are Duncan, Vanessa and Roger. From upstairs comes the sound of Clive pulling the plug of the WC.' She was taken with the Bell boys, Julian and Quentin, 'very intelligent, always laughing, very young, very serious about everything they do'. On the Friday, they had all gone over to the Keynes' house, Tilton, to watch Lydia and Duncan perform a play by one of Clive's mistresses, Bobo Mayor. There they found the Woolfs and E.M. Forster so that 'the Old Regiment became almost complete – every rank present, all the old uniforms and the old medals displayed'. Maynard was in a fuss because they were late and also because of the chilly weather; the play was to be done outside. When someone said it was raining, 'No it's NOT said Maynard, a second Canute'. So they sat huddled in their coats on wet chairs. The play was not as enthusiastically received as it might have been.

However, Frances went on, the evening gave Virginia and Forster plenty of scope for their 'whimsical irony' as the occasion was thoroughly analysed the next day. There were many jokes about how six people were expected to eat one duck – 'Maynard's stinginess is a standing joke' – and how when Virginia asked for some skin Maynard had said triumphantly as he passed it, 'There you are Virginia and what's more there's some flesh clinging to it.' The next day they visited Bobo at Steyning in Clive's hired Daimler, and that evening Frances found herself deep in 'a grand full blast aesthetic argument' over dinner. She was not sure what came over her; maybe it was the wine. 'I actually dared attack the Old Brigade on the very root principle of their beliefs, the bed-rock, their belief in the objectivity of aesthetic judgments. They think, you see, that one can say a picture is good without feeling it – that one can in fact know that one's aesthetic judgments are wrong. Whereas I feel that it is as impossible to think "I like Murillo but I know he's a bad artist" as "I like caviare but I know it's nasty".' They argued for hours, and Frances felt she had not done too badly. 'I had to receive a battery of Roger and Vanessa and Clive's best attacks and didn't give in a tittle nor convince them of a tittle.' Frances admired Old Blooms-bury, but she was not prepared to believe everything they said.

What struck her most on this first visit – and she would always emphasise this aspect of Charleston life – was 'the feeling of passionate activity ... it makes one feel a sloth, a dilettante to watch this fervour for creation'. She felt envious of Duncan's talent in particular. 'Oh to be able to do one thing supremely, instead of most things rather well!'

That autumn, Frances established a new routine. She was pleased not to be tied to the bookshop, but she was not suited to a life of leisure, floating free without the ballast of work to keep her steady. In the morning, she worked on the Plutarch proofs at home; then after lunch she and Ralph went off to the British Museum, where they were brought the volumes of the original Greville Diaries and settled down to what became almost ten years of detailed work on notes and index. She enjoyed the work hugely, and was amazed to discover how similar the courtiers and statesmen of the mid-nineteenth century were to her Bloomsbury circle: 'really', she told Phil, 'you would hardly believe the number of celebrated Victorians who were buggers or hermaphrodites or both'. She gave him a sparkling account of a Ham Spray weekend in September, with Roger Senhouse, Raymond, Julia and Tommy, when conversation rattled along and topics included 'The Royal family and how many equivalents there are for the adjective "fucking" in French – then telepathy, the Scientific Method, Education, Scepticism and Disbelief, Public Schools, whether there can be such things as mute inglorious Miltons.' Everything was much as usual, but if she and Ralph were content with the pattern of their life, Lytton and Carrington evidently were not. Early in November, Lytton dropped another bombshell. He wrote a careful but firm letter to Ralph in which he made it quite clear that he and Carrington would like to see rather less of Frances.

My dearest, I am writing this without telling Carrington, and perhaps you may think it best not to show it to Frances. But of course you must do just as you like. I have felt for some time rather uneasy about F – but have been unable to bring myself to say anything. What worries me is her coming down here with you so much, and staying for so much of the time you are here, so that we see so little of you alone. It is not quite what I had expected would happen – and I think not exactly what you intended either. I am afraid you may suppose that this indicates some hostility on my part towards F, but this is far from being the case. Can you believe this? I hope so. I hope that you will trust that I am telling the truth, and believe in my affection for you, which is something I cannot describe or express. I feel it too deeply for that. I know that this must be painful to you, but it seems better that I should tell you what is in my mind than that I should continue indefinitely with a slight consciousness of a difficulty not cleared up between us.

Lytton's letter could be seen as a brave demonstration of the Bloomsbury principle of facing the truth whether it hurt or not; but it was also a subtle attempt to manipulate the situation to suit himself.

If you feel that you cannot answer this either by writing or in talk, do not do so. I will say nothing more about it, and all will be well between us. But conceivably it might be possible for you to suggest to F that it would be better if she came down rather less often – and if that could be managed the situation would be very greatly eased. It is for you to judge what you can do. I trust your judgment. I only feel that you may perhaps have allowed things to drift from an unwillingness to take an unpleasant step. I don't know. And please do not do anything under a sense of 'pressure' from me. I press for nothing. I only ask whether perhaps it may be possible, without too much pain, to make me happier.

I say nothing about C – she does not say very much to me about these things, and does not guess that I am writing now.

The letter ends with Lytton suggesting that Ralph come to see him in London a day or two later, and ends 'With all my love, my dearest, your devoted Lytton.'

This letter, which Ralph immediately showed to Frances, hurt her and infuriated Ralph. This was, she wrote later, 'the only occasion I have ever seen him really furiously angry with Lytton'. The situation at Ham Spray was not ideal for her either – as she always said, her position there was tricky, being neither host nor guest – but she had accepted it for almost three years, believing it was the best solution for everyone concerned. Now, Lytton was suggesting that he, and by implication Carrington, be made happier at her expense. The truth of the matter was that she was tolerated at Ham Spray, not welcomed. A less level-headed and more selfish woman might well at this point have declared the experiment over and forced Ralph to choose between Ham Spray and her; but that was not her nature. For once, though, Lytton had miscalculated; Ralph was deeply attached to him, and loyal to the way of life they had set up together, but he loved Frances, and refused to give way. As a result, Frances recalled, 'things went on much as before, except that both Ralph and I stayed away from Ham Spray rather more'.

On the surface, then, nothing changed. Writing to Phil in New Zealand two weeks after Lytton's letter, she only sounds mildly out of sorts. She was feeling dull, she told him from the train on the way back from Ham Spray, and 'rather depressed at the thought of the unchangeability of one's character and the more and more fixed state of one's opinions ... A change of self – my kingdom for a change of self.' Was it herself, or her situation, she wanted to change? She could not admit it to herself, and still less to Phil, but at the end of 1928 she was once again in a trap. This time it was not the weather but Ralph's commitment to Lytton and Carrington that trapped them both. The strain was beginning to tell; over Christmas, back at Ham Spray, Frances fell mysteriously ill and retired to bed. It was to be some time before she was herself again.

Nine

Darkness at Ham Spray, 1929–1932

The malaise that began to affect Frances just before Christmas 1928 lingered for much of 1929. Later she decided that it had been largely psychosomatic, and related it both to Lytton's letter and to suppression of her maternal instincts. Now that she had found her mate she wanted to have his child; but both she and Ralph felt unable to go ahead while they were unmarried, and the prospect of introducing a baby into Gordon Square or Ham Spray was unimaginable. Whether she recognised her true feelings at the time is hard to tell. She had to a considerable extent adopted the anti-family, anti-child idiom of Bloomsbury; but her letters to Phil are sprinkled with half-wistful references to their mutual friends who were busy marrying and producing children, and she was approaching thirty, which at the time seemed older for childbirth than it does today.

The symptoms she described at the time suggest that she was as much emotionally as physically ill. She had no appetite, she lost weight, her pulse was irregular; above all she had no energy, and felt weak and lethargic. Early in January, she went back to Brunswick Square in a state of collapse to be nursed by Mam. Her pocket diary records days spent in bed, consultations with doctors, visits from nurses, daily checks on her temperature; by the middle of February she was considered strong enough to spend ten days in bracing Brighton with Ralph, and go on to Ray and Bunny at the even more bracing Hilton, whence she wrote to Phil explaining her long silence. She had been, she told him, 'without any energy or desire or pleasure in doing anything – feeble as an earwig, irritable, odious, dim'. Being back at home with Mam and Eleanor had driven her nearly mad, and she had nearly driven Ralph mad in turn; he had demonstrated, she wrote wryly, 'the normal desire of the healthy animal to crush and kill the sick animal, which he vented upon me by fits and starts and by fits and starts was full of repentance'. Gradually she started to feel better, and to mark her recovery she took up skating. Her father had been a great skater, after all, and now Frances' spirits rose as she whirled around the ice in Regent's Park or on the frozen fens near Hilton. Then and later, Frances closed the lid firmly on too much examination of her psychological state. She enjoyed analysing emotions and behaviour, including her own, but she did not like to brood and she always maintained that all the medicines and doctors had been useless, and that she had cured herself by taking vigorous exercise. At ice rinks in London after the thaw, if she could not take a friend as partner – Arthur Waley, the Chinese scholar, and Raymond Mortimer were regulars – she could always pay a professional, dressed in a dark blue uniform, to dance with her for 2/6d an hour.

Frances was resilient; she was not by nature someone to pine for what she could not have, or could not change. Slowly, her appetite for life returned. From Ham Spray over Easter, though, she told Phil that she was still getting thinner 'and my heart occasionally breaks out'; however, she had been well enough to spend a recent evening with Ralph as Clive Bell's guests at the Gargoyle Club, along with Eddie Gathorne-Hardy, Mary Butts and Clive's latest flirt, Elizabeth Ponsonby. The Gargoyle, run by David Tennant, was then the height of fashion and frequented by the higher bohemia and the Bright Young Things. Bloomsbury and this other tribe, not often bracketed together, sometimes overlapped; Elizabeth Ponsonby, the wild upper-class girl usually considered the model for Agatha Runcible in Evelyn Waugh's *Vile Bodies*, was an exact contemporary of Frances. They did not, however, make friends; Frances called her 'my pet aversion'. She described a gruesome scene when Elizabeth Ponsonby got so drunk that she was sick into a plate of mushrooms.

In early July, Frances took off again for a few days by herself, exploring the Norfolk coast while Ralph was travelling in Holland with Lytton and Carrington. In the wake of Lytton's letter, such separate holidays were tactful, if not essential; Frances did not complain, but every letter she wrote to Ralph told him how much she loved and missed him.

During the summer of 1929 Young Bloomsbury was bitten by the amateur film-making bug, then all the rage. First at Hilton, then at Ham Spray, Frances, with some reluctance, was drawn into several days of frenzied activity, organised by Alec and Beakus Penrose, with the help of Bunny Garnett and Carrington. Beakus (whose real name was Bernard) was the youngest of the four Penrose brothers, a clever family brought into Lytton's orbit via Cambridge, and had been Carrington's lover since the previous year. He was ten years her junior, an enigmatic, silent character with a passion for the sea, who took her sailing, slept with her when it suited him and undermined her fragile confidence by his elusiveness.

Ralph was in Holland during the Hilton filming, which Frances thought was probably just as well. Beakus operated his new camera, Bunny, in a special white peaked cap, was the director, and the story was based on a Penrose anecdote about two aunts destroying the family's stock of wine. Ray Garnett and Frances' friend Lettice Ramsey were the aunts, Frank Ramsey played the family butler and Frances herself was cast as Alec's virtuous girlfriend. It was a cold grey day and the proceedings seemed interminable. 'I simply had to spend my time merrily running through hayfields and scampering over fences, or bounding into Alec's arms – and very silly I looked, too,' she wrote to Ralph. She annoyed the others by refusing to continue when it got dark, and decided that acting was not for her.

Frances did a lot of letter-writing during her solitary week. Her correspondence, like her diary, was important to her, as a form of conversation; she had also taken to photography, another way of capturing time and celebrating friendship. Bloomsbury, Old and Young, took to the camera with enthusiasm; Ottoline Morrell and Virginia Woolf were keen photographers and life at Ham Spray was recorded in albums by Lytton and Carrington as well as by Frances herself. As well as to Phil Nichols, she wrote long, entertaining letters to Gerald, now back in Spain. 'You may wonder what I am doing here,' she wrote from a boarding house in Hunstanton on the Norfolk coast, surrounded by old ladies and commercial travellers. 'I wonder it myself. Well the truth is I have run away from Ralph, unable for another instant to stand his overbearing egotism.' Admitting that this was merely a tease, she went on: 'When you return to England you will be forced to look at endless cinema films of your friends, idiotically prancing ... I consider it a very grave menace in our midst.'

Even so, she was drawn into another two-day film session at Ham Spray later in the summer. Lytton kept away, but Ralph was there, along with Saxon, Rachel MacCarthy and Stephen Tomlin. This time, the film was set in a lunatic asylum, run by a sinister Doctor Turner, played by Saxon. Rachel was the innocent heroine, shown wearing a daisy chain in her bath while Dr Turner leered at her round the door; Frances performed as a deranged inmate, crawling around the grass with a daft expression on her face and riding boots on her arms. Ralph annoyed Carrington, who had made all the masks and props, by asking everyone to stay for Sunday lunch.

By the end of August, Frances felt well again and told Phil firmly that she was 'as happy at times as I've ever been in my life'. She and Ralph had decided to go back to Spain in September and visit Gerald in Yegen. Whatever he was thinking about in New Zealand, she herself, at Ham Spray, was preoccupied with 'madness, buggery and whether there's an absolute standard of value in literature'. Her recovery, apparently, had led her to contemplate the life going on around her with a fresh eye; the latest goings-on in the homosexual world surrounding her prompted her to fury. Buggery, she informed Phil, was having a drastic and deleterious effect on civilised life, because 'it usually causes the middle-aged and intelligent to fall in love and subjugation with the young and merely pretty ... The middle-aged intellectuals give up supporting their intellectual standards, and lose all power of criticism – and if they do, so does everyone else.' They had often argued about why she liked the world of Bloomsbury, and how

> the Blooms stood for the things I valued and were the only sort of people I wanted to be with. Well Bloomsbury is dead. Swallowed up in a sea of Buggery, all the old Bloomsbury standards which *were* good whatever you may say – of courage, independence, passion for the truth and reality instead of romance and hyppocracy [*sic*] – have been replaced by snobbery, sillyness and a passion for fancy dresses ... it shocks me that all these young men have no solidity whatever, can't read a book and burst into tears if they are left alone for more than half an hour on end.

Since she greatly liked both Roger Senhouse and Dadie Rylands, Lytton's constant companions and loves at the time, it was probably the newer hangers-on, such as John Banting, Stephen Tennant and Brian Howard, who were much given to camp posturing, who provoked her. Her irritation did not last long.

Frances was not alone, though, in sometimes finding the flamboyant younger generation of homosexuals annoying. Virginia Woolf was also unnerved by the way the discreet intellectual or artistic buggers of early Bloomsbury, whose dress and speech rarely, at least in public, revealed their sexual preference, were now surrounded by brighter, shriller young men, like a flock of drab old owls being mobbed by parakeets. In particular, she deplored what she saw as the bad influence of these new arrivals on her friend Lytton – both on his character and on his work. When Lytton's *Elizabeth and Essex* came out in 1928, Virginia found it to be a 'lively superficial meretricious book' and blamed, in part, 'the Carringtons and the young men' around him. At Bloomsbury parties she sometimes found the homosexual men present 'giggly and coy' with their gossip about clothes and pretty boys: 'This all made on me a tinkling, private, giggling impression ... As if I had gone into a men's urinal.'

The atmosphere was very different at Charleston, where Frances spent another late summer weekend in 1928 while Ralph visited his mother in Devon. This time she found Duncan particularly fascinating and easy to talk to, whereas Vanessa still made her feel shy; but the beauty and creativity of the place impressed her all over again. She herself made a strong impression on Vanessa's daughter Angelica, then aged ten, who found Frances' good looks and vitality a refreshing change from her statuesque mother. Angelica was growing up in the belief that Clive Bell was her father; Bloomsbury's passion for openness and truth-telling did not extend to her paternity, although everyone around her knew the truth. Charleston liked Frances, christened by Angelica 'Miss Marshall, to whom we are partial'.

By mid-September, Frances was in Spain with Ralph. From Gerald's house in Yegen, she wrote Phil an ecstatic letter. 'How would you like to sit on a flat roof in the sun, rocking backwards and forwards in a rocking chair, with the whole world, or half of it at least, spread out in amazing panorama around one, with a nest of white roofs round one on the side of the hill covered with pimientos and figs drying on straw mats, with mules jingling up the cobbly streets, and raucous voices of Spanish children from the courtyards ... I'm drunk with the worst kind of drunkenness for writing letters, drunk with everything I see.' The village 'floats among the clouds rather than being built on the slopes of the Sierra Nevada'. Apart from the intoxicating beauty of the place, she was riveted by the dramas swirling around 'Don Geraldo' and his 'curious horde' of retainers, all of whom appeared to be tortured by elemental emotions, especially jealousy, 'which it seems to me is to be found here in its purest, most essential state. In the midst of it all Don G himself, comic as ever, and as charming, in an orange dressing gown, distracted, machiavellian, enjoying it all in a way, laughing at himself, throwing the meals and the plates out of the window one moment, giving his last penny to one of the retainers the next.'

After the suppressed jealousies and tensions of Ham Spray, it was refreshing to be part of a household where emotions were rampant and undisguised. She was greatly amused by Juliana, the young servant girl Gerald had made his mistress, who refused to get out of his bed in the morning, thus driving the other staff 'half mad with fury and jealousy'; and by Black Maria, Queen of the Fleas (they all spent a lot of time scratching), 'a splendid character, nut brown face and wicked black eyes, dances like a fairy, rails and screams like a shrew, squeaks with high spirits as she tells one how dreadful it is that her daughter will do nothing but pray, pray, pray and have toothache'. Frances revelled too in the remoteness, cut off from all news, unsure even of the date. But above all she was thrilled by the huge landscape, the thin, cold air, the mountain pools, the wild mushrooms, the stony hillsides where 'filthy handsome shepherds show one enormous underground caves full of bats'. Spain released something in Frances, overrode her cool, rational, well-behaved side; she felt free. 'Oh you would love the evenings when the village comes in and there is dancing. Young men of incredible beauty sit around the walls sipping aguardiente and as stuck as pigs, till the guitars begin to thrum, and then suddenly they rise proudly to their feet and begin dancing the Malaguenas with the girls, breaking out into their harsh hysterical singing as they dance . . . Oh what excitement. This whole country gets into my blood, under the toe-nails – it's like hundreds of tom toms as soon as one crosses the frontier.' She was happy and well, she told Phil, and sounded at last as if she meant it.

After two weeks at Yegen, Frances and Ralph spent a few days in Barcelona on their way home, meeting up with Clive Bell and Raymond Mortimer. The city was crowded with visitors for the Great Exhibition held there in 1929; they wandered through coloured fountains, admired Gaudi's extra-ordinary glittering façades and had their photograph taken at a fair as flamenco dancers, each head poking incongruously through a hole above a cardboard costume.

The carnival atmosphere and Frances' exhilaration could not last. Not long after they returned to England in October, they found themselves dealing with two pieces of bad news. First, James and Alix had decided to reclaim the first floor of No. 41 to use as consulting rooms, and asked them to move out by the end of the year. Frances was sad to leave their first home, but before long they found somewhere else nearby, in Great James Street, where Francis and Vera Meynell rented them the top two floors of the Queen Anne house which also accommodated the Nonesuch Press. The other problem was more serious, and, although Frances never spoke or wrote about her deeper feelings on the matter, must have troubled her rather more. Carrington, to her horror and despair, was pregnant by Beakus Penrose. Both Lytton and Ralph talked to her at length about her pre-dicament and agreed that 'her abhorrence of the idea had reduced her to a suicidal state and that something must be done'. The child would have been legally Ralph's; and after her attempts to end the pregnancy by strenuous rides failed, a termination (then an illegal operation, expensive and hard to arrange) was organised and paid for by him. All Frances could do was to stay out of the way, which she did, observing later that Lytton had been so nice to her as a result that she felt her efforts to be accommodating 'had not been in vain'. She did, however, visit Carrington in the nursing home, a remarkable gesture of solidarity and kindness in the circumstances. Everyone concerned, especially Beakus, appears to have heaved a sigh of relief and felt nothing but gratitude to Ralph; any emotional repercussions were ignored. But against this background, the next letter Frances wrote to Phil about a month later, just before Christmas 1929, reads oddly. Naturally, she did not mention the episode; but after giving him news about the weather (depressing) and what she had been reading (she sent him Svevo's *Confessions of Zeno*, saying she rated it as highly as Proust) she went on: 'A great deal of giving and taking in marriage goes on, and still more of baby production. In fact it's a bumper year for babies and people who have been struggling to conceive for years have suddenly succeeded – something in the air I suppose . . . one spends one's life visiting happy mothers in nursing homes.' Letters, especially to someone safely on the other side of the world, can construct alternative, sunnier versions of a darker reality. In the late 1920s, Frances was obliged to control or suppress many of her emotions in order to make a success of her life with Ralph. She loved him, but there was a price to pay.

No sooner had the move to Great James Street been accomplished in January 1930 than Frances was caught up in another painful crisis. Since Frank Ramsey had married Lettice Baker, her friend from Bedales and Newnham, she had become a frequent visitor at their house in Cambridge. She admired Frank's passion for abstract thought and his love of music, especially Beethoven's late quartets; and she was amused by his large, ungainly appearance, his big head and wispy, untidy hair. Lettice had told her that neither partner was faithful, and that she had been tempted to have an affair with Ramsey's brilliant friend, his handsome, tortured Viennese protégé, Ludwig Wittgenstein, who had been back in Cambridge since 1929. Through the Ramseys, Frances saw a certain amount of Wittgenstein, recognised his 'towering intellect' and acknowledged genius and observed his many peculiarities. 'In mixed company his conversation was often trivial in the extreme, and larded with feeble jokes accompanied by a wintry smile. I was aware of suppressed irritability in him.' She liked the way he enjoyed his own silly jokes, as well as detective stories, films and concocting strange alcoholic drinks, and saw that he needed such trivial amusements as a release from his intense nature and powerful mental processes. Above all she liked him for his devotion to Frank, whom she really preferred to Lettice.

When, towards the end of January 1930, a prolonged attack of jaundice turned out to be something more serious and Frank Ramsey was admitted to Guy's Hospital in London in a terminal condition, Lettice turned to Frances, whose diary for the next few days shows how she had by this time discovered that describing unnerving events as precisely as possible helped her to get them, and her own emotions, under control.

She found Lettice in a hot little room, 'compulsively writing postcards and crying a little now and again. Very sensibly she asked me not to be sorry for her – in words at least – as it only made her lose control.' They talked a lot about Frank's condition; he was lying nearby, his breathing distressingly laboured. Frances decided not to go down to Ham Spray with Ralph but did not want to be alone; she went home to Mam in Brunswick Square, where Lettice had also lodged for a while. The next day was mostly spent at the hospital, and Wittgenstein arrived to see his friend. Frances felt they shared 'intense sympathy for Lettice'; but she found the way he disguised his emotions beneath 'a light, almost jocose tone' disconcerting. She went back to Brunswick Square for the night; in the early morning Mam came in to tell her that Frank was dead and Lettice needed her. 'I found her lying red eyed on a tousled bed looking dreadfully forlorn, and only after I had taken her hand and kissed her and we had both burst into tears did I fully realise that it was *Frank* who had died – my friend Frank, the engaging, original, brilliantly clever Frank.'

Frances attended the funeral at Golders Green Crematorium, which she found both horrifying and grotesque. She noted the comic clumsiness of the pall-bearers, the coffin, Lydia Keynes' self-consciously tragic expression, and the way Lettice's aunt's sobs were replaced by gay smiles on the bus afterwards. This was the first funeral she had ever been to and it made her resolve to avoid ever going to another. 'I know that I want none of it for myself or anyone I dearly love.' Oddly, she had noted in her diary before Frank's illness a conversation with Lettice when Frances had tried to envisage her own death, and Ralph's, and wondered whether anything could make it acceptable. She came to only one conclusion: 'I hope to God I die before Ralph does.'

Frances did her best to help Lettice in the aftermath of Frank's death, although she flinched at her friend's new dependence on her; when Lettice suggested they go abroad together, Frances arranged a retreat nearer home and took her for a week to Ham Spray. From there she brought Phil up-to-date. She was desperately sorry for Lettice, but their melancholy life at Ham Spray made her feel torn between selfishness and unselfishness and 'I think selfishness is going to win.' All they did was rest, walk, read and play ping-pong. Frances was reading *Oblomov,* and finding it 'a most soothing book'; she could sometimes cheer Lettice up by reading *Memoirs of a Fox-Hunting Man* aloud.

Frances never allowed sadness to dominate her life for long; she always fought back. On 15 March she turned thirty, and found her first grey hairs; she did not, she wrote, greatly care. She and Ralph were still enjoyably at work on the Greville Diaries; she began to wonder what she would do when the task came to an end. In London during the week they went to a great many parties, and gave a small house-warming party themselves, which Frances felt too preoccupied to enjoy; she had to fend off embraces from various men including Oliver Strachey. Then Alix Strachey and her great friend Nancy Morris gave a bigger party, where most of the guests were homosexual. 'Young man after young man pushed his pretty face round the door, and a crowd of truculent Lesbians stood by the fireplace, occasionally trying their biceps or carrying each other round the room.' Since Frances was no longer interested in hunting for a partner, she found she much preferred evenings with old friends. There was a tea party in Duncan's studio, with Vanessa and Clive, and dinner at Rules, before yet another Bloomsbury gathering where she saw Frankie Birrell, Julia, Tommy, Alec and Beakus Penrose. Frances was taken aback to be told by Adrian Stephen that several of his patients, two women in particular, talked about her during their psychoanalytic sessions. 'Almost everyone you know is being secretly analysed,' he told her, 'and we have meetings where everyone and everything is discussed.' Then there was the Great Hermaphrodite Party, which Frances summed up in a letter to Gerald: 'Almost all the young men had the same idea which was to make themselves look as lovely and seductive as possible, with the result that none of them had ever looked more hideous ... Over-excitement made the buggers shriek so loudly that one could not hear one's nearest neighbour's loudest remarks.' Arthur Waley looked really beautiful in a huge pink poke bonnet, while Ralph, in a red wig and Spanish shawl, 'failed to look in any way feminine'; Frances herself sported a bowler hat and a tiny moustache. One of the hosts, Eddie Sackville-West, became tearful when a young German he fancied refused to dance with him, and enlisted Frances' help: 'Now come on, my dear, just take him by the hand and *throw* him into my arms.' The German asked her to dance instead.

Parties, she decided, were all very well, but what she really enjoyed most were the times she and Ralph could be alone together, as they never were at Ham Spray. They managed a weekend at Noel Carrington's country cottage, where they talked and played chess and lit a fire in their bedroom. Frances lay in bed and watched the flames flicker, thinking about pleasure. Was it, she wondered, just 'biological bait? to ensure the survival of the species?' Being close to Ralph, physically and emotionally, gave her the greatest pleasure she had ever known.

Not even the return of Phil Nichols from New Zealand, and his final attempt to persuade her to leave Ralph and marry him, upset her for very long. A couple of scribbled, anxious notes during the summer confirm her published diary: seeing him was, she wrote, 'a ghost resuscitated; I saw it and was afraid. With enormous gratitude I realised the delights of the happy reciprocal love Ralph and I have enjoyed for the last four years.' They met, he told her he still loved her and asked her again to marry him; in return she could only offer him a loving friendship. This time he gave up. It was not long before he did what Frances had been urging him to do in her letters for some time and found someone who could make him happy. In 1931 he married a beautiful, well-connected and wealthy woman, Phyllis Spender Clay, and went on to have three children and a highly successful career as a diplomat. He was the only man who ever presented a challenge to Ralph for Frances' love, and although they did their best and the forms of friendship were observed, neither man ever really liked the other. In her old age, Frances acknowledged that she had truly cared for Phil, adding that Ralph had encouraged her to go to bed with him, believing that she would not get over him unless she did. But by that time the years when her life still contained uncertainties, before her love for and belief in Ralph ran like a calm river on a settled course, were very far away. All she would say when reminded that she might have married Phil Nichols was that she thought being an ambassador's wife would not have suited her.

In choosing Ralph, she had chosen not only an unconventional situation but a man with no interest in a career and a great interest in the odder aspects of human nature. She came to share his growing fascination with unusual, even extreme behaviour, which provided much material for enjoyable discussion and the application of Freudian terminology. That summer, when Gerald came to stay they were entertained by his tales of sexual intrigue in Spain, where Juliana was now alleged to be pregnant by him. Overwrought by this possibility, he would prowl the London streets picking up girls, and report back to Ralph and Frances; once they found him up on the roof with binoculars, convinced he could see a naked girl in the bath. Ralph could only see an elderly man; Gerald always had a strong streak of the voyeur. Frances and Ralph also relished the endless vagaries of human sexuality and the stranger aspects of human nature. They both loved detective stories, and reading accounts of the trials of famous criminals; and, around this time, they became briefly caught up in the louche adventures of one Hayley Morris of Pippingford Park.

Hayley Morris was a rich man who in the late 1920s fell foul of the police and the British public in a spasm of outraged morality. He had been sent to prison for sleeping with an under-age girl in his employ; the press ran lurid tales of the tycoon who enticed young women to his estate in Sussex by promising them jobs looking after his exotic menagerie and held orgies of sexual licence. Frances and Ralph came across Morris by accident, one hot weekend when, staying with Leo Myers in Sussex, the party decided to go for a swim in Morris' lake nearby. They assumed he was away – perhaps even still in gaol. As they were approaching the lake – with Myers' two daughters and Rachel MacCarthy – they saw a small figure leaning on a bridge. Ralph went to enquire, and came back to say it was the owner himself, that they were welcome to go swimming, and that Hayley Morris had asked them back to his house for tea.

The consequence of this encounter was that both Leo Myers and the MacCarthys were appalled at the idea of their daughters having any connection with the scandalous gaolbird, and that Ralph and Frances went out of their way to befriend him. After all, as Frances wrote, 'Here was a man who had done what? Gone to bed with a few pretty girls? Of which of one's friends could not the same be said? . . . He had served his sentence, but still was not to be treated with common decency by people of advanced views. He had become to us much as an ill used animal is to the RSPCA.' For about a year, they kept up with him, stayed with him at The Crow's Nest, his house at Pippingford, admired his flocks of strange birds – the place was a haven for cranes – and other unexpected animals. 'Once, coming back to the Crows Nest we were confronted by a squat muff of fur on short legs. It was a wombat.' They learned that the showgirl from the Savoy who had been the first of his alleged harem was in fact a lesbian, and that it was she who had brought other girls to the house by advertising for kennel maids for the wolfhounds. It was all amusing for a while, but they were not really sorry when after about a year Morris married, and they felt he did not need their company any more. Much later, Frances' sparkling account of this strange episode was one of the first autobiographical fragments she wrote.

After spending what by now was her annual weekend at Charleston in mid-August, Frances and Ralph, accompanied this time by two younger girls, Rachel MacCarthy and Lytton's niece Janie Bussy, spent most of September back in Spain. Gerald was in England, where that summer he met the American poet, Gamel Woolsey, who was to become his wife; this time, instead of the mountains they chose the coast at Cadaqués, on the Catalan border. The party would set off every day with books and picnics in their rucksacks, in search of deserted coves where they could swim and sun themselves naked. Frances took many photographs of these outings, often showing Ralph displaying his large but splendid rowing man's torso. Janie Bussy, the daughter of Dorothy Strachey and the French artist Simon Bussy, was a plain girl with a lovely figure, who became a favourite of them both – and developed, for a while, a marked crush on Ralph. Frances never appeared to mind the fact that Ralph liked to have pretty young women around him; she seems to have found it entirely natural that he should be drawn to them, and vice versa. Anyway, as some of the photographs show, her own figure was easily good enough to stand comparison.

So Frances' thirtieth year ended better than it had begun. No-one gathered at Ham Spray for Christmas 1930 could have imagined that the year ahead was to see the familiar pattern of life there gone for ever. Looking back, a series of ominous events, like small clouds gathering to darken a bright landscape, appear; but for Frances 1931 began cheerfully enough. In the first half of January she saw the Marx Brothers' new film, *Animal Crackers*, visited Rodmell for the weekend, went skating with Carrington and to a party of Clive Bell's. Since the previous autumn, Clive had been suffering eye trouble and Frances had endeared herself to him even more by cheering him up with frequent visits and reading aloud; luckily he was successfully treated in Zurich and made a full recovery. Frances wrote him gossipy letters, which he relished. One of them contained the unlikely news that Carrington had 'got off' with Harpo Marx at a cocktail party and was to paint his portrait.

After the abortion Carrington's affair with Beakus Penrose had resumed, but her own sporadic diary shows she was far from happy. She knew he was not in love with her, she hated getting older and finding herself often alone at Ham Spray. Lytton, too, was still obsessed with Roger Senhouse but finding him elusive; he was often low and unwell. Carrington was drinking too much; she slept badly and had appalling nightmares. She was often angry with Ralph, who found her moods infuriating; they would have explosive rows, often about money. But she and Frances managed their relationship well; another entry in Frances' pocket diary reads 'Turkish Bath and lunch Carrington'.

Ham Spray continued to draw new friends into the circle, like Rosamond Lehmann and her second husband Wogan Philipps, now living not far away at Ipsden. Frances knew Rosamond slightly from Cambridge, and they had a mutual friend in Dadie Rylands, to whom Rosamond had dedicated her first novel, *Dusty Answer*, which appeared in 1927 and established her as a young writer of great promise. Through Dadie, Rosamond met Lytton and Carrington, both of whom approved of her; Lytton found her admiring and eager to learn, while Rosamond became one of the beautiful young women who brought out Carrington's playful, flirtatious side. Both Frances and Ralph also became fond of Ros and Wog, while never taking them entirely seriously. Rosamond's writing was too romantic for them, but they appreciated her good looks and sweet nature. Another well-connected beauty of the day, Diana Guinness, one of the already celebrated Mitford sisters, lived nearby at Biddesden with her husband Bryan; she too became rather a favourite of Lytton and Carrington's, though Ralph and Frances found her deceptively blank blue gaze and affected speech annoying and nicknamed her Dotty Di.

Just occasionally, Frances was sharply reminded that for the world outside Bloomsbury Carrington still had the status of Ralph's legal wife. During the summer, his mother suddenly became seriously ill, and it was Carrington he took down to Devon to visit her; the letter Frances wrote just after he left tells its own story. 'Did you think me very grumpy this morning? I couldn't get used to the idea of parting from you in such a short time . . . but I am horrified to think how grumpish and growlish I was. Carrington was so nice to me.' But such moments passed, and by September she and Ralph were off again together to the South of France. Meeting up with Eddie Sackville-West in St Tropez, they were amused by the antics of the smart set, 'who shrieked at each other in the bars and bôites, dressed in striped sailor jerseys and the shortest possible shorts, and painted their toenails silver or green'. This was not their style, but they loved to observe it.

As always, life at Ham Spray revolved around Lytton, and as winter approached his health took a worrying turn. Never robust, in recent years he had been increasingly prone to fevers and stomach problems; at first, he seemed no iller than he had often been before. Already, a plan had been launched to close Ham Spray for the winter and for the household to move to Málaga to avoid the cold; Lytton had approved, and Ralph had begun to make enquiries. But by early November, it was clear that Lytton was not up to any such journey. He took to his bed at Ham Spray.

There now began a time of particular difficulty for Frances. Doctors came and went, nurses were installed, and Ralph's presence was required. There was little that Frances could do except, once again, withdraw to the sidelines; she accepted this with her usual realism and common sense, while at the same time longing to be able to help Ralph. No-one knew better than she did how emotionally vulnerable he was, however strong and competent he appeared. Over the next weeks, they wrote to each other almost every day, a stream of loving, anxious letters which chart the ups and downs of Lytton's condition and Carrington's mounting desperation. They also spoke regularly on the telephone, but the telephone was not in those days private enough to be safe.

Ralph knew that it was up to him to keep Carrington as calm as possible. His letters to Frances go into great detail about Lytton's symptoms and the different opinions offered by the specialists, who ordered endless tests and came up with assorted diagnoses. None of them discovered the truth, which was that he had advanced stomach cancer. Ralph badly needed to share all this with someone level-headed, as it was impossible to do so with Carrington; so Frances received page after page of information about Lytton's temperature, pulse, diet and 'motions'. With her, he could be frank about the doctor's opinions; Carrington had to be protected, but Frances could help him face the truth. When, on 10 December, he asked one of the specialists whether Lytton's life was in danger, the answer was 'Whatever it may be it is dangerous'; but, Ralph went on, 'I have told Carrington that he said it might *become* dangerous. All yesterday she went about as if L was dying and she had killed him by going up to London last week, so I had to tell her something quieting.' Both he and Frances knew that Ralph could not leave Ham Spray, for Lytton's sake. 'He asked me this morning how long I could stay and I said I would stay until he was better. Carrington cries every moment she goes in to see him as soon as she gets out.' Evidently, Ralph was sharing a bed with Carrington. 'We had a very disturbed night sleeping very light – and every time Lytton's bell rang Carrington stiffened in every limb – she can't relax enough to get off soundly to sleep.' He knew that Frances would understand. 'I hate our being separated, lovie one, but you shall come here if it goes on by some means or other ... our lives are all short and precarious, but I shall love you as long as I live with all my heart.'

Frances' letters, at first, show her trying to amuse and distract Ralph with news of London life, reminding him that although she missed him terribly he need not worry about her. She was seeing Rachel and catching up on gossip about Cyril Connolly and his first wife Jean, neither of whom were popular with Bloomsbury although Desmond MacCarthy had been one of his early literary mentors. Leo Myers took her out to lunch and talked about his love life; he had a secret arrangement with them to rent a room at Great James Street for assignations. As she often did when Ralph was away, Frances fell back on her family; she would spend occasional nights with Mam and Eleanor at Brunswick Square, and weekends with Judy and Dick at Owley. She also kept Ralph informed about her dealings with the gynaecologist Dr Helena Wright, one of the handful of sympathetic women doctors at that time who would provide women, married or not, with contraception. She found the whole business awkward and absurd.

Meanwhile at Ham Spray Lytton was no better, and Ralph and Carrington had to deal with the constant enquiries and visits of his friends and, especially, of his relations. Ralph was particularly irritated by Dr Ellie Rendel, Dick Rendel's sister and Lytton's niece, whose profession entitled her to confuse the picture still further. He did his best to protect Carrington from her gloomy predictions, and let off steam in his letters to Frances. From Owley, Frances wrote back crossly: 'What a fiend Ellie is.' She was not much enjoying 'the Marshall atmosphere', she told him, and had had a bad night fretting about Lytton and Helena Wright, a bizarre combination. Ralph wrote back telling her that Lytton had not given up, and was still talking of Málaga. He had managed to persuade Carrington to spend a day at Biddesden where Bryan and Diana Guinness had been very kind to her. Pippa Strachey was staying, and James and Alix were in close touch; Mary Hutchinson, Raymond, Rosamond and Wogan kept ringing up for news. As for him, he reached for a telling analogy. 'I feel back in the trenches myself, there are the same orders for the day to carry out, telephone messages from HQ, visits from the colonel and staff, NCOs to question and tell to carry on with what they do infinitely better than ever you could, and at the back of one's mind the anxiety at night, the possibility of something unexpected and certain to be unpleasant being sprung upon one. I sleep as lightly as a feather.' He had been warned that in a crisis, he would be required to give Lytton a blood transfusion: 'the only way I could ever be sent over the top in this campaign'.

By the middle of December a group of Stracheys had taken up residence in the Bear Hotel at Hungerford, and Frances was planning to join them. All she wanted, she told Ralph, was to be at hand should he need her. Not long before Christmas, as she had done so many times before, she arrived at Hungerford station where Ralph met her. 'Always an emotional man,' she wrote later, 'easily moved to tears, and deeply devoted to Lytton, he had been left with his powers of resistance reduced to practically nothing by the constant strain of trying to support Carrington in her even more agonising state of dread. During the drive from Hungerford to Ham Spray he talked and wept without stopping, and though I've never been prone to tears my own soon began to flow in sympathy.' She was still tearful when they arrived at the house, where she found her old College Principal, Pernel Strachey, sitting calmly doing the crossword with Oliver, Pippa and Marjorie. 'I had no idea what she thought of my relationship with Ralph, and I was almost ashamed of the reluctance of my tears to stop oozing from my eyes. So I was grateful that she greeted me with marked kindness' – a rare indication from Frances that she could occasionally feel self-conscious about her position as Ralph's mistress.

After a few days at the Bear, the Strachey atmosphere – gloom and anxiety relieved by sudden shrieks of laughter, as when a telegram arrived for Pernel addressed to The Principal Bear – and the expense became too much for Frances, and she found a room above the post office in Ham, close enough to walk up to Ham Spray. There she tried to help Carrington with domestic tasks, and to get Ralph out of the house occasionally so that they could talk. 'Our conversation hinged on two vital points: how likely was Lytton to die, and whether Carrington would kill herself if he did?' Ralph felt virtually certain that she would; he had found an ominous torn-up letter in the library wastepaper basket. He was determined to do everything he could to stop her, and to surround her with those who loved her. Gerald was enlisted, and Tommy and Julia.

For three weeks after Christmas Lytton hovered between life and death, and three times he was thought to be dying but rallied. Carrington left a simple, detailed and intensely moving account of how he lay on his death-bed, sometimes semi-conscious, sometimes surprising them all with a flash of humour. She was hugely comforted by hearing him say to himself, as she sat at his side, that he wished he had married her. Still the visitors came, from the Bear or from London; bulletins appeared in the newspapers. Frances was at the Bear when the expected telephone call brought the news, on the afternoon of 21 January 1932, that Lytton was dead. She did not speak to Ralph until the next morning, when he rang to say he was coming to fetch her, 'the tone of his voice suggesting further unspeakable horrors'. She went for a walk along the canal with Gerald, and later recalled that they both found some comfort in the beauty of the winter morning and the release of Lytton from suffering.

As Ralph drove Frances to Ham Spray he told her what had happened on the night of the 20th, when Carrington finally understood that there was no hope for Lytton. She had crept out of the house in the small hours and waited in the garage until the sound of the milking machines at the farm would mask the sound of the car engine. Then she switched it on and lay down on the back seat to die. But the milking started later than she had expected, and Ralph woke earlier, heard the sound of the car and found her unconscious. He was just in time, so that, as Frances put it, 'the poor creature had the cruel fate of witnessing what she had so longed to escape: Lytton's death'. That afternoon, Carrington sat by the deathbed; Ralph sat on the floor. At one point, she left the room to be sick; he brought her a basin. As Lytton's breathing stopped, she stood watching with Pippa. Ralph and James stood behind them. When it was over, she wrote, 'Ralph brought me some glasses of brandy and some sal volatile to drink. A blackbird sang outside in the sun on the aspen.' They left the room; Ralph brought tea. Later, he went back to see Lytton with Carrington. 'I went in and kissed him. Ralph came with me. He was colder than when I kissed him before.' Ralph told Frances every detail.

When they reached the house, Ralph took Frances up to Carrington's room. Frances' powers of observation did not fail her. 'She lay in her bed very still and white, but with the hectic colour in her cheeks that comes from inhaling gas. I felt more sorry for her than I had ever felt for anyone in my life. As we kissed I felt the thick softness of her hair against my cheek.' When they were alone, Frances urged her to let Ralph take her abroad for a while. 'Perhaps conceitedly,' she wrote later, 'I didn't have a moment's fear that any temporary separation could endanger our relationship.' Even so, it was a generous offer. But Carrington told Frances that the most helpful thing she could do was to take Ralph away and look after him, as his grief for Lytton made her own even harder to bear. As she wrote of Ralph: 'He is too near. He understands so much. I can hardly bear his sorrow added to mine.'

Ralph asked Frances to go to Lytton's room, where his body still lay, the wreath picked by Ralph and made by Carrington around his head, and she agreed, although, as she was to write many years later, 'I hated and feared the idea.' For her, the ceremonies of death were pointless and, as far as possible, to be shunned. The next day, Ralph decided it would be best to take Carrington for a walk in Savernake Forest so that she should not be in the house when the undertakers came to remove Lytton's body. Frances went too; she always remembered how Carrington could hardly walk.

With Lytton's death, Carrington had lost the love of her life; and Ralph had lost the man he always called his dearest friend, his mentor, the man who had changed his life, expanded his mind and opened his eyes in so many ways. Stoicism was not part of Ralph's nature, and Frances found his grief 'almost mad, frightening and violent'. They went away for two days, to Llansteffan, Wogan Philipps' family house in Wales, where Ros soothed them both by her kindness; Carrington remained at Ham Spray with Julia and Tommy. On Friday, 29 January, a week after Lytton's death, Ralph and Frances returned to Ham Spray and the task they both knew awaited him: to prevent Carrington from killing herself.

That this was her aim was never really in doubt; everything she wrote confirms it. The only hope was to stop her from carrying out her intention for as long as possible in case she might change her mind. Ralph extracted a promise from her not to try again for at least a month; but he had more reason than anyone to know that she was not to be trusted, especially when put under pressure. He then began a series of what Frances called 'elaborate plans to pin her to life, playing for time, and devoting unflagging concern to the smallest detail that might help to prevent her finishing what she had so bravely tried to do'. These plans involved making sure that she was never alone for very long and that the days and weeks ahead were mapped out so that she saw she had a future.

The trouble was that Carrington did not want a future without Lytton. For all Ralph's assurances – that Ham Spray (of which he now became the owner) was her home as much as his, that he would always look after her – she knew that his future, like his heart, belonged to Frances. Lytton had left her most of his capital, some £10,000, and all his pictures and natural history books; his other books were divided between his brother James and Roger Senhouse. Materially, then, she was provided for; but emotionally she was destitute. During the next few weeks, she found the John family, especially Dorelia, the greatest comfort, and spent several days with them at Fryern at the beginning of February, thus releasing Ralph to London and Frances. She saw a good deal of Julia and Tommy (although Ralph found Tommy increasingly intolerable) and a certain amount of the Guinnesses; when at Ham Spray with Ralph, she filled her time writing sad letters to friends, giving away small tokens of Lytton, and tending the garden where she had hoped his ashes would lie. There had been no funeral; after he was cremated his brother James took the ashes to the family plot.

Meanwhile, the Carrington question was much discussed among Lytton's old friends. Virginia Woolf saw the problem all too clearly. 'They can't leave Carrington alone,' she wrote on 30 January. 'She says she will kill herself – quite reasonable – but better to wait until the first shock is over and see. Suicide seems to me quite sensible.' On the same day, Ralph wrote to Gerald: 'Nothing can really console her and any attempt to pretend there is consolation is a fraud. I hate life.'

Frances' role in the drama was also, inevitably, under discussion. Early in February, the Woolfs dined with Clive Bell in Gordon Square, along with Vanessa, Duncan Grant and Roger Fry; the next day Virginia recorded part of the conversation. Evidently Roger Fry had wondered whether the solution might be for Ralph and Carrington to resume married life. Clive Bell put him right. 'No, Roger, I don't think you understand. Nothing, humanly speaking, is more unlikely, in fact impossible, than that R[alph] should go back to Carrington. He opened his heart to me once.' Duncan Grant joined in. 'Well, I'm fonder of Frances than of any of them; but I think as a human being, she might have behaved differently. I think so.' Clive tried to explain. 'But you don't understand, Duncan. She was passionately in love – is still – with R. So when it came to the point – I mustn't come this weekend – one shade of pressure from him – how could she resist it?' Duncan meant, presumably, that Frances should have kept away from Ham Spray, given Carrington's desperation and her need of Ralph; what neither he nor Clive could appreciate was Ralph's need of Frances. Her sanity, as much as her love, was essential to him.

Even so, during much of February, with the first intense aftermath of death fading and the dull grey misery of acceptance beginning, Ralph remained at Ham Spray with Carrington while Frances stayed in London. From there, she answered a letter from Clive Bell, sounding bleak and practical.

> About Ham Spray, it will be kept on, though necessarily I suppose in rather a reduced style. At present we have not made any definite plans, because the difficulty is to induce Carrington to think it possible to live anywhere or anyhow. Tommy says she must be forced to leave Ham Spray and never mention the word 'Lytton' again – or words to that effect. All right, if he simply wants to murder the poor girl why not say so. I imagine what will happen is something like this – Carrington will live at Ham Spray, with R and I having a permanent weekend nest there and probably going there rather more in the middle of the week. She will come up to London more in mid-week, and have friends to stay with her when she doesn't. But oh dear, Clive, it is all very gloomy indeed, and Ham Spray is a haunted house, and my poor old Ralph is more crushed than I can bear to see him. I wish I could think of something more cheerful to tell you, but can think of nothing except that the more of one's friends who choose to die the more one discovers how extraordinarily fond one is of those who aren't dead.

On top of everything else, Frances was worried about her sister Ray, who had discovered a lump on her breast; she was being treated by Geoffrey Keynes, Maynard's doctor brother – who while maintaining that it was not cancer was recommending 'radium treatment'. And it cannot have been altogether easy for her that while she was surrounded by anxiety and grief, Phil Nichols married Phyllis Spender Clay, who, Clive Bell told her, was 'a worthy successor to Fanny in beauty, intelligence, charm, spirit and general loveableness'. Frances did not go to the wedding; but, she wrote back to Clive, she had seen Phil just before, found him in the best of spirits, and was hoping to see the couple before long. 'I sent him rather an unsuitable wedding present, but it was the only thing I could find in a hurry – the first edition of *Liaisons Dangereuses*'. In a hurry or not, it seems a significant choice – one of Bloomsbury's favourite texts, and a book that had played its part in Ralph's seduction of her. Even allowing for the special tone of Frances' correspondence with Clive, which was always light-hearted, this letter reads like an exercise in self-control, a deliberate refusal to sound uncertain or vulnerable. Her letters to Ralph were, not surprisingly, very different.

Three weeks after Lytton's death they were writing to each other daily. He shared every detail of Carrington's moods with Frances; she tried to sound calm. The trouble was, as they both knew, Frances herself was part of the problem, and Ralph's commitment to her limited the reassurances he could make to Carrington. The fact that she was waiting for him in London could only increase Carrington's feeling that her life was pointless. Just as in the past she had hated knowing that Ralph discussed her with Frances, now she began to resent the way that, as she saw it, they were spying on her and trying to control her. In a ghastly parody of the past, when love letters arriving at Ham Spray were smuggled upstairs, now Frances and Ralph had to take steps to hide their letters about death.

On 10 February, Ralph reported that although DC was 'not entirely self-destructive outwardly', he did not trust her. She kept saying she wanted to be left alone, and urging him to go abroad; and she was much preoccupied with her will. By the next day, he had become convinced that when she seemed more cheerful it was only because 'she has some desperate plan up her sleeve. Please don't refer to any of this when you write, as she may sneak a look at your letters in my coat when I'm sawing wood – she's so sly she'd manage anything – she asked if she could see your letter this morning offering me one from Beakus in exchange and as there was nothing but news in it I showed it to her. But her object was probably to see if I would show it to her, or if we were in some secret league against her.' He advised Frances to go to Owley: 'DC did not urge you coming here.'

He found himself having ominous conversations with Carrington about his future life at Ham Spray. 'She won't discuss any future but mine, or yours and mine,' he told Frances, 'and that idea of your having a child is a suicidal compensation for her, I'm convinced ... The substratum of truth in what she says makes it plausible, but where does she come in? She comes in by just going out, and leaving her money to me and thinking she is procuring your happiness as she can't procure any for herself.' As for the will, 'if she's in a hurry to get it signed over the weekend her plan is fixed'.

He may not have intended it, but such a letter was bound to make Frances feel some responsibility for Carrington's plight. Nor can it have been easy for her to learn that her desire for a child was under discussion, as if such a matter were in Carrington's gift. And now Ralph, the truth-teller, had begun to deceive Carrington about his feelings. 'I must stay on with her if I can, and I must assert that you and I are not all sufficient to each other, or all is lost. I hope you see that, dearest – the truth is negligible now – it is silly to kill her by inability to tell a lie – you and I can manage all right, but she can't. Remember only to write news – I know what you feel in your heart and that gives me support which I need, but don't refer to it. Now she's calling, so I must fly. The bonds that unite us are real enough, but we must make light of them at present.'

Frances kept her letters restrained and cheerful while admitting to 'a turmoil of sympathetic emotions'. Always, she sent her love to Carrington. She was busy doing some research for Bunny's new book on Pocahontas (eventually published in 1933 and dedicated to her). It was very cold; she missed Ralph's warmth in bed. His next letter was frantic. He felt that no-one except he was taking the situation seriously enough. He had begun to question his own position. 'If I left a loaded revolver or an ounce of opium on the table, and went for a long walk, there is little doubt what I should find on my return – and I'm well aware that DC has just made a will leaving me £10,000 and there's Wuzzle [his pet name for Frances] who'd like a child, and who minds me being away from her day after day – far too many motives to enjoying [sic] a long walk.' He had even begun to wonder if his fear somehow made Carrington's death more likely, if his obsession with her suicide might 'put it into her mind when she'd quite forgotten it. Everything is so double edged.'

These confused letters broke Frances' nerve. Her next letter included a secret PS. 'This bit of letter can you please smuggle away and burn – show C the rest. I don't know how to write lovie – I feel you may rather I didn't at all, or anyway that I should write in a distant sort of way – please tell me what to do in your next letter – One thing absolutely certain is that C opened and looked at your last letter.' Since Carrington was reading his letters and must have known that he did not believe her promises, why not have it out with her, perhaps in front of James and Alix on their next visit? 'I feel terribly worried darling by your anxieties – you must get help in bearing them ... you must not be alone, for her sake as well as yours – do summon aid, Tommy, Dorelia, or get Alix to stay – please darling ...'

Her agitated letter brought a calmer, but not altogether reassuring, reply from Ralph, who after talking things over with James had decided that it was safe after all to leave Carrington for a couple of days midweek and come to London.

> I got your smuggled letter. Sweetie, you mustn't get over anxious. I had to tell you what I thought, but DC's disease – for it is a disease – is not necessarily fatal ... I have a certain philosophy, which makes the prospect

anxious but not desperate – if she can't bear it she will relieve herself of a great deal of misery and she will have had only happy memories of Lyttoff and herself – she will make my misery greater but she will herself be well out of it. I shall wait for that misery to materialise before I try myself to see if I can bear it . . . It is sad all day long – I hope when I die I shan't leave such cruel gaps in other people's lives. And now courage, my sweetie – how I love you!

When Frances reread this letter half a century later, she added a footnote. 'The appalling strain which R was constantly under explains this uncharacteristic remark, which was tantamount to putting me in a similar position with regard to him as he was in vis a vis DC.' In other words, she feared he too might become suicidal. She was deeply sorry for Carrington, but she was also determined to protect Ralph, and indeed herself, from the contagion of Carrington's despair. Her next letter made this clear. After apologising for her outburst – 'I am sorry to have written so frantically, I was out of my wits with anxiety which had no outlet' – and admitting that she had written to James begging him to give Ralph more support, she urged him to persuade Carrington to come up to London. 'I don't think being alone with you at Ham Spray is good because it doesn't present a feasible future.'

Carrington did not want to leave Ham Spray, but Ralph did; and by the end of February she had persuaded Ralph that he could safely leave her alone there for a few days each week. 'It's the only thing to do after such a conversation,' he wrote, 'as if I stayed it would show such a mistrust and desire to thwart her that she would be intractable.' Friends came and went; everyone did their best; nothing, in the end, made any difference. The last time Frances saw Carrington was on Saturday, 5 March, when she drove down with Bunny Garnett to Biddesden for the weekend. A photograph taken at a picnic shows Carrington and Ralph holding a pony's head. She is looking away from Ralph, whose gaze is fixed on her. Frances recalled that it was during this picnic that Carrington asked to borrow a gun as she wanted to shoot the rabbits ruining her garden. She had done so before, from her bedroom window. 'We all heard the request, but it was rather vaguely given.' No gun was produced, but a few days later she went back by herself to fetch one. Ralph and Frances returned to London; on 10 March Leonard and Virginia Woolf drove down to Ham Spray to see her. Virginia wrote: 'She was pale, small, suffering silently . . . Her wrists seemed very small. She seemed helpless, deserted, like some small animal left.' She was alone in the house, but not for long: on 12 March she was due to leave for France with Dorelia and Augustus John.

Early on the morning of 11 March, when Ralph and Frances were still asleep, there was a telephone call from Ham Spray. The gardener had arrived to find Carrington on the floor of her bedroom, alive but terribly wounded. She had shot herself in the side, aiming for her heart. Ralph telephoned the doctor in Hungerford and a nurse in London; then Bunny Garnett, who was staying in the room he rented above their flat, drove them as fast as he could down the Great West Road. They picked up the nurse on the way. When they arrived, Carrington was still conscious; the doctor had not dared to move her. She had told him it was an accident and offered him a glass of sherry. She told Ralph she wanted to die; changeable to the last, when she saw his 'agony of mind' she promised to try to live. That afternoon, she died. Afterwards, Frances wrote much later, she was shocked by Carrington's tiny, waxen face. To Bunny Garnett, it seemed that she had a look of great pride.

Ten

Marriage and Motherhood, 1933–1935

In Frances' engagement book for 11 March she drew a cross, like a gravestone. She wrote: 'Carrington died. Alix and James came. Gerald came.' They were all at Ham Spray over the weekend, and the inquest was held on the Monday; the coroner accepted the story that her foot had slipped as she leaned out of her bedroom window to shoot rabbits, and the verdict was accidental death. Suicide, like divorce, was regarded as shaming in 1932. Carrington, so fiercely unconventional in life, was shielded from censure in death. Once again, there was no funeral, and no details of who attended her cremation are known; Frances was vague on the matter. Many years later, Ralph told a close friend that he had done as Carrington wished and put her ashes in the earth at Ham Spray in the grove of trees she loved. The day after the inquest, Frances and Ralph left Ham Spray for the Weld Arms, a hotel near the Brenans' rented cottage at Lulworth on the Dorset coast.

Frances always found it painfully hard to recall the immediate aftermath of Carrington's death. Ralph was not the only one 'tortured by a sense of failure'; if he was close to breakdown she was not much better. Now it was her turn to be on watch: 'I thought of nothing night and day but how I could save him from his self torment.' With hindsight, she felt that he had never been the suicidal type: 'the life-instinct was in fact very strong in him'. At the time, though, she could not be so sure.

All around them, their friends were trying to make sense of what had happened. Gerald wrote to tell Alix Strachey that Carrington had died wearing Lytton's purple dressing gown; his conclusion was that she killed herself 'mainly, I think, to emphasise Lytton's death', an act he found 'childish and thoughtless and pitiful'. Virginia Woolf found herself angry with Lytton. 'Lytton's affected by this act. I sometimes dislike him for it.' Vanessa Bell, no fan of Ralph's, wrote to Clive about him: 'I believe he is in the most awful state, but evidently no-one could have prevented it.' Death always brings guilt in its wake, and although Frances chose not to dwell on it, she felt her share. Before long, too, she realised that there were some who thought her in part responsible for Carrington's death. As she later said, it was not surprising that they thought so because, considered dispassionately, there was some truth in it. But she also knew that she could hardly be blamed for the fact that she existed and that she and Ralph loved each other; and she was too busy worrying about him to care much about what was being said about her.

They were back at Ham Spray for two nights over the Easter weekend at the end of March. By that time they had decided to follow the advice of most of their friends and leave England for a while. Ralph seized on a suggestion from James and Alix Strachey, and agreed to drive their car down to the South of France and hand it over to them at Avignon; he then came up with a dramatic idea. On the way south he would take Frances to the battlefields in France and Belgium where he had fought and nearly died during the war. He felt, and persuaded her, that by revisiting the horrors of what had been, until recent months, the most traumatic experience of his life he might regain some perspective. Frances described this melancholy expedition as Ralph's search for the antidote to his despair.

On 31 March, after a night at the Rendels', Frances and Ralph took the ferry from Folkestone to Boulogne. For the next five weeks, her engagement book records their movements day by day, and she had also resumed her diary. The journey did not start well: they had gone to bed the night before 'sodden with drugs and despair' and Ralph had woken in low spirits; 'It needs very little to convince him that life is not worth living. I resolved to be more cheerful at all costs.' Disembarking at Boulogne she heard a cry of 'Fanny!', and turned to find that Vanessa, Duncan and Angelica had been on the same boat en route for their house at Cassis, near Marseilles. Frances was touched when Vanessa pressed her arm kindly and urged them to visit La Bergère.

For the next three days, in a cold drizzle, Frances and Ralph revisited the places where he had lived and fought fifteen years earlier. He had one particular destination in mind. Not all his memories of the war concerned death. Soon after he arrived in Flanders he was billeted with a farmer's family at Oosthove. There he had slept with a girl who, he told Frances, had begged him to give her a child. He had done his best, and moved on; he had no idea whether he had left her pregnant or not. Now, he wanted to find out.

On Friday, 1 April, after spending the night at Armentières, they drove across the border – where a small boy hoping for a tip sang 'It's a Long Long Way to Tipperary – into Belgium, looking for Oosthove. Ralph could not recognise the landscape; Frances was struck by the visible signs of the war, the absence of trees, the shell holes, the unfilled trenches and rusting barbed wire. When eventually they found the farm, they were warmly welcomed, and invited into the kitchen for a glass of red wine; but when Ralph asked after Berta, the girl who had wanted his child, there was little response; she had moved away. There was a girl at the farm of about the right age, and Frances 'rather thought she might have been' Ralph's daughter; but nothing was said, and later she reflected that if she had been his daughter, and he had then turned up, surely there would have been a request for money. Frances took some photographs before they left: two stout drab women, two small boys and an older girl stand smiling in a muddy farmyard, while Ralph, pipe in mouth, hat on head, towers over them with an air of vague geniality. Then Frances and Ralph drove off to have lunch at Ypres. They were surprised and touched by the 'genuine human warmth' with which they had been received. The matter of Ralph's possible daughter was not pursued any further. Afterwards, Frances would never write or speak of this episode with much interest or emotion. Asked, some seventy years later, what she would have done if a child of Ralph's had indeed materialised in 1932, and whether she had been unnerved at the prospect, she smiled wryly, said it had never really seemed very likely and changed the subject.

She was, however, deeply and permanently affected by her first direct exposure to the landscape and consequences of war. She spent three days with Ralph thinking and talking of little but his wartime experiences. On the road to Ypres, she saw 'the astonishment in his face as he tried to identify different places whose configuration had once literally been a matter of life or death to him, his amazement as he looked at a gently sloping turnip field and realised that it was to gain possession of this tiny area that he and his fellows had fought so bitterly for weeks on end, and been ready to die or kill'. Everywhere they went there were grim relics; bones were still often brought to the surface by the plough. They passed two tin hats by the side of the road where a body had just been disinterred. In a cold cellar at the museum in Ypres they studied photographs of dead men piled in heaps. Frances felt it was her duty not to flinch, but 'to look the results of modern warfare full in the face, once and for all'. Then they drove on in search of the exact place where Ralph had been buried alive.

In the end, he could not find it, although he pored over the map and paced the ground peering at the earth 'like a dog searching for a rabbit hole'. Instead he relived the experience by telling her all over again what he had felt when his agonised lungs filled with soil and his tongue was forced from his mouth. Then, in heavy rain, they drove on to Vimy Ridge, where they visited trenches forty feet down. 'It was beyond anything I had expected, and it gave me a glimmering of what being in a war must be like.' They spent the night at Verdun, where they were briefly distracted by a wedding in their hotel; but, Frances wrote, 'it was the battlefields that filled my dreams'. Next day, after taking a look at the blasted landscape north of the town, where shrapnel still hung in the trees, they turned south. They reached Nancy, where they had a good dinner and went to the cinema. At first, it seemed the antidote was working; the battlefields were behind them and the sun came out. For three or four days Ralph did not mention Carrington; but when, after a bad night, Frances decided to try to get him to talk, he was so desperate that she found herself thinking that things would never be the same again.

They drove on down the Rhône Valley, through olive groves and blossoming fruit trees, heading for a hotel at Beaumes de Venise beneath Mont Ventoux recommended to them by Gerald. Arriving on 7 April, they were based there for the next two weeks. On the 9th they drove to Avignon to hand over the car to the Stracheys; the next ten days were spent resting, reading and going for long walks in the spring sunshine. It grew hotter; the wild flowers on the hillside were in full bloom. Frances' mood depended on Ralph's; he would often wake badly. A batch of letters reached them, and plunged him into gloom, especially one from Gerald, the one person he knew who fully shared his sense of loss.

Before leaving England Ralph had told Gerald how he simply could not believe that Carrington was gone. When he went into her room and the truth began to come over him, 'for several hours I felt I could not go on living – exactly what she must have felt about Lytton. There was no alternative; the desire to escape the pain by unconsciousness was overwhelming.' Now Gerald wrote that he felt the same 'complete inability to believe that she is dead', but that he had terrible dreams, 'which show me that in one part of my mind at least I have understood her death only too well'. Ralph's reply gives some idea what Frances was up against. Driving the car was a useful drug; but 'otherwise I have no object in this voyage except to pass the time until it is less oppressive. I have not succeeded so far. She accompanies me everywhere and yet she is nowhere.' He did not mention Frances; he asked Gerald to write again.

They decided to take up Vanessa Bell's invitation and visit La Bergère, and went to tea with Vanessa and Duncan on 20 April. A fragment of a letter from Vanessa to Virginia shows her regretting her impulsive invitation. There had already been too many visitors; 'But to crown all the Partridges arrive tomorrow – did you ever hear such horrors? I really think this place is becoming impossible.' Stephen Tomlin was also around, which was awkward as he and Ralph disliked each other; and 'why any of these people after all they've suffered from each other these past few months should rush to the same place here one cannot conceive. I feel pursued by the very people one longed to get away from. The Partridges will be the worst. I can't stand Ralph as you know.' When Vanessa was displeased she could be 'cold as ice and as withering as gall', but the visit was tolerable enough for the tea party to be repeated the following day.

On 30 April they collected the car from the Stracheys at Avignon and 'turned reluctantly towards home and its problems'. They stopped in Lyons, admired the Romanesque basilica at Autun, and, to round off their death-haunted journey, spent the last day visiting the immense cemeteries of the Somme. Frances found the endless rows of white crosses, the neatness and the mown grass and flowers even more appalling than the trenches; the clean and tidy memorials, with their religious and patriotic symbolism, struck her as simply an attempt to disguise reality. By 7 May they were back at Owley; two days later they went to London to see Mam and have dinner with Oliver Strachey. Then on 12 May they went down to Ham Spray, to begin the rest of their lives.

In theory, the great question facing them was whether or not to go on living there at all. For some of their friends, the answer seemed obvious: Ralph should sell up and start again. In practice, there never appears to have been any serious consideration of such a move. All Frances wrote and said on the matter was consistent; Ralph wanted to stay at Ham Spray, so they stayed. It had always been his house as well as Lytton's; it was dear to him, he had helped to find it and make it, and he did not want to live anywhere else. If Frances ever questioned, even to herself, whether it was wise to stay in a house so full of Lytton and Carrington's presence, or if she ever longed to change it, to replace Carrington's taste with her own, she left no hint of it. She, too, liked it as it was; there were never to be any serious alterations. All she would ever admit to was an occasional flash of irritation when people still assumed, decades later, that everything delightful about the house and garden was due to her predecessor.

Frances did, however, acknowledge that getting back to Ham Spray in 1932 was not easy, although the sun shone, the garden was full of polyanthus and narcissi and Olive the maid and Tiber the cat were pleased to see them. She worried about getting onto a new footing with Olive and the other staff, about taking over the house 'without in any way seeming to try and supplant Carrington, but without letting standards fall'. She had to achieve a difficult balance – 'Not to change anything and yet continue "being myself"' – and she also knew that Ham Spray meant much to many of

Lytton and Carrington's friends and relations, who would all feel they had a right to come down as before, and have their eye on her. At times, she wrote with unusual vehemence, the problems and difficulties facing her seemed 'insoluble and appalling'.

Most of all, though, she worried about Ralph. She knew that she tended to be over-anxious about him, but she also knew how vulnerable he was and dreaded making a false step. 'I got into the way of never saying or doing anything without first thinking how it was likely to affect him, what reverberations it would set going on his feelings ... it was a tremendous strain.' All she wanted was for him to be happy again and to regain his appetite for life. After all the drama, above all they needed some peace.

As for Ralph, as soon as he got back to Ham Spray he wrote again to Gerald, asking him to visit them. The next day would mark nine weeks since Carrington's death. 'I don't dread tomorrow at all – a Friday, the ninth of the series. How many more? My fondest love always.' Soon he took up the sad task of managing with the aftermath of two deaths: dealing with two wills, sorting Lytton's books and papers, most of which were going to James, going through Carrington's letters and notebooks, all of which were now his, deciding what to do with her paintings, and Lytton's. Everything she had inherited from Lytton – money, books, pictures, furniture – now belonged to Ralph. He tried to do what she had wanted, although he did not feel able to mark the spot where her ashes lay. Before long he needed company, and through the summer the visitors arrived in waves – the Brenans, the Garnetts, the Penroses, Noel and Catherine Carrington, and numerous Stracheys. As Lytton's executor and other principal heir, James, with Alix, was a constant presence. It was hot, and there were picnics on the downs, and expeditions to favourite swimming places; sometimes, Frances thought, Ralph's high spirits verged on hysteria. Gradually they settled down. They decided on something new, to suit themselves: a swimming pool. Frances had her first driving lesson.

In August she went off alone as usual to Charleston, driven there by the Rendels, who had been spending the weekend at Ham Spray; Alix and James stayed behind with Ralph. Separated only for a few days, their particularly long and loving letters show that they had become closer than ever, as couples do when they come through terrible times together, especially when they sense that not everyone around them understands or approves. 'I do not at all like this separation,' she wrote, 'and I had an owlish desire to burst into tears when I saw you looking so sweet and left behind me on the drive.'

Not that Frances felt any disapproval at Charleston. Her letters to Ralph are full of the amusement and appreciation she always felt when she was there; she loved the garden bright with zinnias, walks and talks on the downs with Clive, the charm of the thirteen-year-old Angelica in her scarlet dress. As for Vanessa, Frances was struck all over again by 'her beauty and nobility'. She felt part of the family as she sewed name tabs onto Duncan's silk pyjamas. The only drawbacks were the wasps, and the fact that Julian Bell had taken up with Lettice Ramsey, who was there with her children. Frances found Lettice overdressed and annoying; she was usually on the side of lovers, but something in her remained unamused at her old school friend's romance with Clive's much younger son. Her thoughts kept turning towards Ralph. 'Oh dearest Towser what are you doing, I desperately want to know how you are.' She received a letter from him so full of love that it made her cry. 'My darling,' she wrote back, 'it is constantly a wonder to me how with all the misery you have to bear you manage to be so sweet to me.'

One afternoon she and Clive visited Leonard and Virginia at Rodmell. The sun shone, they played bowls, and the Woolfs were at their gentlest and best. 'Virginia knows how to be utterly charming if she likes, and today she did. Playing bowls she is the cracked Englishwoman, with an old felt hat on top of her head and long pointed canvas shoes ... It was so lovely on the bowling lawn, I wished you were there. The sun shone through the grass in dazzling emerald colours. Two dogs sat about, in the way a great deal.' What meant most to Frances was her conversation with Virginia on the way back to Charleston in the Woolfs' car.

I cannot describe to you the kindness as well as fascination of everything she said – about the beauty of Ham Spray, about life in the country and its charms, about you and how she believed you could write if you wanted to. I got a feeling she was really fond of you. She sent you her love and asked us to come and see her whenever we were in London. I felt she really meant this. She wants you of course to write something about Lytton – and she said he had told her how good Carrington's letters were, and she wanted you to think of publishing some of them some day. In all this, though direct, there was not a hint of exploitation and the 'taste' was perfect. I felt she really wanted this fascinating Ham Spray life not to be altogether lost, but for her own sake wanted it preserved. I was bowled over by her irresistible cracked charm.

Virginia, though not positively hostile to him like Vanessa, had her reservations about Ralph, and was never especially interested in Frances, but at this critical moment she knew intuitively how to make both of them feel better.

Back at Ham Spray, as the autumn began, they planned the new swimming pool – to be sited to the right of the garden behind some shrubs – and picked mushrooms. In October, they were in London for Rachel MacCarthy's wedding to David Cecil, the slender, brilliantly clever younger son of the Marquess of Salisbury, at St Bartholomew, Smithfield, an event in which they felt they had played some part, as confidants both of Rachel and her mother. David as well as Rachel was to be a lifelong friend. The next day, Frances lunched with the faithful Colin Mackenzie.

Seasons trigger memories; it cannot have been easy to be at Ham Spray as winter approached once more. Ralph's mood, as reflected in another letter to Gerald, sank. 'The most humble cottage pie life goes on here, and that is the best I can do for myself.' On their trips to London, he felt misanthropic; parties seemed pointless. Worse, girls no longer excited him; 'Were they ever worth having? I have no desire to have them now. You see how I feel – very extenuated and dimsy about everything except Ham Spray and Tiber and the aspen tree.' He had started to go through Carrington's letters, a depressing task. He particularly disliked reading his own: 'They are utterly unsympathetic, and yet there was never a time when I didn't feel as if I was inextricably involved with her ... Where did my love for her go? Did she have to deduce it always from my criticisms and abuse?' His letter to Gerald was controlled enough; but there were times when he lost control, and Frances needed help. One day, around this time, she had to summon Wogan Philipps from Ipsden; he described what he found to the Woolfs. 'We talked of Lytton and Carrington last night,' wrote Virginia afterwards. 'Wogan sent for, 30 miles, twice one day to master Ralph, who emerged from the bushes, where he was skulking, threatening suicide. And had barricaded his door against Frances.' As when he had made emotional scenes at the Hogarth Press, Virginia's reaction to Wogan's account of Ralph is full of a fascinated distaste. Wogan, she went on, 'said Ralph play-acted; was a lonely, but boring man; brings you tea stark naked, a bull among heifers. They're all naked, they all comment eternally on "parts" and "breasts" – a kind of rough parody of the old Ham Spray – Lytton acted in the kitchen.'

Virginia and Leonard, in fact, had never played much part in the old Ham Spray, where louche talk, and a touch of nudity, were commonplace; and it cannot have become quite such a caricature as she suggested, for none of the true Ham Spray regulars stayed away. It was remarkable, in fact, how the old rhythms were maintained. In late November, Ralph and Frances had a visit from E.M. Forster, staying nearby; and Saxon and Oliver Strachey spent Christmas with them. Then on Boxing Day, Rosamond and Wogan themselves came over from Ipsden for dinner. They brought a guest with them, Barbara Ker-Seymer, who was for a time an unsettling presence in Frances' life.

Ralph ended 1932 claiming that he was in no mood to be interested in girls. Even so, during 1933 he was to have a short, sharp love affair with Barbara, a stylish professional photographer in her thirties and a close friend of Julia Strachey's, who was working as an assistant in her studio at the time. If this was the first time he was unfaithful to Frances since they had started to sleep together in 1925, it was not to be the last, but this was one of the few of his affairs to leave significant traces. Part of diary for 1933 and 1934 survived among Frances' papers, describing a sequence of events in her marriage that she decided not to make public, concerning her relationship with Ralph and her hopes for a child.

In the summer of 1933 she became pregnant, but the happiness she felt was brief. 'I open the book after another year has passed', she wrote, 'and am reminded what a bungler I am by spilling my bottle of green ink all over it, over my dress, over my hat. I sometimes feel I bungle everything, and the last thing I have bungled is a baby.' In early July, she had begun to suspect she was pregnant, and 'an extraordinary peaceful feeling came over me'. The thought that her body contained 'some blended elements of R and me' made her feel specially loving and grateful towards him. At the same time she felt slightly 'ridiculous' to know so little, at thirty-three, about pregnancy; and in retrospect she blamed herself for her ignorance and for not taking more care. 'So, uninformed, I bathed and dived backwards and forwards, swam and leapt as usual, and the baby came to an end.'

After describing the unpleasantness of the curettage she underwent at a London nursing home she turned back to the events of early 1933. 'The main event of last winter was the making of our wonderful swimming pool. We continued our life very much as usual. In February we gave a grand party at No. 41.' (They were still renting a room in Gordon Square.) Then comes a brief reference to an event that for most people would rank higher than a new pool: 'On March 2 we were married at the St Pancras Register Office, Alix and Bunny being our witnesses. With the addition of James we had lunch afterwards at the Café Royal and then R and I went to see a dreadful film of Early Christians being thrown to the lions.'

Frances would say, when asked about her wedding, that she had considered herself married to Ralph since 1926, and that they had only gone through the formalities because they wanted to share a cabin on a boat to Spain; she would, if pressed, also concede that as she was hoping for a child they thought it best to marry. While not disapproving as strongly of weddings as she did of funerals, the ceremony meant little to her. She and Ralph chose to have as little fuss as possible, and certainly no family from either side were present. She kept no photographs of the occasion, and had long forgotten what she wore or had for lunch. They sailed for Gibraltar two days later, and were away for a month, first with Gerald and Gamel at Yegen and then in Morocco. It seems unlikely, though, that the marriage and the pregnancy were unconnected; at some point Helena Wright's equipment must have been discarded.

By the late summer of 1933 she admitted that she was 'almost entirely preoccupied with the idea of having a child. My recent experience has roused feelings in me which make me fling all my old caution and anxieties to the wind. I simply feel an absorbtion in the idea which would make any vision of the future which didn't allow of it intolerably empty – and yet I am as completely satisfied with my love for R as ever.' The contradiction in the last sentence was uncharacteristic. What was entirely characteristic was the way in which she tried to ignore the unhappiness which the failure of a longed-for pregnancy brings, although she admitted to feelings of 'dimness and lack of energy' (the same symptoms she had recorded in the winter of 1928–9). She hated being in low spirits and felt humiliated at the way small irritations reduced her to tears: 'I am sick of passivity but feel too morally feeble for activity ... I told R how I despised myself and he was exceedingly sympathetic. With great intuition he suggested a walk together.' Frances could always be cheered by a walk and a long, close talk with Ralph.

She was not just preoccupied with her own problems that summer. She and Ralph enjoyed mulling over the romantic entanglements of their friends, and in 1933 and 1934 Julia Strachey's complicated love life gave them plenty to discuss. Carrington's death had brought Julia closer to Frances again and the slow disintegration of her marriage to Tommy made her more sympathetic to Ralph. 'Julia has again come to the forefront of our lives,' wrote Frances. 'Ralph has suddenly relaxed his hostility and feels most warmly to her. I feel that she is the female for whom I always have felt most affection in my life.' Julia's first novel, the delicately satirical *Cheerful Weather for the Wedding*, had been published by the Hogarth Press in September 1932; Virginia Woolf considered it 'astonishingly good,' and it brought her a modest fame. Meanwhile she had been having a serious love affair with Wogan Philipps for at least a year, during which Rosamond had become pregnant with their second child. By the summer of 1933 Wogan was frantic with guilt, Rosamond was frantic with jealousy and Julia was longing to leave Tommy once and for all. Frances cast a cool eye on them all: Wogan she regarded as a natural bohemian, while Rosamond needed 'a lady's life, padded and sweetened and bourgeois'. As for Julia, Frances felt that her prospects of winning Wogan were slim, and worried about her; 'Her unsatisfactory life with Tommy leaves her constantly very lonely – and she longs for support.' Frances did her best to supply it.

'Well then,' Frances continued, 'the other love affair this summer has been R's with Barbara Ker-Seymer, a gay, amusing but very neurotic character. It is now ended.' Only the fact that she was writing after the affair was over makes Frances' detachment understandable. She did not describe when or how she first became aware of it, let alone how she felt; but Barbara appears in her engagement book before, during and immediately after the unsuccessful pregnancy, and even as a visitor to the nursing home on 22 July. Frances' attitude by the time she wrote about the affair was calm, if faintly malicious. At Ham Spray, Barbara 'made herself very agreeable, except for a habit she had of retiring to her bedroom immediately after dinner'. This Frances ascribed to her being intellectually out of her depth. As for her effect on Ralph, 'After she left R was in a ferment about her – more I think than I realized, for I could not somehow take her quite seriously.' Then, 'they had some evenings together in London and she began to tease him a good deal'. The affair was no secret; Bunny Garnett (a later lover of Barbara's) was in the picture as well as Julia. She and Frances talked it over at length, as did Frances and Ralph. One night, Ralph returned to the attic flat in Gordon Square at about 2 a.m., 'in a great state of mind'. Frances was still awake – but, in no sort of 'state' herself, she emphasised. Indeed she soon fell asleep, but Ralph, 'poor dear', had a miserable night. Over breakfast they discussed the situation, whereupon 'it came out by chance that what I had half suspected was true – he was identifying Barbara with Carrington – and hence her power to torture him and the strange force of the hook she had sunk in his flesh. When this was openly said at the breakfast table, he burst into tears, and at once saw the truth of it.' Having arrived, with Frances' help, at this interesting conclusion, Ralph went off to share it with Barbara herself, only to discover that she had just started an affair with Tommy. Like Carrington, she knew how to drive Ralph to distraction; otherwise, Frances reflected, 'Barbara's actual similarity to Carrington is dim indeed. She has vitality, she has blue eyes, she is elusive and slips away when you try to hold her, but she has none of Carrington's genius, imagination or complexity.' Soon afterwards, Ralph decided he had had enough, and told Frances, 'I've done with Barbara for good'.

The affair does not seem to have left much of a mark, though for a while Ralph had 'revenge fantasies' about Barbara – especially when Julia kindly informed him she was telling other people things he had told her. But, Frances wrote, 'Since the preoccupation waned R has overwhelmed me with sweetness and affection; not that at any moment throughout the affair we did not get on perfectly well. I was for some reason only very slightly jealous and we talked over every single thing. Also the extreme interest of the Carrington identification made it easy to put up with. That, rather naturally, began to wane as soon as it was recognised.'

At this point Frances moved on to 'another love affair of this summer: Leo [Myers] and Iris Origo. It is a very grand passion indeed.' Just as Iris had heard a great deal about Colin Mackenzie's pursuit of Frances, now the roles were reversed: Frances became Leo's confidante about Iris. Luckily the two women liked each other, though they only met a few times.

Frances' diary is not the only evidence of Ralph's brief infatuation with Barbara Ker-Seymer. A handful of his letters, written between July and September 1933, reveal a man with no sense of guilt at openly pursuing another woman while his wife is trying to hold onto a baby. If anything, he treated Frances' plight as a justification: the romance was 'the only alternative to thinking about hospitals and surgeons', as he told Barbara in mid-July. Ralph's letters show him trying to convince a sceptical Barbara that his reputation as a 'lady's man' was undeserved; they are full of argumentative teasing and protestations about the sincerity of his feelings. Certainly he found her physically attractive, but that was not all; anyway, 'I've never felt at ease and friendly with anyone, male or female, in my whole life, to whom I wasn't "drawn" as they sometimes say – and the only pain I've ever received was from the same class of people.' The more she declined to believe him – she seems, not surprisingly, to have reckoned that what he was after was a fling, not a serious relationship – the more pressing he became. 'You continually threaten not seeing me any more, and that throws me into a frenzy of agitation'; 'Dearest, please be glad to see me – I adore you.' Disconcerting though these echoes of his letters to Frances are, love letters are bound to have a certain sameness, and the affair did no lasting damage. Asked how much it troubled her at the time, Frances replied that of course she had not liked it, but that she never doubted that it was her Ralph needed and loved. She had never thought that sex was the most important element in marriage.

After her account of the three summer love affairs, Frances' diary changed gear, as if to remind herself of what really mattered. 'Here is one dull day in detail,' she wrote, just as she had in 1927, and proceeded to describe 'a very warm and affectionate waking' on a grey and drizzling autumn day, and Olive bringing them tea and the post in bed. Breakfast, though, was less harmonious: they found themselves having 'a conversation about hostility and the ups and downs of one's feelings for other people. It grew rather heated, as I always find myself attacking R's hostile and sadistic side which fills me sometimes with alarm.' This mention of a side of Ralph she did not care for is the nearest she ever came to criticising him. Others recall Ralph as warm-hearted and kind, but capable of ferocious criticism of his friends' behaviour and sudden outbursts of irrational rage, when Frances would be the only person who could calm him down.

The rest of the day was peaceful and domestic; Frances ordered the meals, (shepherd's pie for lunch) and they went for a chilly walk in the afternoon, hand in hand. Then there was gardening, and sewing, and reading by the fire (Gertrude Stein) and a concert on the wireless after dinner. It was, she wrote, 'a very quiet but very nice day indeed'.

During November they went up to London most weeks for a night or two, and Frances went down to Brighton to see Frankie Birrell, who had recently had an operation for a brain tumour. She found him pale but quite himself, thrilled to have had a visit from Margot Asquith. Back in London they had lunch with Hayley Morris at the Café Royal and went to the new film of Charles Laughton as Henry VIII; and that evening Frances had one of her tête-à-tête dinners with Clive Bell. This time, after an agreeable dinner and a certain amount of drink, the conversation took an unexpected direction.

'Clive was a little drunk,' she wrote, 'and it was very late, and suddenly he began to shower me with compliments, connected with my happy life with R, and what pleasure it gave people to see us so happy together.' Then his tone changed. 'He started on old times, and his constant talks with Lytton about me and my relations with Ham Spray. He said how Lytton had spoken of my ultimatum when I wanted to live with R – and how he had described me as "very tactless" when afterwards I came so often to Ham Spray.' What followed was worse: 'he then in so many words said that of course many people thought me directly responsible for Carrington's death'. As an example Clive cited Aldous Huxley's wife. 'As Maria Huxley said to me as we drove across France in her Bugatti: "There must have been a villain in the piece, and it's clear the villain was Frances Marshall". For of course he went on to say that if Carrington had felt that anyone really cared for her she would not have committed suicide.'

Frances responded with great self-control. She tried to reason with Clive, pointing out that many people did love Carrington – the point was that she could not love anyone but Lytton, and that her suicide was 'a logical and reasonable act'. She refused to allow herself to become angry or emotional. 'I was interested in what Clive said, and I wanted to speak the truth and convince him that it was the truth. But I saw by the puzzled and frustrated look in his eyes that he not only believed me responsible, but did not want to believe otherwise.' She did manage to make him concede one, comparatively trivial, point: 'that if R and Carrington had been divorced in 1926 like conventional people no-one would have held me responsible'.

Again Frances waited until the dust had settled before writing about Clive's attack. She was not inclined to use her diary as an instant outlet for bursts of emotion or anger. She looked beyond the particular to the general, and ascribed Clive's behaviour to 'a substratum of hostility and savagery' in human nature. The conversation shifted to a discussion of suicide, and when Frances told him that if Ralph died she hoped she would have the courage to kill herself Clive professed himself shocked. Only once she was at home in bed – no mention of Ralph – was she suddenly 'assailed by a feeling of misery. What had upset me was his desire to hurt me which, brushing aside any obstacles, came battering back again and again.' The next morning, though, she had recovered, 'and discussed it with Julia that same night, dispassionately and with interest'. Clive, she concluded, had not consciously decided to cause her pain, but his unconscious urge to do so had taken over, and given him what she called 'his curious "savage pig with little eyes" look'. There is no sign that she held his outburst against him; the friendship continued. The following day she and Ralph dined with James and Alix and went on to a dance, where Frances 'felt in tearing spirits and ready to laugh at anything'.

In her response both to Ralph's affair and Clive's provocation, Frances showed herself capable of an almost unnatural composure. Perhaps, after eight years, her sexual feelings for Ralph had begun to wane; certainly many of their friends took it for granted that while he was highly sexed she was not. As for Clive, here Frances demonstrated how deeply Bloomsbury's approach to friendship had affected her. Friends were not expected to cushion each other, or try to protect each other from hurt or criticism. Perhaps her knowledge of Freudian concepts helped too; she believed he was right in saying that aggression lurked in everyone, and could surface in subconscious ways.

At all events, she was able to maintain her equilibrium. As winter approached, there were more snug days by the fire in the library at Ham Spray, writing and reading; Ralph was still working on the notes for Greville, now that Roger Fulford was to succeed Lytton as editor. The Brenans came over one day, much preoccupied with whether or not to adopt Juliana's daughter by Gerald. They both liked Gamel, a sweet-faced, melancholy poet from the American South, although she sometimes seemed an unlikely wife for Gerald. After they had left, Frances and Ralph went for a walk; 'R told me several times I had never looked more beautiful, and that was very nice.' Each month Frances wondered if she might be pregnant and was disappointed when she was not. But, she insisted, she and Ralph were perfectly happy. In her last diary entry for 1933, the year of their marriage, his affair with Barbara and her miscarriage, she wrote firmly: 'It is just about ten years since I first met R, eight since we first went to bed together and since when we have continued steadily to go to bed together. I am all the same as much or more in love with him than ever before. Yesterday he said the same of me.' By writing it down, she reaffirmed their happiness.

Over Christmas 1933 they had Oliver Strachey, Saxon and 'the lovers' – Wogan and Julia – in the house. Frances recorded the misty 'artichoke soup' weather, some hilarious evenings and hearing Wogan creep into Julia's bedroom every night. Rosamond had given birth in December, but Frances' sympathy with her was limited; her loyalty was to Julia, who had decided finally to leave Tommy, although 'her relations with Wogan are not altogether satisfactory ... It is independence from Tommy and freedom to write that she is fighting for more than love.' Frances' own mood varied; but when she was low, Ralph could usually cheer her up, although she sometimes thought that their approach to life was fundamentally different. For her, it was essential to be active, consciously experiencing life to the full; her nature was positive and optimistic. Ralph she saw as 'much more defeatist and passively pessimistic', and this difference bothered her. However, she wrote, 'I can't see that if we can talk about it, and have no taboos, it should upset our relations.' This point of view was central to their marriage.

In the spring, Frances, Ralph and Julia went to Portugal for a holiday with the Brenans, and the diary lapsed. She took it up again in June, feeling 'well, lively and rather fat'. She and Julia remained close; by this time Julia had separated from Tommy and was drifting towards an affair with Bryan Guinness, whose wife had left him for Oswald Mosley. That summer, Frances, Ralph and Julia all went to stay with Bryan at his house near Dublin; in August, James and Alix came to stay at Ham Spray as usual. 'Their visit has given me almost undiluted pleasure', Frances wrote, 'but in some way they cause me to have an "inferior" feeling and I'm particularly aware of my lack of initiation of ideas.' She was never quite sure whether to kiss them goodbye. More Stracheys were on the way – the Bussy family, Simon, Lytton's sister Dorothy and Janie. Evidently Janie's infatuation with Ralph had become serious, and perhaps he had responded; Frances felt she was regarded as 'Janie's successful rival' but was determined that the visit should go well.

Abruptly, again, she discloses that Ralph had been having another affair. 'Had rather an interesting conversation with R about his sexual life and what it is that forces him to run after girls like Phyl Page (here last weekend) and then cool off just as they are warming to their work. He says he has a craving for crude sex in an indecent form – pure smut which I don't provide him with, and yet as soon as he sees "something is expected" of him his heart fails and he fears he won't rise to the occasion. This conversation produced a great many hilarious jokes.' Afterwards 'I spent a long time picking and arranging quantities of flowers.'

All marriages are a closed book to outsiders, especially where sex is concerned, but Frances' detachment seems extraordinary. Ralph's inability to perform with Phyl struck her as 'a little mysterious and I do not understand what holds him back.' It is almost a relief to find her adding 'I can't help being glad about it nevertheless.' However, Ralph managed to overcome his problem; towards the end of the year Frances returned to the subject. 'R got a long letter from his Phyl this morning. We read and discussed it in bed. I am quite amazed to find how utterly all jealousy of her has left me, and how I seem to be able to think about the subject and discuss it quite dispassionately. It may be because the balance of feelings is so much on her side and not on his and because I do take in now that it has made no effect on his feelings for me. In fact I think his having actually been to bed with her has exploded a mirage (the attractiveness of infidelity) in much the same way as my going to bed with my Phil did for me several years ago.' Phyl, like Barbara, was not in the end very important.

As the end of another year approached, Frances remained concerned about Julia's unhappiness and even more so by the news that Frankie Birrell was dying. She managed to finish a short story she had been working on for some time, and showed it to Bunny and to Julia who were both very encouraging. This was not the first story she had written, but an earlier one had drawn such criticism from Leo Myers that she had felt crushed and discouraged. Later Frances would always insist that imaginative writing was beyond her; and the pages that survive indicate that she was right. Before long both she and Ralph began to write regular book reviews for the *New Statesman*; she used the name Francis Bird, and reviewed mainly children's books, while Ralph wrote on nineteenth-century history as well as detective stories.

Early in December she found herself feeling sick, and consulted her London gynaecologist. When he examined her, he told her she was probably six weeks pregnant, and that a mouse test – then the usual way of establishing pregnancy, involving injecting the mouse with the woman's urine – would confirm it. 'He also said I had been trying hard to miscarry and prescribed a most stringent regime to avoid it, and off I tottered to tell R who took it amazingly well and has been ever since incomparably sweet and charming.' Frances lunched at the Café Royal that day with Dadie Rylands and Raymond, and discussed *Hamlet*; they dined with Clive, Frances feeling that her refusal of alcohol might have alerted him to her condition. Bunny was there, being a bit ponderous; Clive teased him a good deal. 'In his own way no-one can be more malicious than Clive. Still I am fond of him.' The social round continued: next day she had tea at Claridge's with Iris Origo, and discussed their mutual admirers: Colin Mackenzie, who had recently decided he was in love with a much younger girl, and Leo Myers' curious relationship with his wife, known to him as Mum. Frances liked Iris, finding her intelligent and very beautiful.

On the following day she had lunch with her mother and a quiet dinner alone with Julia. 'R was out with Phyl. I told Julia of my possible pregnancy and she appeared to be pleased.' She also told Frances that both Alix Strachey and Wogan had already guessed, 'which makes one feel very naked and exposed'. Julia then launched into her own desire for a facelift, which Frances thought was risky; in the end Ralph paid for the successful operation. When Frances went back to Ham Spray, she travelled alone; Ralph had other plans. She went straight to bed, feeling fragile: 'There I was really happy, with sweet Olive lighting fires and bringing hot water bottles and my supper on a tray.'

When Ralph arrived two days later she found him 'rather disgruntled and prickly, unsettled by my possible pregnancy which at first he had taken so smoothly'. When the news came on 19 December that 'the mice have squealed yes', Frances was not sure quite what she felt. 'I still feel dazed about this child and poor R almost more so. There are many problems to be considered, but for a little I feel this blotting paper daze is perhaps a good thing and will break the shock.'

Although Frances had long wanted a child, it was hardly surprising that she had mixed feelings. Nothing would alter life at Ham Spray more dramatically than the arrival of one of the 'petit peuple'; neither she nor Ralph had ever been much drawn to small children, and were given to deploring the disruption and boredom they brought in their wake. Above all, she must have known that a child would require a readjustment of her emotional priorities. For almost ten years, Ralph had been the centre of her universe; this would now have to change. The change began at once; on the day the confirmation arrived Ralph wrote to Gerald to cancel a projected visit to Spain, where the Brenans were moving into a new house. His letter was breezy but non-committal. 'As a possible father I feel very out of it. Nobody wants my urine; I wasn't even given a pig's testicle for supper.' For the next three months, Frances led a very quiet life, determined not to take any risks. By May, she was allowed to be more active, and they went on a holiday to Devon; but as the date for the birth approached, her gynaecologist informed them that it would not be straightforward. Because Frances had fibroids, he felt a caesarean would be best, so that he could deal with the problem at the same time. As Ralph explained briskly to Gerald, he had been looking into the matter. 'If he can guarantee to do the whole thing within 15 minutes it will be safe enough.' There were advantages: the timing would be clear, the 'damage and horror of birth of the child' would be minimised, and there would be 'no laceration of female genitals with consequent frigidity (such as every normal mother seems to suffer from for years if not permanently)'. The caesarean was scheduled, and on 3 July Frances went to London to prepare herself. On Monday, 8 July, her engagement book notes: 'Burgo. 10.50 pm'.

She remained in the nursing home in Bentinck Street for three weeks, and was kept in bed for two. After the first week, she was allowed visitors, and her diary lists them: her sisters Judy and Ray, Julia, Alix, Oliver, Rosamond, Helen Anrep, Iris Origo, Maroussa (the companion of the Russian mosaicist Boris Anrep), Raymond, Saxon and Clive, to whom she also wrote a letter of thanks for a present of delicious fruit. 'I feel extraordinarily well and cheerful, if hot – and Partridge minimus seems to thrive and cause no anxiety.' He was named, she explained, for the dashing Burgo Fitzgerald, a dissolute charmer in Trollope's novel *Can You Forgive Her?* a favourite of hers and Ralph's. This was, however, his second name; his first was Lytton.

By 1 August Lytton Burgo Partridge and his parents were safely home at Ham Spray, with a nurse and Mam in attendance.

Eleven

Ostrich Tendencies, 1936–1939

Some time before the arrival of Burgo at Ham Spray, the large room with the sloping roof at the far end of the house, which had been Carrington's studio, was turned into the nursery, and a bedroom was allocated for his nanny nearby. The significance of the cradle displacing the easel would not have been lost on anybody, nor the fact that Carrington's vision of the future had now come true. Like most couples in the 1930s with enough money and space, they wanted nursery life kept separate, and Frances and Ralph set up Burgo's quarters well away from the rest of the house. Frances dearly loved her little son, especially as she was advised against having another child, a decision that did not, she would later say, trouble her very much. Neither the pregnancy nor the birth had been easy for her, and she sensed that one child was enough for Ralph. Fatherhood was unlikely to be straightforward for someone who had never been close to his own father, and who had chosen Lytton Strachey as mentor. They agreed from the start that Burgo should call his parents Ralph and Frances, a sure indication of an unconventional approach to child-rearing. Both of them would flinch if a nanny ever made the mistake of referring to them as Mummy or Daddy.

If Frances kept a diary at all during Burgo's first five years it has not survived, and he features little in her surviving correspondence; but her photograph albums after 1935 are full of happy pictures of the little boy, who was not at all like his blue-eyed father but dark-eyed and dark-haired like his mother's family, and had a large domed forehead like hers, beaming in her arms, pottering about the garden or playing on the grass with other small children. Frances took pains to organise gatherings of friends with offspring the right age, and there would always be a traditional tree and a party with presents for local children at Christmas. After Burgo was born, Mam came to stay regularly; she was a doting grandmother. Burgo's life at Ham Spray with his nannies (there was a certain turnover) was ordered and secure; he grew up accustomed to his parents going away without him and to the presence when they were at home of their many friends, most of them less than enchanted by childish ways. One friend who was at Ham Spray constantly when Burgo was small never found him an easy child, and sometimes felt sorry for him; his behaviour was always under scrutiny, as if he were a Freudian case study in child development, and often discussed in front of him. His toys and games never lay around downstairs, but were confined to the nursery, as if Lytton's strictures about 'le petit peuple' still held sway.

By the spring of 1936, after a quiet year with no travel, fewer visitors and fewer trips to London, Ralph and Frances were ready for another journey to Spain. Gerald was urging them to visit his new house, at Churriana, a village in the hills above Málaga; there was, he joked, plenty of room for Burgo and 'Nursie' as well. He also assured them that the political situation in Spain was not as alarming as recent reports in the English press claimed; and as he was on the spot, they believed him. On 3 April they sailed to Lisbon, and made their way via Gibraltar and Algeciras to Churriana.

When looking back on the 1930s, the decade now regarded as a time when any intelligent, principled person must have recognised that the good times of the 1920s were giving way to unease at the rise of fascism in Europe and the possibility of another war, Frances would acknowledge that she remained almost deliberately unaware of such dangers. She would admit, not with pride, to having 'ostrich tendencies'. Pressed, she would speak of her preoccupation with Ralph, the long recovery from the deaths of Lytton and Carrington and the impact of finally having a child. Ham Spray, she claimed, was remote from the news and opinions and arguments of London; it was easy, there, to be oblivious of the outside world. Certainly her diary fragments and surviving correspondence from the 1930s concentrate almost entirely on her personal life.

But if Frances kept her head in the sand, Ralph was a different matter. He read *The Times* and the *New Statesman* regularly and took a keen interest in world affairs, if only because he played the stock market and needed to keep himself informed. His correspondence with Gerald Brenan, about the situation in Spain and then about the build-up to war, makes his attitude to the international situation clear. For him as well as Frances the great issue was not how to counter fascism, but how to avoid another war. Their pacifist convictions intensified as war drew closer. The only politician he admired, Ralph told Gerald, was George Lansbury, the Labour Party's leading pacifist MP.

Despite Gerald's reassurances, they arrived in Spain to find him and the other British residents in and around Málaga in a state of some uncertainty. Since the election of the left-wing Popular Front government in February

1936, there had been sporadic violence from both the left and the right; wild rumours circulated about communist plots, a right-wing coup, the murder of priests and unprovoked attacks on workers. Gerald was a romantic; party politics bored him, but his sympathies were with the new government. 'Spain is my country,' he wrote airily to Ralph 20 March, 'revolution or no revolution, and if it goes red I must try to change my colour too.' At the same time, he remained on good terms with the impoverished Spanish aristocrat who had sold him the house and the expatriates near Málaga who held very different views from his. For the moment, he sustained this precarious balance and went his own way.

Anyway, it was not interest in Spanish politics that took Ralph and Frances to Churriana. They were in search of the warmth and pleasure they always found in Spain and the stimulation of Gerald's company. When they arrived, they found the Brenans' house enviably beautiful. Dating from 1840, it had seventeen well-proportioned rooms and a huge walled garden full of tall trees – palms, avocados and fifty-foot bamboos, as well as orange and lemon trees, vines, a water tank just big enough to swim in and a fine view down to the sea. When the Brenans moved in, the place was so overgrown and dilapidated that it reminded Gamel of a decaying southern plantation. They restored it, turning three small outbuildings into a cottage for the servants (or helpers, as Gamel preferred to call them) transplanted from Yegen – Rosario, Maria and Antonio – to look after them and Miranda, Gerald's daughter by Juliana, now aged five. The move had been partly motivated by Gerald's wish to remove Miranda from her mother and bring her up himself.

After the remote harshness of Yegen, the gentler climate and easier life of Churriana were seductive. Since the eighteenth century, Málaga and the surrounding hills had attracted foreign residents – French and German as well as British – and by the time the Brenans arrived there was a settled expatriate community, sometimes linked with the grander Spanish families by marriage. Gerald's local friends were almost entirely foreigners, and for the rest of his life, most of which was to be based in Andalucia, it was this community, along with a steady stream of friends from Britain, who formed his circle. The dramatic, uncomfortable but romantic life of Yegen was replaced, for him and for regular visitors like Ralph and Frances, by a beguiling, eccentric, pleasure-loving social scene. In the mid-1930s the English around Málaga were still wearing sola topees, the badge of Empire, and were precisely the kind of people Gerald had left England to escape; but in Spain he just laughed at them.

His own presence, though, soon attracted a number of less conventional characters to Churriana. Bertrand Russell and his third wife, Peter, came to stay for six weeks; Molly MacCarthy's niece Clare Sheppard and her family took the house next door. And it was through Gerald that Ralph and Frances first encountered, in April 1936, a family who became a vital part of their lives. In 1935, while back in England, Gerald had decided to find a tenant for Yegen. His advertisement – 'House to let in Southern Spain. 3000 feet altitude facing sea ... library of 3000 books ... servants ... beautiful country, living cheap ... rent £2.10 a month' – had caught the eye of a young brother and sister, both aspiring writers, Mark and Angela Culme-Seymour. When he met them, Gerald was so taken with their charm and good looks, especially Angela's, that he quickly decided to let them have the house for nothing. In 1936 Angela's mother, Jan Woolley, and her half-sister, Janetta, arrived to stay at Torremolinos, then a small white village with a windmill east of Málaga. Janetta, a schoolgirl of fourteen, made a particular impression on Gerald, who told Ralph that she had 'set his heart on fire'.

On 12 April, Frances noted: 'Walked to Torremolinos ... Tea with Mrs Woolley and Janetta and walked back.' Mother and daughter also made an instant impression on both Partridges. Jan Woolley was a slender, delicate woman whose first husband had been killed in the war, and who afterwards married his brother officer, Geoffrey Woolley, who had won the VC at Ypres. He was the father of Janetta and her older brother, Rollo; but by the time the Partridges met Jan in Torremolinos the marriage was effectively over. Geoffrey Woolley was a clergyman's son and a man of firm religious and moral conviction who was himself ordained in 1921. He believed strenuously in the Church of England, the Empire and the public school system; since 1932 he had been Chaplain of Harrow. The values, let alone the behaviour, of Bloomsbury were anathema to him. Meanwhile, his wife had begun to spend most of her time abroad, partly to help her serious asthma; and his children regarded him as old-fashioned and oppressive. Jan and Janetta, by the time Frances and Ralph met them, had, like the Brenans and the Partridges before them, turned their backs on conventional family expectations and were immediately welcomed, not just because they were attractive but because they were recognised as kindred spirits.

Frances and Ralph fell for mother and daughter on their first meeting. They were especially struck by Janetta, who as well as being lovely-looking, with dark blonde hair and long legs, was a girl of unusual strength of character. She in turn was drawn to them, by Ralph's handsome, warm presence, by Frances' intelligence and energy and above all by their independence of mind. When, after two weeks of walks in the hills, picnics by

the sea and long evenings in Málaga or Churriana the Partridges moved on
to Seville, it was with the expectation of seeing the Woolleys again. Their
stay with the Brenans had been such a success that Ralph was now seriously
considering buying a house nearby.

The simmering unease in Spain does not appear to have affected the
holiday mood. In Seville, they were joined by Rosamond and Wogan
Philipps, and spent three days happily going to the fairs, visiting the vast
and gloomy Gothic cathedral and the fine Islamic courtyards and mosaics
of the Alcázar; Frances declined to join the others at a bullfight. They went
on to Madrid and a whole day in the Prado with the Goyas and then to
Barcelona, whence they took a fast train that got them back to London via
Paris in twenty-four hours. At Ham Spray Burgo, according to Ralph, was
'quite unaffected' by either their absence or their return; by 17 May Frances
was able to note the first bathe of the season.

As the summer at Ham Spray wore on, Ralph and Frances worked in
their garden, swam (always naked) in their pool, and invited their friends
and relations (Burgo's birth prompted an unusual round of family visits) as
usual. Frances' attention was taken up with her son's first birthday, and also
with the decline of Nan, who had been frail for some time and whose death
in July she noted sadly. Meanwhile, Ralph was receiving regular letters from
Gerald about the rising tide of violence in Spain, where Málaga was in the
grip of strikes, troops were on the streets and revolution seemed imminent.
He relayed to Ralph the views of the American journalist Jay Allen, who
lived in Torremolinos and was predicting a socialist-led terror and the
liquidation of the upper and middle classes: 'It sounds almost incredibly
stupid and barbarous but I feel that in these days anything may happen,'
wrote Gerald on 8 May. 'I shall send out a lorryload of books and furniture
when the arming of the workers begins.' Ralph wrote back about his own
war on ground elder and meeting Elizabeth Bowen at dinner with Ros and
Wog. A month later, Gerald reported that they were still living quietly, while
'Every day in Málaga the Communists and Anarchists kill one another.' At
the beginning of July, three local landowners told him that a right-wing
coup led by the army was imminent. 'If this rumour is true it is most
dangerous.' Gerald could not quite believe that such a coup would succeed;
he thought it more likely to lead to a communist revolution. Either way, 'if
you wish to buy a house here I recommend waiting till November'.

Through Gerald, Ham Spray must have been one of the better-informed
houses in England about the political chaos in Spain on the eve of the Civil
War. Perhaps it was partly this personal, local knowledge that made the
Partridges reject the simplistic attitudes – Rightists always bad, Leftists

always good – that were increasingly adopted by many in their circle; they felt, as did Gerald, that such polarisation, with its tendency to dehumanise opponents, was partly what made war acceptable.

On 18 July 1936 Gerald was in Málaga collecting his trousers from the cleaners. He bought a newspaper, and saw that the army had mutinied in Morocco two days earlier. Within a few days Málaga was in flames. Janetta and Jan were caught in the city, and were lucky to get back safely to Torremolinos; some days later the Governor of Gibraltar, a relation of Jan's, sent a British destroyer to pick them up. The Brenans asked Jan to take Miranda to safety; they themselves would stay. After pausing in France, Jan Woolley and the two girls were back in England and staying at Ham Spray by the end of August.

Over the next six weeks, Gerald described their situation in a vivid series of letters to Ralph. The night the destroyer left the bombing began; soon Málaga was a Republican enclave cut off by Franco's rebel forces from the rest of Spain. Gerald and Gamel were notably brave; they sheltered panic-stricken villagers, regardless of their politics, and took in their Falangist landlord and his family, though it was well known that those who were found harbouring Fascists were likely to be shot. Through Bertrand Russell, Gerald was writing an occasional column for the *Manchester Guardian*; he could bicycle into the shattered town and watch the bombing from his roof. Ugly reprisals were under way; he told Ralph that forty people had been killed in Málaga in one night.

Early in September, Gerald decided it was time to leave. It was plain that Málaga could not hold out, and he was was running out of money. Giving what he had left to Antonio, Maria and Rosaria, and entrusting the house to their care, the Brenans left for Gibraltar. By mid-October, after a chaotic few weeks as a journalist and a short visit to Morocco, he and Gamel headed for home. On 22 October they landed in Plymouth, penniless, and wearing djellabas. They went straight to Ham Spray.

Because of Gerald – who arrived back from Spain a man obsessed, determined both to campaign for support for the Republicans and to make the war the subject of his next book – Frances and Ralph could not avoid the intense argument of the next three years over whether or not the British government should intervene on the government side. By the mid-1930s, the pacifist leanings of Bloomsbury had largely crumbled; Leonard Woolf especially was alert to the threat of Nazi Germany, not just as a Jew but as someone passionately concerned with international relations, and Julian Bell, Vanessa and Clive's elder son, like many of his generation of young, left-wing intellectuals found the Spanish cause heroic and irresistible. Much of Bloomsbury, Old and Young, had recognised that war might after all be the lesser of two evils, and that fascism, if not checked in Spain, might overrun all Europe. For Ralph and Frances, however, this change of heart was anathema. If Ralph's pacifism was fundamentally emotional, derived from his war experience, Frances always maintained that hers was strictly rational, the consequence of thinking clearly about how to avoid violence and preserve life. Hers was always the cooler head; some of their friends believed that her commitment to pacifism was stronger than his. Nothing, to Frances, could ever be worse than war which, she deeply believed, only spread violence, never ended it. To support one side against another could only intensify conflict; the answer was to refuse to fight at all. Of their close friends, Clive Bell shared their uncompromising view, as did Julia – despite the fact that she was emotionally involved during the 1930s with more than one young man of passionate anti-fascist opinions.

The most important result of the Partridges' visit to Spain on the eve of the Civil War was not political but personal: their encounter with the Woolleys. While Gerald campaigned, spoke at pro-Republican meetings and worked on his book *The Spanish Labyrinth* (published to great acclaim in 1943), Frances and Ralph's life at Ham Spray expanded to include Jan, Rollo and Janetta. They liked Jan – it did not seem to trouble Frances that she became, briefly, Ralph's lover – and were always kind to Rollo; but for both of them, there was something irresistible about Janetta. When, before long, the restless Jan decided to return to France, leaving her children at school, Ham Spray became, and remained, Janetta's base, her English home. In Frances and Ralph she found a couple who offered her the stability, affection and sympathy of family life without the disadvantages. She went to Ham Spray for half-terms and holidays; Frances advised her about her reading and her essays, discussed her wish to go to art school, and cut her hair. Already, rising fifteen, she was mature for her age; from the start Frances and Ralph treated her not as a child, but as an interesting, attractive character in her own right.

It is easier to see why Janetta was drawn to the Partridges than why, from the beginning, they were so drawn to her, and tempting to suggest that there was a gap in their emotional life that she was destined to fill. They were perhaps one of those couples whose relationship works best when it includes strong feelings, not necessarily sexual, for another person; and unlike the kind of love affair Ralph had previously drifted into, which excluded Frances, a quasi-parental love for a beautiful, strong-minded girl on the threshold of adulthood was something they could share. Instinctively, too, Frances may have recognised that the way to prevent Ralph acting on the sexual attraction he was bound to feel sooner or later for such a girl was to build a strong, loving bond with her. The ways of friendship, like love, cannot always be explained; what is certain is that from 1936 onwards, Janetta became one of the most important people in Frances' emotional life.

All three Woolleys came to Ham Spray for Christmas 1936; early in 1937 Jan left for the South of France, Janetta went back to school, Málaga fell to the rebels and the Partridges went to Kitzbühel to ski. There, they met up with Raymond Mortimer and his partner Paul; they also befriended a ski instructress, Jenny, who later, with Ralph's help, came over to London (she was partly Jewish) and became his mistress. After Easter at Ham Spray with Bunny and Ray, their sons Richard and William, and Janetta, almost the whole of April was spent in Greece and Turkey, joining David Cecil and his parents, Lord and Lady Salisbury, on a cruise. While they were away, the Germans supporting Franco bombed Guernica, greatly strengthening the argument for intervention, but not causing the Partridges to reconsider. On the way home they visited Jan in Toulon.

For the rest of the year, Frances' engagement book is sprinkled with Janetta's name and school arrangements. In July, Ralph spent five days fetching her back from France; two days after he arrived home, on the 21st, they heard that Julian Bell, who had gone to Spain as an ambulance driver, had been killed. The tragedy of his death at the age of twenty-nine was not mitigated for them by any feeling that he had died for a noble cause. Frances, who had known Julian since boyhood, felt deeply for Vanessa and Clive, neither of whom had wanted him to go. Janetta and Rollo joined them for Christmas again that year, along with Julia, and helped decorate Burgo's Christmas tree.

With hindsight, the approach of war seems to have been inexorable during the late 1930s, and the hope that peace could still be maintained, as Hitler's demands increased, appears weak and deluded. But it is natural to want peace, to hope against hope that war can be averted; Ralph and Frances, during 1938, continued, like most people in Britain, to do so. The year began with Rachel and David Cecil and Colin Mackenzie joining the Ham Spray party; Colin and Frances had never entirely lost touch, and now that she was a married woman with a child he found he could get on perfectly well with Ralph. He was still unmarried, living in Scotland in a beautiful house on Skye, which became one of Frances' favourite places. She and Ralph liked to travel in spring or autumn; that year the whole of April was spent in France, driving slowly through the Dordogne to Toulouse, eating well, visiting Romanesque cloisters and churches; for some of the time they had Raymond Mortimer with them, one of their favourite travelling companions, lively, energetic and with a great knowledge of France. Janetta was visiting her mother, now living in Cassis, and they met her in Mont-pellier; by this time, for reasons Janetta could not later recall, they were calling her by a nickname, Wolfers or Woolfie. They lingered in Provence, where Frances hunted for wild narcissus while Janetta painted; they went walking and picnicking in the Luberon. By 1 May, they were back at Ham Spray for the summer, apart from short trips to Skye and to Wales, to give Burgo a holiday by the sea.

During the spring of 1938, Frances wrote a long letter to Julia, whose social and emotional life was a constant source of amusement and anxiety to her. Julia's latest young man (he was ten years her junior) was Philip Toynbee, then at the height of his communist fervour and passionately pro Republican Spain, where his friend and fellow public-school rebel Esmond Romilly had gone to fight. Julia was about to spend a few weeks with Philip in the country; Frances gave her sensible advice. 'Don't expect too paragon-like behaviour of Philip,' she wrote, 'by which I do not mean to imply that he is not one, but only that in young men as in other things I fear you have in your mind a more than human ideal of perfection.' She went on to report a visit to the Brenans who, unable to return to Spain, had found a house at Bell Court in Aldbourne, a mere ten miles from Ham Spray. She and Gamel had been for a peaceful walk; Frances was genuinely fond of her, despite her dreamy, mystical tendencies. It sounds as if she was also pleased to avoid listening to Gerald arguing with Ralph; this meeting, not long after the Anschluss, when Hitler annexed Austria, was potentially explosive. Gerald, largely through his involvement with Spain, had come to believe that Hitler had to be stopped, by force if necessary; he could not resist provoking Ralph by trying to get him to agree. 'The international situation', Frances told Julia, 'gets R and Gerald invariably shouting at each other louder and louder, which nothing will stop, and then they go home and write each other poems signed "Cassandrus" or "Old Crow".' So far, these sessions had done no real damage, and Frances had come to an interesting conclusion. 'It is more fun for R than Gerald as I have just discovered he *likes* such shouting arguments as these. After living with him all these years in which I thought he did it because he couldn't help it, like other people!' As for her own views, she was 'an absolutely adamant pacifist ... Nothing, nothing is more awful than war, and more senseless for it never does any good only produces new wars. And Spain is far more sickening now to contemplate to my mind than Austria, for that reason.' This comment encapsulates Frances' attitude to Hitler's advance. As she saw it, the situation in Spain (where Franco was doing increasingly well) was worse than the takeover of Austria because there was open violence and death there. The intolerable nature of Hitler's ideology, the vile behaviour of his regime, the repression, the anti-Semitism, the broken promises – none of this was as bad, to Frances, as war.

For Frances and Ralph, then, appeasement was never a dirty word. Chamberlain and his supporters, who were seeking at all costs to keep the peace, were to be admired; those who backed Winston Churchill, who was pressing for rearmament and urging the government to stand up to Hitler, they regarded as warmongers. It was predictable, therefore, that during the third week of September 1938, when it became clear that Hitler's next move was to dismember Czechoslovakia, the fear of war mounted and Chamberlain flew to Munich to negotiate with him, they would find themselves out of step with a number of their closest friends – Raymond Mortimer and Bunny Garnett now among them – as well as Gerald. There was bound to be another row; but when it happened, it was of a different order from their usual sparring, and involved Frances as well.

Janetta, who was staying at Ham Spray at the time, remembers not so much what was said as how terrified she was by Ralph's uncontrollable, purple-faced anger. Gerald himself wrote a long verbatim account of the scene to Bunny Garnett the following day, which, even allowing for Gerald's inventive powers, rings true. He wrote on 27 September, describing how he had driven up to London the previous day to see if he could get nation-alisation papers for a German friend. There, he observed the trenches dug in the parks, dined with Helen Anrep ('acid about Chamberlain') and discussed how many refugees he and Gamel could take; on his way back he telephoned Ralph from Hungerford. Two days earlier Ralph, sounding 'very emotional', told Gerald that he had been at Cranborne talking to David Cecil's older brother, Robert Cecil (Lord Cranborne), who was Par-liamentary Under-Secretary for Foreign Affairs at the time, about the situ-ation and would like to tell him about it, 'if we could meet without disagreement'. Now Gerald drove on to Ham Spray, with some misgivings. 'I thought it safe to go,' he told Bunny, 'as Janetta was there – also I was curious to hear what Cranborne had to say.'

At first, all was well; but when Gerald ventured to question Ralph's account of his talk with Cranborne, the trouble began. 'Ralph told me that Cranborne was in favour of our standing out and also that he had written Eden's last speech. I said I could not see how these two things were com-patible' (a reasonable point, since Eden had resigned over Chamberlain's foreign policy). Ralph accused Gerald of behaving like Hitler, trying to browbeat anyone who opposed him, and presenting them with ultimatums.

He got more and more worked up. 'This began as a joke,' Gerald admitted, 'but suddenly as he talked the joke was gone and I *was* Hitler. And he began to talk to Hitler as I am afraid Chamberlain never dared to do.' Unable to resist hitting back, Gerald said: 'The thing that seems to me absolutely intolerable is that people should project their annoyance upon the Checks [*sic*] and let the Germans go scot free.' Ralph said, 'I entirely agree with them. The Checks' attitude has been unspeakable. Why didn't they offer to return the Sudetens to Germany long ago?' The Germans living in the Sudetenland had, in his view, been treated 'abominably' and Hitler had been 'perfectly reasonable'. At this point, Frances pointed out that Hitler was unreasonable too, but it was too late to restrain Ralph. 'Well, the Checks are most to blame,' said Ralph. Gerald's riposte was lethal, not least because it contained elements of truth: 'You say you are a pacifist and I respect pacifism and have nothing to say against it. But what I do find outrageous is that you should distort the whole course of events and project your annoyance upon the Checks, as though they were to blame for upsetting Ham Spray. You use the words "truth" and "reason" a hundred times every day and yet your attitude over this crisis has been the most unjust and unreasonable possible.'

This accusation was too much for Frances as well as Ralph, who now lost all control and accused Gerald of longing for war. '"You will never be happy", he shouted "till there are two or three million dead. You *loved* the last war and are *longing* for another." And Frances said: "Who asked you to come and air your opinions? We loathe your opinions here. Get out of the house."'

Trembling with emotion, Gerald started to leave. Then, remembering that some of his possessions were still stored in the boxroom, and convinced that he would never set foot in Ham Spray again, he thought he had better collect them. He heard Frances say: 'You'd better help him with the baggage.' When Ralph appeared, Gerald burst out again: '"You call yourself a pacifist ... and yet you don't scruple to call your oldest friends murderers and turn them out of your house merely because they do not entirely agree with you." I thought Ralph would have a fit – then I thought he would knock me down. But he only said "Get out quick".'

Drama turned to farce as Gerald loaded his car with trunks, boxes, jugs and plates. Janetta appeared and 'very sweetly' took his hand. Then he drove away, feeling, he told Bunny, increasingly sad at what he thought had to be the end of more than twenty years of friendship. He added a telling memory. 'Indeed it is a little more than 24 years ago since I remember a rather similar scene, in which Ralph told me pacifists were cowards and should be shot, and I defended them. My opinions are exactly what they were on this point – Ralph's are diametrically the opposite. But the heat of his feelings has not changed.'

Brooding on the whole humiliating episode, Gerald found himself seeing Ham Spray in a new light; it now became 'that house of violence and hysteria'. He was particularly shocked that Frances, usually so balanced, so sane, had lost control. 'I find the peculiar malignancy with which Frances turned on me hard to forgive.'

Frances, looking back, ascribed her own fury with Gerald to the way in which he would deliberately bait Ralph, whom he knew perfectly well was easily roused. She also always felt that although Gerald was certainly the more creatively gifted of the two, Ralph was better-informed and had a clearer mind, and that it was Gerald who argued from emotion, always shifting his ground. Her reaction on this occasion is not hard to explain; such an attack on Ralph was an attack on her. But the storm had blown itself out. Both Ralph and Gerald quickly realised that they had gone too far. Frances and Gamel had a word; rueful, conciliatory letters were exchanged. On Friday, 30 September, she noted, Peace Declared. For the time being, like Chamberlain's, it held.

In approving the Munich deal, Frances and Ralph were in accord with most of the country, which was swept by relief and hope when Chamberlain returned with his piece of paper. They were also in accord with Clive Bell, who wrote to Frances on 4 October after dining with Raymond Mortimer and his great friend, the MP and writer Harold Nicolson, neither of them Chamberlain supporters. Ham Spray, far from being a backwater, had excellent sources. 'The state of our friends' minds was curious,' wrote Clive. Harold Nicolson was anticipating war and 'said it was going to be far more horrible than anyone had dreamed; was bound to last four years'. Nicolson, who also made regular broadcasts on foreign policy, had recently seen the Russian Ambassador, and learned that the Russians were unlikely to take a stand against Germany; 'Why should they?' asked Clive. 'Their proclaimed policy has always been to get Europe thoroughly war-weary and then cash in with a bloody revolution.' When he asked why, given all this, Nicolson still predicted war, '"We must fight!" was the gallant reply of our BBC foreign affairs expert, and Raymond seemed to agree.' Clive's tone of jocular superiority to the infinitely better-informed and more politically experienced Nicolson reads badly today.

It's lucky that curates and housemaids have so much stronger a sense of reality than the professional intellectuals. What seems to me important is that the people of France and England have said quite deliberately – of course it's a national humiliation, a loss of honour and prestige and all that, and tough on 'gallant little Czechoslovakia', and a diplomatic defeat, and none of us (except of course Mr Duff Cooper) can ever hold up his head again – and what the hell does it matter compared with general war. If, as I surmise, the Germans and Italians have been saying much the same, we really are getting somewhere.

He assumed that Frances and Ralph agreed with him; he was probably right.

New Year 1939 at Ham Spray included Julia (her romance with Philip Toynbee already over), Colin Mackenzie, Janetta and Jenny, Ralph's Austrian refugee mistress. As Janetta remembers, there was never any secrecy about Ralph's trips to London to make love to her; indeed, in true Bloomsbury fashion, he would return eager to tell Frances all about it. She put up with this until the day when Jenny sent her a present, whereupon Frances lost her temper and made one of her very rare scenes. Perhaps this put an end to the affair; Jenny was not included in another skiing trip arranged for late January, this time to St Gervais in the French Alps. The party was to be Ralph and Frances, Janetta (who had just turned eighteen) and another couple, Heywood and Anne Hill. The Hills were originally friends of Julia's, who had written about them glowingly to Frances soon after they opened their bookshop in Curzon Street in 1936. Julia reckoned they would all like each other, and she was right. Another lifelong friendship was formed.

Frances was not often ill; since the mysterious malaise of 1929 she had suffered nothing worse than a cold. But four days before they were due to leave for France, she was struck by giddiness severe enough to put her to bed. Her balance and her eyes were affected; she could hardly move, or read, without feeling dizzy and sick. It was obvious that she could not leave for France as planned, but she insisted that Ralph should go without her and that she would join him when she recovered; the doctor felt that after a few days' rest she would be fine. Ralph offered to stay, but she was adamant, and on 25 January he set off, leaving Frances not only dizzy but snowed-up, with the telephone down and Ham Spray almost cut off from the outside world.

Since 1932, Ralph and Frances had never been apart for any length of time; now, for the next couple of weeks they wrote to each other almost every day. Both of them felt guilty: Ralph because he was leaving his ailing wife alone in the snow, Frances because she hated spoiling his pleasure. It sounds as if Ralph had not been entirely sympathetic to her collapse. 'My sweetest love,' he wrote from London en route for France, 'I have been so beastly and disagreeable to you – do try to forgive me . . . as I'm going I shall try to enjoy myself.' Janetta added a PS (rather as Carrington used to do): 'Ralph is pink and miserable looking and I do feel it's all so awful your being left there . . . Ralph's in despair and I'm ready to burst into tears.'

Frances' letters were staunchly reassuring. He was to have a good time and not worry about her; she was improving and determined to join him. She told him every detail of her progress – the local doctor was treating her with liver pills, she found dark glasses useful, she was snug with the wireless, listening to concerts, Burgo was building a snowman, Nannie was helpful, as were the two maids and the gardener – and she hoped he and Janetta were having fun. 'I am so so glad you have Wolfers to keep you company,' she wrote, 'because no-one could be better.' He wrote back to tell her how much he missed her. 'I am not cut out to go away from your side . . . without you I'm quite lost and hopelessly discouraged.'

As soon as she felt well enough, Frances set off through the snow for London. By the time she reached the hotel at Paddington, she knew she had made a mistake; she was so giddy that she could hardly stand up. For once her strength failed her; she wrote a seven-page wail of misery to Ralph. 'Darling oh sweet lovely towser how I wish you were here at this moment. I do want you so badly – I suddenly feel so lonely and discouraged.' She broke off to see a doctor recommended by Mam; he told her what she knew already, that she could not possibly make the journey. Otherwise he was reassuring; the condition would disappear with time and rest. Frances wired Ralph immediately, and then wrote a four-page PS. 'Please darling do not be disappointed and do not not not <u>think</u> of coming home. Just keep on enjoying yourself with sweet Wolfers.' The next day she wondered whether to send the first letter at all, but decided to do so. After consoling visits from Mam and Rachel Cecil she took the train home and went back to bed.

For the next week, telegrams and letters whizzed between Ham Spray and St Gervais. At first Ralph decided to return; then he decided to stay. His skiing was going well; Janetta was fearless and making good progress. Frances apologised for her desperate letter; she felt guiltier than ever for being so feeble. 'I feel now I somehow have failed you badly.' But she knew she was right; the quiet life of Ham Spray was all she was fit for and she was once again on the mend. There had been more snow; the ilex tree had lost some branches. Miss Huth (the daughter of their crusty neighbour) had come round to talk about billeting refugee children at Ham Spray 'in the next war'. They had agreed on three, or two and a teacher. Frances followed the news, and wondered what the French made of Hitler's latest alarming speeches; she listened to Chamberlain, still boasting about his piece of paper and ignoring the collapse of Spain. She also kept Ralph up-to-date with news of Jenny, to whom she had sent what sounds like a regular sum of money. 'I sent Jenny her cheque yesterday, pretending I could scarcely write. Oh my, wouldn't she have thought it a chance for her to come in my place?' Jenny, she went on, was 'rather down on Janetta, who she obviously resents bitterly as her successor'.

This linking of Jenny and Janetta suggests that Frances knew quite well, and that Ralph knew she knew, that Janetta was becoming increasingly important to Ralph and that he was attracted to her. Given Ralph's susceptibility it must have occurred to them both, as Janetta grew up, that another triangle might take shape. Perhaps the intensity of Frances' anxiety about dropping out of the skiing trip, as well as Ralph's guilt, derived from the unspoken realisation that for him to be in Janetta's company without Frances for two weeks could be a turning point. As Janetta recalls, Ralph had genuinely longed for Frances to join them; but when it was clear she could not, his behaviour changed towards her, becoming tense and irritable. When one night he suddenly came to her room, threw himself on top of her, burst into tears and told her he loved her, she was appalled and deeply embarrassed. Somehow she persuaded him to leave, and he left for England as soon as possible.

What Janetta could not know was that he had already begun to complain about her in his letters to Frances. 'I don't really get on very well with her,' he had written. 'She's such a child and not a real companion ... selfish, cross and vain, redeemed by occasional flashes of real sensitiveness and sweetness.' Frances wrote back calmly. 'Wolfers appears to be irritating you – why, I wonder?' After wiring to Frances that he was coming home he wrote her a long emotional letter, telling her enough of the truth to clear his conscience. Janetta's behaviour had become intolerable. 'I hardly believed the day would come when I would want her to go away and stay away. You are the only person I can talk to so I have to pour out everything.' After a long account of Janetta's moods and inconsistencies, he came to the point. 'If I'd stayed another week W and I would either not have been on speaking terms or lovers, so it's a good thing from that angle too that I'm leaving. She's rather a cock-teaser and I would have been worked up to reprisals.'

The only indication of Frances' reaction to all this is a line at the end of her final letter before, on 7 February, Ralph arrived back at Ham Spray. After telling him how much she was longing to see him, and hoping he wouldn't find her too dull and plain, she wrote: 'Don't be too cross with

Wolfi. I dare say her position had its difficulties too.' Whatever he may have told her on his return, ten days later Janetta was also back at Ham Spray, where everyone behaved as if nothing had happened.

By all accounts, Ralph accepted after this that Janetta would never go to bed with him. Before long, he also had to accept that his role in her life would be that of confidant and adviser when she found lovers nearer her own age; despite spasms of jealousy he played this part well. In the years ahead, Ralph's affection and understanding were of great importance to her; indeed, she often found him easier to talk to about her emotional problems than Frances. Being frail himself, he was more tolerant of human frailty. As for Frances, Ralph's attempted seduction of Janetta in St Gervais was something she acknowledged but preferred not to discuss.

But if the three people concerned managed the episode with discretion, there was nothing to be done about the rumours that sped around in its wake. The Hills were great gossips; they would have talked to Julia; before long the story was – and remained – that Frances' anxiety about Ralph and Janetta had made her ill, indeed that she had gone temporarily blind – probably as a result of declining to see what was going on. This version of events lingered for years. In fact, Frances' giddiness passed in due course and never recurred; it was probably just a commonplace viral infection.

It took Frances a while to recover completely, but by the middle of April she and Ralph were once more off to France. This time they paused in the Loire Valley before driving down through Bordeaux (and lunching at Ralph's favourite restaurant, the Chapon Fin) to the Pyrenees, where they went for long walks among the spring flowers near the Spanish border. By now the Spanish Civil war was over; they avoided the grim camps on the French side, full of Republican refugees. They were back at Ham Spray by mid-May. The last summer of peace saw a steady flow of guests, including Rosamond Lehmann and her new lover, Goronwy Rees, the Cecils, Dick and Esmé Strachey, and the Brenans. Mam came to stay, moving on to Tom Marshall and his second wife Nadine, now living not far away near Thame. There was renewed worry in the family about Ray; her cancer had returned, and probably Frances already knew that Bunny, like Ralph not given to controlling his sexual impulses, had for some time been pursuing his former lover Duncan Grant's still unacknowledged daughter, Angelica Bell.

On Sunday, 20 August, Frances noted: 'Crisis Looming'. Two days later: 'Full Crisis. Mam arrives.' On the 26th they were visited by Phil Nichols – as a diplomat, he was able to keep them abreast of the slide to war – and Julia, Gerald and Wogan Philipps. Frances wrote 'Crisis' every day until, on 3 September, war was finally declared. That day, they entertained two of

Ralph's fellow veterans of the trenches. Gerald and Gamel Brenan came to lunch; Noel and Catherine Carrington to tea. Then in their twenties, now in their forties, two out of the three men fully intended to join the fight in whatever way they could. For Ralph, and for Frances, it was to be a different kind of war.

Twelve

Trials of War (1), 1939–1942

During the last months of 1939 Ham Spray filled up with mothers and children from London, braced for German bombs as soon as war was declared. Frances described it as 'a congested and gruelling time . . . at the worst we had six children, three nannies, parents at weekends and two adults'. 'Le petit peuple' had arrived at Ham Spray in force; but at least these were not the scared bed-wetting children from the East End, packed onto trains and billeted on strangers, but those belonging to friends like the Nichols. Phyllis Nichols, who shared the Partridges' pacifist convictions, moved in with her two children, and Janetta was usually around at weekends; she had recently fallen in love with the man who became her first husband, Humphrey Slater, a communist journalist and veteran of the Spanish Civil War. Ralph and Frances welcomed him for her sake while thinking him hardly good enough for her. Mam and Julia also made lengthy visits; Julia was by now in love with a talented art student, Lawrence Gowing, lanky, stammering and seventeen years her junior. He was to become the centre of her life.

During the next few months the war barely touched Britain. While Ham Spray, along with the rest of the country, held its breath and waited, Frances had to face the imminent loss of her favourite sister. Towards the end of September Ray and Bunny came for a night after a disastrous trip to Ireland, when Ray had collapsed with terrifying seizures. The cancer she had been treated for ten years earlier was now spreading fast. With the outbreak of war Bunny, his pacifism as far behind him now as his homosexuality, took a job with the Air Ministry; his work, and his increasingly intense relationship with Angelica (no secret from Ray), meant he was often in London. This visit, noted in Frances' pocket diary, was to be the last time she and Ray saw each other. Back at Hilton as the winter approached, Ray was soon bedridden and desperately ill.

The winter of 1939–40 was fiercely cold. During January – Frances and Ralph saw the New Year in alone, drinking nips of neat whisky – there was much exhilarating skating on the frozen ponds and canal, in what Frances called 'ice-madness'; the cold, and the tension, seemed to intensify her appreciation of the small pleasures all around her. As the first full year of war began, her diary shows her resolving to focus on what made her life worth living – her love for Ralph and Burgo, her friends, her house, her garden – and to appreciate 'small sensual things, pots of cyclamen, the shine on holly berries and cat's fur'. She was determined to maintain her own values, not just her hatred of war but her suspicion of sentimental patriotism.

All her life Frances dreaded apathy almost more than anything. 'All experience,' she believed, 'whether painful or pleasant, can have an essence squeezed out of it which is the main source of happiness ... the process of tasting can be good and valuable even when what is tasted is not.' She tried to hold on to this conviction, but sometimes it was impossible. 'I dreamt of Ray and her illness,' she wrote on 5 January 1940, 'and in the dream all I had suppressed of the reaction to her horrible situation came out ... I woke and lay in the dark, very miserable and oppressed by the thought of death.'

Meanwhile, daily life at Ham Spray went on much as usual. Burgo's nanny was a trial, always complaining; Joan, one of the two resident maids, was preoccupied with a soldier boyfriend; Frances found that listening to music made her too emotional, but that writing reviews for the *New Statesman* was a distraction. They saw much of their local friends, especially the Cecils ('no-one is better company') and the Wests, a younger couple living nearby; Anthony, a writer and the son of Rebecca West and H.G. Wells, was uncertain whether to adopt the pacifist position, or join up; when he did so, the friendship was unaffected. Meanwhile Gerald had joined the Home Guard; he and Ralph maintained an uneasy truce. Clive Bell came to stay, bringing his washing; he had written to Frances after war was declared predicting that England would soon be as barbarous a country as Germany. He remained in favour of making peace, and thoroughly approved of all moves in that direction. Alix and James Strachey arrived, full of the latest feuds in the Freudian world, and bringing the alarming news of a proposal to publish Lytton's letters. (The idea got nowhere; a selection was finally published in 2005.) Frances and Ralph even managed a couple of trips to London, where they ate oysters and plovers at the Ivy and went dancing.

All this time, the news from Hilton was getting worse. Bunny's letters inflicted on Frances what he could not share with anyone else: Ray was in agony, not just from pain but from fear. She begged him to stay with her and reassure her; but she also told him not to lie. 'It is not easy to remove the fears: indeed it is impossible, though I try.' Mam, Judy and Eleanor took turns helping him look after her; Frances wrote offering to visit, or to have Richard and William to stay; she sent detective stories and jigsaw puzzles and a box of spring flowers – small pink cyclamen, grape hyacinths, freesias. Soon two nurses were required, and Ray was given heroin for the pain. Bunny wrote back: 'She has had several morphia dreams in which you were coming or had come to see her. But she, in the daytime rational hours has said often that she wants to write to you to tell you not to come. Seeing anyone for the last time is useless and terrible and that she probably would not be fit to see you.'

In Frances' published diary, Ray's illness is mentioned once, in a footnote, and Frances' own feelings are never mentioned. But unpublished fragments show that she sometimes found Ralph unsympathetic. In January, after a letter from Mam had upset her, 'A painful conversation followed between R and me, as it often does on this subject because of his hostility to the family element in this drama. I generally in the end hit back with instances from his own behaviour during Lytton's illness. I was depressed all day as a result.' Such moments of difficulty between them were rare, and usually occurred when something or someone appeared to Ralph to be taking her attention away from him. He needed to be the focus of all her thoughts and emotions; most of the time, he was. Two days later she recorded how happy they were together; throughout the war, indeed, she felt that they were closer than ever. 'Outer bleakness has intensified this very great happiness.'

Frances turned forty on 15 March, but felt 'nothing particular' about it. Ten days later, Ralph took the phone call from Bunny to say that Ray had died in the night. 'That's a very good thing' was Ralph's reaction. For Frances, it was more complicated. She went off by herself, feeling 'sulky and frozen'; Ralph, she went on, 'suspects my feelings about Ray ... he would like me to see her death and herself more detachedly or cynically than I do. I therefore shrink a little into myself and don't discuss it with him.' Frances had to deal with her grief for Ray while feeling at odds with her husband, who always counted on her complete sympathy when his own emotions overflowed. A few days later, Bunny brought his sons to stay, and poured out to Frances and Ralph the terrible details of Ray's last days and hours. He told them how she had begged him to help her to die. Frances could hardly bear it. 'I can't forgive him that he didn't. What barbarous cruelty to keep the poor creature alive.'

The next day, on a walk, Bunny confirmed to Frances that he and Angelica had already been lovers for two years, and that he intended, now that Ray was dead, to make her his wife. They discussed the reaction at Charleston. 'Duncan's attitude is cold disapproval, Vanessa's slightly warmer,

but Bunny thought they would behave all right ... I can't help thinking
Bunny underestimates the opposition he will meet at Charleston, especially
if marriage is his aim.'

Never, at the time or looking back, did Frances show any hostility towards
Bunny for taking up with Angelica while Ray was enduring cancer, nor did
she find it difficult to discuss his remarriage plans within days of her sister's
death. Asked whether she had felt any anger, she looked faintly surprised.
'No, not really,' she answered. 'We all knew what Bunny was like; Ray had
been ill for a long time.' Pressed, she added 'Ralph and I were always on
the side of lovers, especially if they met with disapproval.' Not that they
took an over-romantic view at the time; Frances noted 'When he is 60 she
will be 36. Surely she won't stay with him for ever.' Before long, Bunny
brought Angelica to Ham Spray; both of them regarded Frances and Ralph
as allies. Charleston took some time to accept the inevitable.

As the spring advanced, so did Hitler's armies. Frances read Madame du
Deffand, listened to Monteverdi, her spirits lifted by the primroses and
violets in the hedges and the first two red tulips in the garden; but try as
she might, she could not keep the war out of her head. She was discovering
that pacifism did not bring detachment. 'A conversation about the nature
of our interest in the conduct of the war,' she wrote. 'A few weeks ago we
thought very little about it, now we are absorbed in the strategic drama of
the Norwegian campaign, and are of course delighted when our troops do
well.' She put the crucial question to Ralph. 'If we so much want the Allies
to win, shouldn't it logically follow that we ought to help them to?' He
answered with an analogy. 'It's as if all our money had against our wills been
put on a certain horse in the Derby. We may hate horse racing, disapprove
of it even – yet we still want that horse to win. If we are to remain sane we
must follow the news with interest, and we must mind what we hear.'

Ralph maintained this attitude throughout the war. He followed events
in detail through newspapers and the radio; he pinned up huge maps
and traced the movements of troops; he thought about strategy, and his
predictions were often accurate. To Janetta, who witnessed all this, it was
quite clear that he wanted Germany to be defeated, as she did. Frances, as
her diary shows, was for some time less sure of her position.

On 10 May, Gerald rang Ham Spray with the news that the Germans
had invaded Holland. 'I felt a grip of emotion, fear and excitement, as if a
giant's hand had seized me violently round the waist, where I stood by the
telephone, lifted me up and then dropped me again.' All day, she and Ralph
followed the news; they only left the radio to take Burgo to the station to
meet Mam. That evening they listened to Chamberlain's 'abdication speech'

as he handed over to Winston Churchill. The next day, Gerald bicycled over to tea, 'in pensive mood, very charming' except when he suddenly announced that as pacifists were now on the same side as fascists they should be interned. One of the things that maddened Ralph and Frances about Gerald was his inconsistency. They were never, if they could help it, inconsistent.

Over the next few weeks, as the Germans advanced across Europe and an invasion of Britain seemed increasingly likely, Frances' diary shows her struggling to keep her head above the waves of panic and rumour. New tennis rackets arrived from Harrods. Julia came to stay, and, when during a walk a pheasant almost flew into Frances, said 'perhaps it's a disguised parachutist'. Frances found the stories about Germans landing in Holland dressed as nuns absurd: 'How amazing to think of these sinister air-transports filled with fancy dress figures.' But when she answered the door to three men in clerical garb with beards and German accents, she thought 'aha!' until they revealed that they were Christian Pacifists from a community near Swindon in search of Phyllis Nichols. Over tea, she told them she was a pacifist too. 'Are you much persecuted?' they enquired. To Frances, it was 'the maddest of mad hatter tea parties'.

Such comic moments were few. As the Germans approached Paris, Frances felt sick with fear. She could not see how invasion and defeat could be avoided: 'I still feel it is likely that we lose the war, though a painful ray of hope is struggling within me.' She and Ralph lay in bed one morning discussing suicide. 'I suddenly thought of Ray as lucky and enviable, and felt a longing to have some safe way of dying within my power.' Ralph envisaged all three of them gassing themselves in the car (as Carrington had tried to do); Frances had a strong preference for drugs and began to think how to acquire some. 'I feel it would be the greatest possible help to know that we had death in our power.'

Not surprisingly in these circumstances, both Mam and Julia, their constant companions, sometimes irritated Frances. Mam was no pacifist, and she never doubted that the war would be won; her simple patriotism and optimism grated on her daughter and infuriated Ralph. There were fierce arguments; Frances recalled Mam saying, 'with some truth, "There's no-one so bellicose as a pacifist".' With Julia, it was a matter of what Frances called 'this difficult, teasing old triangle'. Julia, she sometimes felt, instinctively disliked happy, harmonious couples. She liked to stir up trouble, and told Frances she indulged Ralph too much. 'You spoil him. More than any mortal man.' She was also inclined to lecture Frances on her appearance and how she should try harder to make the most of herself.

Julia believed in make-up, hairdressers and following fashion; Frances, as photographs show, relied on her natural good looks.

By the end of May, neither the foaming blossom and cow-parsley in the hedges, nor Mozart's Clarinet Quintet, nor a conversation about aesthetics over breakfast ('quite like old times') could keep reality at bay any longer. The first bombs fell on English soil; a neighbour told Frances that defeatists were to be shot on sight. Then came the news of Dunkirk; all Frances could think of was that with 300,000 men brought safely home, at least there were 'hundreds of individual happy endings'. Raymond Mortimer, perhaps the most passionately Francophile of their friends, invited himself to stay. He was not a pacifist, but regarded Ham Spray as a good place to hear bad news. It was hot; 'Sitting in the cool of the evening among the exuberant pink roses and tall valerian on the verandah, we talked to Raymond about suicide.'

Everyone in Britain had reason to be afraid, and to wonder whether death might be preferable to Nazi occupation; but not many, then or later, admitted to feeling as hopeless as Frances. On 13 June, she wrote: 'We can't win this war. Oh, if we could then lose it quickly.' Next day, the Germans marched into Paris. 'It's very difficult to imagine. But it's a good deal less painful than to think of Paris and Parisians being burnt and destroyed by bombs. I am certain the French will make peace in a few days. But will we?' Clive Bell reappeared; he, like her, would have made peace even now; but as this possibility receded, he, like her, remained determined to go on enjoying life as best he could.

Over the next weeks, while Churchill's speeches rallied the nation and the RAF fought the Battle of Britain over southern England, Frances found herself more and more out of tune with the national mood. Never Churchill admirers, she and Ralph greatly disliked his sonorous rhetoric. She positively hated the spate of Churchill-inspired letters to *The Times* 'all saying in their different ways, "just see me die, how dashingly I'll do it"' and 'the balderdash uttered by politicians. Lord M says "if we must die let's die gaily and Lord C that we must do it On Our Toes".'

She also felt increasingly out of tune with her mother. It was a matter of principle to Frances and Ralph not to allow themselves to feel, let alone express, any pleasure when the RAF brought down large numbers of German planes; they hated Mam's excited reaction. After news of a particularly successful night during the Battle of Britain Frances and Ralph grimly agreed that 'it would be a good idea to take this news to Mam, to gratify her, and show also that we could recognise "good news" when we heard it. R said "It will give her a good appetite for her breakfast, to think of a lot of young Germans being slaughtered".' Frances felt ashamed when she realised Mam sensed she was causing tension. She poured her resolutions to be kinder into her diary.

At night, they watched the searchlights hunting for bombers over the downs; Alix Strachey now told them she had abandoned pacifism and decided the war had to be won. When Hitler was said to be starting a peace offensive Frances found she no longer had any hope that it might happen. 'There's no shadow of doubt we will reject any such suggestion. Now I suppose Churchill will again tell the world that we are going to die on the hills and on the sea, and then we shall proceed to do so.' As fear of invasion receded, fear of German bombers increased. Marjorie Strachey had already suggested taking Burgo to America; now the Nichols decided to send their children across the Atlantic. Frances could not bear the thought; surely he would be safer at Ham Spray, even though they often heard planes going over and a German plane was brought down nearby. But when she went to London with Ralph early in August, to see an exhibition, a film and dine with Raymond, who had left the *New Statesman* for the Ministry of Information, London was quieter at night than Ham Spray. Frances had learned that fine weather meant danger; but it was hard not to relish the hot days when they could all swim naked, and have tea on the lawn. Janetta came down again with Humphrey, and there were fierce political arguments. Frances' love for Janetta had not diminished. She was 'someone I am fonder of and more closely linked to than anyone except R and Burgo.' And her physical loveliness was a constant pleasure. 'She has the most beautiful female body I have ever seen.'

In mid-August Frances and Burgo, walking on the downs, saw four German planes roar directly over their house. Bombs fell near Newbury; Nanny spent most of the day in an air raid shelter. By the end of August, Mam had returned and Saxon in his white silk suit was on his annual visit. They were both safely at Ham Spray when, on 7 September, the blitz on London began. That night, 430 people were killed and 1,600 wounded, and a new wave of refugees began to arrive in Wiltshire; two bewildered families, one from Wandsworth and one from Bexhill, moved into Ham Spray. 'With a sinking heart', wrote Frances, 'I feel what remains of me being submerged under the tide of practical arrangements, just as it was last winter, only with infinitely more painful events happening.'

The refugees had moved on by late October, but the flow of friends and children continued. All that winter, and indeed throughout the war, Frances managed the practicalities of running the household in increasingly difficult conditions as best she could. She and Ralph between them worked hard to look after all their refugees, friends or strangers, and shared everything they had; they tried not to upset anyone, while making no secret of their pacifist views, but they both, and especially Frances, found it hard to be optimistic. To be pessimistic was widely considered defeatist, unpatriotic, almost treacherous; but 'to us it seems as if in the long run it hardly matters who wins ... we are pessimistic because the war is horrible in itself, because it is solving no problems and doing no good to anyone, but on the contrary making endless new problems and doing infinite harm to countless people'.

She meant, of course, problems on the national and international scale; but on the more local scale there were plenty to deal with. Around Ham Spray, as all over the country, there were rumours of spies and fifth columnists; anyone with German connections or anti-war views came under suspicion. Prominent among them was Ralph and Frances' former neighbour Diana Mosley; they had seen nothing of her since she had taken up with the Fascist leader Oswald Mosley. Frances noted her arrest on 29 June without comment.

Ironically, Gerald Brenan was in trouble, reported for possibly signalling to the enemy after Helen Anrep had failed to close her blackout curtains properly; then when he flashed a torch while out on Home Guard duty, he was reported again. Scotland Yard sent detectives down; to make matters worse, they had found Gerald's name and address among papers taken from Mosley's former headquarters. By chance, Ralph arrived at Bell Court while the police were there, and spoke up for Gerald, who was then called before magistrates in Marlborough; Ralph rallied local worthies on his behalf, including Clive Bell's highly respectable brother Major Cory Bell. With Major Partridge and Major Bell on his side, let alone the fact that he was able to show that he had written to *The Daily Telegraph* calling for Mosley to be imprisoned, the matter was dropped and Gerald went off to London to spend a month as an air raid warden.

Ham Spray followed the harsher impact of the war through their friends. Boris Anrep told them all about his escape, with Maroussa, from occupied Paris. From Julia and Janetta, both of whom were still London-based, Frances learned what air raids felt like. Janetta admitted that she was terrified, and that if it were not for Humphrey she would leave London. Her brother Rollo was now training for the RAF; when he visited Ham Spray in October, Frances wrote, 'the effect of his airforce uniform was electric', especially on Burgo and Mam. Rollo appeared to have no illusions about the war; he told them he saw little difference between Nazis and communists. She was touched by his courage and by his confusion; Ralph thought that Rollo 'fully realises the suicidal nature of his career'. Both

Frances and Ralph found the deliberately cultivated romantic image of the young fighter pilots suspect; Ralph especially was outraged at the way those too old to fight were always eager to send young men to their death. Many of Ham Spray's fiercest arguments revolved around this point, which derived directly from Ralph's own war experiences.

Throughout Frances' war diary, she wrote of Burgo with great love and tenderness. He was growing up to be an original little boy, imaginative and with a precocious way of talking; but he still climbed into bed with his parents in the mornings and tumbled around with Ralph. She tried not to be over-anxious about him, but she could not help fearing for his future as she recorded his funny, charming sayings and doings, and when that autumn of 1940, aged just over five, Burgo went to school, it soon became clear that the uncomplicated years of his early childhood were over.

Burgo did not take kindly to school, and Frances soon found herself dealing with a tearful child who clung to her and pleaded with her not to make him go. This in itself was neither unusual nor unexpected; what she found more painful was that she and Ralph could not agree on how he should be handled. When she told Ralph how miserable such scenes made her, she soon wished she had not; 'He became greatly agitated and said my coaxing methods were all wrong and that if Burgo wouldn't go to school without coaxing he must be made to suffer for not going.' Frances felt they were drifting towards 'a dreadful indeterminate state of disapproval and punishment on our side and sense of failure on his'. When she tried to comfort Burgo with hugs and kisses, Ralph objected; 'he often speaks of my "slobbering over" him which is really more what he himself does ... I sat almost silent, a feeling of misery welling up within.'

One of the other children at the old-fashioned dame school in Hungerford recalled his arrival. To her, Burgo seemed scruffy and peculiar. 'One morning, Miss Richens came in with a lady dressed in trousers with a small boy in tow. He was crying and was introduced as Burgo Partridge. I was told to move up a place and look after him. He was a most unfortunate looking child in thick corduroy shorts and oversized jumper.' He never settled down, cried constantly and soon left, never to reappear. His classmate still felt sorry for him half a century later.

This glimpse of Burgo confirms what Frances was beginning to perceive – that the transition from home to school was going to be particularly hard for him. Ham Spray was an unusual household, and Burgo was an unusual child; he looked different, with his big head, long curling hair and intense dark eyes, and he had grown up in a household where not many concessions were made to childishness. Frances and Ralph were delighted to be rid of

Nanny, but perhaps her departure left Burgo feeling insecure and unable to be childish at all. 'I realise', wrote Frances, 'that we have been led away by the pleasure of seeing Burgo be grownup, and not realised what an effort it has all been to him.'

When Burgo, perhaps not coincidentally, became quite seriously ill that autumn, Nanny was recalled to help nurse him; at one point, feverish and hysterical, Burgo terrified his parents by telling them he was going to die. 'I suppose I shall remember that harrowing moment all my life,' wrote Frances, adding that Ralph had been 'dreadfully upset' and that if Burgo were to die, she would kill herself. After three weeks or so, he recovered, but now he told Frances that the thought of going back to school terrified him; 'he said that he somehow only felt *safe* with Ralph or me'. In the wake of all this, they decided to find another way to educate Burgo in the New Year.

Burgo's troubles had blotted out the war for a while, but not for long. On 4 November bombs fell on Ham village; luckily no-one was hurt. In London, Duncan Grant's studio in Fitzroy Street, where Frances and Ralph had danced at so many parties, had been demolished, and Gerald, back from his spell as a warden, was full of dramatic tales of narrow escapes. The news of the destruction of Coventry dented even Mam's optimism, and Frances lay in bed trembling all over as bombers droned overhead. 'How degrading to lie here afraid, and how degrading to have cause to be afraid.'

As the year drew to a close, a little light relief was provided by Isobel Strachey's tales of the love affairs she was enjoying in London, where danger heightened emotions and the blackout provided exciting opportunities. Frances was amused rather than envious, but she still thought that middle-aged women should accept their limitations. 'The fatal mistake', she wrote, 'is to makeup, dress, behave and show that they think of themselves still as potential general lust provokers.' She certainly did not; her main worry was that she and Ralph were so seldom alone any more. On the other hand, there is no hint that he was continuing to bed other women.

She sent in a review of children's Christmas books for the *New Statesman*, read Lytton on Voltaire and found herself talking wistfully about the old days with Ralph, comparing the Ham Spray of the past with the grim present. Perhaps the war marked the end of 'Old Bloomsbury'; even though now, Frances reflected, she could see that it was already past its peak when she first knew it. Even so, 'how inspiring and exciting all the same were its standards ... Old Bloomsbury, Ralph and I agreed, was the only society we could think of comparable to the 18th century.' War or no war, they would do what they could to keep those standards alive.

Before Christmas they had a visit from an old friend who had never much cared for Bloomsbury: Colin Mackenzie, bringing his new and much younger wife, Aileen Meade, known as Pin, to stay for the first time. Burgo was fascinated by his wooden leg; Frances was not altogether surprised when her old admirer announced that all Germans should be sterilised. Julia and Lawrence came for Christmas; there was a goose, and a tree, and paper hats. Soon afterwards Burgo, suffering from earache, lay in their bed considering Carrington's portrait of Lytton. He told them he thought it was a picture of a dead or dying man, and asked what became of him after he was dead. Frances did not record her answer.

Perhaps because so much that had gone into it was painful, Frances wondered, as the year turned, whether her diary was worth keeping at all. 'I don't believe I shall ever read this one through again ... as for the war, there can hardly be anyone in England who is less affected by it than I am, so I am the last person who ought to keep a war diary.' But the habit of diary-keeping, founded as it was on her determination not to let life drift by unobserved, and her need to shape and control her thoughts and her reactions, proved stronger than her misgivings. The 1940 diary was the longest of the wartime sequence, running to 376 typed pages; the complete document runs to just over 1,000. As the war ground on, she found her energy for writing it sometimes flagged, but she never gave up; in itself it is testimony to her refusal to allow the war to take her over. After 1940, Frances' attitude to the war changed little. She loathed it, and never accepted that it had to be fought, but she had no choice but to adapt her way of life to the new conditions it required. Her thoughts she declined to adapt.

The problem of Burgo's schooling was solved when Mr and Mrs Padel, a gentle couple of elderly pacifists living in Inkpen, agreed to teach him at home, along with two or three other children. Frances was encouraged to find that their house was full of musical instruments and books, and not at all put off to discover that they were communists. It was a great relief when Burgo settled down. It was also a relief, when she and Ralph went up to London in February for the first time since the blitz, to find the city less shattered than she had feared, and to have a jolly lunch at the Ivy with Clive, Raymond and Boris. In March they went down to Ralph's family's house in Devon, where Frances was amused by the Anglo-Indian atmosphere and appreciated the warm welcome they received from several elderly Partridge aunts and cousins living nearby. Even Ralph, she observed, was touched (although he avoided his sisters, whom it amused him to describe as Goneril and Regan, with himself as Little Cordelia). They went for walks by the sea, where the defence preparations along the shoreline struck them as pitifully inadequate, as Frances wrote to Clive.

While they were in Devon, word reached Frances from her sister Eleanor that their mother had been taken to hospital and found to have advanced lung cancer. 'I suppose I must have been expecting it,' she wrote bleakly, 'for the news hardly came as a shock.' Ever since Ray's death, her mother, now seventy-eight, had been failing. Ralph was kind but brisk, reminding her that 'we are all dying'; Frances found it best not to talk to him about it very much, but 'the terrible loneliness of dying' filled her mind. 'As I walked along admiring the fans, spears and twirls of the shells, I thought of Mam and wondered how much courage it needs to die.' She sent her a big box of huge, sweet-scented Devon violets, but did not go to her bedside. Back at Ham Spray, on 22 March Burgo brought up the post to her in bed. When she opened a letter from Eleanor, she read, 'with a stifling, choking sensation and the sudden stoppage of my heart (then to go on with a gallop) the words "she died"'. Mam had not survived an operation two days earlier. Eleanor maintained she had sent Frances a telegram at once, but Frances did not believe her; she already felt sure that with Mam's death the family would disintegrate, and did not much care. She attended a gathering about the will – no mention of a funeral – and afterwards complained of the 'dead, apathetic, sub-human atmosphere of the family conclave of Marshalls'. But her feelings for her mother were different: 'I owe her a great deal of happiness.' To the end of her days, Frances wished she had been kinder to Mam in the last years of her life.

Not long afterwards, Frances opened *The Times* and read that Virginia Woolf had been missing for several days and was presumed to have drowned in the Ouse, near Rodmell. She had been a figure in Frances' landscape since her girlhood; now her death, which Frances knew to be the result of her fear of madness, seemed to have an 'Aristotelian inevitability' about it. Clive and Frances exchanged sad letters; 'I can't be sure she was unwise,' he wrote. Frances rather agreed: 'It is impossible not to think of the dead (I at least find now) without a certain envy, but for all of you, and for numbers of others in lesser degree, the loss and pain must be immeasurable.' She pressed him to visit them again, and mentioned that since the death of her 'aged mother' she had been finding distraction from gloomy war news in sorting family papers, 'reading curious letters written to my father by Charles Darwin on the subject of Earth Worms and Butter-wort'.

By now, Frances found that she did not react quite so strongly against Churchill's rousing speeches as she used to; she wondered if it was him who had changed, or her. Probably, she decided, her; she recognised that she felt 'both more detached and more fatalistic than I did last year'. Clive came to stay, bringing Angelica – the first time she had seen Frances since Ray's death. They played the piano and sang together; Frances found her beautiful and gifted. Rollo Woolley paid them another visit; he still felt the war was not worth fighting, while being ready, even willing, to risk his life with the RAF. Frances was moved by his vulnerability, as she was by the desperation of their household help, Joan, whose soldier lover was being sent overseas. When Joan announced that she felt she must leave Ham Spray and go to work in an aeroplane factory in Newbury, Frances and Ralph were both upset – not just because it was inconvenient for them but because they felt so sorry for her. At the same time, Frances knew she would badly miss Joan's help. 'Our life gets more domestic and agricultural, and when Joan goes it may get more so. If only I could cook!' The fact was that Frances, like almost all women of her background, had never yet had to clean or cook for herself. All over the country such women were finding out what a servantless existence was like, and not much liking it. The two girls who replaced Joan did not turn out well; Frances found them lazy and dishonest, and exploded in the diary: 'I'm sick to death of them ... having — and — in the house is like having worms.' But the thought of doing without help was almost as bad.

On the night of 17 June, Frances and Ralph were woken in the night by the sound of armoured cars and lorries; for the next twenty-four hours, they were surrounded by a large contingent of soldiers. At first, Frances felt resentful; but when she went for a walk and found the young soldiers asleep in their vehicles all down the drive, her hostility evaporated. Two days later they had gone and she was off for a cheering day in London, where she bought Parmesan cheese in Soho, visited the tailor for a new tweed suit, took in an exhibition of Vanessa Bell's work at the Leicester Galleries and ate salmon, asparagus and zabaglione with Clive at the Ivy. Afterwards she walked down Gerrard Street, but it was so full of rubble that the old bookshop was barely recognisable. Such outings were a mixture of pleasure and pain, but never, to Frances, a source of guilt. To enjoy herself was to triumph over the hated war.

Towards the end of June, out of the blue, a letter arrived for Ralph from Gerald. Since the beginning of the war the Partridges and the Brenans had met frequently and amicably; Ham Spray and Aldbourne were only a bicycle ride apart. Now, prompted partly by Hitler's sudden invasion of Russia and partly by his recent return from a Home Guard camp in the West Country, Gerald's emotions about the war overflowed into a fierce attack on his old friend. As he wrote in a notebook, he considered that the war could have been avoided, or won quickly, had Britain confronted Hitler earlier; such thoughts led to 'a rage I can hardly contain against Chamberlain, Baldwin, appeasers – and, unspoken, Ralph'.

It was not unspoken for long. First Gerald made a statement calculated to disgust Ralph and Frances, proclaiming that 'every German woman and child killed is a contribution to the future safety and happiness of Europe'. Next, he attacked pacifists: 'poor creatures, I think . . . they feel sad because they are cut off by their beliefs from other people'. Frances and Ralph decided that the best way to deal with the letter (and to annoy Gerald) was to ignore it. Over the summer, the Partridges continued to send the Brenans fruit and vegetables; mutual friends like Julia reported that Gerald would enquire keenly about Ralph's reaction to his attack and seem disappointed when told that he had found it rather funny. When Julia told Gerald in September that the Partridges assumed he did not want to see them she stirred up another broadside. 'Your particular brand of calling yourself a pacifist, and at the same time associating yourself with the aggressors rather than with the attacked, is very disagreeable to me,' wrote Gerald to Ralph on 28 September. 'I think your ideas need sorting . . . you would feel better if you had some work to do and left your seat in the stalls.' He advised Ralph to take a turn as a fireman or an air raid warden, 'because danger is a tonic to you and the tremendous warmth of your feelings in this war is in part, I believe, due to a repressed desire to be an actor in it'. Ralph, he concluded, was among the 'pacifist isolationists, who I consider by their folly and shortsightedness have helped to produce this war'. Even so, 'there is not the slightest diminution in my affection for you and Frances'.

At this point, Ralph and Frances decided that contact between the two households had to cease. Frances fumed in her diary, and admitted that she felt sad as well as angry; she could hardly believe 'that the only person to pillory us in any way for our pacifist views is Gerald, almost Ralph's oldest friend'. It was certainly ironic, but not altogether surprising. Gerald's long-standing rivalry with Ralph, the tangle of memories and jealousies they shared, and his nervous, volatile temperament, drove him towards confrontations as much for personal as political reasons. Frances remained determined not to lose touch with Gamel; they exchanged letters, and even met once or twice for lunch in Hungerford, but Ralph and Gerald did not meet or communicate again until the war was over.

During the autumn, Frances and Ralph managed a holiday at Solva, in South Wales, with Burgo, where they went seal-spotting and swam naked, and the war seemed wonderfully far away. Ham Spray's fruit and vegetable harvest was splendid; Frances gave the Padels thirty pounds of plums.

By the river and the pool: Frances, Ralph and Lytton

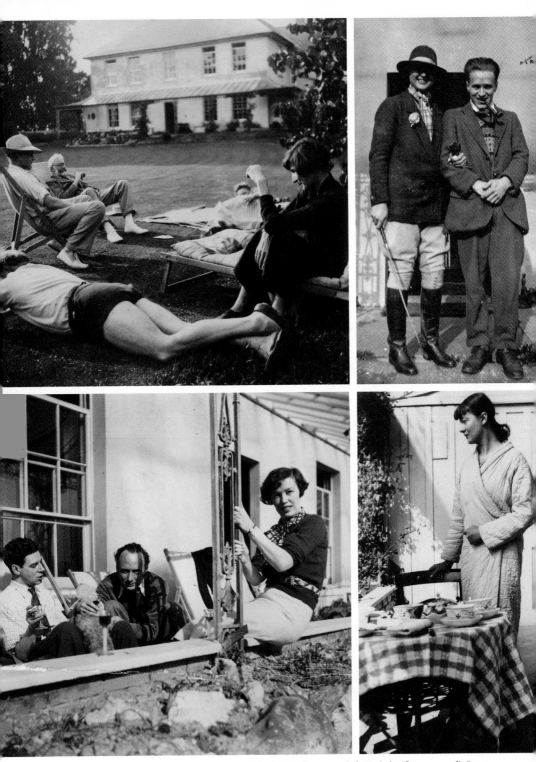

On the grass and the verandah, Ham Spray. *Clockwise from top left:* Ralph (foreground) James Strachey (with beard) Alix Strachey (in black); Henrietta Bingham and Stephen Tomlin; Julia Strachey; (left to right) Raymond Mortimer, Patrick Kinross, Frances

Ham Spray games. *Clockwise from top left:* tea by the pool with Catherine Carrington (centre); Alix Strachey takes aim; Frances and Ralph at bowls; Frances with parasol; Julia Strachey, Stephen Tomlin and Carrington in the shrubbery

At Charleston, summer 1928: (left to right) Frances, Quentin Bell, Julian Bell, Duncan Grant, Clive Bell, Bobo Mayor, Roger Fry (with glasses) and Raymond Mortimer

On the beach in Spain: Rachel MacCarthy, Ralph, Janie Bussy

On the rocks: Frances (top) and Rachel

The photographers: Barbara Ker-Seymer, Ralph, Frances

Return to the battlefields: Ralph and the La Roy family, April 1932. Frances thought the girl on the far left could have been his daughter

Frances and Ralph, 1930s

Ralph, Frances and Janetta Woolley, late 1930s

River bathing with Augustus John's daughters, Poppet (left) and Vivien

Cutting Janetta's hair, Ham Spray 1936

Lytton Burgo Partridge, born 1935. *Clockwise from top left:* with his mother; with Janetta and Eddie Sackville-West (captioned by Frances, 'Music, Poetry and Innocence'); with Tiger; with his grandmother, Mam; with his father

War at Ham Spray. *Clockwise from top left:* bandage practice with Anne and Heywood Hill; the Nichols family; Burgo mushrooming with Rollo Woolley; Julia Strachey and Lawrence Gowing

Encouraged by their musical life, she took up playing the violin again; having given up lessons at the age of thirteen, she found it hard at first, but was soon looking forward greatly to their sessions.

At the beginning of December 1941, it was announced that men aged between forty and fifty-one were to register for military service, and Frances' heart sank. Ralph, at forty-seven, was faced with a decision. 'I rather feel I must testify as a conscientious objector,' he told her. 'It's a bore, and one can't guess how it will affect our local life.' Soon afterwards came the news of Pearl Harbor, bringing America into the war; to Ralph, this was exciting and positive news, while once again Frances could only feel despair. As the war expanded, all she could see was that 'the possibility of pacifying this vast inflammation must surely become even more remote'. Another winter closed in and the last of Ham Spray's domestic help disappeared. 'I am now doing all the housework,' wrote Frances, 'which fills me with a glow of virtue and makes me enormously warm.' Julia annoyed them both by complaining bitterly about the cold.

Two good things happened in January 1942: Frances bought herself a violin, and Alice came to work at Ham Spray, bringing with her a small boy and a husband on leave from the army. Even so, life was dreary; food and petrol rationing dominated conversation, and she felt herself becoming mentally lazy – a condition she abhorred – and worrying that she was boring company for Ralph. She felt the war machine grinding towards them, but when she tried to talk to Ralph about what they should do his reply was to wait until something actually happened. Meanwhile he was reading books about the care of pigs, as Ham Spray was about to acquire two from the Biddesden estate. She concentrated on looking after any friend who needed them: Boris and Maroussa came from London exhausted and tense (he was working as a Russian translator) and Janetta, whose relationship with Humphrey Slater was in trouble. In late April, Jan Woolley reappeared, thinner and more fragile than ever; she had made her way back to England from France via Lisbon. She recovered at Ham Spray before moving to London.

Early in May 1942 Ralph and Frances were suddenly summoned to London by Bunny to be witnesses at his marriage to Angelica. They set off not knowing whether Vanessa, Duncan or Clive would be there; but Bunny and Ray's younger son William was the only other guest at the Ivy for lunch before the register office. Some weeks later at Ham Spray Clive told them about Bunny's arrival at Charleston to announce the marriage. This was the first time, Frances wrote, that Clive 'dropped all pretence that Angelica was his daughter'; he described Duncan as full of resentment and Vanessa as desperately hurt. When Angelica had telephoned her parents to tell them the wedding was the next day, Vanessa said it was too short notice for them to attend. Frances had always thought the conspiracy of silence a mistake, but she felt for Vanessa. 'R said she hadn't a leg to stand on, and no more she had, but I see her as painfully caught in the pincer movement of Duncan's resentment and Bunny's victory.'

There was something disquieting about the marriage. Everyone in the Charleston circle had watched Bunny's advance on the beautiful adolescent he had known since birth; they all knew of his early love affair with her real father, Duncan Grant; they had all helped to support the fiction, maintained until Angelica was eighteen, that her father was indeed her mother's legal husband, Clive Bell. Those most concerned with Angelica – Vanessa, Clive, Duncan and Virginia – were all troubled when they realised Bunny was in earnest; but although they hated the idea and feared for Angelica's future happiness, they were caught in the trap of their own long-held and long-practised beliefs in non-interference, and the superiority of love over convention. By the time this passiveness had allowed Angelica to fall in love with Bunny, the damage was done; only if she had known the whole truth from the start might she have thought differently about his ardent pursuit of her. As she herself was to write, reflecting on the whole story, her parents – all three of them, for Clive always behaved to her as a father – chose, by their withholding of the truth about their relations with each other and with Bunny, an oddly timorous and conventional path, which was to lead to great emotional difficulties in the future.

Meanwhile, Angelica and Bunny were happy, and after their eldest daughter Amaryllis was born in 1943 relations with Charleston were soon mended. As for Frances and Ralph, their instinctive support of beleaguered lovers was strengthened by their equally instinctive loyalty to Bunny as an old, even if sometimes deplorable, friend. The links between Ham Spray and Hilton remained as strong as ever.

They continued to discuss the war with Clive, who had been seeing Maynard Keynes, who was much involved with the war effort and 'very thick' with Churchill. Both of them, Clive reported, were full of optimism about the war. For all Frances' admiration for Keynes' intelligence (she would always say he was the cleverest man she ever knew), she was not impressed when Clive quoted him as saying the war had to last at least another year 'because we haven't got our plans for the peace ready'. She was finding her music a great comfort and distraction; she would pedal off to rehearse in the Padels' quartet with her violin in a rucksack. 'If this is to be a regular feature of life it is going to make a great difference to it.'

Their other pacifist friend, Lawrence Gowing, already registered as a conscientious objector, had now decided that he would accept Civil Defence work when required; and when Frances was summoned to register for National Service she too complied. In fact, only the most absolutist among pacifists refused to obey any orders that might further the war effort. Of the 60,000 or so conscientious objectors of the Second World War (four times as many as in the First), only about 3,000 were granted total exemption, usually on religious grounds; the rest were required to accept noncombative duties like ambulance driving, or whatever civilian duties they were assigned to. If they declined, they could be sent to prison; about 6,500 were, and they were often badly treated. Taking Burgo into Hungerford, Frances waited her turn with the other women. She was asked about her household and how many people she catered for, and informed that if directed to a job she would be legally obliged to take it. In fact, she never was; having a child of seven was usually considered exemption enough.

Although it was rare, in the Second World War, for pacifists to be considered pariahs, not everyone in Ralph and Frances' circle regarded them kindly. When the opinionated Marjorie Strachey came for a weekend in August, Frances was 'slightly afraid of a skirmish . . . she had evidently heard of our views and was I think surprised not to find us more provocative'. All was well until the last day, when Marjorie suddenly announced that 'all conscientious objectors ought to be dropped by parachute in Germany since they wish to be ruled by the Nazis'. Ralph refused to rise and a row was averted; but later Frances felt indignant. 'Does she ever remember that both Lytton and James and most of their closest friends were COs in the last war and would she want them to be treated likewise?' Marjorie was too eccentric to be taken seriously, but Ralph and Frances sometimes sensed an undercurrent of criticism from others. After a particularly busy few days, entertaining Raymond, the Hills, the Nichols (none of them, except Phyllis Nichols, pacifists) and a stray American sergeant, they found themselves reflecting on their position. 'There is, we conclude, very little pleasure in hospitality to those who disapprove of us, and don't want us to have the very things we are trying to share with them. Eating with relish our home-grown honey and fruit, they will with equal relish imply that we shouldn't be allowed to have it.'

By early in October, Alice had moved on. The pattern all over the country was the same; women wanted to do their bit, and preferred the companionship of factory work to domestic service. From then on, Frances took over the cooking. Ralph was kind about her efforts, remarking helpfully, 'For a woman not to be able to cook is like impotence in a man.'

Saxon came to stay as usual; Frances noted his frayed suit, black button boots, and how he would carry a volume of Pindar around with him. One evening Ralph opened a bottle of Corton Charlemagne 28 in honour of one of Lytton's oldest and gentlest friends.

At last, in late October, Ralph was notified that he was likely to be called up for military service, perhaps the Home Guard. He put off his decision about how to respond until after the killing of the two pigs, a gruesome event which involved everyone at Ham Spray. After the extraction of the entrails – 'strange marine looking objects, pink and frilly' – they all sat up late making brawn, 'like the witches in Macbeth', picking out eyes and teeth – before the carcass was stored in the bath, in what became known for ever after as the Pig's Bathroom.

Frances was well aware that her 'very busy practical existence' made it easier for her not to think too much about difficult matters – principally how Ralph should behave now that he was being put on the spot. In fact, she felt that she should not try to influence him, and it was only when he asked her directly for her opinion over the washing-up that she realised exactly what she did think. 'I hoped he would refuse, not because I fail to realise that it may well lead to local awkwardness, nor because the matter has much significance; indeed it would be far less trouble to accept. But because it seems somehow not *digne* to act in a way that doesn't correspond to principles that are seriously held.' Anyway she regarded the Home Guard as faintly ridiculous, with its hats decorated with leaves, and why should her Ralph become just another sausage in the sausage machine?

Feeding themselves and their friends lavishly on pork and bacon, they waited to hear what would happen next. Ralph sent off a form stating that he was a conscientious objector, and received a letter asking him to state his reasons. During November, the defeat of Rommel in North Africa made a successful outcome seem possible for the first time in a year or more, and Frances confessed herself 'profoundly moved' when the French fleet at Toulon destroyed itself rather than surrender to the Germans. They began to prepare for another Christmas; the local postman, who doubled as a conjuror, Professor Frisco, was booked for Burgo's Christmas party. Then Ralph received a letter summoning him before a tribunal in Bristol that very day. He said he was not 'consciously' worried about it; Frances certainly was.

The weekend before the tribunal, Frances' soldier brother-in-law Dick Rendel came on a rare visit. She well recalled his unspoken anguish as a young infantry officer in the First World War; he was now a colonel in the Second. Stationed at Dover during Dunkirk, he told them of the dazed and staggering wounded and boats awash with blood. Now, he was part of a board interviewing would-be officers, where one of his colleagues was Frances' old admirer Adrian Stephen, whose psychoanalytic skills were required and who referred to the soldiers as patients. When they discussed Ralph's position and the tribunal they found Colonel Rendel 'tolerant, sensitive and understanding'.

When the time came, Professor Frisco was a great success, though for Frances the day was 'unreal and dreamlike' after Ralph set off early for Bristol. When he came back, his first words were 'no luck at all'. He had found the judges 'hostile and angry'; he had not been given a chance to explain his views. Instead they lectured him on the Treaty of Versailles and told him that he was obviously just 'a war-weary veteran of the last war'. After only ten minutes, the tribunal rejected his application to be registered as a conscientious objector. Next morning, after a bad night, Ralph and Frances decided not to give up. Frances felt that he had not been properly prepared: 'How I wish we had discussed it more, and rehearsed the statements he must get out.' The next day Ralph wrote to their solicitor and friend, Craig Macfarlane, about launching an appeal.

Thirteen

Trials of War (2), 1943–1945

The first weeks of 1943 were dominated, for Frances, by her determination that this time she would not stand back but would do all in her power to help Ralph with his appeal. It had been foolish, she realised, to assume that no tribunal could possibly doubt his sincerity; and when they talked the matter over with their advisers, Julia and Lawrence, who had found lodgings nearby, they pointed out that Ralph's solid appearance and his broad-shouldered, pipe-smoking, confident manner had probably counted against him. The important thing now was to work out how to enable the judges to fit Ralph into one of their preconceived categories, which meant convincing them of the moral and ethical strength of his beliefs. Craig Macfarlane encouraged them to round up references and letters of support.

Meanwhile, on 11 January the cost of war was brought home to them in the sharpest way possible. Rollo Woolley had gone missing in North Africa, and his father, who was on the spot, believed he had been killed. 'I felt no surprise,' wrote Frances sadly, 'Rollo always seemed to have a doomed air.' They went up to London and saw Jan and Janetta, whose courage was exemplary. Janetta had left Humphrey Slater for Kenneth Sinclair Loutit, a young left-wing doctor, also a veteran of the Spanish Civil War, and she was now pregnant. Frances was worried about her, and also about Burgo, who had learned too much about death too early; one day when he could not find her, he thought she was dead and burst into tears. Grimly she cleaned baths and peeled potatoes (from now until the end of the war they only had occasional help with the house and in the garden; they were luckier than most) and repeated stubbornly in her diary her 'absolute conviction that progress can never be achieved by force or violence, only by reason and persuasion'.

While Ralph collected testimonials – from Clive Bell, Phil Nichols (now Ambassador to the Czech government in London, he told Ralph he would write anything he liked), Colonel Rendel, and Lord David Cecil – the Padels came up on their bicycles to express their solidarity. By now, Ralph's rejection by the Bristol tribunal had been reported in the local press; on the whole, Frances thought, it was 'comforting to be able to appear in our true colours'. She felt defiant; it was up to them to 'keep the good old flag of Bohemia flying and realise that what "the world" thinks of one matters not at all'. Julia, meanwhile, had also been interviewed and declared herself willing to undertake agricultural or civil defence work; but when she revealed that she was writing a book, she was granted a postponement. Ralph's appeal was set for 8 March in London.

February was not a good month. On the Russian front, the siege of Stalingrad brought horrific details of death and starvation; at home, bombs fell on Newbury, hitting a church and a school and killing around twenty people. Julia was suddenly summoned to look after her father, Oliver, who was now working with the codebreakers at Bletchley; he had collapsed with a heart attack. Frances and Ralph did their best to console a distracted Lawrence, and once again found themselves discussing the limits of family loyalty. Frances reaffirmed the Old Bloomsbury credo. 'I agree with R', she wrote, 'in questioning the rights of the moribund over the young and strong, and of blood relations over the friends of one's choice.'

Then on 16 February, Janetta rang up to say that her mother had died in hospital after a bout of flu. Although Jan was never strong, her death was unexpected; but, as Frances wrote, 'there had been no more news of Rollo, and she had clearly lost the will to survive'. Janetta and Kenneth spent the following weekend at Ham Spray. Hopelessly alienated from her father, Janetta had within a month lost her mother and probably her brother, and neither Frances nor Ralph felt Kenneth was the right man for her. They had good reason for feeling that she needed them, and the security that Ham Spray represented, more than ever.

By this time, for all her brave words, Frances was uncomfortably aware of a coolness in local feeling since she and Ralph had been exposed as pacifists. It was a younger friend, Judy Hubback, who brought it home to her, reporting an exchange with one of the local grandes dames, Mrs Hill. When Judy mentioned that she was giving Burgo extra lessons, she provoked a rant. 'You, a serving man's wife, teaching the child of a conscientious objector! I'm going to have nothing more to do with them myself.' The news of Mrs Hill's disapproval bothered her and Ralph more than she later cared to admit, giving them 'a dose of persecution mania'. It was not pleasant, she discovered, to be disapproved of, even by people whose standards you despised. 'I had half-guessed Mrs Hill would react in this way, though I never dreamed she would include Burgo in her ostracism. But she seemed a nice and humorous character, who genuinely liked us I'm sure, and whom we liked. We have quite gone out of our way to be nice to her in the past

... I suppose that if she talks to everyone in the village in this strain she will work up feeling against us.'

Unsettled by all this, when on the following day another group of soldiers on manoeuvres arrived at Ham Spray, Frances could hardly bear it. Because she is normally so level-headed, even in her diary, her moments of irrational emotion stand out. She loathed the sound of their 'bestial muffled shouts' and felt a visceral distaste at the thought of their physical presence in her house. 'They would make a fearful mess and smell, use our sponges and leave VD on the towels and our charming Ham Spray would be sullied by them.' But again Ralph, who sympathised with soldiers, calmed her down, and she found herself feeling almost fond of them by the time they left.

At last, on 8 March, the day of the appeal arrived. Both Frances and Ralph were very nervous; she tried to hide her anxiety in case it made him feel worse. They took the train to London and met Craig Macfarlane and Raymond for lunch at the Ivy; it was particularly good of Raymond to support his friend despite disagreeing with his opinions. After lunch Frances went to see Janetta in her new flat overlooking Regent's Park, shared with Cyril Connolly and his girlfriend Lys Lubbock from *Horizon*, where Janetta occasionally worked. She waited for news, watching as air raid sirens shattered the peaceful scene – nannies, children, swans on the lake. When Ralph appeared, his first remark was 'Perfect – money for jam.' This time the judges had been courteous, understood his statement and believed it. They asked him a few simple questions, he made them laugh. 'It was over.'

Ralph's statement to the appeal tribunal was short and clear. He had become a pacifist after the last war out of 'a conviction that wars never lead to peace but only to the next war'. He believed war to be 'wicked as well as irrational ... wrong in itself and all its consequences'. The organised violence of war, moreover, was 'infinitely worse than individual acts of violence because for political reasons it is exonerated by the state and even glorified'. He respected the authority of the state, but 'I claim the right to refuse to take lessons in murder'. Finally, he had no objection to taking part in civil defence, but felt that he was more use to the community 'producing and distributing food' in the 'remote part of Wiltshire' where he lived. This is what he proceeded to do. Frances was tremendously proud of him, and would say, to the end of her life, that she agreed with every word. She had, after all, helped him to write it.

Frances had never doubted that it was right for Ralph to stand up for their joint beliefs, no matter what the consequences. In fact, local reaction turned out to be mild, and although Frances noted, a week after Ralph's triumph, that she disliked feeling 'embarrassment, and the thought that

I might not be able to pass off an unexpected meeting with Mrs Hill', there were never any difficult confrontations. The strongest local reaction was entirely positive and came from the Padels, who were delighted to greet the Partridges as kindred spirits, and began to try to tempt Frances with communist literature – a hopeless venture, as she soon made clear to them. As for Gerald, silence reigned.

With the tension of Ralph's tribunals receding, Frances resigned herself to the routine of Ham Spray life and her domestic duties. Burgo's company gave her great pleasure; they would dig away happily together in the garden or on the downs, where he hoped to find prehistoric treasures. Around the tenth anniversary of her marriage, in March 1943, she found herself reflect-ing on how their lives had changed, and how they had become 'much more securely embedded in it, like nuts in toffee'. Then, they lived for pleasure, 'and a very good thing to live for'; only sometimes it had been hard to know whether the country or London could best provide it. Much though she disliked housework and cooking, she had come to find a certain satisfaction in not always depending on other people. 'The fact is I am now an ordinary person with a job, just as I was in bookshop days. If you think of domesticity as a job only, the groans of modern housewives seem exaggerated, because after all what could be pleasanter, more under one's control and interlarded with off moments.' Frances had always been good at making the best of things, and despised self-pity.

It was often some remark of Julia's, whose originality delighted her, that led Frances to personal ruminations in her diary. Thus although Julia too was taken with Burgo at this age (he was eight that summer) and told Frances how delightful he was, it was also Julia who talked of mother love 'as if it were some prehistoric monster' and felt that women who chose to have children had no right to complain about what a burden they could be. Julia also took it upon herself to discover about the menopause and enlighten her friend, rather as she had done about the facts of life when they were children. The news was not good: 'I've been collecting facts about it, my dear, and it's evidently terrible what we have in store.' Middle age was advancing on them, and although Frances, more secure than ever in Ralph's love (and from now on all traces of infidelities disappear from the record, so if he continued to have affairs it was with more discretion), minded much less than Julia, she pondered that summer on the difference between sexual and maternal love, and whether the one inevitably displaced the other.

She had been disconcerted to find, while dancing with Phil Nichols at a nightclub in London after the two couples had dined together, that 'a flash of mutual attraction' passed between them. This, she soon decided, was 'more sentimental and nostalgic than physical' – and Frances deplored sentiment and nostalgia; soon she was feeling 'sheepish' and longing to discuss her feelings with Ralph. She decided not to, however, and by the time the Nicholses next came down to Ham Spray she was able to note firmly in her diary that she now found Phil 'totally unattractive'. Frances' fidelity to Ralph was absolute.

With Janetta's baby due in the early summer, Frances felt more protective towards her than ever. There are signs, too, that the transformation of Janetta from free spirit into mother unnerved the Partridges; certainly Frances' diary shows a preoccupation with the disadvantages of motherhood. Janetta herself shared – or had learned – some of these reservations, telling Frances that she was determined not to become a tiresomely adoring mother. 'One finds very few people these days to hold out against children and say they aren't suitable company for adults,' observed Frances approvingly. Wartime summers followed a pattern: a visit to Devon, a weekend with Raymond Mortimer and his friend Eardley Knollys, a handsome man then working for the National Trust, on the Thames near Henley, and many visitors at Ham Spray. Ralph taught Burgo to swim; he had a new friend, a dull little girl whose visits depressed his parents. 'Childishness as such is boring except in certain kittenish aspects,' wrote Frances firmly. They rejoiced in James and Alix's annual visit; James was now complaining that there was a dearth of neurotics, and that those there were tended to be snapped up by the many refugee analysts. Alix entertained them with tales of her eccentric old mother, a crusader against the modern lavatory.

During 1943, it gradually became apparent that the tide of the war was turning in the Allies' favour. Bells rang for victory in North Africa; the Allies landed in Italy; Judy Hubback's husband came home on leave. In October, Bunny and Angelica had a daughter, the first of four. Nicholas Henderson, always known as Nicko, Barbara Bagenal's nephew whom they had known since boyhood, visited his parents nearby on leave from Cairo and told the Partridges that Ham Spray was known to remain 'the only civilised house in England'.

It was not only civilised, it was unusually well-informed. On 1 November, as Frances wrote in her diary, 'I opened a letter from Bunny at breakfast and out fell a bombshell.' He was writing to ask if Angelica and the baby could come to Ham Spray, as he had a 'hunch' about something and wanted them to be out of London. Frances and Ralph immediately realised the implications: Bunny, working at the Air Ministry, had secret information, about a new German attack. She felt in an impossible position. There were others in London she would want to warn – Janetta and her baby, and Julia, who had anyway heard most of the letter as Frances read it aloud before realising what was in it. 'Damn it all,' wrote Frances, 'we aren't playing this beastly war game of Bunny's.' Nevertheless, she wrote immediately to Bunny to say that Angelica and her baby could stay as long as they wanted.

In the event, they decided to go to Charleston instead; and Frances did not have to decide whether or not to warn other friends, as rumours were already rife about a German secret weapon, perhaps a giant rocket to be launched from the French coast. Lawrence christened Bunny's hunch Bunny's hutch, and soon Frances was writing, 'I am beginning to suspect that Bunny's Hutch is everyone's Hutch.' Talk of the secret weapon gradually died down, to be replaced in the press by great agitation over the release of the Mosleys from prison. Frances' only comment was: 'As neither Ralph nor I accept the principle that people should ever be shut up for their principles or imprisoned without trial, the question doesn't arise for us.'

At the beginning of 1944, spirits at Ham Spray were low. They all had colds, and their daily developed flu and left, never to return. When Ralph attacked Frances for reading the *New Statesman* at breakfast rather than talking to him, she snapped; if he wanted her to be human, she told him, he had better find her some help. To her amazement, he soon did; 'What joy! What comfort!' Her music was her lifeline; she played quartets regularly with the Padels, and when Angelica came to stay they managed the Bach Double Violin Concerto together. London was still being battered by bombs. When they went up to London for another Ivy lunch with Bunny, Angelica, Clive and Raymond, they found the familiar Great Western Hotel at Paddington boarded up and their London friends under great strain. The whole country was on edge, waiting for the Second Front.

Then, early in May, something totally unexpected happened. Noel Carrington was by now working for Penguin's founder, Allen Lane, and through him Frances was approached to write the text of a new complete Flora of the British Isles, to accompany illustrations by a talented young botanical artist, Richard (Dicky) Chopping. Frances had been a keen amateur botanist since Bedales, and all her friends were used to her collecting and identifying wild flowers wherever she went; she was instantly drawn to the idea, especially after she met her prospective collaborator, who turned out to be a tall, good-looking, amiable young man not long out of art school. Frances and Ralph liked him at once, and he liked them; it was the start not just of a working relationship but of a true friendship. Dicky was already in a relationship with another young artist, Denis Wirth Miller; he seemed to Frances to show 'all the practical companionability of many buggers without their silliness'. On his first visit he and Frances sat up late planning how they would work, keen to get down to it as soon as possible. Looking back, Frances was aware of her lack of qualifications: 'I can't imagine how I was bold enough to take on the job.'

Back in Devon that summer, Denis and Dicky joined them. During their stay at the farm they heard the news that the Second Front had at last begun, and that the British and Americans were crossing the Channel to Normandy. They spent peaceful days walking and plant-collecting, but there was renewed trouble between her and Ralph over Burgo. These rows had a pattern: Burgo would annoy Ralph, who would come down very hard on him; he would naturally turn to Frances, who would find it hard to resist him. This would annoy Ralph even more; he was beginning to find his son over-sensitive, and too dependent on his mother. Frances was torn between them; she would later say that the only bad times in her relationship with Ralph were over Burgo. It would have been better, she sometimes thought, had their only child been a daughter. Ralph could not help wanting his son to be more like him, less nervous and more sporting. Frances knew Burgo's faults; she could see that he had 'an anxious and rather hysterical nature' and was inclined to be lazy; but then Ralph could be 'unreasonably fierce and unforgiving'. The row died down; there were to be more in the future.

When they got back to Ham Spray, their London friends were ringing up with the unnerving news that the city was now under attack from pilotless aircraft. Hitler's new weapon, the V-1 rockets (nicknamed doodlebugs), were also known to Ralph and Frances as 'chaps' after the *New Statesman* reported a remark from an English village: 'and then I looked up and there was another chap coming along'; but they felt like the last straw, and another wave of refugees began. For Frances and Ralph, this meant Janetta, her new baby Nicolette, and Julia settling in with them again, and others coming and going; much though they loved them all, they sometimes longed for time off. Burgo showed signs of being jealous of Nicolette, and Julia could be maddening, reminding Frances that she too knew what it was to run a household without help when married to Stephen Tomlin (just the two of them in a small cottage with a resident maid, as Frances could not forbear to observe). It was a tense summer: a doodlebug fell to earth a mile from the house, and Ralph had a violent row with the farm next door over their shared water tank. Everyone's hearts lifted when Paris was liberated in August, but there were new rumours of a final horror to be unleashed by Hitler – another kind of rocket, or perhaps gas. And early in September, Janetta learned that Rollo's body had been found. She fell into a state of quiet despair; even Frances found her sadness 'almost oppressive'. As for Burgo, it was time to send him to a proper school, and he was to start at Newbury Grammar in September.

Soon the tearful scenes began again, and Frances was at her wits' end. This was not a situation where reason could help her much; nothing is less reasonable than a frantic child. This time, though, Ralph was at his best: patient, kind and supportive. She stood firm with Burgo; no matter how many hysterical scenes he made, he had to go to school. Faced with her furious son, Frances retreated into music. 'The happiest time today was spent with my fiddle. Burgo's obstinacy and hostility to me are a great weight on my spirits.'

As the year declined, and the sixth winter of the war closed in, Frances found herself more conscious than ever that her youth was over. She compared herself to Janetta, who for all her melancholy was so young and so beautiful; then she was found to need a minor gynaecological operation. Frances tried hard to be realistic and positive about growing older, but everything she wrote around this time indicates sadness and unease. The power to attract men could not last; but 'it must be appalling not to be able to convert it into the pleasure of being liked, or interest in other people, or enjoyment of the attractiveness of the young. It's as impossible to regret the passing of youth all the time as it is to grieve all the time for someone dead.' Impossible, but not unnatural. Another pig was killed, and the year ended with a wave of friends to help eat it: the Cecils, Boris and Maroussa, the Wests, Dicky Chopping. And Burgo, to his parents' delight, emerged from the ordeal of his first term with flying colours, judged to be intellectually three years ahead of his age.

The start of 1945 was once again fiercely cold. Burgo went back to school without too much fuss; Frances fretted about Janetta, whose relationship with Kenneth was looking uncertain, especially after he was sent out to Belgrade. She consoled herself by reading Milton, and with a new cat, Tiger. Isobel Strachey amused them with louche stories of her American lovers, one of whom sent her pornographic letters and suggested she masturbate during his absence, 'but I'm much too laaazy'. The Russians advanced on Berlin, and Ralph and Frances had a conversation about which one of them would die first, which made them both cry. But her spirits lifted with the 'vegetable rush' of early spring and the knowledge that the end of the war could not be far off.

The last stages of the war forced her to face the horrors she had managed to ignore for so long. On 16 March, Frances recorded her reaction to the news reports that reached Britain when the American forces arrived at the concentration camps. She was confronted with 'appalling revelations of German atrocities now coming to light: mass execution of Jews in gas-chambers.' Anyone who remained a pacifist during the Second World War had to face the question: when did you first realise what Hitler was doing to the Jews? To the end of her life Frances' answer to this was the same: not until the end of the war. If pressed as to whether, had she known earlier – and plenty of people in her circle did – she could have remained a pacifist, she would reply that she would have been in favour of assassinating Hitler, but not of going to war, which she regarded as another name for mass murder. Sometimes she would add that there was evidence, after all, that it was the war that led Hitler to decide to exterminate the Jews. In March 1945, she discussed the matter with Phil Nichols, who was on his way to Czechoslovakia. He expressed astonishment that 'the man in the street' had not reacted more strongly to the horrifying discoveries at Belsen and Auschwitz. 'Probably because the world has for several years been one huge atrocity,' was Frances' response. To her and Ralph, there was little difference between the man who controlled the gas chambers and the man who dropped bombs on German cities. Both were obeying orders, and both were murderers.

A few weeks later, on her way with Ralph and Burgo to a picnic by a mill-pond, she picked up the newspapers in Newbury and was confronted by photographs showing piles of naked, emaciated corpses. They arrived at the millstream, and sat eating their hard-boiled eggs and watercress. 'The day was unbelievably beautiful, the grass positively sparkled, heat poured from the blue sky – but none of this could dispel the horror and disgust brought from the newspapers. They haunted me all day. I feel as though the world's sanity had received a fatal blow, and I can't stop thinking of it and all it implies.'

As the 'vast Wagnerian finale' to the war ground on, Saxon came to stay as usual. The blackout was lifted, Ralph sat over the wireless, and on 1 May came the news that Hitler was dead. Saxon went on discussing the runners in the Guineas. On 7 May a neighbour, phoning Frances about the school run, told her that Churchill would announce the end of the war in Europe the next day. 'So here it was at last,' wrote Frances. 'Oddly enough, the news of peace actually brought a *sense* of peace, very refreshing like a good drink of water to a thirsty person.' On VE Day in Newbury the flags were out, and all the little girls had red, white and blue bows in their hair.

The next three months were in some ways a phoney peace, a time of waiting, to match the Phoney War of 1939–40. Until Japan admitted defeat, the war was far from over; and although it was wonderful to be able to use petrol just to go off for a picnic, Frances felt agitated and unsettled. Burgo's mind was still running on death; after a walk round a churchyard he couldn't stop talking about it. 'Why I'm interested in dying is that I simply can't imagine it and long to know what it can be like.' She was eager to emerge from the Ham Spray cocoon, and wrote to Julia, 'We rustic mice feel very much out of the way now that civilisation has begun again in London. I suddenly feel there are so many things I want to do, exhibitions of pictures to see, Britten's new opera to hear.' Julia told Frances that she felt drained by the war, 'like a sheet of old newspaper or pressed dried grass'; Frances agreed that the advent of peace had been 'a severe shock to all our nervous systems'. Up in London, Bunny met Janetta at a party and was bowled over by her beauty; Angelica had just given birth to their second daughter, Henrietta.

Frances and Ralph reacted to the arrival of peace in different ways. She felt 'possessed with a demon of relentless energy' while he, she noticed, was in low spirits. Perhaps, she thought, he had inherited his father's tendency to melancholy; but she sometimes wondered, too, if the lack of an occupation, of any 'creative effort' in his life was bad for him. He had been too busy in practical ways during the war for this to matter; what was he going to do now? Meanwhile he did not appear to mind staying behind to look after Burgo, who had measles, so that Frances could take Janetta to the new Britten opera, *Peter Grimes*, at Sadler's Wells in mid-June. She was thrilled by the music and interested by what she instantly perceived as the underlying theme, 'a plea for the freedom from persecution of homosexuals' – a cause she found entirely sympathetic.

It often struck those who knew him well that Ralph put so much energy and warmth into his friendships precisely because he did not have a demanding enough occupation. Certainly he spent much of his time keeping up with friends, in correspondence and conversation, and now it was the arrival at Ham Spray of a promising newcomer that cheered him as much as anything. On 23 June, Nicko Henderson brought a friend who had just emerged from three years in a prisoner-of-war camp, to supper.

A friend of Nicko's from Oxford, Robert Kee was a thin, dark, vital young man, strikingly attractive and intelligent; both Ralph and Frances took to him immediately. He made his prison experiences sound funny, reducing Ralph to helpless laughter; but it was evident that he had been through a great deal. Now he wanted to write, perhaps about the war. Almost at once, Ralph and Frances found themselves wondering if he and Janetta would like each other. 'That's the man for her,' was Ralph's comment. Soon Nicko introduced them at a party in London, and word came back to Ham Spray that they were seeing each other; Kenneth meanwhile wanted an increasingly reluctant Janetta to join him in Belgrade with their daughter. Frances had never really liked Kenneth, or believed he could make Janetta happy; now, she decided that Robert and Janetta were meant for each other. 'I find myself craving to bring these two together in an obsessional way.'

In the general election of July 1945 she and Ralph voted Liberal, as they felt the local Labour candidate had no chance of winning; they were agreeably surprised when Churchill was thrown out and the Labour government elected. Janie Bussy came to stay; she had spent the war in France, and astonished Frances by her bitter hostility to collaborators and especially to Pétain, the disgraced leader of the Vichy regime. To Frances, he was just 'a gaga old man of ninety whose crime is that he made peace'; to her, leaders who preferred peace to war were to be admired, not condemned. Equally, when William Joyce, known as Lord Haw-Haw, who had broadcast German propaganda during the war, was condemned to death for treason Frances did not approve. To her, his only crime was 'to utter his sincere views'. Neither then nor later could Frances understand that such views struck many people as both ignorant and offensive.

At the beginning of August, the Partridge family, accompanied by Dicky and Denis, set off for a combined holiday and botanical expedition to the Scilly Isles. They flew from Penzance, and Frances found the first flight of her life (as it was for all of them) more soothing than alarming, inducing in her 'a most satisfying fatalism'. They hired a boat and explored the islands, delighted by the silvery sand, the wide, empty beaches and the 'unspeakably pure and ice-cold turquoise blue water'. They all swam naked, as usual, though Burgo, now ten, asked Frances anxiously what he should do about his 'personal parts'. She also observed that he had started 'an intoxicated flirtation' with Denis. Although she and Ralph both liked Denis, he was a less sunny character than Dicky, and the young men's relationship was stormy. And already, much though Frances liked her collaborator and respected the perfectionism of his exquisite botanical paintings, she had begun to worry about the time he took to finish each one. 'If Richard is unable to go quicker I shall be dead before the book is finished.'

Then, on 5 August, came the news that the Americans had used a terrible new weapon against Japan. It was clear at once, as Frances realised, that the atomic bombs dropped on Hiroshima and Nagasaki had effects 'incomparably more horrible than anything yet'. They were still in the Scilly Isles a week later, when it became plain that the Japanese were about to surrender; Ralph and Frances were half-asleep when the noise of celebrations in the street made them realise that peace had been declared. Burgo appeared, and snuggled into bed with them. 'The whole world is now at PEACE!' they said to each other, and joined in the celebrations the next night with bonfires and a torchlight procession.

But it was hard to feel truly happy about peace when so much of the news was so ominous. Like many others, Frances found that her belief that humanity was fundamentally decent had been profoundly shaken by the revelation of what the Nazis had done to the Jews; and now, any hope that the world might be safe for a while from the horrors of war was undermined by the implications of the use of atomic weapons. Back at Ham Spray Frances was appalled by the details coming out of Hiroshima and Nagasaki, and by the thought of Burgo growing up into a world which could be so easily destroyed. 'My own instincts lead me to love life,' she wrote, 'but as I read on a desire welled up in me to be dead, and out of this hateful, revolting mad world.' She saw nothing ahead but fear and danger, and 'the earth reduced to a few meteorites and moons circling round in empty space'. As the postwar world looked likely to be even more dangerous than before, what had been the point of the war at all? 'This, then, this great joyless prospect seeded with ghastly explosives, is what the world has torn itself in pieces to produce.' Something in Frances never quite recovered from the realisation; it coloured her outlook for the rest of her life. But for all her lack of confidence in the future, her appetite for life remained exceptionally strong, and she learned, as most thinking people must, to enjoy the good and pleasurable things in life while they lasted.

The end of the war meant that the way was now clear for Ralph and Gerald to mend their friendship, which they did by an exchange of letters towards the end of August. This was followed up by a brief visit to Aldbourne, during which, wrote Frances, 'We talked as if nothing had happened … I can't say I feel very much about this reconciliation, but I am glad it happened.' Through the Brenans, the Partridges now became better and better friends with the writer and critic Victor Pritchett and his wife Dorothy, who were now living near Aldbourne. VSP, as he was known, and Gerald had been drawn together by their mutual passion for Spain; he was a leading light on the *New Statesman*, to which both Ralph and Frances were regular contributors in the postwar years. Though Frances found VSP odd-looking, and wished he would not refer quite so often to his humble origins, she recognised his quality as a writer and, almost more importantly for her, as a talker. Frances had absorbed, from Bloomsbury, the capacity to be sharply critical of her friends; regular visitors to Ham Spray, like Janetta, still recall the alarming way everyone's foibles and weaknesses were exposed and mocked mercilessly by both Ralph and Frances, often while a letter from a victim was read aloud at the breakfast table. Everything and everyone was grist to the mill.

Someone who annoyed Frances around this time was Phil Nichols. As he advanced in his career at the Foreign Office, Frances found him becoming steadily more conventional in his views. When the Nichols came for a night in September, on leave from Prague, a fierce argument broke out over public schools and the Empire, on both of which contentious topics Phil's line was far too 'ambassadorial' for Frances. They also talked a good deal about conditions in Prague, where the Russian presence (Phil described them as 'childlike barbarians') meant Phil's job was of considerable interest and significance.

Later, Frances analysed her aggressive feelings towards her old love in her diary. 'On thinking over my last night's clash with Phil, I think this is what underlies it: it is as if Phil was all the time saying, "You see what a good, valuable, important life I'm leading. Don't you wish you'd had the sense to share it with me?" And I: "I wouldn't have it for worlds and I disrespect all your values."' Even so, Phil's successful public life must have contributed to Frances' half-acknowledged desire for Ralph, whose intelligence and vigour she so admired, to find something constructive to do. Later, she would express her regret that he never really found a proper outlet for his gifts and energies, always ascribing his striking lack of ambition to his experiences as a soldier. Although this reaction was not uncommon in the aftermath of both wars, the fact also remained that between them Ralph and Frances had enough inherited capital for him not to have to work in order to live. He managed their investments successfully, and they both made a little from reviewing and other literary odd jobs, but they managed to live well without needing to earn serious money. Inevitably, this meant they sometimes appeared to be insulated from reality.

Her botanical researches, and Burgo's delightful company (he seemed resigned to school at last), soon cheered Frances up. She was happiest, she knew, with a working routine, and would try to sit at her table upstairs in Lytton's library, where she and Ralph both liked to retreat to read or write, every morning. After a tearful scene with Dicky Chopping (he had calculated that the best he could manage would mean that the Flora would take twelve years to complete, and had so informed Allen Lane). Frances decided to stop fretting and accept the situation. It was enough for her to be able to write, 'the morning flew by studying violets'.

During the autumn, Frances and Ralph realised that their fantasy about Janetta and Robert was becoming a reality with unnerving speed. 'It seems too odd,' she wrote, 'that when one considers two people made for each other, they also should think so.' Kenneth, having realised that something was up, now decided to come to London himself to confront Janetta, and a full-blown emotional drama blew up. Frances and Ralph were as involved in this particular version of the eternal triangle as anyone not directly concerned could possibly have been.

When Janetta arrived at Ham Spray, desperate to discuss the muddle she was in, she soon sensed that Frances and Ralph were not only on her side, but on Robert's. They had both, it seems, fallen for him as quickly and lastingly as they had fallen for her nearly ten years previously, and were already willing this particular love affair to have a happy ending. In any contest between love and duty, there was never much doubt where Ralph and Frances' sympathies would lie; indeed, Frances was surprised to find that Janetta was genuinely still in doubt about what to do. 'She asks why shouldn't one be happy making a life with a person one likes but doesn't love? And she is 23!' (the age, as it happens, when Frances first fell in love with Ralph). Although Janetta wanted their advice, Frances felt they had to be careful not to be 'interfering or dominant', and tried to offer her support whatever she decided to do; but her real feelings overflowed into her diary. Love, she wrote, was by far the most important thing in life – not just the ecstatic love at the start of a relationship, but the quieter, deeper love that a lasting commitment can bring. 'I feel', she wrote, 'Janetta to be capable, if anyone I know is, of such a relation.'

Frances could not help identifying Janetta and Robert with herself and Ralph; to help them on their way to happiness was to relive and validate her own experience. She and Ralph, after twenty years, had moved into the calmer waters of a settled marriage, but it was thrilling to be caught up in the turbulence of an early passionate affair. For Ralph, who had accepted with some difficulty that Janetta could never be his, the identification was more complex, but still strong. If he could not have her, he wanted her to go to a man he considered worthy of her, a man he liked and admired, a younger man he could be close to, even influence. Janetta went back to London to face Kenneth, and Frances prepared for Burgo's half-term. She had invited some young Stracheys for the weekend and a Guy Fawkes party. When, on 2 November, Janetta rang to say that she had decided to leave Kenneth and asked if she and Robert could seek refuge at Ham Spray, the answer was yes.

For the next two weeks, while Janetta disentangled herself from Kenneth, Frances was exhilarated. 'There is something very touching, moving and disquieting', she wrote, 'about having these two young people enacting their drama of All for Love in our house.' She found herself fibbing to Kenneth about Robert's presence; he suspected as much, and found it hard to forgive her. The more they saw of Robert, the more they liked him; never, Frances observed, had Ralph taken so strongly to a younger man. As for Robert, he told Ralph how good it was to feel he had an ally, and wrote to Frances after they all left to say he would go on being grateful to her for the rest of his life. By the middle of November they were gone, to try to make a life together. Ham Spray was peaceful again, but Frances felt sad; she knew perfectly well why. 'In some odd way I feel that this wave of depression derives from the intense emotions and interest caused by Wolfers and Robert and their love affair.' Janetta's happiness and well-being had become more and more important to Frances over the last ten years; now, she invested many hopes and emotions of her own in the success of Janetta's relationship with Robert Kee.

Fourteen

Problems of Peace, 1945–1954

With the war at last over, Burgo managing rather better at school, congenial work to do and Janetta's course set in a new and hopeful direction, Frances had reason to hope that some calm and productive time lay ahead. But it was not long before she realised that peace brought problems all its own. The country was exhausted and impoverished; rationing and restrictions remained severe. Love affairs might have happy endings; wars never did.

The first summer of peace brought Janetta and Robert back to Ham Spray. At first, Frances felt pure delight. 'The presence of Robert and Janetta, both so beautiful and charming, enhances everything for both Ralph and me, and in exactly the same way.' But one day, observing them as they stood talking in the fields, she realised that all was not well. From then on, their relationship was to have dramatic ups and downs, quarrels and rec-onciliations; even after they decided to get married early in 1948, and their daughter Georgina was born, it was clear that the marriage was unstable. Frances knew that she cared almost too much about them, and wondered why. 'Both Janetta and Robert', she wrote, 'still haunt my mind like a tune that half delights and half drives me mad. I don't recognise any other human situation that has in my life affected me in exactly this way; and I find I am unable to sort out the threads which comprise it, nor decide which refer objectively to them – and which more or less to myself, that is to feelings about my own youth.' Her passionate preoccupation with the Kees and their marriage was to persist in a way that could be uncomfortable for her and disconcerting for them.

Through Janetta, Cyril Connolly now reappeared in their lives. He had pursued her since before the war, given her work at *Horizon* and was now sharing the house in Regent's Park with her. There were mixed feelings on both sides, dating back to the 1920s and Cyril's involvement with the MacCarthy family; since then Cyril and Ralph had recognised each other as rivals for Janetta's favour. Cyril nicknamed Ralph the Berkshire Bull, thus neatly suggesting a hefty bucolic seducer; to the Partridges, Cyril appeared physically grotesque, pleased with himself and not to be trusted. Moreover, since editing *Horizon* Cyril's status as a writer and critic had soared, and he had come to represent a fresh, modern intellectual and artistic world which had moved on very distinctly from Bloomsbury (even though an early postwar *Horizon* carried an article in praise of Lytton Strachey). But these worlds were never entirely separate; and Ham Spray, in the later 1940s and 1950s, was a place where they sometimes met.

Through Connolly's friendship with Janetta, the Partridges were put in touch with two new neighbours in the spring of 1948. Mary and Robin Campbell had bought a rambling farmhouse, Stokke, near Great Bedwyn; they had both been married before, and she had two daughters by Philip Dunn, son of the Canadian millionaire Sir James Dunn. Robin Campbell was a handsome, well-connected man from a diplomatic family who had worked for Reuters in Berlin before the war, in which he joined SOE and lost a leg in a famous attempt to kidnap Rommel in North Africa. He ended the war in a prison camp, and had emerged determined to be a painter. Mary, who came from a grand Scottish family, was full of warmth and energy. They all soon began to see a good deal of each other, and Frances was delighted when Burgo made friends with Mary's daughters, Serena and Nell. When the Kees were not at Ham Spray they would stay with the Campbells, along with other mutual friends like Philip Toynbee.

Cyril Connolly was another Stokke regular. Brought over to Ham Spray for tea one weekend, he did not endear himself to Frances by telling her how much he had admired Carrington; after he left she reflected disapprovingly on his self-indulgent approach to life, and how 'the modern smart intellectual falls so far below Old Bloomsbury, who knew that personal relations came before money, good food and luxury'. Another friend of Cyril's and the Kees whom Frances never really liked was Sonia Brownell, also a *Horizon* girl, who was to marry the dying George Orwell in October 1949. Robert and Janetta went to the wedding at his hospital bedside, and told Frances how moving it was; others were more cynical about Sonia's motives, and Frances considered any marriage to a terminally ill man 'as near to no marriage at all as it is possible to get', noting in her unpublished diary that apparently Sonia had only been to bed with Orwell once, some time earlier, 'and hated it'.

Not for the first time, or the last, Frances found herself increasingly concerned about Julia. After the war, she and Lawrence Gowing were finding it hard to decide how, or if, they could go on living together; deeply attached though they were, their relations were always platonic and neither of them was ready to accept a sexless life. Both of them had brief affairs, which led nowhere; Julia, as always short of money, became a reader for the publishers

Secker & Warburg, where one of her bosses was Lytton's old love, Roger Senhouse. Above all, Julia wanted to write another novel, but she found the process more and more agonising. When Lawrence was appointed Professor of Fine Arts in Newcastle in 1948, Julia stayed in London; she was deeply unhappy. 'I've been trying desperately to get married these last few years,' she told Frances, 'and now I must realise it – I've failed. And I must face spinsterish old age, with my hateful writing as chief interest.' Frances tried her best to look after her troubled, demanding friend, who was always welcome at Ham Spray; they exchanged long letters, and from time to time she sent her a substantial cheque. 'Oh my dears my dear my dears!!!!!!' wrote Julia on one such occasion. 'Was there ever such a handsome present! ... Somehow one takes and takes and takes from you both – spiritual support, physical support, financial support, every kind of up-bolstering, my dears, comes from Ham Spray in a steady stream down the long years.' In return, Julia tried to comfort Frances over Burgo's difficulties, pointing out that to rebel against school could be regarded as an excellent sign.

Meanwhile, Frances worked away on the Flora, making good progress herself and encouraging Dicky. June 1946 saw an important meeting take place at Ham Spray between Frances, Dicky and Allen Lane himself. Frances and Dicky were both nervous, as Noel Carrington, the instigator of the project, had warned them that paper was scarce and Penguin likely to question the scope and ambition of their plans, let alone the timetable. Frances was curious to meet Allen Lane again; she could just remember him as a young travelling salesman from her Birrell and Garnett days, trying to flirt with her as he presented his wares. When he arrived, sweeping up the drive in a large Bentley, accompanied by the printer, she found him irritatingly tycoon-like in a smart grey suit, and cheerfully ignorant of the subject under discussion. She and Dicky presented their plans, which were for twenty volumes, each illustration having a page to itself. 'When he at last brought himself to discuss the book we got our way on most points,' Frances recalled, 'except for the very important one of scope, and here he irritated us greatly by saying we mustn't include trees.' In vain did Frances point out that trees, shrubs and herbaceous plants were all part of the same botanical family: Lane would not budge. To Frances, this was 'as silly as it was ignorant'; but she conceded defeat. He did make one constructive suggestion, that they should find a professional botanist to advise them, and Noel Sandwith, an expert from Kew, joined the team. A gentle, scholarly figure, his expertise was invaluable and he soon became a regular at Ham Spray with whom they went on enjoyable plant-hunting expeditions.

That summer Ralph and Frances took Burgo abroad with them for the first time, on their first trip to Europe since 1939. They travelled by train across France to Switzerland, a country where they would not have to encounter the consequences of war; in their hotel on Lake Lugano they were joined by three senior Stracheys: James, Alix and Marjorie. Frances took a touching photograph of Ralph and Burgo about to go for a swim, Ralph's broad shoulders and strong legs looking massive beside his small, slender son. At home, rationing persisted; in Switzerland, they found croissants and real coffee and cherry jam.

The holiday was 'blissful'; but more trouble was approaching for Burgo and his parents. At eleven, it was now time for him to go to prep school, with a view to Eton in due course; Frances regarded prep and public schools with distaste, it was Ralph who wished to see his son receive a traditional upper-class education. In September, off he went as a weekly boarder to a school at Kintbury.

There now began a time of wretched unhappiness for Burgo and great strain for Frances and Ralph. Away from home for the first time, Burgo began to be tormented by the thought that in his absence his parents might have died. Gripped by this fantasy, his anxiety would rise to such a pitch that he was compelled to do something about it; he took to running away and heading for home. Sometimes he would manage to telephone before the school realised he had gone. His parents would collect him; relief that he was safe would soon become anger, or at best a reproachful silence. They would take him home, talk to him, and take him back to school to try again.

This pattern began in the autumn of 1946, and was to be repeated over and over again. It was bad enough to know that her son was so desperate, but almost worse was the fact that his troubles caused such tension between her and Ralph. Ralph was for taking a strong line, Frances for trying gentleness and persuasion. There were many difficult discussions between the two of them, and with their friends and with the schools concerned. Eventually they called in Dr Edward Glover, the Freudian psychoanalyst most trusted by Bloomsbury, who treated Burgo and corresponded with his parents over the next few years. Glover told them that such fears and fantasies were quite common in adolescents, and they all struggled on; sometimes Burgo would seem a bit more settled, but then just as they were beginning to relax the phone would ring again. The anxiety, not to mention the guilt felt by all parents, especially mothers, when a child's unhappiness seems insoluble, made Frances unable for a while to keep up her diary. As she later wrote, 'Angst is not something one enjoys recording.'

The diary breaks off altogether between mid-1946 and January 1948, and thereafter only touches on Burgo's troubles occasionally. After her death, a small packet of his letters came to light; several of them make painful reading now, and must have been devastating for her at the time. 'Dear Wuz,' he wrote to Frances in the summer of 1948, when he was thirteen, 'I am sorry but I cannot bear it. I shall go mad if I do not know that you are alive. I shall have to run away from this beastly place. I don't know why you sent me here ... I cannot stay here and stay sane any longer than Thursday morning. I shall have to run away.' That autumn, they moved him to Millfield, a school with a reputation for handling awkward boys; all thoughts of Eton were abandoned. For a while, Burgo seemed better; he wrote stilted but normal letters about plans for outings, nasty school food or trouble over a bicycle. But a letter of January 1949 shows that his problems were far from resolved. 'Dear Ralph and Frances,' wrote their fourteen-year-old son, 'I am afraid that I must ask for your help again. My old worries have come back. First the one then the other. I would not say that the one about you being dead is any stronger than the one about you not being my parents. Also I feel generally depressed and wretched and feel I need your help. Will you please do something to help me as soon as possible. Yours truly, Burgo.' Evidently they hurried down to see him; a week later he thanks them for coming and bringing him some fudge, adding 'The worry came on after you had gone, but it is not as bad as it might be.' When they saw him at half-term, he seemed better but Frances knew it would be a mistake to think his, or their, troubles were over. 'There's no such thing as calm water in life,' she wrote, 'and somehow or other we have now reached an age when people suddenly die for no reason, so that I think we both expect to do it ourselves, or perhaps Burgo's anxieties about our deaths have made us conscious of the possibility.'

There can be no doubt that Frances was deeply shaken by Burgo's unhappiness during the late 1940s and early 1950s, nor that her marriage was troubled by it; but the fact that she resumed her diary in 1948, as well as the busy, energetic and stimulating life she chronicled, indicates her determination not to let herself be overwhelmed. The Flora was a help; by now she had joined the Wiltshire Botanical Society, which led to several useful contacts and discoveries. There were enjoyable expeditions: an eccentric colonel took her to find the beautiful scarlet Adonis cannua, or Pheasant's Eye, and Noel Sandwith showed her other local rarities, like the Bath Asparagus lurking in a copse only half a mile from Ham Spray. And she would always remember with particular delight an outing with the Brenans on 30 April 1948 to the hills above Streatley, where Gerald, a keen amateur botanist himself, had told her that he had once seen Anemone Pulsatilla, otherwise known as the Pasque Flower, with its purple flowers and golden heart surrounded by feathery grey foliage. After trundling up steep chalk tracks they reached open downland, where two shepherds directed them across a valley to a large patch of the flowers Gerald had remembered for thirty years. 'Specimens were speedily conveyed to Richard,' wrote Frances, 'and then back I went to my botany books and the long solid oak table in the library where I used to work.' Everything about her botanical researches pleased her: the expeditions, the beauty of the plants, their history and the precise descriptions she was required to write.

Frances also began, during the late 1940s, to write, tentatively at first, about her own life. She was prompted to do so by being elected to the Memoir Club, now over twenty years old, which had resumed regular meetings since the end of the war. The club, started in 1918 by Molly MacCarthy in the vain hope of prompting her husband to write a novel, had originally consisted of the core of Old Bloomsbury: the Woolfs, the Bells, Duncan Grant, Keynes, E.M. Forster and Roger Fry; by the time Frances joined, Roger, Virginia, Lytton and Keynes were dead, and Bunny Garnett, Adrian Stephen, Oliver Strachey, Janie Bussy and Quentin Bell had been elected. The thinking behind the club, which held meetings two or three times a year in a member's house after dinner in a Soho restaurant, was, as Frances put it, 'that papers should be both confidential and completely frank, and that no-one should take offence at anything read'. At her second meeting in January 1948, wearing a new black silk suit trimmed with gold braid (Frances very seldom mentions anything to do with her appearance, but she was pleased with this outfit, which she had designed herself), papers were read by Desmond MacCarthy and E.M. Forster ('a very long and slightly boring one about his aunts') and she was asked to prepare one herself. This first paper, which she had great difficulty writing, was an account of the strange friendship she and Ralph had made in the early 1930s with Hayley Morris of Pippingford Park; but in November 1949 she started planning another about her early childhood, and found she rather enjoyed allowing her memories to surface.

She liked the Memoir Club, while deploring the way the old guard, especially Duncan and Vanessa, resisted bringing in new blood; she was especially interested to hear Leonard Woolf read parts of Virginia's diaries, and Vanessa Bell on the sisters' childhood. The Memoir Club signalled the early stirrings of Bloomsbury's wish to record and celebrate itself at a time when its stock was low; many of the papers were to reappear in published memoirs and autobiographies. Younger members who eventually made it through Charleston's barrage of blackballing included Julia Strachey, Olivier Bell and Angelica Garnett. It was definitely a sign of Old Bloomsbury's approval to be elected. Ralph was never a member, though he did belong to the Bloomsbury-based, all-male Cranium Club, set up in the mid-1920s by David Garnett to stimulate good conversation.

In the summer of 1949 Dicky gave Frances ominous news from Penguin. The first volume of the Flora was in proof and publication supposed to be imminent; now they learned that the future of the project was in doubt. It was simply uneconomic. For Frances, who was already embarking on the text for volume five, this was a blow; she had been counting on several more years of work. Then, at a meeting in Allen Lane's office, furnished with black leather armchairs from the German embassy, he told them that he was not going to bring out even the first volume. 'It seemed entirely suitable', Frances observed, her sense of proportion failing her badly, 'that we should receive the death sentence in seats where Goebbels and Goering had probably sat.' She was furious as well as miserable: 'I shall try and squeeze the uttermost financial compensation out of the brutes. They have not hitherto suggested paying me a penny.' For a while, she and Dicky looked into other publishing possibilities, but in the end they had to admit defeat. With the help of the Society of Authors, Frances eventually received £1,500 for her five years' work, which was some comfort; and she came to realise that the aborted Flora had been a valuable education in a subject she loved and pursued for the rest of her life. She always treasured the original painting of three cornfield plants that Dicky framed and gave her – not to mention their friendship, which was never to fail.

Both Frances and Ralph had become very fond of Dicky, but they had also come to realise that his relationship with Denis was difficult. Both young men drank too much, and then there would be violent rows and hysterical accusations of infidelity, even threats of suicide. They did what they could to calm them down, but Frances was sometimes exasperated. She was also conscious that Burgo, in his early teens, was at an age where his developing sexuality could make him attracted by, and attractive to, homosexuals, and this made her wary. She later said she would not have minded at all had he been homosexual by nature, but she did not want him influenced, when still a child, one way or the other. She discussed the matter with Raymond, who told her firmly that 'buggery declared itself very early', even before a boy first went to school. One day, Dicky asked her what she really felt about sex between men; she told him that she 'could see nothing wrong in it' – but when he then acknowledged finding Burgo attractive, she did not like it. 'I confess that all this gave me rather a turn.' But she

trusted Dicky and Denis, and she was right; they were always kind friends
to Burgo, but no advances were made. Not many parents in the 1950s would
have been as relaxed.

For his part, Dicky Chopping felt sorry for Burgo, who was growing up
under pressure from his father to be a different kind of boy. To Dicky, it
seemed likely that Ralph, whom he liked and admired for his kindness,
humour and vitality, was a man whose own youthful homosexual tendencies
had probably been stronger than he liked to recall, which explained both
why he took such an interest in his homosexual friends' sexual and emotional
lives, and at the same time wanted his son to be straightforwardly manly.
Dicky was also bemused, and rather shocked, by Ralph's emotionalism, and
the way he could explode over small things; once, when they were all driving
to the cinema in Hungerford, Burgo, aged about thirteen, gave his mother
a playful punch on the arm. Ralph, purple in the face, stopped the car and
shouted at Burgo in a fury: 'Nobody hits my girl!' Dicky reckoned that
Ralph was jealous of anyone with a claim on Frances, even their own son.

Perhaps because of Burgo's age, or Dicky's rows with Denis, or the
emotional and sexual turbulence going on among her friends, Frances found
herself reflecting on the boundaries and categories of sexual experience. She
always considered that no-one was exclusively male or female, but that each
sex had some attributes of the other, recognised or not; as she wrote in 1949,
both she and Ralph positively preferred people 'with a touch of androgyny'
and she declared herself in favour of 'as much variety in human relationships
as possible'. On the other hand, she was increasingly out of sympathy with
the view that any girl who had dinner with a man should automatically go
to bed with him; this seemed to her to be not freedom, but a new obligation,
and 'a drastic limitation of the range of human pleasures'. Bloomsbury had
believed in sexual freedom, but not in casual promiscuity. It was a principle
for her and Ralph never to be shocked by sexual behaviour; their tolerance
was tested, though, when Gerald, in a state of euphoria, arrived to see them
and announced that he was 'in love' with his teenage daughter, Miranda,
and therefore 'obliged, so he told us, to toss himself off several times a day'.
Long discussions followed about whether, as Gerald maintained, 'there are
no morals in love'; Frances and Ralph agreed that they found their old
friend's latest sexual obsession (confined, as they realised, in his head), most
interesting, but Frances was struck by his inability to see that his attitude
to his daughter could be damaging to her. It was more often Ralph who
received Gerald's sexual confidences, often by letter; he would reciprocate,
and it is likely that some parts of their correspondence were later destroyed.

Three days later, and, as she observed, 'somewhat in tune' with her previous entry ('Hurrah for homosexuality, and also for the happy friend-ships between buggers and women and vice versa!') Frances set off with Ralph in October 1949 to spend a weekend, the first of many, in a homo-sexual household recently set up at Long Crichel, a Georgian rectory near Wimborne in Dorset, by three friends: Eardley Knollys, Desmond Shawe-Taylor and Eddie Sackville-West. They were soon to be joined by Raymond Mortimer. All four had jobs in London, using Crichel as a retreat where they could relax together, garden, walk, play croquet and entertain their mutual friends. The house was full of books and music: Desmond and Eddie were both music critics, and evenings were often spent listening to and arguing about opera, or whatever book Raymond was reviewing (he was now, along with Cyril Connolly, a lead reviewer on *The Sunday Times*) or art; Eardley was soon to give up working for the National Trust and devote himself to painting. Each of them had furnished his own room – Eddie's with a large crucifix and imposing furniture from Knole – the food and drink were delicious, there was always a cook and sometimes even a butler. Conversation flowed; Frances compared the four hosts' different tones and voices exploring a theme to a string quartet. Crichel was exactly the kind of house and atmosphere she most enjoyed.

On this first visit, though, she found being the only woman slightly daunting, especially as she and Ralph had been put in separate rooms. Looking through the visitors' book, she observed that previous female visitors had usually been mothers or sisters; she felt uncharacteristically self-conscious about her sex. 'I feel that it is quite a job for them to swallow a heterosexual couple into the house,' she wrote. 'It's not that they don't like women, they don't like love between man and woman, and whenever a marriage is discussed it is always a marriage of convenience. They like to think of people marrying for good sensible reasons, money, companionship, care for each other's orphaned children – but not for love.' She sensed she was not perhaps the kind of woman they preferred – motherly, nice women, or 'elegant and ultrafeminine and bosomy'. She worried about making 'some bloomer offending to their sensibilities. They don't for instance like women to talk too much like men, and I fear I sometimes do. But they have been very charming to both R and me.' Later she felt rather ashamed of herself for having such thoughts, and in fact she was to become one of Crichel's most regular and appreciated guests.

Just as Frances' Flora was approaching its depressing end, a new oppor-tunity opened up for Ralph – oddly enough, again through Dicky Chop-ping. Ralph had always been unusually interested in violent crime; as well as reading and reviewing detective stories he would study real murders, unsolved crimes and famous trials and analyse the psychology of criminals. Something in him, and to an extent in Frances as well, was fascinated by the darker side of human nature. When Ralph learned that a cousin of Dicky's, Dr Stanley Hopwood, was the Superintendent of Broadmoor, the asylum near Reading for the criminally insane, he showed such interest in every detail of what went on there that Dicky arranged with his cousin for his friends to visit.

Early in April 1948 Ralph and Frances made the first of a series of expeditions to Broadmoor. Her descriptions of the place and the patients are extraordinary, unflinchingly observant, disconcerting in their cool precision. They were taken round by Dr Hopwood and several large male nurses with clanking keys hanging from their belts, who 'produced a spice of danger by closing in round us whenever we entered a building'. The red-brick buildings reminded her of Euston station, and she was impressed by the fine views and extensive grounds where patients were rolling a bowling green, while a group of older men sat nearby. 'Some of their faces were as vacant as most old men's, others had a curious mask-like beauty as if all expression had been washed away from them. Most of them had some distortion or imperfection in their appearance . . . In the great bakery the male murderers were making bread; in the laundry murderesses washed the clothes and sheets . . . the scene was dramatic rather than dull, as if their madness was a form of originality which must make them far from boring for the admirable people who looked after them.'

They were treated on this first occasion to a theatrical performance of a jolly musical called 'The Earl and the Girl'. The curtain went up on 'a row of mostly young, tall and strong murderers dressed in hunting pink singing the opening chorus at the top of their voices'. The performance, she felt, was 'absorbingly strange; it could never have been mistaken for a show put on by normal amateurs'. The hero of the piece, 'a small neat young man with a rosebud mouth' and 'the typical sloping forehead', she found terrifying. 'One could easily imagine him suddenly changing a caress into strangulation.'

Dr Hopwood was a humane, progressive man who had introduced many reforms at Broadmoor and improved conditions for the inmates; Ralph and Frances were impressed. He willingly answered all their questions, which suggests that it was unusual, and encouraging, for him to have visitors who took an intelligent interest in what he was trying to do. As a result, when in September the following year Ralph was commissioned by Chatto & Windus to write a book about Broadmoor, Dr Hopwood, according to Frances, was all in favour of the idea. But while she was genuinely pleased for Ralph, who returned from another day at Broadmoor 'in a state of great excitement and activity, bringing a lot of papers about the relation of insanity to crime' which they pored over together, she could not help feeling envious. 'I am humiliated having no work to do,' she wrote.

During the next three years, Broadmoor visits made a strange counterpoint to Ham Spray life. One of the more peculiar social events of Frances' life was surely the Broadmoor dance, where, she wrote, 'I felt a certain alarm at the thought of dancing with any madman who asked me, however repellent.' Dressed 'unfestively' in green corduroy and rubber-soled shoes, she was soon asked to dance by a red-faced old man in a dinner jacket, 'whose speciality was raping little girls. He taught me the Boston Twostep, remarking that he hoped he had given me something to think about when I went home.' She had several more partners, including a nice young man who had been in the RAF during the war, cracked up and killed his girlfriend. 'All said and done I was glad to have taken part, but ashamed to realise how little insight I had into these abnormal minds.'

Not long afterwards she and Ralph stayed for two nights with Dr Hopwood in the Superintendent's House, which she found somewhat of a social strain (Dr Hopwood being not quite a gentleman; though she disliked snobbery Frances was aware of such gradations) and where she slept badly. 'All night long I was aware where we were, and that a narrow if high wall separated us from the Parole Block of male lunatics.' They attended a sports day, organised, Frances wrote, by the Blackheath Murderer, 'a kindly looking man', and she shook hands with several 'famous monsters'. The next day she went for a walk, looking for interesting plants, and found herself 'ludicrously rattled' when she saw a man approaching on a bicycle; she turned down a side track to avoid him and 'went through all the sensations of being attacked and strangled in my imagination. After which I returned, hating the moor and wanting nothing of it.' It was a relief to get back to Ham Spray, where their guests the next weekend, who included the Kees, Nicko Henderson and a Foreign Office friend of his, Donald Maclean, encouraged them to recount their Broadmoor experiences. Later Janetta told Frances that Maclean had been sent back from the embassy in Cairo after trying to kill his wife in a drunken rage. Frances had found him charming.

As 1949 ended, and a new decade began, Frances surveyed her world and recorded more than usually mixed feelings about it. Her most serious and fundamental anxiety remained Burgo, though she had hopes that the worst of the crisis was behind them; she badly needed some sustained work of her own, but on the other hand Ralph was enjoying his Broadmoor researches and it gave her real pleasure to see him happy and occupied. But all around them, people she cared about were in emotional difficulties, seemingly unable, even when they found a partner, to find a way to live happily together. She recognised that sometimes she became too caught up in other people's dramas. 'It is unsatisfactory', she observed, 'to exist as a sort of mistletoe on the life blood of others.' Always, she appreciated how lucky she was to have Ralph. 'These reeling cracking menages', she wrote, 'have I think made both R and me thankful for the rocklike stability of our own. It seems that even hard words get rarer and rarer as time goes on, and elderly as we are [they were forty-nine and fifty-five respectively] there is the most exquisite happiness in our days together and our nights snug beside one another in bed.'

During 1950, as Frances and Ralph were uncomfortably aware, the Kees' marriage began to reel and crack in earnest. That summer, while the Partridges, along with Esmé Strachey and her daughter Vicky, were on holiday in northern Spain, Janetta left Robert and her two small daughters and went to France. She wrote to Frances that she longed to be free; meanwhile Cyril Connolly was pressing her to marry him – even though he was in hot pursuit of his second wife, Barbara Skelton – and soon the news reached Ham Spray that she was also being pursued by Derek Jackson, the rich, eccentric and extremely right-wing scientist and amateur jockey. Frances was distressed, both because she felt Janetta did not realise the effect of her disappearance on her children and because she thought very little of Derek Jackson, whom she had known slightly for years, first as the husband of Augustus John's daughter Poppet and then when he was married to Pamela Mitford. She described him crisply as 'Very substandard, with little to commend him as far as I can see except money and perhaps enthusiasm.' Meanwhile, Robert was intensely unhappy and in need of support; she felt for him too, and found herself quite unable to give up hope that the relationship could be mended. She and Ralph did their best to tread the fine line between advice and interference, and spent many hours in intense discussion. 'I really feel', she wrote, 'both R and I have put all we know about the human heart and its sensibilities into our dealings with both Robert and Janetta in all this.' Soon other friends were drawn into the drama. Frances was irritated with the Campbells for seeming to favour Derek Jackson, and with Julia for repeating to Robert something Frances had told her in confidence; Julia, she thought, having never really found what she wanted from a man, was inclined to be hostile towards them and could not help being glad when a marriage collapsed. By December, it had all become too much. 'I am almost tired', she wrote, 'of setting down accounts of the life and death struggles of our friends with their mates.'

During the next few months, it became clear that Janetta was indeed involved with Derek Jackson; and in March 1951 she asked Ralph to talk to Robert about a divorce on her behalf. Slowly and reluctantly, Frances came to terms with the situation, and with Derek; the Partridges made a joint expedition with him and Janetta, the Campbells and Philip Dunn to the south of France in the late spring. As Frances wrote to Dicky soon after her return, this holiday was not a total success; Janetta was 'not the old Janetta, though she looked quite happy – but so thin, tense, jittery'. There was too much drinking for her taste, and she disliked Derek's habit of doing loud imitations in French. She christened Dunn and Jackson 'The Tycoons'; their idea of foreign travel, she told Dicky, was 'to blaze about in huge cars making a great noise, épateeing the bourgeoisie'. She could not believe that Janetta was really in love with Derek; nevertheless, after the divorce from Robert came through in 1952 she married him. Later, Frances tried to analyse her instinctive dislike of Janetta's new husband. 'To be honest I believe that jealousy was partly responsible,' she wrote, '– a jealousy with regard to Janetta that had been completely absent in Robert's case ... Almost a stranger, Derek carried Janetta off into a world of very different values from our own, and during her years with him she appeared to Ralph and me to be less "herself" than at any other time.' Janetta minded Frances' disapproval and disappointment. It was Ralph, she later said, whom she could really talk to at this time of great confusion and unhappiness, Ralph who was unshockable and who understood the complications of her emotional life without judging her. Frances had higher expectations than he did of the people she loved.

While his parents were on holiday in France, Burgo had another bad anxiety attack. Once again, Dr Glover was much in play; he still felt that full-scale analysis was not called for, and that time and patience would resolve Burgo's problems. However, 'He also says that if R and I were not so devoted to each other Burgo's troubles might not have arisen! So really poor parents nowadays are neither allowed to part ('broken homes') nor get on well, but I suppose only to stay together endlessly bickering.' By the end of the year, Burgo was not doing any better. He came home from Millfield for Christmas very low, saying that his obsessive worries had been bothering him again; he went back to school in January, but early in February Ralph took a phone call from the headmaster to say he had disappeared. Half an hour later, Burgo rang to tell them that he was all right, but refused to tell them where he was unless they promised not to take him back. They did so, and set off to fetch him from a hotel in Devizes; 'the journey there passed in thoughtless relief, the journey home in gloom'. All he would say was that he felt desperate, that the other boys were unbearable, they were so 'animal'.

It was not easy to decide what to do next. Ralph, she wrote, was 'floored by the whole affair, and, though managing with a supreme effort to behave reasonably to Burgo, he is filled with what I can only call wounded pride'. She felt certain that this time it would be wrong to try to force Burgo back to school, and so she decided to organise an alternative in London. Ralph did not oppose her, but neither did he agree; he simply withdrew from the whole business. The situation made Frances wretched: 'I have found it unbelievably strange', she wrote, 'to have to take all the decisions and carry them out unaided.' She arranged for herself and Burgo to see Glover – who approved her plan – drove to Millfield to collect his things, arranged for him to lodge in Chelsea with Isobel and Charlotte Strachey, and found tutors. Meanwhile, she and Ralph were living 'like strangers for the first time in our lives. Not quarrelling – that might have been easier to bear.'

Gradually, they recovered their equilibrium. Frances knew that fundamentally her husband and her son loved each other – although, as she wrote, 'where there is love there is also jealousy'. They discussed it all at length with their friends, asking them what they would have done in a similar position; none of them, to Frances' relief, said they would have made him return. Janetta wrote loving, sympathetic letters: 'It seems to me so awful you feel you must blame yourselves so much about Burgo.' Julia was more bracing: 'His behaviour, though inconvenient, is very healthy and normal ... Burgo has developed into the most charming, sweet and intelligent fellow, as I observed with my own eyes and ears, and just because he is so intelligent and emotional he is very naturally causing trouble in these difficult years. I hear from Isobel that he is turning communist.'

Unable to talk freely about their son to Ralph, Frances exchanged long letters about him with Dicky, to whom it seemed quite clear that sex, and probably repressed homosexual tendencies, lay behind Burgo's troubles and he told Frances so. Early in 1952, she wrote a thoughtful reply. Sexual guilt was not, she thought, the real problem – although, she conceded, 'in the sort of Freudian sense it is always sex au fond'. Burgo, unlike her generation or even Dicky's, was used to the adults around him talking openly and graphically about sex; he had lately begun to show an interest in girls, especially pretty Nell Dunn.

When I said his trouble was connected with non-functioning it was something I've noticed in him all his life from a tiny boy and long before puberty – compared to other children he always seemed to be defeatist and stepping back from even the things in life which interested and attracted him ... I always look on it as a good sign if he 'steps forward' into some active response to life. Thus I was pleased when he became a communist; am pleased if he makes a friend on his own; was pleased because he was keen on Nell. NOT my dear as you obviously think because I thought Ah, he's not queer – but because he was actively responding to life.

Evidently, Dicky had told her that he too had been keen on a girl when he was a boy, and look at him now. Frances was quick to reject what this comparison implied. 'Well! Goodness me, in the sense I meant all right, you are perfectly all right now. If Burgo could end up so well, I should be delighted. You have hosts of friends, earn your own living, are frightfully good at your work, enjoy it, lead a fairly full sex life and are not inconveniently neurotic!!!'

From time to time during all this, Frances found herself turning back to philosophy, looking perhaps for some clarity and rigour as a respite from personal dramas. Her mind needed exercise; tinkering with papers for the Memoir Club, writing the occasional book review and helping Ralph with his Broadmoor book were not enough. In the spring of 1950 she met the young philosopher A.J. Ayer at Stokke; Freddie Ayer was was not only brilliant but fashionable, talkative and charming; he was a social success, especially with women, but Frances wanted to talk philosophy with him. Soon she was reading *Logical Positivism*, 'with great pleasure and interest', finding it made her want to reread her earlier favourites, Berkeley, Hume and Mill, and 'sort out' what she really believed. She took to keeping notes again, not just to summarise what she was reading but to argue with herself and whichever philosopher she was tackling. 'The more philosophy I read,' she wrote, 'the more amazed I am by its inexhaustibility.' Because of her Cambridge education, and her early friendships with Ramsey and Wittgenstein, Frances was not frightened of philosophy or philosophers; something in her needed to grapple with their arguments and concepts. She kept notes on her readings in philosophy for the rest of her life.

She liked Freddie Ayer, whom she met again with the Campbells, and in the spring of 1953 he came to Ham Spray for a weekend. They found him a delightful, easy guest; he sat in the music room working in the mornings, saying that he could think better with people about, and he and Frances had a most enjoyable conversation about solipsism and whether it was possible to know what went on in other people's minds. 'I think

I'm almost able to prove that we do have knowledge of them,' he told her.

But by this time, Frances had embarked on a new and demanding project of her own. In May 1952, James Strachey asked her if she would undertake the indexing of his translation of the complete works of Freud, which the Hogarth Press was proposing to publish. With the experience of the index to the Greville Diaries behind her, and her familiarity, gleaned over many years of conversation and argument with James and Alix, with the central themes and the idiom of the Stracheys' version of Freud, she had no hesitation in accepting. Now, she was able once and for all to dispose of the remains of the Flora. The notes and typescripts were all burned on one of Ralph's mighty bonfires; and on 28 May she cleared her table in Lytton's library of all traces of botanising, 'to make way for my Freudian indexing for James'. Frances was both modest and matter-of-fact about this huge task, which occupied her on and off for twelve years. Whatever the arguments as to the merits of Strachey's version, it was to be central to Freud's followers for most of the twentieth century. Only a careful, reliable index can make such a vast edition on such complex matters useful and accessible; anyone who has ever used it owes Frances Partridge a debt.

Meanwhile, Ralph was still working away on his Broadmoor book – sometimes, Frances thought, not quite hard enough. Then, in the summer of 1952 he was galvanised by the Straffen case, when a Broadmoor patient who had strangled a little girl escaped, and before being caught strangled another. This horrible event focused press and public attention, and led to calls for security at Broadmoor to be reviewed; Frances and Ralph felt for Dr Hopwood, who was on the point of retirement. He, like Ralph and Frances, was strongly opposed to capital punishment, and they had attended a session of the commission looking into abolition when he appeared before it in 1950; Straffen's crimes set the cause back considerably. When Straffen went on trial in Winchester in July, Robert Kee (by then working on *The Spectator*) arranged press tickets for Ralph. On the second day Frances went with him.

Frances' account of the trial was written as it was taking place, and is a striking piece of reporting. She noticed everything: the little grey flapping tails of the barristers' wigs, one of the jurors, 'a small fat cad in sandals and a tiepin', flirting with another; Straffen's mother and sister, 'a couple of debased sheepfaced women', and the downy outline of Straffen's head in the dock. His head, she decided, was 'very abnormally shaped, a high thimble, microcephalic and with no back, his fair hair cut in a short bob ending suddenly above his long neck, like an Italian baby'. It was a hot afternoon; the lawyers' faces shone with sweat; various witnesses seemed to Frances to be rather enjoying the spotlight. As for the victim's mother, who was young and pretty, 'her demeanour and charm are not entirely artless, though her grief is of course genuine'. She admitted to being 'shocked to find in myself little human sympathy – only intense interest' – a function, she thought, of the clinical atmosphere of the court. Straffen claimed he was innocent; it seemed likely that he was not. His expression, Frances noted, was one of 'lost, abysmal sadness'.

One day was enough for her, but Ralph went back several times, taking Burgo with him and then Julia, who pronounced Straffen 'marvellously good-looking'. Even so, he was convicted and sentenced to hang; the verdict was much discussed at Ham Spray, where Alix and James were spending the weekend. 'Alix thought it might be necessary for him to be hanged so as to satisfy the bloodlust of the public ... the old question as to whether savagery and violence are increased by being fed or starved came up once again, and was tossed about for a while.' Straffen was duly executed; capital punishment was not abolished until 1965.

Later that year a curious incident brought the question of murder closer to home. Burgo, who to his parents' huge relief had just passed the necessary exams to enable him to apply for a place at Oxford, was hustled off the street outside the house where he was staying in London by five large armed plain-clothes policemen. They were looking for a young man who had pushed his parents off a cliff; his description matched Burgo closely – an ex-public-school boy, very dark, long hair. Later that night the right man drove up to a house in the same street and was promptly arrested. Frances and Ralph were amazed to find that Burgo, their jumpy son, took this strange experience in his stride. This incident, which of course made a very good story, fed into the rumour already circulating among Burgo's friends that his relationship with his parents had been so awful that he had not only harboured fantasies about killing them but had once been discovered digging a grave for them in the woods near Ham Spray. This story persists; those who knew that Burgo had been tormented as a boy by fears that his parents were dead, inevitably speculated that this meant that he wished that they were. Ralph and Frances and their neurotic son were the subject of a good deal of enjoyable amateur analysis and speculation. They were also, though they never knew it, a source of inspiration for their neighbour V.S. Pritchett.

Decades later, Pritchett published a story built around recollections of the years in the late 1940s and 1950s when his children played at Stokke and Ham Spray with the Dunn girls and Burgo. Written from the viewpoint of

Sarah, a fourteen-year-old girl, it suggest how the Partridges (called the Shorts in the story) were regarded, in the postwar years, by at least some of their neighbours. The house is said to be haunted; there were sightings of a tall man with a black beard, and tales of the suicide of Major Short's first wife. The narrator's father, also a military man, has strong views about the Shorts and their friends: 'Gang of traitors. Pacifists, longhaired pansies, atheists, bathing stark naked in that swimming pool. Friends of Hitler and Stalin. Calls himself a major.' Her mother, who plays in a string quartet with Mrs Short, protests mildly that surely the Major had been decorated in the First World War. 'Got himself blown up. Some fool dug him out.' Thereafter, Sarah always thinks of the Major as 'a kind of fair-haired elephant, with a huge chest, lying under tons of French mud'. As for the Shorts' twelve-year-old son, Benedict, who shares his mother's black hair and 'sunburned toasted skin', he is reputed to be very odd. Her father blames the Major. 'Sends his boy to a god awful boarding school in Dorset run by pansies and refugees wearing sandals, where the boys live in trees. No wonder the little bastard runs away.'

Sarah, a dutiful schoolgirl, is fascinated by tales of the runaway boy and the naked bathing at the traitors' house, and takes to walking past the bottom of the garden hoping to see something interesting. She merely observes Mrs Short gardening, and guests sitting on the verandah in basket chairs or playing croquet; then one day she bumps into a frantic Benedict, who has just shot a bird. She helps him bury it; suddenly they are caught in a thunderstorm and drenched to the skin, and she runs with him back to the house. The Major's wife is standing there calmly, and then the Major comes out. 'Ah,' he says in a calm, insinuating, conspiratorial voice. 'The frightful Benedict, and who has he brought with him?' Mrs Short tells Benedict what a bore he is and takes Sarah up to get dry; she brings her some shorts and a jumper. 'Now you're a boy; what do you think of that? Rather fun?' Downstairs, Sarah is taken into a large room with a music stand and a violin propped against the wall, a big table spread with books and newspapers and a large, unfinished jigsaw puzzle. 'And that is how I remember Emma Short always: a small woman with small, brown, brilliant eyes, as dark as Benedict was, wearing a plain but pretty dress, chattering and eagerly questioning herself as she stands before the large puzzle ... "How beastly they are to put so much water in these things. It's cheating. What a bore. Ah, now – here, do you think?"' After tea, they all play the chasing game called Cocky Olly, hunting each other all over the house.

Sarah makes friends with Benedict despite his peculiar ways, his tendency to 'screech' and caper about and whisper about witchcraft, the devil and, above all, death. One day she overhears the Major talking on the telephone about his son: "'I fancy that Oedipus is coming into the open,'" he says. "He is digging a grave in the garden – indeed, two graves.'" Outside, Benedict was digging two long rectangular shapes, saying they were for a Pharaohs' tomb. It is generally agreed that Benedict is 'quite mad', but through Sarah's eyes we see a vulnerable, highly strung boy, with a tendency to macabre fantasy, whose eccentricities are indulged at home but lead to ridicule and bullying at the school he hates.

The climax of the story comes when Sarah finds herself stuck with Benedict on the wrong train back from school. When the police turn up, it is not to help them but to check Benedict's identity; a boy answering to his description had released the handbrake on his parents' car so that they rolled off a cliff and were killed. When Benedict, thrilled with the drama, starts telling Sarah the devil did it, she teases him back. '"There was a devil on this train – it was you," I said, and gave him a push.' Back at the house, Mrs Short is standing over another jigsaw.

'Cocky Olly' gives a great writer's distilled impression of Ham Spray, Frances, Ralph and Burgo during the difficult years of his adolescence. As parents, the Shorts appear detached, busy with their friends and occupations while their son grapples with demons. Burgo/Benedict is a touching boy, loveable but unnerving, who plays with thoughts of death as a child plays with fire. Frances, who could have read the story when it appeared in 1989, does not seem to have done so; certainly she never mentioned it. All she would say, when asked about Pritchett, was that she always preferred his conversation to his writing.

During 1952, a number of landmark events took place. As well as Janetta's marriage to Derek, Julia and Lawrence decided, after twelve years of sporadic cohabitation, that they would get married and live together in Newcastle. Frances was touched by Julia's relief and happiness. In the same year, Julia's second novel, *The Man on the Pier*, partly inspired by life at Ham Spray, was published. She was also pleased when Quentin Bell, whom she had seen grow up and of whom she was really fond, married Olivier Popham; it was good to see another Charleston generation beginning and made up a little for the sadness she felt when Desmond MacCarthy died that year. Often, these days, Frances found herself comparing the approach to life of her Bloomsbury friends, old and young, with the smarter, richer circles now frequented by Janetta and, after he took up with Oonagh Oranmore, a bohemian Irish aristocrat, by Robert Kee as well. Sometimes, on a trip to London, the Partridges would be swept up by Janetta and Derek into a raffish, drunken evening at the Gargoyle, where they were likely to meet

Sonia Orwell, Lucien Freud and Francis Bacon (the latter, whose paintings Frances admired but found too horrifying for her taste, was also a great friend of Denis and Dicky). It was not really a world where they felt at home; increasingly, Frances agreed with Ralph that London social life was too frenetic and ultimately unsatisfying, with never enough time to pursue an argument or an idea. It was not just a matter of age, they felt, but of values.

Even so, when they were invited to stay with Oonagh at Luggala, her enchanting house on a peat-brown lake at the foot of the Wicklow Mountains south of Dublin, they accepted, along with Robert, the young writer Francis Wyndham, Lucien and Kitty Freud and Claud Cockburn. Beguiled though they were by the beauty of the place, not to mention the comfort and the many servants – 'Irish voices ministering seductively to our needs', as Francis put it – they were relieved to be back at Ham Spray, discussing their reaction with Lawrence and Julia. 'Mainly attractive, even romantic', was Frances' verdict on Luggala, 'and such shadows as it possesses are thrown by childishness, insensitivity and competitive drinking. And after sojourning in other civilisations it is very pleasant to feel alive again in our own.' Some people, Francis Wyndham among them, found Frances' confidence in the superiority of her own values verged on smugness.

In January 1953, Frances started work on the Freud index. 'I am resolved', she wrote, 'never to be without work again while I can totter about or wield a pen.' For the next fifty years, she never was. But Freud alone was not enough, as there would be long gaps between volumes, and by February she was taking Spanish lessons. Since discovering the fascination of comparing the French and English versions of Proust she had been thinking that she might like to try translation herself. Now that Burgo was all set for Oxford – after some anxious moments, he took the exams for Christ Church, his father's old college, and was accepted – and Ralph's book was finished and due for publication in the spring, Frances was able to find new confidence and energy. That spring, they drove down to southern Spain for the first time since the war, taking Burgo and Pippa Strachey, heading for Málaga and Churriana; the Brenans had given up Bell Court and returned to Spain early in 1953. On the way back, via Tarifa and Cádiz, they paused in Seville, where they caught a glimpse of Franco, 'the fat hand of fascismo' waving from a car; then on their way through France they visited the caves at Lascaux and bumped into E.M. Forster, who appeared pleased to see them and was particularly nice to Burgo.

Everything was going well, and at the end of April Ralph's book was published at last. Asked why he had undertaken it, he wrote: 'No serious book about Broadmoor had ever been written before, Stanley Hopwood wanted his life's work appreciated, and once I found out what homicidal maniacs were really like I wanted the outside world to get them in better perspective.' The book combined a history and description of the institution and several case histories with a study of the legal and medical thinking behind it; it was admirably clear and unsensational, and received some excellent reviews. C.H. Rolph, the ex-policeman who was the *New States-man's* expert on such matters, was particularly glowing; he praised Ralph's 'neatness and restraint', adding that 'his narrative carries the facts along so easily and flowingly you need to remind yourself at intervals how cheaply sensational such a book could have been ... Broadmoor and the entire mental nursing service are very greatly in Mr Partridge's debt.' Acclaim for Ralph gave Frances the greatest pleasure; she hoped that this success would lead to others, and that, like her, he would realise that to be productive, to use his gifts, would make him happy.

The trouble was that Ralph had not been feeling very well. For some time, he had lacked energy; now, two weeks after his book came out, something happened which neither of them could ignore. She asked him to remove a dead hedgehog from the empty pool, and he got into it to do so; but he found it a great struggle to heave himself out. 'An upsetting conversation followed, one of those that lay a chilly hand on the heart,' wrote Frances. 'It seems that poor Ralph has been feeling so feeble as to become seriously anxious about his state of health. I blame myself exceedingly for not seeing what I didn't want to see. It shocks me that there should be any watertight doors between two people as intimate as we are.' Ralph hated seeing doctors, but she insisted; they went to London for tests which revealed that he had developed diabetes. He spent a week in the London Clinic, after which he and Frances faced up to a change of diet, regular urine tests and, before long, insulin injections. He soon started to feel better, and life resumed much as before; but Frances, who for thirty years had assumed that Ralph was as strong as he appeared, was never to feel entirely safe again.

For the moment, there was not much cause to worry. In July, she read her paper about her childhood to the Memoir Club, and was pleased at its reception; Bunny took a copy away for his children, wanting his sons to learn more about the Marshall side of the family. In late August they went up to Edinburgh, to stay with Colin and Pin Mackenzie at their fine house in Heriot Row for the Festival, where Frances revelled in the beauty of the city and some wonderful music – *Idomeneo*, and Bruno Walter conducting Brahms.

During the summer, Frances was thoroughly distracted from her anxiety over Ralph's health by shocking news about Janetta and Derek. Out of the blue, on the day she gave birth to their daughter Rose in hospital, he telephoned to tell her that he was now living with her older half-sister, Angela. Looking back, Frances was blunt. 'Ralph and I felt very far from objective about this harrowing situation, and it was some time before the seed of relief that the marriage was over could develop into a thriving plant. We had never happily accepted it.' They gave Janetta all the support they could while she set up house with her new baby and her two small daughters in London. At least, as Ralph wrote to Gerald, Derek's millions would ensure her a measure of security. In mid-September, Janetta came to stay for five days at Ham Spray, and in long talks while blackberrying Frances began to feel they were growing close again.

That autumn, Burgo went up to Oxford. For Frances and Ralph, to be able to deliver him to his new rooms, with his name painted on the door, and hear his scout take charge – 'Are you Mr Partridge, sir? I shall be looking after you now' was a huge relief, though it was hard for them to shake off the years of anxiety. He seemed to settle in satisfactorily; David and Rachel Cecil kept an eye on him. That Christmas, during his first vacation, they broke with tradition and went to Paris for a few days, staying on the Left Bank, drinking at the Deux Magots and visiting Boris Anrep's studio. Over a lavish dinner on their last night at Lapérouse, a conversation about values took place, Ralph and Burgo siding together against Frances' 'high-mindedness'. It was all a great success, but while they were there Ralph read in *The Times* that Molly MacCarthy was dead. They had both loved her since the early 1920s, and felt very sad; especially when they found a farewell letter from her awaiting them at Ham Spray thanking them for all the lovely times they had had together over the years. Molly and Desmond both dead; Maroussa ill with cancer; Raymond Mortimer facing an operation; Ralph's health in doubt for the first time in his life: no wonder that Frances sometimes felt that 'Postman Death' was knocking on their door. 'I notice our generation talk a great deal about old age and death, because they have come within range and we talk about everything,' she wrote a little later, adding 'but I'm not sure the young enjoy seeing us gesticulating and even laughing on our way to the tomb.'

Fifteen

Facing Fear, 1954–1960

By 1954, it was exactly thirty years since Ralph and Lytton had bought Ham Spray, the house found by Carrington, and Frances had helped them paint it and move in; and over twenty since it had become her own. Ham Spray's past had never been ignored, much less rejected. Visitors, many of whom had known it as long as Frances had, were often struck by how little the place had changed, with Carrington's decorations (including a lampshade she had made and decorated one Christmas), Lytton's library, the paintings and the Spanish plates all as they had always been. Behind the scenes, too, Ham Spray was stuffed with memories – old letters and papers, put away since 1932. Early in 1954, Frances decided to tackle a large trunk of letters to Carrington; it made her 'dreadfully sad ... many of the writers dead though their voices go on screaming silently'. She threw away a great many: 'mounds of parental love and scolding, or girlfriends' meaningless high spirits', and tried to organise the best, such as those from Alix; there is no mention of letters from Ralph. She did not enjoy the task; when it was done, she sank back into reading Gibbon's *Decline and Fall of the Roman Empire* with a feeling of relief.

That spring, Frances was beset by unease. Waking in the small hours one night, she had 'one of those unexpected and acutely painful "moments of truth". In a flash I saw the precariousness of happiness – of mine, of Ralph's and Burgo's – and saw it very clearly.' She went downstairs and sat in the music room with Minnie, her latest cat, trying to think things through. She considered herself a hedonist, whose guiding principle in life was the pursuit of happiness for herself and others. Now Ralph, the basis of all her happiness for thirty years, was threatened; where did that leave her? 'I thought that to be a practising hedonist was an enormous gamble; happiness to him fulfils the same role as faith plays to the Christian, and loss of happiness is like loss of faith.' Characteristically, she did not just let this thought go, but started rereading John Stuart Mill, and making notes.

From now on, like everyone newly aware that someone they love is vulnerable, Frances watched Ralph. He hated her to fuss, so she tried not to. For the moment, he seemed well, and his doctors were satisfied with him. He was following another sensational trial taking place in Winchester: three men, Peter Wildeblood, Michael Pitt-Rivers and Lord Montagu of Beaulieu had been accused of homosexual acts by two younger RAF men, and the press were having a field day. So, too, was Ralph, who wrote long, sardonic, bawdy letters to friends like Gerald Brenan and Victor Pritchett. Frances and Burgo went along one day, but she did not stay long; she found the humiliating ordeal of the three in the dock cruel and 'morally wrong'. Now, Ralph was approached by a publisher to write a book about homosexuality based on the trial; Frances rather wished he would, while suspecting that he would decline. He toyed with the idea for a while, but she was right: 'I feel my rough methods are hardly suited to such an eggshell subject,' he wrote to Gerald, adding that it had long been clear to him that 'hatred of homosexuality derives from prudish inability to face one's own homosexual tendencies'. On meeting E.M. Forster at a party at Hilton, Ralph asked him whether he should proceed with such a book: 'and he wagged his head like a bird in a zoo aviary – a toucan perhaps – and said No'. Old Bloomsbury was still understandably nervous on the subject.

Ralph's letters to Gerald suggest that he too was in a sombre and reflective mood. Frances had also been sorting out letters from Gerald, which reminded Ralph that they had been friends and correspondents for forty years. 'I want to say now', he wrote, 'that the attachment on my side has been one of the great pleasures of my life.' It was easier for him to grumble to his old friend than to Frances; he did so now about Burgo, and 'that unending match which the older generation is forever losing', and about himself. 'I am a bad father, a tiresome husband and an unfruitful man – and I shall never be anything else. Lack of spirit is at the bottom of it.' By spirit, he perhaps meant energy; he certainly had less than a healthy man of rising sixty leading a quiet life in the country might have hoped to have. Meanwhile, Frances was also writing to Gerald, resolutely cheerful letters thanking him for some Spanish orchids he had sent her and relaying the current jokes about the Montagu case. Duff Cooper: 'What are the police doing? Surely they know we would all rather be buggered than burgled?' Churchill, on what should happen to the accused: 'They ought to be thrown into a bottomless pit.' As for Ralph: she described him as 'pretty well I think, but liable to get depressed about himself'.

Frances kept her own spirits up by working on the Freud indexes and pursuing her musical life. In May, she was invited to join the Newbury Orchestra, which suited her well as her quartet life had dwindled; she found the orchestra hard going at first, but loved it. It was Burgo's first summer term at Oxford, and Ralph put on his Leander tie to go to Eights Week, and show his son the oar with his name on it hanging in the Christ Church boathouse; it was all great fun, but followed another setback when Ralph was struck by agonising pains from a kidney stone. Not long after, Janetta was taken to hospital with peritonitis; she came to Ham Spray to convalesce. Frances and Ralph loved to look after her; they tried to remain detached from her complicated love life, although they could not help it when their hearts lifted at the slightest sign that she and Robert might be reconciled. When Janetta recovered, she needed someone to help her drive down to the South of France, where she had taken a house for the summer. Her latest conquest, Ralph Jarvis (it was all rather awkward: his wife was a cousin of Anne Hill's, and his daughter a friend of Burgo's), was a possibility, as indeed was Robert, but in the end the task fell to Ralph. Frances was not fooled by his simulated reluctance: 'He is inclined to preen himself on travelling with a lovely young woman who will be taken for his wife. "More likely your daughter" I say snubbingly', adding that although she hated him flying or driving long distances without her, 'it is the right thing and it is mainly my doing that he goes'. While he was away, she had three young musicians to stay – her nephew William Garnett, Pippa Strachey and Burgo's former tutor, Alan Tyson, who played the viola and composed a piece to be played to Ralph on his return. (Tyson was a brilliant young man, a philosopher as well as a Mozart expert, who was also helping James Strachey with the Freud Standard Edition.) When Ralph got back, she gathered that Janetta had struck him as 'a somewhat exigeante princess'. Janetta and her love affairs are mentioned quite often in Ralph's letters to Gerald in the 1950s, always fondly, sometimes a touch cynically; he professed relief that his own life was not so complicated. 'Don't you congratulate yourself at times at being out of the hurly burly of sex?' In fact, Gerald sustained a keen interest in sex as he grew older, and rather enjoyed making this plain to his old rival.

After a typical Ham Spray summer, with a visit from Saxon ('blanched as an almond, fragile as old lace') and a weekend with the Nichols in Essex, Ralph and Frances took off at the beginning of October for Italy. After a taste of Florence, last seen by Frances in 1924, they went on to Rome. This was the first visit there for them both, and they were intoxicated. Characteristically, Frances' diary evokes not just the beauty of the city, its ruins and fountains, but the experience of taking a Roman bus, which she likened to being a mouthful of food working its way from the mouth through the gut 'so as to be ready to drop out of the arse at the psychological moment'. They drove back through Italy, pursuing Piero della Francesca's paintings from Urbino to Sansepolcro and Arezzo. It was, they both decided, their best holiday for many years.

During the mid-1950s, regular Memoir Club meetings kept the flame of Bloomsbury flickering away. Not only did it bring the survivors together two or three times a year, it stimulated them to look through their letters and diaries and begin to shape and define their recollections. Although Bloomsbury's stock was low – Janetta recalls how irrelevant it all seemed at this time – a trickle of books had begun: Leonard Woolf published the first taste of Virginia Woolf's diaries in 1953, and both Bunny Garnett and Gerald Brenan were embarking on autobiography. Frances recorded the first approaches to Ralph and herself by American academics; at first, she found the confident way they spoke of 'Lytton' or 'Virginia' disconcerting, but she soon got used to it.

Ralph, never tempted to write any kind of memoir himself, ruminated occasionally on Bloomsbury in his correspondence with Gerald. His tone in these exchanges was detached, ironic, impersonal; he gave no hint that his own encounters with Bloomsbury had changed his life. Like Frances, he admired the Virginia Woolf diary, while having not much to say for her as a novelist nor, looking back, as a person. 'She was a remarkably heartless woman,' he wrote, 'living in an auto-erotic world of her own imagining, and engaged in a lifelong struggle with words in preference to people.' In 1956, Ralph was a contributor, along with Vanessa and Quentin Bell, to a radio programme about Virginia. In light, clipped tones he recalled her pleasure in teasing the young, and how she could make young men feel foolish. Leonard omitted most of Virginia's criticism of Ralph during his time at the Hogarth Press, apart from her anger when he failed to get her novel to the reviewers on time in 1922. Ralph called it 'a reprimand from the grave', and added that of course 'Bloomsbury prestige has sunk into the trough along with George Meredith'. Later he returned to the theme of Virginia's deficiencies, adding that not only had she always craved recognition as a great novelist but that in general 'ambition was the worm in Bloomsbury, riddling their fine ideals with its insatiable progress'. Although Frances sometimes regretted his own lack of ambition, to Ralph it was no failing.

When the Memoir Club members – described by Frances as 'this wood of old trees in whose shade I came alive myself – gathered again in April 1955, Frances was struck by how impervious those present were to insult or neglect. There had just been a fierce attack on Bloomsbury's elitism and irrelevance in the *New Statesman*, and Frances had wondered how the old guard would react; but Vanessa, Duncan and E.M. Forster showed what she called 'their usual, really rather sublime indifference to what the world thinks of them'. She admired them for it, and for their refusal to give in to old age (she was wryly amused by Bunny's excited account of his new novel, *Aspects of Love*, about how young girls were always falling in love with men in their sixties, which became his most successful book since *Lady into Fox*). More and more, Frances appreciated the courage and consistency of Old Bloomsbury, the way they held onto their standards. She felt this particularly when her own were challenged, as they were that spring over a weekend at Mottisfont, the fine house in Wiltshire where Maud Russell, a great friend of Boris Anrep's since the death of Maroussa, held rather demanding house parties, and Frances had a brush with the formidable Liberal politician and grande dame, Lady Violet Bonham Carter. Friendly though she was, Frances felt that 'beneath her social gifts lay a system of worldly and conventional values which set my teeth on edge, nor was I mollified by hearing her say to Clive that she would rather both her sons had been killed in the war than fail to play their part in it'.

Frances' own son (who agreed with his parents about pacifism, and who had been excused National Service after an appeal to Dr Glover for a statement) was happier at last, she thought, beginning to enjoy himself at Oxford and to make new friends. The trouble was that although she wanted him to be independent, she fretted if he was out of touch, especially when she was concerned about Ralph, who nowadays often struck her as 'shockingly short of vitality'. But that summer, they were all swept up in a plan with Janetta to share a house in Spain. This time they did not head south, but rented a handsome old villa at San Fiz, near Coruña on the Atlantic coast. The basic party – Janetta, her three little girls and a nanny, Ralph, Frances and Burgo – were looked after by three cheerful maids and other friends came and went, including two of Burgo's contemporaries, Jonathan Gathorne-Hardy and Caroline Jarvis, and the Brenans. Two months were spent swimming and picnicking on the wide surf beaches, dancing and drinking and watching fireworks at local fiestas; Janetta went off to Portugal for a few days with Burgo, Jonny and Caroline. When they got back, it was not long before the sharp-eyed Frances realised that the exceptionally good-looking Jonny, aged twenty, was falling for Janetta, and that she was taken with him. Complications ensued, not least because it irritated Ralph to see her charmed by a handsome youth under his very nose; but they could not help liking Jonny, who as well as being handsome and clever was nice to Burgo and got on especially well with Gerald, who Frances felt was not best pleased to find the Partridges settled into a Spanish life of their own. He felt better when he decided that where they were was not really Spain at all.

All that year, Frances had either a Freudian index or a translation from Spanish in hand. As word got around that she was available, a small but steady stream of work came her way. She had finished one index in July, before leaving for Spain; back at Ham Spray in October, she started another. Translation, like indexing, suited Frances; she was both scrupulous and delicate in her use of words. Nineteen fifty-six started quietly, although it was an exceptionally cold winter. Vanessa and Duncan came to stay for the first time, their reservations about Ralph forgotten, and proved appreciative and entertaining guests. In the spring, Frances and Ralph took Janetta with them for a short holiday in the Pyrenees, where they picnicked among the spring flowers on the mountainsides; she gave them some grounds to hope that in the end she and Robert would be together. Burgo was facing Finals, and it was touch-and-go as to whether he would lose his nerve and pull out; when he did not, Frances felt he had won a significant victory over himself. That summer he turned twenty-one; at a gathering at Hilton, she noticed how 'little Henrietta', the loveliest of the four Garnett girls, now eleven, seemed to have fallen for Burgo, and sat holding his hand with a romantic expression on her face. There was something romantic about Burgo too, with his dark curling hair and brooding, Byronic air. He celebrated his birthday at Ham Spray with three of his men friends from Oxford, including Frances' favourite, Simon Young, Serena Dunn and Quentin Bell. Frances had begun to think it was time he fell in love, but there was no sign of it as yet.

It was in September, when they were in Ireland staying with Eddie Sackville-West, that Frances began to fear that Ralph's health had taken a turn for the worse. When they got home she insisted he see a doctor; the verdict was angina and heart disease. Ralph's chest pains came and went; he was told to rest and put on a strict diet. Frances tried valiantly to keep panic at bay and face facts. 'Any strength I possess is available for Ralph's illness,' she wrote, 'my task is to explore every cranny of the situation, however agonising, and somehow come to terms with it as best I can.' As she well knew, the position she was now in was commonplace, but that did not make it easier to bear. No-one has written better than Frances about the sickening anxiety endured by those who find themselves watching for signs of recurrent illness in the person they love best, walking on thin ice, waiting for the next crack to open while trying to lead a normal life. Janetta came to Ham Spray to cheer them both up; Frances found her gentle touch the greatest help and comfort. The local doctor, known at Ham Spray as

Sawbones, was painfully heavy-handed. When Frances bumped into him outside the fishmonger's in Hungerford, 'with a grin on his face he told me straight out that he thought I ought to know that Ralph might die at any moment'. No wonder that Frances drove to orchestra practice that night feeling 'terribly sad and lonely'.

After Janetta left, Robert came to stay for a few days. He and Ralph had long discussions about the looming Suez Crisis; after Nasser seized the Canal, Israel invaded Egypt, France and Britain issued their ultimatum and war became inevitable. When Robert was abruptly sent off by *The Observer* to report from Israel, Frances could hardly bear it. The British actions were repulsive to her, and in the wake of what Sawbones had said she had been planning to consult Robert about how much to tell Ralph. Accustomed as she was to relying on him to put her worries in perspective, now that he was the source of her anxiety she did not know what to do.

Slowly, Ralph got better, and Frances' fears subsided. They went for gentle walks together; she built in more stops than usual to look at plants, hoping he would not notice. Burgo came down; it is not clear how much she confided in him about his father's illness. She was pleased to find him 'thinking hard' about the Suez fiasco, to which he was vehemently opposed. Bunny also came, bringing Amaryllis and Henrietta; even though he was pro-Eden and talked for seven hours about himself, it was good to see him. Early in December Ralph saw his heart specialist in London and was told that he had recovered pretty well and advised to reduce his smoking and drinking, which caused Frances' heart to sink. He had smoked a pipe all his adult life; it was one of his greatest pleasures. For once, Janetta irritated her by telling Ralph she did not see why he should not drink if he wanted to.

Now they decided it would do them both good to spend the coldest part of the winter in Spain. They booked flights to Gibraltar for mid-January 1957, and wrote to the Brenans to see if they could stay with them while looking for a house to rent. Gerald's answer was half-hearted, and Frances began to feel doubtful about the whole enterprise. When Janetta offered to go with them, suddenly everything seemed possible again. 'Ralph and I said to each other that she is our best friend. I certainly lean on her more than anyone else, young as she is.' Julia, Lawrence and Burgo were at Ham Spray for Christmas; Frances found her son 'angelically helpful, genial and talkative'. By early January, the Brenans were still prevaricating; Ralph became so alarmingly furious that Frances feared Spain might not be a good idea after all, 'if Ralph and Gerald are going to get so worked up with each other'. Her spirits sank still further.

In the end, some friends of Mary Campbell's, whom Frances and Ralph had met once or twice at Stokke, came to the rescue. Bill and Annie Davis were hospitable Americans with plenty of money who had a large and comfortable house, La Consula, outside Churriana. Annie's sister Jean had been Cyril Connolly's first wife, and they had remained on good terms with him; he was frequently at La Consula himself.

By late January, after a few days with the Davises, the Partridges found a house. Buena Vista stood above the road between the Davises and the Brenans, and when Frances and Janetta had made it warm and comfortable she began to feel better. The beauty all around them soothed her; they hired a small car and drove into the hills to hunt for wild flowers, the almond blossom was out, the sun shone and there was snow on the mountain tops. The Campbells were staying at La Consula, and before long Cyril arrived. Frances tried to like him better, and sometimes succeeded; but she remained irritated by the way everyone deferred to him, and the way he took this for granted. The fact that, as Janetta told her, he was in despair because Barbara Skelton was carrying on with George Weidenfeld did not seem to her an excuse, and she was struck by his grotesque appearance. 'With his great round head passing necklessly into his body, his torso clad in a flashy American beach shirt, skiing trousers and fur-lined boots, he looked like some strange species of synthetic man or Golem.' Frances preferred the company of a handsome, charming young Spaniard, Jaime Parladé, whose family had property in the area and who was evidently much taken with Janetta. Gerald took them to visit Málaga cemetery, where he planned to be buried; meanwhile he was working himself into a state of romantic anticipation over the imminent arrival of Noel and Catherine Carrington's twenty-year-old daughter, Burgo's childhood playmate Joanna. Now a fair-haired beauty and a painter, Joanna had spent a weekend at Ham Spray that autumn, where her projected visit to the Brenans was much discussed. In a long letter to her mother, Joanna, who had known the Partridges and their friends all her life, looked at them with fresh eyes. 'One can't help liking Ralph and forgiving him,' she wrote, 'but dear me he is so malicious, tears people apart in the most destructive manner.' He filleted people like a fish, alarmingly quick to spot the worst in everyone. 'But at least he enjoys and probably loves best all the people he is beastliest about.' Robert Kee was present, and Joanna found him alarmingly cynical, more so than Ralph, who could be 'rather little boyish and loveable at times'. Robert struck her as 'in complete sympathy with Ralph and always supports him and in many ways is rather like him'. She really liked Julia, finding her 'gentle and restrained, shrewd but not malicious, sad but not bitter' while Frances was 'terribly sweet and kind and somehow protective'. They all went over to Stokke for drinks and Joanna, observing the older generation at play, was struck by how 'desperate' they all appeared, and wondered what the point of it all was. Overall, she sensed 'an undercurrent of frustration and disappointment'. As for Frances and Ralph, they privately agreed that Gerald was bound to identify Joanna with her aunt and fancy himself in love with her.

The winter escape to Spain seemed like a miracle. Within a month Frances felt that Ralph was stronger, and when they returned to England at the beginning of March they were already planning to come back later in the year. Frances took back with her some interesting Spanish plants, warmly received by the Natural History Museum; she was encouraged to do more. She settled down to a new Freud index, without finding it meant much to her: 'I sometimes wonder', she confessed, 'if my "work" is not the frantic leg movements of a spider just before it hurtles down the runaway hole in the bath.' Ralph had ups and downs; he hated feeling feeble. When they argued, their normally enjoyable discussions could become fractious. A disagreement about communism ended with Ralph shouting at her; she thought she might faint. She felt deeply tired and apathetic; but although she recognised that in Freudian language she was suffering from a withdrawal of libido (Frances very seldom used such terms, but 'libido' was one she found useful, denoting appetite for life) she still recorded moments of pure delight, observing her garden or her cat drinking a saucer of milk.

They decided to take Buena Vista again for three months from the beginning of December. Frances went back to the Natural History Museum, where she was delighted to be treated like a professional, given a press for her plant specimens, and asked to look out for a particular Spanish dianthus for Kew. When she received a cheque for her last index and a request from Robert to review some children's books for *The Spectator*, she noted 'a spurious sense of being a going concern'.

This time, they set off confidently to drive out to Spain by themselves. All went well – as usual, they made a special stop in Bordeaux for a huge meal – until, pausing for a night in Madrid, they found themselves, by chance, in the hotel last visited on their first trip as lovers in 1925. When Frances pointed this out to Ralph, the contrast between his past and present condition made him miserable and furious; again, he reduced her to tears. Calling on the Brenans on the way to Buena Vista, they found Joanna Carrington in residence and Gerald in a state of high tension. He told them how wonderful he felt, how close he was to Joanna and how she had rejuvenated him.

Before long, trouble broke out between the Brenan and Partridge establishments after Ralph and Frances dropped in on Gerald and Gamel one morning, a time they liked to reserve for work. Gerald wrote Ralph one of his stinkers, whereupon Ralph stopped all visits and a frosty silence fell. Joanna's letters home convey her amazement that two grown men should behave so childishly; she thought they were both at fault. She felt sorry for Frances and for Burgo, who arrived for Christmas to find his father refusing to speak to his old friend; and when Burgo went to the Brenans to see Joanna, Gerald forbade her to ask him in. By this time, Joanna had realised that the Consula crowd were as malicious as Ralph; she reported that Burgo's arrival had not been greeted warmly, not because he was disliked but because 'he unbalances Ralph and consequently Frances'. Slowly, relations improved. Christmas Eve was celebrated together with games and a visit from local musicians, and the Partridges spent Christmas Day at La Consula. Joanna, who knew all about his early difficulties, found Burgo calmer and his occasional stammer less pronounced; they gravitated towards each other, shared reservations about the frantic socialising of the expatriates and were soon going off together to the clubs and bars of Torremolinos. Burgo told her how alienated he felt from his parents and their talk of values. 'I have never had illusions,' he said. 'I have been disillusioned since I was ten. I believe in nothing.' It was Gerald who was now unbalanced by Burgo; he hated everything Torremolinos stood for, and resented Burgo's claim on Joanna's attention. Once, Ralph had won and kept Carrington; was Ralph's son now cutting him out with Carrington's lovely niece? Joanna's departure for London calmed him down, for the moment. Later, he would claim that they had slept together; she always denied it.

Robert Kee arrived to stay with the Partridges; he was soon drawn into La Consula's orbit, which as usual revolved around Cyril's moods and wishes. Already, Frances felt strong reservations about the social round; she much preferred days collecting plants or working on another Spanish translation, and quiet evenings with Ralph over their olive-wood fire. Before Burgo left in mid-January, they took him and Robert on an expedition to Yegen, last seen in 1933. It was extraordinary, and poignant, to be there again, to see the same view over the white rooftops and breathe the clear, sharp air.

In February, Raymond Mortimer came to stay. They took him to dinner at La Consula on Cyril's last night – 'rather orgiastic', Frances wrote, with a great deal of drink and even some hashish. 'I resent being made drunk against my will,' she wrote crossly. 'It's as if someone deliberately passed me on their infectious disease.' Beneath her disapproval lurked her fear that such indulgences were bad for Ralph; and she was also uneasy when he and Gerald had a fierce exchange about the way he had been portrayed in

Gerald's first autobiographical book, *South from Granada*, just published. Taxed with showing his friend in an unflattering light, Gerald's response was hardly soothing. 'Oh, it wasn't unkind at all. I merely made you out a dashing philistine who slept with actresses – just what everyone would like to be. Anyway I sent it to you and you passed it for publication.' Ralph hit back; he told Gerald that although he had not interfered his lawyer had considered the portrait libellous, but that what he really objected to was the way Gerald showed himself as behaving admirably, 'when really what you were after was seducing my wife'. Cornered, Gerald launched into an attack on Lytton, asserting that his writing had suffered because he wrote to make money; to prevent Ralph boiling over, Frances stepped in. Neither Lytton nor any Old Bloomsbury writer wrote for money, she insisted, 'and I challenge you to prove the contrary'. To Raymond's relief, the conversation settled down; but it was the first shot in a campaign that was to reverberate for years.

The drive back was not easy. They took Raymond as far as Barcelona; the wind was cold and Ralph's angina bothered him. It was a cold spring at Ham Spray, too, and Frances felt it had perhaps been a mistake to leave Spain so early; and they had returned to find the neighbourhood agitated by the arrival of American planes carrying nuclear weapons at an air base near Newbury. She and Ralph approved, naturally, of the growing anti-bomb movement; to Frances, it was obvious. 'How can people ask "Ought we to renounce nuclear war?" Of course we ought to.' As for their friends, when they saw Janetta it became clear that her situation with Robert was as hopeless as ever. Although neither of them was happy, and none of their other relationships had worked, neither could quite trust the other enough to start again. The Pritchetts were also having problems: Dorothy was drinking too much and VSP was having an affair. At least Robin and Mary Campbell, after a bad patch, seemed to be back together again. And Burgo had been commissioned by his friend Anthony Blond, the dynamic young publisher, to write a book about orgies. His parents had their doubts about this idea, which seemed to them to verge on sensationalism and vulgarity; but at least he was hard at work.

In April, a letter arrived from Gerald, who had evidently been brooding. He maintained that Ralph had been unjust, that it was he who had behaved worst during the Great Row of 1922. Talking it all over, Frances found herself fascinated by the way time brought out new elements in old emotional dramas. 'We all knew, even before Joanna went out to Spain, that Gerald would identify her with Carrington,' she wrote. 'Her own parents do it, Ralph sometimes does; I always feel it's rather hard on this beautiful young girl to be saddled with the very unusual and potent personality of an aunt whom she never even met.' Frances was right, and Joanna resisted the identification, but it was striking the way that her letters resembled her aunt's, with drawings sprinkling the text. Frances and Ralph decided that in Spain, when Gerald told Ralph about his closeness to Joanna, what he was really saying was that he had got Carrington after all. By June, however, Gerald was off on a new tack. He wrote triumphantly to tell Ralph that he had a new girlfriend, Hetty, one of the wandering hippies who had started to make their way to southern Spain, who was proving sexually obliging. Ralph was irritated; Frances rather felt for Gamel, and promptly invited her to stay.

During that summer, Frances and Ralph learned that Robert Kee had taken up with someone new. Cynthia Judah met him through television, where she was working on the production team of 'Tonight'. A slender, pretty, dark-haired girl in her twenties, before long she was seriously in love with Robert. He had inconclusive talks with Ralph about the pros and cons of 'settling down', and before long brought Cynthia to Ham Spray. It cannot have been an easy occasion for anyone, least of all for Cynthia, who much later put her first impressions into a novel, giving an unflattering but instantly recognisable view of the house and its owners.

In the novel Harold, an attractive, tormented man, takes his girlfriend Victoria for a weekend in the country with an older couple he admires and loves. 'He would not want Guy and Vivian, sharp as needles, to think badly of him . . . They had probably almost certainly never met a working woman before, certainly not one who worked in television. Come to think of it they had almost certainly never seen a television set.' Victoria is surprised by the shabbiness both of the house and the woman who opens the door to them. 'She was wearing shapeless trousers, a top of indeterminate cut and colour and a necklace of what looked like dull silver teeth around her neck. Her face was creased, her eyes round and brown and her grey hair thin, wispy and short. Behind her stood a big burly man with a red face and a rumbly voice. They were both laughing and clucking as they greeted Harold with pats, hugs, handshakes and kisses.' Victoria observes the couple's peculiar lilting voices and frequent emphasis on unexpected words: 'Speaking seemed to be a sort of game to be played with initiates; an odd word here or there, a cue for general amusement.' The house strikes her as cold and uncomfortable, with threadbare rugs and ugly, clumsy pictures, worn sofas and chairs, dim lamps with painted parchment shades and a fireplace surrounded by painted tiles above which hung 'a strange picture of a very long thin man in a yellow suit lying back and holding the tips of his attenuated fingers together before him'.

Victoria feels excluded as the others launch into private jokes and anecdotes over glasses of wine that they have bottled themselves. 'No-one took the slightest notice of her.' Guy gives her some wine; she decided that he 'looked nice, but not very, and was obviously less important than Vivian and Harold'. Over dinner (toad-in-the-hole, Brussels sprouts and fried potatoes), when they learn what she does, they are not impressed. '"Television," said Guy, as though he were tasting an early strawberry and lowering his voice several registers on the third syllable.' All through the novel, Victoria is made to feel an outsider; Vivian describes her as 'a strange little creature from another planet'. But Victoria is not altogether a victim; she keeps her head, and her job, and by the end it seems that her competence and kindness may win Harold over.

Long afterwards, discussing the novel, Cynthia stood by her first impressions. Bloomsbury meant little to her; what she noticed was an atmosphere of social and intellectual superiority, and an idiom that seemed to her faintly ridiculous. As time went on, Ham Spray became part of her life, but looking back she recalled how little she liked some of its habits: the joking about the servants, Mrs Hoare and Wilde (Madame la Putaine and Monsieur le Sauvage), the dismissal of television, the malicious reading-out of letters over breakfast and the embarrassing naked swimming. She also remembered feeling sympathy for Burgo; he too seemed not to fit in, unlike Robert, who certainly did. To someone like Cynthia, Frances and Ralph could appear snobbish, affected and unkind. To them, she represented not only an uncongenial contemporary world but a threat to their hopes of seeing Robert and Janetta reunited.

Despite efforts on both sides, Frances and Cynthia never really took to each other. Soon after the visit, Frances found it a relief to be reminded of the solid, if eccentric, characters and values of Old Bloomsbury by a visit to James and Alix at Lords' Wood, their house at Marlow. She found them 'as ever true to themselves ... though admitting that Bloomsbury was now in the trough they were convinced they would rise again.' Frances was not so sure: 'Their figures have become very small, like those of people rapidly disappearing down a road, but whether this is perspective or their actual size I can't be sure.' Marjorie Strachey, never a small figure, came for a weekend; now seventy-six, she was still impressively full of energy.

Later that summer, Robin and Mary Campbell's marriage finally collapsed. Frances and Ralph were saddened, but followed their rule of not taking sides and remained friends with both of them. Burgo, meanwhile, had finished his book and gone abroad with Anthony Blond, who had just married Charlotte Strachey; after surviving a bad car crash in Yugoslavia, he was spotted by Bunny in Venice, who wrote to tell Frances that her son was looking 'handsomer than I've ever seen him, and obviously happy, not a care in the world'. Good news of Burgo made Ralph and Frances especially sympathetic to their old friend Rosamond Lehmann, whose daughter Sally had died suddenly of polio in Jakarta. They asked her to stay; she had already told them that she was convinced that Sally was still in touch with her, and although they were equally sure that this was total nonsense, they were moved as well as puzzled by her certainty.

As the winter wore on, Frances found herself recording both her complete happiness with Ralph when they were alone together – she called it 'perfect relaxation without dullness' – and her fearful battles with her anxiety whenever he seemed tired, in pain or out of sorts. Looking back, she always wondered whether she should have tried harder to talk to him about the possibility of his dying suddenly and before her; she rather wished she had, but at the time it was just too difficult. It was hard for her, rational as she always tried to be, to accept that on some deep level she felt that if she tried hard enough she could keep him alive and at her side, as if by ignoring death she could keep it at bay. She felt low as the year ended, and the successful publication of Burgo's book barely rated a mention in her diary, although she recorded a mixed review by Cyril Connolly. In fact, the book was well received on the whole, with a mention in *The Spectator* and a long review in the *New Statesman*, which called it 'highly entertaining'. It sold well and was the saving of Blond's struggling publishing venture. Like his father, Burgo's approach was more academic and historical than crude or sensational, but it was unusual at the time to write openly about sodomy, rape and group sex, even among the ancient Greeks.

Although Frances and Ralph were due to return to Buena Vista in January, sharing the house this time with Janetta and her two youngest daughters, they had decided that four weeks in Spain would be enough, and planned to go on to spend three more by themselves in a quiet hotel at Praia da Rocha in Portugal. Frances felt increasingly out of tune with the expatriate social life around La Consula, the parties, the drinking, the gossip and speculation about everyone's love life, not least Janetta's; she called the cast of characters 'a company of voyeurs flambéed in alcohol'. She even found herself displeased with Janetta, who tended to be swept along on the Consula tide, and worrying about Georgie and Rose; 'having seen how desperately they long for her company I marvel at her blindness'. She particularly disliked being interrogated about Janetta and Robert by Cyril, who had heard rumours that they were on the point of setting up house together again. Robin Campbell had brought the art student who later that year became his wife, Susan Benson, to La Consula; here was another strange young woman to deal with. And she took a strong dislike to Hetty, the girl who had now moved in with the Brenans. She hated feeling so disapproving, but could not help it: 'I wish we'd never come here', she found herself writing, after a month had passed.

But when they moved on to the quiet, old-fashioned hotel at Praia da Rocha, still in those days an unspoiled seaside village in the Algarve, she picked up. Back at Ham Spray towards the end of March, Frances wrote out for herself a 'charter for living', based on her strong feelings about their time away. Social life should be kept to a minimum; she wanted peace and privacy with Ralph, and some interesting work to do. She was back with Freud, and found herself as a result wondering whether her resolutions represented a Freudian 'flight from reality'; but surely, she concluded, they signified an acceptance? One night early in April, she woke with the words 'It's a case of Mournful Prementia' on her lips; it amused her to have invented 'an ailment that [with its suggestion of melancholy and prediction] somewhat conveyed my mood'.

Her amusement did not last long; by the middle of April it was clear that Ralph was significantly worse. With the support of Janetta and his doctors, and after some horrible sleepless nights, she persuaded him to go to bed and stay there. He had suffered a second heart attack, and it was a full month before he was able to lead a more or less normal life. His first outing was a visit to Stokke, where they sat in the sun talking to Freddie Ayer about Bertrand Russell, Madame de Staël and Duncan Grant's painting. That evening, Frances started reading and making notes on Russell's latest book.

The summer passed peacefully enough. Clive came to stay, with his new chosen companion, Barbara Bagenal. Frances continued to find her a trial, but recognised that she looked after Clive very kindly. By now, Frances had been appointed Secretary of the Memoir Club, at Vanessa Bell's suggestion; she started to plan another paper. In June, they managed a weekend away at Crichel, where Raymond entertained them all with an account of a recent visit to the Churchills at Chartwell. Winston, he reported, was quite gaga. On a visit to London, they went to see Robert in his new flat in Percy Street, where they watched *Panorama* on his brand-new television. Frances was not impressed. 'It certainly riveted one's attention in a horrid compulsive sort of way, yet I was bored and rather disgusted.' When Robert told them that they were watching one of the great television personalities, 'the

best-known face in England' (perhaps Richard Dimbleby?) all Frances saw
was 'a charmless countenance with the manner of a Hoover salesman'.
Television, she decided, was definitely not for her, even though Robert loved
it and was well on the way to becoming a star.

In July 1959 Frances organised her first Memoir Club meeting. Dinner
for fifteen was followed by Julia's paper, 'Animalia' (dragged out of her by
Frances and later published by the *The New Yorker*) and Leonard Woolf's
on religion, at Leonard's house. But the event of the summer for Frances
was that Burgo brought a girlfriend home, a 'pretty puss' called Jane. Frances
was delighted, calling it more important than his getting a degree. The
weekend went well; 'even Ralph said he thought my manner to her was
exactly right, and inferred that he'd been anxious about it. I rather think he
has always thought I would be crabbing and jealous ... I feel nothing but
gratitude to her.' Through Anthony Blond, Burgo had made another good
friend, the novelist Simon Raven. Frances and Ralph considered the louche,
humorous Raven good for Burgo, whose confidence had definitely grown
since his book came out. 'His liberated vitality makes even his hostility
quite funny,' she observed. 'As when he said to me: "Don't take yourself so
seriously – you treat yourself like a sort of cathedral".'

The autumn found Frances indexing Freud on jokes, and wondering,
after observing how differently she and Ralph reacted to the news of the
suicide of an acquaintance, about the nature of sympathetic emotion. She
sometimes thought she had too much, while recognising how she counted
on it in others – Janetta most of all. She kept anxiety at bay with music –
an evening with her orchestra always restored her, even though Ralph did
not much like it when she left him alone – and plunged into reading the
Memoirs of Saint-Simon in nineteen volumes. She also read the latest literary
sensation, Nabokov's *Lolita*, which she liked, not finding it in the least
pornographic. A visit to the Nichols was not a great success; Ralph was not
feeling his best and Phil had been suffering from depression. On the way
home, they agreed that the two men had never really liked each other; Ralph
blamed Phil's 'inability to blot out the past', but it was probably mutual. At
Crichel again, Frances had an unusual crisis of confidence. 'There is a sense
in which I always feel a fraud,' she wrote. 'A fraud as a violinist, a fraud as
a car driver and cook, perhaps ultimately I feel a fraud as a human being.'
Sonia Orwell and her new husband, Michael Pitt-Rivers (of the Montagu
trial), came for dinner; Sonia, Frances thought, had developed 'a bloated,
tart in a night club look'.

Over Christmas, Ralph appeared 'dispirited and tired' and she began to
lose her nerve about going back to Spain in January. They were once again

driving out; she wondered if he was really up to it. 'I dread lest any small mishap common to journeys might affect him, and can think of no magic talisman to quell my fears except the one word COURAGE, which I have written on every page of my pocket diary.' She was not so rattled, though, that she failed to reflect on the Freudian significance of Cynthia's Christmas present to Janetta, who had organised a gathering at Stokke: a key, or Kee-ring.

Frances needed all her courage for the journey to Spain in January 1960. She fretted about Ralph 'guzzling' rich meals on their way through France, and in Madrid, when they tried a stroll together before dinner, he felt so weak that he had to give up; back at the hotel, 'he sank into an armchair. After a pause he said: I'm all right now. I'm as right as rain.' Then, sotto voce: 'No, not right as rain. I shall never be as right as rain again. That's the worst of it.' Later, he fell asleep at once; but Frances lay awake, 'penetrated and saturated by grief'.

They had decided against Buena Vista that winter, choosing a quiet hotel in Alicante instead. It was unusually cold at first, but when milder weather arrived they were able to walk along the seafront under the palm trees. Ralph admitted to what he called 'trouser panic' when she tried to prevent him doing anything strenuous. Janetta arrived to see them, and Gerald, who was at his affectionate best. The time passed. It was a relief to get home in the spring, although Frances sometimes felt close to despair. 'Is this fag end of one's life going to be worth having really?' she asked herself. 'Ralph and I are no longer of interest except as a sort of background, cardboard wings in other people's theatre.' When one night Robert came to tell them that Cynthia was pregnant and that they were getting married, she could hardly bear it. 'It was as if someone had died, and this I still feel. Janetta and Robert's past, present and potential relationship has always been something I highly valued and now it's dead, I think.' Janetta took the news well; Cyril Connolly told Robert to look on the marriage as a three-year contract. After the wedding in April, Frances summed her feelings up in her diary. She could not comprehend how Janetta, someone of 'extraordinary distinction', could be replaced by anyone else. She minded so much that it was almost as if she herself had been superseded.

Luckily she had plenty of work, and she was finding the latest Freud index – to *The Psychopathology of Everyday Life* – particularly interesting, and 'the agility, profundity and virtuosity of Freud's mental processes' more impressive than ever. Another of Bloomsbury's household gods, Mozart, reached her in a new way; listening to the *Requiem*, written as his own life approached its end, she briefly caught a glimpse of how great art can make even death acceptable. That summer brought death very close: Oliver Strachey, Julia's clever, eccentric father, died in a nursing home and Janie Bussy was asphyxiated in Gordon Square by a faulty gas heater. On a short trip to Ireland with Janetta on a plant-collecting expedition, filling in ten-kilometre squares for the *Cambridge Atlas of British Flora*, Frances recorded a strange dream. She was upstairs at Ham Spray at night, when 'with an explosion of fear and wonder I saw Carrington with the electric light shining on her hair and Lytton sitting motionless and block-like ... I knew that they were dead'.

But the summer was not entirely death-haunted. There was another weekend at Crichel, where Frances' sharp eye lit on Cecil Beaton: 'a slightly comic figure ... his smooth pink face like some sly gnu's or moose's. Slit by a narrow little grin. Not really a nice character I feel, selfish and vain, malicious and merciless at times.' And by July she was writing her new Memoir Club paper, based on her wartime diary. She had decided to write it as testimony to 'my only strong belief – the futility of war'; it was disconcerting when Janetta's response to the idea was 'Oh dear, how boring', but encouraged by Ralph she pressed on. Two days before she had to deliver it she read it to him: 'he is my severest critic,' she wrote, 'and if it passes him I gain a little confidence'. It did, and she went up to London to deliver it on 27 July. It was odd to be in the hotel at Paddington on her own: 'the cell-like isolation terrified me ... How do people manage who have to live alone?' But the paper was a triumph. She was told it was brilliant and moving, and even Julia 'said kind things which I think she meant'. This was an important moment for Frances as it marked, she noted, 'the first appearance of any part of this diary, and hopelessly though I had cut and hacked at it to make these extracts, I would I think have felt discouraged had it been a complete failure'.

All that summer, she and Ralph were as close and happy as they had ever been. 'It really isn't nonsense to say that I have never in all my life felt more loved. What can be the reason for it? It almost makes me a little anxious.' And their endless conversation, sustained now for almost forty years, never flagged. A discussion of Freud's *The Interpretation of Dreams*, which Ralph was reading, led them to compare the way their minds worked; to Frances, Ralph's was the more creative: 'he could theoretically – had he more energy – be an innovator. My mind on the other hand is always analysing and subdividing and it is the complexities rather than the simplifying generalities that obsess me.

'I realise', she went on, 'how much I have all my life been influenced by the Psychology I read at Cambridge so long ago, and have founded on it a picture of an almost raw sensitised human surface continually and simultaneously assaulted by sensory stimuli like a swarm of bees.' Ralph did not share this feeling at all; Frances rather envied him.

That autumn, Ralph was called for jury service in Marlborough. Frances realised that it was important for him to accept and for her to let him go by himself. She was missing Burgo, who had not been to see them for two months; he was still seeing a great deal of Simon Raven, and had been much caught up with Charlotte's divorce from Anthony Blond and subsequent remarriage to the journalist Peter Jenkins. Towards the end of October she had another ominous dream; this time it was that she and Ralph had decided to commit suicide together, and despite concern about Burgo and Janetta had done so. 'The dream was impregnated with mingled desire for oblivion and nostalgia for life.' Worried about not having enough to distract her, she had written to various publishers asking about translation work. She was greatly pleased when she heard that there was a chance of a new edition of Casanova's memoirs. 'Enough work to last me for years!' She plunged into a sample and sent it off.

When Burgo surfaced towards the end of November she was delighted, and when he arrived for the weekend on 26 November, bringing Simon Raven, she felt 'relieved and released by B's independence and aliveness and friendliness'. They had already invited Eddie Sackville-West, and Frances was not best pleased with their old friend when the company of two young men prompted a stream of graphic 'bugger talk ... Surely heterosexuals never go on quite so boringly about their physical needs and sensations?' On the Sunday night, while she was cooking dinner, she realised Ralph had disappeared. Writing the next day, she described how she ran upstairs to find him lying down. He had suddenly felt a tightness in his chest; he had taken his pills, felt drowsy and could not face food or company. Telling herself that all this had happened before, Frances went down, finished cooking and sat through another graphic conversation about sex, like a parody of early Bloomsbury boldness. 'On it thundered; female orgasms, the clitoris and its part in sexual life, all discussed with heavy don-like portentousness.' She does not say if she told Burgo what state his father was in; eventually she was able to go to bed, to lie beside Ralph but not to sleep.

Next day she drove Burgo, Simon and Eddie to the station. She cannot have told Burgo much, if anything; he was, she observed, 'delightfully freed from any melancholic tinge'. All day, she 'sank slowly into the pit'. She realised that Ralph must have had another heart attack, but he refused to admit it, 'fighting a desperate rearguard action against admitting himself ill' and becoming frighteningly angry and upset at the thought of seeing a doctor. When Frances insisted, he was indignant. '"I can never tell you about my sensations if you behave like this." I couldn't tell him that it was impossible to face another night of desperation and fear, lying with beating heart listening to his short difficult breathing.' When the doctor appeared he said Ralph must remain absolutely still; 'a sort of perversity' made him disobey. The night of the 29th was even worse.

On 30 November, Frances wrote to Gerald, a calm, factual letter about Ralph's latest attack. 'The thing itself was almost painless ... but it has left him in a state of utter exhaustion, breathlessness and without the energy to do the smallest thing.' She tried to sound positive. 'It was only three days ago and there has as yet been no chance to recuperate.' Their plans for Spain after Christmas had to be changed; 'Of course this means at the very most optimistic postponing our journey abroad for several weeks later than we'd planned.' Would Gerald kindly cancel their arrangements? She pressed him to keep in touch with Ralph. 'He talked of writing to you himself, but I really don't think he has the energy.'

What happened that same evening was described in a later letter to Gerald. 'On Wednesday he seemed livelier, ate more and read more, and my desperate anxiety began to let up a little – and then about 9.30 when he was dozing came the last fatal attack. It was so awful that I longed for it to end; and I suppose it could have only lasted ten minutes. I was alone with him – he didn't want me to leave him – and yet I had to dash to the telephone for the doctor. I was tortured afterwards by the fact that there seemed no way I could make it less dreadful for him, and by the feeling that perhaps something could have been done to save him.' In her diary, there are a few more details. Ralph kept a stick by his bed to bang on the floor if he needed her; she was downstairs listening to Berlioz' *Symphonie Fantastique* on the radio when she heard 'that dreadful thump, thump, thump'. He died in her arms. She spent the rest of the night alone with him, and in the morning made the arrangements for his body to be taken away and cremated. 'The moment he was dead,' she told Gerald, 'he was utterly irretrievably gone to me. What remained was not him at all.'

Sixteen

Return to London, 1961–1963

There was never any question of a funeral or a grave for Ralph. His body was taken away by undertakers and disposed of. Frances did not recall how she told Burgo that his father was dead, or how he reacted. Friends were telephoned, and the news spread; the first to arrive at Ham Spray were Noel and Catherine Carrington, soon followed by Robert from London. He sent a telegram to Janetta in Greece. She flew back immediately. Frances spent a few days with Julia and Lawrence at their house in Lambourn, and then went up to London to stay with Janetta. Ralph had been much loved, and a strong presence in many lives; letters poured in. Frances destroyed most of them, but a few survived among her papers. Eddie Sackville-West, the last of their friends from the old days to see him alive, told her that she and Ralph 'were among the very few of my contemporaries who made a true marriage'. From Kitty West she learned that Ralph had once said to her that if Frances were to die, he would not go on. The *New Statesman* printed a tribute by Raymond Mortimer to their contributor of thirty years. As well as acknowledging his skill as a reviewer and an expert on nineteenth-century history, his contribution to the Greville Diaries and his book on Broadmoor, Raymond evoked Ralph's paradoxical nature. 'He was remarkable for combining cool judgment with hot blood – passionately sceptical, intolerant towards the enemies of individual freedom, quick to anger in support of non-violence ... he endeared himself as a great enjoyer, a most stimulating companion and a most affectionate friend.'

Frances decided almost at once to accept the Gowings' suggestion that she should accompany them on their forthcoming journey to the South of France, and help them sort out the paintings, books and papers at La Souco, the Bussy villa at Roquebrune. Her instinct told her to retreat for a while before starting to build what she knew already would have to be a completely different way of life. She needed company and she needed an occupation; the plan was perfect. On 16 December, two and a half weeks after Ralph died, Janetta drove her, her eyes full of tears, to Victoria to meet the Gowings on the Golden Arrow. Burgo was to join her for a while; she intended to stay away from England till March.

As soon as she reached the Hôtel Mas des Héliotropes on 17 December Frances sat down to write to Gerald. She explained why she had come to France rather than Spain: she had thought of doing so as planned, 'but then I realised I was just acting like a poleaxed sheep, and that I couldn't bear it'. She went on: 'I believe you'll want to know how things happened' and wrote it all down, in an act of respect for the great friendship he and Ralph had shared, and because she needed to tell someone. Gerald was deeply sad; he too had lost a part of himself. 'Ralph has been the only man I really loved', he told her. One of Ralph's last letters had been to Gerald, who himself had just finished a long letter back when Annie Davis brought the news. 'Even during our periods of estrangement I have loved him as much as at other times – I simply didn't want to see him and quarrel with him.' Over the next weeks and months, and for some years to come, Frances wrote more freely and regularly to Gerald than to anyone else, and he reciprocated; this was the start of a correspondence which fulfilled his need to write a running commentary on his own life. 'Starting with letters to console her in her desolation, he gradually replaced Ralph with Frances.'

At the hotel, Frances replied to letters of condolence and wrote her diary, which became the safe place where she could freely discharge her agonising feelings of loss and grief. Powerful though these feelings were, she remained able to deploy her powers of observation. She watched herself in the process of surviving, while at the same time wondering whether there was any point in going on living at all. She thought about suicide; 'It seems to me so much more logical and dignified and altogether respectable than continuing to struggle as I seem to be doing,' she told Gerald. 'I don't understand it myself. Perhaps it's partly the memory of the agony it was trying to circumvent Carrington's suicide, perhaps partly not wanting to deal another blow to Burgo' – who 'has been sensitive, kind and practically helpful and efficient'. She was aware that she was still numb from shock, as people are when the blow has just fallen: 'Some part of me has not and will not come out of the anaesthetic ... but the fact remains I am fighting desperately to keep my worthless life going.'

Even now she was able to notice, record and even enjoy natural beauty and the eccentricities of her friends. Her letters as well as her diary are never just wails of pain. 'Julia in a deep black extinguisher of a straw hat hissed into my ear as we got into the Golden Arrow: "I must fight against my terrible desire to be taken for a millionaire duchess. Too shaming!"' She appreciated the hotel, with its terraced garden of roses, geraniums, palm trees and cacti and its swarm of cats; she loved the views and the 'mild, soft light over the silvery sea', and found the work at La Souco absorbing, as Lawrence sorted paintings and she and Julia discovered letters to the Bussys from Matisse, Valéry and Henry James. Work, she wrote, 'hammered me for a while into a sort of unconsciousness'; but when she was alone at night she stared into an abyss. Even then, she analysed her emotions. 'Compared to the torture of being on the rack, the deadly fear of losing everything – having lost it, utter desolation is a state of calm. I have nothing to lose, I care about nothing.' She was grateful for the great kindness of her friends, but at the same time she felt 'painfully aware that I am a street accident exuding blood on the pavement, and it's a ghastly strain for each of them personally to be with me. They do want to help (and God knows they do) but if they could know my wounds were tied up and the blood stopped, they would naturally be happier away from me.' She used the image of feeling like a victim of a street accident more than once.

The friend she counted on most of all was Janetta, but she worried about needing her too much. She toiled away at replying to condolence letters quite calmly, but Janetta was different. 'When I even begin to think of all you've done and been to me these last days I simply burst into tears,' she wrote, 'which are things I try and stave off as much as possible ... there's no-one in the whole world I love more than you and want to see ... I dread to think what an exhausting draining weight I must have been to you, who have so many others.' On the whole, she was getting on better than she thought she would, although 'I've felt worried that I was trying to bear the unbearable and would wake up and find I just couldn't, and go off my head.' She longed to hear from Janetta: 'You mustn't mind if I write to you often – and please write to me.'

On 20 December Burgo arrived, and kept his mother company at the hotel for almost a month. She appreciated his presence very much, found it bracing – she did not intend to burden him with her grief – and told Janetta that he was being 'human and kind'; they went for brisk walks together along the coast and talked about books and his plans for the future. He was awaiting word from Simon Raven about meeting him in Tunisia, where he planned to write some articles for *Time & Tide;* he told Frances that when he had tried to talk to Simon about Ralph, all his friend said was 'You never liked him, did you' which, as Frances remarked, was 'very obtuse'. Ralph, in his last letter to Gerald, had described lunching with Burgo in London, finding him in high spirits, 'and I believe he quite liked me and I liked that'. As Burgo grew older and more confident, his relations with both his parents became easier. His letters to his mother after his father's death show a son trying his best to be affectionate and responsible.

The work at La Souco complete, Frances started on a translation and tried not to mind that nobody ever mentioned Ralph. She knew that Julia and Burgo were getting on each other's nerves; both were being unnaturally patient. Dick and his cousin John Strachey turned up, agitated about their inheritance; their behaviour, and Dick's extraordinary appearance, amused her. By the middle of January 1961, Burgo's plans were made and the Gowings were on their way back to England. She cried when Burgo left; he had been 'as sweet, kind and thoughtful as possible . . . none the less, I hope he will soon make himself a life apart from me, chiefly for his sake'. She had decided to move on to Menton, where she knew she would find Clive Bell and Barbara Bagenal on a winter holiday, and where Raymond was expected.

As soon as she arrived at the Hôtel des Ambassadeurs, she became ill, coughing and feverish, and found herself thinking hopefully of death. She retired to bed under the care of a local doctor, and saw no-one for a few days – which was almost a relief. Raymond arrived, filled her room with carnations, and acted like a tonic; she had been finding Clive and Barbara a trial, and greatly disliked the 'nursery intimacy' between them, the baby talk about false teeth and potties and constant fussing. It was sad, she and Raymond agreed, to see Clive so reduced by age and anxiety. Frances herself remained far from well; she lost her voice and had moments of black despair. When Clive fell and cracked a bone in his leg, Barbara begged her to share a flat with them, and help look after him, but Frances felt barely able to look after herself; she began to think of flying back to England. But this seemed too much like running away, and she moved instead to yet another hotel nearby. 'My bid for independence has set me up quite a little,' she wrote. 'I must now contrive to take that independence.'

The next six weeks were hard. Exhausted and weakened by her illness, alone, at sixty-one, for the first time in almost forty years, she took what amusement she could from the company of her elderly, ailing fellow residents, paid dutiful but depressing calls on Clive and Barbara, worked at her translation (a glum book by a French doctor about alcoholism), went for more long walks and tried to peer into the future. She discussed the big question, whether or not to stay on at Ham Spray, in letters to Gerald, and to Janetta; Ralph's executors, Noel Carrington and Craig Macfarlane, were already urging her to sell it and making gloomy noises about her finances. They calculated that she would have about £1,500 a year to live on. She told Gerald she had thought of dividing Ham Spray into two, but realised this could never work; she would have to sell it and move to London. Lawrence and Julia were in favour of this plan and, she wrote, 'I'm not really against it provided I could have trees and a view and some sun.' Raymond, on the other hand, told her living in London was horrid and urged her against it.

Then she received a letter that touched her deeply. Janetta wrote to suggest that both Ham Spray and her house in Montpelier Square could be sold and that they should look for a house in the country to share, big enough for them to be as independent as they wished while living alongside each other. 'I'll say at once', Frances replied, 'that though of course lots of utterly unreal visions of my future life will come worming their way into my mind when I try not to think how I'm going to make an existence without Ralph, this is the only one to which I could attach any libido. But but but . . .' It was true, she confessed, that her inclination towards London was more because the alternative, once Ham Spray was ruled out, would be a country cottage and that would be 'too lonely' than for any more positive reason; she knew she would miss 'the sights and sounds of country life' badly, and rather dreaded the rush and racket of the city. Maybe the plan could work; but she felt it must only be temporary, as surely Janetta would sooner or later take up with a man, and should not be tied to an elderly friend. She did not reject the idea, but she did not rush to embrace it either.

Having written so staunchly to Janetta, she battled on, her walks getting longer and longer. Doggedly, she noted what she saw in her diary: a madwoman in a fur stole, a little girl carrying a cat (sometimes Frances longed for her own black cat, Dinah) and, 'at the upper cemetery, a widow in deep black dabbing her eyes with a handkerchief and confiding in her taxi driver'. Such ritual consolations were not for her. Sometimes, she walked into Cap Martin, but the sight of couples arm in arm almost reduced her to tears, whereupon she became 'rather panicked about being unable to steer my thoughts, until by dint of walking I stupefied myself into one big eye'. More and more, she wondered what she was doing, on her own in a hotel, and whether she was perhaps punishing herself for failing to keep Ralph alive. She worked at her translation, like a 'scribbling schoolgirl'; Clive and Barbara wittering on, full of self-pity, drove her mad; her small bedroom was 'full of the sour aroma of sorrow'. By 7 February, she was desperate. 'I'm terrified of trying yet another change only to find I can't stand it – for the real fact is I can't bear living without Ralph. But I must stop saying that. I've got to bear it and a lot more, too, or get out.'

It was at this point, she realised later, with Ralph two months dead, that she reached her lowest ebb. Her diary and her letters make painful reading; her friends were worried about her; she was worried about herself. Slowly, one step at a time (like the alcoholics in her translation) she rediscovered her courage. On 15 February she was taken out of herself by witnessing a total eclipse of the sun. Putting a skirt and fur coat over her nightdress, she watched over breakfast on the glassed-in terrace as the sun rose in the clear lavender sky, then was gradually covered until darkness engulfed the earth. She went up to her room to write about it 'in a state of catharsis. It's the first thing I can say I've enjoyed for itself.' Later, she likened the darkening of the sun to her own total eclipse, the absolute, black recognition that the light had gone out for her with Ralph's death and would never return. She knew she had to accept this fact emotionally as well as intellectually, and resolved to do so with the only weapons known to her, endurance and self-discipline.

After a flurry of social life, as the spring weather brought more visitors to the coast – the Nichols, Eddie, John Banting – and she was invited out by local residents like the Graham Sutherlands, she left by train for Paris on 10 March. Through Mary Campbell, now having an affair with him, she had arranged to stay at Derek Jackson's luxurious flat. Anne and Heywood Hill joined her, and she had two busy days with them before travelling back to London alone on 14 March. Her base was to be with Janetta, at Montpelier Square, for the next few months.

Given how rapidly the business of selling Ham Spray was set in train, she must have returned from France with her mind made up. Most people, after such a bereavement, are advised not to make any quick decisions; and many are in no fit shape to do so. But Frances was strong, she hated to be passive and she had decided that to live on there without Ralph would be intolerable. A smaller country house could only be a travesty. Most of her friends took their line from her; the only one to protest strongly was Boris Anrep, who wrote her a letter that upset her very much. 'To abandon the house where you lived so long and where happy memories supersede the sad ones is a terrible uprooting of your life. Is it wise?' Ham Spray had been, and surely could remain, 'a centre of loving hospitality and enlightenment and the greatest English civilised taste in all things. To ruin all this will be a disaster for all of us and primarily for you and Burgo.' Her decision was indeed very hard for Burgo, who had never known another home; but while she sympathised with him up to a point, she also found it ironic he should want to cling to a place he had often said he detested.

In London, she dealt with lawyers and bankers and put the house on the market with composure, but when Janetta took her to *Fidelio* she was swamped with emotion. She went back to Ham Spray for the first time from Lambourn, driving over with Julia; she was less upset than she had anticipated. It was just a house, and 'houses are impassive things', but it was not until the end of the month that she spent her first night there; Janetta and Burgo kept her company. 'Our bed has become my bed,' she wrote, 'and I have faced the great shock of return.' She planned to spend Easter there, with Janetta, Rose and a Spanish nanny. When Janetta left briefly for London, and she found herself in the evenings alone downstairs, she felt panic-stricken, her heart beat loudly, and she drank whisky until it was time to go to bed. Looking back, Janetta always felt that Frances took the decision to leave Ham Spray too quickly, almost 'violently'. It was an example, to her, of the way in which Frances sometimes used her determination to act rationally to the detriment of her deeper feelings, and those of others – in this case, Burgo. At the same time, she recognised that Frances was showing great courage, and did more than anyone to help her.

After Easter, events moved fast. Agents and prospective buyers roamed Ham Spray; on 11 April Frances was informed that the house was sold at the asking price of £9,500. 'I felt my heart drop like a stone, and from then on the agony swelled and swelled.' Burgo was staying, and found the news hard to bear. Frances went to bed that night feeling like a murderer, to the sound of her son shouting 'Fuck' and tramping up and down the music room. Two days later this sale fell through after the buyers took a closer look at the condition of the house, but another couple, a well-connected Major Elwes and his wife, viewed it and fell in love with it. Soon the deal was done. It had been, she told Gerald, 'a fortnight's intensive horror' during which 'Burgo supported me most gallantly and efficiently, especially as he thought selling the house was a mistake'.

The next few months were spent between Montpelier Square and Ham Spray, facing up to the huge task of sorting out and packing up. Burgo was with her most weekends, and continued to be 'sweet and helpful'; he had just been made film critic of *Time & Tide*. James and Alix came on a last visit to discuss the fate of the remains of Lytton's library and papers. Some weekends she spent with friends – the Cecils, Dicky and Denis, the Crichel boys, the Nicholses all tried to look after her. In London, she went to see Boris Anrep at work on the mosaics in Westminster Cathedral; he looked, she thought, like 'a magnificent crumbling ruin among what he believes to be his last works'. She worried about him, and about the fate of his mosaics at Ham Spray; Mrs Elwes had already said that they, and most of Carrington's decorations, were not to her taste. (Eventually they were first covered over, then removed. Years later Frances came across the mosaic he had made her and Ralph as a wedding present, which they had in their bedroom, in a London gallery.) In London, she met two friends of Janetta's whom she greatly liked, and who both took to her: Magouche Phillips, an American whose good looks and warmth impressed her, and Julian Jebb, a voluble young man of great charm.

At Ham Spray, she found herself rereading the letter left by Carrington for Ralph along with her will, in which she asked him to promise to live at Ham Spray always. She recalled Ralph's resentment at this attempt to control their lives, and how they had both decided that 'we were going to live at Ham Spray because it was his and we wanted to', and that they certainly would not place a bust of her by Stephen Tomlin over the place where her ashes lay in the shrubbery. 'In his own will,' she wrote now, 'Ralph made no stipulation or request for me to live at Ham Spray. He was too rational not to see that this was my choice – and I have made it.' Gradually, as the summer wore on, she dismantled not just her own life but the almost forty years of Ham Spray's identity as the base established by Lytton, Carrington and Ralph in 1924. She wrote to Gerald, offering him Carrington's portrait of him – he accepted – and asking what she should do with the letters he had written to Carrington, which were now her property, though the copyright was his. She gave several more paintings away, to Burgo and Janetta and to Bunny, and some were sold. For herself, she kept Carrington's portrait of Lytton, a Yegen landscape and a Wiltshire snow scene and two Duncan Grants, bought by Lytton in the 1920s: *Juggler and Tightrope Walker* and a still life of a Greek head. She also kept Lytton's favourite chair and a walnut cupboard he had bought in France, a framed tapestry cat and the Spanish plates; but most of the furniture was sold at auction. She was pleased when Nicko Henderson and his wife Mary bought several items for their house nearby.

By mid-June, most of the work was done, and she retreated to her childhood haunt, the Lake District, to stay with her brother Tom and Nadine in their whitewashed stone house at Skelwith Fold. The familiar landscape soothed her; she was finding it hard to sleep, even with pills, but 'the greenness and beauty has cast a temporary veil over my sharpest pangs'. After a week she went on to the Mackenzies on Skye, and then to a new acquaintance, nicknamed 'The Lairdess', she had made in France. This, she soon realised, was a mistake; she was not up to dealing with kind strangers, and felt out of her element, swamped by feelings of panic and despair.

Burgo and Janetta spent the closing days of Ham Spray with her in early July, staying at Stokke. When at the last minute Janetta, who had rented a chalet in Austria for the summer, suggested that Frances join her there as soon as she could, she accepted. By 24 July she was able to write in her diary: 'Ham Spray is a closed book'. She left no record of the moment of departure, the last time she closed the door and drove away. A month later, back in London and starting to look for a flat, she was able to write a long account of it all to the Brenans. The last weeks at Ham Spray, she told them, had been 'absolute hell'. Barbara Bagenal had managed to infuriate Frances yet again by writing to Noel Carrington complaining of feeling left out because she had not been given one of her best friend's paintings, adding that she thought it a shame that 'Carrington's memorial to Lytton' should be destroyed. 'It is very odd', as Frances put it, 'when one has spent thirty years of one's life in a house, and the best and happiest too, to be told it is anyone's memorial to anyone else. But this is all finished now and the relief of having it behind me is immense.'

Not surprisingly, Austria had been a mixed success. Frances stayed in a small hotel near Janetta's chalet; she took against the folksy wooden buildings, the 'cuckoo clock' culture and the picture postcard alpine scenery. The presence of Arthur Koestler (a friend and an admirer of Janetta's, he had arranged the visit) nearby was not much help, but the general 'nursing home atmosphere' she found suitable for recuperation and the translation she was trying to finish. She helped to look after Rose, then aged six, and found the company of two of Janetta's younger friends – Julian Jebb and someone else new to Frances, Georgia Tennant – a real pleasure. 'What a splendid girl!' she wrote. 'Intelligent, warm-hearted, brilliantly funny and fine to look at.' Georgia and Julian were both greatly under Janetta's influence, which Frances did not find hard to understand. The Campbells came to stay, and Derek Jackson paid a visit; he and Koestler argued fiercely. Frances found the mountains (like everything else in her life at the time) a personal challenge, and set off on her last day on a solitary climb of six thousand feet. She did it 'mainly to prove that I could and because I thought I never should again. I enjoyed it.' She did not tell Gerald about a nightmare in which she dreamed of Ralph's death, and that she was standing in her half-empty bedroom at Ham Spray, 'feeling a creeping paralysis of loneliness and cold'.

By the end of August, Frances had found a London flat. She chose to re-start her life not in Bloomsbury, but in Belgravia, in a fine white stucco house in West Halkin Street, between Belgrave and Cadogan Squares. It was small, with only one bedroom, but the rooms were high-ceilinged and well-proportioned and she decided to paint them in the colours she liked best: the bedroom in soft grey and white, the sitting room in warm pink, mustard, green and purple. There was room for her piano. While the flat was being decorated and shelves built for her books and Spanish pottery, she moved back to Montpelier Square, bought a car – a white Mini – and embarked on a series of visits: to the Gowings, to Crichel, to Cranborne to see the Cecils, to Stokke. She also went to Hilton, where she was struck by how beautiful Henrietta Garnett had become; of all four girls, she was 'the most dazzlingly attractive'. On 1 November 1961, she moved into 14 West Halkin Street, and her new life in London began.

From the start, this life was lived on two levels. Even those closest to her had been amazed at the energy and determination she had shown in making the move so quickly; now, with no pause for readjustment to such a dramatic upheaval, she sought out more translation work, began to invite friends for drinks or meals, started going regularly to concerts and the opera, sometimes alone, and decided to take up the violin as soon as possible. She applied her own principle of being active, not passive; disliking the idea of being pitied as much as she did any hint of self-pity, she embarked on a sociable, busy, productive life. Her letters, and her diary, reflect this; but only her diary shows the other dimension, the darkness always present behind the bright, firm construction. Frances experienced to the full, and expressed with unusual eloquence and precision, the emotional see-saw of the grief-stricken, the unsteady balancing act they have to perform between relief at being able to manage life and desperation at having to manage it alone. London, she decided, was like an iron lung, 'which grips one and forces one to go through the motions of a living being almost against one's will'. Within two weeks of moving into West Halkin Street, she survived a Memoir Club meeting at Charleston – where she slept in Vanessa's icy bedroom (Vanessa had died that May) – absorbed the 'potent Bloomsbury atmosphere' and listened with keen interest to readings from the indiscreet Lytton Strachey–Keynes correspondence. But a few days later, she was at a very low ebb. 'Death is always in my thoughts now, and tears make a highwater mark in the inside of my head ... After almost a year of bereavement, in which everyone has been infinitely kind and I have probably seemed well on the way to recovery, how can anyone possibly realise that it's worse now than ever, or if they do, how can they fail to be bored by the fact?' She knew why she felt so desperate: 'All this last year I have been preparing to live my new life, by demolishing the old. Now I've got to begin doing it and it's a ghastly mockery.' For all her moments of despair, the life instinct was strong in Frances. This time, and many times to come, her mood was quickly lifted by the combination of a sunny day and the arrival of Janetta.

With the first anniversary of Ralph's death approaching, her friends were anxious and watchful. They knew she needed a project, something more engaging than another index or translation; there had already been talk among the Cecil and MacCarthy families of publishing Desmond Mac-Carthy's letters, and she was pleased when they asked her to take this on.

The Nichols asked her to Lawford for the last weekend in November, where their neighbour Randolph Churchill came to dinner and became boringly drunk, but Frances found what she most needed: 'relaxation with company'. She spent the evening of the 30th at the cinema with Isobel Strachey; they saw *The Innocents*, the disturbing film version of *The Turn of the Screw*. On 1 December, Janetta came to the rescue; she took Frances up to Chatsworth by train to stay with her new admirer the Duke of Devonshire, along with Patrick Kinross and the painter Adrian Daintrey. The beauty and grandeur of the house and its treasures were almost overwhelming; Frances and Adrian, who struck her as a likeable, amusing, communicative man, spent hours looking through Rembrandt drawings while snow fell softly on the terraces and fountains. Back in London, she found two letters awaiting her: one from Eardley Knollys, suggesting they drive out to Spain together in two weeks' time, and another from Gerald, who had not forgotten 'the saddest of anniversaries'. After a demanding literary dinner party with the Kees, where Robert irritated her by asserting that he and Cynthia had decided that she was really enjoying the London rat-race, she took off for Spain, retracing with Eardley the familiar route through Bordeaux and Salamanca. By the end of December she was installed with the Brenans at Churriana, where their company, the winter sun and the familiar views of Málaga and the mountains more than made up for a certain amount of discomfort. Frances never required luxury – in fact she rather deplored it – but even she was taken aback by the more squalid aspects of life chez Brenan, the dust everywhere, the smelly lavatories and the way Gamel's adored cats were allowed to make messes in the house and lick the butter on the breakfast table. She was also not best pleased when Hetty and her son Jason reappeared; Hetty was so plain, with her orange hair and suet-coloured face, although Frances did allow that she was good-natured and cheered Gerald up.

During January 1962 she found herself, at Gerald's request, revisiting Ralph's and her own past history. He asked her to read his new volume of autobiography, due out later that year, containing an account of himself and Ralph during the First World War; when she did so, she was taken aback. When they discussed her reservations, she felt Gerald must have 'a deep unconscious need to discharge on me everything he had felt and thought about Ralph all his life long'; it was painful for her, barely a year after Ralph's death, to listen to him. He was, she decided, 'blind as a bat to other people's feelings ... the effort to respond with temperate, balanced remarks exhausted me'. And it was not just the war he wanted to talk about; soon he was justifying himself all over again about Carrington, and blaming

Ralph for unreasonable jealousy. It was a relief to be able to retreat and work on Desmond MacCarthy's letters.

Next, Gerald presented her with all Carrington's letters to him. These Frances read with mounting admiration. They reminded her of Carrington's best qualities, and told her much that she had not known at the time. Not only did the letters – and she would have been the first person apart from Gerald to have read them – strike her as extraordinarily vivid and original, they revealed Carrington's vulnerability, her ambivalence about being a woman, her dislike of marriage as a form of ownership and her determination not to have children. When Frances reached the letters written during the early stages of her own relationship with Ralph, she was struck at first by how 'marvellously unresentful' Carrington appeared to have been. Only after opening a letter on its way from Ralph to Gerald and realising that the all-important triangle formed with Lytton was at risk had she panicked and begun to try to win Ralph back.

Whether he meant to or not, Gerald had done something important by showing Frances Carrington's letters. Still at the stage when she needed to talk about Ralph, it helped her to revisit the early stages of their love affair and to remember how eventually they worked out the way to be together without destroying Carrington's life. She had no regrets. 'Looking back, I still think the decision we found was a civilised one.' This was the start, for Frances, of a long and fruitful process of reassessing the past, during which she and Gerald would often disagree; but for the moment she was purely grateful to him. 'My historical interest in seeing things I lived through from the other side has carried me along, and the result has been not only that I am the wiser about certain things in the past but a certain catharsis has spread its benign force and warmth, invading areas of more recent pain.' All Frances' old admiration for Carrington flooded back; she saw her as 'a golden character, remarkable, a near genius'. Carrington's letters, she decided, were her masterpiece, and a great deal better than Desmond MacCarthy's.

Back in London in February, Frances decided to apply herself to 'the technique of being alone'. The flat had begun to feel almost like home; she even managed to spend one or two evenings there by herself. She found a violin teacher and looked around for an orchestra to join, took up her Memoir Club duties again, and went to Hilton for Bunny's seventieth birthday celebrations in March; she went back to Ham Spray with a concerned Mary Campbell. To her surprise, she felt only 'detachment and interest'. Then in April, she gave a small drinks party, inviting Cyril Connolly as well as some of the younger generation like Jonny Gathorne-Hardy and Julian Jebb. When Burgo arrived, he brought with him Henrietta Garnett, now seventeen and on the point of leaving Dartington, where she had been studying drama. Frances soon realised that something was going on between them. 'Rather unexpectedly they had the demeanour of a pair of lovers. I admire his good taste. "None of my business" is my feeling, but I'm not sure if Bunny and Angelica would agree.'

Before long it was clear that Burgo and Henrietta were indeed in love. Their relationship seems now to have had a certain inevitability about it, as yet another link in the chain of Bloomsbury entanglements. As Henrietta would recall, there had never been a time when she did not know Burgo and his parents, or Hilton and Ham Spray to be closely linked through her half-brothers, Richard and William, Frances' nephews and Burgo's first cousins. As for Burgo himself, she had adored him for as long as she could remember. The stormy adolescent had been a romantic hero to her; when he stopped treating her as a little girl, all her dreams came true. It must have been wonderful for him, too, to be the first love of such a beautiful and trusting girl. Henrietta was tall and slender, with luminous grey eyes like her mother's, a wide, full-lipped mouth and a magnetism inherited from her grandfather, Duncan Grant. Frances' only reservation was Henrietta's extreme youth, although Bunny seemed untroubled by it. 'I am very happy about Henrietta by the way,' he wrote, 'because she is happy – and Burgo seems so too in his genial way. He is like Ralph.' She was pleased that he thought so, and to hear that Henrietta had described Burgo as 'the kindest man in the world'. For the older generation, the love affair must have seemed like an extraordinary new flowering on the old root stock of Bloomsbury.

Frances' life was beginning to take on a new pattern. At Ham Spray, for almost thirty years she and Ralph had been among their circle's favourite hosts. Now, although she continued to have people for lunch or dinner regularly in London, she became a favourite guest. That spring and summer, she started a round of visits to friends in the country which was to be repeated regularly during the years ahead. In April she was back at Crichel, where her mother's old lodger and her husband's old admirer E.M. Forster impressed her more than ever before with his 'enormous humanity and tolerance'. Not long afterwards she went to Stowell, or 'The Tycoonery' as she took to calling Philip Dunn's large Wiltshire house. Mary Campbell was always on good terms with her ex-husband (whom she later remarried) and it was she who drew Frances there repeatedly, even though Dunn's extravagant right-wing views, combined with what Frances regarded as neglect of his guests' basic comforts, made her cross. 'All these servants and an elderly lady can't have breakfast in bed?' Like his great friend Derek

Jackson, Dunn enjoyed baiting Frances with remarks about the lower classes.

In June, she and Janetta went to Aldeburgh for the festival, the Hills' house at Snape was to be another favourite refuge. She was staying with them when Gerald's autobiography, *A Life of One's Own*, came out. Seeing it in print, Frances realised that although he had done some of what she had asked after reading it in Spain – mainly taking out facetious quotations from Ralph's early letters – she remained unhappy with the general impression. 'I still feel that there is a certain maliciousness in the picture. Some element of hero-worship, as he says but more desire to make fun of him that he's aware of and I find this hard to tolerate.' She was pleased to find that the Hills felt 'exactly as I do ... and think it gives no notion whatever of his mental calibre'. In August, she joined Janetta and a group of her younger friends in Spain and then went on to stay at Philip Dunn's house in Majorca; the excellent swimming made up for finding herself once again among a group whose watchword appeared to be 'Down with the intellectuals and up with the millionaires'. The question arises as to why, given that her diary shows so much disapproval of the way of life of her richer friends, she continued to accept their hospitality. The answer has to be that she was deeply attached to the two younger women, Janetta and Mary, who drew her into their pleasure-loving world, where comfort and luxury were to be enjoyed, not regarded with suspicion. Frances could never resist an invitation to spend time with either of them.

Burgo and Henrietta spent the summer together, and by the autumn it was plain that they were more in love than ever. Their happiness delighted Frances, and helped take her mind off the plight of several old friends. Saxon, Clive and Phil Nichols were all seriously ill, and Julia's marriage was under threat. Lawrence had fallen in love with a young art teacher, and was proposing, Bloomsbury-style, that they try a ménage à trois. That autumn, though, personal concerns were suddenly overshadowed by the Cuban Missile Crisis. Frances, like the rest of the world, held her breath, and thought of 1939; 'There's a hideous familiarity about everything,' she wrote, 'even the way that one gets used to the very horror itself ... I thought of poor Henrietta's face yesterday ... I can't forget the difference between the attitudes of the young to their unique and precious lives and ours to our old done-for, worn-out ones.' But the crisis passed, and Frances found herself in a curious state of mind. 'I see that I'm really disappointed at not being atomized, though deeply relieved that Burgo, Henrietta, Georgia and Rose are not. No need for logic in the id.'

At the beginning of November, Boris Anrep brought her the most wonderful present. He had made her a mosaic fireplace for her new flat, showing a large black cat sitting gazing into golden flames against a bright green background. It cheered her greatly, and she gave a small party to celebrate, despite being very cast down by a visit to Phil in hospital and the news that Clive had been operated on for cancer. But when she heard that Saxon, Lytton's old friend who had remained part of Ham Spray life to the end, had died, she felt only relief. 'The release of the old and sick is a thing one must welcome,' she wrote firmly, adding 'The way out! Oh where is it, for the old and decrepit?' Even so, she was shocked and very sad when she heard not long afterwards that Phil Nichols was dead. He had loved her once, and had been the only man apart from Ralph to touch her heart.

Before the end of the month, around the time of the second anniversary of Ralph's death, Burgo came to tell her that he and Henrietta had decided to get married as soon as possible. Frances' first reaction was 'intense joy . . . this is something entirely good and positive for Burgo'. She also trembled for him; Henrietta was so very young, and love and life so very fragile. As for herself, 'I now feel I have a stake in the world, and the only steadying thing I felt before was that I hadn't. Perhaps I might be some use to them both.' That winter, London was in the grip of one of the last of the classic pea-soup fogs, which crept into Frances' flat and made her think of poison gas, but when Burgo and Henrietta appeared for dinner it was 'as if an exotic flower, an orchid perhaps, had suddenly bloomed in the London fog and I shake with terror at what might happen to it. But it is a happy agitation.'

Henrietta's parents were in France, from where they both wrote to Frances. Bunny was matter-of-fact. 'I hope you are as happy about the marriage as about the love affair. I am.' Angelica admitted to reservations. 'Of course I can't pretend personally that my feelings aren't mixed – that is to say that theoretically I am not in favour of anyone marrying at Henrietta's age – she is only just 17 and apart from knowing others has so very little knowledge of herself either as yet.' However, she agreed with Frances that it must be right for them to seize their chance of happiness, and 'they do both seem so delightfully, charmingly happy' and expressed delight at the prospect of having Burgo as a son-in-law, 'not least because he is your and Ralph's son, and to be connected with you seems to me a luxury'. Frances summed up her own feelings to Gerald. 'It has made a new man of Burgo, hopeful and responsible . . . if they have a year or two of happiness in this grey and uncertain world this is something. It confirms my view that B has a great deal of potential lovingness and protectiveness bottled within him – and though I shall naturally feel anxieties about this little boat setting out to float, and watch for lists or leaks, I am profoundly grateful.'

Burgo and Henrietta decided on a very small family gathering at their flat after their register office wedding on 22 December. Meanwhile Frances had already arranged to spend three weeks over Christmas with Julia at Lambourn while Lawrence was with his new love, and duly set off there on 14 December. She did not expect it to be easy, and she was right. At first all went well; they both worked for several hours a day (Frances had another translation on hand) and went for brisk cold walks. But she soon realised that she had to watch her step; Julia was unnerved if the conversation took an argumentative turn and would reprove Frances if she failed to follow the house rules and rituals – which windows to open, how the stove should be lit, how to make the coffee. For all their long friendship, they were very different characters, and both were struggling to adjust to painful changes in their lives.

It must have been very hard for Frances not to have Ralph with her at their son's marriage to Bunny's daughter. 'Everything about the wedding was to me deeply touching and charming and it has left me in a state close to anguish,' she wrote, back at Lambourn the next day. 'I hadn't expected that I would hardly get to sleep last night for the passionate longing I felt for Burgo and Henrietta's happiness.' Thoughts of Ralph and her own lost happiness filled her mind; within a few days she was feeling desperate, and when heavy snow threatened to cut them off altogether she could hardly bear it. Tired of being addressed by Julia as if she was 'a halfwitted housemaid whom she was hoping to train but despairing of, instead of an elderly highbrow', when Julia announced that as a 'creative writer' she didn't have time for friends in her life Frances replied that if she didn't value friendship she would shoot herself. They soon made it up, but it was with great relief that Frances managed to drive her Mini through the snow and reach London to face the new year. Burgo and Henrietta gave a party in London to celebrate their marriage on 10 January 1963; Frances noted that it was 'an unqualified success'.

Although West Halkin Street was round the corner from Burgo's flat in Cadogan Square, Frances knew that she must not expect to see too much of her son and daughter-in-law. As the third year of her solitary life began, she recognised that she was feeling less acutely unhappy; but she still felt that without Ralph she was in danger of becoming 'a thin grey husk'. Her way of coping with loneliness was to be as busy as possible, and she was hurt when Julia attacked her for living in a social whirl. It does not seem to have occurred to her that Julia may have been jealous; she felt she had been 'written off ... as a futile member of the rat race unworthy to mix with serious people like her and Lawrence'. She found herself looking back over their friendship, 'and wondering how much rivalry there is in it – on either side – and how much I am over-critical of her. Why isn't it easier just to appreciate people for what they are ... rather than dissect them so remorselessly?' The trouble was that both Frances and Julia, conditioned over their Bloomsbury years to regard criticism and mockery as aspects of friendship, were finding it impossible to adjust to circumstances in which both were too vulnerable for such treatment.

As always, work and music made Frances feel better. Through the Penrose family's medical connections, she joined an orchestra which was to become an important part of her life for the next two decades. The Medical Orchestra was one of the top amateur groups in the country, and when Frances joined the second violins in March 1963 she found herself rehearsing for a concert to be held at the Central Hall, Westminster, under Sir Adrian Boult and with Hephzibah Menuhin as soloist. She loved the hard work required, the discipline, the sense of being part of something, the release from her own concerns into a joint enterprise. It was pleasing, too, when her latest translation, *The President*, by the Guatemalan Nobel Prize winner Miguel Asturias, brought her praise and congratulations from the publishers, Gollancz.

In September 1962 Frances had received a letter which, though she could not know it at the time, signified the beginning of a literary project which was to lead her away from translation and transform the rest of her life. Michael Holroyd, then twenty-seven, had recently finished (but not yet published) his first book, a biography of Hugh Kingsmill, a writer said to have been influenced by Lytton Strachey. Having discovered that no biography of Strachey existed, Holroyd was now proposing one, and wrote to ask Frances' advice. She told him that he should first of all approach James Strachey, and that she herself, if James approved, would help him as much as she could. Now, having gained James's support and started work on the huge collection of Lytton's papers at Lords' Wood, Holroyd, who was as assiduous as he was handsome and agreeable, was working his way around other Strachey friends and relations; he had been to see Julia to discuss Carrington, her feelings for Lytton and her suicide. Frances realised that Holroyd would be keenly interested in Ralph, and in her own role in the Ham Spray ménage, and that he was likely soon to be asking for her help. Her conversation with Julia disturbed her; she could not help suspecting that Julia's current position, as the wife of a man who preferred someone else, might colour her version of events. 'Carrington is an emotionally charged topic for Julia as well as for me,' she wrote, 'and the charge is different for us both. I'm glad we've broken the long undisturbed ice over the subject, and hope we shall revert to it.'

It was Michael Holroyd who proved the ice-breaker, and it was not long before he came to see Frances. He had already been in touch with Gerald. 'I hear that Michael Holroyd wrote to you, and is longing to accept your invitation to go out and see you,' she wrote. 'I think you'll like him. I did, and so do most others, James and Julia for instance; but a few made reservations. Nobody of course knows whether he can write.' Already, Frances was aware that Holroyd would be hearing different versions from different people. 'Little Barbara has of course stepped forward and announced herself as DC's dearest closest friend and the greatest living authority on Lytton, so Lord knows what sort of impression the poor young man will get. When he came to see me I thought him sensible and intelligent and I gave him all Lytton's letters to R.' She had since been wondering whether or not to give him Ralph's letters to her, 'and DC's to R, all of both of which I have', and had begun to sort through and reread them; in the process, she wrote in her diary, she threw 'quite a lot' away. She could not help finding 'deep sadness in this stale dry dust emanating from the rich and living years'.

But, at the same time as she was beginning to reconsider the past, she had more reason than ever to concentrate on the present and the future. That spring, Henrietta was pregnant; the baby was due in mid-July. By early August Frances was beginning to worry. She tried not to fuss, but she could not help feeling a sense of responsibility, especially as Angelica and Bunny had gone off to France. Suddenly, after supper together at her flat, Burgo rang to say that Henrietta had been taken to hospital with suspected toxaemia; after three days of mounting anxiety, she had a Caesarean, and on 9 August Sophie Vanessa Partridge arrived. Frances visited them in hospital, cooked meals for Burgo, helped him buy a pram and drove them home. She was exhausted, exhilarated and 'obsessed' by it all, and as she often did she asked herself what Ralph's reaction would have been. 'The birth of a child', she imagined him saying, 'tugs at old buried feelings and arouses ghosts from the past on both sides. The navel string is tweaked. But now it is time to get back to the independence of adult human beings. Yes, I agree.' At the same time, she could not help feeling that now she had 'a motive for going on far stronger than any I have encountered during nearly three years of struggle'.

About four weeks later, on the morning of 7 September, Frances picked up the telephone in her flat. It was Peter Jenkins, Burgo's friend and Charlotte Strachey's husband, and he was ringing to say that he was concerned about Burgo. They had been in the middle of a cheerful telephone conversation about a trip to the races when Burgo had suddenly stopped

Janetta, late 1940s

Robert Kee, late 1940s

In France, 1951: (left to right) Janetta, Robin Campbell, Frances, Ralph

Burgo, mid 1940s

CLOCKWISE FROM TOP:

Picnic in Spain, 1956: (left to right) Burgo, Ralph, Gerald Brenan, Joanna Carrington

Burgo on his 21st birthday, 1956

Frances cuts Ralph's hair, Spain, 1955

Ralph and Burgo on the beach in Spain, 1955

CLOCKWISE FROM TOP LEFT:

At lunch in Malaga: Burgo, Joanna Carrington, Gamel Brenan

At Buena Vista, 1956: Robin Campbell, Cyril Connolly, Ralph

Picnic in France, mid 1950s

A visit to the Stracheys, 1960: (left to right) Alix Strachey, Angus Davidson, Ralph, James Strachey. This was the last photograph Frances took of Ralph

Burgo with
Henrietta Garnett,
1963

Henrietta and
Sophie Partridge,
1964

CLOCKWISE FROM TOP LEFT:

In Egypt, 1980: (left to right) Jaime Parladé, Frances, Stanley Olson

Frances in Mexico, 1974

Sophie in West Halkin Street, early 1970s

At the launch party for *A Pacifist's War*, 1978: Sophie and Frances

Stanley Olson, mid 1970s

CLOCKWISE FROM TOP LEFT:

Sophie's wedding day, Tuscany, 1981

Frances and her sister Eleanor outside their childhood home, 28 Bedford Square, 1975

Jaime Parladé and Janetta at Tramores, 1970s

Mary Dunn in Majorca, 1970s

David Garnett and Rose Jackson at lunch in France, mid 1970s

CLOCKWISE FROM TOP LEFT:

Scrabble with Janetta, Al CuzCuz, 1990s

Frances in her bedroom, 1997

At the Bloomsbury Gallery with Sophie and
Henrietta, 2001

Nigel Nicolson and Frances, West Halkin Street,
2001

In the garden at Al CuzCuz with Tony Fry, 1999

Frances at 90, photographed by Snowdon, dressed by Issey Miyake

talking; Peter thought he might have heard a gasp, and the sound of a fall. Then nothing. Frances immediately went round to Cadogan Square; she must have had a key, as when she entered the flat she found Henrietta was in the bath, Sophie asleep in a Moses basket on the bed and Burgo lying on the floor. He was dead.

Seventeen

Towards Recovery, 1964–1970

Burgo's death was caused by an aortic aneurysm, a weakness in the main artery leading from the heart which is symptomless, develops over time and almost invariably, if untreated, leads to rupture and death. It was some small comfort to Frances and Henrietta when they learned that the catastrophe could not have been averted. The details of that terrible discovery are still veiled by shock and grief. Frances took charge. As with Ralph, there was no funeral, no wake, and no grave. At the time, Henrietta was in no state to question this; later, she came to feel sad about it, and at the time some of Burgo's friends were outraged. Anthony Blond claims that Frances rang Harrods' funeral department and instructed them to remove Burgo's body. He had loved Burgo and helped him grow up, and felt that Bloomsbury's chilly parenting had done him harm. He never quite forgave Frances; her own friends, whether they shared her views or not, understood. The person who did share them and who would have understood best, Janetta, was away; she had gone travelling in Greece with Jaime and some other friends. Asked who supported her in the immediate aftermath of Burgo's death, Frances recalled her friend Joan Cochemé (the artist Joan Souter-Robinson, who had painted Burgo as a a small boy) as the first to reach her, followed by Julian Jebb and Robert Kee. When Bunny arrived from France, he could not manage one word about Burgo, but plunged into talk of legal and financial arrangements. It was decided that he would take Henrietta and Sophie back with him to France for a while. Frances was visited by Rosamond Lehmann, who tried hard to convince her that Burgo was not really gone, only translated to the spirit world. Frances found her kind, but absurd.

Not quite two weeks after finding her son dead, Frances left for Italy as planned with Raymond Mortimer. Perhaps nothing else in her life illustrates her capacity for self-control so strongly as this decision; she decided to take herself in hand and drive the hired car round Puglia (Raymond was a nondriver), believing that to be active, not passive, even in the face of such a terrible blow, would help her more than even a short time of quiet mourning. She would later cite a saying of Voltaire's: 'Courage is not enough.

Distractions are also necessary.' As she acknowledged, it was also a 'heroic' act of friendship on Raymond's part to accompany her.

But not even Frances could keep her feelings altogether battened down. When they arrived in Rome they found Janetta there, and an emotional crisis erupted. The days after Burgo's death had passed with no word from Janetta; Frances, knowing that Anne and Heywood Hill had joined the party since the tragedy, could not understand her continued silence. In fact, the Hills had been unable to face telling Janetta what had happened, so that it was not until she arrived in Rome shortly before Frances that she learned of it. Appalled, she wrote a note to Frances at her hotel explaining why she had not been in touch. Frances removed almost all traces of Burgo's death from her papers – not one letter about it survives – and whatever Janetta said, it was not enough. Among the few surviving fragments of diary from those weeks are some desperate lines. Frances could not believe that the Hills had kept quiet; she felt that Janetta must have chosen to stay with Jaime instead of returning to be with her, as she had done when Ralph died. Frances was desperately wounded. At such a time, it seemed that Janetta had put Jaime before her. 'Venus toute entière', she wrote, 'has forgotten for the moment her children and friends.' Over dinner that night in the Piazza Navona, Janetta tried to convince her otherwise, but Frances was beyond reach. 'My heart turned cold as a stone,' she wrote afterwards, 'and I couldn't look at Janetta. I know I'm being unfair to her, but her letter was false, false.' The next day Frances and Raymond took the train to Bari.

Somehow, for the next three weeks she managed to focus on the trip. Her diary returned to normal; her descriptions of the fine churches and charming towns, the *trulli* and the olive groves, are detailed and appreciative. The driving was a strain, but exhaustion kept her numb. Raymond was kindness itself. After the first week, though, she wondered if she could go on; all the beauty and interest of the journey, she wrote, 'lies like scum on the surface of a stagnant pool of heartbreak'. Next day, she felt feverish and ill and had to stay in bed. Among the letters that reached her in Italy was one from Bunny that irritated her very much; he had let Henrietta and Sophie travel back to London alone and was evidently assuming that Frances would be able, on her return, to help his eighteen-year-old widowed daughter rebuild her life. It did not seem to occur to him that Frances herself might need support. After a short stay in Naples and a visit to Pompeii, she flew home on 14 October.

On her first day back, she had Henrietta and dark-eyed Sophie – who already, she thought, had a look of Burgo – to lunch. Later she saw Janetta, and this time she realised how she had misjudged her, and all was well between them. Janetta never forgot how painful and incomprehensible she found the misunderstanding; but she accepted that Frances had been unhinged by shock and pain. As for Frances herself, she felt terrible. 'Guilt about my awful insane mistrust of Janetta in Rome,' she wrote on 16 October. 'Indignation with the Hills for causing it by what was evidently sheer cowardice. Wondering really how much I can count on my own sanity if I could be so awful to Janetta. Can she ever forgive me?' She could, and she did. 'Lovely evening with Janetta,' noted Frances a day or two later. 'I am utterly ashamed of Roman insanity.' As for the Hills, she wrote to Anne to protest about 'the Corfu conspiracy of silence' which had caused her 'huge pain'; Heywood took the blame, and eventually they were forgiven. Almost forty years later, Anne Hill still felt guilty.

With all the strength she could muster, Frances now set about reapplying the hard lessons she had learned since Ralph died. She spent as little time as possible alone, went out and about in London, and accepted a series of invitations to the country. She sorted through more of Ralph's letters for Michael Holroyd, and she took up her violin. She endured the inevitable moment when a member of the orchestra congratulated her on Sophie's birth and asked after Burgo. She kept her anguish out of her correspondence; her first letter to Gerald began with the sights of the Italian trip (no mention of Janetta) and only then continued, 'I think the utter unexpectedness and unwarrantableness of Burgo's death has made it peculiarly difficult to adjust to; even though not such a total earthquake of my own life as R's was.' She did admit to wondering whether there was any point in anything any more. But her diary shows that during November and December she was making repeated 'dips into the suicide well'. Death often seemed like the only solution to her pain and loneliness; but her appetite for life pulled her forward. She considered going to the London Library to research efficient ways to die; but twelve days later she gave a successful dinner party for Julia, Raymond and Adrian Daintrey.

She also saw a great deal of Henrietta and Sophie, and the evident fact that they needed her tied her to life. The strength of her feeling for her granddaughter surprised her; she was, she wrote, 'half-terrified of getting too fond of her'. Henrietta too was bravely trying to restart her life. Two weeks before Christmas, she and the girl who was now sharing the flat gave a party, and asked Frances; she was persuaded by Janetta to spend the evening with her instead. Julian Jebb joined them from the party and described it in glowing terms; later Frances wept as she recalled the happy gathering earlier that year to celebrate Burgo and Henrietta's wedding, and the sight confronting her so recently of 'Burgo's body lying on the floor of that very room. I'm crying now as I write this, and I see plainly that dearly as I love Henrietta and glad as I am for her to be happy, much as I want her to find new love, I shall be deeply sad when Burgo is quite supplanted.' She went back to Lambourn for Christmas, where this time she found not only Julia but Lawrence and his new love, Jenny. To her relief, 'Christmas Day was totally ignored.' The year ended with Frances back in London, dreaming of Burgo and Ralph and waking 'to stare into the deep black hole of their joint absence'.

At the beginning of 1964, Frances contemplated her situation and came to the conclusion that, as her own life was effectively over, the only way ahead for her was to sink herself in the lives of other people. It was not long before one life in particular gave her plenty to think about: Julia Strachey's. Over the next decade, as they both advanced into their seventies, the tragi-comedy of their relationship darkened and intensified, demonstrating that friendship can be as obsessive and tricky as any love affair.

Not surprisingly, the strain of sharing Lawrence with Jenny was unbearable for Julia. Frances tried to help her to make the best of things, without success; 'Julia came to dinner last night and worried me greatly,' she wrote to Gerald in March. 'She can't come to terms with the situation at all, nor I think realises that it has ever happened to anyone else. I am so afraid she'll do or say some reckless thing which will send it up in flames, pitch a hand grenade into the triangle which will make it impossible for her ever to be with Lawrence and Jenny again. And her horror of ever being alone is quite terrifying – she told me she would rather live with anyone than quite alone. I felt I ought to throw up my flat and go and live with her – but I simply couldn't. It would be the death of me.'

Instead, she came up with a plan, of the kind that always helped her when things were bad, and suggested to Julia that they go to Rome together, at her expense. 'She needed no persuading', as Frances later wrote, 'but it was not a success – instead very much the reverse.' Frances set off 'with three resolves: to remember she is desperately unhappy; to treat her fuss as farce (which it is) and try to enjoy it as such; to be as adaptable as I can'. Joan Cochemé, whose husband worked in Rome, had found them a quiet pensione on the Aventino; it was perfect spring weather and the journey went smoothly, but from the moment they arrived Frances realised that Julia was in a bad way, far worse than she had ever known her. After three days she wrote to Janetta: 'I must say at once that I have quickly had to give up my avowed intention of enjoying Julia's fantasies – they are simply no laughing matter, but desperately tragic and I'm ashamed of having ever thought of them in comic terms . . . I can't possibly convey to you the state of perpetual panic she is in. She's ready to die of terror every time she crosses a road, is terrified of losing her way and forgetting the name of where she wants to get to, too frightened to take the lift up the 5 floors to Joan's flat, terrified of bugs in the drinking water, rabies in the dogs – simply everything.' She was also confused and forgetful, incapable of consulting a map or reading a guidebook herself but unable to trust Frances, who found herself answering the same questions over and over again, 'under fire of ceaseless rather school-mistressy heckling: "Yes but are you sure this is the way? How are you sure? Are you sure this isn't another bridge? Don't you think this is a different island?" . . . it's truly pitiful, and knowing me and my irritability you'll realise what a job it is for me not sometimes to snap back.'

Julia almost gave up and went home, but somehow they struggled on, with expeditions to the Villa d'Este and Hadrian's Villa at Tivoli, and to 'the sexiest little church' in Rome (Santa Maria della Vittoria, where St Teresa is shown swooning in orgasmic delight). Joan Cochemé was endlessly kind and hospitable (though Julia did not care for her and grumbled a great deal about her to Frances). By the end of the month, Julia left, having recovered somewhat, and Frances was joined by Raymond Mortimer for a short journey through Tuscany and Umbria. 'What a relief', she told Janetta, 'to have a fellow traveller who knows how to look up a train and consult a guidebook and doesn't endlessly fuss! Poor Julia, I do feel it was a wrong choice to bring her to this great overpowering masterful town.'

At first, when they were both back in London, it looked as if Rome had not done their relationship any harm. Julia wrote thanking Frances for her 'infinite generosity', saying that she was feeling better and apologising for her 'panic fear . . . it must have been too harassing and distressing for words for you'. But a couple of weeks later, when Frances arrived for dinner, she was greeted with frigid hostility. Hurt and bewildered, Frances felt Julia's 'dislike and disapproval hitting me like a wave, implicit in her cold eyes and her mask-like face . . . her manner was artificial in the extreme, like someone going through a part in a play'. Frances found Julia's reaction inexplicable; she lay awake at night wondering if it was her fault. Bearing in mind a maxim of E.M. Forster's that Bunny passed on to her – 'Kindness, more kindness and even after that more kindness – I assure you it's the only hope' – she decided to keep trying; but all her efforts only placed her more firmly in what she recalled Ralph used to call Julia's very large doghouse. When she received a letter in which Julia asserted that for some time she had felt hostility beneath all Frances' kindness, that her face and manner were 'tart and unfriendly' and that it was time to accept that their feelings towards each other were 'ambivalent', she was deeply upset. For a time, they avoided each other.

Over the next months and years, the problem of Julia preoccupied Frances a good deal. Something in her could not stop trying to help her friend, even when whatever she did seemed to make matters worse; and something in Julia remained dependent on Frances. A pattern established itself: after a period of estrangement Julia would summon Frances, in search of help and comfort, fail to find what she wanted, then turn on her and banish her again. This behaviour, Frances knew, derived partly from boundless insecurity, dating back to Julia's childhood and magnified by Lawrence's desertion, and partly from an increasing addiction to amphetamines, the purple hearts she had been accustomed to take occasionally and was now taking all the time. Julia was also drinking too much and needed sedatives to help her sleep, and the combination was disastrous, leading to waves of paranoia and confusion. When she was herself, her charm and originality were as sparkling as ever and she and Frances still had good times together; but it was never long before Julia's thin skin and her lack of interest in anyone's life except her own would lead to trouble. From the Rome trip onwards, Frances' letters and diaries are full of the Julia problem; and while the situation was funny as well as sad, and the latest news of Julia's impossible behaviour made entertaining reading for Gerald and Janetta, during the later 1960s Julia's plight, and her own inability to help her, often made Frances feel guilty and inadequate. In 1967 Lawrence finally asked Julia for a divorce, and eventually he and Jenny got married and had a child; they never excluded Julia from their life, but she felt more than ever, she told Frances, like a stray cat, allowed in other people's homes on sufferance. Frances tried to tell her that she was a stray cat too, but Julia became more desperate and demanding than ever. Frances never gave up; she supported Julia as best she could, including financially, but sometimes she felt Julia really hated her.

Feeling a failure with her oldest friend made Frances even more appreciative of those who did not reject and criticise her. Janetta's concern and affection were more vital than ever, although much of her time was being spent with Jaime in Spain; but when she was in London, Montpelier Square was Frances' second home, especially as Dicky and Denis were now renting the basement flat. She valued two new friends, Iris Murdoch and John Bayley, whom she met with the Cecils; she liked their devotion to each other, and the way they would discuss serious matters in an unpompous way – Iris about philosophy (she was a don at St Anne's, Oxford, at the time) and John about Shakespeare, both favourite topics for Frances. She tackled Iris' philosophical writings, and they exchanged letters about Plato and the Good. Burgo's death brought her no closer to her family; apart from an annual visit to Tom and Nadine in the Lake District, and an occasional dinner in Cambridge, she saw little of the others.

It was different, of course, where Henrietta and Sophie were concerned. Frances loved them both, but before long she began to find that the generation gap was catching up with her. Having herself been liberated by Bloomsbury from many of the stuffier conventions of her time she was now to have her own tolerance tested. During the 1960s, another wave of rebellion against conformity and parental expectations swept over the young, who set off once again in search of social and sexual freedom. Frances strongly believed that the younger generation should question the standards of the world around them; but at the same time she could see Henrietta's particular vulnerability in the wake of Burgo's death, and as the Swinging Sixties gathered momentum she worried a great deal about her, and even more about Sophie.

Early in 1964, Henrietta decided to try living in Spain for a while, and set off for the coast near Marbella, where to Frances' relief she was within Janetta's orbit and not far from the Brenans. 'I hope you and Gamel may see a little of her,' she wrote to Gerald, 'I needn't, I know, ask you to be kind to her. I'm deeply fond of her – she's a girl in a million in that she has a character of great natural sweetness and spontaneity . . . She's very romantic and will probably fall in love with a number of young men; I only hope they'll be kind ones. I think her life in London was pretty nightmarish after Burgo's death and she deserves a little happiness, she was so good and unself-pitying.' Frances felt that Henrietta needed help with Sophie, and was ready to pay for it; over the years she would contribute substantially to her granddaughter's upbringing and education, as although Henrietta had inherited Burgo's capital as well as the flat, her finances were always pre-carious.

That summer, Frances went back to Spain herself, based this time with Nicko and Mary Henderson in a house near Marbella, anxious to see how Henrietta and Sophie were getting on. What she found was not reassuring. Along with Henrietta's sister Nerissa, they were living at a small hotel where they helped out in return for their keep. Frances arrived to find Henrietta away in Málaga, caught up in an unpleasant drama after a girlfriend had been attacked by her drunken lover and ended up in hospital. It was ferociously hot, Sophie was pale and listless, and Frances disliked the way they were all 'living in a nightclub', working all night and sleeping all day. Friends, especially the kind and well-connected Jaime, came to the rescue,

Henrietta returned to recover by the Hendersons' swimming pool and Sophie's first birthday was celebrated at La Consula; with Frances' help Henrietta and Nerissa decided to leave the hotel and rent a small house of their own. The first anniversary of Burgo's death found Frances in cooler, calmer Portugal with Janetta, where Frances was relieved to hear Jaime, who had been occasionally employing Henrietta in his decorating business, praise her and Nerissa for their beauty and originality and true bohemian attitude to life.

Frances returned to London to find that Clive Bell was near to death. She steeled herself and went to the hospital, where she found him weak but entirely himself, wanting her to read to him from *The Times*; but two days later, when he died, she could only feel glad for him. Almost his last words, Barbara told her, weeping in her arms, were 'Give my love to Fanny'. As the ranks of Old Bloomsbury dwindled, Frances found herself reflecting on the difference between their standards and aspirations, and those of Henrietta and her circle; and when, not long after Henrietta came back from Spain in October, she drove her and Sophie down to Charleston to stay with Sophie's great-grandfather, Duncan Grant, she realised all over again how much she respected what Charleston stood for. She felt contented there, and thought Henrietta did too, in a place where 'real values have been aimed at and achieved, something lovingly created and kept alive. Even now when nearly all of them are dead, it is the same.' She was encouraged to hear Duncan say that a younger generation of painters were beginning to appreciate his work. The sweep of the downs, long walks through wintry mist, the familiar painter's clutter of the house, the ease and charm of Duncan's conversation, the sight of Sophie pottering about pointing at her great-grandparents' pictures gave Frances intense pleasure. It was all so much more congenial to her than the sunny expatriate nightclub life of southern Spain, or the dreamy idleness of the hippies.

Over the next few years, Frances did her utmost to give Henrietta and Sophie love and security. She gave Henrietta curtains from Ham Spray for her new flat (admitting to her diary that it irritated her when Henrietta, admiring the fabric, assumed that they had been Carrington's choice) and was genuinely pleased whenever an amiable boyfriend appeared on the scene. She loved her little granddaughter's visits, and started to read her stories and teach her the piano; Sophie's alertness, her bright dark eyes and curly hair were a touching reminder of Burgo. But as time passed, and Henrietta's admirers came and went, and she seemed unable to settle – there were more extended trips abroad – Frances began to feel uneasy. She did not want to clip Henrietta's wings, but when she heard, in the autumn of

1965, that Henrietta was thinking of leaving Sophie behind in a communal household to go travelling she intervened. 'I must fight for Sophie over this,' she wrote, and she did. She felt this responsibility for her granddaughter all the more because neither Bunny nor Angelica appeared ready to share it; Bunny was always a non-interventionist, and during the later 1960s he and Angelica were having difficulties of their own.

Where Sophie's well-being was concerned, Frances could be fierce; and she was not afraid to argue with all her younger friends, including Henrietta, about drugs. They did not feel any need to hide their experiments from her; but while she was not easily shocked, she did not pretend she approved. To her, drug-taking was boring and mindless, a way of blotting out reality. Pressed by Henrietta – 'perhaps there were wonderful new sensations one ought to try?' – Frances was crisp: experiments were all very well, 'but it was a mad world, a world of the bored and futile, and of the lunatic asylum'. At the same time, the last thing she wanted was to drive Henrietta away, or to become the representative of the conventional world. She believed that the young should be encouraged to reinvent themselves and the world, and often admired them for it; 'Make Love, Not War' was a slogan bound to appeal to her. After a weekend at Hilton in March 1967, she observed with affection how 'Henrietta cooked magnificently, played Bach on the piano slowly and lovingly and spoke in favour of Buddhism and marijuana.'

However, by 1968, the year that Sophie reached the age of five, it was becoming clear that Henrietta's way of life was increasingly incompatible with her daughter's needs. That summer, she had taken to the road in a caravan with her friend Mark Palmer and three other young men, five horses, a goat and a dog; this cavalcade, much reported by the press, drifted around the countryside in tattered velvet and silk, tinkling bells and a haze of woodsmoke and marijuana, dedicated to peace, love and the simple life. It was all very well until the autumn came and the question of Sophie's education became pressing. At this point, after much agitated discussion, Frances' eldest nephew, Richard Garnett, and his wife Jane offered to have Sophie to live with them and their children in Islington, so that she could have a family base and start school. Henrietta would see her daughter at weekends, and in the holidays; she agreed to the plan, which lasted for a number of years while Sophie was growing up; Frances was much relieved, although she well knew – and Julia was there to remind her – that small children really ought not to be separated from their mothers. She summed it all up to Gerald: 'A child of five is not a parcel that can be transferred from one home to another, and though her new one is excellent she sometimes has fits of speechless sobbing. I hope it won't be damaging in the

long run – also that Henrietta, who has so many gifts and so much beauty
and charm, will find some more practical and happier way of life.' There
were to be more difficult moments, but Henrietta and Frances never lost
touch and always appreciated each other's best qualities.

It was during the mid-1960s, as the double bereavement that had altered
her life changed, as all such losses do in time, from being an open wound
to a dull, familiar ache, that Frances began to contemplate her own mortality.
Not long after her sixty-fifth birthday a visit to Lawford reminded her how
much she missed Phil Nichols, although the sight of his grave only confirmed
her conviction that it was 'terrible ... to preserve the mouldering remains
of a dead person thus in an exact position and put a little bunch of white
carnations on it'. A few days later she recorded her conviction that she now
had, at the most, 'ten years of dwindling sensibility' left to live, and wished
she could know exactly how long there was to go so that she could 'make
appropriate arrangements'. With Eddie Sackville-West's death that summer,
another friend of her youth was gone; 'Life', she wrote sadly, 'suddenly
seems a mere antechamber to the tomb.' From then on, thoughts of death
were never far from her mind. It became one of her maxims that the only
way to deal with the terror and the mystery of death was to become familiar
with it, not to keep that door closed but to open it regularly and have a
good look round the room. Her own health remained good, apart from one
short episode when chest pains sent her to the doctor; a cardiogram revealed
nothing serious, although she was advised to take better care of herself. She
told Julia, whose concern for her surprised and pleased her, and Janetta,
who troubled her by suggesting that she was perhaps too wound-up and
restless; but the anxiety passed, and anyway Frances disliked thinking about
health, which she regarded as like drains – vital but distasteful.

Somehow, she pressed on energetically with her life. She had no intention
of giving up work; if she ever found herself without a task to structure
her days around, it caused her something like panic. She had joined the
Translators' Association, and was always on the lookout for more work; she
did not mind much how dull it was, she loved the distraction of the task
itself. Between 1956 and 1978 she had thirty translations of books and articles
published (see Appendix B). Meanwhile, after some twelve years, James
Strachey's edition of Freud was finished; Frances compiled her final index
in 1965, and attended the grand banquet held to mark the completion of
the great work in October 1966. She was struck by the unexpectedly 'glossy,
stylish, confident look' of the four hundred or so psychoanalysts gathered
there, 'with their clever Jewish faces'. (Frances was not shy of remarking on
Jewish or Negro attributes in the manner of her generation; her references

read oddly today, but were more anachronistic than racist.)

Frances had always been a good traveller, and during her sixties and seventies she found travel the perfect distraction and an antidote for loneliness. Janetta and the Brenans drew her back to Spain at least once a year, especially after Janetta established herself at Tramores, the beautiful house she created around a ruined Moorish castle in the late 1960s. Sometimes Frances travelled with a couple – to Cyprus with the Hills or Austria with the Penroses – more often with a woman friend or one or two of the Crichel boys. These journeys were a vital outlet for her physical and mental energy, and gave her unflagging powers of observation full range. Her diaries show her great gifts as a travel writer, alert, humorous, always curious, whether about history, architecture or human nature. Two journeys she made in the late 1960s stand out: to Russia with Kitty West in September 1965, and to Sicily with Rosamond Lehmann in the spring of 1967.

Frances had been excited by the idea of Russia since her sister Ray's time there before the First World War. In 1965, only two years after the Cuban missile crisis, it was neither usual nor easy to go to Russia as a tourist; Frances and Kitty joined a culturally acceptable, if notably well-connected and well-heeled, group organised by the Irish Georgian Society, run by Desmond and Mariga Guinness (the son and daughter-in-law of Diana Mosley and her first husband Bryan Moyne, known to Frances since the early days of Ham Spray). From the start, Frances found it all thrilling. They flew to Leningrad via Paris and Moscow, drinking vodka and eating caviar; their hotel was the faded but splendid Europa, just off the Nevsky Prospekt, where she had a huge room with a writing desk and large bathroom. 'Hurrah!' she wrote on her first night there, so excited that she could hardly sleep.

Frances was delighted by the wide skies and magnificent architecture of the city, so delicately coloured in pale yellows, pinks and greens, and she naturally approved of the fact that as the state was atheist ('stimulating thought') the many churches they visited were treated as museums. Far from finding Russia grim or oppressive, she positively enjoyed signs of austerity, and considered the people she observed in the streets 'a good deal jollier, less hag-ridden and apathetic than London crowds'. The critical comments of her companions annoyed her; unlike them, she was pleased by the way that the regime was 'turning what were once private parks of the rich into public gardens available to all'. Frances' instinct for low living and high thinking, her distaste for opulence and suspicion of the rich found satisfaction in what she thought she discerned in Russia: an egalitarian society where the best of art and culture was available to everyone. As for the dark side of Soviet life, she seems hardly to have been aware of it; as she reported to Gerald, 'Probably overcrowding is still the worst hardship … it's quite untrue that there are no bathplugs, lavatory paper, chocolate, fruit … the odd thing about this regime based on dialectical materialism is how un-materialistic it is.' She disliked the Marxist jargon, and in Moscow she declined to view Lenin's embalmed body, but then there was *Boris Godunov* at the Bolshoi, and the Oistrakhs playing Bach's Double Violin Concerto. She returned to London exhausted, but in a state of excited Russophilia.

It was soon clear to Frances, when she set off to Sicily with Rosamond Lehmann in the spring of 1967, that she was to be 'acting husband', and she accepted her role with good grace. She did not mind the sniggers of the Sicilians at Rosamond's purple-tinted hair and billowing figure, nor the fact that she had to do most of the driving; she positively enjoyed capturing the absurdity of it all. 'The queenly figure bends her head like a swan and smiles sweetly from beneath her sunshade; the little companion looks beadily and inquisitively about her.' What she did find trying were Rosamond's mystical ramblings about the afterlife and repeated attempts to persuade her that, like her daughter Sally, Burgo was not beyond reach. Such 'comforting rubbish' was not for Frances. The last week of the trip was overshadowed by a letter from Alix Strachey telling Frances that James had died of a sudden heart attack. It was a blow she had not expected; he had somehow seemed immortal. She arrived back in London wondering sadly how best to help Alix bear the unbearable.

During these years, Frances, even more than most people approaching seventy, found herself often taking on the role of comforter to the bereaved. She was, as she ruefully acknowledged, something of an expert; but it was not just that. Her friends knew she felt deeply for them, and understood what they were going through; but they also knew that she abhorred melodrama and sentimentality, so that her kindness was never over-emotional and her advice was likely to be practical and realistic. Also, she was proof in herself that it is possible not just to survive grief and loss but to continue afterwards to explore life's possibilities and pleasures. Her company was bracing as well as comforting.

At the beginning of 1966 Frances needed all her resources when her brother-in-law Dick Rendel died and she was asked to help look after her sister Judy in Kent. 'The family have cast me for the role of support, thankfully and as if they were calling in an expert on bereavement as they would a plumber. I may be one, but this only makes me know only too acutely what she is suffering.' Her family never brought out the best in Frances, funerals were anathema to her and she had just started work on a

new translation: 'With my torturing thoughts for Judy, how can I concentrate on work?' Even worse, she had recently received alarming news
about Janetta, who was suddenly coming to London for an operation. She
did her best, helped by her nephew Jim Rendel, a professor of genetics who
had moved to Sydney. As Judy could not face the funeral, Frances was able
to avoid it by keeping her company; even so, she found the gathering
afterwards with its 'congealed family atmosphere' 'intolerably suffocating'.
She explained to Judy why she would have to leave her for a few days to see
Janetta, describing her as 'the person I was fondest of in the world who had
done most for me and utterly propped me in my times of trouble'. When
Judy expressed guilt that she and Dick had done nothing for Frances when
Burgo died, Frances thought to herself: 'No, they didn't, but nor I suppose
did I want them to.' But her sister's grief brought them closer, and when
Julia's reaction to Judy's plight was more than usually unsympathetic Frances
was furious: 'it almost seems like jealousy that anyone else's troubles should
be considered and cared for'. Nor was Julia concerned about Janetta; this
upset Frances even more, and their estrangement deepened. 'I almost feel
my affection for her has gone, and almost, too, my respect,' she wrote, but
then added, 'I expect both will revive.' It was an enormous relief when
Janetta's operation was safely over. 'This operation', wrote Frances, 'has
made me aware of how deeply I love Janetta . . . I have been seized by mortal
dread on her behalf . . . it is always frightening to realise one's dependence
on another human being.' But Janetta's fragile beauty as she lay in bed
surrounded by spring flowers had 'irradiated my days'.

Frances was surprised to find how much Alix Strachey needed her after
James died. For all the forty years of friendship since she and Ralph had
lived in Gordon Square, the many visits to Ham Spray and the confidence
shown in her as their preferred Freud indexer, she had never quite known
where she stood with them. But from her first visit to Lords' Wood after
James's death in May 1967 any doubts vanished. They talked for hours about
the past; Frances could not bear to tell Alix what she really thought, which
was that the pain got worse 'for at least a year'. Such conversations were hard
on Frances; she lay awake that night, her heart racing; 'the delayed effect of
my pain for Alix zoomed out of the darkness like a huge crow and clutched
me with its claws and beat its great black wings at me'. She worried for
some time about whether she was doing all that she could to support Alix.

It was not just because she was a comfort in distress that Frances' friends
loved her, as the Crichel boys showed her after Eddie Sackville-West's death.
The future of Crichel looked uncertain; Eardley had already decided he
wanted a place of his own. Now, Desmond and Raymond asked her if she

would consider sharing it with them. Although she was touched and pleased, she knew at once that she could not accept; she never wavered from her conviction that after losing Ralph she could only live alone. As for love affairs, there was no question of that either, as she told Bunny when he raised the matter with her: '"How do you manage, darling?" I considered the question and wondered how I could convey the sense that so large a part of me is torn away, such a miserable remnant remains that it would be a mockery to provide it with such "intimate excitement" even if available.' Love, for her, had to be 'on an entirely different plane from the past'. Frances in her sixties made little effort with her appearance; she let her hair go grey, and bothered less than ever about make-up or clothes. She found something pathetic about women (like Julia) who tried to disguise their age, and who made it clear that they longed to find a man with whom to share their lives. And when, after dining at her flat one night with Isobel Strachey, Adrian Daintrey made a tentative advance, she was scathing. 'He's all right in company, amusing even. But when he lingered on and slobbered over me and said he thought he was a little in love with me I was not at all amused. Shall avoid him in future. What an old juggins.'

Her own detachment from romantic and sexual entanglements made her an ideal confidante and adviser to her more confused friends, of all ages and both sexes. Sometimes she felt drained and exhausted by their emotional dramas; but the human tragicomedy never bored her. And her circle continued to provide plenty of scope. Janetta was beginning to find happiness with Jaime, but Robert's marriage to Cynthia was often stormy, Mary Campbell had married a difficult American, Gerald was tormenting Gamel with various hippy girls, Margaret Penrose was agonised when Lionel found a Polish girlfriend, and Angelica was to leave Bunny for good in 1969. Richard Chopping and Denis continued to have dramatic rows and re-conciliations, and Julian Jebb, who longed to find love, was often worryingly low. Frances had always given homosexual love as much respect as het-erosexual, and believed that male couples had the right to live together openly. At last, in early 1966, almost nine years after the publication of the Wolfenden Report, the Sexual Offences Act made sex between consenting male adults over twenty-one legal. Frances paid her first visit to the House of Commons with Dicky to hear the crucial debate. Her account is char-acteristically sharp and amused:

> There we sat in the gallery of this Gothic brown interior looking down on the green benches where a scanty, frightfully bored looking crowd sprawled among their order papers ... nobody said anything of the

smallest interest, but there was much talk ... of these 'unfortunate people' (buggers) as of creatures horribly deformed but perhaps needing pity. Roy Jenkins spoke in fine ringing tones ... there were a number of shocks of long, greying hair; the square pale clever face of a Foot (I think) stared up at us women, Queers and Indians in the gallery.

Dicky, over-excited, pursued Lord Arran, who had introduced the Bill, to thank him: 'So you think I did right?' said Arran. 'I've LOATHED every minute of it.' They were joined by a man in knee-britches who announced at the top of his voice that he used to be in the Navy, 'and in my view there were three things you should never have on your ship – rats, buggery and thieves'. They left before the vote, and Frances drove Dicky home to Wivenhoe and Denis in her Mini. Later, they heard that 'the ayes for buggery' had won. 'Modified jubilation,' wrote Frances. 'I wonder very much whether quite a few who get a kick from being outsiders and rebels won't feel a sort of disappointment and perhaps have to try some new eccentricity.' Denis, she found, rather agreed with her.

Looking back, though, Frances acknowledged that it was a relief to be able to stop worrying about the risks run by some of her oldest friends whose sex lives had involved them in criminal activity, like Dadie Rylands, whose life as a pillar of King's College, Cambridge, and a leading Shake-spearean scholar was punctuated by alarming episodes when he would get very drunk and go off around parks and pubs in London in search of partners. Now, although he would still be risking his reputation and his career, he and others like him were free of the threat of prosecution and less vulnerable to blackmail; but if the Sexual Offences Act had at last made homosexuality legal, it had by no means made it respectable.

Exposure, to the likes of Rylands and many others in Frances' circle, whose love lives were no secret to their friends but had always required concealment from the outside world, was still a terrifying prospect; and those of them whose lovers had included Lytton Strachey were about to find out what it was to be exposed. It had always been Michael Holroyd's intention in writing about Lytton to deal openly with his emotional and sexual life; he believed, like his subject, that 'discretion is not the better part of biography', and was aiming to write a 'modern biography' which made 'no moral distinction' between homosexual and heterosexual behaviour. He was confident that James Strachey had no wish to conceal his brother's homosexuality. But as publication of the first volume (taking Lytton's life up to 1910) approached, he came to realise that, for all his admirable intentions, he was in for trouble.

Early in 1965 Frances had been to see James and Alix at Lords' Wood where she found them highly critical of Holroyd's first draft. James, who controlled all Lytton's copyrights and so had the power to stop Holroyd in his tracks, told Frances that he was insisting on many changes. Although Frances suspected that James's hero-worship of his brother was affecting his judgement, she felt apprehensive as she prepared for her own next interview with Holroyd. 'Do I want this young man to have access to any of it?' she asked herself as she sorted through her papers. 'Should people who were in no way concerned with feelings that were private, tender or painful have access to them?' She wished she could consult Ralph; there were moments when she was tempted to burn all the papers she had.

In the end, of course, she did no such thing. The book was a reality; she would try to make it as accurate as possible, especially about Ralph. The evening with Michael Holroyd went well; she gave him extracts from Ralph's letters and her diaries, and showed him photographs of Ham Spray in the early days (she had inherited all Lytton and Carrington's albums from Ralph). She told him that she believed that although Lytton had been in love with Ralph, her husband had been 'hopelessly heterosexual' and that they had loved each other as devoted friends; she found no reason 'to suppress the truth' about anything, including Carrington's affair with Beakus Penrose and how Ralph had paid for the abortion. She herself had nothing to hide.

About a year later Holroyd showed her the draft of his second volume, covering her relationship with Ralph and its consequences for Lytton and Carrington. She read it 'at first with horror, then with a sort of amazed admiration . . . Perhaps he has probed too unmercifully, even the bedrooms and beds are explored for data; but he has relied enormously on written materials.' Frances now found herself in the curious and unsettling position of learning from a biographer details she had not known before, especially about Lytton's last illness and death; she found Holroyd's account very moving. As for his portrait of Ralph, she found it, as she had expected, 'unsympathetic', closer than she would have liked to Gerald's portrayal of a handsome philistine; but it was only the account of Watendlath and the Great Row that she found inaccurate. 'I shall try and put him right on that.' Overall, though, she was greatly impressed. Holroyd had made her 'see Bloomsbury with slightly fresh eyes', and recognised the qualities in Lytton and his friends that she valued most: originality, 'working out their own standards', intellectual integrity and fearlessness.

By the following summer, however, Frances had come to realise that others were finding the draft biography alarming. She had a visit from an agitated Duncan Grant, and an awkward conversation with Angelica who felt strongly that it was wrong to publish such things about living people. Frances, who had decided that the only valid reason for concealing the truth was if it caused pain, was surprised to discover that it was fear of shocking people that worried Angelica most; and even more taken aback when Bunny turned out to be in favour of 'wholesale repression' on the same grounds. She accused Bunny of allowing himself to be influenced by the opinions of 'colonels and old ladies', and pointed out that his own memoirs had been full of personal revelations (although not about his own homosexual past). She wished, afterwards, that she had mentioned the pain he had caused her and others in her family by publishing some of Ray's agonising deathbed letters, which Alix Strachey considered the most disgraceful revelation she had ever read; and she linked Angelica's reaction to the lingering secrecy about her real father, which Frances had long considered foolish and pointless.

Frances was disappointed with such nervous reactions to Holroyd's truth-telling. 'There was always that foot fumblingly advanced by Bloomsbury towards the conventional and aristocratic enclave,' she observed tartly, 'their Victorian childhood perhaps coming to the surface in a way totally inconsistent with their defiance of idées reçues.' She wanted them to have the courage of their convictions, and it surprised her, too, that homosexuals should want to conceal their sexual activities just at the moment when 'their position seems about to be legally ratified'. Bunny, on the other hand, feared that publication of Holroyd's book might even turn public opinion against the legalisation of homosexuality. For Frances, it was simple: 'One must stand up for what one believes.' She did appreciate, though, that it was not so simple for Duncan, who disliked the thought of his youthful love life being made public and even wondered if he might be arrested; she wrote him a thoughtful letter, suggesting that he had every right to ask Holroyd to remove any details about himself he found upsetting. 'As I rather gathered that you didn't mind Lytton's feelings for you being apparent, or anyway realised that they were a very important element in his life, perhaps you could see what it looked like if you cut out anything you minded.' He followed her advice, and Michael Holroyd agreed to consider all such representations carefully. To his great relief, in the end Duncan only asked for minor alterations and the removal of one reference to copulation; one or two of Lytton's other amours were given pseudonyms (as was Beakus Penrose) and Maynard Keynes' affair with Lytton was represented as a close friendship, in deference to his widow Lydia's feelings. Looking back, Holroyd acknowledged that at the time he underestimated the alarm caused by his book and the courage required by those concerned, and paid tribute to Frances' support: 'It was fortunate for me that she felt strongly in favour of unbowdlerised biography.'

That summer, Frances was back to Spain, staying with the Brenans and Janetta. She had been corresponding steadily and affectionately with Gerald, and given him a brisk summary of the Holroyd ructions – 'He has been too outspoken for the buggers'; but it was not long before he managed to upset her all over again about Ralph. He showed her his novel *The Story of Poor Robinson*, a satirical version of his affair with Carrington, in which Parrywag, the Ralph character, is depicted as a handsome, doltish womaniser. 'I find it infuriating', wrote Frances, 'that Gerald has launched this myth of Ralph as a lumbering carthorse, only faintly civilised by Lytton.' It was one thing for Frances to support publication of an accurate account by a scrupulous outsider like Holroyd, but quite another when someone she had long considered an unreliable, self-interested witness set out through Holroyd to damage Ralph's image and reputation. She was hardly reassured to learn that Gerald was intending to press on with his second volume of autobiography. It was not an easy visit, and Frances left Spain aware that Gamel was drinking too much and looking far from well. Early the next year it became clear that she had cancer; and although Gerald was deeply upset, he was also showing signs of falling for another young woman, Lynda. Frances and Janetta exchanged worried letters about the increasingly bleak situation at Churriana.

By the time the first volume of Holroyd's biography was published, in September 1967, the Sexual Offences Act had become law and James Strachey, having agreed the text, was dead. The book was instantly recognised as masterly, combining depth of research with humour and humanity; it was greatly admired, even though some reviewers – notably Malcolm Muggeridge – took the opportunity to attack the morals and pernicious influence of its subject and Bloomsbury in general. In *The Sunday Times*, Raymond Mortimer (who was in a position to know how accurate it was) praised its quality and courage, calling it 'the first post-Wolfenden biography', and the literary world began to understand that Holroyd, like his subject before him, had broken new ground and reinvented biography itself. Frances had Holroyd round for another evening that month, and they discussed the whole book; much though she praised his achievement, she was not happy with his account of how Carrington acquired the gun to kill herself, which indicated that she had brought it back to Ham Spray from the Guinnesses under Ralph's nose. When she told him that she was certain, and Bunny, Gerald and Julia agreed, that Carrington had returned in secret to get the gun, she learned that it was Gerald who had informed him otherwise. 'But didn't you realise how uninterested Gerald is in the truth?' she asked. It was hard for her to accept that, like all biographers, but especially those whose subjects are living or recently dead, Holroyd was bound to hear different versions of the same story, and to consider them all before writing his own. Frances was enviably, sometimes alarmingly clear about what truth was; and she never doubted that she knew the truth about Ralph.

Increasingly irritated though she was by Gerald, her heart went out to him as Gamel's condition deteriorated. He spared her no details, writing her immense, graphic letters (one was thirty-eight pages long) describing Gamel's ordeal and the inadequacy of the treatment; Frances would tremble at the sight of another fat envelope in the familiar writing. She was appalled at the refusal of the Spanish doctors, on religious grounds, to give Gamel enough morphine; and she felt immense relief, as she had done when Ray died, when she heard, in January 1968, that it was all over. Gerald had shown great devotion to Gamel at the end; but, wrote Frances, 'I think his mainspring may recoil quickly and we may soon hear of Lynda again.' She was right.

Frances wanted to comfort Gerald if she could, and began to plan for a spring visit to Spain. The year had not started well: Julia was more difficult than ever, Robert Kee's recurrent unhappiness distressed her. Bunny's separation from Angelica was now permanent (she had recently taken up with the artist George Bergen, another of her father's former lovers). Then, in February, the publication of Holroyd's second volume stirred up another round of agitation. By now it was clear that this was a major literary event; *The Sunday Times* was serialising the book, and inevitably the extracts highlighted Lytton and Carrington's love lives. Frances was shocked by this 'ruthless vulgarisation', the huge pictures and the headlines proclaiming 'Trouble at the Mill House' and 'Abode of Love' (referring to one of her own photographs of Ham Spray). Again, the book was much praised, but Bloomsbury and its morals came in for criticism and derision; Frances found it all much more distressing than she had expected. 'I don't mind the book,' she wrote, 'but I suppose none of us would have produced the information we did had we known it was to be distorted by the Sunday papers into the likeness of a *News of the World* account of the lives of film stars.' Frances was invited to the launch party for the book, but went to *The Meistersingers* with Julian Jebb instead.

All she wanted, in the aftermath of publication, was for the fuss to die down. She longed to get away, but was not sure whether Spain was really a good idea: Janetta might be in Morocco, the weather was bad and she dreaded finding Gerald in an aggressive mood about Ralph. Meanwhile, everyone she met wanted to know how she felt about the book. 'I defend it as best I can, and particularly on the score that it is the first book about Bloomsbury that is not a suppressio veri, like Roy Harrod's on Maynard.' But when, during a weekend with the Carringtons, Julia spoke up for Ralph and said that the book's account of him was 'totally inadequate', Frances was so pleased she could hardly speak. Julia had confirmed Frances' growing feeling that Holroyd's image of Ralph was a travesty, and as she wrote, 'This image is of course Gerald's creation, and had it not been for interpolations of mine it would have been further still from the truth.'

Her spirits rose when Janetta sent her a welcoming cable, and she flew to Málaga early in March to be met by Gerald, 'looking years younger'. Lynda was already installed; Frances found her intelligent, gentle and lovely to look at, but the house was cold and smelled strongly of cat and she had to sleep in the bed where Gamel had so recently died in agony. Gerald she found quite cheerful and obsessed with Holroyd's book. 'He half identifies with him, feels he has written the book or at least contributed most of the material, is delighted with his own portrait in it.' He told her that he had recently made Holroyd, whom he had not yet met, his literary executor (displacing Julian Jebb and Jonny Gathorne-Hardy; the latter was later to be restored, and eventually to write Gerald's own biography). He did not tell her that he was still sending Holroyd long letters about Ralph; one went off a few days before Frances arrived: 'I strongly suspect Ralph of having gone to bed with Lytton a few times in the early days. He was ready for experiments and had a lot of sexual vanity. In Italy during the war he had an incomplete homosexual experience with an Italian who made up to him. His actress mistress in London was unspeakably stupid and very vulgar, but very sensual, which was all he wanted.' Gerald's interest in his dead friend's love life was unbridled; he had already told Holroyd about Ralph and Barbara Bagenal, and now went on to assert that Ralph had always felt intense sexual rivalry with Bunny, at one time over Frances herself. After four days, Frances was more than ready for the serenity of Tramores and Janetta's sympathetic company.

In the wake of Holroyd's book, Frances and the others whose early lives would never be altogether private again had to accept that the revival of interest in Bloomsbury was not diminishing but growing, and that it was focused not on its members' contributions to art or literature but on their personal lives. There were rewards for this as well as penalties: the Bloomsbury revival meant that the market in private papers, carefully cultivated since the early sixties by two American dealers, the Misses Hamill and Barker from Chicago, became more tempting. That summer, Frances began negotiations with them over Lytton's letters to Ralph, which she had been told could be worth as much as £2,000 (around £14,000 today). When they offered £750, she declined; but the following year she was happy to accept £844 (after they had deducted their usual twenty-five per cent). According to their records, Hamill and Barker paid Frances the equivalent of around £17,000 between 1962 and 1970. Carrington's letters were also of growing interest to collectors, and Frances held the copyright; now Noel Carrington asked her if she would like to edit a selection for publication. Much though she admired the letters, she knew at once that she did not want to do so, and the job was handed on to Bunny.

'I can't face playing with the past for several years' was Frances' reaction to the Carrington letters proposal; but the past was not to be so easily dealt with. For the rest of her days, she would be more and more sought after as a source for and controller of material, as the people she began to call the Bloomsbury hounds came to her for advice and information. More often than not, Frances was ready, even happy, to help; but when she decided against doing so, she was a formidable adversary. One of her fiercest and most effective battles was the first. Before the end of 1968, she heard that the BBC had commissioned Ken Russell to make a film about Lytton based on the Holroyd biography. Frances still despised television, and Russell was known for his wildly inventive, fantastical treatment of his subjects; the press was hinting at 'sensational casting'. The prospect of a Russell version of Ralph, and perhaps of herself, was unbearable. Frances contacted the Society of Authors about her powers as holder of Carrington's copyrights, and summoned Michael Holroyd; she was not best pleased to learn that he had encouraged the project and had presented it to Alix on the basis that it would increase the sale of Lytton's books. Left in no doubt that Frances was angry and upset, he apologised for 'obtuseness' and promised to try to get it stopped. The BBC tried to persuade Frances of Russell's brilliance and good intentions; she remained unconvinced, and wrote Norman Swallow, the BBC executive concerned, a polite but exceedingly firm letter:

> It must surely be obvious to you that, from the point of view of friends and relations, a 'dramatisation' as you call it is a totally different thing from a documentary ... None of the people chiefly concerned (Carrington's brother Noel Carrington, Alix Strachey and myself) would in the least object to a documentary based on Holroyd's book, but we are deeply distressed at the idea of our sisters, husbands, relatives and friends

fictionally – for no actor's performance, however good, can be other than grotesque to those who knew the originals intimately . . . whereas we were prepared to co-operate in a literary history, and did so fully to the best of our ability, we are not ready to take the same attitude to a dramatisation.

She cited Raymond Mortimer, David Garnett and Rosamond Lehmann as writers who felt 'absolute horror at the vulgarity of the idea', enquired whether Russell proposed to represent Ralph and herself, as well as Lytton and Carrington, by actors, and if the painful topic of Carrington's suicide would feature in his film. Finally, 'I am afraid that, as you will realise, I am very far from giving you approval and support. You say that Michael Holroyd is allowing you to refer to his biography. The book is of course largely made up of quotations from copyright material in the form of letters and diaries: the copyright in nearly all these belongs either to Alix Strachey (in the case of Lytton) or myself (in the case of Carrington). I think I should state here in writing that neither of us is prepared to give permission to the BBC to use any of this material for a dramatisation.' The battle dragged on for some weeks; Frances would not budge, and moreover roped in Robert Kee, by then a BBC star, to write to David Attenborough, then Director of Programmes, on her behalf. In the end, the project collapsed and Frances was left wondering why she had minded quite so much. The answer was not hard to find: 'What am I protecting so tigerishly? Ralph, I believe.'

The fight with the BBC left Frances feeling agitated and vulnerable. She tried to cultivate serenity, as Janetta advised, but found it hard. In April, she set off with Bunny to drive to Tuscany; they were to stay with Magouche and her daughter Maro, married to Stephen Spender's sculptor son Matthew, in Tuscany. At seventy-seven, Bunny was hoping for a romance with Magouche, which Frances found both endearing and alarming, as he pushed himself and her to get there as quickly as possible. That summer, she lost another very old friend when Boris Anrep died a few days after they spent a weekend together at Mottisfont, when he reminded her of how he had urged her not to hesitate about committing herself to Ralph. As her seventieth birthday approached, she feared that old age was beginning to affect her; she would catch herself humming away, and recalled how Burgo used to tease her about it. Reaching seventy, she contemplated 'the increasing obscenity of old age' and took comfort in the thought that at least she did not have much further to go.

Eighteen

Bloomsbury Revisited, 1970–1978

New Year melancholy often afflicted Frances, and it was particularly hard for her to feel positive at the start of her eighth decade. Later, she would advise younger friends to make the most of their sixties, as after seventy they would begin to feel the limitations of age. She herself remained strikingly active and energetic, but two concerns weighed on her more and more: her general responsibility towards the friends of her youth, as the Bloomsbury revival continued, and in particular the pitiful decline of one of those friends, Julia Strachey. Inevitably, as interest in them gathered pace the survivors faded and their ranks dwindled; Frances, in her seventies, was not just one of the youngest and fittest but remained, as she had always been, one of the more approachable and sensible. Her basic sanity had long been apparent to those around her. As Angelica Garnett would say, perhaps with a slight edge, 'dear Frances: she always had such a healthy mind'. Now she became more and more in demand as Bloomsbury's spokeswoman, which, although flattering and often stimulating, could also be a burden. When early in 1970 the Strachey Trust was conceived, at the instigation of Michael Holroyd, Paul Levy (a young American writing about Bloomsbury's founding philosopher, G.E. Moore) and Lucy Norton (French scholar and sister of Lytton's friend Harry) to ensure that Lytton's papers, and later other Bloomsbury material of value and interest to future generations, should be acquired and protected, Frances was asked to help, and especially to encourage Alix Strachey to donate her large and valuable collection. Frances had reservations; she did not much care for Lucy Norton, who was, Frances feared, failing to consider Alix's best interests. Sometimes she could not help feeling suspicious of the increasing number of people staking a claim to the records of the past. 'I hear the music of the three conspirators straight from Ballo in Maschera,' she wrote after one meeting. Meanwhile, though, she continued, quietly, with her own profitable dealings with Hamill and Barker.

As for Julia, she was increasingly a worry to all her friends. As well as Frances, the Kees, the Campbells and Margaret Penrose did their best, and Lawrence and Jenny Gowing tried nobly to include her in their family life, but she was more and more erratic and self-destructive. Her writing was permanently stalled, as she wrestled with a memoir that would include the collapse of her marriage. The practicalities of everyday life were beyond her; she looked more and more peculiar, with her hair dyed too dark and her skirts too short. The drink and the purple hearts continued; sometimes she sounded quite mad, claiming to be persecuted by a marauding cat and that shrimps emerged from her taps. Frances could never bear to leave her struggling, and sooner or later would go to the rescue – taking round expensive food that Julia then rejected, organising domestic help, collecting her pension – only to be treated with contempt. Frances' kindness, her reliability, above all perhaps her sanity, brought out the worst in Julia. 'She really is most horribly disagreeable to me,' wrote Frances sadly. She resolved, not for the first time, never to be trapped into such a demeaning position again. It was easier said than done.

For the time being, she escaped into another journey to Russia. This time she travelled with Janetta, and Magouche joined them; the trip began in style, with a visit to the Hendersons, now at the embassy in Poland. As guests of the Ambassador they were shown round in the official Daimler with the Union Jack fluttering on the bonnet; Frances felt faintly embarrassed, unlike Janetta who never pretended not to relish special treatment. While approving the careful restoration of Cracow and the Poles' pride in their culture, she found the country grey and oppressive; and when they travelled on by train to Moscow she soon realised that her enthusiasm for Russia was waning. It was partly the fierce cold, partly that the fresh excitement of her first visit was lacking, but most of all because she found herself out of tune with Janetta and Magouche, whose reaction to the Russian scene was far more critical than hers. She felt responsible, having told them how wonderful it all was, and began to wish she had not come; it was a relief to be back in London on the eve of her birthday, even though she did not much look forward to passing the milestone. But Janetta organised lunch at Wheeler's, with Jaime, Robert and Cynthia; Margaret Penrose took her to *Uncle Vanya*, the Campbells sent flowers, and Frances felt better. 'The dread occasion has been eased past as it needs to be, and this great and friendly kindness has made it tolerable.'

But she came back to a Julia crisis. While Frances was away, she had been taken to the psychiatric ward of St Pancras Hospital. Frances went straight there; she found Julia looking gaunt, but although muddled not as evidently deranged as the other patients. In a way, Frances thought, she appeared relieved to be looked after. Over the next weeks of visiting Julia in hospital and talking to her doctor, Frances realised, perhaps for the first time, that her friend really was ill, in mind as well as body. This should have stopped her feeling she had failed; but somehow it did not. 'I feel so terribly guilty now for past irritation with her and for not taking her sometimes impossible behaviour just as a symptom that she is extremely ill.' She offered to pay for Julia to spend time in a comfortable nursing home when she left the hospital in May, but Julia refused; back in her flat it was not long before she began to relapse. By this time, she had been diagnosed as suffering from dementia. Although she had seemed pleased to see Frances in hospital, she soon turned on her again, returning what Frances called 'my usual cheque' with a cold letter. Frances found she hardly minded. 'I think Julia has had some satisfaction in rejecting my present, and repeating in writing that she doesn't want to see me.' Frances' standards of friendship remained high, and she expected a lot from those she loved; but she also expected a great deal of herself. When, in April, Isobel Strachey's daughter Charlotte Jenkins died from leukaemia, Frances found the echoes of Burgo hard to bear; but she stayed close to Isobel, who appeared fragile but whose courage was admirable. Frances knew better than most how the bereaved fear that their company is a burden to their friends.

Frances drew the strength she needed from familiar sources: her music, some translation work, and discussing Chomsky and neo-Kantianism with Paul Levy, whom she met often with the Cecils and liked more and more. In April there was a trip to Alderney with Dadie Rylands and Eardley, where the sea and the wild flowers and the energetic company revived her; in June she was at the Aldeburgh Festival with Dicky and Denis, and by mid-July back at Tramores with Janetta. She visited Gerald, now established at his new house in Alhaurin with Lynda. Frances wondered how long such a lovely girl would tolerate 'platonic marriage' with Gerald; she found him more than usually argumentative, stirred up by the prospect of the publication of Bunny's edition of Carrington's letters.

During August, back in England, Frances read the letters in proof. She admired them as much as ever; Frances was always generous about Carrington's originality and talent. If she was irritated by what Carrington wrote to Lytton about Ralph when he first entered their lives – that, although kind and handsome, he was dull and held conventional anti-pacifist opinions – she did not say so, and nor did she comment on the small phrase in Carrington's letter to Lytton of May 1921 that was before long to cause her much trouble, referring as it did to 'that night when we were all three together'. That summer, a different ménage à trois took up much of her attention: Lionel and Margaret Penrose and his Polish girlfriend, Dunyusha – 'as awkward a situation as I remember, yet such a familiar one,' she wrote. 'Everyone always eagerly administers blame; but as usual I see three people in a knot that none of them has deliberately tied.' The only answer, she felt, was to make the best of a bad job. She was cheered by seeing something of the spry and ageless Duncan Grant, veteran of his own ménage à trois and now involved with a married bisexual, Paul Roche. She took him to see *Carmen* and back to her flat for supper. A few days later she found herself Georgia Tennant's guest at *Oh! Calcutta!*, Ken Tynan's revue exemplifying the younger generation's determination to celebrate sexual experiment. Frances was beady-eyed and unimpressed, finding it neither funny nor pornographic enough, and while some of the naked bodies were beautiful, 'there was something inevitably phony in the assumed lustfulness of their movement and dancing, when no male had the ghost of an erection'.

When the Carrington letters appeared in November, Frances found herself back in the front line. Raymond Mortimer came to talk to her about Carrington before writing his (highly favourable) review; it pleased her to find that he had been moved by the crucial exchange of letters between her and Carrington in 1926, as she had not found it easy to agree to Bunny publishing them. Not everyone was beguiled by Carrington and the further revelations about Bloomsbury; when Frances met the literary editor of *The Sunday Times*, Jack Lambert, at a party for Iris Origo, he launched into a tirade. 'Of course I've always found Bloomsbury infuriating. They were so supercilious, they despised everyone ... There's nothing to them at all. No-one now cares about anything they did.' Even Keynes and Virginia Woolf? Frances wondered. Iris, though, was gratifyingly friendly, telling Frances she had always regarded her as 'a life-giver'.

Publication of the letters coincided with the first exhibition ever held of Carrington's paintings. The Upper Grosvenor Gallery was crammed with familiar faces; Frances dodged Julia, only to be confronted by her Cambridge admirer Raisley Moorsom, reminding her how unhappy she had made him some fifty years earlier, and embarrassed by David Eccles, then a Lord and a leading Tory politician, who in his speech opening the show boasted how he had once bought a book from Frances Marshall in his youth. She was so irritated when he went on to disparage Carrington as an amateur painter and Bloomsbury in general as an overrated bunch that she wrote him a stiff letter. Slowly but inexorably, Frances was becoming the representative and defender of the friends of her youth.

Her seventieth year ended with candles in the blackout caused by Heath's battle with the unions, Bunny opening his heart to her about romantic trouble with Magouche, long depressing talks with Robert about his marriage and an anti-Franco demonstration trailing past her window. She had a new translation of interviews with Spanish writers on hand; 'I keep on worrying about finishing, or not finishing tasks; but behind all this lies the inescapable fact that what I'm really busy finishing is my life.' For Christmas she was rescued by the Cecils, and spent it contentedly with the loving, voluble family gathering at Cranborne, wondering about David's Christianity, trying to understand Wittgenstein, taking chilly walks with Rachel in the snow, and reading *Hamlet* and *Othello*. The Cecil children always remembered Frances' visits with pleasure. She would talk to them as equals, and when Laura, at seventeen, took up with a man her parents did not care for, she felt instinctively that Frances was on her side.

Throughout her seventies Frances maintained one clear purpose: to correct the impression of Ralph created by Gerald and Michael Holroyd, and to protect him, along with Lytton and Carrington, from further distortion. She saw it as a simple matter of truth and justice, of defending as best she could the reputation and standing of the man she had loved; but she was also defending herself. To belittle Ralph was to reduce her, too; if he had been merely a hearty philistine, where did that leave her? In the end, after a series of skirmishes, she was to realise that there was only one way to counter what she always regarded as the Brenan version of Ralph, and that was to present her own.

But in the meantime, she found herself dealing with a new wave of Bloomsbury hounds, some of them more congenial than others. She had dealings for a while with an aspiring writer and broadcaster, Catherine Dupré, who had become fascinated by Carrington; Frances found her too eager to please. Michael Holroyd and Paul Levy she had already begun to regard as friends; now, another young man sought her out for advice. Stanley Olson was an American postgraduate writing a thesis on the early years of the Hogarth Press, and his first visit to her flat in June 1971 marked the beginning of the most important new friendship of Frances' later years, even though his initial letter had struck her as so 'obsequious' she almost declined to see him at all. In the event, they took to each other at once. Apart from his intelligence, which was considerable, she was impressed by his equally considerable eccentricity, perceptiveness and humour. Above all, though, she was beguiled by his interest in Ralph, whose role at the Hogarth Press he was anxious to explore. Olson's timing was good; he found Frances at the very moment when she was most likely to welcome a researcher prepared to do Ralph justice. He went away carrying her last copy of Ralph's book.

Stanley Olson was a curious and slightly mysterious character. Like a figure from a novel by Henry James, a writer he loved, as did Frances, he had left America to reinvent himself, looking for a more stylish, cultivated way of life than his rich, conventional Jewish family could provide. By the time Frances met him, he had been in England for two years and was well on the way to establishing himself in literary London. His subject had already led him to make friends with Michael Holroyd, and with a young woman who was to play a significant part in the next stage of Frances' life. Gill Coleridge was then working at Chatto & Windus, owners of the Hogarth Press, and had been so taken with Stanley that she found him a desk in her office. Stanley was good-looking, if on the stout side, with thick black hair and blue eyes behind heavy, dark-rimmed spectacles; he was highly articulate, emotional, loved gossip and had soon lost all trace of his American accent. Generously subsidised by his long-suffering father, he was able to cultivate expensive tastes: he liked hand-made shoes and shirts, grand stationery from Smythson's ('to write to all the old Bloomsburyites on') and dining at Claridge's or the Connaught. He had a passion for Wagner, whose music made him cry, and for his spaniel, Wuzzo, who was trundled round London in a specially made Harrods tricycle. Despite her puritan tendencies, Frances was amused rather than put off by Stanley's extravagances; she liked his idiosyncrasies and his kindness, his good brain and his vulnerability. He admired her likewise, writing in his diary, 'Her humour, and the originality of her mind, its quickness and deftness, is remarkable and a marvel to witness.' He also recognised her more formidable side: 'And speak of brute will power and strength of character – she's got it all.'

Frances' diary for the next fifteen years is full of Stanley. She understood his mixed feelings about his parents and approved of the fact that he had loathed the military school they made him attend; nothing pleased her more than his independence of mind. 'He loves thinking, that's everything.' During those years, he sustained her more than anyone, always excepting Janetta, in her constant battle against loneliness. He gave her many treats, but as well as taking her to Covent Garden he would make sure her heating was turned on when she came back from abroad. She helped him too, by introducing him to her friends (several of whom, including Janetta, became his), and to Henrietta and Sophie, who both came to love him, listening to his troubles (prone to depression and sexually confused, his love life was never satisfactory) and by advice on his writing. It was a true friendship, based on respect, affection and need.

Not long before Stanley arrived on the scene Janetta and Jaime had decided to get married. As a joke, Frances offered to be a bridesmaid, only to learn that Julian and Magouche were to be in attendance at the register office; she sent flowers, feeling conscious of her own 'insignificance'. Immersion in natural beauty, especially in the spring, always revived Frances; that year she stayed with Bunny at his house at Charry in the Lot, among the red squirrels and the wild orchids. She and Bunny shared a passion for the natural world; their friendship deepened as they grew older, and she greatly admired his stoical, unresentful attitude to his solitary life. They worked every morning, walked or made expeditions later – she always remembered the splendid Romanesque carvings at Moissac – and discussed writing, love and loneliness over whisky by the fire at night.

As so often happens, she returned to a new set of problems. Joan Cochemé's husband had died suddenly, Julia was suicidal, and Magouche was concerned at Robert Kee's state of mind, sending Frances something he had written about death. Sometimes, Frances felt barely strong enough to advise or console; she too thought about death all the time, and although, ten years on, she could sometimes remember Ralph with more pleasure than pain, the thought of Burgo could still pierce her to the heart. 'Oh, poor human beings,' she wrote sadly. 'How they are put through hoops.' That summer, she joined Janetta and Jaime in Corfu. She was happy in their happiness, while feeling a little excluded by it. She went on to Italy to meet Raymond and Dadie for some energetic sightseeing. They travelled well together, although she could not help noting Raymond's obsession with guidebooks and Dadie's embarrassing interest in handsome waiters. Of Piero della Francesca's great *Resurrection* in Sansepolcro she wrote: 'I come nearer to understanding religious emotion when I'm looking at that painting than at any other time' – quite an admission, for Frances.

Soon after she returned to London, Stanley Olson came to see her again, eager to talk further. The night before the visit she had a painful dream in which she searched for Ralph in vain; was it really right to trust this strange young American, show him private letters, and encourage him to pursue his researches? 'One may tend to assume', she wrote, 'these young addicts of Bloomsbury get it more right than they do. And what is right, anyway?' She consulted Robert Kee, who had recently touched her very much by saying he would like to write something about Ralph himself; he too felt that the man he had loved and admired had not been fairly portrayed. Now she put him in touch with Stanley, knowing that Robert would back her up. Meanwhile, though, Stanley had taken it upon himself to write to Gerald about Ralph. Stanley on the page was less beguiling than Stanley in person. 'He irritated me intensely by writing me several letters in which he tried to make me say that Leonard was a shady character with very little business sense,' Gerald told Frances later. 'Then, when I was already very irritated by this man, he asked me whether R was not in 1918 a very cultivated and literary man, who fitted into Bloomsbury from the first moment like a glove, so I burst out … What business have these Americans to get so worked up about our petty domestic affairs?'

Gerald wrote at length to Stanley, giving his usual view of Ralph as an aggressive philistine, and kindly sent Frances a copy. Naturally she was furious; but she felt better after several more long sessions with Stanley, which left her sure both of his good opinion of Ralph and of his sympathetic intelligence. From then on, although Frances sometimes found Stanley exhausting, she trusted him. He became, along with Michael Holroyd and Paul Levy, one of her 'Bloomsbury Boys' (although her secret name for him was 'The Wombat'), and she relied more and more on his attentiveness and kindness, his jokes and confidences, his admiration, the almost daily telephone calls, his company at parties or concerts, and most of all the exhilarating sense he gave her that it was possible to have a meeting of minds with someone young enough to be her son. He helped a little to fill the enormous gap in her life caused by Burgo's death.

As she became fonder of Stanley, she became crosser with Catherine Dupré, who was now talking of a play about Carrington starring Jill Bennett, not an actress Frances admired. It was a relief to discover that Noel Carrington agreed with her, and they decided to present a united front against the project, using Frances' control of Carrington's copyrights if necessary. Before the end of the year, another menace appeared on the horizon: word reached Frances that an established playwright, Peter Luke, author of a recent highly successful play about Hadrian VII, proposed a new play about Lytton and his circle. Half against her will, for she was beginning to realise that although she had won the battle over Ken Russell, the war against the fictionalisation of Bloomsbury was probably unwinnable, she tried to find out more.

Before long two things became clear: the play was already written, and Peter Luke was a well-connected adversary. He lived in southern Spain and was a friend of Janetta's half-brother, Mark Culme-Seymour; Janetta, primed by Frances, went to call and found him alarmed and indignant, protesting that he had disguised Ralph as a naval officer and given him a different name. She advised Frances to request a copy of the play. Luke's agent stalled, but admitted that the whole point was 'to highlight Strachey and his contemporaries in an identifiable form', adding unwisely that it would probably be called 'Poor Lytton' or 'Poor Ottoline' or 'Poor Virginia'. Alix Strachey, when Frances gave her the news, said: 'I don't like the sound of Poor Lytton'; but neither she nor Noel Carrington thought much could be done. Frances, dreading the prospect of a travesty of Ralph on a London stage, could not help trying.

For the next two or three years, Frances fought for Ralph on two fronts. In the wake of Carrington's letters (which he managed to review for the *New York Review of Books* without revealing how well he had known her), Gerald was now determined to proceed with a second volume of auto-biography, in which Frances knew he would justify his relationship with Carrington at Ralph's expense; and the Luke play slowly gathered momentum. Sometimes, she felt extremely low; she was finding it harder than ever to sleep, and two minor health scares in her early seventies (an angina attack and a kidney infection) frightened her. Whenever anything reminded Frances of her own mortality, she would observe in her diary how little she really minded the prospect of death. One day, in the London Library, she spotted a volume by someone named Partridge entitled *The Technique of Dyeing*; she opened it eagerly only to find that it concerned textiles. Meanwhile her busy round continued: Cambridge, Skye, Crichel, Snape, Stowell, France with Desmond to visit the haunts of Proust and George Sand, Majorca with Mary Dunn, Madrid and Tramores with the Parladés. Her heart was always lifted by the arrival of Sophie, who was now old enough to be interested in Frances' many photographs of Burgo. Sophie remembers how reassuring she always found her visits to Frances' flat, how they would sing together at the piano and then walk round to Harrods to look at the puppies and kittens in the pet department.

Music remained essential, and so did her need to exercise her mind. She read and made notes on Stuart Hampshire's book on Spinoza, then proceeded to compare his views with Bertrand Russell's and brood about his analysis of sentimentality, an emotion she had always deplored. 'With a supposedly painful emotion, such as regret, remorse or sympathetic pain,' she wrote, 'he thinks that enjoying the idea that you are feeling it constitutes sentimentality. I worked this out for myself long ago – but I think there's also room for sentimentality with emotions that are not painful.' She missed discussing such matters with Ralph; 'No-one does it much now – is it because we're all too old? I must try them on Stanley.' When Lionel Penrose died she mourned him not just as a dear friend but because she had always relished their conversations about scientific theories. Although her last translation, a collection of essays in Spanish including one by Borges, an author she had long respected, was particularly well-received, and she was invited to a reception to meet the great writer, she could not manage to line up another, and began to feel that her translating career was over and that she must perhaps accept the end of her working life. Much though she loved her friends, and entered into their lives and crises, it did not really satisfy her to feel that her own life was now focused mainly on personal relationships. Even so, she found herself after a long gap making contact once again with Julia. It was a relief when the olive branch was accepted and Julia came to dinner, drank only water and although full of complaints about her life showed no sign of hostility.

Both Frances and Ralph worked at friendship and were good at it; it was ironic that, in Julia Strachey and Gerald Brenan, each of them regarded as their greatest friend someone who caused them as much pain as pleasure. By the 1970s, Frances, who in the wake of Ralph's death had found Gerald such a comfort, was increasingly infuriated by him. When, in February 1973, he sent her his latest account of Ralph, she decided that this time she would fight back. She was tired of tolerating his compulsive need to revisit the same old themes, tired of being calm and patient. Encouraged by her supporters – the Hills, Janetta, Noel Carrington and Stanley – she wrote him a long and forceful letter. 'I have felt quite ill and been unable to sleep at nights', she told him, 'as a result of your continued misrepresentation of certain aspects of Ralph's character.' She took him through his assertions one by one.

First, she questioned his portrayal of Ralph as an undergraduate only interested in rowing. Ralph's contemporaries at Oxford, she insisted, had admired his intellectual capacities and quoted them to prove it. 'I didn't know Ralph in 1913, nor did you, but all these men did and do not bear out your view. You once wrote to me that "but for Lytton, Ralph would never have read a book" and this is absolutely refuted by Noel. If you can't give a more accurate portrait of him at this time, I wish you would leave it out altogether.' Next, Gerald's speculations about how Ralph might have turned out had he not fallen in with Lytton and Carrington were 'hypothetical and irrelevant ... do you really suppose he would have become a farmer in South America?' As for his claim that except for Carrington Ralph would have remained a conventional, even 'sedate' character and married a conventional girl, she found it absurd. 'Good heavens, Gerald!' She took particular exception to the patronising way Gerald went on to present Ralph's life after the war – 'Office boy to Leonard Woolf, bookbinder in a back room at Ham Spray, useful man about the house' – pointing out that these were words 'loaded with denigration', and reminded Gerald about the years of work on the Greville Diaries, the reviews and the book on Broadmoor. She conceded that Ralph was idle, but not that he was ignorant or intellectually dull.

When it came to Ralph as Carrington's husband and the Great Row of

1921–2, Gerald's version was everything she had feared. Ralph was shown as an over-sexed, self-indulgent bully who denied his wife the freedom he took for granted himself. This Frances could not allow. 'I don't believe this to be accurate or fair. Have you any evidence that R was unfaithful to C before Watendlath and YOU had disrupted the marriage?' Gerald cited Ralph's behaviour with Barbara Bagenal; evidently this was not news to Frances, who maintained that this episode also took place in the aftermath of the Great Row. 'Of course he was strongly sexed, but your portrayal of him as having a different standard for C and himself before the break is a further example of your denigration. He trusted C at this period – look how unsuspicious of her he was with you.' Finally she made it plain that she could no longer stomach Gerald's protestations of affection for the man he was undermining. 'You say "he was by a long way my best and closest friend". I believe this is true, and you were certainly his. He was deeply attached to you, and had you died first I wonder if he would have dealt with your character as you have with his.'

Gerald's response to Frances was melodramatic. He claimed that her letter had upset him so much that he had suffered a stroke which caused him to fall into a ditch. He recovered enough, though, to sit down, a week later, to cover ten pages with self-justification and, according to Frances, more 'whopping lies'; but he did not withdraw anything he had written. Indeed, he added more. He quoted Carrington's early letters to prove Ralph's dullness and anti-pacifist views. He went into detail about 'Little Barbara': 'Early one morning she got into R and C's bed. C went down to get breakfast and R had her. It was all done in a high-spirited way. C did not seem to mind and so it was of no importance. But can you imagine what Ralph would have done had some young man got into Carrington's bed?' (as, of course, Gerald himself had been trying to do). He asserted that Carrington had only taken up with Ralph because 'he was a useful bait for holding Lytton. That setup needed three legs to stand on.' He repeated the stories about how when they were in France together Ralph only read *The Times* while Gerald read *War and Peace*. 'I came to the conclusion that he had never read a book for pleasure in his life.'

Finally, 'I find then that your picture of Ralph sailing into Bloomsbury, cultivated, literary, and with real social gifts a pure day dream picture lacking in any sense of reality ... Ralph, when he felt at ease, had his prodigious high spirits and charm, but he had nothing to give in the way of conversation to people who had not his war background. But then Lytton fell in love with him and came to see that he had considerable undeveloped potential.' Nevertheless, he added in a PS, he now intended to expand his account of

Ralph 'and I think you will approve of it'. He also planned, in an appendix, to say that his views had been questioned, and to give his evidence for them. He asked her not to write again, as the sight of her handwriting upset him.

The trouble was that Gerald and Frances were both partly right. During the war, when they first met, Ralph had indeed been a keen young officer from a conventional background; after the war he had indeed been liberated, intellectually and emotionally, by Lytton and Carrington. But Gerald's portrait was both exaggerated and self-justifying. Half a century later, he still needed to prove that Carrington should really have belonged to him. Frances knew this, which was why she was hardly surprised by Gerald's response to her letter. 'I want to stop thinking about the whole affair,' she wrote. 'I've no desire to give Gerald a stroke, but don't regret giving him a few unhappy hours.' A few days later, she had encouraging news from Janetta, 'that knight errant, that unequalled diplomat', who had been to see him. At first 'frenzied and incoherent', eventually she got him to calm down and agree that he should think again about what he had written. 'She was so pleased she could have wept,' wrote Frances, 'he is going to alter a lot and show it to her for her to let me know. It exceeds my wildest hopes.' And there, for the next year or so, the matter rested.

Meanwhile Frances managed to acquire a copy of Peter Luke's play through Dadie Rylands. Dadie was familiar with the theatrical world; he and Luke shared an agent. She read it over a weekend at Stowell, and she was not impressed. The main characters were Lytton, Carrington and Ralph; another appeared to be a combination of herself and Henrietta Bingham, Carrington's American lover. Although Luke had assured her in a letter that he liked the sound of Ralph, and was sympathetic to pacifism, 'it suits his plot to make him a hearty soldier saying "bally well" and "top hole" and that "shirkers should be put up against a wall and shot"'. The play telescoped events, so that the publication of *Eminent Victorians*, the end of the war and a scene of the Tidmarsh trio in bed together coincided; almost worse was that Lytton was shown as reverting to Christianity on his deathbed. Ralph, she told Michael Holroyd, keen to enlist his help, was made to say, 'So the old sinner has been deceiving us all this time. Well, I suppose it's rather marvellous really.' At this point Frances consulted her solicitor, who advised her that her copyrights gave her considerable bargaining power and that she should request cuts. To Dadie, trying to mediate, but telling Frances he thought the play 'disastrous and vulgar', she wrote that Ralph was 'of course the figure I find most distasteful', adding that to show them all in bed together was gratuitous, implying 'that Ralph was at least partly homosexual, whereas the fact was that though adored by and adoring Lytton he simply was not, many friends as he had among the darlings ... well, perhaps it's hardly worth bothering about, but I do. There's also been a lot of tra-la-la about Gerald's forthcoming autobiography, so with one thing and another I hardly get a wink of sleep at nights.'

Then something happened which put all such matters out of her mind. On 26 April, Henrietta rang Frances to tell her that Amaryllis Garnett, the eldest of the four sisters, had been found dead. Aged barely thirty, an actress, beautiful and talented but with a turbulent emotional life, she had been living on a houseboat in Chelsea, and had slipped, or perhaps thrown herself, into the river. Frances found herself bursting into tears, something she very seldom did. In the days that followed she tried to comfort Henrietta and look after Sophie. Again Frances was impressed by Henrietta's courage; she was at her best in the worst of circumstances. She had accompanied her mother to identify the body. Again, a sudden death brought back the past for them both. 'She talked quite a bit about Burgo's death, how much she had loved him, but how different it made it that he had been swept away by fate. A young suicide is a terrible thing to everyone.' Later the same week came the news that Alix Strachey had died after a short illness from which she seemed to have recovered. 'So the tumbrils roll us one after the other to the guillotine,' wrote Frances, shaken to the core. She had loved and admired Alix for nearly fifty years.

She was tormented, too, about whether or not she should go to the funerals, which to her remained meaningless and irrelevant. 'I never expected anyone to go to Ralph or Burgo's, nor had a ceremony of any sort. Why then should I go to these?' Janetta, who knew how Frances would try to disguise pain by trying to be rational, persuaded her that they should go together to Amaryllis' funeral in Golders Green. 'Through the dreadful rain and soused glistening streets we drove to the great red palace of death.' Afterwards, she still could not see the point. It did not occur to her, apparently, to cancel the supper party already arranged for Stanley, Henrietta and her new French-Canadian boyfriend Michel and two other younger friends. They all came; Henrietta was at her most sparkling before collapsing in a faint. Next day, Frances steeled herself again for Alix's funeral, a humanist cremation in Putney, which she found 'a more cheerful green and flowery setting' with good music. She conceded that perhaps the ritual helped the mourners, and 'if one must have a ceremony, this was the best I have ever been to'. Later, she managed to drive Janetta to the opera, though she smashed a headlight on the way. It had been, she admitted, 'a week of exceptional emotional tension'.

Frances had remarkable powers of recovery. She wrote an appreciation –

the first of many such – of Alix for *The Times*, attended a conventional memorial service for Ralph Jarvis ('balderdash') and relished a 'tutorial' with Georgia about transcendental meditation. When she tried Georgia's relaxation technique, she immediately fell asleep; she did not really fancy the idea of emptying her mind. All too soon, though, it was full of a new tiresome rumour. Stanley, who was not above stirring up trouble, told her that a film about Lytton had been in the works for four years, but that he had been sworn to secrecy. Inevitably, she suspected that Michael Holroyd must be involved. 'Well, of course if he stands to make a fortune he doesn't want me interfering.'

Wondering if she was unique in minding about the deliberate mis-representation of those she had loved, she set off on her summer travels, first to Switzerland with Eardley and Dadie, then on to Magouche in Tuscany. Back in London in July, she sent an account of 'the Brenan–Holroyd distortion of Ralph's character' to a new and rather unlikely Bloomsbury hound, a retired major-general at work on his own book. She also tackled Michael Holroyd about the film rumours. Their exchange of letters provides an unusual insight into the afterlife of a successful biography and the delicate relationship between a biographer and a living source. For all their mutual liking and respect, it was not an easy situation for either of them.

Her solicitors, Frances told him, had discovered that John Osborne, the leading playwright of his generation ever since *Look Back in Anger* in 1956, was writing a screenplay based on Michael's biography. As Stanley seemed to think this would be news to him, she hoped he had given his permission and been promised 'a handsome sum'. She was somewhat confused, though, over the copyright position: 'of course I granted you permission to print anything that was my copyright, but I wouldn't have thought that auto-matically passed it on to anyone else'. Yes, Michael wrote back, he had been to see John Osborne about a year before. He had explained the position; that there were living people to be considered, and that he did not control certain copyrights; since then he had heard nothing:

> As I'm sure you must realise, there have been a considerable number of people over the years who've thought they wanted to write a play round the book. I've stuck to the formula we agreed after the Russell fiasco and which we confirmed that weekend with the Dunns: that is, I would head off any people who I thought were either not serious, talented or whose approach seemed to be very wrong. If there was a real writer who wanted to do something with my book I would explain all the difficulties and

complications but not oppose him personally. If he actually produced something after all this, I would see that it was sent to you, and that you were involved in whichever way you decided was best. In other words I would not indulge my own financial interests at the expense of your emotional interests; but I would not scotch all hope of some financial reward.

He could, he went on, have already sold the rights, and a play or film could have gone ahead; 'but only by the wrong people'. Osborne he considered a 'real writer', and if he were to produce something then indeed a 'handsome sum' could materialise; 'but quite frankly I have my doubts'. He thought it inevitable that the story he had told should appeal to dramatists; 'But at no time have I hawked around my book, or sought out anyone to transfer it into a film or play. The first test must be whether the writer is interested enough to think of it himself.' Finally, 'What I think I'd like to know is if you think my policy fair, and still in accordance with what we discussed years ago.'

This reasonable letter brought a quick and equally reasonable response from Frances. 'I think, and always have,' she wrote, 'that your policy about Bloomsbury output is absolutely and impeccably fair.' She often felt guilty about the Ken Russell affair, lest the suppression – 'though heavens how glad I am it was suppressed – may have cheated you of a handsome royalty'. She accepted now that a film or play was likely to happen, and all she wanted was for it to be as accurate as possible, and 'as little distressing to the few survivors, by vulgarity or making figures of fun of their old friends'. Luke's play failed on both counts, although he had in the end been prepared to make all the changes she asked for 'except removing the scene with L, R and C all tucked up in bed together'. The play had so far failed to find a backer, but she knew it still might. Meanwhile she would get her solicitor to point out to Osborne's agent that she still controlled various copyrights, 'by which means I hope to retain a tiny controlling hold ... I only wish Mrs Osborne wasn't so very unlike Carrington and so charmless'. Frances was right; a film was becoming inevitable. Another playwright, Christopher Hampton, was already showing interest, and was to pursue the idea, with Holroyd's full support.

Back at Tramores that summer, Frances had to face Gerald. She did not trust him to have made the changes he had promised, nor believe him when he told her that she need not worry as his publishers, Cape, had asked him not to repeat anything about Ralph that Holroyd or Bunny Garnett had already covered. She disliked the way he treated her 'like a naughty schoolgirl'. When she returned to London she heard that Margaret Penrose was to remarry; Frances was pleased for her, and admitted to envying anyone who had 'someone to live for, a purpose in life'. She saw much of Stanley, who poured out his personal and professional troubles in a way she sometimes found exhausting; they went to two Wagner operas together, which made him weep with pleasure, and argue passionately with her reservations. Frances really preferred Mozart and Verdi, but she also discovered a particular passion for Janáček's *Katya Kabanova*, which she saw three times.

In October, after a stimulating few days with Robert, again as guests of the Hendersons, now at the embassy in Germany, she was depressed to learn that she might have to leave her flat; there was more talk of Jill Bennett as Carrington, and a young journalist friend of Stanley's told her that the younger generation thought Bloomsbury precious and affected. But Stanley also introduced her to Sybille Bedford, a writer she admired; the two women took to each other, although Frances could never really share Sybille and Stanley's passion for good food and fine wines. A reporter from *The Observer* came to interview her about friendship; she was amazed, when the piece was published, to have a call from Julia saying 'I'm proud to be your friend'. The year ended in a flurry of plans for an ambitious journey to the USA and Mexico with Janetta and Jaime, though Frances wondered if it was really a good idea: 'How can they fail to resent my clogging presence?' She retreated for Christmas to The Slade, Eardley Knollys' peaceful house near Alton, where she was able to read and rest and go for walks and where they managed to ignore the festivities.

In January 1974, Frances flew the Atlantic for the first time. She had not been able to resist the thought of avoiding the lowest time of the year in Janetta's company. She took the flight in her stride, and was soon 'astonished and bowled over by New York, its space, light, and sparkling champagne air'. Both Stanley and Desmond Shawe-Taylor, her music critic friend from Crichel, happened to be in New York; with them she did the rounds of the great museums (Frances liked the Frick best), the opera and the Empire State Building. When they flew on to Mexico, at first Frances found the pace too much; she felt exhausted by travel and altitude, and did not much care for Aztec art or ruins. But once they had hired a car and started driving south, staying at small hotels with flower-filled courtyards, playing Scrabble (Frances liked to win and often did), criticising fat American tourists, identifying and collecting plants for Tramores, and buying jewellery, she revived. They went all the way to the Mayan ruins at Palenque, mysterious and grey among the tangled tropical vegetation, and on to the coast of Yucatán where they bathed in the warm Caribbean. After three weeks,

Frances flew back to New York, saw *Rosenkavalier* at the Met with Desmond, made a dash to Philadelphia and the Barnes Collection and then on to London. Neither her energy nor her curiosity had flagged; she felt the New World was now part of her own, though the American people, while nice enough, did not strike her as a very interesting race. It had all been a great success.

The aftermath of 'one of my most exciting travel adventures' was predictably lowering, though Frances was surprised and pleased when the Conservatives lost the March election. Henrietta had gone to Canada with Michel, taking Sophie; life felt 'repetitious', and the only work on offer was a translation so dull she turned it down. Then, suddenly, both Gerald's book and the Luke play came to the boil. No wonder Ralph was often in her dreams; in Mexico she dreamed he was leaving her, and was so changed that she did not love him any more, and back in London he was with her in bed at Ham Spray as they discussed why they had drifted apart. Subconsciously, perhaps, she felt she was failing him, which was also to fail herself.

At last, all Gerald's evasions, not to mention his broken promises, were about to be found out. The new book was now with Cape, and Frances was visited by his editor, David Machin, and a colleague in search of illustrations. She showed them her albums, which excited them very much, and offered them a drink; she also reminded them that Gerald had promised certain omissions, whereupon she observed that Machin looked 'a bit anxious'. Increasingly suspicious, worried that she was becoming boringly obsessed with the subject, under pressure from Cape and beginning to want Gerald to suffer for his betrayal of Ralph, she issued an ultimatum: no photographs unless she approved the text. Gerald told Machin not to show it to her; but when Noel Carrington pointed out that not only the illustrations but the cover, using one of Carrington's paintings, were at stake, he had no choice. When Frances saw the text, she was 'appalled and shocked'. Gerald had not done what he had promised. She made an appointment to see David Machin.

When Frances arrived at the Cape offices, then at 30 Bedford Square, it was 'an odd excursion into the past'. Arriving early, for the first time since her family moved to Hindhead in 1908 she took a good look at the huge plane trees in the square where she had played and the white mouldings around the door which had always reminded her of her father's fur-collared coat. Machin offered to take her into No. 28, now also full of publishers; so Frances found herself back under her childhood roof, looking at the familiar mahogany doors, fine staircase and Adam mouldings, though there was a conference going on in her mother's drawing room. At the top of the house where she had lived with Nan, her old nursery was a warren of small offices. It was all too long ago to be moving; 'it was mainly with curiosity that I looked at the noble house which that other little me had inhabited so many years ago'.

Machin turned out to be perfectly prepared to accept her alterations, and together they removed descriptions of Ralph's 'rolling blue eyes' and 'look of an Oxford hearty' and 'loud Rabelaisian laugh'. Frances was very angry that Gerald had plainly not done what he had promised her and Janetta he would do, which was to give a fuller and more generous appreciation of Ralph's good qualities, the qualities which had sustained their friendship and correspondence through thick and thin. The estrangement between them lasted for six years.

In the middle of all this, Frances heard that Luke's play was coming on and that the actor chosen to play Lytton, Daniel Massey, wanted to meet her. Dadie Rylands urged her to co-operate; she minded that he seemed to have changed sides. She reread the script, which despite some changes still infuriated her, and showed it to Raymond, who agreed that the portrait of Ralph was 'grotesque'. Her greatest supporters, Robert, Janetta, Julian and Stanley, all rallied round, although after Stanley told her of a dream about her and the play in which her mouth was painted bright red, she could not help wondering if he saw her as a vampire 'draining the blood of would-be biographers and playwrights'. She wondered if Michael Holroyd stood to make money from the play (in fact, he was neither acknowledged nor paid). When the producer came to see her, she left him in no doubt about her distaste and sent him away with a copy of Ralph's statement of his pacifist views to the tribunal of 1942. As for Daniel Massey, he turned out to be a charming friend of Julian Jebb's from Cambridge but also quite incapable of seeing what she meant. When she called the play 'vulgar tripe' he replied: '"But Lytton was gloriously vulgar!" I had to explain that by vulgarity I didn't mean obscenity but bad taste.' After this, Frances reluctantly accepted that the play would go on; her one hope was that it would be a flop.

In the end, it was. *Bloomsbury* ran for just five weeks at the Phoenix Theatre in the summer of 1975. The reviews were mixed; the performances, especially Daniel Massey's Lytton – 'a high-voiced and frisky male aunt' – and Penelope Wilton's 'boyish' Carrington – were praised; the audiences failed to materialise. Even the 'jolly but improbable' scene showing them in bed with a soldier made little stir. Frances made sure she was away, in France with Bunny, when the play opened; Raymond and Janetta went to a preview, and reacted as she would have wished, but several others she felt should have known better, including Angelica Garnett and Margaret Penrose (now

Newman), said it made them laugh and was not all bad. When Frances
went to play Haydn trios with Margaret she tried to explain. 'F: "If someone
wrote a play that was an absolute travesty of Lionel and everyone roared
with laughter, do you think you'd be extremely delighted to hear about it?"
Margaret: "No, of course not." This test of imagination is a sort of litmus
paper by which I observe people's sensitivity.' Julia pleased her by hating
the play almost as much as she did; but otherwise their contacts were more
painful than ever. When they met for lunch, Julia kept dropping her
enormous handbag; Frances spotted a note she had scribbled to herself: 'Go
out and buy two bottles of aspirin and kill myself.'

As if she had not had a difficult enough year, Frances learned during the
summer that she would have to move out of her flat before Christmas. She
tried to fight back without success, but as it turned out, her landlords (the
Grosvenor Estate) were able to offer her very similar rooms in No. 14 two
doors down, in the same building as Eardley Knollys. She worried that he
might not like this, but all was well and with the help of Joan Cochemé,
Georgia and Heywood Hill the exhausting business of moving, decorating
and reinstalling Boris Anrep's cat fireplace was accomplished by Christmas.
In the middle of it all, Julia rang. 'I wonder if you'd have a moment. I've
been feeling suicidal. The doctor doesn't send my pills and my sink's full of
dirty washing up and I've no food in the house.' This time, Frances stood
firm. 'I told her I needed support myself, was in as bad a case as she was.'
On Boxing Day, she flew out to Tramores to recover. More than ever, she
needed what Janetta always gave her: a peaceful, beautiful place where she
felt at home, amusing company, love and understanding.

Not long before, during the height of the agitation over Gerald's book
and Luke's play, Janetta had made a suggestion to Frances that was to
change her life, and lead to a truly remarkable late flowering. It had
occurred to Janetta, who hated seeing Frances so preoccupied and
distressed, that she should write her own account of her life, and Ralph,
rather than battle on against other people's. She urged Frances to try,
and presented her with a notebook for the purpose. Frances remained,
for some time, unconvinced. Her diary-keeping was both a pleasure and
a necessity for her, but she had never thought of publishing it, or of
herself as a real writer. However, she always listened to Janetta. 'I have
promised to try,' she wrote, 'in spite of my conviction that there are too
many bad books, and only very very good ones should be written, and
anything else is pure indulgence.'

It took her two more years to decide what she wanted to do. She started
a memoir, but felt half-hearted about it: 'I found myself getting into the

course and development of my beliefs and ideas and I'm not sure if that's a good thing to indulge in.' In the process, though, she reread her old diaries, the incomplete, episodic ones from the late 1920s and early 1930s and then the ones from the war years, when she began to keep them regularly. She had never shown any of her diaries to anyone, not even to Ralph. Now, prompted not just by Janetta but by the increasing flow of Bloomsbury's private papers towards publication – including Virginia Woolf's diaries, which Olivier Bell was editing – she began to wonder what to do with them all. Was the diary even worth preserving after she was dead? She was already starting to cut and prune it herself, discarding material she thought boring or hurtful or too intimate. One weekend with the Cecils, she discussed the question with Rachel and with Iris Murdoch. 'Some talk of diaries. I put my problems: to destroy more or not.' Both Rachel and Iris said keep them, but edit them yourself. Iris Murdoch (also, as it happened, a constant diary-keeper) was particularly insistent. So she continued to do so.

Sometimes, though, she wondered if wallowing in the past did her much good. It was almost a relief when she was asked to do another translation from Spanish, and she was pleased when it got particularly good reviews upon publication in 1976. She even agreed to join the Committee of the Translators' Association; she had never much cared for committee life, but she realised that it was in its way a tribute to the books she had translated over the past twenty years. Another tribute came when Stanley asked if he could interview her for 'some glossy woman's mag'; he was a bit sheepish, but she was rather pleased. Socially, she was always in demand; as her old friends became more eminent, Frances was often included on grand occasions; she could be relied on to keep her end up. When Lawrence Gowing was made head of the Slade in the spring of 1976 she found herself sitting between Noel Annan and Richard Wollheim at dinner after his inaugural lecture. 'Conversation ranged amusingly between philosophy and pornography. I enjoyed it.'

In the summer of 1976, the question of diaries and of doing justice to Ralph was reactivated when Frances, on a visit to Quentin and Olivier Bell in Sussex, read Virginia Woolf's diary of the years Ralph was at the Hogarth Press. Although Virginia's portrait was hardly flattering, Frances was relieved, finding her 'kinder than I had expected'; later she helped Olivier with several editorial queries, and when consulted on whether a certain entry about Faith Henderson, Nicko's mother, was too waspish to be published (Faith was still alive), Frances' advice was to go ahead. 'On general principles,' she wrote, 'I do think a definitive edition of what is obviously a masterpiece shouldn't leave out anything that can be helped.'

She herself, though, remained undecided about what, if anything, to do with her own diary, and being undecided did not suit her. Nor did being without a task to build her days around and provide some respite from the ups and downs of her life and the troubles of her friends. Stanley was having a bad patch; according to Henrietta, who had become one of his closest friends, he was sometimes suicidal. Henrietta herself was worryingly thin, and struck Frances as unhappy and aimless; at least Sophie was safely away at Dartington, but she often feared for her future.

Then, early in August, her mind cleared. If she forgot about writing her own memoirs, and concentrated on editing her war diaries, the focus would be on Ralph, not on her; and there would be another advantage. 'Sudden thought!' she wrote. 'Why not get my own back on Gerald – subtly not violently?' Her account of life at Ham Spray during the war could be a way of presenting Ralph as he really was, a man of warmth, generosity, humour and above all deep convictions, loved and appreciated by his family and friends. Through her diary, she could present and celebrate both her husband and the most fundamental belief of her life. She decided to produce 'A Pacifist's Diary of the Last War'.

Her first readers were Janetta and Stanley, and both were encouraging. She pressed on, sometimes excited, sometimes full of uncertainty. By September she was thinking of showing some of the material to a publisher; Stanley consulted his friend and now his agent, Gill Coleridge, who suggested Norah Smallwood of Chatto & Windus, who agreed to read it. In the meantime, Frances took Stanley on a short jaunt to Paris, to stay with the Hendersons, now installed in great splendour at the Paris embassy. Henrietta turned up too, and they all had a good time; but soon after they returned to London Frances was faced with a tiresome piece of gossip. Joan Cochemé, 'with an extremely malicious and mischievous expression on her face', informed her of a rumour that Stanley and Frances were lovers. Joan seemed almost to believe it herself. 'What a bore,' was Frances' first response, but she was cross too, on Stanley's behalf. 'My reaction is that I'll go about with whomever I damn well like and who likes going about with me. But casting me in the role of Ninon de Lenclos and her grandson isn't really very kind to poor Stanley.' It was true that she was closer to Stanley than ever; he was helping her more than anyone with the cutting and shaping of her diary, but her own worry remained that she must guard against turning him into a 'pseudo-Burgo'. It was a son she missed and needed, not a lover. As for Stanley, whose relationships with girls never came to very much, he had a magic touch with older, stronger women. As well as Frances there was Sybille Bedford, and by the mid-1970s he was also caught up with Rebecca

West. These relationships were certainly emotionally important on both sides, and flattery, even flirtation, no doubt played a part; but romantic they were not.

By November, the word came that Norah Smallwood was 'interested'; but Frances went back to Tramores for Christmas with nothing settled, and a final translation to do. It was not until March 1977 that Frances and Norah finally met for lunch. Frances arrived prepared for, almost ready to welcome, rejection. 'However it seems she thinks it worth publishing, though I wouldn't call her enthusiastic, and it must be cut. None the less I came away I suppose with the idea that some day, somehow, I might publish a book.'

Nineteen

Travelling and Writing, 1978–1990

The decision to publish her diary of the Second World War was the beginning of an unexpected change in Frances' life which would see her, in her eighties and nineties, increasingly celebrated in her own right. She had never sought exposure or acclaim; when the rediscovery of Bloomsbury in the late 1960s brought her the attention of the literary world, she did not welcome it. She published her first book only after much hesitation, and the last thing she intended or planned was to establish a reputation for herself. Later, she would always emphasise her wish to record and explain her pacifist beliefs. At the time, she told Janetta that her main motive was to present Ralph as he really was.

Before she had time to settle down to the final cutting and shaping, she was faced with another family crisis. In the last week of March 1977 Angelica Garnett rang her to say that Henrietta was in Charing Cross Hospital with terrible injuries, including a broken pelvis, after throwing herself off a hotel roof. Shaking with shock, Frances' first thought was for Sophie; the Easter holidays were about to begin, and she quickly arranged to take her to Janetta in Spain, but before leaving they went together to see Henrietta in hospital. Sophie's reaction struck her grandmother as remarkable for a girl of thirteen: 'amazingly sane, unegoistic and tender'. Frances felt desperately sorry for Henrietta, but also angry on Sophie's behalf, and her own. Carrington haunted her all over again. When they got to Spain, the strain began to tell; Sophie, not surprisingly, had bad moments, and Frances felt helpless and inadequate. 'I seem to irritate Sophie, and she shuts her face and is cold and snubbing, sometimes hurting me deeply in spite of myself.' It helped that Georgia, whom Sophie loved, was also there, and soon all was well again. Sophie told Frances she was the nicest granny in the world. Slowly, Henrietta recovered, although she was left even more fragile than before. While she was in hospital, Stanley was one of her most attentive visitors, bringing her flowers and gossip and making her laugh.

It was the middle of the year before Frances was able to deliver her revised diary to be typed. She had decided to explain in an introduction how she felt Ralph had been misrepresented by Brenan and Holroyd, and to give her own short portrait of him. She conceded that after the war he had lost all ambition, but that along with reading, 'thinking, talking and arguing were the breath of life to him', and described him as 'a dedicated rationalist and almost shockingly truthful' and 'a man of deep and strong emotions'. She included the full text of his statement about his pacifism to the tribunal of 1942, even though she had become aware, discussing it with friends, that not all of them thought such views necessarily something to be proud of, or advertised. The pacifists of the Second World War, unlike those of the First, were widely regarded as unrealistic and mistaken at best. There had been fierce arguments at Crichel, and both Mary Dunn and David Cecil expressed reservations; even Robert warned her that she should expect criticism. But Frances was feeling 'unreasonably elated . . . as if I had laid an egg'. When the typescript came back, she left a copy with Robert, and then waited nervously for his reaction. It was entirely positive; he told her it was an important document and urged her not to alter a word. Although she was greatly relieved, her emotions were not straightforward. Early in July she wrote:

> I've been pondering my diary and my wild ambivalence about it. Here have I been writing it for thirty-six years, and I think in a sense it has seemed like my main occupation. Tragedy has struck, travel has whipped through, but there it has been as the thread on which my experiences and thoughts are strung. If I look as coolly as possible into my heart about it, one side of me must rate it quite high . . . Yet there is another side which is horribly unconfident. These last days since it took shape and was in the hands of Robert, my chosen arbiter, I have been positively quivering with strange agitation, and I still find the extremes of depression and elation I have been through thoroughly disturbing.

She was struck by how often, for her, a promising start had led nowhere: the Flora, translating Casanova, editing Desmond's letters: 'I think in spite of my natural optimism I do feel somehow my projects are doomed.' This one, however, was not. Stanley's friend Gill Coleridge now became Frances' agent; Frances found her very pretty and very enthusiastic. She took the book back to Norah Smallwood, and by early August the deal was done. 'The whole thing seems to me extremely strange,' wrote Frances. 'To turn author at seventy-seven!' Strange, but also exciting. Almost at once, Frances began to think of what might come next. 'I must pull myself together and decide what to do with my final years. I think I'm quite prepared for PW to be a total flop, but I rather think it may please a few and annoy more. If so I shall continue with what I have begun – organising and above all cutting the rest of my diary.'

Around this time Frances reread the whole of Proust in French, and reflected on the nature of memory. She copied some lines into her diary, including his famous remark, 'The only way to regain lost time is through a work of art.' As she wrote, this 'is of course the whole of his masterpiece crushed into a nutshell'. Frances would never have put any diary, least of all her own, in the same category as Proust, but she recognised the impulse to capture and honour the past. At the same time, there was life to be lived and more journeys to make; Janetta and Jaime were proposing an expedition to India, a place Frances had always wanted to see.

As 1978 began, Frances was at Charleston with Angelica and Sophie. The house was in a state of 'rather beautiful decay'; as Duncan Grant was by now living with Paul Roche and his family, its future seemed in doubt. Frances and Angelica were drawn closer by their concern for Henrietta and for their granddaughter, and by Angelica's unfeigned admiration for Frances' book, for which she was to design the cover. Angelica herself was far from happy; she told Frances she had begun to think of writing a memoir of her childhood, and the consequences for her of her hidden parentage. She also told her that she now realised that she had never really wanted to marry Bunny, and could not help blaming Vanessa for not telling her the truth. 'We agreed that the mother-daughter relation was well-nigh impossible,' wrote Frances. Her own book was due out in June.

Meanwhile plans for India were going ahead. Before she left, the film rumours resurfaced; Michael Holroyd brought Christopher Hampton to meet Frances and discuss the emerging script. She suspected that the purpose of the visit was to ensure that she would not cause trouble, and felt a wave of hostility towards them both. 'I thought: you're not as charming as you think you are,' she wrote afterwards. When she enquired whether she herself was to feature in the film, the answer was 'Yes, marginally'. She was less concerned about this than about the 'muck-up' she felt sure they would make of Carrington and Ralph; but while she may have appeared compliant and stoical, her diary tells another story. 'I just kept my end up I think with these two fellows, but after they had left I felt as though two crows had been pecking at my carcase ... I wish they would wait till we're dead, even though our longevity may be a nuisance to them.' She talked all this over with the sympathetic Stanley, who understood her reservations; he too was suspicious (and probably a bit jealous) of Holroyd, whose understated English charm was so effective in circles to which Stanley aspired, and whose literary credentials were so unimpeachable. At this moment, feeling as vulnerable as a snail about to be poked from its shell, Frances particularly needed and appreciated Stanley's support.

Then three weeks in India blotted out everything else. Frances found the country more beautiful than she had expected, but also more melancholy. She liked the Indians they encountered, but travelling with a tour meant too much time was spent as a group. She loved the brilliant flowering shrubs and trees, but was not especially moved by Indian temples and sculpture, and positively disliked the famous erotic friezes of Khajuraho; she noted without comment the following exchange with one of the youths who hang around such sites:

Youth: 'Where is your man? Are you a virgin?'
Frances: 'He is dead.'
Youth: 'Where is your son?'
Frances: 'He is dead too.'

She got back in the third week of February to find that kind Stanley had turned the heating on in her flat; a few days later, 'the proofs of my embarrassing book have come'. For the next few days she worked hard on correction and the index; exhausted when the job was done, she asked herself on 2 March: 'Why do I nearly drive myself crazy writing so obsessionally?' This question was to recur, to herself and others, during the years ahead.

For all her nervousness, well before *A Pacifist's War* appeared Frances had turned her attention to what she might write next, and to considering what to do with the next portion of her diaries. She had begun to think seriously of what should happen to her papers when she died; she knew she would either have to prune the diary or destroy it. Paul Levy suggested that she consider leaving her archive to King's College, Cambridge; this possibility had not apparently occurred to Frances before, and at first she thought it odd that he reckoned they would be interested. But the idea grew on her, and she began to cut and edit. She raised her worries over the Holroyd–Hampton film with Paul, who defended Michael and his good intentions; but Frances was not altogether convinced. The trouble was that Paul, like Michael, was professionally interested in Bloomsbury, so that his friendship with her was likewise mixed with self-interest. 'I can't help thinking of him and Michael as vultures,' she once wrote. Her feelings for Stanley were greatly simplified by the fact that once his thesis on the Hogarth Press was done, he moved away from Bloomsbury as a subject; indeed, he became positively hostile to the cult, and was inclined to sound off to Frances on the matter. Sometimes he went too far, but in some ways she agreed with him; and at least she knew that he was not cultivating her because of what he could get out of her.

In April, Frances made another visit to Tom and Nadine at Skelwith. Her mounting anxiety over the approach of publication was pushed aside when, just before she left London, she learned that Stanley and Henrietta were seriously considering marriage. Frances was taken aback. Stanley was a dear, he had been wonderfully kind to Henrietta after her suicide attempt, Sophie was fond of him, but was he really the marrying kind? When Henrietta talked about the episode later she was forthright. Stanley and she had great fun together, and were interested in each other's writing, but she had been surprised when he suggested it. Looking back she reckoned he had wanted to anchor himself in English literary circles with a decorative and well-connected English wife, someone to help him with dinner parties. She was touched, and briefly tempted, but it would never have done. 'What he did not want was sex.' He could not replace Burgo for either her or Frances. As Frances saw it, Stanley soon began to panic; the fact that neither she nor Janetta thought such a marriage could possibly work did not help. It was awkward for a time but before long they both realised it was better to remain as friends.

Chatto had decided to put off publishing *A Pacifist's War* until July. 'So my little dandelion fluff of anti-war feeling is suspended ... the cynical feelings I have about PW are of course mixed with a certain underground excitement.' At Skelwith she went for long soothing walks – one took her to the farmhouse at Watendlath where Lytton, Ralph and Carrington stayed during the fateful summer of 1921 – discussed reading habits with Tom and lay in bed rereading Painter's biography of Proust, relishing his analysis of how 'Proust deliberately developed his writing from memories much of which were unconscious, expanding them from some small sense experience like Japanese flowers in water'. Her thoughts turned again to her own motives in diary-keeping.

'I do it', she wrote, 'because though I can never invent or imagine anything, I have a passionate desire to describe what I've felt, thought and experienced, for its own sake – to express, communicate or both? And I can hardly now bear not to pin down the fleeting moments: it's an activity that has become central to my life.' Writing her diary was a way of validating her continuing existence; gradually, publishing it was to become a lifeline.

Then, on 19 July, Frances recorded the arrival of the first finished copy of *A Pacifist's War*: 'a solid, tangible and on the whole pleasing object'. A week later she was at Tramores, for two weeks' blissful respite; on her return, she braced herself for publication, fending off nerves with self-mockery: 'How ludicrous to be such an ancient debutante.' Word came that Raymond Mortimer was to review the book for *The Sunday Times*, and Philip Toynbee for *The Observer*; two such old friends were likely to treat her gently. *The Times* wanted a young journalist, Caroline Moorehead, to write a profile of her; Frances was alarmed at the prospect, but her neighbours and increasingly good friends, the painter Tony Fry and his wife Sabrina, who knew Moorehead well, reassured her. She spent the weekend before the book appeared with the Campbells at their seaside cottage, taking them the book as a present. 'At first Robin picked it up and I thought he wasn't going to like it. By Monday morning he was quite enthusiastic. "You'll have publishers pestering you for more," he said. "Yes, you'll be like Pepys" said Susan. "Oh, I like it much better than Pepys" said Robin.' She had also given a copy to Cynthia and Robert; she already knew she had Robert's approval, but from Cynthia, she learned that Noel Annan had expressed distaste for 'the pacifism'. 'So that's why he hasn't answered the invitation,' wrote Frances crossly. 'I do object to his rudeness, not his anti-pacifism. Silly old bugger.' On the night before the publication party, Julian Jebb rang. 'You have written a masterpiece', he told her. 'No wonder I am all of a shake.'

By the end of July she was feeling a good deal better. 'Well, it's all over now – the party, the birth of the book, the first reviews – and I don't know whether I feel flat (as Robert foretold) or shaken to my foundations, or simply as if I had given birth.' The party, given by Stanley, Rose and Henrietta, was 'magnificent'. The reviews, apart from one by Peter Conrad in the *New Statesman* ('cultivating their genteel ineffectualness, treasuring their neurasthenic intensity, the Partridges failed to understand the war'), were excellent. Toynbee in *The Observer* called the book 'tough-minded in the best sense'. Frances was especially pleased by Victoria Glendinning in the *TLS*, who wrote that the diary forced the reader 'into examining his own attitudes to aggression, defence and self-defence'.

Caroline Moorehead's interview with Frances for *The Times* was the first of many by journalists over the coming years. Eventually she would take such encounters in her stride, and even learn to enjoy them; but this was the first, and Frances was genuinely anxious about it. As it turned out, they got on so well that she worried she might have been indiscreet; on the day she knew the piece was to appear she woke early and 'felt so shaky before I read the damn paper that I took a tranquilliser, something I almost never do'. To her huge relief, the article was entirely friendly, and even the photograph taken to go with it had, she thought, been given 'such an anti-wrinkle treatment as to bear little resemblance to me'. Her only reservation was that Moorehead, possibly influenced by Holroyd's book, had not understood the strength of Ralph's personality. In fact, Frances wrote, 'he was strong, strong, strong ... Several people – some who never knew him – have emphasised that it brought him to life.'

She found, to her slight surprise, that the fan letters and telephone calls she was getting almost every day gave her real pleasure, although she continued to feel 'bewildered by having suddenly been pushed – or stepped of my own free will – onto the stage in the glare of footlights'. At first she observed that none of her relations had reacted to the book, and wondered if this was another example of the Marshall family's 'chronic undemonstrativeness'; but the next day's post brought her enthusiastic letters from her brother Tom, and from her niece Jill. She also received a fan letter from Diana Mosley. The letter has not survived, but two decades later Frances recalled that she realised Diana Mosley wanted to establish that they had been on the same side about the war, which of course they had not. She noted in her diary that she had received some sixty letters about the book, all of them positive except one. Predictably, the most irritating reaction of all from within her circle came from Gerald, who, according to Noel Carrington, had decided not to read the book. Furious, Frances wrote in her diary 'So he still can't swallow my being a pacifist! Or thinks it impossible to be critical of God Churchill!' Overall, though, A Pacifist's War was admired for its honesty and excellent writing, even by readers who could never concede that pacifism during the war against Hitler was reasonable or right.

By the end of the year, the reaction predicted by Robert Kee was upon her. She turned, again, to sorting through her papers, wondering whether anything could or should come of the King's idea; her first meeting with the librarian had not gone well, as he had expressed mild interest in some of her and Ralph's correspondence but very little in the diaries, and only really perked up at the naked photographs. She missed Stanley, who was on a visit to his family. She felt unwell, with alarming heart flutters. One day she looked out her will, which would need revising when she decided about her archive. She felt she was 'preparing for the tomb'.

In fact, she was preparing for a decade of constant literary activity. The success of A Pacifist's War made her reconsider Janetta's suggestion that she should write an account of her early life. Having launched herself on the reading public as a middle-aged married woman with a mind of her own, she felt confident enough to relate how she had arrived at that point and become that woman. To do so, of course, meant going right back to the beginning, well before she had ever kept any kind of diary, to write about her parents, Nan, Bedford Square, Tweenways, her brothers and sisters, Bedales, Cambridge, Bloomsbury and above all meeting and falling in love with Ralph. Judging by the references to 'the project', as she called it, in her diary, she wrote it with remarkable ease and speed. It was as if there had always been a writer in Frances waiting to be unleashed, once she had accepted the fact that her subject could and should be herself, her circle, her life and times. The discipline required was no problem to her, regular work having been a vital ingredient in her days for years; and she soon found that remembering and pinning down her past was a wonderful distraction from the problems, public and private, of the present. The world was in a vile state; she detested Mrs Thatcher's government; her friends and relations were enduring marital upheavals, breakdowns and one by one growing old and fragile, and she was greatly needed as a support and adviser by them all – but her writing gave her a focus, a professional identity, a certain status as a productive and appreciated working person, which suited her well. At an age when most people's energies and achievements begin to fade, Frances was putting out new leaves. As her contemporaries continued to sicken and die, and two of her closest friends, Raymond and Julia, as well as her sister Judy, were both now near the end, Frances was busy recalling and celebrating them in their youth, and hers.

Life looked up again, too, when Stanley returned to London, boosting her confidence in her writing, and when Sophie came to stay, sleeping on the sofa for three happy nights. When Stanley gave a party she even found herself dancing, for the first time in many years; it was 'quite delightful, but without the devilish dervish excitement of early jazz, black bottom and Charleston'. One of the other guests was a young woman called Cynthia Millar, an aspiring musician who was working in Heywood Hill's bookshop; Frances liked her very much, and they were to become close. Frances never lost the capacity to make a new friend.

By the spring, and her birthday in March, Frances was back at Tramores, writing each morning and trying not to mind that she received no cards or presents on the day. Sybille Bedford came to stay, with her friend Lesley Marple, and although Frances found their keen interest in food and drink a bit much, she appreciated Sybille's originality of mind. On the day she returned to London at the end of the month, her oldest sister Judy Rendel, who had been fading for some time, died. Frances noted the event without emotion. She visited the now 'mountainous' Rosamond Lehmann not long afterwards, but their conversation contained 'surprisingly little about the next world'; Rosamond seemed to avoid the topic as her own end approached.

Sometimes, inevitably, 'the project' hit a tricky patch. 'Experimentally I invented new ways of assault,' she wrote at one point, 'like an army besieging a town, and in the end had the satisfaction of getting some slight purchase. It's an odd sensation putting a long spoon into the preserve-pot of my past and stirring it about.' She realised that she could incorporate some of the letters she had exchanged with Ralph, and some pages of her earliest diaries from the 1920s and 1930s, into the book; her engagement books were also very useful.

She went back to Tramores in July, taking Sophie, who had fallen seriously in love with a fellow Dartington pupil from a Swiss-German family, Wenzel Gelpke, and was talking of leaving school, at sixteen, to be with him. Although concerned, for she had hoped Sophie would go to university, Frances was determined not to risk her relationship with her granddaughter; instead of criticising her, she talked to her about her own life, and showed her what she was writing. She was making progress; by mid-August she was embarking on what she refers to as 'my catastrophe chapter', namely the story of the awful winter of Lytton's death and Carrington's suicide. It was not easy to write.

She worked on during the autumn; for the first time she had little urge to keep up her current diary, so absorbed was she in her book. She broke off for a fortnight in October to go to Greece with Desmond, where they managed three-hour walks, much swimming and Frances discovered that she was not too old to dive off the rocks: 'I am pleased to find that I still love cleaving the water.'

On her return, she was met at the airport by Rose Jackson, Janetta's youngest daughter, of whom Frances was especially fond. Rose had come to tell her that Julia Strachey, the strongest link of all with the childhood her book aimed to evoke, was dead. Frances had been expecting it, and indeed had felt for some time that Julia's life was so wretched as to be not worth living; yet still the news came as a profound shock. Why, she asked herself, had she been moved to tears? Perhaps because 'early friends become a part of one, like the yolk of an egg inside one's shell, so that I am not just me but made up of bits of Ralph, Julia, Burgo, Janetta'. She had tried so hard to help Julia in her misery, to remain her friend and put up with her painful, irrational hostility; she never stopped wondering why she had failed.

As the New Year began, Frances observed that she was 'entering the year in which I shall strike 80' and buried herself in finishing her book. It was all she wanted to do: 'suddenly I became obsessed'. On 12 January, the last words were written. She noted the fact, and then turned back to record the death, two days before, of Raymond Mortimer, who had been with her in 1923 when she met Lytton and Carrington for the first time and was 'almost the last great friend who stood between me and the end'. For him, too, it had been time; Frances had found his slow withdrawal from life painful to witness. Slow death appalled her. 'There has always seemed to me something horrible and unreal, something impossible to grasp about the time when someone is dying but not yet dead.' At least, with Ralph and Burgo, she had been spared that.

But now, having left the typescript of the new book with Gill Coleridge, she was off on her travels again. She was joining Janetta and Jaime on another package tour, this time to Egypt; and Stanley was coming too. They visited the pyramids, and the museums, and flew to Luxor to take a cruise on the Nile; it was a mixed success, as Frances found Egyptian art and architecture more interesting than beautiful and they all disliked being herded around by guides. Her diary gives a detailed and wryly comic account of Stanley as a travelling companion; he was, she decided, much the most critical and snobbish of them all, finding the other tour members beneath his notice and the quality and presentation of the food repulsive. She took him to task for being rude to waiters, and they also disagreed fiercely about the aesthetic value of what they had seen. Stanley was keeping a diary too; he did find Egyptian art beautiful, but knew he would not convince Frances. On their last night they decided not to go to a belly-dancing performance with the group, but dined in their hotel and continued the argument. 'What a way to finish a tour of Egypt,' wrote Stanley in his own diary; 'we can't even decide how to classify what we have seen.' As for Frances, she got stuck in the shower and, 'for the first time in my life, shouted Help!'

Early in February, Frances heard from Gill Coleridge, who to her huge pleasure and relief showed 'genuine enthusiasm' for the book. Now, perhaps, it might be time to stop working so hard, to take life a bit more easily; she was after all about to be eighty, and death could not be far away. She felt almost resigned to the prospect: 'I think my chief desire is to bring this book of mine to birth and then come what and when it may.' This mood did not last long; as her birthday approached she found herself thinking about Julia Strachey's papers, which she had already promised Lawrence Gowing she would help to sort out. Her eightieth was celebrated on 15 March with a party at Mary Dunn's; Frances bought herself a new dress – cream silk with an Indian pattern – and went to the hairdresser, and mocked herself for getting into 'an octogenarian flutter'. She sat between Robert and Jonny Gathorne-Hardy, and enjoyed herself greatly.

Gill sent the new book – provisionally, if not very excitingly, entitled 'Now and Then' – to Norah Smallwood, but although word came that she was 'very keen' no specific offer followed. Frances became anxious, and Gill decided to try Livia Gollancz, who had expressed admiration for *A Pacifist's War* and an interest in Frances' work. By the end of April, the deal was done; the advance was £1,500 and Frances was delighted. The news came through while she was at Skelwith with Tom and Nadine; on leaving, she remarked that her brother gave her a parting kiss for the first time in her life. She delivered the final version of the book – now called, unmemorably, *Memories* – at the beginning of June, before going off to the Campbells' for the weekend and proceeding to attend three dinner parties, featuring the Spenders, Sybille Bedford and Patrick and Joan Leigh Fermor, great friends of Janetta's. For once, she admitted she might have overdone it, but was not too tired to deal briskly with a young relative, one of her niece Jill's sons, who rang her up with a peculiar request. 'He has turned photographer, and wants to produce a book of elderly people in the nude! (Me?) Well, I can answer that at once, I said. "NO".'

That summer, her task during her three weeks at Tramores was to read through Julia's writings, and to work on a talk she had been asked to give on Charleston. She also went with Janetta to see Gerald, hoping to mend matters between them before it was too late, but the visit was sad; he was so old, and so odd. Her work on Julia's papers, on the other hand, was beginning to fascinate her. She realised all over again what a strange mixture of qualities her friend had possessed; 'her imagination so original and vivid, her writer's technique often so inept'. She began to see what she wanted to do with them; she saw Julia as trapped in a net of her own, partly self-induced, incompetence. 'What I must do is cut away that net while leaving the remarkable observant and speculative human being inside it intact.' She was taken aback all over again by Julia's astonishing self-centredness, and the fact that she could not focus on anyone unless they were emotionally involved with her. 'Having written so much about her in my diaries it is, or should be, a shock to my self-esteem to find myself virtually un-mentioned in hers. As are all her other friends.' She saw that while she had known Julia very well in some ways, she was in others deeply mysterious. 'Familiarity and strangeness mixed.'

In September she finished off the proofs of *Memories*, and once again compiled her own index before making a short journey to Portugal with Eardley Knollys. The book was to appear in January 1981. 'Crossing the grey isthmus into the New Year,' she wrote as she began a new diary, 'I gradually approach my lying-in.' This time, she was less apprehensive. There was to be a party at her flat, and then Robert was organising a dinner; Frances bought herself 'a severe, expensive, quite elegant dress of silver coloured Thai silk' for the occasion and decided to wear it with red shoes and tights. When *The Observer* interviewed her, she took the opportunity to air her political views: 'I should love to strangle Mrs Thatcher.' She disliked people assuming that because she was old she must be right-wing; in fact, her opinions moved steadily leftwards. Frances was naturally good at interviews; journalists found her intelligence, her humour, open-mindedness and perfect manners beguiling. She found their attentions flattering, if sometimes comic. After the party, she noted, a story appeared about 'the absurdly beautiful Mrs Partridge, her elegant ankles in red stockings'. *Memories* was well-reviewed everywhere, as a fascinating piece of the Bloomsbury jigsaw and an elegant, atmospheric piece of writing. Frances was surprised not to feel more excited by such praise, and horrified when she heard herself on the radio: 'I sounded like a lady with blue hair and two black poodles, twinset and pearls, strolling down Knightsbridge.'

Among the letters Frances received about *Memories* from old friends was one from Bunny Garnett, telling her that on a first reading he had reservations which on the second melted away. A few weeks later came the news that he had suffered a stroke and soon afterwards that he was dead; her heart, she wrote, 'fell into a desolate black hole'. Bunny had been intimately connected with her life for sixty years; her sister's husband, her employer, her son's father-in-law, her co-grandparent, her friend. 'Tears keep filling my eyes.' She wrote a tribute to him for *The Sunday Times*; increasingly now she would be sought out by editors of the obituary pages for her unsentimental, affectionate appraisals.

Before long, she was fretting about what to do next. She was not sure if she could make a book about Julia work after all, and was more and more inclined to concentrate on her own diaries: 'the only thing I want to tackle'. Stanley suggested she write about old age; Frances was quite indignant. 'My god, why should I? It isn't interesting – it's bad enough to live it. One might as well write about toothache or Tuesday.' Meanwhile, *Memories* was going into a second edition, and Gill reported interest from America; she clinched a deal with Little, Brown, who retitled the book *Love in Bloomsbury* and announced publication for October. Frances began to realise that she was having a real success, and that the book had brought her new admirers. She went to dinner with the Frys and was amused to be kissed by Lord Snowdon, but was even more pleased to get a fan letter from the philosopher Mary

Warnock saying she had never read such an 'utterly truthful' autobiography. That spring she went to Italy, where Sophie was staying with Wenzel's family in Tuscany and studying history and Italian in Florence. Frances felt reassured about her. 'How I adore my darling beloved Sophie! She has given me perhaps the greatest happiness of my latter years and I would like her some day to know it.'

By the late summer, she was back at work on Julia's papers, having decided to combine unpublished autobiographical fragments with extracts from their correspondence and her own diary. In this way she could reclaim the best aspects of their friendship and celebrate the friend she had loved and admired; the sad last years would be recognised, but not dwelt on. Gerald might have betrayed Ralph, but Frances would pay tribute to Julia. It was both generous and necessary. At the same time, she was preparing to travel to America for the publication of *Love in Bloomsbury* in early October. Janetta accompanied her, and after New York they went on to Washington, where Nicko Henderson had moved for his final ambassadorial post. It all went well; *The New York Times* praised the book, Frances gave interviews and held signing sessions, and the Hendersons gave her a grand party at the embassy.

Frances deserved her success, and enjoyed it, but soon she was back in her quiet flat, to face the effort of constructing her book about Julia and more bad news about people she loved. Rachel Cecil was seriously ill, and by the end of the year it was clear that Tom Marshall was failing fast. She was surprised by how upset she felt when he died, and she and Eleanor, together at his cremation, faced the fact that they were the only two of Mam's children left. When she reached Tramores in New Year 1981 for what had by now become her regular winter visit, it was with a powerful need to escape. During her stay the news reached her that Sophie and Wenzel were to be married that summer in Tuscany. 'I shed tears of happiness and emotion,' she wrote – and even then stood back to comment, 'How few tears I ever shed out of misery or anger. If any.' Sophie was married in a simple ceremony in August and Frances, who travelled out with Stanley, was full of pride and delight in her granddaughter's beauty and evident happiness. Although Sophie was so young, Frances felt she knew her own mind, and realised that her lack of a father and her unsettled upbringing had given her a great need to build a life of her own.

Before the end of the year, *Julia* had been accepted by Gollancz and Frances was again thinking about returning to her diaries. With two books published and a third on the way, she had established herself, in four years, as a writer to be reckoned with; at eighty-two, she was invited to become a

Fellow of the Royal Society of Literature, and soon after to join the old Bloomsbury stronghold of the Cranium Club, along with Barbara Strachey, as its first two female members. Now run by Stephen Keynes, son of her sister Ray's doctor, Geoffrey, the current members included several philosophers she admired – Freddie Ayer, Isaiah Berlin and Stuart Hampshire – as well as Quentin Bell and Michael Holroyd. 'What on earth would Ralph have said?' she wondered, recalling that although a member he had never bothered to attend much. She was increasingly sought after for advice on writing; Stanley was embarking on a biography of John Singer Sargent, and Angelica wanted help with her own memoir. Once again, Frances compiled her own index for *Julia*, which came out in April 1983 to another gratifying chorus of excellent reviews, and was hailed by *The Observer* as adding 'an extraordinarily fascinating chapter to the literature of friendship'.

That summer, back at Tramores, Janetta made a suggestion that touched Frances deeply. She and Jaime had recently decided to take over his family's fine old farmhouse, Al CuzCuz, in the hills above the coast not far from Marbella; Tramores was to be sold. For some time, Janetta had been thinking ahead about how and where Frances should live in her old age; she knew better than anyone that for all her remarkable energy and busy social life, there were bad patches when she felt lonely and fearful of what lay ahead. Now, as she had done after Ralph died, Janetta proposed that Frances should come to live with them. 'I was quite undone,' wrote Frances. 'I had turned over the possibility of going to live near them in Spain. But this! Choking back my emotion, I heard her say: "You know I love you more than anyone." Even tho' I know this isn't true, it moved me to the quick.' She promised to think it over, while making it plain that she could only imagine living somewhere close but separate, not under their roof.

In fact, though discussions were to continue for some time, Frances' diary shows that she knew from the first that it would not do. The more she thought about it, the more she realised that she could not bear to be dependent on anyone, even Janetta, and that southern Spain, for all its beauty, would feel isolated and unreal as a place to live rather than visit. Al CuzCuz, like Tramores, would always be vital to her as an escape, but her solitary London base had become her home. She tried to explain this to Janetta: 'I emphasised the necessity, as one grew older and feebler, of keeping going the activities and human contacts that remain, as well as retaining those things into which one's roots have plunged – my books, my violin, my contacts with people, ability to telephone them, *The Times*, the post, the radio. The less of a life it becomes, the more important to sustain it.' But she was tempted, more than once, and Janetta's loving kindness meant a great deal. 'The principal stupendously heartwarming fact is that they should for one moment think they want me. And my astonishment is great that I should all this time have had the desire to be wanted, and loneliness because I felt I was not.' Janetta and Jaime's offer gave Frances a sense of emotional security, a safety net, which made all the difference.

Before the end of the year Frances had decided to return to her diaries for her next book. She envisaged 'a sort of sequel to *A Pacifist's War*, ending heaven knows where'; for a time, the project was even entitled *A Pacifist's Peace*. Over the next year, she grappled with her material, conscious from the start of two main problems: firstly, 'the two deaths', Ralph's and Burgo's, towards which the trajectory of her postwar life inevitably declined, and then how much to include of the story of Janetta and Robert. The first was solved when she decided to finish the new volume with Ralph's death. The second she could only manage gradually, by careful editing and by consultations with them both. The last thing she wanted was to upset or embarrass them. Early on, Janetta looked at some of the material; her reaction was generous and encouraging. Neither she nor Robert wanted to undermine Frances' confidence, and they kept any reservations to themselves. Even so, when Frances came to deal with the end of their marriage and her hostility towards Derek Jackson and everything he stood for, she found herself in trouble. 'The difficulty of dealing with Derek makes me almost want to throw up my task,' she wrote. She had softened towards Derek over the years, and was devoted to his and Janetta's daughter, Rose. All Janetta's daughters were truly fond of Frances, who had often been a source of security to them during their mother's frequent absences as they grew up. Rose would later say that she always felt safe with Frances.

By this time, Frances had established her editorial approach to her diaries. She regarded them as raw material, and felt perfectly entitled to cut and prune; she sometimes altered a phrase or even a few lines which she felt could be better expressed, but she did not add or change anything significant. She took out whatever she found repetitive, dull or, occasionally, too emotional or too sharp. She did not want to be self-pitying, and she did not want to hurt people's feelings; at the same time, her passion for the truth, even if it was uncomfortable, and her adherence to the Bloomsbury conviction that love and friendship should not preclude criticism, allowed her considerable scope. She toned down her distaste for Derek Jackson, but it is still there. The most significant personal omissions from the 1945–60 material concern Burgo, and she explains that herself in the text; and she neither published nor left behind any traces of Ralph's occasional amours after 1939.

Although Frances sometimes felt that her preoccupation with editing her old diaries led to her paying less attention to the current volume, there is little sign of this during her eighties. It was as important as ever to her to capture the passing scene and continue the conversation with herself that replaced the conversations she still missed with Ralph – about people, about ideas and about the problems of the modern world. At the end of each year, she would edit and correct her handwritten notebooks – always lined A4 size – and send them off to be typed by Robert's trusted typist before filing them in sequence in Lytton's walnut armoire in her bedroom and destroying the originals. What they show, as the years pass, is how the publication of the old diaries, both the work involved and the attention stimulated by the process, became more and more necessary to her. More than ever as she aged, Frances needed to be occupied and to apply and exercise her mind. For all her full life, the loyal affection of her old friends and the gratifying attention of new ones, there were many bad moments when she felt lonely and afraid. Then she would reach for her diary to express what she could not say to anyone, even Janetta: 'I hate being so old, I hate the swift disappearance of the years behind me, I hate the state of the world.' More and more, she disliked the moments in the year when people who live alone always feel most solitary – long weekends, Christmas and New Year, the summer holidays.

Occasionally she would wake in the morning to an empty diary, 'silence, and the familiarly recurrent feeling "no-one cares about me, or wants to see me"'. In fact, the silence never lasted for long. On one occasion, shortly before her eighty-fourth birthday, the telephone rang before she got out of bed; Sophie made a date for them to go together to *The Barber of Seville*, Janetta asked her to supper, and a new friend met through the sociable Frys, Lucy Snowdon, rang to invite her to a grand birthday dinner for her husband. Later that day, Channel 4 asked to interview her about Bloomsbury, and arranged to come on 15 March, so that she found herself experiencing 'the most extraordinary birthday in my repertoire', with eight admiring young people ('terribly nice creatures') filming her and then presenting her with a large chocolate cake and a bottle of champagne and all singing happy birthday. Her spirits much restored, her next diary entry reads: 'I've been brooding over the nature of emotion, trying to see its place in the organisation of the human psyche.' She wanted to sort out why she had recently been twice moved almost to tears: once by a Brahms violin sonata, and then by a play on the radio about Siegfried Sassoon and Wilfred Owen.

Perhaps because of her Marshall upbringing, or because for so many years she had been the one to keep her head and her temper while Ralph lost his, Frances was suspicious of waves of emotion. But the struggles of her friends against illness, depression and the fear of death moved her more and more. Since 1980, when she wrote him a sympathetic letter after his daughter died of cancer, she had been back in touch with Gerald, by then eighty-six and enduring a prolonged physical and mental decline. His first letter to her after their six years of estrangement told her he wanted to die; they shared their thoughts on obtaining suicide pills and leaving their remains to medical science (both of which Frances managed to do). Now, on her visits to Janetta, Frances would usually call on Gerald, increasingly bedridden and rambling, who was sharing the house at Alhaurin not just with Lynda but with the man she had married in 1978 and their two small children. He seemed to Frances 'a poor old Goya buffoon'. As Gerald became weaker and more confused, it was decided that he should try a period in a nursing home in London, and Frances found herself, along with Janetta, the Pritchetts and Magouche (who had married Patrick Leigh Fermor's wartime friend, Xan Fielding, in 1978; he was at work on an edition of Gerald and Ralph's correspondence, published in 1986), caught up in the tragicomedy of Gerald's brief stay at a nursing home in Pinner.

Loyally she played her part in finding the home and raising money to pay for it. No sooner had he arrived there in April 1983 than wild rumours surfaced in the Spanish and British press that he was there against his will; Frances found herself translating for Spanish journalists and diplomats now determined to rescue him and take him home. Less than two months later he was back in Alhaurin, where the local authorities had undertaken to take care of the great Hispanophile writer to the end of his days. Frances and Janetta went to call a week after his return, and found him lying in a darkened room waited on by two pretty young girls, who at first did not seem inclined to let them in. When they did, Frances was reminded of 'some strange nocturnal bird'; Gerald's eyes, huge behind thick lenses, stared fixedly at them and his mouth drooped in a grimace of despair. 'I felt embarrassed by the tears that filled my eyes,' she wrote. Although he seemed to recognise her, Janetta was not so sure. Everyone, not least Gerald himself, knew it was time for him to die.

Although the Christopher Hampton film had receded for the time being, Bloomsbury matters were never off the agenda for very long. Angelica Garnett's memoir, *Deceived with Kindness*, was published that autumn, and although Frances had encouraged her to write it, when she read the final version she was taken aback. She had always thought that it was wrong to keep Angelica in the dark about her parentage, but she now felt that

Angelica's resentment towards Duncan, Clive and especially Vanessa went too far; and she questioned, too, Angelica's anger towards Bunny, for seducing his former lover's innocent, ignorant daughter. When she was asked to review the book, she refused: 'It is delightfully, vividly, freshly written and that I could praise – but the underlying psychological pattern is disquieting in its persecution mania. Why should she feel herself so hard done by?' In fact, as Frances must have known, Angelica had been near breakdown for some time after Duncan Grant died in 1978, and writing the book was a deliberate attempt to exorcise the past; it was a brave and, for its time, unusually open account of the damage she felt she had suffered and the price she paid for Bloomsbury's attitudes to love and family life. But to Frances, who was not much given to soul-searching, and who remembered Clive, Vanessa and Duncan as friends, it was too easy to blame them for everything that had made Angelica unhappy in her marriage, and she rather sympathised with Henrietta, who was angry with her mother for some time.

Frances' own new book, though, was taking shape. She had decided to include extra material, short portraits of some twenty of the most significant characters – the Anreps, Cyril Connolly, the Woolfs, the Bussys, E.M. Forster, various Stracheys including James and Alix – evocative, affectionate studies that helped to give substance to the diary and make it as much about her circle as about her. That winter, the volume was retitled *Everything to Lose*, and it pleased Frances very much when Gill, Gollancz and Little, Brown all received her first draft with real enthusiasm. 'I can't disguise that I like thinking of myself as a writer,' she wrote. Her American editor, Ray Roberts, was particularly encouraging; on a visit to London he took her out to lunch and made her promise to embark on another volume. Frances said she would, but privately she was not sure. The death of Burgo seemed too hard to deal with, and she already knew that Henrietta would prefer her not to do so. She was reminded of the particular sharpness of grief at a premature death when the news came that Julian Jebb had killed himself. Like all his friends, she had watched helplessly as he struggled with depression and drink. Sitting next to Janetta at the Requiem Mass in Westminster Cathedral, her sadness was less evident than her instinctive distaste for the ceremony; another mutual friend always remembered how she and Janetta waved away the incense with their handkerchiefs.

After spending Christmas with Mary Dunn in Wiltshire, and observing, not for the first time, that her hostess was regularly drinking too much, Frances settled down to complete *Everything to Lose*. Inevitably, dealing with Ralph's death upset her; alone in London over a freezing New Year, she found herself wondering again whether she should not have been more

open with him about the local doctor's 'grinning death sentence'. Robert
Kee came to dinner and told her he did not think Ralph would have wanted
to know; but she could not shake off a feeling of melancholy that persisted
until the book came out later that year. She was beginning to wonder about
giving up the Medical Orchestra, where a new conductor was not to her
liking, and also to find driving her car, especially at night, something of a
strain; but she dreaded slowing down, and when, back at Tramores for the
last time before it was sold, Janetta tried again to persuade her to move to
Spain, at least for part of the year, explaining that they were restoring a
'casita' in the courtyard of the new house with her in mind, she found
herself almost resenting the implication that she would soon be too old to
cope on her own. It pleased her when Janetta gave the new book her blessing,
although she herself still wondered sometimes why she had done it. In the
end, she decided, it was 'to celebrate my love of life, my love of Ralph'.

To mark her eighty-fifth birthday, Janetta and Jaime took her to the
Canary Islands, and on her return she heard the good news that Sophie was
pregnant; Julia Frances Gelpke was born in October, the same month that
Everything to Lose was published. This time, when reviews were slow to
come, she was worried; but without cause, as they soon became a chorus of
approval. She noted with satisfaction that some papers, including *The
Observer*, compared her diary favourably with the latest volume published
by her contemporary and acquaintance James Lees-Milne – a view, it later
transpired, shared by Lees-Milne himself.

Lees-Milne and Frances had several friends in common, notably Eardley
Knollys and Raymond Mortimer, but they were too fundamentally different
to be comfortable together. She found him, and his world, too snobbish and
right-wing; and he often found her 'godlessness and leftishness' irritating, as
well as her tendency to criticise the idle rich while enjoying their generosity.
'Like all Bloomsberries', he observed, 'she relishes the good life which the
upper crust provides. Yet she makes my own diaries seem adolescent and
lowbrow.' Another writer and diary-keeper, Anthony Powell, an occasional
visitor to Ham Spray in the old days and whose wife, Violet, Frances
counted as a real friend, also rated Frances' diaries highly, calling them 'very
enjoyable, and sometimes so funny that one laughs aloud'; to him, she
was 'free from the overwhelming self-satisfaction that Bloomsbury used to
project'.

It was not long before Frances realised that a diary, even if carefully
edited, is likely to cause trouble; Cynthia Kee was upset at the way she
appeared as a poor substitute for Janetta, and Philip Dunn's daughters,
Serena, now Mrs Jacob Rothschild, and Nell (by then celebrated as the

author of *Poor Cow*), found it hard to swallow Frances' critical attitude to their father's wealth, given how often she had accepted his hospitality. But by this time, Frances was already at work on the next volume, and beginning to confront the problem of Henrietta's reluctance to see anything published about her and Burgo, in particular Burgo's death. It was to take her some time to resolve the matter; and in the meantime she agreed to put together a book of photographs selected from her albums. She intended to record and celebrate her family, Ralph and Burgo, Lytton, Carrington and the rich years of life at Ham Spray; again, there was pain as well as pleasure in finding the right pictures of so many who had been important to her and who were now dead, including, that year, Robin Campbell, David Cecil and Heywood Hill. She was beginning to be asked to give talks at literary occasions, and finding that she rather enjoyed doing so; she spoke on Bloomsbury houses at Charleston, recently restored and open to the public, and prepared a paper on diaries, including her own, for a gathering in Croydon. Sometimes, she realised that she was overdoing it; her balance was not perfect, and she had begun to have migraine headaches which affected her vision, but she was determined to pay such ailments as little attention as possible.

All through the nervous work of publishing *Everything to Lose*, Frances relied more than ever on Stanley Olson's affection and encouragement. In turn, she had helped him finish his biography of Sargent, sending him detailed suggestions for simplifying his convoluted prose, and when it was published in the spring of 1986 she was invited to his grand celebration lunch at Claridge's. Although she could not help noting 'a certain vulgarity in plugging your own book so violently', she was glad that Stanley had found the literary and social success he so badly wanted. Not long afterwards, out of the blue, came the shocking news that he had suffered a major stroke which at first left him semi-paralysed and speechless. This 'ghastly tragedy' left Frances feeling she could not bear to record it, but when he began, slowly, to recover movement and limited speech she went to see him regularly in hospital. Like everyone who had come to love him, she found his plight appalling; but for her, perhaps, it was especially hard. She tried to control her emotions by pinning them down. 'Of course Stanley's position will continue to be acutely painful and agonising for some time, and of course too, just as there is something of Burgo in him for me and always has been, my grief for Burgo – so sternly repressed at the time – has flowed into the present. Perhaps the psychoanalysts are right for once: one cannot do this with impunity. As well as poor Stanley's trouble I am faced with a buried corpse.' When eventually Stanley was able to leave hospital, he was mobile but unable to say more than a few words and phrases. Frances did her best to help him keep a life going, taking him to the cinema and having him to lunch at her flat; but she could not pretend that she did not think it the best thing for him when a second stroke killed him three years later. Her life was sadder without him.

Her own health was remarkably good. On her first visit to the Parladés' new house, in September 1987, she was comforted to find she could manage the steep steps to the swimming pool and swim ten lengths easily; this became her aim on every subsequent visit, to the growing alarm of her hosts. She went at least twice a year from then on, always taking some work, reading a great deal, keeping her diary, playing Scrabble; her only concession to age and late Spanish hours was breakfast in bed. Al CuzCuz, a house of great charm and comfort built around a flowery courtyard with a fountain, a wide terrace and a view down to the sea, was a place where she felt welcomed, safe and at home; but for all Janetta's urging she never changed her mind about living there.

Early in 1987 she decided, after twenty-five years, to give up the Medical Orchestra; but she continued to play quartets with a group of friends for another couple of years before recognising that it was time to stop even that, and sending her violin and her music to Sophie. With her photograph book on the way, she began to think again about how to manage another diary. The grim truth was that she was more and more in demand as an obituarist; both Gerald Brenan and Colin Mackenzie died that year and she was asked to write about Gerald for *The Spectator* and Colin for the King's College journal. Neither death made her particularly emotional, as neither was unexpected, and in Gerald's case she felt it was overdue. 'The corpses of old gentlemen surround me,' she observed, and got on with it. There was, of course, no trace in her piece about Gerald of how badly she felt he had behaved. She was truly saddened when Isobel Strachey died, but she managed to write about her too. She was also beginning to be a favourite with literary editors, especially with Mark Amory of *The Spectator*, whom she had known slightly for some time and very much liked; when they first met he was sporting a beard, and this and his voice reminded her of the young Lytton Strachey. He often sent her books by or about her contemporaries and remembers her as a model contributor, always on time and needing minimal editing. Reviewing gave her a welcome feeling of being 'a going concern'. That year she travelled to Turkey with the Hendersons and the Parladés and to Italy with Dadie Rylands (now a mere eighty-five); she went on to see Sophie in Tuscany, pregnant with her second daughter, Jessica. In November, *Friends in Focus* was published. It was well-received, but she always felt vaguely disappointed with it, and by this time was a seasoned enough author to grumble that the publishers could have tried harder to make it a success.

After much discussion and thought, Frances had now come to a decision. She would go ahead with a diary of the early 1960s. It would be an account of how she recovered her own balance and controlled her misery through the help of her friends and her increasing involvement in their lives; she would take the story up to Sophie's birth in 1963, end it on a positive note and call it *Hanging On*. When she showed some material to Gill in June, the response was positive; but then Chatto turned it down as being too depressing. It took Gill some time to find another publisher, and there were times when Frances felt she might have shot her bolt. Encouraged by Dadie Rylands, she had finally decided to leave her papers, including all her diaries, to King's, and she began to think that all that remained for her to do was to prepare them for their eventual destination and forget further publication. Sometimes she minded this, sometimes she thought it for the best.

She was increasingly busy helping other people with their books; in the late 1980s there were two in particular for whom her help was essential. Gretchen Gerzina was a young American academic who was turning a thesis on Carrington as an artist into a full biography, and then there was Jonny Gathorne-Hardy, now at work on the biography of Gerald Brenan. They both interviewed Frances at length; she read draft chapters and made many detailed suggestions. She enjoyed helping other people; as she rightly observed, 'It's not nearly so agitating as trying to do something of one's own.' Sometimes she drew the line; although she always answered letters courteously, and never refused to see any researcher who sounded sensible, she was not inclined to be helpful to the kind of earnest women who wrote to tell her that, as frustrated artists, they had a special bond with Carrington. She was aware that interest in Carrington (she sometimes called it Carringtonitis) was flourishing, and she was not surprised; there was talk of a new edition of her letters, but when it was proposed that Frances herself should edit and introduce Carrington's journal, including her account of Lytton's death, she firmly declined. When Gerzina's book appeared she decided not to review it herself. 'I feel a sort of resentment at being forced back into the most emotional part of my life by someone else.'

By early 1989 she had finished *Hanging On*, but there was still no publishing deal. Frances tried not to mind, and distracted herself by accepting an invitation to speak at Bedales; she talked about pacifism and the desirability of being unconventional, and the audience laughed at her jokes, but she could not help remembering how little she had liked the school when she arrived in 1915. That spring she went to Spain and later to Greece with Janetta and Dadie; they visited Paddy and Joan Leigh Fermor at the beautiful house they had built, at Kardamyli in the Mani, and Frances bathed in the sea every day. 'I am terribly bad at balancing on the uneven round stones on the little beach,' she wrote, 'oh hateful old age! – but still not too old to enjoy the wonder of being in the clear blue sea-water again.' But in July she was sharply reminded of her vulnerability when she climbed onto a chair to open a window, fell and cut her shin to the bone. Somehow she staunched the blood and got herself to the doctor nearby, to be told that her paper-thin skin meant she needed specialist attention and should go at once to the Westminster Hospital casualty department. She was eventually admitted to a private nursing home in Pimlico, where she spent the next two weeks.

Frances' account of her ordeal was another exercise in what she did best: mastering pain by observing and recording it. Instead of collapsing into shock or complaint she wrote it all down: the 'degraded' magazine they brought her when she asked for a book, the characteristics of the nurses – 'a very charming black Virginia came and washed and potted me like a baby' – and the relief when her cleaner brought her clean clothes, a volume of Trollope and her address book. She rang Robert, who spread the news and came as often as he could: 'a wonderful break of light through darkish clouds'. She amused her stream of visitors with stories of the other inmates, several of whom had lost their wits. Frances, trapped in bed, was visited by one, stark naked, exclaiming, 'Can you help me?' Saying 'You must go back to your room' and summoning a nurse, Frances watched her led away. 'As the short terribly exposed figure turned, her dangling breasts disappeared and we had a sight of her bottom crumpled like tissue paper. This little scene strikes the keynote, sums it all up – the degradation, pathos of the Last Lap.'

Back home, Robert Kee encouraged her to write something for publication. The result appeared in *The Daily Telegraph* on 28 October 1989 under the heading 'Casualties of a Sick System; the biographer Frances Partridge tells of a most unpleasant experience in an NHS casualty department'. She explained how after waiting an hour and then learning it could be another four or five before she saw a doctor, she fled in search of a private doctor. She knew how lucky she was: 'It seemed to me entirely unfair that I owed my rescue to the fact that I could at a pinch raise the money needed, and that the possession of money should now be the criterion of the health care one received, rather than the directness of one's need.' She blamed the

Thatcher government for failing to fund the Health Service properly. Writing the article gave her great satisfaction.

Frances often reflected, as she advanced towards her nineties, on her own last lap. It was not that she did not fear it, or notice the loss of energy and strength, the thinning hair, the papery skin, the deepening wrinkles; but she was able to manage her fear by acknowledging it in her diary and then pressing on with all the possibilities her life still offered her. That summer, in the wake of her accident, she was busy with book reviews and obituaries – Noel Carrington, David Cecil, her old school friend Margaret Newman – remarking to her diary that 'this business of making soup from old bones is what I'm reduced to! Thus also do biographers keep going, I suppose.' Of her sister Eleanor's death, she simply remarked: 'So now brothers and sisters have I none.' Family feeling mattered less than ever to Frances as she grew older.

Then, in late July, came some good news. Gill had placed *Hanging On* with Collins, where a rising young editor, Stuart Proffitt, was enthusiastic about adding Frances to his list. 'A sort of triumph,' she wrote, but also noted 'a parcel of dismay'. She had already begun a smaller project, a short account of her passion for botany in general and her favourite plant, the Pasque Flower, in particular, for a small press in Devon, so it suddenly looked as if her ninetieth year would see two new publications. Another wave of attention was coming her way; when she saw Snowdon again during a weekend at Cranborne Manor, where Robert Cecil and his wife Hannah began to invite her regularly in the wake of Rachel and David's deaths, he told her he would like to photograph her for *The Sunday Times*, and suggested she should be dressed by the newly fashionable Japanese designer, Issey Miyake. 'I hate being a monument, wonderful for my age,' she wrote crossly; but she agreed, and in the end rather enjoyed it all, the fittings, the shapes and colours of the clothes, the kind and reverent attentions of the 'tribe of acolytes' who dressed her and gently trimmed her hair, made up her 'poor old face' and sent her off to Snowdon. He posed her 'with tact and amiability' and got her to look less serious by making her say 'Bloomsberrrrry'. Perhaps being ninety would not be so bad after all.

Twenty

So Old and Still Alive, 1990–2000

As her ninetieth year began, Frances had two things on her mind: whether it was time to give up driving, and how to line up more work. She had not used her car for some time, but she was reluctant to get rid of it, and 'it's hateful giving up things . . . a miniature death'. When the moment came to do so, she did not make a fuss, but kept melancholy at bay by having friends to lunch and writing the entry on Carrington for the *Dictionary of National Biography*. That done, she rang Mark Amory to ask for a book to review for *The Spectator* as soon as possible. A radio programme about heroes prompted her to make a quick list of her own: Wilfred Owen, Pablo Casals, Lord Gardiner (because of his part in the abolition of capital punishment), Piero della Francesca and Boris Anrep. She reflected on the bleak fact that Ralph had now been dead for thirty years, and that she still missed him acutely. *Hanging On* would be the first diary to lack his living presence; when the proofs arrived she regarded them with distaste and wondered if the book could really be worth publishing.

Frances disliked being labelled wonderful for her age, but the fact remained that she was increasingly recognised as such, and that during her nineties her stamina did not fail her. Her ninetieth birthday saw a cascade of flowers and cards, and Janetta gave a supper party for about thirty of Frances' nearest and dearest before taking her back to Spain four days later. It had been, Frances recorded, 'a fabulous day, a day whose significance it's impossible to understand . . . Looking back at its steamroller approach I really believe I had equated it with death, for how could anyone be so old and still alive?' Nervous beforehand, she had, in the end, relished the party, for which she decided to wear the heavy cream silk shirt given to her by Issey Miyake; there was a birthday cake shaped like a book. Of those present, many had known Ralph and Ham Spray well; as well as Janetta and Robert there was Lawrence Gowing, Anne Hill, Nicko Henderson and Dicky Chopping. Henrietta was there and Sophie, over from Italy for the occasion. Many of the guests told Frances how beautiful and loveable they found her granddaughter, 'which brought joy to my heart, detached joy not pride, for it was none of my doing'.

It was not just her old friends who appreciated Frances; her intelligence, humour and responsiveness continued to bring her new admirers. In May, she spent weekend with Paul and Penny Levy in Oxfordshire, where she captivated their small daughters by telling them she did not believe in God. Iris and John Bayley came to dinner and Frances was a great success with Judge Stephen Tumim, whom she had not met before. She told him she admired his liberal approach to prison reform, and was delighted to discover that he knew and approved of Ralph's book about Broadmoor. Later that month she flew to Tours to stay with Anne Hill at her house in rural France; they picnicked by the Creuse, and Frances hunted for orchids in the lush fields.

Hanging On was due in the late summer, but before that Frances was disturbed to hear that dry rot meant she might yet again have to move flats. This news provoked a rare flash of self-pity, 'for if one lives alone without even dog or cat and no major occupation and is very very old one is mated to one's nest and things'. It was some comfort when, after discreet interventions on her behalf with the Grosvenor Estate, she learned that they would find her a third and almost identical flat at the same, very reasonable rent in No. 15. By this time the Estate were aware of Frances' age and distinction, and took pains to treat her well.

Frances had never planned to be a writer, but now, as publication of her sixth book and third volume of diaries approached, she found herself lying awake one night trying to analyse what kind of writer she had turned out to be. Certainly writing had become more and more vital to her: 'I don't know how much ability I have to write, how much skill I put into it, only that I want to do it.' She knew she would go on keeping her current diary, by now as much a companion as a record, and intended to continue editing and polishing previous ones; but she was increasingly uncertain about further publication, mainly because she was aware by this time that some of the people she cared most about, notably Janetta and Henrietta, were not happy at the prospect. She decided that after this one she really would call a halt.

The response from critics and readers to the publication of *Hanging On* in August 1990 was remarkable. Letters poured in, many of them from the bereaved, especially widows, who found Frances' account of her struggles with grief and despair in the wake of Ralph's death both moving and inspirational. Her qualities as a comforter for those in distress were well-known to her friends; now she began to be sought out, on paper and in person, by strangers in need of advice. She responded to them all, at first regarding it as a duty, but gradually finding that it pleased her to be able to help other people.

That autumn, after three weeks recovering from the excitements of publication at CuzCuz, Frances was approached for the first but not the last time by a would-be biographer. Her response was revealing. It was out of the question, she told him, for three reasons: 'the possibility I might publish more, my desire for privacy and independence, and the fact that my papers were my sole source of creative occupation for my remaining days'. The truth was that Frances could not now bring herself to relinquish the sense of purpose, the excitement and the attention that publishing her diaries brought her in her old age. The record of her past life was lending her present life a new significance, to herself as well as to her readers; this in itself made her continued diary-keeping worthwhile.

It would be wrong, though, to show her as entirely preoccupied with herself. She followed the news with attention; in the winter of 1990–91 she was thrilled by the downfall of Mrs Thatcher, approved of the working-class origins of John Major, and was much agitated by the approach of the first Gulf War. When it was over, Frances noted that despite claims of victory Saddam Hussein was not dead or captured, and was said to hold lethal chemical weapons. It horrified her that war should still be seen as the solution to anything. 'World disarmament should be the aim of all civilised countries . . . if not, it's all up with us.'

By the middle of 1991, Frances had returned to working on her diary, although she still felt that the next section, containing Burgo's death, was probably destined for King's rather than for publication. Meanwhile she kept up her reviewing and sharpened her philosophical wits by reading a long biography of Wittgenstein; while she was doing so, over Easter at Crichel, she realised that her eyes were giving her trouble and consulted Pat Trevor-Roper, the world-class eye surgeon, who referred her to an oculist. For the moment, all she needed was stronger reading glasses. That summer, she went back to Skye to see Colin Mackenzie's widow; it was so beautiful there that she wondered seriously whether she should have stayed in the country after Ralph died. But although she had waves of such longing, especially in the spring, she knew she needed her London habits. All through her nineties she relished getting on the bus to the London Library, going to concerts and the opera, and above all being able to see friends easily. Increasingly, she regarded large parties as a challenge (which, however, she seldom declined), and preferred smaller gatherings; best of all was a quiet evening of talk with Janetta, who came to London several times a year, or with Cynthia Millar, to whom she felt increasingly close despite the sixty-year age gap between them. She loved talking music with Cynthia.

Inevitably, she continued to lose close friends. Lawrence Gowing died that year, and Frances spoke at a memorial event at the Slade. An even greater blow fell when Eardley Knollys was found dead of a heart attack in his flat above hers. Since living in the same building they had become increasingly companionable, and she would miss him badly. She mourned the loss of 'the last bastion before complete isolation closes me in its prison'. Soon afterwards, though, she was able to fly out to Pisa to visit Sophie and the girls. Sometimes, these days, she would reluctantly consent to use a wheelchair at an airport, but she continued to ignore her physical limitations as much as possible. When the chauffeur-driven car in which she was travelling to Wiltshire one weekend with Mary Dunn was involved in an accident on the M4, she made so little fuss that it was some time before it was discovered that she had cracked her breastbone and was in considerable pain. She recovered well, and by Christmas was safely back at CuzCuz; perhaps she had been more shaken than she would admit, as despite Janetta's company her spirits were low and her mind played with the idea of suicide. 'Brave Virginia going out to the river with stones in her pockets! Craven Frances, trying to fit in to other people's lives and snatching at a moment of pleasure like a child at play.' She shared such thoughts only with her diary, certainly not with Janetta, whose seventieth birthday was celebrated during her stay.

Such truly dark moments were rare for Frances; she would note them in her diary, and move on. It was not long before her mood changed, especially after she heard from Gill that Collins were definitely still interested in further diaries. The reception of *Hanging On* proved that Frances had now established a readership not just for her Bloomsbury reminiscences but for her personal story of how she had come through grief and loss. In June, Frances learned that Collins proposed to take two further diary volumes covering the 1960s, to be published in quick succession, provided that she would fill in 'the missing year': the gap between the point where *Hanging On* ended, with Sophie's birth in 1963, and where the new material she had shown them resumed in 1964. Burgo's death would have to be mentioned, but it was understood that she would do so briefly in an introduction. This Frances felt able to do; the news, she wrote, 'has had the effect of whirling me back on to the stage I thought I had left for good'. She felt nervous, but elated.

Frances was reinvigorated, but by this time some of her friends were starting to worry about her living alone except for a daily help two or three times a week, and to panic if she did not answer the telephone when they rang. There was talk of her wearing an alarm call button, or accepting daily visits from the social services to help with her morning bath or to put her to bed; when she got wind of this, she was not pleased, and when it turned out that there had been great hesitation about telling her that Sophie and Wenzel's marriage was in difficulty in case the news gave her a heart attack, she was furious. She felt quite capable of looking after herself and she found her friends' concern insulting. 'They seem to harp on my age in a way that has only one conclusion – an old folks' home, and I find it intolerable,' she wrote. 'Fuming over my cornflakes I mutter to myself crossly: "You can all fuck off and leave me to die in my own way!"' Frances' independence of spirit grew fiercer as she grew older. There were more such arguments ahead.

The news that Sophie's marriage was indeed over and that she was returning to England with her daughters saddened Frances, but she accepted it calmly; she had known too many marital disasters to be surprised. 'Must marriages made in youth always crash?' she reflected. 'Only the second try in middle age, when sex is less urgent and so is the desire for adventure, can produce the warm trusting companionship enjoyed by an earlier generation – Ralph and me, Anne and Heywood, the Cecils.' She was reassured when Sophie and the girls came to see her, and to learn that they would be financially well looked after and probably settle in the country. Eventually they found a house near Totnes in Devon, and the times Frances stayed with them there became an increasing joy to her. With them, she was reminded of Burgo in the happiest way; and she represented a link with him that was badly needed. Sophie, like her grandmother, was positive by nature. When she became interested in alternative medicine, and took a course in aromatherapy, Frances was sceptical; but she liked the fact that Sophie was independent-minded. Sophie's relations with Henrietta, whose life was never calm for very long, were often tricky, but with her grandmother she knew exactly where she was. That summer, staying with the Hendersons nearby, Frances revisited Ham Spray, and found that far from troubling her the beauty of the house and the view of the downs gave her 'intense pleasure'. The ilex tree was gone, but the beech on the edge of the shrubbery was larger than ever, Burgo's initials still clearly visible on its thick grey trunk.

All her life Frances had feared physical and mental inactivity. Now she loved nothing more than to feel her mind engaged by new thoughts. When she found herself, unplanned, listening to a discussion about quantum physics on Radio 3, she rushed to take notes; one of the speakers, she realised, was Roger Penrose, son of her old friends Lionel and Margaret, whom she remembered as a small boy. 'I wouldn't have missed it for anything,' she wrote afterwards. 'It seemed to light dozens of sparks inside my head.' Not much later, Iris Murdoch's latest book, the distillation of her philosophical ideas, *Metaphysics as a Guide to Morals*, kept Frances intellectually exercised for months. It was her liveliness of mind, unusual enough at any age, that made her continue to be a sought-after guest at London dinner tables and country house weekends.

She helped Dadie Rylands celebrate his ninetieth birthday, along with some of the actors who had long admired him: John Gielgud, Prunella Scales and Judi Dench. She charmed Barry Humphries, noting that 'in real life he is a tall, quite masculine fellow . . . sharp as needles'. She also charmed Glenys Kinnock and Fiona Millar, who came to interview her for a book on remarkable women; she liked them both, while noticing how they wanted her to be 'more feminist than I am or pretended to be'. Over a weekend with Olivier Bell in Sussex, she also met Denis Healey. At first she thought him 'a little standoffish', but then he 'suddenly advanced and seized hold of me, saying "Shall we dance? You're beautiful" . . . and we did dance a step or two'. The Kinnocks asked her to dinner; she was startled by Neil Kinnock's bad language, but mollified when he sang the theme tune from *Chariots of Fire* (also his campaign theme) at the top of his fine Welsh voice. Frances had decided to vote Labour in the next election; for a time she became a member of the Labour Party.

Early in 1993, with publication of *Other People*, her diaries for 1963–6, due in July, Frances had to prepare for another move. 'The old marionette is being shaken up into a macabre dance.' Full of trepidation on both fronts, she was greatly saddened by the death of Mary Dunn in January, and by the ordeal of a winter funeral; as ever, she found the ceremony more 'barbaric' than comforting, especially as it included the hymn she most disliked, 'Onward Christian Soldiers'. Thanks to her friends, Janetta, Georgia and her husband Paul, and the Frys in particular, the move along the street was accomplished by the end of April. The strain told on Frances; she had migraine headaches, accompanied for the first time by a strange effect when she saw hexagons superimposed on her vision. 'I stop dead at moments, and a voice in my head says: All this is mad. You should be going to a Home.' Her spirits were not improved by reading Cynthia Kee's novel, with its cool portrayal not just of her and Ralph but of Robert and Janetta. Luckily, no-one outside her circle was likely to realise the book's close connection to reality.

Everything in Frances' new flat on the first floor of 15 West Halkin Street was arranged as before. Carrington's portrait of Lytton hung over her desk,

Duncan Grant's calm classical head over Boris Anrep's fireplace, his *Juggler and Tightrope Walker* over her work table, the tapestry cat over her bed and the bright Spanish jugs and plates on the shelves. Only one thing was different: she had finally given in and decided to buy a television. Along with answering machines (too impersonal) and CDs (musically artificial), Frances never really approved of television; but that summer she discovered the joy of watching Wimbledon and gradually also took to watching *Newsnight* in bed.

When *Other People* appeared, at first Frances was disappointed with its reception. But she was cheered by a good review in the *TLS* (by the present writer), by a signing at the newly established Bloomsbury Gallery, where the owner, Tony Bradshaw, was a great admirer and promoter of her books, and by a long interview for the *Observer Magazine* with Naim Attallah, the Palestinian-born publisher, described by Frances as 'a large man with a face that suggested a baby elephant and a very direct manner ... the only interviewer I have ever really enjoyed'.

In fact, *Other People* reinforced the success of *Hanging On*, as more readers discovered her to be an exemplary guide to surviving grief and loss. For them, the fact that she had endured the sudden death of her only son within three years of her husband's death, and managed to haul herself out of deep misery to rebuild her life all over again, was inspirational. That winter, she spoke to an audience of 300 at the Cheltenham Festival, and then attained, as she remarked, 'the peak of celebrity' by being approached to record her *Desert Island Discs*. To her slight disapproval she found Sue Lawley more interested in her personal life than her musical tastes, but the programme brought her a new wave of fan letters. Encouraged, she started to edit another volume. She had been relieved to get a generous letter from Henrietta, who admitted that although she had not found reading *Other People* easy, she recognised its quality, adding 'I know that you went out of your way not to hurt me one iota and you haven't.' Then, at the end of the year, she realised that another surge of interest in her Bloomsbury past was approaching. At last, after nearly twenty years, Christopher Hampton's film, now focused on and entitled *Carrington*, was going into production, and Michael Holroyd's thorough revision of his Strachey biography was to appear around the same time. After the happiest Christmas for some years in Devon with Sophie and her great-granddaughters, Frances returned to London to prepare for a visit from the young actress who was to play Carrington, Emma Thompson. Seventy years after the events the film portrayed, with all the main protagonists except for her in their graves,

Frances was about to be confronted with a film version of the most dramatic emotional experiences of her life.

Over the almost thirty years since she had fought Ken Russell and the BBC, and won, Frances had learned that although she could not prevent the fictionalisation of her friends, her husband and herself, she could exert some influence over the results. Then, she had been unknown outside her own circle; now, she was an admired writer and authority on Bloomsbury, whom it would not be wise to ignore. When Emma Thompson arrived in West Halkin Street, they were soon getting on famously; they looked through the old Ham Spray albums and discussed Carrington's complicated nature. After this, it was agreed that Frances should read Christopher Hampton's script and give her views. She took it with her to CuzCuz in February, where she wrote detailed notes on how each of the main characters came across.

Lytton, she felt, was captured pretty well: 'you have avoided the usual snag of making him purely ridiculous ... he was a shade more selfish than you have portrayed him'. Carrington was less of a tomboy than the script portrayed, 'and you don't suggest her immense fun and fanciful imagination'. As for Gerald Brenan, this was 'not a good likeness'. Hampton had made him seem weak, which he was not. Like Carrington, he was 'devious, no respecter of truth, original, charming, wonderful company at times ... extremely egocentric'. Finally, she came to Ralph, 'of course the person I'm most concerned about'. Here, inevitably, she had more serious objections. 'I realise', she wrote, 'you have tried to mark his change from the brash young major to an interesting man, who people depended on. This has made you ignore his quality at his first appearance.' Once again she explained that although sporting and brave, he was also clever, and that his experiences in the First World War had made him a pacifist. Patiently, she corrected the language put into his mouth: 'He was not an "oaf" nor would he ever call Gerald "old chap" ... and perhaps you can understand why I dislike the remarks about "shooting COs" given to him in the script ... I should be very glad if they could be at least modified.' (They were not.) She pointed out that Ralph had always been haunted by the horror of having to command a firing squad to execute a deserter. Gill Coleridge had suggested to Frances that she should be made a paid consultant on the film, but after reading the script she decided she would rather not. She could not endorse this version of Ralph.

Anyway, while the film was in production during 1994 Frances was busy with the finishing touches to her next volume. She was pleased to find that she could still put in four hours' work a day, and manage her habitual round of visits to friends in the country. That summer, Paul Levy took her to Garsington, which had become the setting for a summer opera season; her only previous visit, she noted, had been in 1928. As her London circle went off for their summers abroad, so her new admirers, especially the Americans, arrived eager for her company. She let them all come, observing wryly, 'Friends may leave London and England, but fans go on marching up my stairs.' She was particularly amused by Oleta, an air hostess, who knew almost more about Bloomsbury than she did. She always answered her readers' letters, taking particular trouble over those from people in distress after losing a husband or a son, and if someone wrote asking for a meeting, she usually agreed. Some of her old friends wondered if this was wise, and were surprised that she did not find her new admirers tiresome; but the fact was that such visits boosted her morale and mitigated her loneliness, and whereas her old friends' concern made her feel weaker, her new friends' – for several of them became so – admiration made her feel useful and independent.

Janetta, who could always sense what Frances needed, now took her back to their French house for two weeks, where Frances settled down to review Michael Holroyd's new edition of *Lytton Strachey*. It was a demanding task. Published in *The Spectator* in August, Frances' essay reassessed the book in the light of Holroyd's revisions, the mass of new material behind them and her own, as well as his, altered perspective. Generous about the book in both incarnations, she declared her own interest: 'I can read it now with more detachment than I could then, and my preference is all for unbowdlerised biography and for the truth if it is not distorted, bearing in mind that distortion can come from omission as well as inclusion.'

In September, *Good Company*, her fifth volume of diaries, covering the years 1967–70, appeared. This time, although her publishers and readers were happy, Frances soon realised that within her circle she had caused consternation. Magouche was upset by Frances' references to her romance with Bunny, and to the way Frances described some of her fellow guests in Italy; and after a series of tricky telephone conversations, Henrietta wrote to her from France, where she was living on a hilltop in Provence with her new partner, Mark, whom she had met when he was working as a gardener at Charleston. 'Darling old F,' she began, 'Although the volumes fascinate me I've never understood your need to publish them especially when, attaching such importance to friendship as you do, you then worry about whether you may have wounded Magouche. It doesn't somehow make sense.' It could indeed be hard on those close to Frances that her diary, as it went on, tended to be as much about their lives and doings as hers.

Inevitably, they felt exposed. When she realised this, she was appalled. 'I must stop!' she wrote, and this time, she told Gill Coleridge, she really meant it. She would occupy herself in other ways. 'Editing unpublished diaries, doing crosswords, reading books that make one think, brushing up my French and Spanish – that could fill my last lap, I suppose.'

Early in 1995 Frances found herself at her desk in London after another family Christmas with Sophie, writing an obituary of Joan Cochemé, and reviewing a 500-page life of Goethe. Then, on 9 February, she went, feeling 'quite scared' but supported by Robert Kee, to see a preview of Christopher Hampton's film, *Carrington*. It was less of an ordeal than she had feared; she was relieved. 'I will quickly say', she wrote the next day, 'that the only thing that created a feeling of travesty and disgust was that HAM SPRAY in large letters denoted a hideous dark crouching house designed by that brute Lutyens, dark and cottagey inside but decorated by a few Spanish plates.' She was amazed at how like Lytton Jonathan Pryce was, not just in looks but in manner; Emma Thompson she found had transformed her appearance, but was less truly Carringtonesque. Overall, though, 'the stars and the production dealt with their relationship in a sensitive and sometimes very moving manner', although it did not seem to her or Robert that the plot was strong enough to grip an audience. Hampton had kept the focus closely on his version of Carrington's love life (omitting, however, any hint of her lesbian tendencies); Frances summed up: 'The four lovers – Gertler, Ralph, Gerald and Beakus – take their turn at rolling about with an enthusiastic Carrington, Lytton dies and she shoots herself with a loud bang.' She herself was played by Alex Kingston, 'a sallow governessy girl', and she found her one big scene, with Lytton at the Oriental Club, all wrong, as the film had him threatening to sell Ham Spray, 'which of course he didn't do, nor could, as Ralph and Lytton shared the price equally. In fact he said, "If you and Ralph do what you suggest I can't promise to stay with Carrington" – much more deadly for her.' Afterwards, she decided, and Robert agreed, that the film was unlikely to be a great success when it was released later that year, adding 'but I no longer fear it'.

By early March, with her ninety-fifth birthday coming up, Frances was back at CuzCuz with the Parladés. Despite having decided to adopt 'a more leisurely tempo', she was incapable of doing so, and occupied herself with writing an article on her musical tastes, reading a biography of Diderot and preparing a talk she had been asked to give at Charleston in the summer: she had decided to return to the subject of pacifism, largely because of the fiftieth anniversary that year of the end of the Second World War. She revelled in the glorious weather – 'a pearl of a day, a nectarine of a day' – and in still being able to beat Janetta at Scrabble. When she reached 'the day I never thought to see, my 95th birthday', she had some good news to celebrate: her editor, Rebecca Wilson, had moved to Weidenfeld and Gill had just negotiated with her for paperback publication of the recent diaries. There were congratulatory phone calls and flowers to mark both the birthday and the deal, and Frances felt rejuvenated. 'How can I not glow with happiness, foolish though I may be?'

Few people in their mid-nineties can ever have been as busy and sought-after as Frances, still comparatively unaffected by her great age. She was reminded, at the Charleston Festival in May, that others were less lucky; John Bayley and Iris Murdoch were also on the programme, and she was shocked by their dishevelled appearance and especially by Iris's lost, miserable expression and inability to collect her thoughts. She wondered if Iris was drunk; but as she later realised, she was showing the symptoms of the Alzheimer's disease which was destroying her brilliant mind and placing her husband under terrible strain. Frances was pleased with her large attentive audience at Charleston (which included her American air hostess fan, Oleta, and three of her colleagues) and felt satisfied that her anti-war arguments had hit a different note from all the VE Day celebrations, which she found excessive. It was always a pleasure for her to stay with the Bells and their family. That summer, she also spoke at the Dartington Literary Festival, spent sociable weekends at Crichel and Cranborne, and attended the first night of a new production of Britten's *A Midsummer Night's Dream* in London with the Frys, the Snowdons and Tom Stoppard (an admirer of her diaries). There was more opera at Glyndebourne and again at Garsington, and another first night with Paul Levy at the Almeida (the young composer Thomas Adès' opera *Powder Her Face*), a Cranium Club dinner where she discussed determinism with Isaiah Berlin and a few days in Denmark with Magouche. At the end of August Janetta drove her back to France through the Eurotunnel; she swam, picnicked and went botanising, all of which took her mind off the wave of publicity prompted by the imminent release of *Carrington*.

Although she had made up her mind that the film was not really too bad, Frances found all the attention that now came her way disconcerting, especially when the press invented a story of difficulties between her and Emma Thompson. To an interviewer for *The Daily Telegraph*, she acknowledged her reservations about how Ralph (played as a handsome, hearty soldier, given to walking through the woods with Lytton's hand on his naked shoulder) was portrayed, and the inaccuracy of the scene between herself and Lytton, unwisely adding that Alex Kingston, in a drab grey suit and hat, gave the impression of a housemaid applying for a job. Staunchly attending the gala opening of the film and the major exhibition of Carrington's work at the Barbican on 20 September, surrounded by people eager to know how she felt about it all, she felt as if she was struggling through thick fog, and was surprised 'that only a very few of my friends realise what a parlous state I am in or hear my suffocated cries of "Help"'. She went back quietly to the Barbican with Janetta a few days later to look at the exhibition of paintings and Ham Spray memorabilia, including the film made there by Beakus Penrose in 1929. There she was, crawling across the lawn with boots on her hands; there was Rachel MacCarthy in the bath and Saxon leering round the door. These reminders of reality were oddly reassuring: 'the effect has been entirely beneficial and helped to put the whole experience in its place'. What she did not much care for was the feeling that she had turned into public property, and that strangers felt they could ask her personal questions. 'This wretched film has made me a celebrity,' she wrote in October. 'Maybe I was half-way there but (humiliatingly) it has pressed the button home.'

There was one unexpected and oddly welcome consequence of all the publicity. A swingeing review of the Barbican show appeared in the *Evening Standard*, attacking Carrington as a 'trifling' painter and as a woman who enjoyed teasing men with her 'obstinate chastity' and was given to 'cruelly abusing the affections of her husband, Ralph Partridge'. Reading this, Frances felt as if a key had been turned in a lock. At last, someone had seen Carrington clearly. 'I for so long had repressed the fact that I too thought she treated Ralph cruelly . . . all through Ralph's life and mine together he often showed his own awareness of it, yet it was something I felt I must keep under hatches. It is two days since I read the *Standard* and I have only just realised it myself but this little piece of psycho-analysis has produced a curious calm. Why? Because I have faced a piece of the truth.'

Every now and then, in her later nineties, Frances used her diary to face another truth: that her death could not now be far away. 'That is something I think about more and more, and more. What a bore,' she wrote. 'But how, when driven relentlessly towards this tunnel, can one help it? However there is a change. It has become more "how" than "when", and sometimes my thoughts verge on panic about not dying soon enough . . . I fear living too long in a decrepit or deranged state, and almost welcome signs of increasing physical feebleness.' Under pressure from her friends, she had finally agreed to have an alarm call button, but refused to wear it, keeping it in a bowl by her bed. She was amused when a friend telephoned in a panic to check a rumour that she had died. 'Of course I realise that everyone must expect me to be the next death. I do myself.' Meanwhile there was work to be done, even if only to write an obituary of the last of the original Crichel Boys, Desmond Shawe-Taylor, and an article about her love of plants for *Gardens Illustrated*, and sometimes tinker with her 1970s diaries, 'the first to be consigned to oblivion till I die'. And a fine day, even in winter, could still make her heart lift. Back in London after Christmas in Spain, she wrote, 'Yes, it's true – even at my age one can still say to oneself "I'm happy!" At what? Because the birds all over London have been singing the last few days, with spring-like sweetness – particularly in a certain corner of my square garden ... the florist's gardener came and filled my balcony pots with bulbs. I had a new telephone delivered and spent the rest of the morning sticking in some of last year's photos. All little humdrum things but there has been blue in the sky, and yes, I've been happy and busy.'

More than ever, Frances needed her routine. She would wake early, around 6.30 or seven, and read in bed or write her diary before getting up and having her daily bath at eight. She would then make her own breakfast, listening to Radio 4, and probably be at her desk by ten, when Vera, her Scottish housekeeper, would arrive. After much persuasion from Janetta and Magouche, Frances eventually agreed that Vera should come every weekday, and as well as cleaning should run errands – to the bank, the cleaners, the shops – and prepare a cooked lunch. On two mornings a week, Georgia Tennant would arrive to help Frances with her paperwork. Frances liked to walk every day, to Cadogan Gardens if it was fine or round the block for exercise even if it was not; she would tend the plants on her balcony, and sometimes sit out there in the sun. She would rest in the afternoons and listen to music; if she was going out alone she would order a minicab and hope to find a taxi driver later to bring her home and help her open the heavy front door. Otherwise Frances would get her own simple supper – soup, cheese or pâté and fruit, always preceded by a whisky or two. With regret – she deplored what she called 'the unhospitability of old age' – she had decided she must give up cooking for friends, preferring them to come to tea or for a drink; although she noted with pride that on the Bank Holiday weekend in the summer of 1996 she cooked a proper dinner for her young friend Richard Shone, who had become a specialist in Bloomsbury painting since meeting Duncan Grant in his old age. She gave him melon, a casserole of poussins, and strawberries and cream and he stayed till 12.15.

All her close friends knew that it was a mistake to show too clearly how much they worried about her; but by 1996, it was hard not to. In April she was burgled and lost a diamond brooch of her mother's and the heavy silver necklace Ralph had given her and which she usually wore. Her eyes bothered her more and more and she began to feel unsteady on her feet; she consulted a neurologist, both about her occasional giddiness and the strange patterns and colours she sometimes found impeded her vision; he found nothing wrong, and told her she was 'fantastic for her age', but even so when she had a short blackout (luckily when she was at home) it seemed likely that she had had a small stroke. 'Slow recovery after a peep into the abyss,' she wrote, but there was no sign of permanent damage. As for her sight, she was told by a series of eye specialists that little could be done; she was simply suffering from 'the defects of increasing age'. Frances observed and recorded the gradual deterioration of sight she dreaded, and the peculiar semi-hallucinations she experienced more and more frequently: the patterns like chicken wire covering what she saw, people floating in the air, the blue roses alongside the red ones in the Crichel garden; she was relieved to be assured that these were not signs of mental disturbance but were simply physical symptoms of macular degeneration.

She never gave up trying to understand and overcome her condition. Stronger glasses, magnifying lenses, brilliant halogen lamps were all brought into play. She was determined to read and to write for as long as she possibly could, and to prove it embarked on a massive new two-volume biography of Bertrand Russell. She was equally determined to carry on walking and swimming, and hated being hovered over by anyone, even Janetta, while she did so. In Spain that summer, she fell on the way to the pool and bruised and cut herself badly; she felt guilty, and ashamed of being a nuisance. 'Back to childhood must be swallowed,' she wrote. 'I have caused quite enough trouble and worry by not facing facts.'

Frances was shaken by these depressing reminders of her frailty, which lowered her confidence to the point where she found herself dreading a book-signing event organised that autumn by the Bloomsbury Gallery, especially after she learned from Tony Bradshaw that several of her fans were flying over from America to be there. At first, Frances felt more hounded than flattered, especially after two or three of them visited her at home and interrogated her for hours: 'Such is the relentlessness of the American male or female in search of their prey.' In fact, as her friends pointed out, she did not have to see them; and their admiration and interest raised her morale. One or two were to become regular visitors and even friends, like Susan Fox, a young woman who had developed a passionate interest in Bloomsbury after reading Michael Holroyd's book and who now came to London once or twice a year to help Tony at the Gallery. She had already started corresponding with Frances, who was amused to find her rather like Barbara Bagenal in appearance, small, dark and pretty, with a gentle voice and sympathetic manner. In the end, the book-signing session was a great success, and Frances was pleased to find that she could sign books and talk to fans for two hours without flagging or seeing any chicken wire, although by the end she was exhausted and needed a reviving whisky.

Towards the end of a difficult year, Frances had begun to feel better. She had a good weekend with the 'darling Frys ... No horrid blunders', who had become steadily more important to her since Eardley Knollys died, as their London flat was almost opposite hers; as well as liking their company, it was reassuring that they were nearby to help when she had trouble with her keys or the front door. Unobtrusively, they kept an eye on her. There was a setback in December when she got flu, but Janetta came to the rescue; more than once, if Frances was ill, she or Robert would stay the night, sleeping uncomfortably on the sofa. Christmas that year was spent at the Parladés' house in France. Despite her eye troubles, she could still play ferocious Scrabble, and she still found it hard to accept being looked after. Reluctantly, she agreed to have breakfast in bed: 'I hope not because I am a threat while up and about.'

Some reviewing work came her way early in 1997, as well as her first meeting with another admirer who became a correspondent and friend. This was Ann Dix, a philosophy lecturer from Sydney, who first wrote to Frances after reading her diaries, and with whom she now conducted an enjoyable correspondence. With Ann Dix, as with Sue Fox, Frances drew strength from the realisation that as they had never known her before her nineties, they did not see her as in decline; what they saw was her intelligence, precision and excellent memory. She was also a fount of human sympathy and wisdom; when Ann Dix's husband became seriously ill, she found Frances' understanding a real help. Such new friendships were bracing and encouraging; Frances enjoyed putting her best foot forward, and even press interviews – and there was a steady trickle as she approached the age of 100 – she felt were good for her. 'My ability to amuse or interest flows much more easily at the touch of a professional questioner.'

Her fans were much less likely than her old friends to make a fuss over her increasing physical frailty, to seize the kettle from her shaky hand or insist on helping her down the stairs; which made it all the more galling when it was Ann Dix, arriving to see her early in February 1997, who found her with a dramatic black eye and a bleeding nose after she had been blown over by the wind in Lowndes Place. Although Frances insisted she was fine, and they spent the afternoon looking at her photographs as planned, Ann

Dix was worried enough at the constant bleeding to ring the doctor who had patched her up and sent her home earlier in the day. His lack of concern prompted Frances to do what her friends had been urging for some time, and change to a private doctor known to Magouche and the Hendersons. Dr Trevor Hudson proved to be just what she needed, prepared to visit her at home and interested in helping her continue to be as independent as possible. She would not listen to her friends, but when he gave her advice, she would follow it.

When her ninety-seventh birthday came round in March, Frances observed that she felt happier and better than she had for some time, even though since the fall in the street she had been forced to use a walking stick and often felt very tired. But she was able to speak at Quentin Bell's memorial service – he had recently died of cancer – before travelling out to Spain with Magouche in April, taking with her several bits of work: a review for *The Spectator*, an article on music for the *Charleston Magazine* and an obituary of V.S. Pritchett for the Royal Society of Literature. And when Labour won the general election in May, Frances was thrilled. 'Into this,' she wrote, 'I could put a lot of libido.' She took another burglary in her stride, even though she lost more jewellery and felt it had been foolish of her to let in the two bogus television repair men who robbed her: 'What a sucker they must have thought me.' After another visit to Skye, in June she gave a talk on James and Alix Strachey at the newly opened Freud Museum in Hampstead, and in July she felt strong enough to take one of her regular minicabs to the Hatchard's summer party, where among the milling throng of writers and publishers she spotted Princess Margaret, 'a stiff little woman doll'. She was observed later alone on the pavement, hailing a taxi in Piccadilly to take her home.

But later that month, as she realised how many of her friends were leaving London, Frances' morale began to droop. Casting around for distraction from a wave of loneliness, she found herself reconsidering her decision not to publish any more of her diaries. 'I suddenly asked myself: why am I wasting the volumes of my diary that stand condemned to death on the shelves of my armoire . . . I took down volumes 1970–72 and saw that they had been corrected to some effect. Some of it was rather good.' Rebecca Wilson, Gill Coleridge and Robert encouraged the idea, but both Janetta and Magouche 'flinched'; Frances resolved to be very careful, but the prospect of a new publication was too attractive to resist. When both Gill and Rebecca told her they loved the new material she felt she was 'back in business', and by the end of the year she had revised the typescript and signed a new contract. 'What have I done? Where will it all end?' The new book, *Life Regained*, was to be published in the summer of 1998.

By this time, although Frances was still keeping up her diary in her A4 notebooks, there were often long gaps between entries and from time to time she would look back at what she had written and find it 'of little value or interest'. Her handwriting in her late nineties was still clear, albeit smaller and shakier than it used to be; and she still took pleasure in exchanging letters, especially with Janetta in Spain, Henrietta in France, Olivier Bell and Catherine Carrington in Sussex. Neither her correspondence nor her diary ever became a catalogue of her ailments and problems, and both are proof of her continuing interest in other people and in everything going on around her. She was with Janetta in Spain when Princess Diana died in Paris, and was fascinated by the aftermath of the tragedy: 'She is becoming beatified . . . an extraordinary manifestation – a peaceful French revolution'. She was still able to swim, although now Janetta insisted on helping her down to the pool and increasingly Frances worried that she was becoming a burden: 'She is perfectly kind to me as an invalid, but she leaves the room whenever we are alone together . . . where is our old intimacy? I fear I irritate her.' It was true that Janetta sometimes found Frances' refusal to accept her limitations trying, and she was also much preoccupied with her daughter Rose, whose second child was giving cause for anxiety, and had felt Frances to be unsympathetic; some of Janetta's friends, like the Frys, occasionally felt that Frances' need for Janetta put her under strain. What Frances could not see was that her determination to live alone with minimal help was increasingly unnerving for those who loved her. That winter, Janetta tried and failed to persuade Frances to arrange for more help, after one or two dramas when she could not get out of her bath. Frances insisted that Vera and the panic button were enough. When she toppled against a bookcase and cut her head badly, she still would not budge. Instead, she resolved to build up her strength, 'do more exercises and take more walks'.

After spending another delightful Christmas in Devon with Sophie and the girls, Frances found January 1998 much improved by several sessions with Rebecca on the new book: 'my idea of a perfect way to spend a dark day . . . I find I desperately need some little form of endeavour and if possible success, so as to counter the endless dégringolade, the "downhill all the way" effect of old age'. But in February, she was again blown down in the street by a gust of wind; she began to be haunted by the idea of a wheelchair, 'and then the old folks' home waiting to scoop me up', but her powers of recovery remained strong, and before long she was able to go to the Festival Hall with Paul Levy and to a birthday dinner given by Magouche, and to record her choices of music for *Private Passions* on Radio 3. A flu-like illness struck her in late March, but she felt better as soon as her proofs arrived, and when the weather improved, she managed several country weekends. Staying with the Frys near Bath, she took particular pleasure in deadheading the roses. With publication of *Life Regained* imminent in July, she was interviewed by BBC television wearing a new red silk shirt and red slippers, and also by *Woman's Hour* and *The Daily Telegraph*, but it seemed to her that 'dead silence' greeted the book's appearance in August and that when reviews did appear they were less enthusiastic than before. But then Hatchard's, Harrods and the Bloomsbury Gallery held book signings, and in September Nicko Henderson gave a party for her at Sotheby's. Not long afterwards Frances was in Cambridge, staying with Nadine and visiting an ailing and bedridden Dadie Rylands in King's. She also visited her old college, Newnham, and took part in a ceremony at which she was formally awarded the degree she had earned in 1921.

Before the end of the year, she learned that Gill and Rebecca were planning a new edition of all her books so that everything she had written would be in print by her hundredth birthday, which was some compensation for her worsening eyesight and unsteadiness. She was also greatly pleased to be taken down to Kent by Stephen Keynes, Maynard's scientist nephew and a descendant of Darwin's, to see round the newly opened Darwin Museum at Down House, where her father had built a new wing for the great man in 1877. The curator even produced a letter: '"my dear Marshall, do you think you could build me a billiard room and study?" . . . I came away greatly stimulated'. She went back to Sophie for Christmas as usual, travelling alone by train, and spent the New Year in Gloucestershire with Janetta and the Leigh Fermors. When the news came later in January that Dadie was dead, she was glad she had seen him so recently, and recorded a moment of envy.

During 1999, with the turn of the millennium and her own hundredth birthday imminent, Frances' diary-keeping finally began to dwindle to almost nothing. This was not just because her eyes grew steadily worse; she had finally agreed, after rejecting several approaches, to work with the present biographer, and their regular sessions discussing her past and present life became an alternative to the writing she found more and more difficult. She managed one or two more book reviews, and never abandoned her diary entirely; she noted a visit to the Garnetts at Hilton, and an early summer trip to Spain, pondered her obsession with swimming, and mentioned visits from Sue Fox and Ann Dix, the two fans she liked most. Most evenings during the week friends would come for a drink, and she could still manage a weekend in the country if a lift was organised, but sometimes London weekends were lonely. There was another fan, a man living in

Essex, who realised this and took to telephoning Frances on a Saturday to see if she would like a visit the next day. They first met after he wrote to her praising her diaries and asking if he could call on her, and she helped him come to terms with the death of his mother, to whom he was deeply devoted. He made several weekend visits, and Frances enjoyed his company; but later it was to turn out that he had acquired some of her possessions, including valuable books and letters and three of her engagement diaries, claiming that she had given them to him. This was the only time, as far as is known, that Frances' openness and kindness to her admirers led to trouble.

As the century through which she had lived came to an end, Frances was confined to her flat with flu, looked after by a relay of nurses organised by Janetta. On 1 January 2000, determined to mark the start of the new millennium, she turned to her diary. Midnight on 31 December found her lying in bed as the television brought her the scene at the Dome, 'with a rather sweet young nurse sitting beside me watching the hopeless confusion made of our passage into the new century by the powers that be'. The New Year Honours brought her the CBE, for services to literature, and she was able to go to the Palace, accompanied by Sophie and the girls, to receive the medal from the Queen. She wore her old fur coat and her stylish fedora, and enjoyed the whole occasion, although she felt it was more a tribute to her longevity than anything. Frances kept an eye on the progress of the Queen Mother, her fellow centenarian, and enjoyed pointing out that as well as being older by six months she herself managed to live alone, rather than being waited on hand and foot. She made a New Year's resolution: 'To go on trying to think and write if possible.' It pleased her that in January 2000 *The Spectator* contained her review of a book by Ronald Blythe about the friendship, at the time of the First World War, between Carrington and her Slade friends, based in part on letters she herself had rescued in 1932. This turned out to have been her last review.

The approach of her hundredth birthday was regarded by Frances with mixed feelings. She wondered if she could rise to the various occasions confronting her, particularly the big party being arranged by Janetta and other old friends at the Savile Club. In the end, she managed it all with striking composure, and found herself soon afterwards recording a series of triumphs and a sense of renewed energy. On 3 April 2000 she wrote in her diary, 'I am dug into my 101st year – surely a good time for fresh starts!' and then summed up the year so far. 'I have passed the following ordeals,' she wrote, and listed the CBE ceremony, a 'state' or courtesy visit from her landlord, the Duke of Westminster, a lunch on 15 March for twelve close friends by Janetta and Jaime, and the next day the 'Grand Birthday Party for about 150 people' at the Savile Club. A week later there was dinner at the Ivy with Richard Shone and Robert Kee and his third wife, Kate, and finally a sale of 'mini-books' at Sotheby's to raise money for charity. Frances had written a short essay on memory, which sold for £400. All this, she added, had left her feeling 'unjustified hope for the future'. No-one who saw her during the celebrations could doubt that she found life still very much worth living. Although she felt exhausted by all the excitement for some weeks afterwards, and her diary petered out again, she was able to say, on 10 April, her handwriting quavery, the lines straggling down the page: 'Strange as it may be "crossing the bar", in other words becoming 100 plus, seems to make me feel more my old self.'

Afterword

2000—2004

As she approached her hundredth birthday I started to visit Frances regularly in preparation for this biography. Our sessions, of about two hours, were usually on Wednesday mornings, and although Frances would greet me affectionately, make sure I had coffee and always show interest in my doings, I knew that my job was not to develop a friendship but to work with her on the story of her life. She was perfectly at ease with my tape recorder, and entirely willing to answer all my questions, even the ones I found it hardest to ask, about Ralph's infidelities and Burgo's troubles. There was only one topic where I felt her mind was closed: the moral dilemma of being a pacifist confronted with Hitler. It was not that she would not address the matter, but that she could not; she had long ago rejected all the arguments I could deploy.

Sometimes I accompanied Frances on an outing, a talk at the Royal Society of Literature perhaps, or drove her down to our mutual friend Anthony Hobson's house near Salisbury for a weekend. One evening I found myself taking her to Tate Britain, where Nicholas Serota had arranged for her to have a quiet private visit to their millennium exhibition, 'The Art of Bloomsbury', curated by her friend Richard Shone, to which she had lent Duncan Grant's *Juggler and Tightrope Walker*, bought by Lytton in Oxford in 1920. She consented to a wheelchair for the occasion, and we had the entire gallery to ourselves; but she could not really see the paintings, and it was no use asking her whether the Grant drawing of a young man with magnificent shoulders, *Seated Male Nude*, 1922, was of Ralph, as had been suggested. We talked of why Carrington's work was not included, apart from one portrait of E.M. Forster; Frances understood why Shone had decided that her style was somehow too individual to make her fit easily with Grant, Bell and Roger Fry, but emphasised that she had always regarded her as a serious artist. We also discussed the surprisingly virulent wave of anti-Bloomsbury criticism provoked by the exhibition, which had revived the old attacks on the group, especially the artists, as elitist amateurs of little real achievement. Frances, who had heard it all before, wondered why people could not just accept that Bloomsbury was never a superior closed circle, but just a loose collection of people who happened to be friends, some more talented than others, who pursued their occupations as much for pleasure and experiment as to make their mark. On the way out, she announced that she would like to see Tracey Emin's *My Bed*, which had been exciting the press so much. I pushed her wheelchair up to the famous object, with its stained and crumpled sheets and litter of intimate detritus. Frances contemplated it seriously before deciding that it hardly seemed like art to her, but that she was glad to see what all the fuss was about.

Over the next few months, as we talked about her past, I became familiar with the pattern of her life in her extreme old age. By this time, her Scottish housekeeper, Vera, had been replaced by Portuguese Elizabeth, who looked after Frances with quiet skill and increasing devotion. Not long before I came on the scene, Frances had asked Georgia Tennant to help her manage her appointments, her finances and her personal and professional correspondence and keep the archive in Lytton's armoire under control; Georgia came in on Tuesdays and Thursdays, and as Frances' sight worsened her help became invaluable, especially when they started working together on the next section of the diary. This had been agreed during 1999, after Frances learned that the publishers could provide her with a special large-print version of the text; slowly, laboriously, with a magnifying glass and bright lights, she applied herself to the familiar task of cutting and polishing. It was a blow when she learned that her favourite editor, Rebecca Wilson, was leaving publishing; afterwards she would discuss points of editing with Georgia, and decided to dedicate the new volume to her.

I grew to recognise the signs that Janetta was in town: there would be fresh flowers in Frances' favourite Victorian jug, often from the Spanish garden, and Frances would be radiant with pleasure. A telephone call from Robert Kee or Nicko Henderson would always make her face light up, as would any prospect of seeing Sophie; she often spoke of Henrietta with concern and great affection. In the summer of 2000, to her surprise and delight, she made it back to CuzCuz; once safely there it was with a sense of triumph that she managed to get down the steps to the pool and into the water, even though she was so weightless that, she told me later, she bobbed about alarmingly, and when she was helped out by Tony Fry he could not help pulling the papery skin off her wrists so that she emerged bleeding. He minded much more than she did.

Later that year, Frances took part in an elaborate Foundation Day ceremony held at the Senate House of London University, a stone's throw from the house where she was born, to receive an honorary degree as 'an individual of particular distinction and achievement', along with Roy Jenkins, Richard Hoggart, Simon Jenkins, Amartya Sen and Aaron Klug. She wore scarlet robes and a mortar-board, and enjoyed talking to Princess Anne about her exact contemporary, the Queen Mother.

In the spring of 2001, she tried to pick up her diary again. 'Notes on the life of FP, 101 in April 2001,' she wrote, but then the page is blank. Nicko Henderson had arranged a small gathering for her hundred-and-first at Brooks's Club, after which she said that really she had enjoyed it much more than the party at the Savile, splendid though that had been. When *Ups and Downs: Diaries 1972–75*, was published that autumn, it was welcomed by her established readership and kindly treated by reviewers, although to some it seemed that the new volume had suffered from Frances' inability to apply herself as before. She was mortified to find that some sharp remarks about one of her kindest friends had slipped through, but even so it was not long before she and Georgia embarked on the next section. She could no longer keep her diary, but she could still, with help, edit it. That same year, an omnibus edition of selections from her diaries from 1939 to 1972 was published in a fat paperback edition. Most reviewers were kind, apart from Peter Conrad, writing this time in *The Observer*. He took her and all Bloomsbury to task for rating conversation and personal relations above 'ideological commitment', especially in wartime, and for disliking house-work. 'The seminars about ultimate value could only proceed if slavish drudges took care of the cooking and cleaning.'

Although Frances found the weekends and evenings when she was alone increasingly bleak, she still resisted any suggestion that she live any other way. Her nephew Richard Garnett and his wife Jane proposed more than once that she move to Hilton, where they had made a ground-floor room ready for her; but although she was grateful for their kindness, and happy to stay with them for a few days, she was adamant. So she was alone at home when she learned of the attack on the Twin Towers in New York in September 2001, an event that shocked but did not altogether surprise her. 'It was rather awful to be alone,' she said not long afterwards. 'I heard it on the news at six, but luckily I was soon in touch with Robert and able to talk about it. I've long felt the world will be brought to an end by something we do ourselves . . . man is a pretty awful creature.' She was terrified at what America might do in revenge, and found herself reflecting on the dangers of patriotic fervour. She still recalled with shame how she had succumbed to the disease herself in 1914 and worn a red, white and blue ribbon, 'but only for about half a day. Ray gave me a cynical look . . . and I was only 14.' Now, at 101, she contemplated the state of the world with something like despair. 'I've felt ever since the Second World War and the dropping of the bomb that we would do ourselves in. The world will end and it will be our own fault.'

Early in 2002, our sessions stopped for a while. My own life was abruptly derailed by the sudden death in a car crash of my nephew, whom I had brought up as my son. Now I, like so many of her friends and readers, found her a guide to survival. When she heard what had happened, she wrote to me at once, on one of her *Juggler and Tightrope Walker* cards: 'Darling Anne, I have only just heard via Georgia the *terrible* news and am not expecting you until you have enough strength regained to find it even some distraction. And of course I have known what such horrors are like. *All* my love.' When we next met she told me that I would slowly find working on this book a help, and that in time memory would be not my enemy but my friend. Perhaps because our work routine had faltered, Frances made one more attempt to resume her diary. By March 2002 her writing was very shaky, but her intention was clear. 'It has struck me that I should keep writing for myself alone – just to keep alive.' But it was no good; she could not do it. The beginning of an entry for her 102nd birthday is illegible; after that, nothing.

Although by the middle of the year we had talked our way through her life, our sessions continued. Apart from the fact that I always learned something more, from the names of the wild flowers I brought her from Oxfordshire to the fact that the chair in her window had been Lytton Strachey's favourite, we had established a relationship in which the professional and the personal found a language and a balance. When her friends hinted that they hoped I would continue, so that a gap did not open in her life, it was easy to reassure them.

Then, in October 2002 came the news that Frances was in hospital after falling during the night and breaking her hip. Luckily, she had not been alone; a respiratory infection had put her to bed, and Dr Hudson had insisted that she have a nurse at night. When she had recovered from the operation to repair the damage, I went to see her; she seemed entirely herself, and had been answering letters with Georgia, who later told me that Frances had been surprised, even put out, that I had not arrived at the hospital for our usual meeting on the first Wednesday after the operation. Within a week she was back at home, and anxious to resume our weekly routine.

There then began a time when I sometimes found my position uneasy. Everyone around her knew that this was the beginning of the end of Frances' life, and part of me felt that no biographer should be hovering at such a time, observing and recording the approach of death. On the other hand it would be worse should Frances think that my withdrawal meant that I was no longer interested in her or that her death was imminent. I decided to act as normally as possible for as long as possible. She deplored the fact that she could only walk a little, with a Zimmer frame, and that she was now always surrounded by helpers and nurses. Elizabeth and her friend Isabel were there all day, but a series of strangers slept overnight in her sitting room. She was often in pain, but she was stoical. 'I want to die,' she said, 'to get out of the world, but I am not sure how to do it. I also can't stop wanting to get well. One has a life instinct, which struggles.'

By this time I was keeping a diary of my own.

December 12. The phone rings and it is Robert, saying F had been taken to hospital, exactly a week since I saw her and we talked of the tenacity of the appetite for life. Apparently the pain had got worse, she was terrified of moving at all and eventually was taken to hospital by ambulance for an x ray which revealed that the bone had simply crumbled ... so she is back in the Chelsea and Westminster awaiting the knife again, and given the ground she has lost and the strain of it all it is hard to be optimistic. Robert says she has been in good and positive spirits, though. When asked if she was comfortable: 'as comfortable as in my own bed – which has not lately been very comfortable'. That's Frances.

A week later, I described 'a curious biographer's dream':

Frances was in the process of dying, in a large modern hospital room, surrounded by people, all her friends and relations standing by. Meanwhile she and I were also sitting at a round table in an adjacent room, observing and commenting on what was happening to her in perfect calm and cheerfulness ... What do we make of this? Wishful thinking? Guilt? A reminder that my job is not to feel but to observe and record? That is after all what she wants of me. Nevertheless if and when I am able to see her again, which I hope to do next Wednesday, it must be as a friend, not as a biographer with a notebook out. There are limits, although of course eventually I shall have to try to learn the manner of her last hours.

I knew my limits had been reached when one day, as I was helping her to eat her hospital lunch, she lost consciousness and I thought she was dying before my eyes. Nurses rushed to her bedside; curtains were drawn;

I retreated and cried. But she came back, and when I said 'Dear Frances, it seems your heart skipped a beat or two', she said, softly but clearly, 'I am not at all surprised.'

When Frances returned to her flat early in 2003, she was, at first, so happy to be home that it almost seemed she might get better. For a while, with the help of Elizabeth and Isabel, she would be up and dressed each day, ready for the doctor, the physiotherapist, and her stream of visitors. Nurses came and went, some more tactful than others; one of them told me that usually with very old patients the problem was that no-one came to see them; with Frances, the problem was to keep us all at bay. When I saw her in late January, I was able to read her an account I had just obtained of Ralph's childhood in India, and she told me he remembered being called Sonny Sahib. We talked of family, and whether Ralph really hated his. He tried to love them, said Frances, and sometimes succeeded; anyway, she pointed out, with families 'Love and dislike go in waves'. Her memory, and her capacity to reconsider, were as evident as ever. But by the time I called again, two weeks later and not long before I was due to leave for a research trip to America, a series of small strokes had taken her to the brink. She was asleep when I arrived, and I did not wake her. It seemed unlikely I would see her again, or that she could live much longer.

In fact, she lived for another year. During that time she hovered between life and death, drifting in and out of consciousness, expertly and lovingly looked after, sometimes able to say a few words. All of us, Janetta especially, knew that her instinct for life held her longer than she would have wished. When I returned from America, I heard about a gathering in her flat for her 103rd birthday, when she blew out three candles on a cake. Later she told her nurses: 'Robert gave me some champagne. It was disgusting.' Robert himself felt that she was not unhappy, and that she was showing in her way of dying the strength that had sustained her through her life. When Sue Fox visited her in the summer, she told Frances how much she loved and admired her. 'How very extraordinary,' was Frances' reply.

'What does one wish for her now?' I wrote in my diary. 'It is as if some force stronger than her is refusing to let her go . . . it does seem that Robert is right, that her way of dying is oddly characteristic of her. She has managed, against the odds, to avoid humiliation.' Even so, everyone who loved her knew that it was time for her to let death take her away at last. Janetta called me on the morning of 6 February 2004, to say that not long after she had left her bedside Frances had died in the night.

Janetta helped Sophie to arrange the funeral, but then, true to herself and to what she had learned from Frances, she left for Spain. On 17 February

I went to Mortlake, where Frances was cremated to the sound of some of her favourite Mozart, Schubert and Bach, in a coffin made of plaited reeds covered with camellias and primroses from Sophie's Devon garden. There was no mention of God; indeed not one word was spoken. Words did not seem to be needed.

Appendices

Appendix A: Value of £ sterling during FP's lifetime compared with value in 2007

1900	£77.58
1910	£73.15
1920	£28.80
1930	£45.32
1940	£39.13
1950	£24.69
1960	£16.59
1970	£11.15
1980	£3.09
1990	£1.64
2000	£1.21

Figures from the Economic History Services website www.eh.net based on the retail price index.

Appendix B: Translations by Frances Partridge

Between 1956 and 1978 FP translated many books, essays and articles from French and Spanish. The following is a selection of her published translations.

Mercedes Ballesteros, *Nothing is Impossible* (Harvill Press, 1956)
Lovleff Bornet, *Something to Declare* (Harvill Press, 1957)
Vicente Blasco Ibáñez, *Blood and Sand* (Elek, 1958)
Vicente Blasco Ibáñez, *The Naked Lady* (Elek, 1959)
Joseph Kessel, *The Enemy in the Mouth* (Rupert Hart-Davis, 1961)
Gabrielle Estivals, *A Gap in the Wall* (Collins, 1963)
Miguel Ángel Asturias, *The President* (Gollancz, 1964)

J.L. Aranguren, *Human Communication* (World University Library, 1967)
Gilbert Martineau, *Napoleon's St Helena* (John Murray, 1968)
Alejo Carpentier, *The War of Time* (Gollancz, 1970)
Gilbert Martineau, *Napoleon Surrenders* (John Murray, 1971)
Alejo Carpentier, *Reasons of State* (Knopf, 1976)
Gilbert Martineau, *Napoleon's Last Journey* (John Murray, 1976)
Gilbert Martineau, *Madame Mere: Napoleon's Mother* (John Murray, 1978)

Note on Sources, and Acknowledgements

The biography of a diarist presents particular challenges. The existence of my subject's detailed, almost daily record of her life from the age of forty, much of it published, has inevitably meant that my account of her life is written with constant reference to her own. Frances Partridge kept a diary from her late twenties to her mid-seventies with no thought of publication. She then began to edit and publish it, while continuing to keep it until she was 102. She did so because she hated the idea of life slipping by unrecorded, and because she found pleasure in the act of writing. I have also come to believe, in the course of working on this book, that she used her diary to keep her life and her feelings under control. Her diary, published and unpublished, is the most valuable source for this book, but I have tried to look beyond it and not to allow my version of her life to be dominated by hers.

When I began this book, I expected that I would be able to work from the original diaries. However, I soon discovered that Frances had destroyed the handwritten originals after editing them, having them typed and then editing the typescripts again before publication. Until 1999 she continued to edit each year's diary before sending it to be typed. Handwritten diaries only exist from 1999. Truthfulness mattered a great deal to Frances; however, as she told me, she did not believe that by pruning and shaping what she had written, and destroying what she had rejected, she was falsifying the record. Indeed, by leaving behind typescripts on which cuts and alterations are clearly visible, she left many traces of the kind of material she decided not to publish, and I have made full use of this in my text.

At the beginning of my researches, Frances was happy for me to remove box files and folders from her flat and work on them at home. Finding the responsibility increasingly unnerving, I was immensely grateful when the then Librarian at the London Library, Alan Bell, agreed to keep successive instalments of files in his office, from whence I would remove them to the Reading Room before returning them to Frances.

After her death in 2004 all her papers, apart from some family material, was given, as she had instructed, to King's College, Cambridge; again, the London Library came to my rescue by housing her entire archive while legal preliminaries took place, during which time I completed my work on it. I owe a great debt of gratitude to Alan Bell's successor, Inez Lynn, for allowing me to do so, at some inconvenience to herself and her staff.

After receiving the bequest the Librarian and Archivists at King's undertook the considerable task of sorting, conserving and cataloguing the thirty-six boxes and twenty volumes of papers and photograph albums, which arrived somewhat battered and are now kept in pristine conditions. My great thanks are due to Peter Jones, Patricia McGuire and Rosalind Moad who have been consistently welcoming, efficient and helpful.

Apart from the diaries, which run to just over 8,000 typed pages and six handwritten notebooks, the principal sources used in this book and now held by King's include her engagement books, especially those from the 1920s and 1930s when her diary was intermittent, and her voluminous correspondence, particularly her letters to and from her husband, Ralph Partridge, and her friends Gerald Brenan and Julia Strachey. Frances kept very few letters from her family apart from her son Burgo. No letters from her mother or her brothers or sisters survive, and only one from her father, sending good wishes for her ninth birthday.

Frances' involvement with Bloomsbury's most celebrated ménage à trois, which she turned into a ménage à quatre, had been much written about long before I started work, and at first I planned to avoid retelling the story of Lytton Strachey, Dora Carrington and Ralph Partridge which had been so comprehensively described by Michael Holroyd and Gretchen Gerzina. However, it proved impossible to understand Frances' story without revisiting the triangle, although I have tried, by returning to original sources, to look at it from a different angle. The correspondence between Lytton and Carrington held in the British Library, and that between Carrington and Gerald Brenan held by the Harry Ransom Humanities Research Center at the University of Texas, proved particularly fruitful. Several people were generous enough to show me letters from Frances, notably the late Richard Chopping, her nephew Richard Garnett (who gave me access to her letters to his father, David Garnett), her daughter-in-law Henrietta Garnett and Janetta Parladé, her friend and correspondent for over sixty years. I should like to express my particular gratitude to them, and also to Michael Holroyd, the most generous of biographers to those who follow in his footsteps, whose correspondence with Frances is now also in the British Library. I am also very grateful to Roger Louis and the British Studies Centre at the University of Austin, Texas, for a visiting fellowship in 2003 that enabled me to spend a month working in their splendid collections, which are especially rich in Bloomsbury material.

No biographer could have had a more generous and patient subject. My greatest debt is therefore to Frances Partridge herself, who as well as allowing me access to all her papers spent many hours talking to me about her life. These conversations, conducted between 1999 and 2003, ranged widely and were invaluable, not simply in establishing or confirming facts but by conveying the qualities – intelligence, integrity, humour, sympathy and courage – that made her such a remarkable woman.

As well as truthfulness, Frances greatly valued friendship. Many of her friends and mine supported me over the years it has taken me to write this book. For help, advice and hospitality I should like to thank: Mark Amory, the late Sybille Bedford, Anne Olivier Bell, Xandra Bingley, Ann Blaber, the late Anthony Blond, John Byrne, Susan Campbell, the late Joanna Carrington, Laura Cecil, Mirabel and Hugh Cecil, Carlyn and Colin Chisholm, Susannah Clapp, the late Marjorie Clark, Catrine and John Clay, Mary Clemmey, Gemma Clive, Beth Coventry, Ann Dix, Virginia Duigan, Nell Dunn, James Fergusson, Magouche Fielding, Anthony and Sabrina Fry, Helen Garner, Angelica Garnett, Jonathan and Nicky Gathorne-Hardy, Gretchen Gerzina, Victoria Glendinning, the late Celia Goodman, Mary and Richard Gray, Selina Hastings, Phyllis Hatfield, Mary Haynes, Nicholas and the late Mary Henderson, the late Anne Hill, Harriet Hill, Anthony Hobson, Vicky Holloway, Rose Jackson, Cynthia Kee, Kate and Robert Kee, Georgie Kee, Jane Kramer, Patrick Leigh Fermor, Topsy Levan, Paul and Penny Levy, Nadine Marshall, Fay Maschler, Christoper Mason, Perry Meisel, Cynthia Millar, Maureen and Francis Nichols, Jaime Parladé, Lyndall Passerini, Wendy Perry, Jean Phillips, Alice Phipps, Kathy van Praag, the late Simon Raven, Philippa Roberts, Ray Roberts, Sally Sampson, Caroline and John Sandwich, Richard Shone, Elizabeth de Silva, Michael Tanner, Georgia Tennant, Polly Toynbee, Jeremy Treglown, the late Patrick Trevor-Roper, Simon Young, Francis Wyndham.

For permission to use copyright material, my thanks are due above all to Sophie Partridge, who read the text on her grandmother's behalf, and the Literary Executor of the Frances Partridge estate. I also thank Richard Garnett and the Estate of the late David Garnett, Henrietta Garnett, Michael Holroyd, Francis Nichols, the Estate of the late Colin Mackenzie, Benedetta Origo, Jean Phillips and the Society of Authors, literary representatives of the Strachey Trust. Extracts from the letters by Gerald Brenan and from *A Life of One's Own* and *South from Granada* are reproduced by

I could not have written this book without the advice and encourgement of the following people: Gill Coleridge, Frances Partridge's friend, agent and literary executor as well as my own agent, has guided and protected me from the beginning. Susan Fox helped me a great deal with my researches, especially in the United States. Caroline Moorehead read the early drafts and made many valuable suggestions. I am most grateful to Douglas Matthews for the index. Ion Trewin, Bea Hemming and Linden Lawson at Weidenfeld & Nicolson have been models of patience and amiability. My special thanks to them all.

My husband, Michael Davie, helped me start this book. I wish he could have helped me finish it. It is dedicated to him and to our nephew Jesse Stoecker.

Anne Chisholm
London, 2008

Source Notes

The following abbreviations are used in the notes:

The author: AC
Frances Partridge: FP
Ralph Partridge: RP
Gerald Brenan: GB
Dora Carrington: DC
David Garnett: DG
Janetta Parladé: JP
Lytton Strachey: LS

Books and diaries published by Frances Partridge:

A Pacifist's War (Hogarth Press, 1978) PW
Memories (Gollancz, 1980) Mem
Julia (Gollancz, 1983) J
Everything to Lose (Chatto & Windus, 1985) EL
Friends in Focus (Chatto & Windus, 1987) FF
Hanging On (Collins, 1990) HO
The Pasque Flower (The Patten Press, 1990) PF
Other People (HarperCollins, 1993) OP
Good Company (HarperCollins, 1994) GC
Life Regained (Weidenfeld & Nicolson, 1998) LR
Ups and Downs (Weidenfeld & Nicolson, 2001) UD
Diaries 1939–1972 (Weidenfeld & Nicolson, 2001)

Unpublished diaries by Frances Partridge: Unpub D

Libraries and Archives:

The British Library BL
King's College Archives KCA

Harry Ransom Humanities Research Center, University of Texas
  HRHRC

Frequently cited books:

Jonathan Gathorne-Hardy, *The Interior Castle: A Life of Gerald Brenan*
  (Sinclair-Stevenson, 1992) JGH
Gretchen Gerzina, *Carrington: A Life of Dora Carrington, 1893–1932* (John
  Murray, 1989) GG
Michael Holroyd, *Lytton Strachey: The New Biography* (Chatto & Windus,
  1994) MH

In the notes for each chapter the main published sources are indicated
first. Other material, all unpublished material from diaries or letters, and
quotations from my conversations with FP are separately noted

Chapter One: Bedford Square and Tweenways, 1900–1914 (pp. 1–21)

My account of FP's family background is taken from the unpublished
memoir written by her mother, Margaret Anne Marshall, known as Mam,
lent to me by her nephew Richard Garnett. FP described her childhood
and her friendship with Julia Strachey in Mem and included Julia Strachey's
recollections of her early life in J. Some details of late-nineteenth-century
Hindhead are taken from W.R. Trotter, *The Hilltop Writers* (Book Guild,
1966).

p. 1   I was always ... FP to AC, March 1999
p. 3   Will Marshall collected ... PF p. 28
p. 17   In fact, Frances ... FP to AC, May 1999

Chapter Two: Bedales and Cambridge, 1915–1921 (pp. 22–37)

Mam's memoir gives a full picture of the Marshall family during the First
World War, and FP wrote her own account in Mem. Details about
Catherine Marshall are taken from Jonathan Atkin, *A War of Individuals,
Bloomsbury Attitudes to the Great War* (Manchester University Press,
2002). Bedales and the Badleys are described in Roy Wake and Penny
Denton, *Bedales School, The First Hundred Years* (Haggerston Press, 1993).
FP's recollections of Bedales, Julia as a schoolgirl and Cambridge appear
in Mem and J.

p. 26   FP's letters from Bedales to her sister Ray are in the possession of Ray's son Richard Garnett

Not caring ... FP's early interest in botany is described in PF

It was Mr Heath ... FP wrote about discovering Bertrand Russell's book, and meeting him, in *The Sunday Telegraph*, 13 March 1999

p. 30   Her Cambridge years ... FP to Stanley Olson, Unpub D, 1979

p. 31   The return of Tom ... FP to AC, May 1999

p. 33   There was a lot of kissing ... FP to AC, May 1999

p. 35   During his last year or two ... DG wrote about the Marshalls in *The Flowers of the Forest* (Chatto & Windus, 1955)

p. 36   Her mother ... FP to AC, June 1999

When Frances ... DG to FP, KCA

p. 37   Through David Garnett ... FP in 'Bloomsbury Houses', *Charleston Magazine*, June 1985

Chapter Three: The Bookshop and Bloomsbury, 1922–1923 (pp. 38–53)

Birrell and Garnett's bookshop, and FP's first reactions to meeting Old Bloomsbury, are described in Mem, and DG described the bookshop himself in *Flowers of the Forest*, op. cit. My account of the Garnetts is based on Richard Garnett's biography of his grandmother, Constance Garnett, *A Heroic Life* (Sinclair-Stevenson, 1991) and for DG's relationship with Duncan Grant I have relied on Frances Spalding's biographies of Duncan Grant (Chatto & Windus, 1997) and of Vanessa Bell (Weidenfeld & Nicolson, 1983). DG's courtship of Ray Marshall and his impressions of the Marshall family appear in *Flowers of the Forest*, op. cit., pp. 229–34. All quotations from LS's letters to his brother James Strachey are taken from Paul Levy (ed.), *The Letters of Lytton Strachey* (Penguin, 2005).

p. 40   Mam, at any rate ... Mam's letter to Constance Garnett is in the possession of Richard Garnett

p. 41   The baby ... FP to AC, May 1999

p. 44   FP's engagement books are in KCA

p. 45   In a letter to her mother ... FP's letter to Mam is in the possession of Richard Garnett

He kept ... FP's letters to Raisley Moorsom are held by KCA

p. 47   Colin was in the throes ... copies of Colin Mackenzie's letters to Iris Origo are in the possession of his descendants. I am indebted to Caroline

Moorehead for drawing them to my attention and to her biography of Iris Origo (John Murray, 2000) for my account of their relationship.

p. 48   Ralph's background ... details of RP's background, early years and wartime experiences are taken from family papers kindly shown to me by his niece, Mrs Jean Phillips

p. 50   Gerald Brenan ... GB's letters to his father and account of RP during the First World War are to be found in Gerald Brenan, *A Life of One's Own* (Hamish Hamilton, 1962)

Chapter Four: The Making of Ralph Partridge, 1918–1920 (pp. 54–69)

p. 56   Their letters ... the correspondence between Carrington and Lytton Strachey is held by the British Library. In DG's edition of DC's letters, *Carrington, Letters and Extracts from her Diaries* (Jonathan Cape, 1970), louche or unflattering references to FP and RP are omitted.

Virginia Woolf noted ... this and all other quotations from Virginia Woolf's diary are taken from Anne Olivier Bell (ed.), *The Diary of Virginia Woolf* (The Hogarth Press, 1979).

p. 57   Carrington was not included ... DG's remark is taken from his introduction to DC's letters, op. cit.

p. 60   An interested observer ... GB's visit to Tidmarsh is described in Gerald Brenan, *South From Granada* (Hamish Hamilton, 1952). GB's nature and complex relations with RP and DC are fully and convincingly analysed in JGH.

p. 64   LS's letters to RP are in the HRHRC collection, as is the enormous correspondence between DC and GB

p. 66   When, at the end ... FP to AC, July 2001

p. 68   Seventy years later ... Mrs Jean Phillips to AC, May 2003

From there, Lytton described ... LS's letters to Mary Hutchinson are in the HRHRC

Chapter Five: Trouble at Tidmarsh Mill, 1921–1923 (pp. 70–83)

RP's time at the Hogarth Press is covered in the fourth volume of Leonard Woolf's autobiography, *Downhill All the Way* (The Hogarth Press, 1967) and in Virginia Woolf's diary for 1920–24. My account of the Great Row is based on JGH, GG, MH, Mem and conversations with FP.

p. 72   The correspondence between LS and his brother James, and between James and Alix Strachey, is in the BL

I have just kissed ... quoted in Hermione Lee, *Virginia Woolf* (Chatto & Windus, 1997), p. 463

p. 76   In the novel ... quoted in Hermione Lee, op. cit., p. 466

p. 79   In her letters ... FP's letters to Colin Mackenzie were kindly made available to me by his descendants

Chapter Six: Frances and Ralph, 1923–1925 (pp. 84–95)

FP gave her own account of the early stages of her relationship with Ralph in Mem, and all surviving letters between them can be found in KCA.

p. 88   Vanessa Bell ... letter to Roger Fry, 22 June, 1924 see Regina Marler (ed.), *Selected Letters of Vanessa Bell* (Pantheon Books, 1993)

p. 93   If he loved you ... FP to AC, September 2000

She described her ... DC's letters to Alix Strachey are in the BL

Chapter Seven: Journey to Spain, 1925–1926 (pp. 96–105)

FP described her journey to Spain and its aftermath in Mem. Her letters from Spain to Colin Mackenzie are in the possession of his family, and those from Philip Nichols are in KCA.

p. 97   Another view ... copies of Colin Mackenzie and Iris Origo's correspondence about FP and RP were kindly made available to me by their descendants

p. 105   All quotations from James Strachey's letters to Alix Strachey are taken from Perry Meisel and Walter Kendrick (eds), *Bloomsbury/Freud, The Letters of James and Alix Strachey* (Chatto & Windus, 1986)

Chapter Eight: Gordon Square and Ham Spray, 1926–1928 (pp. 106–122)

FP described life in Gordon Square in Mem, and the Stracheys and Clive Bell in EL. My account of the arrival of Freudianism in England is based on that given by Meisel and Kendrick, op. cit., on FP's review of that book in *The Spectator*, 15 March 1986, and on 'The Id Comes to Bloomsbury' by Daniel Pick in *The Guardian*, 16 August 2003.

p. 109   FP's account of VW is taken from her essay in Joan Russell Noble (ed.), *Recollections of Virginia Woolf* (Peter Owen, 1972)

p. 111   Frances described ... FP destroyed her diaries for 1927–32 after using extracts in Mem

p. 112   Something in him ... MH, p. 544

p. 114   DC's notebook is in the BL

p. 115   But Frances' diary ... FP's letters to Philip Nichols were kindly made available to me by his son Francis Nichols

Chapter Nine: Darkness at Ham Spray, 1929–1932 (pp. 123–145)

FP's accounts of her indisposition, Carrington's abortion, Frank Ramsay's death and funeral, all based on her diaries, appear in Mem, as does the story of Hayley Morris. My version of LS's illness and death and Carrington's suicide is based on the full and moving accounts given by MH and GG.

p. 134   FP's letters to Clive Bell are in KCA

Frances knew Rosamond ... Rosamond Lehmann's friendship with LS, DC, FP and RP is described by Selina Hastings in *Rosamond Lehmann* (Chatto & Windus, 2002)

Chapter Ten: Marriage and Motherhood, 1933–1935 (pp. 146–163)

FP's account, based on her diaries, of the journey to the battlefields and the return to Ham Spray is given in Mem.

p. 146   Many years later ... private information

p. 148   There was a girl ... FP to AC, September 2000

p. 149   A fragment ... Vanessa Bell's unpublished letter is in the Berg Collection at the New York Public Library. I am grateful to Susan Fox for bringing it to my attention.

p. 150   When Vanessa ... Angelica Garnett as quoted by Frances Spalding, op. cit.

p. 154   Part of a diary ... Unpub D

FP would say ... FP to AC, July 2000

p. 157   A handful ... RP's letters to Barbara Ker-Seymer are in the Tate Gallery Archives

Asked how much ... FP to AC, July 2000

p. 161   Later Frances ... FP's drafts of stories are in the possession of her granddaughter, Sophie Partridge.

Chapter Eleven: Ostrich Tendencies, 1936–1939 (pp. 164–180)

My account of the Brenans in Churriana before and during the Spanish Civil War is based on JGH, and on Xan Fielding (ed.), *Best of Friends, The Brenan-Partridge Letters* (Chatto & Windus, 1986).

p. 167   She in turn ... JP to AC, June 2007
p. 172   FP's correspondence with Julia Strachey is in KCA
p. 173   Gerald himself ... Richard Garnett showed me GB's letter to David Garnett, and JP confirmed his account of RP's fury (Unpublished letter, 27 September 1938 © The Estate of Gerald Brenan c/o the Hanbury Agency. All rights reserved)
p. 175   Clive Bell's correspondence with FP is in KCA
p. 179   As for Frances ... FP to AC, September 2001

Chapter Twelve: Trials of War (1), 1939–1942 (pp. 181–199)

Life at Ham Spray during the Second World War is described in detail in PW, from which all FP's remarks are taken unless separately noted. GB's letters to RP are taken from *Best of Friends*, op. cit.

p. 182   I dreamt of Ray ... Unpub D
p. 183   That's a very good thing ... FP and RP's reactions to Ray's death are taken from Unpub D, as is FP's conversation with David Garnett about Angelica Bell
p. 184   Asked whether ... FP to AC, July 2000
p. 185   There were fierce ... J, p. 167
          With Julia ... Unpub D
p. 186   After news ... FP and RP's distaste for Mam's patriotism is revealed in Unpub D
p. 187   She has the most ... Unpub D
p. 189   He became greatly agitated ... this and the following comments by RP come from Unpub D
          One of the other ... private information
p. 192   While they were in Devon ... FP removed all details of her mother's last illness and death, and her feelings about it, from PW; my account is based on Unpub D

p. 193   As he wrote ... quoted in JGH, p.338

p. 196   As she herself ... Angelica Garnett discussed her childhood and marriage to David Garnett in *Deceived with Kindness* (Chatto & Windus, 1984)

Chapter Thirteen: Trials of War (2), 1943–1945 (pp. 200–214)

Ralph's statement to the tribunal is printed at the beginning of PW.

p. 200   While Ralph collected testimonials ... a folder of documents relating to Ralph's tribunal is in the possession of his granddaughter, Sophie Partridge

p. 201   I agree with R ... Unpub D

A dose of persecution mania ... Unpub D

p. 202   She loathed ... Unpub D

p. 203   Julia also ... Julia Strachey's and FP's remarks on mother love and the menopause are taken from Unpub D, as are FP's feelings about Philip Nichols as described here and on p. 212

p. 205   He seemed to Frances ... Unpub D

p. 206   Frances was torn ... FP to AC, April 2001. FP's anxiety about Burgo and RP at this time appears in Unpub D

p. 207   The happiest time today ... Unpub D

Isobel Strachey ... Unpub D

p. 208   If pressed ... FP to AC, June 2001

p. 210   I find myself ... Unpub D

They all swam ... Unpub D

p. 213   She asks why ... Unpub D

p. 214   She found herself fibbing ... Unpub D

Chapter Fourteen: Problems of Peace, 1945–1954 (pp. 215–236)

Unless otherwise noted, the main source for this chapter and the next is EL.

p. 215   Both Janetta and Robert ... Unpub D

p. 216   JP's account of Orwell's wedding is in Unpub D

After the war ... Julia Strachey's plight is described in J, and in her letters to FP

p. 218   There now began ... my account of Burgo's troubles uses Unpub

D, Burgo's letters to his parents (in KCA and some in the possession of his daughter Sophie Partridge) and conversations with FP

p. 219   And she would ... FP described finding the Pasque Flower in PF

p. 220   The club ... my account of the Memoir Club is based on Hugh and Mirabel Cecil, *Clever Hearts* (Gollancz, 1990)

p. 221   It seemed entirely suitable ... Unpub D
    Both Frances and Ralph ... FP's observations on Richard Chopping, Denis Wirth Miller and Burgo are in Unpub D

p. 222   For his part ... Richard Chopping to AC, May 2001
    It was a principle ... Unpub D

p. 223   On this first visit ... FP's reservations about being the only woman at Crichel appear in Unpub D

p. 226   It is unsatisfactory ... Unpub D
    She described him ... Unpub D

p. 227   As Frances wrote ... the late Richard Chopping kindly lent me all his letters from FP

p. 231   Decades later ... I am grateful to V.S. Pritchett's biographer, Jeremy Treglown, for drawing this story to my attention

p. 234   Asked why ... RP's dealings with his publishers can be found in the Chatto & Windus archives at the University of Reading

Chapter Fifteen: Facing Fear, 1954–1960 (pp. 237–256)

p. 240   RP contributed to BBC Radio's *Portrait of Virginia Woolf,* presented by Derek Parker in 1956

p. 244   In a long letter ... Joanna Carrington's letters were kindly lent to me by her husband, Christopher Mason

p. 246   Already, Frances felt ... FP's reservations about La Consula and the social round in Spain are recorded in Unpub D

p. 248   In the novel ... *A Responsible Man* by Cynthia Kee (Chatto & Windus, 1993),

p. 249   Long afterwards ... interview with AC, April 2004

p. 252   But the event ... Unpub D
    His liberated vitality ... Unpub D

p. 253   Is this fag end ... Unpub D
    She was upstairs ... Unpub D

p. 255   They had already invited ... Unpub D
    On it thundered ... Unpub D

Chapter Sixteen: Return to London: 1961–1963 (pp. 257–275)

Unless otherwise noted, quotations from FP in this chapter are taken from HO.

p. 258　Starting with letters ... JGH

p. 259　He told Frances ... Unpub D

p. 263　Looking back ... JP to AC

　　　　Burgo was staying ... Unpub D

p. 269　As Henrietta ... Henrietta Garnett to AC, July 2003

　　　　I am very happy ... DG to FP, KCA

p. 271　Angelica admitted ... Angelica Garnett to FP, KCA

p. 274　The birth of a child ... Unpub D

　　　　About four weeks later ... FP and Henrietta Garnett to AC, July 2001

Chapter Seventeen: Towards Recovery, 1964–1970 (pp. 276–297)

Unless otherwise noted, quotations from FP in this chapter are taken from OP and GC.

p. 276　Anthony Blond ... interview and correspondence with AC, October 2002

p. 277　But not even Frances ... my account of the misunderstanding between FP and JP is based on Unpub D and conversations with JP and the late Anne Hill

p. 278　Later Frances wept ... Unpub D

p. 284　I must fight ... FP's anxiety over Sophie is recorded in Unpub D and in letters to JP and GB

p. 288　As Judy could not face ... FP's feelings about her sister Judy and JP's operation are recorded in Unpub D

p. 289　As for love affairs ... FP recorded her exchange with DG and her reaction to Adrian Daintrey's advances in Unpub D

p. 290　It had always been ... Michael Holroyd's approach to his sources, including FP, is described fully in the introduction to MH. His correspondence with FP and GB is in the BL.

p. 292　She wished, afterwards ... DG quoted from his dying wife's letters in *Familiar Faces* (Chatto & Windus, 1962), pp. 216–17

　　　　As I rather gathered ... a copy of FP's letter to Duncan Grant is in the Michael Holroyd archive in the BL

p. 294   Frances was invited ... Unpub D

p. 295   He did not tell her ... GB's letter to MH is in the BL

That summer, Frances ... FP's dealings with Hamill and Barker are recorded in their papers held by Northwestern University, Chicago. I am grateful to Susan Fox for tracking them down.

One of her fiercest ... FP's correspondence with MH and the BBC is in the BL

Chapter Eighteen: Bloomsbury Revisited, 1970–1978 (pp. 298–319)

Unless otherwise noted, all quotations are taken from LR and UD. After 1975, all quotations from FP's diaries are taken from Unpub D, KCA.

p. 298   As Angelica Garnett ... Angelica Garnett to AC, July 2001

p. 302   The Cecil children ... Laura Cecil to AC, May 2008

Stanley Olson ... Olson's background and nature are described by Phyllis Hatfield in *Pencil Me In* (André Deutsch, 1994), who also kindly lent me FP's letters to him

p. 306   Sophie remembers ... Sophie Partridge to AC, 2008

p. 309   To Dadie ... FP's letters to George Rylands are in KCA

p. 315   *Bloomsbury* ran ... John Bowden, *Daily Telegraph* review, 11 July 1975

p. 317   Although Virginia's portrait ... FP's dealings with Anne Olivier Bell over Virginia Woolf's diaries are recorded in Unpub D, and in their correspondence, kindly lent to me by Olivier Bell

Chapter Nineteen: Travelling and Writing, 1978–1990 (pp. 320–343)

All quotations in this chapter and the next are from Unpub D unless otherwise noted.

p. 320   In the last week of March ... Henrietta's plight is described in *Pencil Me In*, op. cit., and in letters to JP

p. 329   What a way ... *Pencil Me In*, op. cit. p. 191

p. 338   Like all Bloomsberries ... James Lees-Milne, *The Milk of Paradise* (John Murray, 2005), entry for 10 October 1996

Another writer and diary keeper ... Anthony Powell reviewed HO for *The Sunday Telegraph* in August 1990

It was not long ... interviews with AC

Chapter Twenty: So Old and Still Alive, 1990–2000 (pp. 344–363)

p. 349   She also charmed . . . Glenys Kinnock and Fiona Millar's interview with FP was published in *By Faith and Daring, Interviews with Remarkable Women* (Virago Press, 1993)

p. 350   Naim Attallah's interview appears in *Asking Questions* (Quartet Books, 1996)

Index

Adès, Thomas: *Powder Her Face* (opera), 354
Aldbourne, Wiltshire, 193, 211
Aldeburgh, Suffolk, 270, 300
Alderney, 300
Alice (Ham Spray servant), 195, 197
Allen, Jay, 168
Amory, Mark, 340, 344
Anderson, Elizabeth Garrett, 7
Animal Crackers (film), 134
Annan, Noel, Baron, 317, 325
Anne, Princess Royal, 366
Anrep, Boris, 163, 188, 191, 195, 207, 236, 262–3, 270, 316; death, 297
Anrep, Helen, 163, 173, 188
Apostles (Cambridge group), 35
Arran, Arthur Kattendyke Archibald Gore, 8th Earl of, 290
Asquith family, 5
Asquith, Margot, Countess, 57, 158
Asturias, Miguel: *The President*, 273
atom bomb: dropped on Japan, 210–11
Attallah, Naim, 350
Attenborough, (Sir) David, 297
Austria: Hitler annexes, 172–3; FP visits with Janetta, 264–5
Ayer, (Sir) A.J. (Freddie), 229, 251, 333

Bacon, Francis, 234
Badley, John Haden, 24–6; *Bedales: A Pioneer School*, 89
Badley, Mrs John Haden, 24–5
Bagenal, Barbara, 204, 251, 260–1, 265, 274, 295, 308, 358
Banting, John, 126, 262
Barbican, London, 355
Barcelona: Great Exhibition (1929), 128
Bayley, John, 281, 345, 354
Beaton, Cecil, 254
Bedales (school), Steep, Hampshire, 19, 24–8, 89, 341
Bedford Square, London, 8, 10–13, 314
Bedford, Sybille, 313, 319, 327, 330
Békássy, Eva, 25
Békássy, Ferenc, 25
Bell, Clive: Bunny Garnett meets, 39; view of Ralph, 78, 88; in Gordon Square, 107; on FP's living with Ralph, 113; entertains, 117, 134; at Charleston, 119; argument with FP, 120; in Spain, 128; eye trouble, 134; and Carrington's future afer Lytton's death,

140–1; FP's correspondence with, 141–2; and Carrington's suicide, 146; on FP's responsibility for Carrington's death, 158–9; friendship with FP, 162; pacifism, 170, 182; and Julian's death, 171; and Munich Agreement, 175; visits Ham Spray, 182, 193; prepared to concede peace during war, 186; on wartime London, 191; and Bunny Garnett's marriage to Angelica, 195–6; testifies for Ralph's appeal as conscientious objector, 200; in Menton with Barbara Bagenal, 260–1; illness (cancer) and death, 270–1, 283
Bell, Major Cory, 188
Bell, Julian (Vanessa's son): at Charleston, 39, 119; relations with Lettice Ramsey, 152; in Spanish Civil War, 169; killed in Spain, 171
Bell, Olivier (*née* Popham), 221, 233, 317, 349, 360
Bell, Quentin (Vanessa's son): at Charleston, 39, 119; marriage to Olivier Popham, 233; contributes to radio programme on Virginia Woolf, 240; friendship with Burgo at Oxford, 242; FP visits, 317; membership of Cranium Club, 333; death and memorial service, 359
Bell, Vanessa (*née* Stephen): Bunny Garnett meets, 39; and homosexual men, 56; and Virginia Woolf's kissing Ralph, 72; dislikes Ralph, 76, 150, 152; in Gordon Square, 106–7; at Charleston, 119–20; FP's relations with, 126; and Carrington's future after Lytton's death, 140; holiday in France, 147, 149; and Julian's death, 171; wartime exhibition at Leicester Galleries, 193; and Angelica's marriage to Bunny Garnett, 183–4, 195–6; and Memoir Club, 220, 251; indifference to attacks on Bloomsbury, 240; visits Ham Spray, 242; death, 266
Bennett, Arnold, 115–16
Bennett, Jill, 305, 313
Bentham, Jeremy, 34
Bergen, George, 294
Berlin, Sir Isaiah, 333, 354
Bingham, Henrietta, 90–1
Birrell, Augustine, 41–2
Birrell, Francis (Frankie), 36, 39, 41–2, 46, 80, 97, 110, 113, 116–17, 158, 161
Birrell and Garnett's bookshop, London, 37–8, 41–3, 77, 113, 117
Bishop, Adrian, 47
Blackett, Patrick, 32
Bliss, Arthur, 20
Bliss, Howard and Kennard, 20
Blond, Anthony, 247, 250, 252, 255, 276

Bloomsbury Gallery, London, 350, 357
Bloomsbury Group: Bunny Garnett and, 38–9; FP's
    acquaintance with, 43; sexual activities, 56, 126;
    turns against Ralph, 76, 78; FP describes, 79–80,
    126; and Freud, 108; and rise of fascism, 169;
    decline, 190, 249; and Memoir Club, 220, 240; and
    homosexuality, 238; public interest in, 240–1;
    Ralph's view of, 240; in Holroyd's biography of
    Lytton, 293–5; revival of interest in, 295–6, 298,
    301, 313, 320; Olson turns hostile to, 323–4;
    criticised during Tate Britain exhibition, 364–5
Blythe, Ronald, 362
Boer War (1899–1902), 9
Bonham Carter, Lady Violet (née Asquith), 241
Borges, Jorge Luis, 306
Boult, Sir Adrian, 273
Bowen, Elizabeth, 168
Brackenhurst (school), Hindhead, 14
Bradshaw, Tony, 257, 350
Brenan, Gamel (née Woolsey): Gerald meets, 133;
    letters to Ralph, 149; marriage to Gerald, 159–60;
    life in Spain, 166, 267; leaves Spain, 169; in Spanish
    Civil War, 169; and war threat, 133; and outbreak
    of war, 180; FP maintains friendship in war, 194;
    and Gerald's affairs, 289; drinking, 293; decline
    and death, 294
Brenan, Gerald: settles in Spain, 44, 68; character,
    50–1; friendship and correspondence with Ralph,
    50–1, 151, 153, 165, 168, 238, 258; in Great War, 50–2,
    76; infatuated by Carrington, 60, 90; letters from
    Carrington, 64–5, 74; Carrington's growing
    interest in, 68; affair with Carrington, 74, 92, 308;
    and Carrington's marriage to Ralph, 74–5; in
    Virginia Woolf's Mrs Dalloway, 76; Woolfs visit
    in Spain, 76; Ralph and Carrington visit in Spain,
    81–3; and Carrington in Paris with Ralph and FP,
    84–6; on Ralph's Spanish trip with FP, 96; sees FP
    and Ralph in south of France, 110; and Clive Bell's
    infatuation with FP, 113; correspondence with FP,
    125, 258; FP and Ralph visit in Yegen, 125, 127;
    sexual experiences and affairs, 132, 248, 251, 289,
    293; visits to England, 132–3; marries Gamel
    Woolsey, 133, 159–60; and Carrington's suicidal
    dangers, 138; and Carrington's grief at Lytton's
    death, 140; and Carrington's suicide, 146, 149;
    Ralph invites to Ham Spray, 151; child by Juliana,
    159; holiday in Portugal, 160; moves to new house
    in Churriana, 163, 165; and political situation in
    Spain, 165–6, 168; leaves Spain, 169; in Spanish
    Civil War, 169; writes for Manchester Guardian,
    169; arguments with Ralph over war, 172–5, 193–4;
    on Hitler threat, 172–3; returns to Ham Spray, 179;
    and outbreak of Second World War, 180; in Home
    Guard, 182; attacks pacifists, 185; suspected in war,
    188; and Ralph's successful appeal as conscientious
    objector, 203; reconciliation with Ralph, 211;
    botanical interests, 219–20; confesses love for
    daughter Miranda, 222; returns to Spain (1953),
    234; maintains interest in sex, 239; autobiography,
    240, 267, 270, 293, 306, 310, 314; visits FP and
    party at San Fiz, 241; and FP's trip to Spain (1956),
    243–4; disagreement with Ralph in Spain, 245–7;
    and Joanna Carrington, 245, 247–8; meets FP and
    Ralph in Spain, 253; FP writes to about Ralph's

heart attack and death, 256, 258; FP gives
    Carrington's portrait, 264; FP visits in Spain
    during widowhood, 267, 286, 295, 300; shows
    Carringtons letters to FP, 268; told of Burgo's
    engagement to Henrietta, 271; and Holroyd
    biography of Lytton, 274, 293–5; letters from FP
    on Burgo's death, 278; and Henrietta's move to
    Spain, 282; FP reports on visit to Russia, 287; affair
    with Lynda, 293–5, 300; relations with Gamel, 293;
    and Gamel's death, 294; disparaging account of
    Ralph in autobiography, 302, 307–9, 314;
    correspondence with Olson, 304–5; reviews
    Carrington letters, 306; FP criticises for account
    of Ralph, 307–8; mixed relations with FP and
    Ralph, 307; FP meets in Spain after disagreement,
    312; refuses to read A Pacifist's War, 326; resumes
    relations with FP in old age, 330, 336; stays in
    nursing home in Pinner, 336; Gathorne-Hardy
    biography of, 341; portrayed in Carrington film,
    351, 353; A Life of One's Own, 270; South from
    Granada, 246; The Spanish Labyrinth, 170; The
    Story of Poor Robinson, 293
Brighton, 123, 158
British Broadcasting Corporation (BBC): proposed
    Ken Russell film of Lytton, 296–7
Britten, Benjamin: Peter Grimes, 209; A Midsummer
    Night's Dream, 354
Broadmoor, Berkshire, 224–5, 229–30, 234–5, 307, 345
Brooke, Rupert, 61, 108
Brown, Sally, 341
Brunswick Square, London, 40, 44, 91, 97, 136
Buena Vista (house, Spain), 244–5, 250, 253
Buller, Tremayne, 9
Burt, Cyril, 37
Bussy, Janie (née Strachey), 133, 160–1, 210, 254, 259
Bussy, Simon, 160, 259
Butts, Mary, 124

Cambridge Atlas of British Flora, 254
Cambridge University: FP attends (Newnham),
    28–36, 361
Campbell, Mary see Dunn, Mary
Campbell, Robin: marriage with Mary, 216, 226–7,
    243, 247; marriage collapses, 249; marries Susan,
    251; stays in Austria, 265; helps Julia Strachey in
    decline, 298; friendship with FP, 299, 330; reads
    FP's A Pacifist's War, 325; death, 339
Campbell, Roy: The Wayzgoose, 116
Campbell, Susan (née Benson; Robin's second wife),
    251, 265, 298, 325, 330
Canary Islands, 338
Cape, Jonathan (publisher), 312, 314
Carlisle, Rosalind, Countess of, 29
Carrington, Catherine, 180, 257, 360
Carrington, Dora: and Mark Gertler, 39, 55–7;
    marriage to Ralph, 43–4, 46, 48, 53, 54, 73–4, 102;
    relations with Lytton, 54–7, 62, 67, 85, 114;
    background and character, 55; meets Ralph, 57–9,
    61; visits Spain with Ralph, 59–60, 68, 81–3;
    correspondence with Lytton, 60, 72–3; Gerald
    Brenan's infatuation with, 60, 90; appearance and
    manner, 61, 77; describes Ralph's body, 62; sexual
    relations with Ralph, 62; letters to Brenan, 64–5,
    72, 74, 86–7, 268; and Ralph's relations with

Lytton, 64–5; growing interest in Brenan, 68; Ralph courts, 68, 71–3; Leonard Woolf on, 71; affair with Brenan, 74–5, 92, 308; moves from Tidmarsh, 79; visits Ralph's mother, 80; letters to FP, 81, 98, 101; in Paris with Ralph and FP, 84–5; affair with Henrietta Bingham, 90–1; moves to Ham Spray, 90, 92; co-writes Christmas play, 93; portrait of FP, 93; Lytton threatens to abandon, 99; and Ralph's living with FP, 99–101, 105; and Ralph's proposed marriage to FP, 99–100; life at Ham Spray, 111–12, 114–15; upset by Ralph's happiness with FP, 111; in FP's diaries, 112; indecisiveness, 114; notebook, 114–15; and Lytton's letter objecting to FP's visiting Ham Spray, 120–2; amateur film-making, 124; relations with Beakus Penrose, 124, 291; travels in Holland, 124; pregnancy by Beakus Penrose and abortion, 128, 134; drinking and moods, 134; and Lytton's illness and death, 135–41; suicidal attempts and dangers, 138–9, 142–4; bequest from Lytton, 140; makes will, 143; suicide, 145, 151, 158, 293; FP blamed for suicide, 158; portrait of Lytton, 191, 350; decorations at Ham Spray, 237; letters at Ham Spray, 237; letter to Ralph asking for promise to live always at Ham Spray, 264; in Holroyd's biography of Lytton, 273–4; letters published, 296, 300–1, 306; on threesome with Lytton and Ralph, 300; exhibitions of paintings, 301, 355; FP defends reputation, 302; portrayed in film, 322, 350–1; Gretchen Gerzina writes on, 341; FP writes *Dictionary of National Biography* entry for, 344
Carrington (film), 350, 353–5
Carrington, Joanna (Noel–Catherine's daughter), 244–5, 247–8, 257
Carrington, Noel, 57–9, 61, 91, 131, 180, 205, 217, 257, 260, 265, 305, 307, 326; death, 342
Casals, Pablo, 19, 45
Casanova, Giacomo Girolamo, 255
Castle Howard, Yorkshire, 29, 57
Cearne, The (house), Edenbridge, Kent, 38
Cecil, Lord David: marriage to Rachel, 153, 348; on Greek cruise, 171; supports Ralph's appeal as conscientious objector, 200; friendship with FP, 207, 263, 300, 302; cares for Burgo at Oxford, 236; death, 339, 342
Cecil, Laura, 302
Cecil, Rachel (*née* MacCarthy; Lady David Cecil), 110, 114, 117–18, 125, 133, 153, 171, 176, 207, 236, 263, 300, 302, 317, 321, 328, 332, 355
Cecil, Robert and Hannah, 342
Chaliapine, Feodor Ivanovich, 45
Chamberlain, Neville, 173, 175, 178, 184
Charleston, Sussex: Bunny Garnett at, 39; FP visits, 119–20, 126, 133, 151–2, 266, 283, 322; FP gives talk at Festival, 353–4
Charry, Lot (France), 304
Chatsworth, Derbyshire, 267
Chatto & Windus (publishers): commission book on Broadmoor from Ralph, 224; publish FP's war diary (*A Pacifist's War*), 318, 324; decline FP's *Hanging On*, 341
Cheltenham Festival: FP speaks at, 350
Chopping, Richard (Dicky), 205–7, 210, 212, 217, 220–4, 227–9, 234, 263, 281, 289–90, 300, 344

Churchill, Randolph, 267
Churchill, (Sir) Winston S.: and war threat, 173; premiership, 185–7, 192; relations with Keynes, 196; loses 1945 election, 210; on homosexuality, 238; Mortimer visits, 251
Churriana, Spain, 163, 165–8
Cochemé, Joan (*née* Souter-Robinson), 276, 279–80, 304, 316, 318, 353
Cockburn, Claud, 234
Coleridge, Gill, 303, 318, 321, 329–31, 337, 341, 342, 347, 351, 353–4, 359, 361
Collins (publishers), 342, 347
Connolly, Cyril, 136, 202, 215–16, 223, 226, 244, 250, 253, 268
Connolly, Jean (*née* Bakewell), 136, 244
Conrad, Joseph, 38
Conrad, Peter, 325, 366
Consula, La (house, Spain), 244, 250–1
Cooper, Duff (*later* 1st Viscount Norwich), 176, 238
Corfu, 304
Coventry: bombed in war, 190
Cranborne, Dorset, 354
Cranborne, Robert Cecil, Viscount (*later* 5th Marquess of Salisbury), 173
Cranium Club, 221, 333, 354
Crichel *see* Long Crichel
Croucher, Elizabeth (Nan), 8, 11–12, 44, 97, 104, 315
Culme-Seymour, Angela, 167, 236
Culme-Seymour, Mark, 167, 305
Cunard, Maud Alice, Lady (Emerald), 57
Cunard, Nancy, 91
CuzCuz, Al (farmhouse, Spain), 333, 340, 346–7, 351, 353, 358, 365
Czechoslovakia, 170, 173–4

D-Day (June 1944), 206
Daily Telegraph: FP writes for, 342
Daintrey, Adrian, 267, 278, 289
d'Aranyi sisters, 19
Dartington Literary Festival, 354
Darwin, Charles, 3, 192
Darwin Museum, Down House, Kent, 361
Davis, Bill and Annie, 244
Dench, Dame Judy, 349
Denmark, 354
Desert Island Discs (radio programme), 350
Devonshire, Andrew Cavendish, 10th Duke of, 267
Diana, Princess of Wales, 360
Dickinson, Goldsworthy Lowes, 62
Dimbleby, Richard, 251
Dix, Ann, 358–9, 361
Dobrée, Valentine, 74, 85
Dorothy (Bennett's mistress), 116–17
Doyle, Sir Arthur Conan, 18
Dublin: FP's mother in, 2
Duckworth, George, 5
Duckworth, Gerald, 5
Dunn, Mary (*earlier* Campbell): marriage with Robin Campbell, 216, 226–7, 243–4, 247; marriage collapses, 249; affair with Derek Jackson, 262; revisits Ham Spray with FP, 268; remarries Dunn, 269, 337; FP's attachment to, 270; marries American, 289; travels to Majorca with FP, 306; and FP's pacifist views, 321; celebrates FP's 80th

Dunn, Mary—*contd*
  birthday, 329; FP spends Christmas with, 337; in
  road accident with FP, 347; death, 349
Dunn, Nell, 216, 228–9, 338–9
Dunn, Philip, 216, 269–70, 339
Dunn, Serena (*later* Rothschild), 216, 242, 338
Dunyusha (Lionel Penrose's Polish girlfriend), 300
Dupré, Catherine, 302, 305

Eccles, David, Viscount, 301
Eden, Anthony, 173
Edgar, Louis, 20
Edinburgh, 235
Edward, Prince of Wales (*later* King Edward VII),
  9
Edward, Prince of Wales (*later* King Edward VIII),
  32
Egypt: FP visits with Parladés, 329
Elizabeth the Queen Mother, 362
Elizabeth (FP's housekeeper), 365, 368–9
Elwes, Major and Mrs: buy Ham Spray, 263
Emin, Tracey, 365
Eton College, 80

fascism: in Spain, 165, 169
Fawcett, Millicent, 7, 25
Fermor, Joan Leigh, 330, 342, 361
Fermor, Patrick Leigh, 330, 342, 361
Fielding, Agnes (*née* Magruder; *then* Phillips;
  'Magouche'), 263, 297, 299, 301, 303–4, 311, 336,
  352, 354, 356, 359–60
Fielding, Alexander (Xan), 336
Fitzroy Street, London, 46
Forbes-Robertson, Sir Johnston, 5, 8
Ford Place, 16, 27
Forster, E.M.: supports Birrell and Garnett bookshop,
  42; at Tidmarsh, 78; in Brunswick Square, 91; at
  Tilton, 119; visits Ham Spray, 153; reads paper at
  Memoir Club, 220; meets FP and family at
  Lascaux, 234; on homosexuality, 238; indifference
  to attacks on Bloomsbury, 240; on need for
  kindness, 280; Carrington portrait of, 364; *A
  Passage to India*, 91
Fox, Susan, 357–8, 361, 369
France: FP and Ralph visit, 110, 135, 147, 149–50,
  171–2, 179; defeat (1940), 186; FP visits after
  Ralph's death, 257–60, 345
Franco, General Francisco, 169, 172, 234
Freud, Kitty, 234
Freud, Lucien, 234
Freud Museum, Hampstead, 359
Freud, Sigmund: in London, 108; Stracheys translate,
  108; published by Hogarth Press, 109; FP prepares
  index of works, 142, 230, 234, 238, 245, 251–3, 285;
  The Interpretation of Dreams, 109, 254
Fry, Roger: sends children to Bedales, 24; gives
  furniture to Birrell & Garnett shop, 42; lectures,
  46; and Ralph's exhibitionism, 88; conversation
  with FP, 113; at Clive Bell's, 117; at Charleston, 119;
  argument with FP, 120; and Carrington's future
  after Lytton's death, 140
Fry, Tony and Sabrina, 325, 331, 335, 349, 354, 358,
  360–1, 365
Fulford, Roger, 159

Galsworthy, John, 38
Garden Illustrated (magazine), 356
Gargoyle Club, London, 124, 233
Garnett, Amaryllis (Bunny–Angelica's daughter):
  birth, 196; visits Ham Spray, 243; death, 310
Garnett, Angelica (*née* Bell): birth and parentage, 39,
  127; admires FP, 127; holiday in France, 147;
  Bunny Garnett courts, 179, 181, 183–4; visits Ham
  Spray with Clive, 193; marriage to Bunny, 195–6;
  children, 196, 204, 209; leaves London in war,
  204–5; in Memoir Club, 221; and Henrietta's
  marriage to Burgo, 271; and Henrietta's situation,
  284; leaves Bunny, 289, 294; and Holroyd's
  biography of Lytton, 292; relations with George
  Bergen, 294; on FP's 'healthy mind', 298; enjoys
  Peter Luke's *Bloomsbury* play, 315; regrets marriage
  to Bunny, 322; visits Charleston with FP, 322;
  writes memoirs, 333; anger at Bunny, 337; *Deceived
  with Kindness.*, 336
Garnett, Constance, 38–9
Garnett, David ('Bunny'): marriage to Ray, 36, 40–1;
  runs bookshop, 38; upbringing, 38–9; promiscuity,
  41, 108; view of Ralph, 78; protective of FP, 80;
  relstions with FP, 87; moves to Hilton, 91, 123;
  and FP's Spanish trip with Ralph, 97; FP visits,
  105; at Nonesuch Press, 117–18; amateur film-
  making, 124; writes on Pocahontas, 143; visit to
  Biddesden with FP, 144; and Carrington's suicide,
  145; as witness at FP–Ralph wedding, 154; and
  Barbara Ker-Seymer, 156; Clive Bell teases, 162;
  and war threat, 173; pursues Angelica Bell, 179, 181,
  183–4; wartime work, 181; and Ray's terminal
  cancer, 182–3; marriage to Angelica, 195–6, 322,
  337; warns of possible secret German attack on
  London, 204–5; autobiography, 240; and Suez
  crisis, 243; FP gives paintings to, 264; seventieth
  birthday, 268; and Henrietta's attachment and
  marriage to Burgo, 269, 271; and Henrietta at
  Burgo's death, 276–7; attitude to Henrietta's
  situation, 284; Angelica leaves, 289, 294; opposes
  Holroyd's biography of Lytton, 292; opposes BBC
  film of Lytton, 297; romance with Magouche, 297,
  301, 352; edits Carrington's letters, 300–1; house in
  France, 304; account of Ralph, 312; death, 331;
  praises FP's *Memories*, 331; Angelica's anger at, 337;
  Aspects of Love, 241; *Lady into Fox*, 42, 46, 82–3
Garnett, Edward, 38, 42
Garnett, Henrietta: birth, 209; falls for Burgo, 242,
  268–70; visits Ham Spray, 243; beauty, 265;
  marriage to Burgo, 271–2; pregnancy and birth of
  daughter, 274; and Burgo's death, 275–8; FP cares
  for, 278–9, 282, 283; finances, 282; moves to Spain,
  282–3; experiments with drugs, 284; lifestyle,
  284–5; fondness for Olson, 303, 318; and sister
  Amaryllis's death, 310; in Canada with Michel,
  314; loses weight, 318; visits Paris with FP, 318;
  injured in suicide attempt, 320; troubled state,
  322; Olson suggests marriage to, 324; gives party
  for FP's *A Pacifist's War*, 325; anger with mother
  over biography, 337; reluctance to appear in FP's
  published diary, 339, 345; at FP's 90th birthday
  party, 344; relations with daughter Sophie, 348;
  writes to FP on published diaries, 350, 352; in

France with Mark, 352; relations with FP in old age, 360, 365

Garnett, Jane (Richard's wife), 284, 366

Garnett, Nerissa (Henrietta's sister), 282–3

Garnett, Rachel (*née* Marshall; FP's sister; Ray): birth, 8; relations with FP, 18, 26; marriage, 36, 38, 40–1; finances, 40; Duncan Grant portrait, 41; pregnancy and stillborn child, 41; illustrates Bunny's book, 42; supposed virginity, 88; children, 91, 118; moves to Hilton, 91, 123; and FP's Spanish trip with Ralph, 97; and FP's decision to live with Ralph, 103; FP visits, 105; lump on breast, 141; visits FP after childbirth, 163; cancer returns, 179, 181–3; death, 183, 292

Garnett, Richard (FP's nephew), 118, 269, 284, 366

Garnett, William (FP's nephew), 118, 195, 239, 269

Garsington, Oxfordshire, 55, 61, 352, 354

Gathorne-Hardy, Edward, 124

Gathorne-Hardy, Jonathan, 241, 268, 295, 330; biography of Brenan, 341

Gelpke, Jessica (Sophie's daughter), 340

Gelpke, Julia Frances (Sophie's daughter), 338

Gelpke, Wenzel (Sophie's husband), 328, 332, 348

General Election (1945), 210

General Strike (1926), 105

Germany: as war threat, 173–6; advance in west (1940), 184–6; secret weapons against Britain, 204–6; atrocities revealed, 208, 211

Gertler, Mark: and Dora Carrington, 39, 55–7, 353; view of Ralph, 78

Gerzina, Gretchen, 341

Gibbings, Miss (schoolteacher), 14

Gielgud, Sir John, 349

Glendinning, Victoria, 325

Glover, Dr Edward, 218, 227–8, 241

Glyndebourne, 354

Gollancz, Livia, 330

Gollancz, Victor (publisher), 273, 332, 337

Gordon Square, London, 2, 104–8, 128

Gowing, Jenny (Lawrence's wife), 279, 281, 298

Gowing, Julia *see* Strachey, Julia

Gowing, Lawrence: Julia Strachey's relations with, 181, 216–17; wartime activities, 197; amd Ralph's appeal against rejection as conscientious objector, 200; and Oliver Strachey's illness, 201; on Bunny Garnett's hunch about German secret weapon, 205; marriage to Julia, 233; FP accompanies to France following Ralph's death, 257, 259; favours FP leaving Ham Spray, 260; infidelity, 270, 272, 279, 281; divorce from Julia and marriage to Jenny, 281; helps Julia in decline, 298; appointed head of Slade, 317; and Julia's papers, 329; at FP's 90th birthday party, 344; death, 347

Grant, Duncan: daughter (Angelica) by Vanessa Bell, 19, 195; paintings, 36; Bunny Garnett meets, 39; anger at Bunny's marriage, 41; in Fitzroy Street, 46; relations with Lytton, 54; in Gordon Square, 107; imitates Caruso, 114; at Charleston, 119; FP admires, 120, 126; and Carrington's future after Lytton's death, 140; holiday in France, 147, 149; opposes Bunny's marriage to Angelica, 183; studio demolished in war, 190; in Memoir Club, 220; indifference to attacks on Bloomsbury, 240; visits Ham Spray, 242; FP discusses paintings with Ayer,

251; magnetism, 269; FP visits with Henrietta and Sophie, 283; and Holroyd's biography of Lytton, 292; and Paul Roche, 301, 322; Angelica's resentment towards, 337; death, 337; FP owns paintings, 350; works exhibited at Tate Britain, 364

Great Hermaphrodite Party, 131

Great James Street, London, 128–9

Great War (1914–18): outbreak, 19, 21–2; Marshall family activities in, 23; Ralph serves in, 49–52

Greece: FP visits, 342

Greville, Charles: diaries, 118, 120, 130, 159, 257, 307

Gruner, Miss (schoolteacher), 14

Guernica: bombed, 171

Guinness, Bryan (*later* 2nd Baron Moyne), 134, 137, 140, 160, 287

Guinness, Desmond and Mariga, 286

Gulf War (first, 1991), 346

Ham Spray House, near Hungerford: Ralph acquires share in, 79, 81, 84–5; Ralph moves to, 90; Lytton and Carrington in, 98; Ralph continues in with Lytton and Carrington, 102–3; FP visits, 111; life at, 111–12, 114, 120, 135, 153; Lytton objects to FP visiting, 120–1; film-making at, 125; Lytton's illness at, 135–6; Ralph owns after Lytton's death, 140; Ralph and FP occupy, 150, 153; swimming pool, 151, 153, 168; nursery, 164–5; wartime refugees at, 181, 187–8; life in wartime, 182, 187–8, 194–5, 197–8, 202, 204; character, 237; Cynthia Kee depicts in novel, 248–9; FP sells, 260, 262–5; disposal of contents, 264; FP revisits, 268, 348

Hamill and Barker, Misses (Chicago manuscript dealers), 296, 298

Hampshire, (Sir) Stuart, 306, 333

Hampton, Christopher, 312, 322–3, 336, 350–1, 353

Harrison, Jane, 20, 30

Harrod, Sir Roy, 295

Healey, Denis, Baron, 349

Heath, (Sir) Edward, 301

Heath (philosophy teacher), 26–7

Henderson, Mary (Lady), 282, 299, 313, 318, 340, 348

Henderson, (Sir) Nicholas (Nicko), 204, 209, 225, 282, 299, 313, 318, 332, 340, 344, 348, 359, 361, 365–6

Hetty (Brenan's lover), 248, 251, 267

Hill, Anne, 176, 179, 239, 262, 277–8, 286, 307, 344–5, 348

Hill, Heywood, 176, 179, 262, 277–8, 286, 307, 316, 348; death, 339

Hill, Mrs (Ham Spray neighbour), 201, 203

Hilton, Cambridgeshire, 91, 123–4, 182, 265, 268, 361, 366

Hindhead, Surrey, 5–7, 13, 18

Hiroshima, 210–11

Hitler, Adolf: as war threat, 171–4, 178; advance in west, 184; peace offers, 187; invades Russia, 193; death, 208; persecution of Jews, 208

Hobson, Anthony, 364

Hogarth Press: Leonard and Virginia Woolf run, 42–3; publications sold at Birrell and Garnett, 42; Ralph works at, 69, 70–1, 73; Ralph leaves, 75; publishes Freud, 109, 230

Holroyd, Michael: biography of Lytton, 64, 273, 278, 290–5; letters from Brenan, 295; and proposed

Holroyd, Michael—*contd*
  BBC television film of Lytton, 296–7; instigates
    Strachey Trust, 298; on Ralph, 302, 312; friendship
    with Olson, 303; friendship with FP, 305; and
    proposed film on Lytton, 311–12, 322–3; and Peter
    Luke play on Lytton, 315; membership of Cranium
    Club, 333; revised edition of Lytton biography, 350,
    352
homosexuality: Lytton's, 54, 56, 290; FP's views on,
    125–6, 221–3, 238; Mortimer on, 221; Churchill
    on, 238; legally permitted, 289–90
Hopwood, Dr Stanley, 224–5, 230, 235
Horizon (magazine), 215–16
Horsley, Pamela, 49
Horsley, Sir Victor, 49
Howard, Brian, 126
Hubback, Judy, 201, 204
Hudson, Dr Trevor, 359, 367
Humphries, Barry, 349
Hutchinson, Mary, 68, 116, 137
Huth, Miss (Ham Spray neighbour), 177
Huxley, Maria, 158

India: FP visits with Parladés, 322–3
Ireland, 234, 242
Italy: FP visits, 90–2, 239, 276, 279–80, 297, 304, 340

Jackson, Derek, 226–7, 233, 235–6, 262, 265, 269–70,
    334
Jackson, Rose (Janetta's daughter), 236, 250, 253, 270,
    325, 328, 334, 360
James, Henry, 42, 259
Jarvis, Caroline, 241
Jarvis, Ralph, 239, 311
Jebb, Julian, 264–5, 268, 276, 278, 289, 294–5, 303,
    315, 325; suicide, 337
Jenkins, Charlotte (*née* Strachey; *then* Blond), 228,
    250, 275, 300
Jenkins, Peter, 274
Jenkins, Roy, Baron, 290, 366
Jenkins, Sir Simon, 366
Jenny (Ralph's Austrian mistress), 171, 176, 178
Joan (Ham Spray help), 193
John, Augustus, 9, 144
John, Dorelia, 140, 143–4
John, Poppet (Mrs Derek Jackson), 226
Johnson, Fanny, 35
Johnson, W.E. ('Willy'), 34–5
Joyce, William ('Lord Haw-Haw'), 210
Judah, Cynthia *see* Kee, Cynthia
Juliana (Gerald Brenan's servant and mistress), 127,
    132, 159, 166

Kavanagh, Sally (*née* Lehmann), 250
Kee, Catherine (*née* Trevelyan; Robert's third wife),
    363
Kee, Cynthia (*née* Judah), 248–9, 253, 267, 289, 299,
    325, 338, 349
Kee, Georgina (Robert and Janetta's daughter): birth,
    215; misses mother, 250; stability, 270
Kee, Robert: meets Janetta, 209–10, 212–15; marriage
    and child with Janetta, 215; visits Ham Spray, 225;
    marriage to Janetta ends, 226–7, 247; attends
    Straffen case, 230; and Oonagh Oranmore, 233–4;

sent to Israel to report on Suez crisis, 243; in Spain,
    244; relations and marriage with Cynthia Judah,
    248–9, 253, 289, 294, 301; shows TV to FP, 251–2;
    entertains FP, 267, 331; and Burgo's death, 276;
    and FP's objections to proposed BBC film of
    Lytton, 297; helps Julia Strachey in decline, 298;
    lunches with FP, 299; meets Olson, 304;
    preoccupation with death, 304; wishes to write on
    Ralph, 304; visits Hendersons in Germany, 313;
    supports FP over Peter Luke play, 315; encourages
    FP's publishing diaries, 321, 334, 359; and FPs *A
    Pacifist's War*, 325–6; celebrates FP's 80th birthday,
    330; and Ralph's death, 338; visits FP in nursing
    home, 342; at FP's 90th birthday party, 344;
    accompanies FP to preview of *Carrington* film,
    353; visits FP in old age, 358; celebrates FP's 100th
    birthday, 363; telephones FP in old age, 365; FP
    discusses 9/11 attack with, 366; on FP's final
    decline, 368–9
Ker-Seymer, Barbara, 154, 156–7
Keynes, Geoffrey, 141
Keynes, John Maynard: influenced by Moore, 33; at
    Cambridge, 35; and Duncan Grant, 39, 54; advises
    Birrell and Garnett, 42; teaches Mackenzie, 47;
    marriage to Lydia Lopokova, 104; owns Gordon
    Square house, 107, 243; entertains, 113–14; at
    Tilton, 119; in World War II, 196; correspondence
    with Lytton, 266; in Holroyd's biography of
    Lytton, 292; Harrod's book on, 295
Keynes, Stephen, 333, 361
Kingsmill, Hugh, 273
Kingston, Alex, 353–4
Kinnock, Glenys, Lady, 349
Kinnock, Neil, Baron, 349
Klug, Aaron, 366
Knollys, Eardley, 204, 223, 267, 288, 300, 311, 313, 316,
    330, 338; death, 347, 358
Koestler, Arthur, 265

Labour government: elected (1945), 210
Lake District, 264
Lambert, John W. (Jack), 301
Lane, Allen, 205, 212, 217, 221
Lansbury, George, 165
Laughton, Charles, 158
Lawley, Sue, 350
Lawrence, D.H., 38
Leathes, Margaret, 26, 28
Lees-Milne, James, 338
Lehmann, Rosamond, 32, 134, 137, 139, 154–6, 160,
    168, 179, 250, 286–7, 297, 327–8; *Dusty Answer*,
    134
Leigh Fermor *see* Fermor
Levy, Paul, 298, 300, 302, 305, 323, 345, 352, 354, 360
Levy, Penny, 345
Little, Brown (publishers), 337
Lloyd, Alice (FP's aunt), 2, 12
Lloyd, Charlie (FP's uncle), 2, 20–2
Lloyd, Dora, 2
Lloyd, Edith (FP's aunt), 2
Lloyd, Fred (FP's uncle), 9
Lloyd, Humphrey, 2
Lloyd, Maurice, 22
Lloyd, Winifred, 22

London: wartime blitz, 187; FP visits in war, 191, 193; attacked by V-1 flying bombs, 206, 276
London Library, 278, 346
London University: awards honorary degree to FP, 365
Long Crichel, Dorset, 223, 252, 254, 288, 321, 354
Lopokova, Lydia (Lady Keynes), 104, 113, 119, 130
Loutit, Kenneth Sinclair, 200–1, 207, 210, 213
Loutit, Nicolette (Janetta's daughter), 206
Lubbock, Lys, 202
Lucas, Peter, 117
Luggala, Ireland, 234
Luke, Peter: writes play on Lytton (*Bloomsbury*), 305, 309, 314–15
Lynda (Brenan's lover), 293–5, 300, 336

Mabel (FP's servant), 110
MacCarthy, (Sir) Desmond: friendship with FP, 110, 114; encourages Connolly, 136; death, 233; published letters, 266–8; reads paper at Memoir Club, 336
MacCarthy, Michael, 118
MacCarthy, Molly, 110, 220, 236
Macfarlane, Craig, 199–200, 202, 250
Machin, David, 314–15
Mackay, Dot, 31–2, 45
Mackenzie, Aileen (*née* Meade; Colin's wife), 191, 235, 264, 346
Mackenzie, Colin: relations with FP, 47, 79–81, 88–94, 96–102, 104, 110, 157, 162, 171, 176, 191, 235; death, 340
Maclean, Donald, 225
McTaggart, John McTaggart Ellis, 34
Magouche *see* Fielding, Agnes
Major, (Sir) John, 346
Margaret, Princess, 359
Mark (Henrietta's partner), 352
Maroussa *see* Volkova, Maroussa
Marple, Lesley, 327
Marshall, Catherine, 22, 69
Marshall, Eleanor (FP's sister): birth, 8; childhood, 10; and FP's disbelief in God, 17; relations with FP, 18; plays cello, 19; at Cambridge, 28; war work, 29; failed musical career, 44–5; holiday in Dolomites, 45; and FP's illness, 123; in Brunswick Square, 136; nurses sick Ray, 182; reports mother's lung cancer to FP, 192; at brother Ton's cremation, 332; death, 343
Marshall, Horace (FP's brother): birth, 5, 8; schooling, 10; relations with FP, 18; career, 20; marriage, 20; in reserved occupation in Great War, 21
Marshall, Jill (FP's niece), 326
Marshall, Margaret Anne (*née* Lloyd; FP's mother; Mam): and FP's birth, 1, 9–10; memoirs of own life, 1–2, 19; marriage, 2–4; social life, 4–5, 8; life in Hindhead, 6–7; children, 8; independence of mind, 8; FP's relations with, 13; local activities in Hindhead, 18; supports votes for women, 18–19; passion for music, 19–20, 44; in Great War, 24; home in Brunswick Square, 40, 44, 91, 97, 136; and Ray's marriage to Bunny Garnett, 40; Labour sympathies, 46; FP's nickname for (Queen of the Forest), 82; and FP's decision to live with Ralph, 103; nurses FP in illness, 123; and FP's dizziness,

176; visits Ham Spray, 179, 181; nurses sick daughter Ray, 182; attitude to war, 185; reaction to Battle of Britain, 186; lung cancer amd death, 192
Marshall, Marjorie (*née* Thomson; *later* Joad), 78, 80, 85, 87, 97
Marshall, Nadine (Tom's second wife), 179, 264, 282, 324, 330, 361
Marshall, Rachel (Horace's wife), 20
Marshall, Thomas (FP's brother): birth, 8; schooling, 10; as mother's favourite, 18; interned in Germany, 20–2, 28, 31; at Cambridge, 31, 44, 46–7, 67; home in Brunswick Square, 44–5; teaches at London School of Economics, 46; singing, 82; and Marjorie Joad, 85, 87; visits Italy with FP, 90, 92; marriage to Marjorie, 97; and FP's decision to live with Ralph, 103; marriage to Nadine, 179; FP stays with in Lake District (Skelwith), 264, 282, 324, 330; praises *A Pacifist's War*, 326; decline and death, 332
Marshall, William Cecil (FP's father): marriage and family, 1–4; career and activities, 3–5, 7, 9; home in Hindhead, 5–7; relations with FP, 11; retirement in Hindhead, 12, 18; ill health, 20, 28; death, 35; supports Society for Psychical Research, 108; builds new wing at Down House for Darwin, 361
Massey, Daniel, 314
Matisse, Henri, 259
Mayor, Bobo, 119–20
Medical Orchestra, 273, 338, 340
Memoir Club, 220, 229, 235, 240, 251, 254, 266, 268
Menton, France, 260–1
Menuhin, Hephzibah, 2273
Mexico, 313
Michel (Henrietta's boyfriend), 310, 314
Mill, John Stuart, 34, 237
Millar, Cynthia, 327, 347
Millar, Fiona, 349
Miller, Denis Wirth, 205–6, 210, 221–2, 234, 263, 281, 289–90, 300
Millfield school, 219, 227
Miranda (Gerald Brenan's daughter), 166, 169, 222
Mitford, Pamela (Mrs Derek Jackson), 226
Miyake, Issey, 342, 344
Montagu of Beaulieu, Edward Douglas-Scott-Montagu, 3rd Baron, 238
Moore, G.E., 33–4, 298; *Principia Ethica*, 33
Moorehead, Caroline, 325–6
Moorsom, Raisley, 33, 45, 301
Morrell, Lady Ottoline, 55, 62, 78, 114, 125
Morris, Hayley, 132–3, 158, 220
Morris, Nancy, 131
Mortimer, Raymond: at Tidmarsh, 78; affair with Nancy Cunard, 91; at Clive Bell's, 117; at Charleston, 119; at Ham Spray, 120; in Spain, 128, 246; and Lytton's illness, 137; friendship with FP, 162, 204; in Kitzbühel, 171; in France with FP and Ralph, 172; and threat of war, 173; on Munich Agreement, 175; visits Ham Spray during war, 186; in wartime London, 191; supports Ralph as conscientious objector, 202; on homosexuality, 221; at Long Crichel, 223, 288; reviewing, 223; operation, 236; visits Churchill at Chartwell, 251; obituary tribute to Ralph, 257; visits FP in Menton, 260; opposes FP's leaving Ham Spray, 261; travels in Italy with FP, 276–7, 280, 304; FP entertains,

Mortimer, Raymond—*contd*
    278; praises Holroyd's biography of Lytton, 293;
    opposes BBC film of Lytton, 297; reviews
    Carrington letters, 301; on portrayal of Ralph in
    Peter Luke play, 315; reviews FP's *A Pacifist's War*,
    325; decline, 327; death, 329; friendship with Lees-
    Milne, 338
Mosley, Diana, Lady (*née* Mitford; *then* Guinness),
    134–5, 137, 140, 188, 205, 286, 326
Mosley, Sir Oswald, 160, 188, 205
Mountbatten, Admiral Louis, 1st Earl ('Dickie'), 32
Mozart, Wolfgang Amadeus: *Requiem*, 253
Muggeridge, Malcolm, 293
Munich Agreement (1938), 173, 175
Murdoch, (Dame) Iris, 281–2, 317, 345, 354;
    Metaphysics as a Guide to Morals, 349
Murray, Gilbert, 29
Myers, Frederic William Henry, 7, 108
Myers, Leo, 108, 113, 132, 136, 157, 161

Nabokov, Vladimir: *Lolita*, 252
Nagasaki, 210–11
Nan *see* Croucher, Elizabeth
Nation, The (journal), 109
National Union of Women's Suffrage Societies, 7
Nettleship, Edward, 5
Nettleship, Ethel, 12
New Statesman (journal): FP contributes to, 89, 161,
    190, 211; obituary tribute to Ralph, 257
New York: FP in, 313; Twin Towers attacked, 366
Newbury: bombed in war, 201
Newbury Orchestra, 238
Newman, Margaret *see* Penrose, Margaret
Nicholls, Mrs (of Dawlish), 52
Nichols, Philip: relations and correspondence with
    FP, 47, 79, 93–7, 99, 101, 103, 110, 115–20, 122–6,
    128–9, 131, 203–4; marriage, 132, 141; visits Ham
    Spray, 179; evacuates children to America in war,
    187; as ambassador to exiled Czech government in
    war, 200; provides testimonial for Ralph's appeal
    as conscientious objector, 200; on Nazi atrocities,
    208; FP disagrees with, 212; in Prague, 212; FP
    visits in Essex, 239, 252, 266; depression, 252; visits
    FP in south of France, 262; illness and death,
    270–1, 285
Nichols, Phyllis (*née* Spender-Clay), 132, 141, 181, 185,
    262, 266
Nichols, Robert, 47, 115
Nicolson, Harold, 175
Nonesuch Press, 117–18, 128
Normandy: D-Day invasion (1944), 206
Norton, Harry, 34
Norton, Jane, 90, 97
Norton, Lucy, 298

Oh! Calcutta! (revue), 301
Oleta (air hostess), 352, 354
Olive (Ham Spray maid), 157, 162
Olivier, Noel, 108
Olson, Stanley: friendship with FP, 302–7, 310–11,
    313, 315, 317–18, 323, 339; suicidal impulses, 318;
    and older women, 319; visits Henrietta in hospital,
    320; view of Holroyd, 322; suggests marriage to
    Henrietta, 324; gives party for FP's *A Pacifist's War*,

325; visits family in USA, 326; encourages FP's
    writing, 327; accompanies FP on trip to Egypt,
    329; suggests FP write on old age, 331; attends
    Sophie's wedding, 332; writes biography of Sargent,
    333, 339; strokes and death, 339–40
Omega Workshop, 42
Oranmore, Oonagh. Lady, 233–4
Ord, Boris, 32, 47
Origo, Iris, 47, 92, 97, 99–100, 103, 157, 162, 163, 301
Orwell, George, 216
Orwell, Sonia (*née* Brownell; *later* Pitt-Rivers), 216,
    234, 252
Osborne, John, 311–12
Owen, Wilfred, 335
Owley (house), Kent, 101, 136–7, 142, 150
Oxford University: Ralph at, 49, 59, 63; Burgo at, 231,
    234, 236, 239, 241

Padel, Mr and Mrs: teach Burgo at home, 191; FP
    gives plums to, 194; and Ralph's appeal as
    conscientious objector, 200, 203; music playing,
    205
Page, Phyllis, 161
Painter, George, 324
Palmer, Mark, 284
Panorama (TV programme), 251
Paris: FP joins Ralph in, 83–6; falls to Germans
    (1940), 186; liberated (1944), 206; FP and Ralph
    visit, 236; FP visits Hendersons in, 318
Parker, Sir Roger, 32
Parladé, Jaime: relations with Janetta, 244, 276, 289,
    299; helps Henrietta in Spain, 282–3; marriage to
    Janetta, 303–4; FP holidays with, 306; holiday in
    USA and Mexico, 313; trip to India with FP,
    322–3; trip to Egypt with FP, 329; in Turkey with
    FP, 340
Parladé, Janetta (*née* Woolley; *then* Slater; *then* Kee;
    then Jackson): Brenan meets, 167–8; at Ham Spray,
    170–1, 176, 181, 187, 242, 263; FP's attachment to,
    170–1, 252, 259, 266, 288, 316, 333; in France, 172;
    and Brenan's expulsion from Ham Spray, 174; on
    skiing trip to St Gervais, 176–7; Ralph's attempted
    seduction and criticism of, 178–9; relations with
    Humphrey Slater, 181, 187–8, 195; and Ralph's view
    of progress of war, 184; in London air raids, 188;
    relations and child with Kenneth Loutit, 200–1,
    204, 207; and Rollo's fate in war, 200, 206; on
    mother's death, 201; in wartime London, 202;
    moves to Ham Spray with baby, 206; Bunny
    Garnett meets in London, 209; meets Robert Kee,
    209–10, 212–15; on FP's frankness in criticism,
    211–12; marriage and child with Robert Kee, 215;
    on Donald Maclean, 225; marriage to Robert
    breaks down, 226–7, 247; relations with Derek
    Jackson, 226–7; on Burgo's quitting school, 228;
    marriage to Derek, 233; Derek leaves for half-sister
    Angela, 236; complicated emotional life, 239, 250;
    peritonitis, 239; and Ralph Jarvis, 239; shares
    rented house in Spain with FP, 241; holiday in
    Pyrenees with FP and Ralph, 242; and Jaime
    Parladé, 244, 276–7, 289; in Spain, 250, 253, 270;
    and Robert Kee's marriage to Cynthia, 253;
    disparages FP's Memoir Club paper on pacifism,
    254; returns from Spain on Ralph's death, 257;

proposes sharing house with FP, 261; FP stays with in London, 262; FP gives paintings to, 264; and FP's sale of Ham Spray, 264; takes FP to Chatsworth, 267; silence at Burgo's death, 276–8; FP visits in Spain, 286, 295, 300, 306, 316, 340, 347, 353–4, 358; in London for operation, 288; visits Russia with FP, 299; friendship with Olson, 303; marriage to Parladé, 303–4; supports FP in criticism of Brenan, 307; persuades Brenan to modify account of Ralph, 309, 315; accompanies FP to Amaryllis Garnett's funeral, 310; holiday in USA and Mexico, 313; supports FP over Peter Luke play, 315; encourages FP's publishing diaries, 316, 318, 320, 326, 334; trip to India with FP, 322–3; trip to Egypt with FP, 329; accompanies FP to USA for publication of *Love in Bloomsbury*, 332; invites FP to live with in later years, 333–4, 338; moves to Al CuzCuz (farmhouse), 333, 340; in FP's diaries, 334; attends Requiem Mass for Julian Jebb, 337; in Turkey with FP, 340; in Greece with FP, 342; gives party for FP's ninetieth birthday, 344; opposes FP's continuing to publish later diaries, 345, 359; seventieth birthday, 347; and FP's decline in old age, 357–8, 360; FP writes to, 360; gives party for FP's 100th birthday, 362; visits FP in London, 365; and FP's final days, 369

Partridge, (Lytton) Burgo (FP–Ralph's son): birth, 163–4; appearance, 164, 189; childhood and upbringing, 164–5, 168, 176, 189, 198; FP's devotion to, 182, 189, 203, 212; at Ham Spray in war, 187; character, 189–91, 206; schooling, 189–91, 207, 212, 215, 217; illness as chid, 190; preoccupation with death, 191, 200, 209, 218–19, 231; and FP's wartime activities, 197; learns to swim, 204; parents disagree over upbringing, 206; measles, 209; friendship with Serena and Nell Dunn, 216; absence at boarding school, 218–19; first trip abroad, 218; treated by psychoanalyst, 218; depressions and emotional disturbance, 219, 225, 227–9; letters to FP, 219; sexual orientation and interest, 221–2, 228–9; runs away from Millfield school, 227–8; applies for and admitted to Oxford, 231, 234; attends Straffen trial, 231; mistakenly arrested for murdering parents, 231; in Pritchett short story, 231–3; attends Oxford University, 236, 238, 241; in Paris with parents, 236; Henrietta Garnett falls for, 242; view of Suez crisis, 243; writes book on orgies, 247, 249–50; brings girlfriend Jane to Ham Spray, 252; visits parents, 255; and father's death, 257–9; relations with parents, 259; in Roquebrune with mother, 259–60; and FP's selling Ham Spray, 262–4; as film critic for *Time and Tide*, 263; FP gives paintings to, 264; in love with Henrietta, 268–70; marriage to Henrietta, 271–2; birth of daughter, 274; death from aortic aneurysm, 275–6, 334, 337, 346–7; in FP's published diaries, 334, 337, 339, 346–7

Partridge, Dorothy (Ralph's sister), 48–50, 52, 59–60, 68, 81

Partridge, Frances Catherine (*née* Marshall): birth, 1, 9; family background, 1; childhood and upbringing, 10–13; scarlet fever, 10; swimming, 11, 168, 187, 328, 340, 360; schooling, 12, 14, 19, 24–8; violin playing, 12, 19, 45, 195–6, 205, 207, 238, 268,

316, 340; appearance, 16, 27, 77, 289; loses belief in God, 16–17; early interest in sex, 17; pacifism, 22, 27, 170, 172–3, 176, 184, 197, 364; in Great War, 23–4; social life at Hindhead, 28; wins place at Cambridge, 28–9; attends Cambridge University (Newnham), 29–36, 73; independence of mind, 29; as land girl in Great War, 29, 57; finances, 31, 212; dancing, 32, 45, 93; degree, 33, 36; reads Moral Sciences, 33–5; employment, 36–7; works at Birrell and Garnett bookshop, 37–8, 41–4; acquaintance with Bloomsbury Group, 43; keeps diary, 44, 111–12, 115, 159, 191, 219, 239, 316, 324, 360, 361; meets Ralph, 44, 69; early admirers and suitors, 45–7, 79–80, 93–4; Ralph courts and corresponds with, 61, 71–3, 77–83, 86, 88–91, 93; on nature of Ralph's relations with Lytton, 65; visits Tidmarsh, 78; experience of Bloomsbury, 79–80; singing, 81–2; with Ralph in Paris, 83–6; virginity discussed, 88; reviews for *New Statesman*, 89, 161, 190; and Ralph's move to Ham Spray, 90; sexual preferences, 90–1; visits to Italy, 90–2, 239–40, 276, 279–80; Carrington portrait, 93; Philip Nichols' interest in, 93–5; Spanish trips with Ralph, 94–6, 125, 127–8, 133, 165–8, 234, 243–7, 250, 253; interview with Lytton over relations with Ralph, 98–9; makes decision to live with Ralph, 98–104; moves into Gordon Square flat, 104–6; socialises with Woolfs, 109–10; entertaining, 110, 131; life at Ham Spray, 111–12; attitude to Lytton, 112; emotionally liberated by Ralph, 112–13; Lytton's relations with, 112, 120–1; leaves Birrell and Garnett, 113, 117; and Phil Nichols' departure for New Zealand, 115–16; correspondence with Phil Nichols, 116–20, 122–6, 128–9, 131; and life with Ralph, 116; practical jokes, 117; helps Lytton edit Greville diaries, 118, 120, 130; Phil Nichols attacks, 118–19; commitment to Ralph, 119, 124, 132; visits Charleston, 119–20, 133, 151–2; illness (1928–9), 122–4; desire for child, 123, 129, 142, 154, 160; skating, 123, 134; amateur film-making, 124–5; on buggery, 125–6; moves to Great James Street, 128–9; and Frank Ramsey's death, 130; and Phil Nichols' marriage and career, 132; and Lytton's illness, 135–8; and Carrington's condition at Lytton's death, 139–44; concern over Ralph's health, 142–3, 237, 255–6; correspondence with Ralph after Lytton's death, 142–4, 151–2; and Carrington's suicide, 145–7, 151, 158–9; visits Flanders and southern France with Ralph, 147–50; occupies Ham Spray, 150; learns to drive, 151; marriage to Ralph, 154–5; pregnancy and miscarriage, 154–5, 160; and Ralph's infidelities, 157, 161, 176; holidays in Portugal, 160, 250–1, 283; marriage relations, 160, 182–3, 226, 245, 250, 254; pregnancy and birth of son, 161–3; short story writing, 161; and son Burgo's upbringing, 164, 168, 206, 218; lacks interest in rise of fascism, 165; meets Woolleys in Spain, 167–8, 170; fondness for Janetta, 170–1, 252, 254, 266, 288, 316, 333; skiing, 171; expels Brenan from Ham Spray for war views, 174–5; giddiness, 176–7, 179; and outbreak of war, 180; accommodates wartime refugees, 181; wartime life at Ham Spray, 181–2; fortieth birthday, 183; and sister Ray's death from cancer, 183; on Bunny's marriage to Angelica, 184; and conduct and

Partridge, Frances Catherine—*contd*
progress of war, 184–9; considers suicide in war, 185–6; and Burgo's reluctance to attend school, 189, 207; wartime visits to London, 191, 193; and mother's death, 192; reliance on domestic help, 193; and Brenan's wartime attack on Ralph, 194; cooking in war, 197; registers for National Service, 197; supports Ralph in appeal against rejection as conscientious objector, 199–202; unsettled by soldiers at Ham Spray, 202; on motherhood, 203–4; writes (aborted) Flora of British Isles for Penguin, 205–6, 210, 212, 217, 219, 221; acquires cat (Tiger), 207; awareness of middle age, 207; and revelation of Nazi atrocities, 208; pessimism at war's end, 211; supports Janetta's liaison with Robert Kee, 212–15; and Burgo's emotional troubles, 218–19, 225, 228–9; first post-war trip to Europe, 218; edits and publishes diaries, 220, 316–18, 326–8, 333–5, 351–2, 359–60, 366–7; views on homosexuality and sexual freedom, 221–3; visits Long Crichel, 223; visits to Broadmoor, 224–5; interest in philosophy, 229–30, 281–2, 300, 306; attends Straffen trial, 230–1; burns work on projected Flora, 230; indexes James Strachey's translation of Freud's works, 230, 234, 238, 242, 245, 251–3, 285; in Pritchett short story, 231–2; visit to Luggala, Ireland, 234; joins Newbury Orchestra, 238; on Montagu homosexual trial, 238; rents house at San Fiz, Spain, 241; reviews children's books for *The Spectator*, 245; opposes nuclear war, 247; portrayed in Cynthia Kee novel, 248–9; dislikes television, 251–2; as Secretary of Memoir Club, 251–2; dream of Carrington and Lytton in death, 254; dream of suicide with Ralph, 255; and Ralph's death, 256–9, 261–2, 266; visit to France after Ralph's death, 257–61; correspondence with Brenan after Ralph's death, 258; sells Ham Spray, 260, 262–5; translations, 260–1, 266, 273, 285, 288, 302, 306, 317; witnesses eclipse of sun, 262; in Austria with Janetta, 265; moves to West Halkin Street, London, 265–6; nightmare of Ralph's death, 265; social life in London, 266–7, 269, 272, 278, 349; visits Spain in widowhood, 267, 270, 282, 293, 295, 320, 340, 358–9; reassesses Carrington on reading letters to Brenan, 268; and Holroyd's biography of Lytton, 273, 291–5; joins Medical Orchestra, 273; and Burgo's death, 275–9, 339; in Italy after Burgo's death, 276–7; difficulties with Julia Strachey, 279–81; concern over Henrietta's lifestyle, 284–5; sense of mortality, 285; travels and travel writing, 286, 306; visits to Russia, 286–7, 299; indifference to love relationships in later years, 289; opposes BBC's proposed film of Lytton, 296–7; sells Lytton–Ralph letters to Hamill and Barker, 296, 298; cares for Julia Strachey in decline, 299; and renewed public interest in Bloomsbury, 301–2, 305; defends Ralph's reputation, 302, 306–7, 312; friendship with Olson, 302–3, 305–6, 313, 318, 323, 339; preoccupation with death, 304, 306; stays with Bunny Garnett in France, 304; and Peter Luke play on Lytton, 305, 309, 315–16; and proposed Osborne film on Lytton, 311–12; visits USA and Mexico with Parladés, 313–14; moves flats in West Halkin Street, 316, 345, 349; serves on committee of Translators' Association, 317; publishes war diaries, 318–21, 323; trip to India, 322–3; disposal of papers, 323, 326, 341; literary success, 323–4, 330–3; interviewed by journalists, 325–6, 331, 350, 361; will, 326; celebrates 80th birthday, 329; in USA for publication of *Love in Bloomsbury*, 332; declines invitation to live with Parladés in later years, 333; suspicion of emotion, 336; portrays friends and acquaintances in published diary, 337; gives up Medical Orchestra, 338, 340; visits Canary Islands with Parladés, 338; compiles and publishes photographs of life and friends, 339–40; suffers migraines and lack of balance, 339; talks to literary groups and festivals, 339, 345, 350; reviews for *The Spectator*, 340, 344, 352; hospitalised after injuring shin, 342; photographed by Snowdon for *The Sunday Times*, 342; writes on Pasque Flower, 342; ninetieth birthday, 344; eyesight deteriorates, 346, 357–8, 361, 365; cracks breastbone in road accident, 347; acquires television, 350; reviews Holroyd's revised *Lytton*, 352; routine in old age, 356; burgled, 357, 359; health decline, 357–8, 362; letters in later life, 360; interviewed on TV, 361; awarded CBE, 362; hundredth birthday, 362–3; male fan steals from, 362; author visits and records, 364–8; in wheelchair, 364; honorary degree from London University, 365–6; breaks hip in fall, 367; death and cremation, 369–70; *Everything to Lose*, 337–9; *Friends in Focus*, 340; *Good Company*, 352; *Hanging On*, 341–2, 344–5, 350; *Julia*, 332–3; *Life Regained*, 360–1; *Memories* (in USA as *Love in Bloomsbury*), 330–2; *Other People*, 349–50; *A Pacifist's War*, 323–4; *Ups and Downs: Diaries 1972–75*, 366

Partridge, Jessie (*née* Sherring; Ralph's mother), 48, 135

Partridge, Jessie (Ralph's sister), 48

Partridge, Ralph: marriage to Carrington, 43–4, 46, 48, 53, 54, 73–5, 97; Frances meets, 44, 69; dancing at Fitzroy Street, 46; courts and corresponds with FP, 47–8, 77–83, 86, 88–91, 93–4; background, 48–9; relations with Lytton, 48, 53–4, 58–9, 61, 63–7, 69, 97, 102–3, 300, 308; military service in Great War, 49–52, 65; friendship with Brenan, 50–1; meets Carrington, 57–8, 61; visits to Tidmarsh Mill, 57, 60–2, 64; emotional/intellectual change, 59, 64; returns to Oxford after war, 59, 63; visits Spain with Carrington, 59–60, 68, 82; sexual relations with Carrington, 62; sexual inclinations, 63–6; character, 67; courts Carrington, 68, 71–3; declines invitation to row for Oxford, 68; works at Hogarth Press, 69–71, 73; pacifism, 71, 170, 174–6, 197, 321; affair with Valentine Dobree, 74; and Carrington's affair with Brenan, 74–5; in Great Row over marriage breakdown, 74, 247, 307–8; leaves Hogarth Press, 75–6; promiscuity and affairs, 75, 77, 80, 85, 133, 157, 160–1, 176, 308, 334; bookbinding, 76, 87; acquires Ham Spray House, 79, 81, 84; singing, 81; FP joins in Paris, 83–6; sexual exhibitionism, 87–8; moves to Ham Spray, 90, 92; on E.M. Forster, 91–2; co-writes Christmas play, 93; jealousy of Philip Nichols, 93; Spanish trips with FP, 94–7, 125, 127–8, 133, 165–8, 234,

243–5, 250, 253; and indecision over life with FP, 98–101; and FP's decision to live with, 104; in south of France with FP, 110; liberates FP, 112–13; and Lytton's letter barring FP from visiting Ham Spray, 120–2; and FP's illness, 123; travels in Holland, 124; and Carrington's pregnancy by Beakus Penrose, 128; dresses as Spanish woman, 131; and Lytton's illness and death, 135–9; and Carrington's suicidal attempt, 138; stays with Carrington after Lytton's death, 141–3; correspondence with FP after Lytton's death, 142–4; revisits Flanders and southern France after Carrington's death, 147–50; occupies Ham Spray with FP, 150, 153; inherits from Carrington, 151; invites Brenan to Ham Spray, 151; Virginia Woolf's view of, 152; reaction to Carrington's death, 153; affair with Barbara Ker-Seymer, 154, 156–7; marriage to FP, 154–5; rages, 158; works on Greville diaries, 159, 307; marriage relations, 160, 182–3, 226, 245, 250, 254; reviews books for *New Statesman*, 161, 257; and FP's pregnancy and birth of son, 162–4; interest in world affairs, 165, 168, 172; meets Woolleys in Spain, 167–8, 170; view of Spanish political situation, 168–9; relations with Janetta Woolley, 170–1, 178–9; skiing holidays, 171, 176–7; arguments with Brenan over war, 172–5; and outbreak of Second World War, 180; unsympathetic to Ray Garnett's cancer, 183; and conduct of war, 184, 186, 188–9; visits family in Devon, 191; Brenan attacks in war, 193–4; on FP's cooking, 197; summoned to conscientious objectors' tribunal amd rejected, 198–9; appeals against rejection as conscientious objector, 199–202; and Burgo's upbringing, 206, 218, 222; and Burgo's resistance to school, 207; reconciliation with Brenan, 211; unfulfilled life, 212; in Cranium Club, 221; and homosexuality, 222; visits and writes on Broadmoor, 223–5, 229–30, 234–5, 307, 345; and Burgo's school difficulties, 228; attends Straffen trial, 231; in Pritchett short story, 231–3; develops diabetes, 235–6; complicated relations with Brenan, 238, 308; suffers kidney stone, 239; visit to Rome, 239; angina and heart trouble, 242–3, 246, 251, 255–6; depicted in Brenan's *South from Granada*, 246; disagreement with Brenan in Spain, 247; portrayed in Cynthia Kee novel, 248–9; jury service, 255; death and cremation, 256–7, 266, 334; relations with Burgo, 259; will, 264; in Holroyd's biography of Lytton, 291, 295, 326; Brenan informs Holroyd of love life, 295; FP sells letters from Lytton, 296; FP defends reputation, 302, 306–7; Olson's interest in, 304–5; in Peter Luke's play on Lytton, 305–6, 309, 315; in Carrington letters, 306; Brenan's portrayal of, 307–9, 312, 314; in FP's published diaries, 321, 334; in film on Lytton, 322; death recorded in FP's published diary, 337–8; portrayed in *Carrington* film, 351, 353–4; relations with family, 369

Partridge, Reginald (Ralph's father), 48, 63, 71
Partridge, Sophie Vanessa (Henrietta–Burgo's daughter): birth, 274; appearance, 277; FP's attachment to, 278, 282–4, 306, 365; in Spain as baby, 282; lives with Richard and Jane Garnett as child, 284; and mother's lifestyle, 284; fondness for

Olson, 303; at Dartington, 318, 328; and mother's injuries from fall, 320; visits Charleston, 322; visits FP in London, 327; falls in love with Wenzel Gelpke, 328, 332; marriage to Wenzel, 332; studies in Italy, 332; attends opera with FP, 335; children, 338, 340; FP sends violin to, 340; at FP's 90th birthday party, 344; FP visits in Italy, 347; lives in Devon, 348, 350, 360; marriage ends, 348; FP visits in Devon, 360–1; accompanies FP to Buckingham Palace for medal award, 362; arranges FP's funeral, 369
Pearl Harbor, 195
Pearsall Smith family, 6, 27, 31
Pearsall Smith, Logan, 16
Pearsall Smith, Louise (Aunty Loo), 16
Penguin Books, 205, 217
Penrose, Alec, 124, 286
Penrose, Bernard ('Beakus'), 124, 128, 134, 142, 286, 291, 353, 355
Penrose, Lionel, 117, 286, 289, 300, 306
Penrose, Margaret (*née* Leathes; *later* Newman), 26, 28, 289, 298–300, 312–13, 315–16, 342
Penrose, Roger, 348
Pétain, Marshal Philippe, 210
Philipps, Wogan, 134, 137, 139, 153, 155–6, 160, 162, 168, 179
Pitt-Rivers, Michael, 238, 252
Pollard, Graham, 105, 116–17
Pollock, Sir Frederick, 6
Ponsonby, Elizabeth, 124
Portugal: FP holidays in, 160, 250–1, 283, 330
Powell, Anthony, 338
Powell, Lady Violet, 338
Praia da Rocha, Portugal, 250–1
Pritchett, Dorothy, 211, 247
Pritchett (Sir) Victor S.: meets FP and Ralph, 211; short story based on Partridge family, 231–3; affair, 247; FP writes obituary, 359
Private Passions (radio programme), 360
Proust, Marcel: FP considers translating, 234; FP rereads, 322; and memory, 324; *A la recherche du temps perdu*, 42
Pryce, Jonathan, 353

Queen's College, Harley Street, 10, 12

Raleigh, Sir Walter Alexander, 5
Ramsey, Frank, 35, 125, 129–30, 229
Ramsey, Lettice (*née* Baker), 35, 125, 129–30, 152
Raven, Simon, 252, 255, 259
Rees, Goronwy, 179
Rendel, Dick, 17, 23–4, 36, 136, 198–200; death, 287
Rendel, Elinor, Lady (*née* Strachey), 14–15
Rendel, Dr Ellie, 136
Rendel, Jill (FP's niece), 23
Rendel, Jim (FP's nephew), 288
Rendel, Julia (*née* Marshall; FP's sister; Judy): birth, 8; marriage and children, 17, 23; relations with FP, 18; home at Owley, Kent, 101, 136; visits FP after childbirth, 163; nurses sick sister Ray, 182; FP cares for after husband's death, 287–8; decline and death, 327
Richards, I.A., 32
Ritchie, Philip, 90–1

Roberts, Ray, 337
Roche, Paul, 301, 322
Rolph, C.H., 235
Rome, 239, 277, 279–80
Romilly, Esmond, 172
Rommel, General Erwin, 198, 216
Roquebrune, France, 257, 259–60
Royal Society of Literature: awards Fellowship to FP, 333; FP attends, 364
Ruskin, John, 3–10
Russell, Alys (née Pearsall Smith), 6
Russell, Bertrand: meets Pearsall Smiths, 6; Catherine Marshall works with in peace campaign, 22; in Churriana, 167; and Spanish Civil War, 169; FP studies, 251, 306; FP reads biography of, 357; *The Problems of Philosophy*, 27, 33
Russell, Ken, 296–7, 305, 311–12, 351
Russell, Maud, 241
Russell, Peter (Bertrand's third wife), 167
Russell, Rollo, 6
Russia: FP visits, 286–7, 299
Rylands, George ('Dadie'): FP meets at Cambridge, 32, 47; performs in play at Ham Spray, 93; visits Ham Spray, 112; life at Cambridge, 114; friendship with FP, 126, 162; Rosamond Lehmann dedicates *Dusty Answer* to, 134; homosexuality, 290; trip to Alderney with FP, 300; in Italy with FP, 304, 340; and Peter Luke's play on Lytton, 309, 315; in Switzerland with FP, 311; encourages FP to leave papers to King's College, Cambridge, 341; travels to Greece with FP, 342; ninetieth birthday, 349; health decline and death, 361

Sackville-West, Edward, 113, 131, 135, 223, 242, 255, 257, 262, 288; death, 285
Sackville-West, Vita: friendship with Virginia Woolf, 110; *Seducers in Ecuador*, 42
Saddam Hussein, 346
St Gervais, France, 176–7
San Fiz, Spain, 241
Sandwith, Noel, 217, 219
Sargent, John Singer, 333, 339
Sassoon, Siegfried, 335
Scales, Prunella, 349
Scilly Isles, 210
Sen, Amartya, 366
Senhouse, Roger, 90, 93, 112–14, 126, 134, 140, 217
Serota, Sir Nicholas, 364
Sexual Offences Act (1966), 289–90, 293
Shaw, George Bernard, 6
Shawe-Taylor, Desmond, 223, 288, 313, 328, 356
Sheppard, Clare, 167
Sheringham, Norfolk, 10
Shone, Richard, 356, 363
Sicily: FP visits, 286–7
Sieveking, Geoffrey, 33, 36, 45, 79–80, 93
Skelton, Barbara, 226, 244
Skye, Isle of, 264, 346, 359
Slade, The (house), near Alton, 313
Slater, Humphrey, 181, 187–8, 195
Smallwood, Norah, 318–19, 321, 330
Snape, Suffolk, 270
Snowdon, Antony Armstrong-Jones, 1st Earl of, 331, 342, 354

Snowdon, Lucy, 335
Society for Psychical Research, 108
Solva, South Wales, 194
Souco, La (house, Roquebrune), 257, 259–60
Souter-Robinson, Joan see Cochemé, Joan
Spain: Carrington and Ralph visit, 59–60, 64; FP and Ralph visit, 94–7, 125, 127–8, 133, 165–6, 234, 243–5, 250, 253; rise of fascism, 165, 168; outbreak of Civil War, 169–70; and conduct of Civil War, 172–3; FP visits in widowhood, 267, 270, 282, 293, 295, 320, 340, 358–9; Henrietta moves to, 282–3; see also CuzCuz, Al; Tramores
Spectator, The (journal), 245, 340, 344, 352, 359, 362
Spender, Maro, 297, 330
Spender, Matthew, 297, 330
Spinoza, Baruch de, 306
Spring Rice, Catherine, 3
Sprott, Sebastian, 35, 104
Staël, Anne Louise Germaine, baronne de, 251
Stein, Gertrude, 20
Stephen, Adrian, 16, 39, 107, 113, 131, 199
Stephen, Karin (née Costelloe), 16, 107
Stephen, Sir Leslie, 5
Stephen, Thoby, 54
Stokke (farmhouse, near Great Bedwyn), 216, 264
Stoppard, Sir Tom, 354
Stowell (house), Wiltshire ('the Tycoonery'), 269
Strachey family, 14
Strachey, Alix (née Sargent-Florence; James's wife): courtship and marriage to James, 61, 72; friendship with Ralph, 61; in Gordon Square, 88, 128; Carrington disparages FP to, 93; FP and Ralph live with, 104; friendship with FP, 107, 249; Freudianism, 108–9; visits Ham Spray, 111–12, 146, 151, 160, 182, 204, 263; gives party for homosexuals, 131; and Lytton's illness, 134; and Carrington after Lytton's death, 143; witness at FP's wedding, 154; and FP' pregnancy and birth of Burgo, 162–3; abandons pacifism in war, 187; in Switzerland, 218; and Straffen's execution, 231; and James's death, 287–8; and Holroyd's biography of Lytton, 291–3; opposes proposed BBC film of Lytton, 297; preserves collection of private papers, 298; and Luke's play on Lytton, 305; death, 310; FP gives talk on, 359
Strachey, Barbara, 333
Strachey, Dick, 179, 260
Strachey, Dorothy, 160
Strachey, Esmé, 179, 226
Strachey, Isobel, 190, 207, 228, 257, 289, 300; death, 340
Strachey, James: childhood, 14; and Bunny Garnett's marriage, 40; at Tidmarsh, 57; and Alix Sargent-Florence, 61; marriage, 72; and Ralph's impending marriage to Carrington, 73; FP and Ralph live with, 104; on Carrington at Ham Spray, 105; friendship with FP, 107; Freudianism, 108–9; marriage relations, 108; and psychical research, 109; visits Ham Spray, 112, 114, 160, 182, 204; in Gordon Square, 128; and Lytton's illness, 137; inherits books from Lytton, 140; and Carrington's condition after Lytton's death, 143–4; as Lytton's executor, 151; joins FP and family in Switzerland, 218; translation of Freud, 230, 239, 285; and Straffen's execution, 231;